Anglo-Saxon Studies
in Archaeology and History

15

Edited by
Sally Crawford and Helena Hamerow

Oxford University School of Archaeology

Published by the Oxford University School of Archaeology
Institute of Archaeology
Beaumont Street
Oxford

Distributed by
Oxbow Books
10 Hythe Bridge Street, Oxford, OX1 2EW, UK
Tel: 01865 241249   Fax: 01865 794449

Distributed in North America by
The David Brown Book Company
PO Box 511, Oakville, CT, 06779, USA

www.oxbowbooks.com

ISBN 978 1 905905 10 2
ISSN 0264 5254

A CIP record for this book is available from the British Library

Cover image: Belt buckle from Updown, Eastry, Kent. Courtesy of Martin Welch.

Typeset by Oxbow Books
Printed in Great Britain by
The Short Run Press, Exeter

Foreword

Anglo-Saxon Studies in Archaeology and History is an annual series concerned with the archaeology and history of England and its neighbours during the Anglo-Saxon period.

ASSAH offers researchers an opportunity to publish new work in an interdisciplinary and multi-disciplinary forum which allows for a diversity of approaches and subject matter. Contributions which place Anglo-Saxon England in its international context are as warmly welcomed as those which focus on England itself.

Papers submitted to *ASSAH* must be comprehensible to non-specialist readers. They must, furthermore, conform to the journal's house style. A copy of the style-sheet is available on-line, at: http://web.arch.ox.ac.uk/assah. A hard copy can be obtained from the Editors. All papers are peer-reviewed.

The Editors are grateful to the contributors to this volume for their prompt and efficient responses, and to those peer reviewers who have taken the time to read and comment upon the papers in this volume. Thanks also go to the Marc Fitch Fund and to SLR Consulting for generous subventions towards the costs of the publication of this volume of *ASSAH*.

All papers for consideration for future volumes should be sent to the Editors:

Dr. Helena Hamerow and Dr. Sally Crawford
(Helena.hamerow@arch.ox.ac.uk, Sally.crawford@arch.ox.ac.uk)
ASSAH Series Editors
Institute of Archaeology
34–6 Beaumont Street
Oxford
OX1 2PG

Contents

Contributors

Steven Bassett
  Department of Medieval History, University of Birmingham, Edgbaston, Birmingham B15 2TT

Simon Draper
  The Victoria County History for Gloucestershire, Gloucestershire Archives, Clarence Row, Alvin Street, Gloucester GL1 3DW

Dawn Hadley
  Department of Archaeology and Prehistory, University of Sheffield, Northgate House, West Street, Sheffield S1 4ET

Laurence Hayes
  SLR Consulting, Mytton Mill, Forton Heath, Montford Bridge, Shrewsbury SY4 1HA

Jane Kershaw
  Institute of Archaeology, University of Oxford, 34–36 Beaumont Street, Oxford OX1 2PG

Timothy Malim
  SLR Consulting, Mytton Mill, Forton Heath, Montford Bridge, Shrewsbury SY4 1HA

Martin Welch
  Institute of Archaeology, University College London, 31–34 Gordon Square, London WC1H 0PY

Report on Excavations of the Anglo-Saxon Cemetery at Updown, Eastry, Kent

Martin Welch
with contributions by
Corinne Duhig and Beth Rega, Elizabeth Crowfoot, Glynis Edwards,
Carole Morris and Gareth Williams

*Dedicated to the memories of Mary James (died 21 April 1976)
and Sonia Chadwick Hawkes Petkovic (died 30 May 1999)*

The Anglo-Saxon cemetery at Updown (Eastry III) was located by air photography on 4 June 1973 and was attributed correctly to the seventh century.[1] It consists of inhumation graves orientated east-west, many being enclosed by penannular ditches. The visible cropmark zone (as recorded photographically) was scheduled as an ancient monument (no. 298) in 1975, but the eastern cropmark edge did not mark the actual eastern limit of the cemetery. Excavation in March and April 1976 of thirty-six graves under the direction of Mrs S. C. Hawkes in advance of a water pipeline confirmed dating within the seventh century. In the zone immediately to the east of the designated scheduled monument, the width of the excavated area was doubled from c. 11 m to c. 22 m. Not every feature recorded at subsoil level was excavated due to time constraints and an additional child-sized burial (76:37) was cleared by workmen constructing the pipeline in June 1976, a short distance to the east of the excavated area. The total sample of thirty-seven burials belonged to a prosperous, but not excessively rich community. This cemetery is located a short distance to the south of Eastry, documented as a royal regional centre in the seventh to eighth centuries.

In September and October 1989 the excavation of adjacent and overlapping areas of the 1976 site was conducted by the Kent Archaeological Rescue Unit (KARU) in advance of the Eastry A256 bypass.[2] This revealed a further forty-one graves, as well reopening thirteen of those first excavated in 1976, bringing the total investigated to seventy-eight graves. This excavation also established a northern edge and a less well defined southern edge to the cemetery, just as the 1976 excavation had provided western and eastern limits along the pipeline.

A total of nineteen certain or probable penannular ring-ditches were recorded, each of which contained at least one grave. Some of these have a posthole marking the causeway entrance on the east side and it is presumed that each of these ditches enclosed an earthwork feature such as a low mound. Evidence for ancient grave robbing was noted for a single burial each in both the 1976 and 1989 excavations. Differences in the orientation of two inter-cutting graves excavated in 1976 within a ring-ditch suggest that the earlier burial pre-dates the grave for which the ring-ditch was constructed (76:32 and 76:33). Similarly one of two burials within a ring-ditch investigated in 1989 probably predates the ring-ditch and its associated grave (89:44 and 89:39). In only one case, again from 1976, does a ring-ditch overlap with and cut another ring-ditch (76:16 probably, but not certainly post-dating 76:15). The combination of this evidence implies a two-phase sequence, though not necessarily implying time gaps any greater than a single generation.

By combining information derived from grave assemblages with their orientation, it is suggested that certain burials can be attributed to either an earlier phase (1) within the first half of the seventh century or to a later phase (2) of around the middle and second half of the same century. Burials containing weapons are relatively common, but are difficult to attribute to a specific phase unless accompanied by a distinctive buckle worn at the waist. Silver-inlaid iron buckle sets and Kentish-type triangular buckles are among the key artefacts attributable to Phase 1, but a much wider range of object types help us define later burials. International contacts are indicated by finds such as the inlaid iron belt sets that include imports from the Frankish continent. Other Frankish imports are wheel-thrown pots and there is a gilt copper-alloy copy of a Merovingian gold coin used as a pendant in a female dress assemblage. Amethyst beads and a buckle manufactured within the Byzantine Empire are amongst the more exotic finds from the Mediterranean world beyond the Frankish realms.

The variable alkaline soil conditions were not conducive to good bone preservation. Nevertheless it is possible to match skeletal evidence of the age and/or biological sex for sixty-two individuals. In the remaining sixteen cases, however, we need to rely on grave dimensions to differentiate between children and adults. In the main there is a reasonable match amongst the adult population between biological sex from the skeletal remains and gender indicators from the grave-find assemblages. These seventy-eight graves probably represent at best one quarter of a cemetery population estimated to be above 300. As yet no trace has been detected of an associated settlement and insufficient graves have been excavated to indicate the overall date range for the cemetery, establishing its earliest and latest burials. These may well take us back into the later sixth century or forward into the early eighth century.

INTRODUCTION

Site Location

The Anglo-Saxon cemetery occupies a field called Sangrado's Wood, formerly covered by trees. This lies to the west and northwest of Updown House and is less than a kilometre south of Eastry at NGR TR 3115 5373. A series of air photographs taken by David R. Wilson, University of Cambridge on 4 and 11 June 1973 revealed numerous cropmark features. Interpreted as revealing individual inhumations with a significant number of graves enclosed by ring-ditches, one photograph (Plate 1 middle) was selected for publication the following year with a commentary identifying it correctly as the site of a previously unknown Anglo-Saxon cemetery of seventh-century date.[3] An oblique view taken from the north, it shows graves extending down to the tree-filled hedge that separated the west side of the field from the main road running north to south. The linear cut-off part way across the field parallel to the main road marks the edge of the cemetery cropmarks. As should have been suspected (and from subsequent excavation we now know) the cemetery continued on much further east up to and alongside the main woodland area to the east and south-east of the visible cropmarks.

Its publication aroused immediate interest for Sonia Chadwick Hawkes, Lecturer in European Archaeology, University of Oxford, as she had excavated a nearby sixth- to seventh-century Anglo-Saxon cemetery in the 1960s at TR 3256 5347, named after the hamlet of Finglesham in Northbourne parish.[4] In 1974 she was collating the available archaeological and historical evidence for Eastry and its region in order to demonstrate that Eastry must have been an important regional centre for the administration of Kent as early as the sixth century. The Finglesham site was some two kilometres to the southeast of Eastry, but the new site at Updown provided an undisturbed burial ground within a kilometre. In turn the Finglesham cemetery was only one and a half kilometres east of Updown, so there was obvious potential in comparing the two cemeteries.

In 1975 the cropmark area of the Sangrado's Wood field was scheduled as an Ancient Monument (no. 298), but the scheduled area did not include the eastern part of the cemetery, which had not shown up in aerial photographs due to an overlying crop of barley. Having obtained the landowners' co-operation, Hawkes was able to investigate the non-scheduled half of the field in 1976.

Geographical location, geology and topography

The Sangrado's Wood, Updown cemetery lies directly south of the modern village of Eastry and its southern extension at Buttsole occupying a triangular field. The ground slopes upwards to the east and south-east from the main road (the old A256) beside the western field boundary. Along its north-east edge runs Buttsole Lane, a minor road that takes a south-easterly direction past the entrance to Updown House and on in the direction of Northbourne. The cemetery is centred on NGR TR 3115 5373 and occupies sloping ground at a height of between 33–35 m above Ordnance Datum. Its topsoil covers upper chalk bedrock along a north-west to south-east axis with occasional patches of clay occupying shallow hollows in the bedrock. The western edge of the cemetery towards its southern end does not extend as far as the old A256 and along the sector excavated in 1976 graves were located well to the east. The road here is very straight and seems to be following the line of a Roman road connecting the coastal fort at Richborough on the Wantsum to the equivalent fort in Dover.[5] Similarly, the cemetery does not extend as far east as Buttsole Lane, which links Buttsole to Northbourne. The 1976 excavation did demonstrate, however, that the cemetery overlapped with the then remaining timber cover of Sangrado's Wood to the east. So it seems that the eastern edge of the cemetery extends here for up to 90–100 m beyond the cropmarks visible in 1973. On the basis of the air photographs, it has been estimated that some 300 graves occupied an area of around 150 × 80 m, though this should probably be regarded as a minimum figure. Two successive ditches running from north-west to south-east were recorded in 1989 a few metres to the north of the most northerly excavated graves, and it seems probable that the cemetery was demarcated in several places by ditches.[6] Indeed similar linear features can be observed on the 1973 air photographs and probably represent pre-existing field boundaries visible to the population developing the burial ground. It should be noted that so-called 'Celtic'-field lynchets may similarly explain patterns of dense burial within the late fifth- to early eighth-century cemetery at Buckland near Dover.[7]

Eastry as a regional centre in Anglo-Saxon Kent

A combination of place-name and documentary evidence demonstrates that Eastry was an important regional centre throughout the Anglo-Saxon period and appropriately the present village occupies a dominant hilltop position. Eastry has an administrative unit, a lathe, named after it in the *Domesday* Book of 1086 (*Lest de Eastreia*) and in 1085 it was held by the Archbishop of Canterbury, having been a manor of Christ Church, Canterbury since the ninth century. Prior to that, however, it had been a royal *villa* or *vicus* administered by a reeve or *praefectus*. A land diploma or charter of 805 x 807 survives in a contemporary copy and records a gift of land by Cuthred, to the *praefectus* Æthelnoth.[8] We have two other contemporary copies of early ninth-century charters which relate to Eastry in 811[9] and 825 x 832.[10] In these documents Eastry is referred to as (*to*) *Eastorege*, (*on*) *Eastergege* and (*ad*) *Easteraege*, combining Old English *easter*, meaning 'eastern' in an archaic and early form, with Old English *gē*, again an early form meaning a 'region, district, province' and related to modern German *Gau*.[11]

Comparable place-names occur elsewhere in east Kent, implying that Eastry was one of at least four such centres. The name of Sturry beside the river Stour to the north-east of Canterbury describes a 'centre for the Stour region', while Lyminge was a 'centre of the Limen region', even though it was located within the North Downs and some distance from the former Wealden river, the Limen and its estuary, after which the region was named. If the northern and southern centres for east Kent were represented by Sturry and Lyminge, then Eastry implies a 'Wester-ge', and a plausible candidate is provided by Wester in the parish of Linton near Maidstone.[12] This western centre seems to have been very short-lived indeed.

Then there is the legend of royal murder at Eastry and a subsequent miracle linked to the foundation of a royal nunnery at Minster on Thanet. If the tradition preserved in the *Passio sanctorum Ethelberti atque Ethelredi* (also known as the Mildrith Legend) is accurate, Eastry was certainly a royal centre within the third quarter of the seventh century.[13] According to this document, King Eadbald (616/18–640) had two sons, and one of these, Eorcenberht (640–664), succeeded him. Eorcenberht appears to have been the younger brother, but the older brother Eormenred had predeceased him and left his sons Æthelbert and Æthelræd under Eorcenberht's protection. When in turn Eorcenberht died, it was his son Egbert (664–673) who replaced him and then had his own cousins murdered at Eastry. The murder of two cousins, the sons of a pre-deceased uncle, whose very existence threatened a new king may be shocking, but not particularly surprising. On the other hand, it is not often that a series of accounts record such an event and its aftermath. According to the tradition, Æthelbert and Æthelræd were martyred innocents, yet they are unlikely to have been the young boys portrayed

Plate 1. Air photographs of Updown, Eastry in the summers of 1973 (top and middle) and 1976 (bottom)

in the texts. Rather they were adults whose branch of the family had been bypassed in the royal succession.[14] It seems Egbert felt remorse and settled the blood feud within his own kin by payment of a substantial *wergild* in the form of the foundation endowment of Minster on Thanet. If the niece of the murdered princes, Mildrith, had not ruled as its abbess in the early eighth century and ensured that the legend was recorded, we might well have been none the wiser.

The contribution that Sonia Hawkes made here was to add a compelling archaeological case for Eastry's development as a royal centre as early as the sixth century.[15] She pointed to the existence of four significant burial sites located in and around Eastry. The most central of these was the Eastry House site (her Eastry II) with its isolated female burial revealed in 1970. This woman wore a Scandinavian bow brooch datable to the second half of the sixth century.[16] It remains unclear whether this grave forms part of a cemetery, although the discovery in 2003 of a sixth-century sword, spear, shield, buckle and knife in a grave just across the main road and less than 50 m to the south-east of the 1970 find should be noted.[17] On the other hand, a different site also just 50 m south-east of the 1970 grave revealed no trace of other Anglo-Saxon burials, so the 1970 and 2003 burials may represent isolated graves rather than components of a substantial cemetery.[18] Further, as both are located near the highest point in Eastry, immediately west and east of the Roman road, either of them might have been marked by a prominent barrow mound.

The Buttsole cemetery (Eastry I) occupied the south-east corner of Eastry village extending from Eastry Cross and Brook Street in the north. Graves were recorded here as early as March 1792 and again around 1860–1, while more recently a fifth-century handmade pot containing a copper-alloy ring was discovered when a tree blew down within the garden of Cross Farmhouse in October 1987. The pot seems to have been associated with human bone, implying a grave here.[19] Grave finds suggest that burial in the Buttsole cemetery was centred on the sixth century. Then there is the Eastry Mill (Eastry IV) site discovered in 1969 some 800 m west-south-west of Eastry Cross. One of the four burials revealed in a chalk pit face within a garden close to the Mill was accompanied by a knife. A further three unfurnished inhumations some 95 m to the south share the same grave orientation, so it seems reasonable to suggest that together they form part of a larger cemetery. Hawkes recognized that this western burial site might have been more peripheral to the royal centre than the others. That leaves the Updown cemetery (Eastry III), the subject of the present report. Located some 900 m south of Eastry Cross and some 700 m from the nearest recorded graves belonging to the Buttsole site, this burial ground may well be a seventh-century replacement for the Buttsole cemetery.

To the finds listed by Sonia Hawkes in 1979, we can add a 1987 metal-detector discovery of a brooch, probably manufactured in north-west Germany within the middle third of the fifth century, found to the north or north-east of the village.[20] This cast supporting-arm brooch or *Stützarmfibel* has chipcarved designs comparable to those found on Saxon equal-arm brooches of the Nesse Type.[21] Another is a sixth-century small triangular gilt copper-alloy mount ornamented in Salin Style I found to the west of Buttsole Pond.[22]

As yet, however, there are no recorded postholes or trenches belonging to timber buildings in or around Eastry that might represent contemporary Anglo-Saxon settlement. Hawkes did suggest that Eastry Court, occupying the site of a medieval stone house that formerly belonged to Christ Church, Canterbury, might be the location for an Anglo-Saxon royal hall.[23] Chris Arnold seized an opportunity to test this hypothesis, though without consulting Hawkes first. He directed a small excavation in 1980, but found nothing of relevance.[24] The Channel 4 Time Team seems to have had no more success in 2005. Nevertheless, KARU excavations within the Roman coastal fort at Dover revealed the foundation trenches of two successive large rectangular timber halls both probably of seventh-century date, though these have been interpreted by KARU as parts of a multi-phased monastic timber church.[25] Future opportunities will occur within Eastry to recognise and excavate earthfast features from building types as represented at Cowdery's Down (Hampshire) in its phase 4C.[26] More modest timber structures with rectangular arrangements of postholes and trenches or the pits and postholes of sunken-featured buildings (*Grubenhäuser*) may also be located near the various Eastry cemeteries, including the Updown site, as has been the case at a rural site near Church Whitfield to the north of Dover.[27]

Other Anglo-Saxon sites in and around Eastry

There is a wider hinterland for Eastry and its four principal burial sites along the lower dip-slopes of the North Downs.[28] Not every recorded contemporary site will be discussed here, but reference has already been made to the Finglesham cemetery a short distance to the east of Updown at TR 3256 5347.[29] Further to the south-east is the published sixth-century cemetery at Mill Hill, Deal associated with a prehistoric round barrow at TR 3631 5074, though this is only one of several burial sites in the Deal and Northbourne area.[30] To the north of Eastry, there is the high-status cremation complex from a barrow at Coombe to the north-west of Woodnesborough. The records of this find are poor, but it contained two swords (including one with later sixth-century ornament), a Frankish bronze vessel and part of a sixth-century Kentish small square-headed brooch.[31] This is the nearest we have to an elite burial site within Kent for this period. The very existence of a village that still incorporates Woden's name some two kilometres north of Eastry is also worthy of note.[32]

A particularly exciting find is the cemetery centred on an Early Bronze Age barrow near Ringelmere Farm, quite

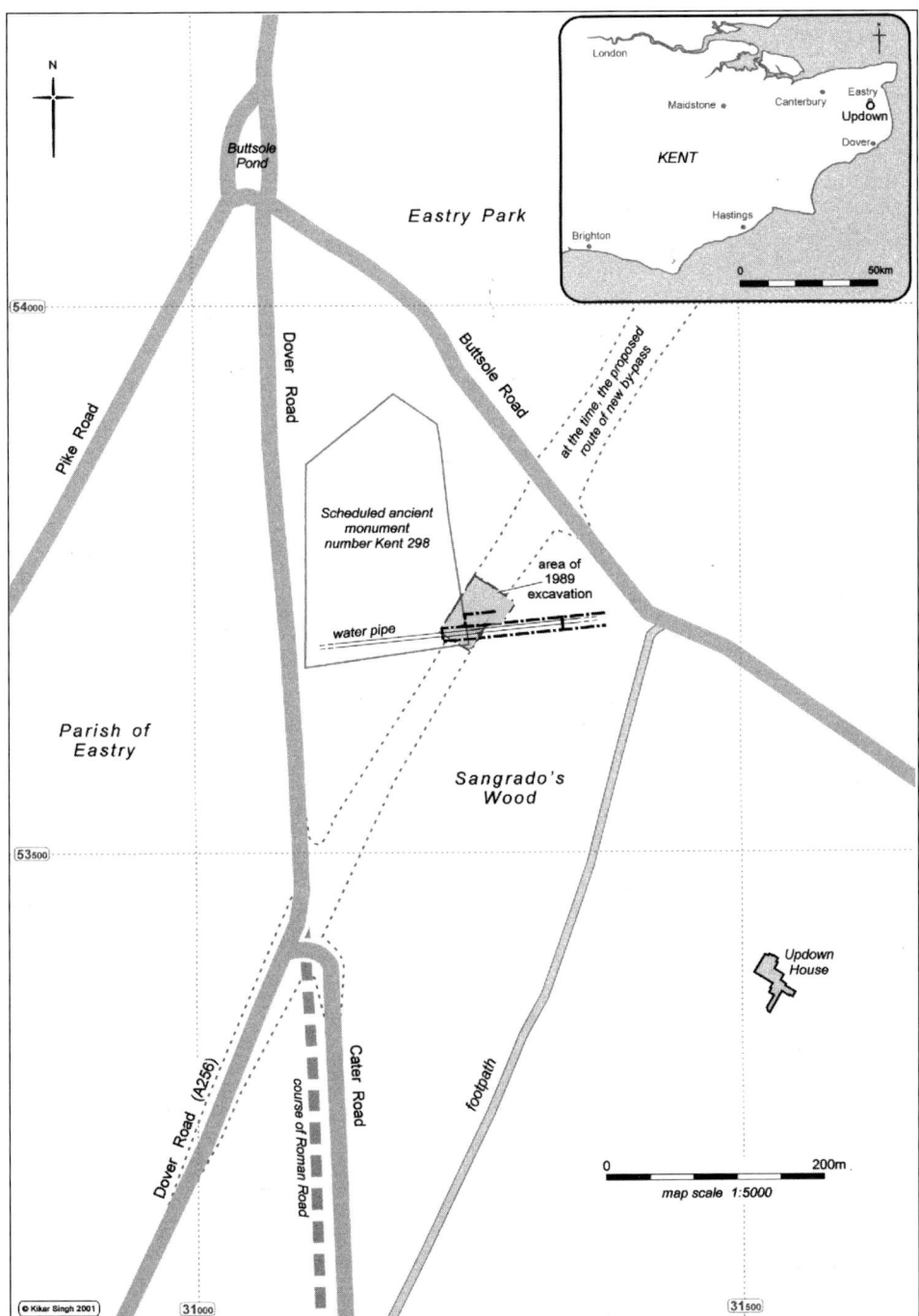

Figure 1. Site location maps (K. Singh)

close to Coombe. Partially excavated, it has revealed both Anglo-Saxon urned cremations and inhumations. There are finds datable to both the fifth century and the sixth century with the inhumations, and a sunken-featured building on the opposite side of the barrow suggests an adjacent settlement.[33] It seems this site may help us define fifth-century phases to match those established for sixth-century Kent through the research of Birthe Brugmann.[34] At present, however, the only published cemetery in east

Kent for which the seventh-century burials have been phased successfully is that at Buckland near Dover.[35] This site overlooks the Dour valley from the north, but is a significant distance to the south of Eastry, though admittedly connected by the Roman road that passed close to the settlement near Church Whitfield.[36]

Finally, mention must be made of the cemetery at Gilton (or Guilton), Ash to the north-west of both Woodnesborough and Coombe. This sixth- to seventh-century cemetery was revealed through sand extraction on a site adjacent to a major east-west Roman road.[37] It was explored extensively in the eighteenth century by the Rev. Bryan Faussett, but has also been subject to a few modern discoveries as well.[38] North and east of Ash we enter a coastal landscape that was formerly dominated by the Wantsum channel separating the mainland from the Isle of Thanet.[39] By the middle of the seventh century, the former Roman fort at Richborough had been replaced by the trading port of Sandwich. Unfortunately we have yet to locate the earliest Sandwich through fieldwork and it seems virtually certain that the present town on its late medieval site occupies a very different location.

This brief survey is sufficient to confirm that Eastry was indeed centrally placed in a territory that extended across the lower dip-slopes of the North Downs. It was linked by road to the east coast and northwards to the more sheltered waters of the Wantsum.[40] The route north to Ash also provided for easy access westwards by road to Canterbury. Equally important must have been the road south to the port of Dover, as has been confirmed in recent research by Stuart Brookes examining the economic development of Kent between the late fifth and eighth centuries.[41] It should be noted, however, that doubt has been cast recently by Parfitt as to the navigability of the streams which flowed from the vicinity of Eastry and Finglesham into the Wantsum.[42] It seems we should not assume too readily that Eastry itself could have been reached by boat from the Wantsum in the sixth to seventh centuries. To see how the Eastry region fitted into the overall organisation of the kingdom of Kent, the reader is referred to several recent surveys of the archaeology of Kent.[43]

THE EXCAVATIONS

The water pipeline and the 1976 excavation

The proposal by the East Kent Water Board for a water pipeline to be taken across this site was made shortly after its scheduling as an Ancient Monument. A way-leave with a width of 10 m was established and the topsoil cover removed by machine from east to west right across the southern edge of the site. The pipe itself would then be set into a trench in the chalk bedrock. It was aligned close to and parallel to the woodland down from Buttsole Lane and then continued on downhill across the centre of the field. Its function was to transport water pumped out of the Betteshanger group of collieries. Clearly this development required archaeological excavation in advance to record all archaeological features and lift the contents of any graves within the way-leave. It would provide an opportunity to establish both the date range and the western and eastern limits of this sector of the cemetery. As the landowners, Major and the Hon. Mrs James, wished to see an archaeological investigation, Sonia Hawkes received a great deal of practical assistance. She and Mary James planned a small-scale rescue excavation for a four-week

period within the Easter vacation of 1976. Everything was managed on a shoestring. Hawkes borrowed or otherwise acquired equipment, boxes and packing materials, assisted by a grant from the Kent Archaeological Society. The water authority was persuaded to use its machinery to remove the topsoil for an additional area beside the way-leave before the main excavation team arrived, and fully reinstated the field after the pipe laying. The widening of the excavated area to the east of and beyond the scheduled area effectively doubled the width of the land cleared. Although priority was given to recording and excavating archaeological features along the way-leave, one grave was missed and subsequently located just beyond the excavation. Unfortunately it was emptied by the workmen laying the pipeline (76:37) before Hawkes saw the pipeline for herself. Nor were all the graves, ring-ditches, postholes and other features observed in the northerly extension investigated. Those marked on the 1976 plan as 38, 39, 40, 41 and 42 were left unexplored that Easter. A greater area had been cleared than the team available had the time and resources to excavate, but fortunately this same area was to be systematically excavated in 1989.

If Mary James had lived, various opportunities to secure independent funding for further excavation might have been explored in the late 1970s. Nevertheless, Hawkes kept tabs on proposed planning applications in and around Eastry, but concentrated her efforts on the essential post-excavation tasks for the 1976 graves. Apparently this did not include the drafting of a grave catalogue text, and more seriously, the individual who had undertaken to report on the human remains left for Australia the following year without either fowarding a report or returning the skeletal material to Oxford. It was not until 1997 that these remains were relocated, still in their original boxes at an English Heritage store near Nottingham. They were subsequently transferred to English Heritage stores in Acton (London) and then Portsmouth (Southsea Castle), before it became possible to arrange for them to be properly studied in Cambridge (Appendix I). Within the next five years, Hawkes also published studies drawing on the Updown evidence. The first assessed the early Anglo-Saxon archaeology of Eastry and its immediate hinterland, taking as its starting point the 1970 grave from Eastry House.[44] The second examined several silver-inlaid iron buckles and belt sets dating to the seventh century.[45] It used material from her excavations at Finglesham (graves 25 and 123), as well as five of the Updown burials (graves 76:5, 76:16, 76:24, 76:29 and 76:31). Thereafter the Updown publication project was put on hold and the larger-scale projects of preparing Finglesham and Kingsworthy for publication were given priority.

The Eastry Bypass and the 1989 excavation by the Kent Archaeological Rescue Unit

Hawkes had hoped that a long-standing proposal to build a bypass for the A256 from Sandwich to Dover to

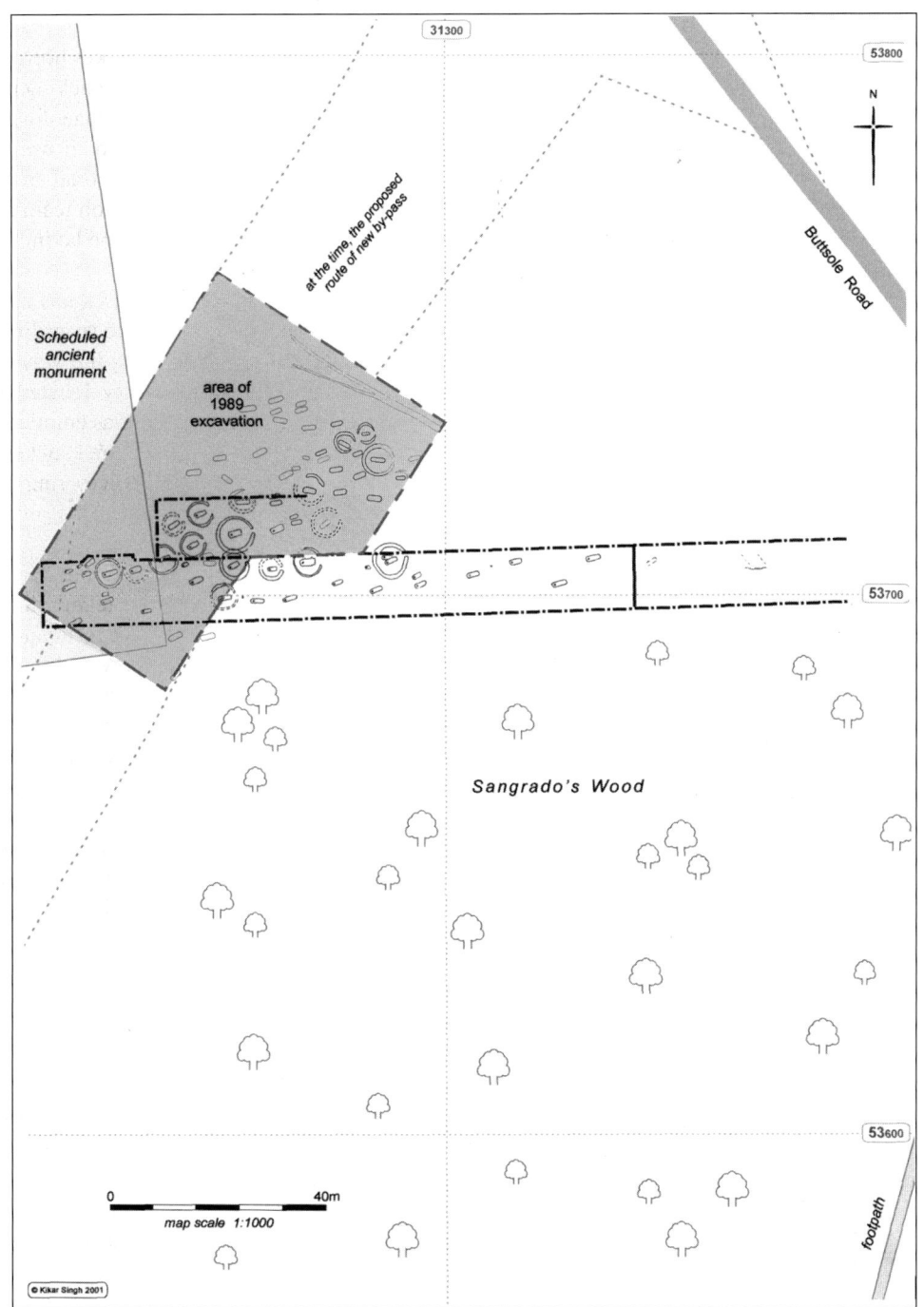

Figure 2. Map showing the inter-relationship of the 1976 and 1989 excavations (K. Singh updated by Faith Vardy)

pass around the east of Eastry and cut across Sangrado's Wood might provide an opportunity for further excavation at Updown. By the end of the 1980s, however, rescue archaeology in England had changed radically from the situation in the mid 1970s. Competitive tendering by professional archaeological units was the norm and there were fewer opportunities for part-time, low budget university-based teams to undertake rescue excavations. Although the legal framework requiring developer funding

as part of the planning process (PPG16) had yet to be established, the need for a regulated system to manage the process was already obvious. The contract to excavate sites along the Eastry bypass was awarded to the Kent Archaeological Rescue Unit (KARU) under the direction of Brian Philp, and an area of about 1,500 sq. m was excavated at Sangrado's Wood during a twenty-eight day period in September and October 1989. A total of forty-one new graves were recorded out of fifty-four uncovered. Just

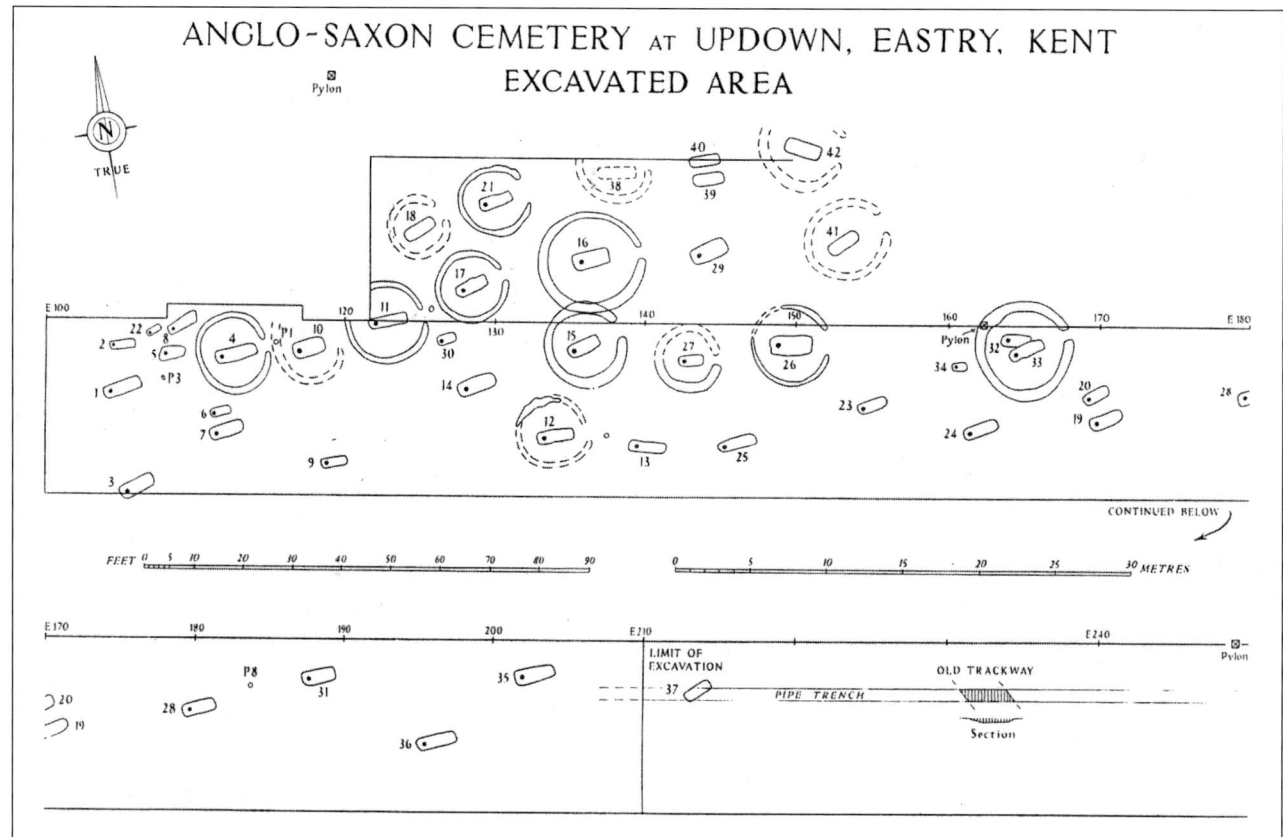

Figure 3. Plan of the excavated area investigated in 1976 (M. Cox)

three of these were within the scheduled monument area and thirteen of the fifty-one graves excavated outside the scheduled area had already been dug in 1976.[46] The total sample of graves excavated thus rose to seventy-eight, if we include Grave 76:37.

By publishing its report independently, KARU introduced a new grave numbering series running from 1–54 to put alongside the graves 1–42 recorded on the still unpublished 1976 plan. Rather than start again and create a third series of numbers running from 1–78, the present author has added a year prefix code (76 for 1976 and 89 for 1989) and a correlation table of the 1976 and 1989 numbers (Table 1). The 1989 excavation seems to have established northern and southern edges for this sector of the cemetery, just as an eastern limit was determined in 1976 with the location of Grave 76:37 a short distance to the east of Grave 76:35. The distance between the northern and southern limits of the burial ground is around 50 m at this point in the cemetery. As already noted, successive ditches beyond the northern edge of this cemetery were planned and excavated in 1989 (ditches F17 and F18), and were possibly associated with a set of five postholes (F19–F23). The relationship of such ditches and postholes to cemetery organization and burial structures needs to be explored further as and when we find opportunities to excavate other sectors here.

The excavation methodology adopted in 1976

Although the underlying geology is chalk and all the graves, postholes and penannular ring-ditches had been dug into its bedrock, there are occasional patches of clay covering the chalk and occupying hollows in the chalk. The topsoil was removed by machine along the length of the way-leave covering a strip of roughly 110 × 11 m, and over a widened area of around 35 × 13 m outside the scheduled area. Hand clearance with forks and shovels was used to loosen and remove any remaining compacted topsoil, and then the chalk bedrock was cleaned with brushes. The graves, ring-ditches, postholes and any other visible features in the bedrock were then recorded, numbered and planned. Ring-ditches and postholes were sectioned as well as excavated in plan. Finally, each grave was excavated, usually by a team of two. Unfortunately, the patches of compacted clay proved stubborn to remove and the process of hand clearance took longer than was desirable. Although priority was given to cleaning and recording the length of the way-leave, particularly during the first two weeks, a few graves were indeed missed. The 1989 excavation revealed three burials in two substantial hollows filled with clay along the pipeline way-leave (89:15, 89:16 and 89:18).[47] The enforced end to the 1976 excavation provides only a partial excuse for the failure

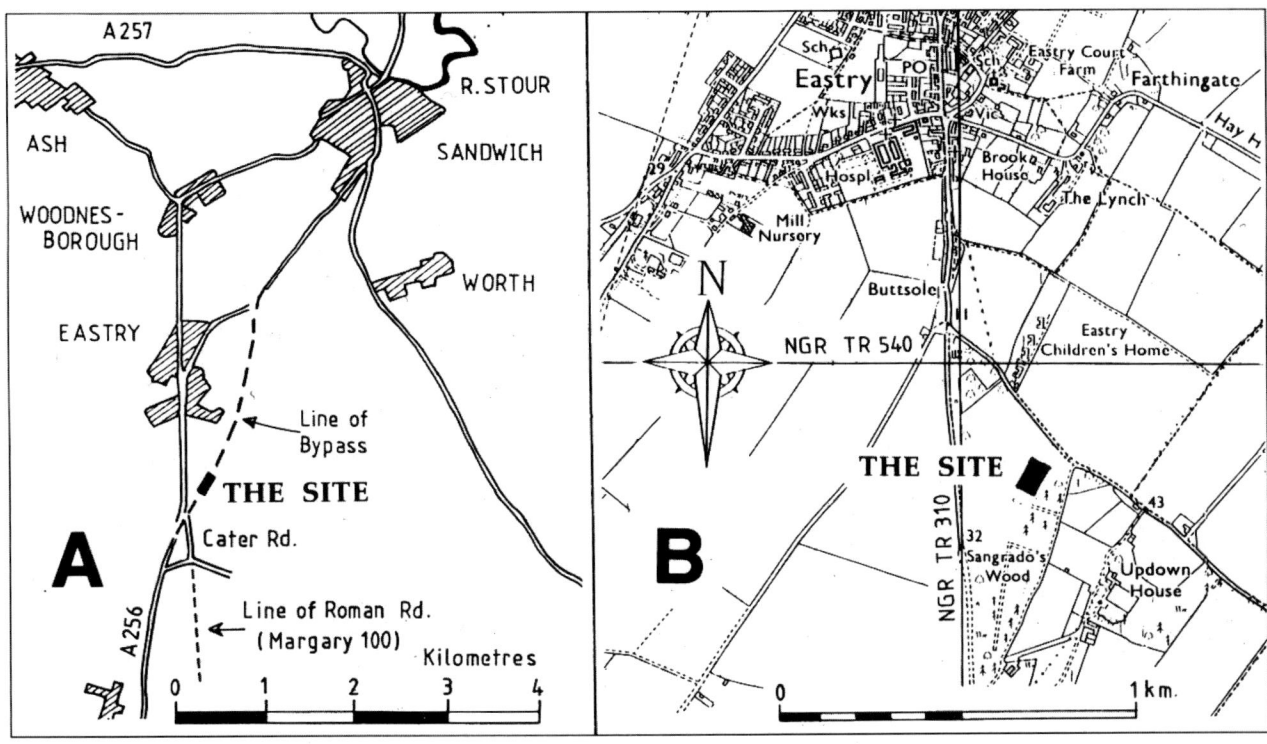

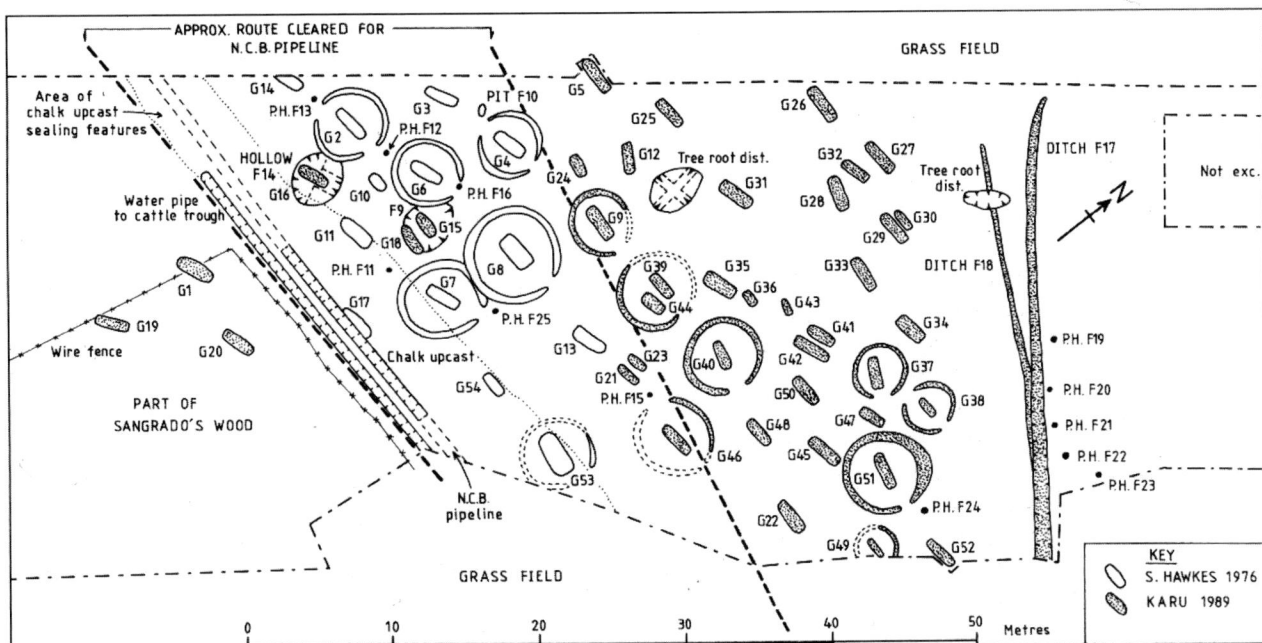

Figure 4. Site location maps and cemetery plan: KARU 1989 excavation (after Philip and Keller 2002)

to explore these two hollows more fully, and perhaps they were too easily dismissed as natural features in 1976. Fortunately the pipeline trenching did not cause any disturbance to them in June 1976 and these three graves were to be fully recorded in 1989. A further two burials (89:21 and 89:23) were located in 1989 within the 1976 extension to the north of the way-leave between those

planned as 76:29 and 76:41. The failure to identify and plan these in 1976 can probably be attributed again to the hurried end to the season and to a lower priority placed on excavating graves beyond the area to be subject to pipeline disturbance. Finally, as already mentioned, an isolated child's burial was uncovered by the pipeline contractors in June 1976 (76:37) within three metres of the eastern end of the way-leave excavation. No further graves were revealed to the east beyond this point along the way-leave as far as Buttsole Lane.

Fortunately, the 1976 and 1989 investigations together provide a comprehensive view of this corner of the site. It seems highly improbable that many more graves were missed within the two overlapping excavated areas. A total of thirty-six graves were excavated from the forty-two identified and planned in the 1976 season, and the only burial from the 1976 season that can be regarded as inadequately recorded is that of the presumed child in 76:37. A total of thirty-two graves were excavated within the way-leave itself (76:1–15, 76:19–20, 76:22–28 and 76:30–37) along a strip of around 110 × 11 m. The area to the north measured 35 × 13 m and contained five graves excavated in 1976 (76:16–18, 76:21 and 76:29), and a further five that were first planned then, but actually excavated in 1989 (76:38–42, the equivalents of 89:9, 89:44, 89:39, 89:46 and 89:40).

The 1989 excavation investigated an approximately square sector of the cemetery covering some 56 × 56 m. This included a restricted area to the south of the 1976 pipeline and way-leave which contained three well-spaced burials (89:1 and 89:19–20). These appear to mark a southern edge for the cemetery. It may be that a few more graves could have been located if the area immediately to the west of these three graves had been cleared, but no more than five or six graves might have been missed here. As already mentioned, the excavators in 1989 re-investigated thirteen of the thirty-seven graves previously dug in 1976 (76:10/89:14, 76:11/89:2, 76:18/89:3, 76:14/89:11, 76:30/89:10, 76:17/89:6, 76:21/89:4, 76:12/89:17, 76:15/89:7, 76:16/89:8, 76:27/89:54, 76:29/89:13 and 76:26/89:53). The remaining burials recorded in 1989 include the three concealed within clay hollows (as mentioned above: 89:15–16 and 89:18) and two to the east of 76:29/89:13 (89:21 and 89:23). All the others were located to the north or north-east of those investigated in 1976, but did not extend as far east or as far west as those along the 1976 way-leave. Of course, the 1989 excavation was limited by the demands of rescue excavation to investigate all of the archaeological features on a site about to be removed by heavy machinery for the construction of a dual carriageway bypass. It is particularly fortunate that the excavation revealed a convincing northern limit to this zone of the cemetery. It can further be argued that the cemetery does appear to be thinning out to the south of the way-leave, implying we are on or very near its southern edge.

MATERIAL EVIDENCE: PART 1

Grave structures and evidence for burial practice

All the burials were single inhumations deposited in individually-cut trench graves, each aligned east-west with the head placed at the west end. They were dug through the topsoil and on into the chalk bedrock. All grave depths were recorded in relation to the top of the bedrock, whether in 1976 or 1989, so we have no secure basis for estimating the original ground surface in the seventh century. Grave dimensions from the 1976 season ranged upwards from 1 m × 0.5 m and 0.16 m deep (76:34 child-sized burial) to 2.85 × 1.13 × *c.* 0.85 m deep (76:29 for an adult male aged 25–35 years). These measurements are comparable to those recorded in 1989 from 1.15 × 0.70 m and 0.90 m deep (89:36 child-sized) to 2.80 × 0.87 × 0.92 m deep (89:5 for a probable male aged 36–38 years accompanied by female-gendered artifacts). Absolute limits for grave cuts are 2.85 m length (76:29), 1.41 m width (76:26) and 1.02 m depth (89:52). It has been argued that grave dimensions and especially their depth indicate the contribution in man hours of preparing a grave, and thus provide an indicator of the relative importance of the individual placed in it. This information can then be compared to the assemblage of finds recovered from the grave.

Another significant feature is the visible presence of either a wooden lining to the grave or of a coffin. Twenty seven graves (35%) produced indications of coffin-like structures, including four iron cleat fittings in the case of the adult-sized 89:31 and iron nails in 76:1 and several other burials, while at least one grave produced evidence suggestive of a wooden base (76:26). The use of cleats as coffin fittings has been considered by Vera Evison in relation to Buckland, Dover and the Sutton Hoo mound 1 ship burial.[48] If we turn to the textile evidence (Appendix II), there is additional, but limited, evidence from 76:28 for the use of grass to line the coffin as part of the burial tableau, the display visible to mourners before the grave was backfilled.

Grave 76:4 was excavated in quadrants for the upper layers above the body space to seek evidence of ancient grave robbing and also traces of a wooden coffin and packing materials in the upper fill that might indicate a mound constructed over the grave. Grave robbing was not an issue in this particular case, though there were two examples elsewhere in 76:18 and one of the 1989 graves, possibly 89:31 with its coffin cleats.[49] The practice of contemporary grave robbing may have been introduced from the Frankish continent and has been noted for other east-Kent cemeteries.[50] The existence of a rectangular coffin with vertical sides and approximate dimensions of 1.90 m by 0.55 m was demonstrated in 76:4, and it had possessed a collapsed top lid. The chalk bottom of the grave cut was very uneven, however, and suggested that the coffin had originally been positioned on a plinth of flint nodules. It was also possible to distinguish the fine, loose chalky soil fill within the coffin from packing around the coffin and also from a layer above the coffin consisting of hard chalk blocks in marl, much disturbed by roots.

The single case of inter-cutting of two differently aligned graves (76:32 and 76:33) enclosed by a penannular ring-ditch proved relatively straight-forward to separate, as one corner of 76:32 had been truncated by 76:33. As 76:33 was aligned with the eastern causeway of the ring ditch, it seems reasonable to suggest that 76:33 was associated with the ring-ditch structure and had accidentally disturbed the earlier and forgotten burial of 76:32. Eleven of the thirty-seven graves excavated in 1976 that produced coffin traces were enclosed by penannular ring-ditches. The ring-ditch itself was orientated east-west and normally had the causeway set to the east. In some cases there was also a posthole placed still further east and aligned on this causeway (76:4, 76:11, 76:12 and 76:15). A total of twelve graves with possible or certain ring-ditches were recorded in 1976 (76:4, possibly 76:10, 76:11, 76:12, 76:15, 76:16, 76:17, possibly 76:18, 76:21, 76:26, 76:27 and 76:32 and 76: 33), and a further eight in 1989 (graves 89:9, 89:39 and 89:44, 89:37, 89:38, 89:40, 89:46, 89:49 and 89:51), though one of them appears to have had its causeway and posthole set instead to the west (89:46). Together these represent over 25% of the excavated graves. In the KARU report it was observed that four of the ring-ditches had been badly plough-damaged and that the generous spacing around some other graves might have permitted them to be enclosed by a shallower ring-ditch. A similar case can be made for the 1976 graves, and partial survival of ring-ditch sectors around graves 76: 26, 76:27 and 76:12 should be noted. Again, possible ring-ditches were indicated on the 1976 plan around both 76:10 and 76:18. The KARU report also argued that four of the ditches had western as well as eastern causeways as indicated on the 1989 plan for 89:2 (76:11), 89:4 (76:21), 89:38 and 89:46.[51] This seems to reflect the different depths to which the ditch sections were dug as well as subsequent plough damage. The published plan is particularly ambiguous in the case of 89:46, seeming to indicate that the western entrance is marked by a posthole (F15) instead of an eastern entrance. Nevertheless, it seems that an eastern causeway entrance was the norm at Updown.

The largest of the penannular ditch structures enclosed 76:16 (89:8). Its ring-ditch was around 7 m in diameter and overlapped with, and possibly cut, that for 76:15 (89:7). The smallest had a diameter of 3.4 m and enclosed 89:49. John Shepherd commented in detail in the 1976 Field Notebook on three of these ditched structures (76:4, 76:15 and 76:16). In the case of ring-ditch 76:4, the information from the sections proved inconclusive in assessing whether soil was entering in greater quantities from the inside or the outside of the ditch. The presence of a mound, bank or berm immediately within the ditch ought to be indicated by the profile of the fill nearest the inner edge. Similarly there was no clear evidence for postholes or stake holes within the ditch relating to a palisade there. All that could be stated with any confidence was that natural silting took place into the ditch from soil outside the ditch rather than any deliberate back-filling. In the case of ring-ditch 76:4 there was also a posthole (P1) with dimensions of 0.35 × 0.35 × 0.20 m deep. This was positioned opposite and to the east of the causeway

entrance and contained a small iron object in its fill, quite possibly a deliberate deposit. It was noted, however, that the causeway, the posthole and the grave axis were not precisely aligned, so the grave itself had probably been backfilled before the ring-ditch was dug. Additionally, it was observed that the very lumpy layer of chalk fill in the ditch fill was extremely similar in composition to the top of the grave fill. This might imply that this soil had been introduced into the grave fill when the coffin collapsed. It was argued therefore that the spoil from the ditch was heaped over the already backfilled grave in the form of a mound, and that this would have obscured the precise east-west alignment of the grave. It was further noted that excavated chalk expands at a ratio of 1:1.5–1.75 when removed from the bedrock and spread. Finally, the varying levels along the ditch floor suggested that three people dug it simultaneously, each having to adjust their section to correspond with that of their partners.

The intersection of the ditches for 76:15 and 76:16 required particular attention. In one section (A–B) the ring-ditch for 76:15 is noticeably deeper than that for 76:16. The ditches are seen as converging at another section (C–D) and they seem to be sharing the same channel in a third section (E–F). It was not possible, in Shepherd's opinion, to show conclusively which ditch was dug first, though he concluded that 'it would be reasonable to suppose that the ditch for barrow 16 was cut subsequent to the ditch for barrow 15'. A preliminary opinion on the mollusc shells recovered from the ditch fill was that they were typical of open-landscape species, an observation that fits the evidence for field ditches just beyond the northern edge of the cemetery.[52] Similar evidence was noted in the description of ring-ditch 76:4 regarding silting into the ditch from the area within the ditch, implying a mound inside. A half-hearted case was also made here for the presence of wattle revetment along the inner edge of the ditch to assist the retention of the mound (or berm) material.

Similar ring-ditches have been noted in many other cemeteries within the Kent chalk-lands in the seventh-century period. A recent example is at Cuxton overlooking the Medway, but geographically the closest is the Finglesham cemetery.[53] The fullest discussion of these and related features utilized the evidence from St Peter's Tip, near Broadstairs, Thanet.[54] This produced evidence for numerous stake holes (2in–6in diameter) in the lower fills of the deeper penannular ditches, implying fencing of close-set stakes set within each ditch. That such convincing evidence was not observed or recorded at Updown is probably due to the extensive tree-root activity on this former woodland site.

While it is commonly assumed that an annular ditch would imply the construction of a central mound, using the up-cast material from digging out the ring-ditch (though the mound might be round-topped or flat-topped according to preference), it is not so obvious what the shape of the upstanding earthwork would have been when enclosed by a penannular ditch. As we have seen, in 1976 Shepherd thought a low mound over the grave was probable, helping to explain minor variations in the alignment of grave, ditch entrance and marker post. We need to consider why a causeway gap (or gaps) was needed. There may have been a mystical reason, but it is also possible that some limited access onto the monument was permitted, in contrast to annular ditched enclosures. Presumably a fence set into the ditch deterred access other than over the causeway, while the marker post (where present) may have presented a spiritual barrier in front of the causeway. Such a post might have been carved, painted or inscribed. It might have supported an emblem, even perhaps a skull or other remains of an animal sacrifice. We should note though that in a Christian-period seventh-century context, the display of animal remains would have surely been viewed by any passing priest as inappropriate pagan symbolism. Further, if there was a penannular earth bank or berm, instead of an overall mound, that would leave a hollow interior at, or perhaps above, ground level that might possibly have been entered by authorized mourners. A further alternative would be a relatively low flattened mound with a relatively gentle ramp from the causewayed end to provide for the possibility of access.

In any case, it is reasonable to suggest that burials enclosed by ring-ditch earthworks might have been considered to be more important members of the community than the majority deposited in ordinary grave cuts. Standard graves were marked at best by a temporary low mound of up-cast material, which then gradually sank back into the grave, as the corpse and coffin decomposed and then collapsed. Despite this possibility, there seem to be no obvious divisions in terms of grave assemblages between those buried in ordinary graves and those enclosed by a ring-ditch, though this will be explored in more detail below.

Grave Catalogue

Grave and feature numbers beginning with 76 followed by a colon and a number refer to grave numbers assigned by Sonia Hawkes in 1976 (1–37 excavated and 38–42 planned at subsoil level) and those in italics with the prefix 89 refer to grave and feature numbers (1–54) assigned by the Kent Archaeological Rescue Unit (KARU) in 1989.[55] These are cross-referenced whenever a grave has been assigned a number in both 1976 and 1989 and a concordance table is appended to this catalogue.

Each grave description gives first the grave number, next a summary of the skeletal data if available (see Appendix I) including sex, age and stature, followed by a description of the grave (dimensions given in metres as length, width and depth) and any coffin together with the positioning of the skeleton, then a description of the positioning of artefacts within the grave and finally descriptions of the grave finds themselves in numbered order. Spears are classified following the system established by Swanton,

shield fittings the schemes published by Dickinson and Härke and knives on the typology developed by Evison.[56] Reference is also made to the earlier publication by Hawkes on the inlaid iron buckles from the 1976 season, to a publication by Werner relating to a Byzantine buckle type and to others by van Bostraeten and Evison for an imported Frankish pot type. Pin types follow the scheme from an unpublished thesis by Ross.[57]

GRAVE 76:1 (Figs 14 and 25)
Male, 25–30 years, stature could not be calculated, (preservation category 3).
E–W grave, 2.14 × 0.80 × 0.55 at head end and 0.60 m deep at foot end, with three sides visible of a four-sided coffin stain, coffin *c.* 0.50 m wide, packed outside with clay on the right of the corpse. Adult skeleton placed in a supine position with its arms at the sides and the legs straight. The skull is at W end of grave and the skull faces to its right. Spearhead (1) is at the left side above the skull, high up in the fill above the coffin, blade sloping as if originally laid on the coffin and then collapsed when it disintegrated; the knife (2) lying at the left side of the waist, point towards the shoulder, parallel with the arm; with two coffin nails on the north and two more on the south upright side wall of the coffin (3) at the right side of the hip on the coffin line with the head on the grave floor and point upwards, presumably fastening the bottom board to the side wall, (4) on the left side of the left lower leg outside the coffin line, (5) at the left side of the humerus on the coffin line, head down, point up (as no. 3 above), and (6) at the bottom of the grave at the right foot corner, nailing the base to the sides; plus a body potsherd (7) from the grave fill.

1. **Spearhead**, iron, very heavy and solid leaf-shaped blade with a split socket, 265 mm L (tip missing), 30 mm W (blade), Type C2.
2. **Knife**, iron, curved back and straight cutting edge, 120 mm long, 14 mm wide, Type 4.
3.1 **Nail** or clench-nail, iron, with rounded head and rectangular-sectioned shaft, 85 mm long, 22 × 21 mm diameter (head). 3.2 **Nail** or clench-nail, iron, with rounded head and round-sectioned shaft, 71 mm long, 28 × 24 mm diameter (head). 3.3 **Nail point** with square section, iron, embedded in wood, 13 mm long, 4 mm sq., overall 27 mm long. 3.4 **Nail** or clench-nail, with (damaged) rounded head and square-sectioned shaft, 59.5 mm long, 17 × 15 mm diameter (head).
4. **Pottery**, body sherd, coarse flint-gritted fabric, probably Iron Age (see 76:25) [not illustrated].

GRAVE 76:2 (Figs 14 and 25)
Sub-adult, 4–8 years, (preservation category 1), dental epigenetic trait of Carabelli's cusp and dental enamel hypoplasia (see also grave 89:39).
E–W grave, 1.75 × 0.55 m maximum width at the middle of the grave × 0.30 m maximum depth at head end and no trace of a coffin. Sub-adult was in a supine position, as indicated by the position of the skull at the W end of the grave and of the two femurs. Buckle (1) is positioned

in what is presumed to be the waist area, above where the pelvis should be located.

1. **Buckle and plate**, iron, with oval loop, single tongue and a rectangular belt plate wrapped round the loop with a rectangular opening for the tongue, most of the upper plate missing and no trace of rivet(s) to attach the plate to a leather belt, with mineralised textile impressions on the back of the lower plate, 31 mm L (overall), 22 mm loop width, tongue 12 mm L, plate 21 × 15 mm.

GRAVE 76:3 (Figs 14 and 25)

Male, 17–25 years, stature 1.77 m, (preservation category 5), arthropathies of vertebrae and dental epigenetic trait of congenital absence of molars.

E–W grave, 2.43 × 0.96 × 0.40 m max. depth, with no trace of a coffin. Adult skeleton in a supine position with the right arm slightly bent and the hands over one femur. Skull facing to its left at W end of grave. Spearhead (1.1) is close to and above the left side of its skull; with a capsule-like ferrule (1.2) high in the grave fill, disturbed by roots or animal activity, above the right knee.

1.1 **Spearhead**, iron, with a broad leaf-shaped blade with a short split socket and traces of mineralised wood, 285 mm L, 5 mm wide (blade), Type C2. 1.2. **Ferrule**, copper-alloy, overlapping sheet fastened by a copper-alloy rivet, traces of mineralised wood, with a cross partition, 18 mm diameter with central perforation 3–4 mm diameter, 12 mm height.

GRAVE 76:4 (Figs 5, 15 and 26)

??Male (i.e. a few sexing characteristics suggest but do not determine the sex), 25–30 years, stature could not be calculated, (preservation category 2).

E–W grave, 2.80 × 0.90 at E end and 0.75 at W end × 0.68 m deep at the head end, with four-sided coffin stain with packing material at the head and foot ends defining the original height of the coffin, which was weighted with four chalk blocks above the head end and two above the north corner at the foot end. An adult in a supine position is indicated by the skull at the W end and the straight position of both the femurs and the tibiae. Enclosed by a penannular ring-ditch, 5.2 (N–S) × 5 m (E–W), with the causeway marked by a posthole, 0.35 m diameter (PH1), aligned with and beyond the east end of the grave. Spearhead (1) lies at the right side of the head, outside the coffin and at a higher level than the skeletal remains, sloping down; a nail shaft (4) located on the corner of the coffin at the right side of the head at a depth below the chalk of 40cm; a knife (2) located at the left side of the chest, point towards the shoulder; with an iron buckle (3) at the left side of the waist, with the loop towards the skeleton's left, implying the individual was left-handed.

1. **Spearhead**, iron, broad blade with angular shoulders and a long tapering socket almost as long as the blade, socket broken across, 660 mm long, 57 mm wide (blade), Type E3.
2. **Knife**, iron, curved back and curved cutting edge, probably horn on tang, 149 mm long, 16 mm wide (blade), Type 1.
3. **Buckle**, with iron oval loop and single tongue and copper-alloy rectangular belt plate wrapped round the loop with a

rectangular opening for the tongue, with five small rivets to attach the plate to the leather belt, and with traces of mineral-preserved textile on the loop and the underside of the loop and plate, 41 mm long (overall), loop 44 mm wide, tongue 20 mm long, plate 33 × 23 mm.
4. **Nail**, coffin nail fragment, iron, with a lozenge cross-section, 37 mm long, 9 mm × 10 mm. (section).

POSTHOLE 76:1 belongs to Ring-Ditch 76:4 and Grave 76:4 with artefact placed vertically in the centre of the posthole:

5. **Object**, iron, rectangular, 88 mm L. [not illustrated].

GRAVE 76:5 (Figs 14 and 26)

?Male, 60+, stature 1.61 m, (preservation category 5), arthropathies of vertebrae, dental abscessing and ante-mortem tooth loss, evidence of habitual activity in the arms and one area of non-specific infection.

E–W grave, 1.75 max. × 0.90 × c. 0.40 m with three sides visible of a four-sided coffin stain. Adult skeleton with the body twisted over onto its left side from the waist up. The skull is at the W end of the grave and faces to its left, with its lower right arm bent at right angles and its fingers over the knife at the waist below its left elbow, while its lower left arm is doubled up with its fingers clutching the nape of the neck. Its legs are slightly bent and turned slightly to the left side with its ankles and feet extending over the bottom end of the coffin. A knife (1) is at the left side of the waist, pointing towards the feet, under the right hand; and a triangular buckle (2) is at the centre of the waist, underneath the right forearm, the loop on the right side, otherwise lying horizontally.

1. **Knife**, iron, with a curved back and a straight cutting edge, probably a horn handle, point missing, 165 mm L, 13 mm wide, Type 4.
2. **Buckle and plate**, iron, with an oval loop, a large rounded shield-shaped tongue, a triangular U-shaped belt plate with three rivet holes and a rounded terminal, with probable traces of keying for inlaid ornament, and a great deal of mineralised leather and textile traces surviving, 113 mm long, loop 53 mm wide, plate 78 mm long, 46 mm wide.[58]

GRAVE 76:6 (Figs 15 and 27)

?Subadult. No skeleton lifted (preservation category 0).

E–W child-sized grave, 1.40 × 0.50 × 0.28 m (below the chalk surface) and no trace of a coffin, or of skeletal remains. A cast jewelled disc brooch (1) occupies a central position, which originally would have been the probable chest area with the pin pointing towards the head, textile attached to the pin implying that the brooch was fastened to the clothing and a piece of charcoal (2), which would originally have been to the left of the skeleton's pelvic area.

1. **Brooch** (Updown Brooch), silver, gilt upper surface, with one central large round cell, the domed shell setting in place, but lacking its *cabochon* stone (probably garnet) and surrounding this central cell three smaller round cells, one still with its shell setting but no *cabochon* stud and the other two empty, alternating with three wedge-shaped keystone cells, with only two of the keystone cells still containing their garnet settings, while the fields between the outer cells contains symmetrical triple line interlace designs in

Salin's Style II, the iron pin possibly a replacement fitting on what seems to be an old piece when buried, diameter 47mm across pin axis by 48 mm along axis at 90 degrees to pin axis.
2. **Textile fragments** [not illustrated].
3. **Charcoal lump** [not illustrated].

GRAVE 76:7 (Figs 16 and 27–30)
Male, 30–40 years, stature 1.73 m, (preservation category 4), arthropathies of vertebrae, ante-mortem tooth loss and epigenetic dental trait of incisor shovelling (see also graves 76:15 and 76:31).
E–W grave, 1.90 × 0.90 × 0.40 m, no trace of coffin. Adult skeleton laid on its right side, with both its legs gently flexed to the right, with its right arm straight and its left arm bent at the elbow across its waist with its hand originally above its right pelvis. The skull is at the west end of the grave and faces to its right. A knife (1) is lying horizontally across the waist, with the point towards the edge of the grave; an iron fragment from a bucket (3.12) above the left pelvis and the remainder of the two buckets (3.1–11) are positioned in the NE corner of the grave below and to the N of the original position of the feet.
1. **Knife**, iron, with a curved back and a straight cutting edge, probably a horn handle, 193 mm L, 17 mm W, Type 4.
2. **Pottery**, wheelthrown sherd, orange-red sandy fabric, probably Roman [not illustrated].
3.1–12 Two **buckets**: scattered remains of two iron-bound stave-built wooden buckets, the larger being parallel-sided and the smaller apparently having a larger base diameter than its mouth diameter: Bucket A: parallel-sided with two (or perhaps three) iron bands, the upper being 19 mm wide with a diameter of 22–23cm and the middle or bottom band 12 mm wide with a diameter of 23 cm, the overall height of the vessel probably being 20–22 cm (*i.e.* slightly less than its maximum diameter); Bucket B: sloping sided with two iron bands, the upper band with a diameter of 16–16.2 cm, together with a handle of 16 cm, and with a bottom band with a diameter of *c.* 21.4 cm, the overall height of the vessel probably being 17–19 cm.

GRAVE 76:8 (Fig. 16)
Female, 25–35 years, stature 1.63 m, (preservation category 5), arthropathies of vertebrae, dental caries and ante-mortem tooth loss and one inexplicable pathological feature, a 'whittled' hand phalanx.
E–W grave, 2.40 m at the top of the grave cut (but the head-end edge slopes inwards) × 0.75 max. at the foot end and 0.60 m min. at the head end × 0. 60 m max. at the foot end, with no trace of a coffin. Skeleton regarded as possibly female in 1976, supine with skull at W end of grave, with the right hand against the grave wall and with the right foot over the left, but with no associated surviving artefacts.

GRAVE 76:9 (Fig. 16)
Sub-adult, 7–11 years, (preservation category 2).
E–W grave, 1.88 × 0.60 × 0.35 m (below the chalk surface), which is much larger than it need be for the sub-adult buried here and with no trace of coffin. A sub-adults's supine skeleton occupies the central area of the grave with the legs gently flexed to the right and with the right arm bent at the elbow with the hand originally above the left upper arm, while the position of the teeth confirm that the skull was towards the W end of the grave, with no associated surviving artefacts.

GRAVE 76:10 [Grave 89:14] (Figs 16 and 27)
??Female, 25–35 years, stature could not be calculated, (preservation category 1: skull and legs only).
W–E grave, 2.27 × 1.00 max. and 0.84 min. × 0.60 m, three sides visible of a four-sided coffin, 0.55 m wide, but the coffin ends not well defined. Skeleton in a supine position with the skull at the W end, right arm placed across the pelvic girdle and the left arm straight. Possibly originally enclosed by a penannular ring-ditch, its causeway being marked by a posthole aligned with the causeway of the ring-ditch around Grave 76:4. Two beads (1 and 2) are located either side of the neck; a knife (3) was lying horizontally by the hand at the left side with its point to the waist; and an iron tool (4) immediately below the knife; with two chatelaine linked bars (5.1 and 2) at the left side, hanging from the hip; and a buckle (6) at the left side of the waist with the tongue upwards.
1. **Bead**, glass, long square-sectioned cylinder, brick-red (terracotta) opaque with yellow spots, 19 mm long, 5 × 5 mm square sectioned.
2. **Bead**, glass, disc-shaped, opaque white monochrome, 5 mm long, 7 mm diameter.
3. **Knife**, iron, with a curved back and a straight cutting edge, probably a horn handle, 131 mm long, 12 mm wide, Type 4.
4. **Tool**, iron, with blade and tang, probably a horn handle on the tang and traces of textile on the blade, 85 mm long.
5.1 **Chatelaine**, iron, pair of linked flattened bars with looped ends, with traces of mineralised textile impressions, 65 mm long, 4 mm wide. 5.2 Chatelaine, iron, section of **rod** with mineralised textile impressions, 34 mm long, 2 mm diameter.
6. **Buckle and plate**, iron, with oval loop, tongue, and rectangular doubled-round belt plate with a central long slot to take the tongue, 37 mm long, loop 20 mm wide, tongue 12 mm long, plate 26 mm long, 14 mm wide.
POSTHOLE: 28 × 28 × 24 cm deep, possibly the last remnants of a penannular ring-ditch feature enclosing Grave 76:10, with the posthole marking the entrance through the ring-ditch.

GRAVE 76:11 [Grave 89:2] (Figs 6, 16 and 31)
Male, 25–35 years, stature 1.71 m, (preservation category 4), arthropathies of vertebrae, dental caries and abscessing.
E–W grave, 2.60 × 0.65 × 0.60 m max. at foot end, set within a ring-ditch (76:11), with a four-sided coffin. Adult skeleton in a supine position with lower right arm bent placing the right hand across the pelvis, legs straight. The skull is at the W end of the grave and faces to its right. Enclosed by a penannular ring-ditch, 5.8 m (N–S) by 5.5 m (E–W), with a causeway aligned with the east

end of the grave marked by a posthole 0.35 by 0.30 m diameter and 0.13 m deep (PP1) and a second posthole 0.28 × 0.24 m diameter and 0.24 m deep (PH0) is located outside and to the west of the ring-ditch, though the latter need not be contemporary with Grave 76:11. A spearhead (1) is located inside the coffin, above the right side of the skull and lying flat on the grave floor; a knife (2) is at the left side of the waist, point towards the shoulder, just below the left elbow; the larger triangular buckle (3) is at the centre of the waist with its loop against the left edge of the lumber vertebra, its plate towards the left; and a smaller rectangular buckle (4) is on the left ilium; while a possible gaming-piece (6) is in the grave fill at the foot end; a potsherd is in the grave fill (5) and a further potsherd and flints are recovered from the fill of the penannular ring-ditch 76:11, which encloses this grave.

1. **Spearhead**, iron, leaf-shaped blade with ancient break just below the junction of the socket and a split socket with remains of mineralised wood, estimated 347 mm long, 38 mm wide (blade), Type D2.
2. **Knife**, iron, with angled back and straight cutting edge with blade tip missing and traces of what was probably a horn handle, 161 mm long, 23 mm wide, Type 5.
3. **Buckle and plate**, copper-alloy, with plain oval cast loop, shield-shaped tongue, the shield ornamented with an outer border of spaced miniature circlet punch-marks and within these spaced triangular punch-marks, a triangular cast belt plate with a border framed by the same spaced miniature circlet punch-marks enclosing the same spaced triangular punch-marks with one smaller domed rivet cover along each long side, one of which retains a nicked washer element and a third domed rivet head at the apex, and a matching plain sheet triangular back-plate, 75 mm long, loop 36 mm wide, shield tongue 26 mm long, plate 32 mm wide, rivet depth indicates a leather belt up to 2 mm thick.
4. **Buckle and plate**, copper-alloy, with plain oval loop, plain tongue wrapped around the loop bar and a simple sheet rectangular metal belt plate wrapped around the loop with a long slot to take the tongue fastened at the far end by three spaced rivets, 18 mm long, loop 16 mm wide, tongue 11 mm long, plate 12 mm long, 12 mm wide, rivet thickness indicates a leather belt up to 2 mm thick.
5. **Pottery**, wheelthrown sherd, thick red fabric, probably Roman from the grave fill [not illustrated].
6. Possible **gaming-piece** or pebble, stone disc with a plano-convex section, 24 mm diameter, 12 mm T.

RING-DITCH 76:11:-
7. Pottery, two wheelthrown sherds, red fabric, probably Roman and two worked flints from the ditch fill [not illustrated].

GRAVE 76:12 [Grave 89:17] (Figs 7, 17 and 32)
? Male, 25–35 years, stature could not be calculated, (preservation category 3), arthropathies of foot and dental enamel hyploplasia.
E–W grave, 2.46 max. × 0.85 max. × 0.48 m max. with the SW corner of a four-sided coffin having left a clear stain, with three large pieces of flint placed over the north edge of the coffin opposite the head and shoulders of the adult skeleton. This occupies a supine position with the right arm

straight and its hand on the thigh and its left arm semi-flexed with the hand over the right hip. The right tibia and foot has externally rotated and apparently the left foot is flattened probably due to animal disturbance. The skull is at the W end of the grave and facing to its left. Enclosed by a penannular ring-ditch estimated to be 6 m in diameter, with a causeway marked by a posthole 0.26 m diameter and 0.20 m deep, beyond and aligned with the east end of the grave. Buckle (1.1) is the right side of the waist, loop to the right, lying horizontally and the underplate (1.2) is over the middle of the waist; with a knife (2) immediately to its left (the north), lying obliquely across the left side of the waist with its tang over the spine and point towards the left elbow; and twin plates (1.3) from the belt set are on the lumbar vertebrae level with the buckle; while iron fragments probably representing shoe fittings (3 and 4) are present on the outer sides of the two ankles.

1.1 and 1.2. **Buckle and plate**, copper-alloy, cast heavy oval loop with parallel incised short lines radiating around the outer area, a heavy shield tongue with three ring-and-dot motifs either side of the tongue proper, attached to an elongated triangular belt plate with an angled nicked ornament in the outer border matched by the angled nicking around the bottom edge of the rivet caps part of the way down the long sides and the larger rivet cap with an empty central setting (probably for a garnet 3 mm diameter) and an inner border running within the two long sides with more spaced ring-and-dot motifs, the underside covered by a thin sheet metal plate again ornamented with the same spaced ring-and-dot motifs along the two long sides, the gap between the two plates implies the belt leather as around 3 mm thick, overall 65 mm L, loop 34 mm W, 21 mm deep, shield tongue 20 mm L, cast plate 49 mm L, 24 mm W, sheet metal back-plate 47 mm L, 18 mm W. 1.3. Twin belt **plates**, openwork rounded triangular-shaped fittings, copper alloy sheet: one pair sharing a semicircular form and matching semicircular openwork element with three copper-alloy rivets attaching the two sheets together, the upper plate decorated with seven spaced ring-and-dot motifs fitting a leather strap 2–3 mm thick, 16 mm L, 18 mm W; the other similar but more triangular in shape with just six spaced ring-and-dot motifs, 15 mm L, 17 mm W.
2. **Knife**, iron, with an angled back and a straight cutting edge, probably with a horn handle, and traces of leather on the blade, 180 mm L, 18 mm W, Type 5.
3. and 4. Two **fragments**, iron, possibly shoe or garter fittings, 9 mm L [not illustrated].

GRAVE 76:13 (Figs 17 and 32)
Male, 45+, stature could not be calculated, (preservation category 2), ante-mortem tooth loss.
E–W grave, 2.50 × 0.65 × 0.51 m deep, with three sides visible of a four-sided coffin, with cleaner chalk packing between the coffin and the grave cut. Adult skeleton placed in a supine position with its arms to the sides, its left knee under the right knee on the right side and with the skull at the W end. A spearhead (1) is at the top right (NW) corner of the grave, high in the fill; a knife (2) is point upwards under the right elbow; and a buckle with a triangular plate (3) at the left side of the waist, aslant with the tongue towards

the left elbow; with another copper-alloy object (4) over the left hip near the buckle and presumably associated with the waist belt; as well as an iron object possibly part of a spear ferrule (5) on the line of wood on the left side of the legs (the N side wall of the coffin); and some animal bone (identified as ox) by the feet in the left bottom corner of the grave as a food offering.

1. **Spearhead**, iron, with a leaf-shaped blade (tip missing) and a split socket with remains of mineralised wood, 223 mm L, 24 mm W (blade), Type C5.
2. **Knife**, iron, with curved back and curved cutting edge, probably with a horn handle, 182 mm L, 20 mm W, Type 1.
3. **Buckle and plate**, copper-alloy cast, with an oval loop decorated with sets of angled incised parallel lines and ring-and-dot motifs, a heavy cast shield tongue fitting also decorated with both incised lines and with ring-and-dot motifs, an elongated triangular belt plate with angled nicked lines along the outer edges and an inner frame containing a row of spaced ring-and-dot motifs parallel to the long sides and around the two plain rivet caps set part way down these long sides, with two additional rivets near the top corners of the plate and a relatively enormous almost spherical rivet head at the terminal of the plate, with no trace of the original bottom plate surviving, but with very well preserved textile on the back (see Appendix II), overall 96 mm L, loop 39 mm W, 13 mm deep, shield tongue 27 mm L, plate 78 mm L, 32 mm W.
4. **Strap fragment**, copper-alloy sheet, with an iron rivet at one end, 28mm L, 7.5 mm wide, 1 mm thick.
5. Curved **band**, iron, incomplete fitting, possibly from a spear ferrule or socket, with wood adhering on the interior, 17 mm by 14 mm.
6. **Animal bones**: ox shoulder [not illustrated].

GRAVE 76:14 [Grave 89:11] (Figs 17 and 33–4)
Adult, 25–45 years, sex and stature unknown (preservation category 2: cranial vault and limb fragments).
E–W grave, 2.55 L × 1.08 W × 0.65m deep (W end) and 0.80 m deep (E end) and with a four-sided coffin. Adult skeleton placed in a supine position, with the skull at the W end. Spearhead (1.1) is at the right side above the head with its point at a depth of 0.39 m and its socket at a depth of *c.* 0.35 m; with a copper-alloy ferrule (1.2) at the right side at the foot end on top of the coffin packing at a depth of 0.41 m; with a shield probably placed on the coffin lid consisting of a tall straight cone shield boss (2.1) at the right side of the legs inside the coffin with the boss hard against the side at a depth of 0.43 m at its knob, with its hand grip (2.2) together with three iron shield studs (2.3–2.5) either side of the boss; a copper-alloy rivet (3) located beside the right knee; with a textile fragment (13) nearby; an iron buckle (4) possibly associated with the shield immediately E of the shield boss at a depth of 0.58 m; and a further iron mount (5) close to one of the shield studs at a depth of 0.63 m; a buckle with a triangular plate (6) is located at the right side of the waist with its loop to the right; with a smaller iron buckle (7) adjacent to it; together with a copper-alloy plate (8); a small copper-alloy buckle (9); an iron tool (10); and two knives (11 and

12); a wood fragment (14) is located between the lower legs; while in the SE corner of the coffin is the remains of a wooden turned vessel (15) marked by wood fragments and copper-alloy fittings (15.1) including three copper-alloy repair clips (15.2–4); finally an iron nail (16) in the SE corner of the coffin may be a coffin fitting.

1.1 **Spearhead**, iron, leaf-shaped blade and longish socket apparently without cleft, 344 mm L, 48 mm W, atypical version of Type C3. 1.2. Spear **ferrule**, copper-alloy sheet, overlapping band forming a ring fastened by two copper-alloy rivets, with mineralised wood on the inner face, 18 mm diameter, 16 mm height.
2.1. **Shield boss**, iron, tall straight cone with 4 disc-headed rivets set around rim flange, a separately inserted disc on rod at the apex, 138 mm diameter, 172 mm height, outer rim flange 8 mm W, disc-headed flange rivets 6 mm diameter, waist 22 mm high, disc at apex 17 mm × 18 mm diameter. 2.2. **Shield handle**, iron, simple strap type, Type Ia.1, with concave sides 133 mm L, 24 mm W and a large disc-headed rivet knocked over at each end, indicating a shield board 5–6 mm thick. 2.3–5. Three shield disc-headed **rivets**, iron, respectively 20 mm diameter and shank 3 mm deep (broken); 17 mm diameter and shank 10 mm deep; 18 × 22 mm diameter and shank 11 mm deep; 18 mm diameter and shank 12 mm deep.
3. Dome-headed **rivet**, copper-alloy, 27 mm L, head 6 mm diameter.
4. **Buckle**, iron, oval loop and plain tongue, with mineralised textile on the loop, loop 22 mm W, 16 mm deep, tongue 13 mm L.
5. **Strip**, iron, sub-rectangular and incomplete with disc-headed rivet at one end, 24 mm L, 11 mm W, rivet 5 mm deep.
6. **Buckle and plate**, copper-alloy, with an oval cast loop flattened on the base and angled to a ridge with a narrow bar section to attach the shield tongue and the front triangular belt plate wrap round, with three dome-headed rivets with milled borders, the rivet dome at the apex being much larger than the other two, the area between having cast ornament depicting two boar's heads in Salin's Style II linked by a U-shaped common neck and with billets filling the remaining area, the outer two in the corners of the narrow edge imitating the position of square *cloisonné* garnet plates, with a plain sheet-metal base plate attached by the rivets, implying a leather belt 2 mm thick; with textile remains on the back, overall 56 mm L, loop 28 mm W, shield tongue 23 mm L, plate 23 mm W.
7. **Buckle and belt plate**, iron, rectangular plate, with textile remains on the back, 30 mm L [not illustrated].
8. Pair of **belt plates**, copper-alloy, triangular form with a central triangular opening on each plate and three disc-headed rivets connecting the two plates at each corner, implying belt leather 2 mm thick, 16 mm L, 15mm W.
9. **Buckle and plate**, copper-alloy, cast oval loop with rounded section decorated with three angled incised lines either side of the point of the tongue, a plain tongue and a sheet-metal rectangular wrap-around belt plate decorated with transverse incised lines (3 and 2) either side of the two disc-headed rivets which imply a leather belt 1.5 mm thick, 15 mm L, loop 15 mm W, tongue 9 mm L, plate 8 mm L, 9.5 mm W.
10. Rounded decorative **handle**, wood, which had possessed a copper-alloy band around the junction with iron, 37 mm L.
11. **Knife**, iron, curved back and straight cutting edge, probably

with a horn handle, *c.* 170 mm L, 17 mm W, Type 4.

12. **Blade** or bar, iron, in two pieces, 26 mm and 60 mm L.

13. **Textile fragment**.

14. **Wood fragment** [not illustrated].

15.1. **Strip**, copper-alloy, with a rivet at each end, at least 39 mm L, 4.5 mm W. 15.2–3. Two rim **mounts**, copper alloy, wrapped round and fastened by two rivets that imply a thickness of 3 mm for the associated wooden turned vessel, each with a zigzag on the top edge, respectively 8 mm L and 15 mm W, 8 mm L and 12 mm W. 15.4. Strip repair **mount**, copper-alloy clip strip wrapped round, 13 mm W around a 4 mm thick object: all four items listed under 15 are probably repair fittings from a lathe-turned wooden vessel.

16. **Nail**, iron, 49 mm L.

GRAVE 76:15 [Grave 89.7] (Figs 8, 18 and 35)
Sub-adult, 7½–12½ years, (preservation category 4), dental epigenetic trait of incisor shovelling (see also graves 76: 7 and 76: 31) and stress indicator of cribra orbitalia.

E–W grave, 2.27 max. × 0.90 max. width × 0.60 m, deep and with a four-sided coffin, 1.78 L × 0.52m W. Sub-adult placed in a supine position, with skull at west end of the grave. Enclosed by a penannular ring-ditch, 5.8 m (N–S) by 5.4 m (E–W), with a causeway 1.20 m W, aligned with the east end of the grave. This ring-ditch is cut by and must therefore predate Ring-ditch 76:16. Necklace of 20 items (glass beads, linked wire rings and a metal pendant: 1.1–20); an iron tool (2); and a knife (3) at the left side of the waist; with the remains of an iron chatelaine (4) immediately below from the left side of the waist to the hip; and a pair of lace tags (5 and 6) at the front of each foot.

1.1–20 **Necklet** made of linked monochrome glass beads and linked silver or copper-alloy wire rings and a copper-alloy bucket pendant:-1.1. **Bead**, glass, disc-shaped blue semi-translucent, petrol blue or turquoise monochrome, 8 mm diameter, 5 mm high. 1.2 **Wire ring**, silver, 17 × 15 mm diameter, with sliding knot and wire section 1 mm thick. 1.3 **Bead**, glass, double-segmented annular red opaque, monochrome, 5 mm diameter, 8 mm high. 1.4 **Bead**, glass, irregular-shaped pale green translucent, monochrome on a copper-alloy wire ring, bead, 9 mm diameter, 3 mm high, and ring 14 mm by 11 mm diameter. 1.5. **Bead**, glass, disc-shaped grass green opaque, monochrome, 8 mm diameter, 5 mm high. 1.6. **Wire ring**, silver, knotted section missing, 14 mm diameter, with wire section 1 mm thick. 1.7. **Bead**, glass, disc-shaped red opaque, monochrome, 7 mm diameter, 5 mm high. 1.8. **Bead**, glass, disc-shaped green opaque, monochrome, 7 mm diameter, 5 mm high. 1.9. **Bead**, glass, disc-shaped green opaque, monochrome, 7 mm diameter, 5 mm high. 1.10. **Bucket pendant**, copper-alloy, short cylinder sheet with a knotted wire loop fastened through it to permit suspension as a bucket pendant, cylinder 7 mm diameter, and wire loop 14 mm high overall. 1.11. **Bead**, glass, disc-shaped red opaque, monochrome, 7 mm diameter, 5 mm high. 1.12. **Wire ring**, silver, knotted, part missing, 16 mm diameter, wire section 1 mm thick. 1.13. **Wire ring**, silver, knotted 14 mm diameter, wire section 1 mm thick. 1.14. **Wire ring**, silver or copper alloy, knotted in three incomplete sections, 14 mm diameter, wire section 1 mm thick. 1.15. **Bead**, glass, disc-shaped green opaque, monochrome, 7 mm diameter, 5 mm high. 1.16. **Bead**, glass, disc-shaped red opaque, monochrome, 8 mm diameter, 5.5 mm high. 1.17. **Bead**, glass, disc-shaped light green opaque, monochrome, 7 mm diameter, 5 mm high. 1.18. **Bead**, glass, irregular mini-globular white opaque, monochrome, 6 mm diameter, 4 mm high. 1.19. **Bead**, glass, globular yellow opaque, monochrome, 5 mm diameter, 4 mm high. 1.20. **Bead**, glass, disc-shaped, petrol blue (turquoise) semi-translucent, monochrome, 8 mm diameter, 4 mm high.

2. **Tool**, iron, with rectangular section, broken off at the end and a round-sectioned tang for a handle, 67.5 mm L and 12 mm W (main section) with a detached tang.

3. **Knife**, iron, with a curved back and a curved cutting edge and probably with a horn handle, 125 mm L, 12 mm W, Type 1.

4. **Chatelaine**, iron made up of sections of four linked iron bars with mineralised textile adhering: 4.1. chatelaine section of a round-sectioned **bar** with a loop at either end, 62 mm L, 4 mm diameter, connected to, 4.2. chatelaine section of an oval-sectioned **bar** with a loop at either end, 77 mm L and 7 mm × 4 mm diameter, connected to 4.3. chatelaine section of a round-sectioned **bar**, incomplete with a loop connected to 4.2 above, 34 mm L, 4 mm diameter; 4.4. chatelaine section of a round-sectioned **bar** with a loop at either end, one loop being damaged, 36 mm L, 5 mm diameter, connected to 4.5. chatelaine section of a round-sectioned **bar** with a loop at one end, surviving in two sections, 14 mm and 34 mm, 4 mm diameter.

5. **Lace tag**, copper-alloy sheet, fixed by a single copper-alloy rivet near the top of a split socket, 20 mm L, rivet 3 mm L.

6. **Lace tag**, copper-alloy sheet, fixed by a single copper-alloy rivet near the top of a split socket, 21 mm L, rivet 2.5 mm L.

RING-DITCH 76:15:

7. **Pottery**, thin body sherd, dark brown sandy fabric in layer a [not illustrated].

GRAVE 76:16 [Grave 89:8] (Figs 9, 18 and 36)
Adult, sex, age and stature unknown (preservation category 2), tibial squatting facets.

E–W grave, 2.40 × 1.10 × 0.85 m deep and with three sides visible of a four-sided coffin, 1.90 × 0.45 m W. Adult placed in a supine position revealed by leg and foot bones in the E half of the grave with the upper body only present as a trace in a few places. Enclosed by a penannular ring-ditch, 6.8 m (N–S) by 7.1 m (E–W), with a causeway, 0. 70 m wide, aligned with the east end of the grave. This ring-ditch cuts and thus postdates Ring-ditch 76:15 and Grave 76:15. A buckle (1) on the right side of the waist; a knife (2) beside the left waist; and a small buckle (3) on the left side; with a pair of copper alloy staples (4) above the right ankle and a further pair of staples (5) below the right foot. A rectangular dark soil stain was noted in the NE corner of the grave outside the coffined area.

1. **Buckle and plate**, iron, with yellow-coloured copper-alloy (or possibly gold) twisted wire inlaid ornament for both the oval loop and rectangular top belt plate riveted at each corner, with copper-alloy geometric stepped pattern around the outer section of the loop and the rectangular plate design

enclosed within a border with a simple row of steps and a rough quarter-circle around each rivet head, with the main area subdivided into three zones with that closest to the tongue and loop having two opposing and inward-pointing small triangles each within a stepped design and with a semi-circle separating the two with its flat edge against the border at the loop and tongue end, a middle band with two simple stepped designs framing a more complex one placed sideways on at the centre and the third panel with four inward-pointing triangles, separated linked stepped designs on either side, 50 mm L, loop 27 mm W, tongue 12 mm L, plate 22mm W probably; the two plates originally had a 2 mm gap implying a leather belt of that thickness.[59]
2. **Knife**, iron, with a curved back and a straight cutting edge, probably with a horn handle, and traces of a probable leather sheath around the central section of the blade, *c.* 140 mm L, 25 mm W, Type 4.
3. **Buckle**, copper-alloy loop, oval, simple form with iron tongue with textile traces on it, 14 mm W, tongue 9 mm L.
4.1. **Staple**, copper-alloy, 15 mm L, 2 mm W, originally fixed through an object 13 × 4 mm. 4.2. **Staple**, copper alloy, incomplete, 10 mm L, 2 mm W.
5.1. **Staple**, copper-alloy, which appears to have been shaped around a step-sectioned object, 10 mm L, 3 mm high, 2 mm W. 5.2. **Staple**, copper-alloy, matching 5.1, 8.5 mm L, 3.5 mm high, 1.5 mm W.
DITCH 76:16 (Layer 6)
6. **Pottery**, four organic-tempered sherds from a handmade vessel [not illustrated].

GRAVE 76:17 [*Grave 89:6*] (Figs 10, 18 and 36)
?Sub-adult. No parts of skeleton could be lifted (preservation category 0).
E–W grave, 2.30 × 0.40 × 0.90 m deep and with a well-defined four-sided coffin stain, 1.80 × 0.50 m W. Body placed in a supine position indicated by a few surviving bones with the skull towards the W end of the grave. Enclosed by a penannular ring-ditch, 4.8 m (N–S) by 5 m (E–W), with its causeway 0.74 m W to the east. A spearhead (1) within the coffin by the right side of the skull nucleus; a knife (2) near the left side of the waist area; and above this a buckle (3); while pot sherds (4) were noted in the grave fill between the foot end of the coffin and the grave cut edge.
1. **Spearhead**, iron, probably Type B1, miniature with short, straight-sided damaged blade and split socket with mineralised wood, 133 mm L, 14 mm W at socket mouth.
2. **Knife**, iron, with angled back and straight cutting edge, probably with a horn handle, 140 mm L, 13 mm W, Type 5.
3. **Buckle plate**, iron, rectangular, damaged, with organic impressions on one side, 32 mm L, 20 mm W.
4. **Pottery**, sherds consisting of one rim section in three pieces, black ware with red-brown exterior surfaces, gritty textured, probably Iron Age [not illustrated].

GRAVE 76:18 [*Grave 89:3*] (Figs 18 and 36)
Sub-adult or young adult, age range c. *6–c. 20 years. One tooth (preservation category 1).*
E–W grave, 2.25 × *c.* 0.90 × 0.70 m max. depth at W end

and with a four-sided coffin stain. No trace of skeleton with the exception of one molar tooth. Grave appeared to have been robbed in antiquity. A spear socket or ferrule (1) is located within the coffined area on the south side of the grave; a buckle (2) at the centre of the grave with its loop pointing SE; a copper-alloy fragment (3) from the grave fill just outside the south side wall of the coffin; and an iron tang from a knife or tool (4) is on the left side of the body area within the coffin, but near its north side wall.
1. **Spear socket** or ferrule from a spear, iron, with mineralised wood, 53 mm L, socket diameter 24 mm by 21 mm.
2. **Buckle and plate**, copper-alloy, small cast oval loop, plain tongue and rectangular sheet belt plate turned back on itself and fastened by two rivets, loop 13 mm W, tongue 9 mm L, plate 12 mm L by 8 mm W.
3. **Sheet fragment**, copper-alloy, curved form, 7 mm by 5 mm.
4. **Knife** tang, iron, probably with a horn handle, 33 mm L, 18 mm W.

GRAVE 76:19 (Figs 19 and 37)
Late adolescence to young adult, sex and stature unknown, (preservation category 3).
E–W grave, 2.32 × 0.80 × 0.65 m maximum depth at centre of grave and with three visible sides of a four-sided coffin, 1.89 m L. Possible adult placed in a supine position with the lower right arm bent across the body and the skull at the west end of the grave. A spearhead (1) high in the fill outside the coffin at the top left corner of the grave; a knife (2) with its point downwards towards the left hip; possibly from the same sheath as the seax (3) at the left side underlying the knife with its point towards the right shoulder; and an iron nail fragment (4) on the left side to N of the seax.
1. **Spearhead**, iron, with leaf-shaped blade and split socket with mineralised wood, 244 mm L, 25 mm W, Type C2.
2. **Knife**, iron, angled back and straight cutting edge probably with a horn handle, 184 mm L, 15 mm W, Type 5.
3. **Seax**, iron, curved back and curved blade, probably with a horn handle, point of blade missing, 349 mm L, 31 mm W, Anglo-Saxon knife-form Type 1 equivalent of a Frankish small seax; binding, iron, flattened at either end with mineralised textile traces, 117 mm L, max. 9 mm W.
4. **Nail**, iron, with disc-head 14 mm diameter, damaged shank 15 mm L.

GRAVE 76:20 (Figs 19 and 38)
Sub-adult, 3 years 9 months – 6 years 3 months, (preservation category 1: skull and legs only).
E–W grave, 1.82 × 0.70 × 0.61 m maximum depth at centre and E end and with no trace of a coffin. Sub-adult with a crushed skull at the west end and only fragments of the left leg surviving elsewhere. It seems probable that it was placed on its side with one leg slightly flexed. The spearhead (1.1) is at the left side of the skull; with a copper-alloy fitting possibly for a wooden staff or baton (1.2) immediately below the spearhead and aligned with it; a knife (2) is on the left side of the pelvis; with another knife (3) below it; while a buckle (4) lies across the stomach; and there is an iron steel (5) close to and below the two knives.

1.1. **Spearhead**, iron, probably Type B1, small with a midrib from which any blade wings have corroded away, with part of the socket missing and a split socket containing mineralised wood and the shaft below the blade are present, 99 mm L, socket 12 mm W. 1.2. Cusp-shaped **cap end**, copper-alloy sheet with seven split sections each with a rivet originally (2 rivets still in place) and a further rivet hole present in the centre of the cap, from a wooden staff, stick, baton (see suggested reconstruction), but unlikely to represent the bottom end of the associated spear shaft as more than double the spear socket opening at 27 mm diameter.

2. **Knife**, iron, curved back and straight cutting edge, probably with a horn handle, 134 mm L, 13.5 mm W, Type 4.

3. **Knife**, iron, angled back and straight cutting edge, probably with a horn handle, 119 mm L, 13 mm W, Type 5.

4. **Buckle and plate**, iron, with D-shaped loop, simple tongue and doubled round rectangular belt plate fastened by a pair of iron rivets near the terminal, with traces of mineralised textile on the loop, loop 18 mm W, plate 15 mm L, 12 mm W, 23 mm overall length.

5. **Steel**, iron, flat sectioned with tang, 103 mm L, 12 mm W.

6. Organic **fragment**, damaged each end, 23 mm L, 16 mm W [not illustrated].

7. **Pottery**, base-angle sherd, grey ware, soapy sandy fabric, probably late Iron Age (Belgic) from the grave fill [not illustrated].

GRAVE 76:21 [*Grave 89:4*] (Figs 11, 20 and 38–9)

Adult, 25–30 years, sex and stature unknown, (preservation category 2: skull and arm fragments).

E–W grave, 2.33 max. × 0.86 max. × 0.70 m max. with just one edge of a coffin stain (the north side wall) visible. Individual identified as immature in 1976, with skull seeming to face left (N) at W end of the grave, but all other bones of the skeleton missing. Enclosed by a penannular ring-ditch, 4.9 m (N–S) × 4.6 m (E–W), with its causeway aligned with the grave on its east side. A knife (1); a copper-alloy ring or bracelet (2); and a buckle (3) were located together near the probable left waist; with two copper-alloy clips (4 and 5); and an iron disc (6) nearer the middle of the waist area; together with a chatelaine (7.1–14) below these; while near the foot end of the grave are iron fittings for a wooden box or casket (8.1 and 2).

1. **Knife**, iron, angled back and straight cutting edge, probably with a horn handle, 127 mm L, 14 mm W, Type 5.

2. **Bracelet**, copper-alloy wire, knotted with a double turn and a single turn, 66 mm × 60 mm diameter.

3. **Buckle**, iron, with oval loop, simple tongue and doubled round copper-alloy rectangular belt plate fastened by an iron rivet, with traces of mineralised textile on the loop and upper plate near the loop, loop 26 mm W, tongue 14 mm L, plate 20 mm L, 18 mm W.

4. Pair of **plates**, copper-alloy, probably belt counter-plates, 23 mm L, 17 mm W.

5. **Stud**, copper-alloy, 21 mm diameter, 12 mm thick.

6. Disc-shaped **fragment**, iron, with mineralised textile impressions on both sides, 16 mm diameter.

7. **Chatelaine**, iron, consisting of: 7.1. **bar** with hooked terminals and incomplete ring attached at one end; 7.2.

ring, round-sectioned attached by rust to 7.3. **bar** with hooked terminals and 7.4. **bar** with terminals missing; 7.5. two **bars** with hooked terminals attached to the hook of the bar (7.6) and the other pair of hooks around ring (7.2); 7.6. **bar** with two hooked terminals; 7.7. **bar** with hooked terminals; 7.8. **ring** with three bars (7.9, 7.10, 7.11) each with hooked terminals attached; 7.9. **bar** with hooked terminal; 7.10. bar with hooked terminal; 7.11. **bar** with hooked terminal; 7.12. an iron **key** with anchor-like terminals (one missing); 7.13. a short **bar** with hooked twisted terminals; 7.14. another incomplete **ring**.

8. Iron fittings from a wooden **box** or casket: 8.1. **lock** mechanism, iron, 112 mm L, 22 mm W; 8.2. **handle** of twisted iron with hooked ends through iron mounts, implying wood 10 mm thick, handle 82 mm W, 42–45 mm deep.

9. Bar **fragments**, iron, one grooved bar, 22 mm L; second fragment, iron, grooved bar, 34 mm L.

GRAVE 76:22 (Figs 19 and 40)

No skeleton (preservation condition 0).

E–W grave, 1.10 × 0.41 × 0.22 m and with no trace of a coffin. Grave cut appropriate to a child, but with no surviving skeletal remains. Two beads (1 and 2) are in the probable neck and shoulder area and two iron hasps, two angled iron mounts and two split-pins (3.1–5), interpreted initially as fittings for a cart or a wooden bed. They are more probably fittings for a wooden box, placed close to the northern edge of the grave cut, though it is more usual to place a box at the foot end of a grave.

1. **Bead**, glass, pale green, small opaque cylinder-shaped with tube-shaped perforation, 8 mm diameter, 6 mm high.

2. **Bead**, glass, pale brown opaque annular, 6 mm diameter, 4.5 mm high.

3. Iron fittings from a wooden **box** or casket: 3.1. **hasp**, iron, with two flattened bars linked by swivel joints, with each bar originally fastened to wood by two large disc-headed rivets with no complete rivets, 164 mm L, 23 and 24 mm W, longest rivet depth 18 mm. 3.2. Two angled **mounts**, iron, with traces of mineralised wood on interior, fastened by two rivets, 34 mm and 35 mm × 19 mm L, 13 mm W. 3.3. **Split pin**, iron, round-sectioned, 32 mm L, fastened through 16 mm of wood. 3.4. **Split pin**, iron, round-sectioned, 40 mm L. 3.5. **Hasp**, iron, with two flattened bars linked by swivel joints, as 3.1 above, with each bar originally fastened to wood by two large disc-headed rivets, 161 mm L, 25 mm W, with two rivets bent at right angles indicating thickness of the wood was 16–17 mm.

GRAVE 76:23 (Figs 19 and 40)

? Male, age and stature unknown, (preservation category 2), ante-mortem tooth loss.

E–W grave, 2.06 × 0.73 × 0.38 m at W end and 0.50 m deep at E end, with a four-sided coffin stain and a stone placed above the SW corner of the coffin. Adult skeleton placed in a supine position with hands in the lap, the legs parallel to the left side of the grave and the skull at W end and tilted slightly on the right (S) side. A knife (1) is within the left elbow with its tang facing up, its point down and the blade facing the body.

1. **Knife**, iron, curved back and curved cutting edge, blade tip

missing and also the end of the tang with probable horn handle, more than 120 mm L, 14 mm W, Type 1.

2. **Pottery**, grey ware sherd lacking any distinctive features, 280 mm L, from the topsoil over the grave [not illustrated].

GRAVE 76:24 (Figs 20 and 40)

Late adolescence to young adult, sex and stature unknown, (preservation category 1: legs).

E–W grave, 2.40 × 0.84 max. × 0.54 m and with a four-sided coffin stain. A supine position for the skeleton is indicated by the few bones surviving, including the skull at the west end of the grave. A knife (1) is to the left of the waist area with its blade facing the corpse and its point towards the head end of the grave; and a buckle (2) is lying diagonally on the right side of the waist with the loop facing downwards towards the outer side of the corpse.

1. **Knife**, iron, parts of blade missing, but curved back and cutting edge worn concave, probably with a horn handle, more than 100 mm L, 17 mm W, Type 4.

2. **Buckle** and **plates**, iron, with an oval loop, tongue and triangular U-shaped pair of belt plates, whose three rivets have copper-alloy domed heads with crimped borders, the largest domed cap occurring at the terminal, with a groove running parallel to the edge to take wire inlay and mineralised textile on the under plate, overall length estimated as originally 110 mm, but now 70–75 mm, loop *c.* 54 mm W, tongue 27 mm L, plate 60 mm long, 37 mm W.[60]

3. **Pottery**, grey ware sherd (possibly of the same fabric as two other grey ware sherds) in the grave fill [not illustrated].

GRAVE 76:25 (Figs 22 and 41)

?? Female (i.e. a few sexing characteristics suggest but do not determine the sex), 45+ years, stature could not be calculated, (preservation category 2), and dental epigenetic trait of a mis-shapen molar.

E–W grave, 2.66 × 0.80 m W at the centre, 0.60 m deep at the E end and 0.64 m deep at the W end, with a four-sided coffin stain representing wood 80–90 mm thick. Adult skeleton placed in a supine position with its skull at the west end of the grave, but originally possibly lying on its left side, with both legs complete and most of the feet. Chatelaine elements (1.1–3) are located to the SE of the head area; two knives (2 and 3) over the left ribs with the tang pointing to the head and the blade tip towards the feet with the blade edge facing south; an iron ring (4) over the left upper waist; an iron tool (5) is rusted together with another knife (6) set diagonally over the ring (4); and finally iron fragments (7) are indicated by purple stains on the left heel and other foot bones.

1.1–3. **Chatelaine**, iron, three fragments, (2) and (3) being round-sectioned and (1) flattened on one side, with mineralised textile impressions.

2. **Knife**, iron, part of the blade and tang, type uncertain, 65 mm L, 16 mm W.

3. **Knife**, iron, part of the blade and separate part of tang, type uncertain, 20 mm and 33 mm L, 14 mm maximum width.

4. **Ring**, iron, round-sectioned with traces of mineralised textile, 72 mm × 73 mm diameter, ring section 8 × 6 mm.

5. **Tool**, iron, flattened bar of a steel, with damaged tang at one

end and rounded at the other end, 127 mm L, 18mm W.

6. **Knife**, iron, angled back and straight cutting edge with probable horn handle, 97 mm long, 16 mm W, Type 5.

7. **Fragments**, iron.

8. **Pottery**, rim sherd, dark grey fabric, white grit specks (possibly crushed shell) in the fabric, with one finger tip impression, early-mid Iron Age, found in the topsoil over the grave fill [not illustrated].

GRAVE 76:26 [*Grave 89:53*] (Figs 12, 21 and 41–2)

Adult, 17–25 years, sex and stature unknown, (preservation category 1: cranial vault fragments), possible parafunctional tooth wear (thread pulled up and down a tooth).

E–W grave, 2.60 × 1.41 × 0.60 m deep at the sides, 0.66 m deep at the centre and 0.72 m deep at the W end, with a four-sided coffin stain. Part of the skull and some teeth survived at the west end of a presumably supine burial. There were carbon traces in two areas towards the east end. Grave enclosed by a penannular ring-ditch, 5.6 m (N–S) × 4.9 m (E–W), with its causeway 1.60 m W aligned with the grave and to its east. Necklace consisting of four green glass beads (1.1–4) and two amethyst beads (1.5 and 6) and a gold pseudo-coin pendant (1.7) in the probable area of the neck; with an iron pin (2) found between the bracteate and the buckle below it; a buckle (3) in the stomach area near the centre of the waist; and below this again a possible strap tag (4); a knife (5) found amongst the chatelaine elements; a pair of iron shears (6) found at right angles to the knife; and a chatelaine complex (7.1–12).

1. **Necklet** consisting of six beads and a pseudo-coin pendant: 1.1. **Bead**, glass, annular light green opaque, 8 mm diameter, 5 mm high. 1.2. **Bead**, glass, annular light green opaque 7 mm diameter, 5 mm high. 1.3. **Bead**, glass, annular darker green opaque, 7 mm diameter, 5 mm high. 1.4. **Bead**, annular, lighter green and yellowish opaque, 6 mm diameter, 4 mm high. 1.5. **Droplet bead**, amethyst, damaged at upper end with a small slice diagonally broken off, 16 mm L, 9 mm maximum width. 1.6. **Droplet bead**, amethyst, with a tiny piece broken off at the tip of the narrow end, 14 mm L, 7 mm maximum width. 1.7. Pseudo-coin **pendant**, thin gold sheet, with an attached gold loop with five parallel corrugations lengthwise and a peaked terminal on the reverse, copied by impression on a Roman coin showing a helmeted male bust right, representing Emperor Constantine I, with the inscription IMP CONSTA[N]TINVS MAX AVG, 21 mm diameter, 1.186 g weight (see Appendix IV).

2. **Pin**, iron, round-sectioned, part of a pin or part of the chatelaine, 18 mm L, 1.5 mm diameter.

3. **Buckle**, copper-alloy, Trebizond type,[61] a damaged East Roman (Byzantine) cast buckle lyre-form plate whose cast-in-one loop section has been removed and fastened by three rivets to a looped-over sheet plate around a cast elongated oval loop with a flat base and a rounded upper part decorated with six sets of triple incised lines with a narrow section around which the plate is wrapped with a perforation to take a cast tongue similarly ornamented with four tightly spaced incised lines on its upper section, representing an insular repair to an imported plate or originally complete buckle; the plate was originally fastened to the leather belt

with five dome-headed rivets, whose heads are still in place and had formerly had a glass or stone teardrop setting near its terminal; overall 50 mm L, cast plate 40 mm L, 19 mm W, loop 25 mm W, tongue 9 mm long.

4. **Buckle plate**, iron, triangular-shaped doubled over plate, originally fastened by at least five rivets with a rectangular area marking an attached feature now missing, and no surviving trace of the loop and tongue, together with mineralised textile impressions on the front plate, 49 mm L, 23 mm W.

5. **Knife**, iron, angled back and straight cutting edge, probably with a horn handle on its damaged tang, more than 98 mm L, 15 mm W, Type 5.

6. Pair of **shears**, iron, with part of the handle sections missing and areas of mineralised leather impressions on the blades in particular, originally 161 mm L, 32 mm W.

7. **Chatelaine**, iron, consisting of: 7.1. a **bar** and a looped terminal; 7.2. a **ring**; 7.3. a **bar**; 7.4. another **bar**, linked by a ring to; 7.5. a doubled **plate**; 7.6. another **bar**; 7.7. a further **bar** plus additional **buckle** and bar element with interlaced design on organic material; 7.8. a set of three **keys** on a ring linked to; 7.9. another **bar** linked to 7.10., triple **bars** linked by 7.11., another **ring** to two bars and 7.12., a further **bar** together with 7.13., an additional iron **rod** with a looped end grasping a narrower broken piece of iron.

8. **Pottery**, thick body sherd, red surface and black interior fabric with white grits, probably Iron Age, from the upper grave fill [not illustrated].

9. **Pottery**, two sherds, conjoining from the shoulder of a vessel with black fabric, probably Anglo-Saxon from the ring-ditch fill [not illustrated].

GRAVE 76:27 [*Grave 89:54*] (Figs 11, 19 and 43)
Sub-adult, 4–8 years, (preservation category 1: two fragments and teeth).
E–W grave, 170 × 0.67 × *c.* 0.46 m average depth and with a four-sided coffin stain, 1.47 m L, 0.40 m W. Sub-adult placed in a supine position indicated by the few surviving bones, notably part of the left humerus and femur, one rib fragment and sixteen teeth at the west end of grave. Grave enclosed by a penannular ring-ditch, 4.3 m (N–S) by 5 m (E–W), with its causeway 0.65 m W, aligned with the grave to the east. Iron objects (1) on the chest overlain by a rib with a layering of wood and textile; a knife (2) at the centre of the waist with the tang upwards; and two other knives or tools (3 and 4) are found together at the left hip with their tangs upwards; and with a buckle (5) overlying them.

1. **Tweezers** or **chatelaine**, iron, flat bar with looped end by which another flat bar is attached, with traces of mineralised organic material probably textile, 67 mm and 53 mm L, 20 mm and 8 mm W, 5 mm and 3 mm thick.

2. **Knife**, iron, curved back and straight cutting edge, probably with a horn handle on damaged tang, more than 95 mm L, 15 mm W, Type 4.

3. **Knife**, iron, angled back and straight cutting edge, probably with a horn handle on tang and leather on the blade, more than 122 mm L, 15 mm W, Type 5.

4. **Tool**, iron, flat bar with tang at one end and a damaged tool end with leather on the blade, 92 mm L, 10 mm W; possibly in a common sheath with knife (3) above.

5. **Buckle** and **plate**, iron, with D-shaped loop, simple tongue and doubled round rectangular belt plate fastened at the far end by two iron rivets, with traces of mineralised textile on the loop and upper plate near the loop, loop 29 mm W, tongue 13 mm L, plate 28 mm L, 22 mm W, 44 mm overall length.

GRAVE 76:28 (Figs 22 and 43)
Adult, 25–30 years, sex and stature unknown, (preservation category 1).
E–W grave, 2.30 m long at the top of the chalk cut, less than 1.02 m W, *c.* 0.65 m deep, with traces of a coffin *c.* 1.85 m L, *c.* 0.50 m W. Corpse placed in a supine position with the skull at the west end of the grave, but the only well-preserved bones were the left femur, patella and tibia together with one vertebra. A belt complex from the right to the left side of the waist with plates (1.1) to the right of a buckle (1.2), which is on the right side of the waist with the loop facing right; and a strap end (1.3) under the left forearm; a knife (2) at the left hip lying aslant with the tang outward; a copper-alloy fitting (3) at the left side on the femur towards the head; and a possible nail (4) under the left knee

1.1. **Belt plates**, copper-alloy, from a belt set, a pair of plain narrow rectangular sheets with three pairs of rivet holes and three rivets still in place on one side, 35.5 mm and 36.5 mm L, 9 mm and 10 mm W, while the gap for the rivets between each plate implies belt leather 2 mm thick. 1.2. **Buckle** and triangular **plate**, copper-alloy, set with two garnets and with three circular shell settings, from a belt set: the loop is cast in an oval form with a flat base and a rounded upper section and narrows to a bar to provide an attachment point for the triangular belt plates; the shield-shaped cast tongue has its base ornamented with fourteen spaced ring-and-dot punch-marks, but is otherwise plain; the front cast triangular plate has a rectangular *cloisonné* garnet at each corner of the narrow edge and within these are two stylised depictions of animal heads linked to a curved zone delineated by a single and a pair of incised curved lines which match the curvature of the tongue base; most of this zone was left plain, but there are two curved lines placed on the inner edge, presumably representing hips or legs associated with the animal heads, which seem to belong to Salin's Style I rather than the Style II repertoire, while beside each garnet there is a rounded shell setting set within a beaded frame covering a belt rivet, each shell setting having a rounded opening, one of which still contained a small *cabochon* garnet, all these features being matched by the third shell setting again complete with its *cabochon* garnet at the apex of the triangle, while parallel to the long sides and running between the shell settings are two framed bands containing animal designs terminating close to the apex with interlacing pairs of legs in Style II, the right-side or upper band overlaps and partially obscures part of the leg design on the left or lower side of the buckle plate; the bottom sheet plate is fastened over central extension of the main plate which is bent around the narrow section of loop and has a central slot to allow the tongue to rotate around the loop bar; it is decorated with a spaced punch-mark of dots making a shape along the narrow edge and within that and along the two long edges a row of spaced punched circlets; loop 44 mm L, 16.5 mm W, 3 mm thick; shield tongue 30 mm L, 17.5 mm W, 4.5 mm thick; upper plate 119 mm L, 89 mm W, 2.5 mm thick; lower plate 112 mm L, 34 mm W; rectangular garnets 5 mm by 4 mm, *cabochon* garnets 3 mm diameter, gap for the rivets between each plate implies two thicknesses of belt leather each 2.5 mm thick.

1.3. **Belt plates**, copper-alloy, from a belt set, triangular (with rounded corners) pair of counter plates in sheet metal fastened (originally through the belt leather) by three small round-headed rivets (one at each corner): the upper plate has a rounded opening parallel to the narrow edge and is decorated with a band framed by an outer and an inner line of small narrowly spaced punched dots containing a row of spaced punched circlets, which run between the three rivets along the two long sides, while the base plate is plain, but has a larger rectangular opening extending from the narrow edge below the equivalent opening on the upper plate, 24 mm L, 24.5 mm W, longest rivet 2.5 mm diameter (head), 3.5 mm L implying belt leather 2 mm to 2.5 mm thick.

2. **Knife**, iron, curved back and straight cutting edge with probable horn handle on tang, more than 154 mm L, 17 mm W, Type 4.

3. **Catch**, copper-alloy, probably from a purse, consisting of a short cast bar with a flat base and a gable profile with a ridge along its length with an incised line or two before it flattens into an extension at each end with a rivet hole to take a round headed rivet, 23 mm L, 3 mm W, 2 mm thick with longest rivet 3.5 mm diameter (head), 6 mm L, implying that two leather thicknesses amounting to more than 3 mm could be present.

4. **Nail**, iron, with rounded section with organic material, probably wood attached, 42 mm L, 8 mm W, 7 mm thick.

GRAVE 76:29 [*Grave 89:13*] (Figs 23 and 44–5)
Male, 25–35 years, stature unknown, (preservation condition 4), also with ossified cartilage, arthropathies of vertebrae, ante-mortem tooth loss, epigenetic trait of spondylolysis and new bone on spine, perhaps traumatic in origin.

E–W grave, 2.85 × 1.13m at the centre, 0.85 m deep at the foot end and 0.86 m deep at the head end, with two sides visible of a four-sided coffin stain. Adult skeleton placed in a supine position with the skull facing to the right at the west end of the grave and both its arms and legs straight. A wheel-thrown pot (1) at the right of the skull on its side within the coffin with its mouth towards the skull; a spearhead (2) at the left side of the packing at the side of the coffin and parallel to the left arm; and belt fittings across the waist (3.1–7); together with a knife (4) at the left side of the waist with the point upwards; and an iron steel (5) with the tang upwards at the left side of the waist with the knife.

1. **Pottery jar**, wheel-thrown grey-black ware, with slightly hollow base, decorated above the low carination with three parallel raised bands separating zones with incised wavy design, Beerlegem Type,[62] 222 mm high, 87 mm diameter (mouth), 102 mm diameter (carination), 49 mm diameter (base).

2. **Spearhead**, iron, larger triangular blade with a short solid shank and a medium length split socket, 475 mm L, 56 mm W, Type E3.

3. **Belt set**, iron, with silver wire and sheet inlay, with rounded plates and associated copper-alloy plates consisting of:[63]
3.1. Rectangular sheet **plate**, copper-alloy, with four rivet holes set along each long side, decorated on one face with incised lines used to provide a rectangular frame, within which are diagonal lines defining a series of lozenges and triangles at the edges, which virtually all contain a punched ring-and-dot design, though two of them contain two such punch-marks and three triangles contain none, and the short edges have a series of short parallel lines cut from the edge of the plate, which on one side stop short of and on the other meet the incised frame lines, 40 mm L, 22 mm W. 3.2. Rounded sub-triangular pair of **plates**, iron, originally fastened to the leather strap with three round-headed domed-headed rivets with central inlaid motif of interlocking figures of eight set in a cross with parallel wire lines providing a border, originally *c.* 50 mm long, 43 mm W. 3.3. **Buckle loop**, tongue and plate, iron, with traces of wire inlay in parallel lines on the loop, the tongue base which is fastened to a connecting iron plate to the rounded sub-triangular plate which originally had three domed rivets (one missing) and both the form and decoration matches (3.2) above, 85 mm L, loop 52 mm W, tongue 50 mm L. 3.4. Rectangular sheet **plate**, copper-alloy, similar to (3.1) above, but with three rivet holes set along each long side and with up to three punched ring-and-dot designs within each lozenge, 37 mm L, 21 mm W. 3.5. Rounded sub-triangular **pair of plates**, iron, originally fastened to the leather strap with three dome-headed rivets and both the form and the decoration matches (3.2) and (3.3) above, originally 45 mm L, 43 mm W. 3.6. Rectangular sheet **plate**, copper alloy, similar to (3.1) and (3.4) above, but with four rivet holes set along each long side and with up to four punched ring-and-dot designs within each lozenge, 40 mm L, 27 mm W. 3.7. Pair of sub-triangular **sheet plates**, copper-alloy, fastened originally by three rivets, one still in plate either side of belt leather, with one side decorated with the same ring-and-dot punch-marks seen on the rectangular plates (3.1), (3.4), and (3.6) above, 19 mm L, 14 mm W and 13.5 mm L, 14 mm W.

4. **Knife**, iron, curved back and straight cutting edge, probably with a horn handle on its tang, 131 mm L (originally), 15 mm W, Type 4.

5. **Tool** with tang handle and flat-sectioned blade, iron, possibly a draw plate with perforations for drawing wire, 101 mm L, 11 mm W.

GRAVE 76:30 [*Grave 89:10*] (Figs 22 and 46)
?Sub-adult. No skeleton (preservation category 0).
E–W grave, 1. 25 × 0.68 m W across the centre, *c.* 0.61 m deep and with a layer of decayed wood on the floor of the grave. This was intended for a small child, but no visible trace of bone or teeth survived. One glass bead (1) was recovered *c.* 0.15 m north-west from the centre of the grave.

1. **Bead**, glass, annular pale blue/green translucent, 10 mm diameter, 3 mm high, with a 1.5 mm diameter central perforation.

GRAVE 76:31 (Figs 22 and 46)
??Female (i.e. a few sexing characteristics suggest but do not determine the sex), 30–40 years, stature unknown,

(preservation category 2), dental epigenetic trait of incisor shovelling (see also graves 76:7 and 76:15).

E–W grave, 2.30 × 0.85 m, depth not recorded, with two long sides of a coffin visible, *c.* 0.57 m W. Skeleton placed in a supine position with the skull at the west end of the grave and the bones in poor condition. At the centre of the waist is a buckle (1); a triangular iron fragment (2) is at a depth of 45 cm by the left arm; a pouch complex (3) includes a spearhead (3.1) outside the left arm and parallel with the corpse; a knife (3.2) is on the left side of the waist, lying diagonally with the tang upwards; beside a leather pouch complex (3.3–17) over the left waist area.

1. **Buckle** and **plate**, iron loop, tongue and rounded (U-shaped) triangular plate, with a front copper-alloy sub-triangular sheet hinge-plate under the iron tongue shield, turned over the edge of the iron loop over the back and fastened by two rivets to the iron plate close to the junction with the loop. A single rivet covered by a decorative jewelled cover at the end of the plate and two other rivets now missing originally fastened a separate triangular copper-alloy back plate. This back plate is decorated with two sets of parallel frame lines made up of small narrowly spaced punched dots. The upper iron plate was ornamented with copper-wire inlay, now barely visible, consisting of outer frame lines infilled by stepped lines imitating *cloisonné* ornament. There are also three silver-gilt studs each with a *cabochon* garnet set in a beaded collared frame. Two of these appear to be purely decorative, but the third covers a rivet which fastens the back plate through the belt leather to the iron plate. The rounded shield base has similar inlaid ornament to the upper iron plate and there are three grooves to take inlay on the D-shaped iron loop, 54 mm L, 24 mm W, *cabochons* 5 mm or 6 mm diameter.[64]
2. **Fragment**, iron, triangular damaged fragment, 6 mm L, 6 mm W, 1 mm thick.
3. **Pouch complex**, consisting of: 3.1. **Spearhead**, iron, probably Type B1, miniature with blade missing, part of a rectangular-sectioned shaft and only the top part of a split socket surviving, 116 mm L, 12 mm diameter (socket). 3.2. **Knife**, iron, curved back and curved cutting edge, probably with a horn handle on its tang, 116 mm L, 16 mm W, Type 1. 3.3. Cast **stud** or rivet, copper-alloy, with a domed rounded head decorated with an incised cross, 6 mm diameter (head), 10 mm thick (rivet): fastening an object 8 mm deep. 3.4. Cast **stud** or rivet, copper-alloy, with a domed rounded head decorated with an incised cross, 6 mm diameter (head), 11 mm thick (rivet): fastening an object 8 mm deep. 3.5. Round-sectioned length of **iron**, associated with a copper-alloy cast fitting with a copper-alloy rivet at one end, 12 mm L, 1.5 mm diameter (iron), 7 mm L, 2 mm W (copper-alloy), rivet shank 3 mm L. 3.6. Round-sectioned length of **iron**, associated with a copper-alloy cast fitting with a copper-alloy rivet at one end, 19 mm L, 2 mm diameter (iron), 17 mm L, 2 mm W (copper-alloy). 3.7. Cast **fitting**, copper-alloy with rivet at one end plus copper-alloy fragment attached to iron, 11 mm L, 2 mm W. 3.8. Round-sectioned **length of copper-alloy**, associated with a sheet copper-alloy fitting originally with a copper-alloy rivet at each end, one rivet still in place, 18 mm L, 0.5 mm diameter (iron), 19 mm L, 5 mm W (copper-alloy). 3.9. Round-sectioned **length of iron**, associated with a sheet copper-alloy fitting originally with a copper-alloy rivet at each end, one rivet still in place, 25 mm L, 2 mm diameter (iron), 10 mm L, 5 mm W (copper-alloy). 3.10. Rectangular-sectioned **length of iron** and separate round-sectioned length of iron, associated with a sheet copper-alloy fitting with a copper-alloy rivet at each end, both still in place, 26 mm L, 4 mm by 3 mm (rectangular iron), 15 mm L (rounded iron), 18 mm L, 4.5 mm W (copper-alloy). 3.11 **Rivet/pin**, copper-alloy, with a domed head broken with a section of it through a fragment of iron, 6 mm plus 5 mm L.

GRAVE 76:32 (Figs 13 and 23)

Adult ?Female, age and stature unknown, (preservation category 2), ante-mortem tooth loss.

E–W grave, 1.60 m × 0.80 × 0.26–29 m deep, cut by and therefore predating Grave 76:33. Supine position indicated with the skull at the west end. No associated artefacts. Enclosed by a penannular ring-ditch, 6.9 m (N–S) by 6.4 m (E–W), with its causeway to the east, but its orientation does not align with the causeway and this grave presumably pre-dates the ring-ditch.

GRAVE 76:33 (Figs 13, 23 and 47)

Male, 35–45 years, stature could not be calculated, (preservation category 4), arthropathies of vertebrae, enthesopathies, dental caries, ante-mortem tooth loss and dental enamel hypoplasia.

E–W grave, 2.30 × 0.76 × 0.64 m deep, which cuts and therefore postdates Grave 76:32 above. Adult skeleton laid in a supine position with the head facing right (south) at the west end and with the right hand over the pelvis. Enclosed by a penannular ring-ditch, 6.9 m (N–S) by 6.4 m (E–W), aligned with its causeway, 0.80 m W to the east aligned to this grave. A knife (1) along the inner lower left arm with its point upwards; and a buckle (2) above and to the left of the spine at the waist level with the knife.

1. **Knife**, iron, curved back and straight cutting edge, probably with a horn handle on its tang, 140 mm L, 18 mm W, Type 4.
2. **Buckle**, iron, two oval loop fragments and tongue, 47 mm W, tongue 20 mm L.
3. Two worked **flints** from the grave fill.
4. **Pottery**, a handmade black fabric sherd from the grave fill.

GRAVE 76:34 (Figs 23 and 48)

Sub-adult. No part of the skeleton could be lifted (preservation category 0).

E–W grave, 1.00 × 0.50 × 0.16 m maximum depth. Very small child, with no trace of the teeth and only a few fragments of the femurs preserved by the presence of the thread box, but probably orientated E–W and placed in a supine position. A knife (1) is in the probable region of the left side of the waist with its point upwards and outwards; and is above a thread or workbox (2) in the region of the right hip in the middle of the grave.

1. **Knife**, iron, curved back and curved cutting edge, probably

with a horn handle on its tang, 150 mm L, 14 mm W, Type 1.

2. Cylindrical threadbox or **workbox**, copper-alloy sheet with its lid fastened to two linked rivets, one each on the lid and the main cylinder, with two pairs of figure-of-eight links joining a double knotted ring, decoration on lid, base and main panels uses small *repoussé* punched dots, 54 mm height lid, 49 × 50 mm diameter, base distorted at 44 × 52 mm diameter, chain length *c.* 11 mm. For textile contents see Appendix II.

GRAVE 76:35 (Figs 24 and 47)

Late adolescence to young adult, sex and stature unknown, (preservation category 1: skull and leg fragments).

E–W grave, 2.73 × *c.* 0.90 × *c.* 0.74 m deep at the centre with the two long sides of a coffin visible. Adult probably placed in a supine position judging from the skull at the west end, the other bones being almost totally decayed. A spearhead (1) is to the left of and above the skull at a depth of 0.65 m; with an iron pin (2) at a depth of 0.68 m and a copper-alloy rivet (3) between the spearhead and the left side of the skull; a nail (4) to the left of the skull at a depth of 0.60 m; a metal stud (5); at the left side of the waist and inside the coffin an iron ring (6); a knife (7) beside this ring with its tang upwards; and an iron steel (8) at the left side of the waist area beside the knife; and over a copper-alloy plate (9); and two buckles (10 and 11).

1. **Spearhead**, iron, chunky, leaf-shaped blade and split socket, 228 mm L, 25 mm W, Type C2.
2. **Rivet**, iron with traces of wood, 19 mm L, head 6 mm diameter.
3. **Rivet** and washer, copper-alloy, 5.5 mm L, head 3 mm diameter, washer 4.5 mm diameter.
4. **Fragment**, organic material, 10 mm L.
5. **Nail** or clench-nail, iron, with oval-sectioned shaft with wood traces, 17 mm L, head 6 × 5 mm diameter, shaft 3 mm diameter.
6. **Ring**, iron, oval cross-section, 32 × 29 mm diameter, 9 mm ring width.
7. **Knife**, iron, curved back and straight cutting edge with probable horn handle on tang, 169 mm L, 20 mm W, Type 4.
8. **Tool** or steel, iron, with leather and wood traces, 130 mm L, 20 mm W, (damaged both ends).
9. Sheet metal **plate**, copper-alloy, sub-rectangular with two pairs of incised lines for decoration, one fragment with a perforation, 15 mm L, 7 mm W; perforated fragment 15 × 7 mm.
10. **Buckle and plate**, iron, oval loop, tongue and rectangular belt plate with rectangular opening for the tongue wrapped around the plate, 22 mm L, loop 17 mm W, plate 10 mm × 9 mm.
11. **Buckle and plate**, iron, D-shaped loop, rectangular belt plate ornamented with two rows of *cloisonné* garnet honeycomb patterned ornament set in gold cellwork either side of a central raised zone giving the reserved outline of a fish, originally with three decorated rivets at the terminal, one still set with a *cabochon* garnet set in a gold collar, the base only surviving of the central collar and the third now missing, 58 mm L, loop 24 mm W, tongue 14 mm L, plate 20 × 43 mm, gold collar setting 5 mm diameter.
12. **Pottery**, two sherds in grave fill [not illustrated].

GRAVE 76:36 (Figs 24 and 49)

No skeleton (preservation category 0).

E–W grave, 2.77 × 0.83 × 0.75 m deep, with the W end of a narrow four-sided coffin, *c.* 0.45 m W, but with no trace of any bone or teeth of a skeleton. A silver pin (1); is above the gilt copper-alloy coin pendant in the presumed area of the neck; a silver buckle (3) is in the presumed centre of the waist; with two knives (4 and 5) nearby, one at the right side and the other lying diagonally below the buckle; and a third knife (6) is by the left side of the presumed chest area above the chatelaine (7.1–5).

1. **Pin**, silver, with flattened disc head, two incised lines on the rounded shaft just below the head and three incised lines around the middle section, with the point missing, Kingston disc-headed type,[65] 42 mm L, flattened head: 4 mm diameter.
2. **Coin pendant**, gilt copper-alloy, imitation of a Merovingian gold tremissis coin mounted for suspension as a pendant, but most of the loop fitting has been lost, the obverse has a diademed bust right with a fragmentary inscription HΛOA____-S and the reverse has a Byzantine-style cross-on-steps flanked by the single letters C and A together with the inscription RIS____IN, 14 mm diameter, 0.93 g weight (see Appendix IV).
3. **Buckle and plate**, silver, oval copper-alloy loop and silver tongue decorated with two incised lines, with a rectangular sheet with a rectangle cut out for the tongue, with the upper plate terminating in three triangles, the belt plate fastened to the leather with three rivets with two positioned by the loop and tongue and the third centrally above the middle triangle, each head set with a rounded *cabochon* garnet set in a silver collar within a gold collar, 21 mm L, loop 16 mm W, tongue 9 mm L, plate 11 × 10.5 mm, *cabochon* garnet settings 3 mm diameter and the garnets 1–1.5 mm diameter.
4. **Knife**, iron, most of blade and part of tang, probably with curved back and curved cutting edge, probably with a horn handle, 87 mm L, 16 mm W, probably Type 1.
5. **Knife**, iron, curved back and straight cutting edge, probably with a horn handle on its tang, 131 mm L, 13 mm W, Type 4.
6. **Knife**, iron, curved back and curved cutting edge, probably with a horn handle on its tang, plus a rod of iron attached by rust, 140 mm L, 15 mm W, Type 1.
7. **Chatelaine**, iron, consisting of: 7.1. **shaft**, iron, which separates into a two-stranded twisted section attached to a connecting loop at one end, with a loop at the other end through which a section of iron ring is attached, with mineral-preserved textile at that end, 79 mm L, 3 mm diameter; 7.2. **shaft**, iron, round-sectioned, with mineral-preserved textile?, 69 mm L, 8 mm diameter; 7.3 two **sections**, iron, one round-sectioned and the other two-stranded twisted, with mineral-preserved textile, 105 mm L, 7 × 5 mm diameter; 7.4. **shaft**, iron, round-sectioned, broken into two lengths with a hook at one end around another hook, with mineral-preserved textile attached, 94 mm L, 6 mm diameter; 7.5. **shaft**, iron, round-sectioned, 24 mm L, 5 mm diameter, part of a chatelaine.
8. **Mount** or tag, cast copper-alloy, fastened with two centrally positioned rivets to a purse or similar item, 19 mm L, possibly associated with the chatelaine.

GRAVE 76:37 (Fig. 3)
E–W grave, discovered in digging pipe-line, formerly containing the skeletal remains of a sub-adult, but both the bones and any associated finds had been removed by the workmen before the visit of Sonia Hawkes to the site in June 1976.

GRAVE 89:1 (Figs 50 and 54)
Adult (preservation category 1: vault fragment and teeth only), sex not determined.
E–W grave, 2.75 × 0.96 × 0.59 m deep, axis: 065°.
   a. **Knife**, iron, Type 4; b. **Beads**, four monochrome opaque glass.[66]

GRAVE 89:2 see Grave 76:11

GRAVE 89:3 see Grave 76:18

GRAVE 89:4 see Grave 76:21

GRAVE 89:5 (Figs 50 and 54–5)
?Male, 36–38 years, stature 1.71 m, (preservation category 2), vertebral osteoarthritis.
E–W grave, 2.80 × 0.87 × 0.59 deep, axis: 092°, traces of four-sided wooden coffin.
   a. **Pin**, silvered copper-alloy, probably base silver, facet-headed type; b. **Bead**, one monochrome opaque glass; c. **Buckle**, copper-alloy; d. **Knife**, iron, Type 5; e.–g. **Shears**, iron; h./j./l. **Girdle-hanger**; i./k. **Rod**, iron; m. **Fitting**, copper-alloy; n. **Lock-plate**, iron from a wooden box; p. **Nail**; q. **Split-pins**, two iron; r. **Rim**, copper-alloy from wooden drinking-cup in a wooden box or casket; s. **Rim**, copper-alloy from wooden drinking-cup in a wooden box or casket; t.–u. **Nails**, two.[67]

GRAVE 89:6 see Grave 76:17

GRAVE 89:7 see Grave 76:15

GRAVE 89:8 see Grave 76:16

GRAVE 89:9 (Figs 50 and 55) see Grave 76:38 on 1976 cemetery plan (recorded, but not excavated in 1976)
? Female, 35–45 years, (preservation category 2), dental ante-mortem tooth loss.
E–W grave, 2.60 × 83 × 57 m, axis: 088°.
Set within a penannular ring-ditch.
   a. **Knife**, iron, Type 1.[68]

GRAVE 89:10 see Grave 76:30

GRAVE 89:11 see Grave 76:14

GRAVE 89:12 (Figs 50 and 55)
? Female, 20–30 years, (preservation category 2), dental caries.
E–W grave, 2.18 × 80 × 48 m deep, axis: 118°.
   a. **Strip**, iron; b. **Buckle**, copper-alloy.[69]

GRAVE 89:13 see Grave 76:29

GRAVE 89:14 see Grave 76:10

GRAVE 89:15 (Fig. 50)
Male, 21–46 years, stature 1.69 m, (preservation category 3), vertebral osteoarthritis, dental caries and bowed femora.
E–W grave, grave cut not defined with length unknown, width unknown, 0.40 m deep, axis of skeleton: 094°.
   No associated finds.[70]

GRAVE 89:16 (Fig. 50)
Male, 19–34 years, stature could not be calculated reliably from arm bones, (preservation category 3), vertebral osteoarthritis, dental ante-mortem tooth loss and caries, bowed femora, and multiple trauma consisting of parry-fractures of both forearms and a clavicle fracture.
E–W grave, 2.28 × 0.80 × 0.48 m, axis: 066°.
   No associated finds.[71]

GRAVE 89:17 see Grave 76:12

GRAVE 89:18 (Figs 50 and 56)
Female, 25–45 years, stature 1.61 m, (preservation category 4), dental ante-mortem tooth loss and caries with parafunctional wear on teeth.
E–W grave, 2.25 × 0.80 × 0.85 m, axis: 088°.
   a. **Pin**, iron; b. **Pin**, iron; c. **Fragment**, glass; d. **Knife**, iron, Type 4; e. **Key**, iron; f. **Strip**, iron with rivets, copper-alloy; g. **Pin**, iron; h. **Beads**, two clear blue translucent glass and seven polychrome opaque glass; j. **Coin**, Roman brass, Constantine II, AD337–40.[72]

GRAVE 89:19
Adult (preservation category 1: tibial fragments only).
E–W grave, 2.45 × 0.87 × 0.80 m, axis: 046°.
   No associated finds.[73]

GRAVE 89:20 (Figs 51 and 56)
Female, 30–36 years, stature 1.58 m, (preservation category 3), dental epigenetic trait of shovelled incisors, tooth crowding and parafunctional wear on teeth.
E–W grave, 2.45 × 0.83 × 0.44 m, axis: 070°.
   a. Cowrie **shell**; b. **Oyster shells**; c. **Bead**, one translucent glass; d.–g. **Rings**, four copper-alloy; h. **Pin**, silvered copper-alloy, probably base silver, with *cabochon* garnet setting, garnet-set disc-headed type (Ross Type LXI).[74]

GRAVE 89:21 (Figs 51 and 57)
Sub-adult, age cannot be defined closely (preservation category 1).
E–W grave, 1.80 m × 0.63 × 0.40 m deep, axis: 076°.
   a. **Knife**, iron, Type 1; b. **Spearhead**, iron, Type B1, spike-type socketed form; c. **Fragment**, copper-alloy; d. **Strip**, iron.[75]

GRAVE 89:22
?Male, 40–44 years, (preservation category 1).
E–W grave, 2.60 × 0.97 × 0.55 m, axis: 088°.
No associated finds.[76]

GRAVE 89:23 (Figs 51 and 57) see Grave 76:39 on 1976 cemetery plan (recorded, but not excavated in 1976).
Sub-adult, 5–6 years, (preservation category 1: 2 teeth only).
E–W grave, 1.55 × 0.70 × 0.55 m, axis: 072°.
   a. Scutiform disc **pendant**, copper-alloy; b. **Beads**, three monochrome opaque glass; c. **Knife**, iron; d. **Ring**, iron.[77]

GRAVE 89:24 (Figs 51 and 57)
Sub-adult, 4.5–5.3 years, (preservation category 1).
E–W grave, 1.63 × 0.76 × 0.71 m, axis: 100°.
   a. **Knife**, iron, Type 1; b. **Buckle**, copper-alloy; c. **Spearhead**, iron, probably Type B1, spike-type socketed spearhead or ferrule; d. Wooden turned-vessel **repair plate**, copper-alloy (mislabelled as belt-plate).[78]

GRAVE 89:25 (Figs 51 and 57)
Adult, ?female, (preservation category 2).
E–W grave, 2.34 × 0.78 × 0.38 m, axis: 083°.
   a. **Knife**, iron, Type 4; b. **Pot**, handmade in a fragmentary state; c. **Spearhead**, iron, Type C5.[79]

GRAVE 89:26 (Figs 51 and 58)
Adult, (preservation category 1).
E–W grave, 2.77 × 0.98 × 0.46 m, axis: 092° with traces of a four-sided coffin.
   a. **Beads**, fifteen monochrome opaque glass; b. **Bracelet**, copper-alloy; c. **Buckle**, copper-alloy; d. Wooden box iron **bracket**; e. **Strip**, copper-alloy; f. Wooden box iron **bracket**; g. Wooden box possible iron **lock-bar**; h. **Fragments**, copper-alloy; i. and j. **Knife**, iron, Type 1; k. **Knife**, iron, probably Type 1; l. **Girdle-hanger**, iron; m. **Key**, iron; n. **Tanged object**, iron, possibly part of a lock-plate[80]

GRAVE 89:27
Male, 24–30 years, (preservation category 3).
E–W grave, 2.57 × 0.80 × 0.53 m, axis: 080°.
No associated finds.[81]

GRAVE 89:28 (Figs 51 and 59)
Male, 18–24 years, stature could not be calculated reliably (preservation category 3).
E–W grave, 2.50 × 0.90 × 38 m, axis: 108°.
   a. **Knife**, iron, Type 4.[82]

GRAVE 89:29
?Female, 20–25 years, (preservation category 2).
E–W grave, 2.50 × 0.80 × 0.43 m, axis: 083°.
No associated finds.[83]

GRAVE 89:30
Sub-adult, 4.5–6.5 years, (preservation category 1).
E–W grave, 1.65 × 0.53 × 0.55 m, axis: 088°.
No associated finds.[84]

GRAVE 89:31 (Figs 51 and 59)
No skeleton surviving, but grave dimensions imply an adult burial.
E–W grave, 2.53 × 0.95 × 0.53 m, axis: 070° with four iron cleats marking the sides of a wooden coffin.
   a.–d. Coffin clamps/**brackets**, iron, four, no other associated finds.[85]

GRAVE 89:32 (Figs 51 and 59)
Female, 38–42 years, (preservation category 3).
E–W grave, 2.12 × 0.80 × 0.30 m, axis: 068°.
   a. **Bead**, one monochrome opaque glass.[86]

GRAVE 89:33
No skeleton surviving, but grave dimensions imply an adult burial.
E–W grave, 2.67 × 0.90 × 0.58 m, axis: 068° with traces of four-sided wooden coffin.
No associated finds.[87]

GRAVE 89:34 (Figs 52 and 60)
Female, 25–45 years, stature 1.52 m, (preservation category 3), dental ante-mortem tooth loss and trauma of fractured right tibia.
E–W grave, 2.33 × 0.90 × 0.59 m, axis: 082° with traces of four-sided wooden coffin.
   a. **Ring**, cast copper-alloy; b. **Nail**, iron, c. **Knife**, iron, Type 5; d. **Bead**, one monochrome opaque glass; e. **Bead**, one amethyst drop; f. **Knife**, iron, type uncertain; g. **Knife**, iron, type uncertain; h. **Shears**, iron; j. **Girdle-hanger**, iron.[88]

GRAVE 89:35 (Figs 52 and 60)
Single tooth fragment, but grave dimensions imply an adult burial.
E–W grave, 2.50 × 1.09 × 0.56 m, axis: 068° with traces of four-sided wooden coffin.
   a. **Pin** head, copper-alloy, depicts a human head, probably Roman; b. **Rod**, iron; c. **Fittings**, three iron, unidentified; d. **Palm cup**, glass.[89]

GRAVE 89:36 (Figs 52 and 61)
No skeleton surviving, but grave dimensions imply a sub-adult burial.
E–W grave, 1.15 × 0.70 × 0.47 m, axis: 090° with traces of four-sided wooden coffin.
   a. **Bead**, one monochrome opaque glass; b. **Knife**, iron, Type 1; c. **Pot**, globular handmade.[90]

GRAVE 89:37 (Figs 52 and 61)
?Male, 25–35 years, (preservation category 2).
E–W grave, 2.16 × 0.80 × 0.43 m, axis: 118° set within a penannular ring-ditch.
   a. **Seax**, iron.[91]

GRAVE 89:38 (Figs 52 and 61)
Grave dimensions imply a sub-adult burial,(preservation category 1).

E–W grave, 1.50 × 0.62 × 0.48 m, axis: 083° set within a penannular ring-ditch.
　　a. **Knife**, iron, Type 2; b. **Pin**, copper alloy, related to Facet-headed pin type.[92]

GRAVE 89:39 (Figs 52 and 62)
Sub-adult, 9.2–12.3 years, (preservation category 2), dental epigenetic trait of Carabelli's cusp (see also Grave 76:2).
E–W grave, 2.03 × 0.80 × 0.50 m, axis: 086° set within a penannular ring-ditch together with Grave 89:44.
　　a. **Fitting** or mount, gilt copper-alloy; b. **Beads**, three monochrome opaque glass; c. **Knife**, iron, Type 1; d. **Firesteel/pursemount**, iron.[93]

GRAVE 89:40 (Figs 52 and 62)
?Female, 18–21 years, (preservation category 2).
E–W grave, 2.14 × 0.85 × 0.56 m, axis: 100° set within a penannular ring-ditch.
　　a. **Knife**, iron, Type 4; b. **Spearhead**, iron, Type C5.[94]

GRAVE 89:41 (Figs 52 and 63)
Adult, (preservation category 2).
E–W grave, 2.30 × 0.73 × 0.60 m, axis: 066°.
　　a. **Spearhead**, iron, Type C4; b. **Knife**, iron, Type 5; c. **Razor/knife**, iron, Type 2; d. **Rivets**, two copper-alloy.[95]

GRAVE 89:42 (Figs 52 and 63)
No skeleton surviving, but grave dimensions imply an adult burial.
E–W grave, 2.83 × 0.87 × 0.48 m, axis: 067°.
　　a. **Seax**, iron.[96]

GRAVE 89:43 (Figs 52 and 62)
No skeleton surviving, but grave dimensions imply a sub-adult burial.
E–W grave, 1.30 × 0.55 × 0.48 m, axis: 103°.
　　a. **Knife**, iron, Type 1; b. **Strip**, iron; c. **Beads**, one amber, seven monochrome opaque glass, one polychrome opaque glass.[97]

GRAVE 89:44 (Fig. 53)
?Female, 25–30 years, stature could not be calculated reliably, (preservation category 3), dental caries and one malocclusion.
E–W grave, 1.90 × 0.92 × 0.58 m, axis: 070°, set within a penannular ring-ditch together with Grave 89:39, but not aligned with its causeway, so possibly pre-dates the ring-ditch and Grave 89:39. Contracted position on its left side.
　　No associated finds.[98]

GRAVE 89:45 (Figs 53 and 64)
?Female, 16–24 years, (preservation category 2), dental caries.
E–W grave, 2.54 × 0.78 × 0.65 m, axis: 078°.
　　a. **Cowrie shell**, one; b. **Workbox**, copper-alloy;

c. Openwork **chatelaine** fitting, cast copper-alloy (misidentified as a wrist-clasp in Philp and Keller 2002); d. **Knife**, iron, Type 4; e. **Buckle**, copper-alloy; f. **Latchlifter**, iron; g. **Spoon**, iron and **Comb**, bone (probably antler); h. **Ring**, copper-alloy; j. **Beads**, one bone, four monochrome opaque glass; k. **Pendant**, probably a heavily worn, centrally perforated coin, copper-alloy.[99]

GRAVE 89:46 (Figs 53 and 65) see Grave 76:42 on 1976 cemetery plan (recorded, but not excavated in 1976)
?Female, 32–36 years, (preservation category 2), dental parafunctional wear.
E–W grave, 2.46 × 0.85 × 0.50 m, axis: 080°.
Set within a penannular ring-ditch.
　　a. **Girdle-hanger**, iron; b. **Knife**, iron, Type 4; c. **Beads**, nine monochrome opaque glass and one polychrome opaque glass.[100]

GRAVE 89:47 (Figs 53 and 65)
Sub-adult, 10.9–11.3 years, (preservation category 3), dental tooth crowding and prognathic teeth, cribra orbitalia.
E–W grave, 1.92 × 0.52 × 0.34 m, axis: 066°.
　　a. **Pot**, biconical wheel-thrown; b. **Knife**, iron; c. **Spoon**, iron; d. **Comb**, bone (probably antler); e. **Strips**, two copper-alloy.[101]

GRAVE 89:48 (Figs 53 and 65)
Adult, ?Male, (preservation category 3), dental ante-mortem tooth loss, ankylosed cervical vertebrae.
E–W grave, 2.27 × 0.82 × 0.40 m, axis: 083°.
　　a. **Knife**, iron, Type 4.[102]

GRAVE 89:49 *(Figs 53 and 66)*
No skeleton surviving, but grave dimensions imply a sub-adult burial.
E–W grave, 1.52 × 0.52 × 0.34 m, axis: 080°.
Set within a penannular (or possibly annular) ring-ditch.
　　a. **Pot**, globular wheel-thrown; b. **Nail**, iron; c. **Knife**, iron; d. **Spearhead**, iron, Type B1, spike-type socketed form.[103]

GRAVE 89:50 (Figs 53 and 65)
Male, 22–28 years, stature 1.67 m, (preservation category 4).
E–W grave, 2.41 × 0.86 × 0.55 m, axis: 088°.
　　a. **Pot**, biconical wheel-thrown.[104]

GRAVE 89:51 (Figs 53 and 66)
?Male, 35–37 years, (preservation category 2).
E–W grave, 2.69 × 0.93 × 0.82 m, axis: 100°, set within a pennanular ring-ditch.
　　a. **Buckle**, iron; b. **Knife**, iron, Type 4; c. **Spearhead**, iron, Type C3.[105]

GRAVE 89:52 (Figs 53 and 66)
?Male, 30–34 years, (preservation category 1).
E–W grave, 2.52 × 0.73 × 1.02 m, axis: 076°.
　　a. **Spearhead**, iron, Type F1; b. **Buckle**, iron; c. and e. **Knife**,

iron, Type 1; d. **Pin**, iron; f. and g. **Strip**, iron pierced by a nail.[106]

GRAVE 89:53 see Grave 76:26

GRAVE 89:54 see Grave 76:27

MATERIAL EVIDENCE PART 2: THE GRAVE FINDS

The finds are considered individually under the following five headings: weapons, dress fittings, personal equipment, vessels and containers (including boxes and coffin fittings) and finally amulets.

Weapons

A total of thirteen graves from 1976 and ten from 1989 contained iron weapons, in most cases limited to a single spear. One such 1976 burial had been robbed in antiquity seemingly leaving only an iron socket to indicate the former presence of a spear or its ferrule (76:18). Of these burials, two represent sub-adults and a further two individuals were on the boundary between late adolescence and young adulthood from the 1976 season with a further three sub-adults in 1989. So, although eight out of the twelve undisturbed weapon graves from 1976 and seven out of the ten from 1989 represent full adults and two from 1976 occupy the borderline between late adolescence and adult, a significant proportion of the Updown assemblages containing at least one weapon were those of biological children. The five child burials from 1976 and 1989 anticipate the normal transition to adult status in the Anglo-Saxon world around the age of ten.[107] No long two-edged swords of the spatha tradition were present, but during the seventh century these seem to have been replaced over time by the seax, a single-bladed short sword.[108] Although the seax and the spatha were functionally different, both represent weapons of last resort, used when the spear and shield combination can no longer be wielded.[109] One 1976 grave contained a seax with a spear (76:19), but the other two excavated in 1989 contained just a single seax without any other weapon or diagnostic artefact (89:37 and 89:42). There was also only one association of a shield and a spear with an adult, in Grave 76:14. This featured a tall straight-cone shield boss typical of the seventh century in a period when shields had become a rare feature in a cemetery (Table 2).

Seax: 76:19; 89:37 and 89:42

The single-bladed knife-like weapon known as the seax was introduced in the sixth century to southern England from the Frankish continent and becomes a popular weapon in seventh-century Kent. Not one of the three seaxes from this cemetery match the forms defined for the Frankish versions on the continent.[110] All three have knife-blades that are attributable to knives of Evison's Type 1 (curved back and curved cutting edge) and none of the three possess an elaborate pommel or the sheath fittings typical of Frankish versions. It would seem that they represent Kentish attempts to copy the Frankish small seax (*Schmalsax*) rather than weapons imported from the continent. The Frankish small seaxes range in size from weapons 26–48 cm long with a blade length of 22–31 cm (and in the case of the heavy A2 version up to 36 cm long) and with a blade width of 2.4–3.4 cm (and 2.9–4.3 cm for the heavy A2 version). Comparable weapons occur at Polhill (west Kent) Grave 84/85 together with a C5 spearhead and in three Finglesham assemblages in graves 33, 159 and 165.[111] The seax from Grave 76:19 was accompanied by an iron scabbard fitting and was over 35 cm long with a blade width of 3.1 cm and the associated spearhead belongs to class C2 (see below), another typical seventh-century form. Surveys of seaxes in Anglo-Saxon grave contexts have been published by Härke and by Geake, while the function of this weapon has been considered by Gale.[112]

Shield: 76:14

The only shield boss recorded from the cemetery belongs to the tall straight-cone form defined by Evison.[113] The simple short handle belongs to Härke's Type Ia.1.[114] Similar shields are recorded from Breach Down and Chartham Down in east Kent and Portsdown Grave 6 in Hampshire, but other tall straight-cone bosses possess a marked carination not present at Updown.[115] Examples are recorded from Faversham and Sittingbourne in east Kent and from Alton Grave 16 in Hampshire.[116] In the past, this form was viewed as broadly contemporary with the classic curved cone 'sugar-loaf' shield bosses in the mid and later seventh century, but this dating has been reviewed.[117] There is a case now for attributing the Updown shield and others like it to the first half of the seventh century. A relatively early date for the straight-cone bosses may be appropriate in view of the distribution of straight tall cone bosses from graves on the near continent between the lower Rhine region and the Channel coast at Boulogne.[118] The Kentish triangular belt buckle associated with the Updown shield also implies a date within the first half of the seventh century rather than any later. The Updown boss is a particularly tall version, being over 17 cms high compared to the published examples from Bury St Edmunds (15 cms) and Alton (11.2 cms). The boss and handle were accompanied by three substantial iron disc-headed rivets, which had been fastened through the shield boards. The position of these disc rivets implies a probable diameter of 60 cm to 75 cm for the shield board. The associated spearhead belongs appropriately to Swanton's class C3 (see below). It is unfortunate that the most recent surveys of shields and also the general survey by Geake have concentrated on the tall curved cone forms of the classic 'sugar-loaf' form.[119]

It is relatively rare to find a shield boss and related fittings in cemetery contexts later than the early seventh century, even in Kent, and interestingly no such shield was buried at Finglesham. Tall straight cone and convex cone shield bosses are rather more likely to feature in isolated barrow burials as at Alvediston, Wiltshire, Banstead, Surrey, Lowbury Hill, Berkshire and Ford, Wiltshire.[120] The Polhill, Dunton Green cemetery in western Kent produced just one tall straight-cone shield from Grave 1 (1984–86 eastern zone) after the excavation of some 162 burials there between 1839 and 1986, and similarly there is just one from Lechlade, Gloucestershire, Grave 40.[121] Thus the chances in any future investigation at Updown of locating a further shield within the cemetery might seem relatively slim. On the other hand, it is not inconceivable that low-cone shield bosses of Group 6 or even late versions of the Group 3 boss type typical of earlier seventh-century graves might be recovered in future excavations of another sector at Updown.[122]

Spearheads

The typology published by Swanton, despite its weaknesses, still forms the only standard basis for describing the Updown spearheads.[123] A more recent survey of spear forms from seventh-century contexts is provided by Geake.[124] Only two spearheads were definitely accompanied by a ferrule, in both cases made of copper alloy, in order to protect the other end of the wooden spear shaft (76:3 and 76:14). An example of this type of copper-alloy ferrule also occurs at Finglesham grave 133.[125] The section from a socket in Grave 76:18 might represent either part of a damaged spearhead or a ferrule recovered from a badly disturbed grave, seemingly robbed in antiquity. On balance, however, it is more likely to belong to the spearhead. When looking at Swanton's distribution maps, the sheer size of the sample from Kentish sites should always be borne in mind. Nevertheless, it is obvious that all the forms represented in the Updown sample are typical of the region and of a period of burial centred on the seventh century, as Geake's published table confirms.[126] More locally still in a comparison with the Finglesham cemetery in terms of Swanton's types, the close similarities are obvious.[127] There were two examples of B1, both associated there with children (graves 74 and 143), one B2 (grave 117), one C2 (grave 6), one C3 (grave 159), five C5 (graves 82, 83, 133, 144 and 170), two D1 (graves H3 and 181), two D2 (graves 86 and 135), three E2 (graves G6, 107 and 198), one E3 (grave 103), two F1 (graves 95 and 211), one F2 (grave 103), one F3 (grave G2) and one K1 (grave 204), though allowance has to be made for the Finglesham sixth-century burials with spears.

Class B1 spiked spearheads: 76:17, 76:20, 76:31; 89:21, 89:24 and 89:49

Short spiked spearheads similar to those classified by Swanton as his class B1 occur principally in sub-adult graves, with the exception of the mature adult in Grave 76:31. The latter seems to represent a female assemblage,

however, with the spearhead in a bag collection. Lengths range from 9.9 to 13.6 cm and such spears are not out of place in seventh-century contexts in east Kent.[128]

Series C leaf-shaped bladed spearheads represent the most popular form from the Updown cemetery, though it is not always clear to which class within the series they should be assigned. Only the smallest C1 spearheads are not present in our sample and the distribution maps confirm the popularity of these spearhead forms in east Kent.[129]

Class C2: 76:1, 76:3, 76:19 and 76:35

These are defined with a length between 20 and 35 cm, but overlap in this respect with C5 spearheads of 16 to 26 cm long. The examples here have lengths of over 26.5 cm, 28.5 cm, 24.4 cm and 23 cm respectively and seem most probably to belong in the C2 category. Class C2 spearheads are relatively slender with the socket shorter than the blade, whereas the C5 version is very slender and curved with no obvious blade-socket junction.

Class C3: 76:14 and 89:51 (or class C4)

These have a still more slender and lengthier profile than C2 spears with lengths of between 30 and 50 cm, while C4 spears seem to represent a variant of C3 with an attenuated leaf-shaped blade and lengths of between 35 and 50 cm. The Updown spearheads have lengths of 34 cm and 35 cm respectively and the example from 76:14 is associated with the tall straight cone shield boss. Both should be regarded as C3 spears, though the 89:51 example is moving towards a class C4.

Class C4: 89:41 and 89:51 (or class C3)

See above under C3: the Updown spearheads have lengths of 44 cm and 35 cm respectively. On balance, it seems more probable that the spearhead from 89:51 should be classified as a C3.

Class C5: 76:13; 89:25 and 89:40

These three spearheads share the characteristics of this class with a simple curve from the blade tip to the mouth of the socket, without an obvious blade junction. Their respective lengths of 22 cm, 24.5 cm and 21 cm fall within the normal range of 16 to 26 cms. They are particularly common in seventh-century contexts in both west and east Kent at Polhill (graves 84 and 85), Buckland I, Dover (grave 135) and Finglesham (graves 82, 83 and 133).[130]

Class D2: 76:11

A leaf-shaped blade with a socket and solid shank longer than a blade and an overall length of 25–45 cm define this form and the Updown spearhead is estimated to have been 34.5 cm long. Seventh-century Kentish contexts for similar spears occur at the Finglesham and St Peter's Tip, Broadstairs cemeteries.[131]

Class E2/E3: 76:4, 76:29

Straight-side angular blades on spearheads with the blade much longer than the socket with an overall length of 35–45 cm form class E3, whereas E2 spears have lengths of just 20–35 cm. The spearhead from Grave 76:29 has a length of 47.5 cm and is thus reasonably close to the upper limit. By contrast, the example from Grave 76:4 is unusually long at 66 cm. Overall, apart from their dimensions, the Updown spears seem to have more in common with the form of the class E2 spears, which have a more angular blade shape than the E3 spears, but are much shorter.[132] As E4 spears represent a still narrower version of class E3 with maximum lengths of 50 cm, this E2/E3 designation seems to be the most appropriate designation for the two Updown spearheads.

Class F1: 89:52

Angular-bladed spearheads with relatively long sockets and junction pieces of class F1 mostly have lengths of 18–25 cm, and are also represented here.[133] The Updown spearhead has the proportions of a F1 as opposed to a F2 spearhead, though it is 28 cm long. This makes it longer than normal for a F1, but still distinctly shorter than both the typical range of 30–40 cms for F2 and the 33–35 cms range for the special form of F3. Spearheads of class F1 are present in a number of east Kent cemeteries in Swanton's sample, including Finglesham grave 95 with its famous Kentish triangular buckle portraying a naked man carrying two spears with angular-bladed heads.

Dress Fittings

One immediate source for surprise is the near total absence of brooches, though other sectors of the Updown cemetery may yet produce jewelled disc or composite disc brooches and miniature safety-pin brooches, etc. in the future. It should be noted, however, that a total absence of such disc brooches was also recorded from the Finglesham cemetery, so this need not be an anomaly.[134] Nevertheless it remains unusual for an East Kent site in this period. Dress pins are relatively common, suggesting most of the female assemblages can be attributed to either side of the middle of the seventh century. There are also beads and silver-wire rings which form festoons of ornament in the neck area and in some cases may even belong to necklaces, together with coin-like and disc pendants. Bracelets worn at the wrist and buckles follow, together with a fire-steel/purse mount and other items hanging from the waist belt, such as a chatelaine, often including keys and rings. Finally there are shoe fittings including lace tags.

Brooch: 76:6

Only one brooch is recorded from the site and this turns out to be effectively the only find recovered from a child-sized grave (76:6). It is a silver-gilt cast disc brooch of Kentish type with a central domed shell setting, whose *cabochon*

garnet setting is missing. There are three smaller round settings near the outer edge of the main ornamented field, only one of which retains its white shell setting. The three keystone settings, two of which still contain their garnet plates, are equally spaced between the three outer round settings. Three-strand knotted interlace with confronted zoomorphic terminals provide the background to the six outer settings and these can be attributed to Salin's Style II animal ornament.[135]

Unfortunately, the Updown brooch (as Sonia Hawkes designated it) cannot be neatly fitted into Avent's classification of Kentish jewelled cast disc brooches. It may be compared to published brooches from Polhill Grave 37 in west Kent and Winnall II Grave 21 in south Hampshire.[136] In particular, it can be observed that both the Updown and the Winnall brooches appear to depict bird's head terminals between each roundel setting and the central domed setting. In the case of the Updown brooch, however, these terminals have become very stylised indeed. A more recently excavated brooch from Lechlade (Gloucestershire) Grave 17 can again be compared to the Updown brooch, yet this has four (rather than three) triangular garnet settings pointing inwards to its central domed boss and four outer roundels with Style II animal designs between them.[137]

Typologically, the Updown brooch represents a late version of the cast disc brooch, designed to be worn singly and to fasten a female costume near the throat. The fashion for wearing a single disc brooch was introduced into Kent within the last third of the sixth century in Brugmann's Kentish Phase IV, c. 560/70–580/90.[138] It appears to be going out of fashion with the last of the composite jewelled disc brooches around the middle decades of the seventh century. Geake has discussed the occurrences of such brooches and noted that the brooches from Polhill Grave 37 and from Boss Hall (Ipswich, Suffolk) Grave 93 were buried in bags and were no longer being worn as costume fasteners in the second half of that century.[139] Deposition in a child burial may well have taken place around the middle of the seventh century, and if this brooch was a family heirloom, its burial might even have occurred later still within the seventh century.

Pins: 76:36; 89:5, 89:18, 89:20, 89:26, 89:35, 89:38 and 89:52

Pins of the Anglo-Saxon period have been discussed in general surveys and were the subject of detailed research by Seamus Ross.[140] Some three (or perhaps four) of the pins considered here can be related to his typology, but another item seems very unlikely to represent an Anglo-Saxon decorated pin-head (89:35). This piece, claimed to represent the head of a metal pin, depicts a three-dimensional bearded male head. It was probably a Roman-manufactured item, however, depicting a god. Roman metal or bone pins with human terminals range from full-length figures to busts, or just a head and belong to Cool's Group 18 and sub-group A.[141] These typically depict adult females, often with elaborate hair arrangements, so the Updown male bust would be atypical. It may well prove possible to date its manufacture more precisely though stylistic comparisons, but as it had probably been scavenged from a deserted Romano-British site and subsequently treasured as a keepsake, such a date is not particularly significant here. It should be noted in addition that the function of five iron so-called 'pins' from various graves excavated in 1989 seems uncertain and some of them may well represent chatelaine fittings.

Overall, pins seem to have replaced brooches by the middle decades of the seventh century in Kent. It should be noted, however, that they do not have precisely the same function as brooches. Most probably they were used to fasten a head scarf or veil to a tailored dress around the area of the neck or throat. Certainly the Updown pins from graves 76:36, 89:5 and 89:20 came from the throat or neck area, but the pin from 89:38 was found instead on the left side of the body area, probably at waist or hip level. It should be noted that none of the Updown pins formed part of linked pairs, but single pins seem to be particularly popular in Kent during the seventh century.[142] Turning to the defined types of pin, we will discuss Ross's types L, LXXII and LXI and a variant of the facet-headed pin type.

Kingston disc-headed type (Ross Type L): 76:36
Cast pins with a discoid head of 3–6 mm diameter and lengths of 35–60 mm define this type named after the cemetery at Kingston Down.[143] The Updown silver pin is 42 mm long and ornamented with incised lines along the pin shaft. Such pins have been recorded in graves from several east Kent cemeteries, notably at Buckland I (Dover), Kingston Down, Ozengell, Sarre and Sibertswold and manufacture in Kent for these would seem probable.[144] The Buckland I examples include those cast in copper alloy from graves F, 10 and 132, which have been attributed to Evison's phases 3 (AD 575–625) and 5 (AD 650–75).[145] Ross concludes that the earliest pins of this type date to the very end of the sixth or the early part of the first half of the seventh century, while those with hipped shafts belong towards the end of the second quarter of that century. They are occasionally found in male graves (*e.g.* Buckland I: Grave 10), but are mostly associated with female costume as was clearly the case here. A copper-alloy example is recorded from Finglesham grave 57.[146] The Updown pin was associated with a gilded copper-alloy imitation of a Frankish Merovingian gold coin confirming deposition within the seventh century (Appendix IV). Both items were located in what was probably the neck or upper chest area and the burial also contained a rather fine, though small, silver buckle with *cabochon* garnet settings and an iron rod chatelaine.

Facet-headed (length less than 85 mm) type (Ross Type LXXII): 89:5
The Updown silvered (probably base silver) pin belongs

to the Shudy Camps facet-headed sub-type (LXXII.i). This is named by Ross after a pin from Shudy Camps Grave 65 in Cambridgeshire and its pin-head appears to be very similar indeed to the Updown example.[147] In addition, Ross cites local parallels in east Kent from Kingston Down Grave 222 and from Finglesham Grave 163.[148] Overall, the weight of evidence supports a seventh-century date for this pin sub-type, which has been found at sites across southern and eastern England.

Pin with a collar and a small multi-faceted head surmounted by a faceted strip: 89:38
This pin does not seem to belong to any of the types and sub-types defined by Ross and the life-size reproduction in the published report does not permit an assessment of the precise form of the pin head here. It is described as having a small multi-faceted head surmounted by a faceted strip, a rounded tapered shank with the head separated from the shank by a flattened collar. Its dimensions are recorded as 32 mm long, with a 2 mm head, the collar 2 mm in diameter and the maximum thickness of the shank as 1 mm. A comparable copper-alloy pin with a 'thistle-shaped head' was the only find from Finglesham Grave 3, and the Updown and Finglesham pins may represent a local variant of the LXXII facet-headed pins.[149] This would fit the apparently seventh-century context of the child-sized Updown grave containing a knife. Neither pin resembles the 'thistle-headed' silver pin (also described as 'double-axe' shaped) from Buckland I Grave 160.[150]

Garnet-set disc-headed type (Ross Type LXI): 89:20
This silvered (or more probably base silver) pin with a single garnet set in its head appears to be comparable to the silver example from Chartham Down Grave 44 in east Kent.[151] In both cases we observe a discoid head with the *cabochon* garnets enclosed by beaded collars and this type forms Ross's variant LXI.i.b.[152] The grave assemblage contexts of Chartham Down Grave 44 and Sibertswold Grave 180 suggest a date range spanning the two middle quarters of the seventh century, and their overall distribution implies Kentish manufacture.[153] Finglesham Grave 20 contains a copper-alloy pin set with garnets in its head.[154] Although the Updown pin has been identified as a silvered cast copper alloy, a base silver casting seems more probable, and ideally this item deserves to be scientifically assessed along with the pin from 89:5.

Iron pins: 76:26; 89:18 (x 3), 89:26 and 89:52 (?)
Unfortunately it is impossible to offer much in the way of meaningful comment on the items described by Keller as narrow-shanked, round or square-sectioned, tapered iron pins with lengths of between 25–35 mm.[155] We need not assume that they were used as dress fittings, as Keller himself observes. Unfortunately Keller does not suggest an alternative function for them, though he does note that two of the five (but which two and from which graves is not made clear) preserve the remains of an iron link passed

through one looped end. This would suggest that they might belong instead to a rod chatelaine. It is particularly unfortunate that none of them is illustrated in the published report and clearly they would merit further study.

The three 'pins' from 89:18 were recorded as being located at the left shoulder (G), left wrist (B) and right ankle (A) of this adult female burial.[156] Seven polychrome and two plain glass beads and an iron ring, a fourth-century Roman coin, an iron key and a knife are the principal finds here. It seems unlikely that such a dressed corpse would additionally be wrapped in a shroud fastened by these three fittings. Single 'pins' are recorded for the other two burials, located by the left lower leg in the case of 89:26 (possibly at E, but unfortunately this is not labelled as such on the published grave plan).[157] Once again this represents a furnished burial of an adult, clearly of female gender with multiple monochrome glass beads and a bracelet. The remaining single 'pin' occurred, however, by the left elbow (D) of an adult male weapon assemblage in 89:52.[158]

Necklets

Necklets made up of beads with or without wire rings and pendants: 76:10, 76:15, 76:22, 76:26, 76:30; 89:1, 89:5, 89:18, 89:20, 89:23, 89:26, 89:32, 89:34, 89:36, 89:39, 89:43, 89:45 and 89:46.

Glass beads are the most common element in these small necklaces or necklets, but amethyst beads also occur in a minority of cases and there are single instances of amber and bone beads. Metal necklet fittings feature in several graves, most commonly in the form of knotted wire rings, on one occasion with a bead strung on them and also with a bucket-shaped pendant (76:15). There are also single examples of a disc or scutiform pendant, a gold pendant copying a Roman coin and a gilded pendant copying a Merovingian coin.

Glass beads have been surveyed most recently by Guido and Brugmann.[159] The range of beads present appears to fit the seventh-century context of the other finds from the Updown graves, with the possible exception of Grave 89:18. Single colour beads predominated with a colour range dominated by red, green, yellow and white for the opaque beads and green and blue for the translucent versions. There were relatively few polychrome beads and most of these seem to have been red with yellow ornamentation, though what seems to be a white-on-blue spiral occurs on a single flattened annular bead.

Single beads were recorded from five contexts: 76:30; 89:5; 89:20; 89:32; 89:36. The pale blue/green translucent annular bead was the only find from the child-sized grave of 76:30. A flat annular bead in 89:5 was found in the neck area near a dress pin, as part of a full female-gendered assemblage. It is described as monochrome opaque glass, but its colour is not provided in the report.[160] The 'clear blue' translucent annular bead from 89:20 was found with four knotted wire rings at the neck together with a garnet-set

dress pin.[161] A single monochrome opaque annular glass bead of un-stated colour from 89:32 was the only reported find from this adult burial.[162] The final example from 89:36 is an annular monochrome opaque glass bead, again with the colour un-stated, in a child-sized grave, found together with a knife and a handmade pot.[163]

Two beads were found by the neck of the adult in 76:10. One was an opaque white disc-shaped monochrome and the other an opaque brick-red long cylinder bead with yellow spots. At Schretzheim such beads were recorded in burials dated to the seventh century in *Stufe* 4, AD 590/600–620/30 (Grave 506), in *Stufe* 5, AD 620/30–650/60 (graves 393, 437, 488 and 541) and *Stufe* 6, AD 650/60–680 (Grave 628).[164] These were associated with a chatelaine amongst a few other finds that confirmed the possible female sex of the skeleton. Again just two opaque beads were recovered from what was presumably the neck or shoulder area within the child-sized grave cut of 76:22. There was one small and cylinder-shaped in pale green and one pale brown annular bead, which were associated with iron fittings from a wooden box. The two beads from 89:34 are a biconical monochrome opaque glass bead of unstated colour and an amethyst bead: for the latter see below.[165]

Three monochrome opaque glass beads were found with a copper-alloy scutiform pendant in what was probably the neck area within the child-sized grave 89:23. There is again no indication of the colours, but the forms are annular and biconical.[166] Similarly the three beads from the neck area in 89:39 are of monochrome opaque glass, with the colours un-stated, but at least there is a greater variety of forms here. One is a normal biconical, another is a twisted cylinder and the third a damaged elongated barrel-shaped bead.[167] This was a child's burial that also contained a firesteel-cum-pursemount and a knife.

There were four translucent green or greenish translucent glass beads from a necklace in 76:26, together with two amethyst beads and a gold coin-imitation pendant (see below) in a well-furnished female assemblage. Four beads were also recorded in the neck area of the unsexed adult (presumably a woman) from 89:1, the only other find being a knife. These appear to represent the usual, simple biconical and annular forms, are listed as monochrome opaque glass, but as ever with no indication of the colours.[168] Then there were four more similar opaque beads in 89:46, together with a flattened annular bone bead, all found in the neck area of an adult accompanied by a workbox amongst other items.[169]

A total of nine beads were recovered from the neck area in 89:18 together with an iron ring which has rusted around one of the beads.[170] This again forms part of a larger assemblage. Two of these beads are described as fashioned from 'clear blue' translucent vessel glass rim-sherds, hence their unusual forms. There were also seven polychrome opaque beads, though the colour descriptions for the polychrome beads are unhelpful: combinations of brown (probably meaning red), yellow, blue and white. The four drum-shaped beads are presumably red (or terracotta) and yellow combinations of circumferential combed zigzags. These resemble no. 50.8 from colour plate 5 in the Schretzheim report.[171] The same colour combination may well be represented by the two beads with circumferential wide crossing waves, one square and the other globular.[172] That leaves an almost square bead with blobs, which again might combine red and yellow.[173] Beads characterised by Brugmann as belonging to Koch types 49/50 (50.8) are attributed to her Bead Phase A2b with a date range centred on the middle of the sixth century, *c.* 530–80.[174] On the other hand those she attributes to Koch type 34 (similar to 35.3 and 33.14) are in her Bead Phase B2 and dated to *c.* 580–650.[175] While we cannot rule out a date within the second half of the sixth century for this assemblage, an early seventh-century attribution remains plausible.

There were also nine beads from 89:43, seven of which are monochrome opaque glass beads of un-stated colour and annular and biconical forms, one a decorated annular glass bead with a spiral trail, probably white-on-blue or vice versa.[176] This can be attributed to Bead Phases B2–C, *c.* 580 onwards in Brugmann's scheme. This burial also contains the only amber bead recorded to date: see below.[177] These beads come from the probable neck area of a child-sized grave and a further substantial necklace was worn by the child in 76:15. This has five silver or copper-alloy knotted wire rings and a bucket-shaped pendant (see further below), together with a mixture of translucent and opaque monochrome glass beads. There are two disc-shaped blue semi-translucent beads and an irregular-shaped pale green translucent bead on a sixth copper-alloy wire ring. The opaque beads are a double-segmented annular and three disc-shaped beads in red, five in different shades of green, all disc-shaped together with one mini-globular white opaque and one globular yellow opaque.

Ten beads are recorded from 89:46 under or near the skull of this probably female skeleton. Nine of these are standard annular monochrome opaque glass beads, colours un-stated, but the tenth is a biconical decorated bead with circumferential wide crossing waves and dots. The colour combination is not stated, but it is probably red with yellow waves and dots of Koch type 20 attributable to Bead Phase B, *c.* 555–650.[178] Finally, fifteen monochrome glass beads were recovered around the neck area of the adult burial in 89:26. Once again, there is no indication of the colours involved, but the forms are annular and biconical as usual.[179] Other finds include a wire bracelet on the left arm, confirming a female gender.

Amber beads are not a normal feature of seventh-century necklaces, though they are common in many fifth- and especially sixth-century contexts. The other beads from 89:43 confirm that this is indeed an otherwise normal seventh-century assemblage in a child's grave.

Bone beads are also relatively rare and the sole example from 89:45 is in a grave containing other glass beads,

but also a key seventh-century female artefact type: the cylindrical metal workbox.

Amethyst droplet beads represent imports from the east Mediterranean region and are a type-fossil for seventh-century burials.[180] Although widely distributed across England, they are more common in east Kent than elsewhere. Two were recovered from a necklace in 76:26 together with four translucent glass beads and a gold pendant copying an issue of Constantine I (see below). A third occurs in 89:34, again in association with a monochrome glass bead and in an assemblage that included iron shears. They occur in nine assemblages at Finglesham in graves 16, 57, 61, 62B, 96, 132, 157, 182, 187.[181]

A bucket-shaped pendant on a wire suspension loop from the necklet of 76:15 represents an amulet of a type more normally found in Anglian female burials of the sixth century. As Dickinson has pointed out, the Updown example is unusual for being in a female child's burial, for being recovered from a cemetery in east Kent and belonging to a mid to late seventh-century context. Another seventh-century possible example occurs in silver, however, from a teenage female burial at Lechlade, Gloucestershire, Grave 14.[182] It is assumed to be a symbolic object of some importance, probably representing the social role of full-size buckets in serving alcoholic drink and the female serving of drink and food to guests (see 76:7 here). A ritual and amuletic role is implied by such a symbol being worn very visibly, in this case at the centre of a necklace. The child wearing it may well have inherited her social and possibly religious role from her own mother, as may have also been the case with another child accompanied by seven bucket pendants in Grave 22 at Driffield I in the Yorkshire Wolds. The Anglo-Saxons were drawing on a wider and long-established continental Germanic tradition here, that was particularly strong in central and eastern Europe, but also represented in south Denmark and Schleswig-Holstein.[183]

Knotted wire rings are recorded in 76:15 (six rings), 89:20 (four rings) and 89:45 (one ring). These have been discussed by a number of scholars, notably Miranda Hyslop, Sonia Hawkes and most recently by Helen Geake.[184] Although they can occur on occasion in sixth-century female dress assemblages, *e.g.* Alfriston (East Sussex) Grave 43, they are more typical of classic seventh-century female necklaces.[185]

Scutiform pendants in silver are found in both sixth-century and seventh-century burial contexts.[186] Imitating in miniature the form of a buckler-sized shield, these disc pendants doubled as amulets.[187] Ornamented with punched circlets, this example from 89:23 can be compared to local examples in east Kent, notably the gold pendant from Kingston Down Grave 205 and also less closely the silver pendants from Buckland I graves 32, 35, 38 in phase 3 and 67 in phase 5.[188] A number of pendants are also recorded from assemblages at Finglesham, including a scutiform pendant from Grave 174 and disc pendants from Grave 138.[189]

Coin pendants are a key feature of seventh-century dress and the substitution of pendants copying coins is an appropriate response where original coins were not available. The *repoussé* gold copy of a fourth-century Roman coin from 76:26 is described and discussed in detail by Dr Gareth Williams in Appendix IV. It is a copy probably derived from a genuine issue of Constantine I and is provided with a suspension loop that matches one used to mount a Merovingian gold *tremissis* from Sibertswold Grave 172.[190] This loop suggests a date of manufacture around the middle of the seventh century and quite possibly later. It is not particularly surprising that the Roman copper-alloy coin recorded from 89:18 is a Constantinian issue attributed to Constantine II (AD 337–40), as fourth-century coins appear to be commonplace in Anglo-Saxon graves.[191] Presumably it was not pierced for suspension, nor is any kind of mount mentioned in Philp's report. It appears to be part of a group of objects placed inside the left arm and above the waist, perhaps in a bag, with this female adult burial.

Gareth Williams has also assessed the base metal imitation of a Merovingian gold *tremissis* originally mounted as a pendant from 76:36. This lightweight copy need not have been intended to deceive, but was perhaps made as 'costume jewellery'. Certainly the setting of Merovingian, Byzantine and Visigothic coins into pendants was fashionable in seventh-century Kent. The two *tremissis* coins set amongst the gold and garnet and gold and glass pendants from Sibertswold Grave 172 are relevant here.[192] The Updown pendant was either directly or ultimately copied via intermediary coins from a *tremissis* minted at Chalon any time between the 580s and *c.* 670. It was probably cast, gilded and provided with a mount around the middle decades of the seventh century.

Not surprisingly, coin pendants also feature in Grave 7 at Finglesham, though only one of these is a Frankish gold import (a *solidus* of Sigebert II/III), the other being a PADA *thrymsa*.[193] There is also a set of eight unmounted primary *sceatta* coins (*c.* 695–700) from a purse in Grave 145 there.[194]

Bracelets: 76:21, 89:26

The wearing of metal bracelets, typically on the left forearm is recorded elsewhere.[195] The bracelet from Grave 76:21 takes the form of a knotted wire ring, while that from 89:26 is an ornamented cast ring. Both seem to have been worn appropriately enough on the left forearm. The cast ring was compared by Keller to that from Buckland I Grave 141 found above the probable area of the left wrist and assigned there to phase 6 (AD 675–700).[196] A knotted copper-alloy wire ring version is also recorded

from Buckland I Grave 67 attributed to phase 5 (AD 650–675) there.[197] Other examples with sliding slip knots are recorded from Finglesham graves 34, 210 and 180 and Castledyke South (Barton-on-Humber) Grave 138.[198]

Buckles and belt sets: 76:2, 76:4, 76:5, 76:10, 76:11 (x2), 76:12, 76:13, 76:14 (x4?), 76:16, 76:17, 76:18, 76:20, 76:21, 76:24, 76:26, 76:27, 76:28, 76:29, 76:31, 76:33, 76:35, 76:36; 89:5 (small plate G5c), 89:12 (decorated G12b), 89:24, 89:26, 89:45, 89:51 and 89:52

Triangular-plated copper-alloy cast buckles: 76:11, 76:12, 76:13, 76:14, 76:26, 76:28; 89:45

Triangular-plated buckles with shield tongues represent a Kentish version of continental plate buckles dated from the late sixth century onwards. Broadly-speaking the Kentish versions seem to belong within the first half of the seventh century, with the possibility that the earliest go back into the last decade or two of the sixth century. The issue of whether they continue to be worn around the middle of the seventh century remains a problem.[199] Evison assigned graves 149 and 158 containing such buckles at Buckland I to her phase 6 (675–700) on the grounds of the horizontal stratigraphy, though this can be questioned.[200] The recent suggestion that the Finglesham 'pagan' buckle from Grave 95 could be as early as the second half of the sixth century is not provided with a full justification and can be regarded as improbable.[201] On the other hand it need not be as late as the middle of the seventh century. A mid seventh-century date may be correct, however, for the deposition of the burial with a tall straight-cone shield boss at Alton, Hampshire Grave 16, but the Style II filigree ornamented buckle was a damaged and repaired item.[202] Updown Grave 76:14 could be argued to belong to a similar date, as it is also associated with a tall straight-cone shield boss. On the other hand, it is now believed that the straight-cone version of the shield boss developed within the first half of the seventh century, in which case the 76:14 triangular buckle set can be regarded as confirming an earlier date. For the purposes of this report, it will be assumed that triangular buckles define an earlier phase of burial at Updown, extending no later than the middle of the seventh century.

Typically these buckles possess a shield-shaped tongue base and three disc-headed rivets on the triangular plate, the largest marking the plate terminal. Ornamentation varies, but includes animal elements in Salin Style II (graves 76:14 and 76:28). This can be combined with garnet settings, domed shell and garnet settings over the rivets (*e.g.* 76:28). Others are relatively plain, having borders demarcated by closely-spaced punched dots and spaced triangular (76: 11) or circlet (76:12 and 13) punched designs. The former can be compared to a buckle from Finglesham Grave 159 and the latter two buckles are more closely matched still by the Grave 97 buckle.[203] It is reasonable to suggest that these were produced in the same workshops. They are normally worn as waist belt fittings in male graves, often associated with spears.[204] The Updown examples fit the general pattern and spears are associated with the buckles in 76:11, 76:13 and 76:14 (plus a shield).

A cheap imitation of this triangular form in copper-alloy was recorded in Grave 89:45.[205] This can be attributed to Marzinzik's Type 23bii and is comparable to the copper-alloy buckle from Morning Thorpe (Norfolk) Grave 37.[206] Another such buckle in iron which belongs to her Type 23a occurred in Grave 76:26 and was associated there with a repaired imported Byzantine buckle of the *Trebizond* Type (see below), implying burial no earlier than the middle of the seventh century. Geake notes that small and miniature versions do continue into the later seventh century.[207]

Inlaid iron buckles: 76:5, 76:16, 76:24, 76:29 and 76:31

These five silver-inlaid buckles or belt sets were considered in an article by the excavator, in which she argued that the smallest of these from 76:16 with a square plate and loop decorated with silver-wire inlay imitating *cloisonné* cell designs was probably a Kentish version of a continental type.[208] It may yet turn out to be matched in a continental cemetery, however, and could represent a Frankish-made import. There is no doubt that a three-piece belt set with two triangular and one square plate from Grave 76:29 was such an import.[209] A similar case can be made for the buckle with a triangular plate and *cabochon* garnets set over the three plate rivets from Grave 76:31. Traces of silver inlay imitating *cloisonné* designs feature once again here.[210] The Finglesham cemetery also produced a continental inlaid belt set from Grave 25.[211]

A triangular-plated buckle with a set of three disc-headed rivets intact from Grave 76:24 has a groove marking an outer border, but no other trace of inlay.[212] The triangular-plated buckle from Grave 76:5 seems to have been an old and worn item when buried apparently without any rivets to attach it to a belt and with a secondary repair in order to provide a working tongue. There seem to be faint traces of inlaid designs within a central panel and in the outer border of its plate as well as on the tongue of the buckle.[213]

Overall the dating of continental inlaid belt sets with 'monochrome' silver wire inlay, particularly when it imitates *cloisonné* designs, is now placed relatively early. This means the late sixth and the first third of the seventh century (Ament's AMIII and JMI).[214] It is probable that all the Updown inlaid buckles were buried within the first half of the seventh century.

Inlaid cloisonné 'Fish' buckle: 76:35

The iron buckle with a long rectangular plate to which is attached a copper-alloy *cloisonné* garnet plate with a central outline of a fish enclosed by a honeycomb cell background represents an unusual find. Fish motifs occur as components of composite buckles from Crundale

and from Eccles Grave 19 in east Kent.[215] An additional example is a gilt bronze buckle from Faversham in the Ashmolean Museum collection in which the fish is flanked by predatory birds.[216] These are interpreted usually as overtly Christian symbols indicating the beliefs of either the craftsmen or more likely the patrons who commissioned these buckles. The four fish arranged in a cross shape on a box disc mount from Hardingstone, Northamptonshire might support such a case.[217] On the other hand, fish and specifically portrayal of pike appear on shield fittings of the sixth to seventh centuries, so the buckle versions may equally refer to the fearsome qualities of this particular fish.[218] The Updown buckle is an important addition to this small corpus of material and appropriately comes from a weapon assemblage featuring a class C2 spearhead.

Silver-sheet buckle set with cabochon garnets: 76:36

This buckle stands out in the corpus of material, despite its relatively small size. Manufactured in silver and set with three *cabochon* stones with a zig-zag cut-out at the belt-end of its upper plate, this buckle combines a silver dress pin, an imported Frankish gold coin and a chatelaine to mark out one of the richest dress assemblages of the Updown cemetery.

Trebizond Type Buckle: 76:26

This buckle represents an import from the Eastern Roman Empire belonging to a form found in East European contexts dated to *c.* 630 for the Mersin Treasure and *c.* 646 for the Malaja Pereščepina deposition.[219] Its form is a simplified version of one from the Istanbul Museum.[220] The Updown brooch was clearly an old and damaged item, which had lost its lower plate ornamental infill and its original loop and tongue fittings. The upper plate had been cut straight and sheet metal attached by rivets to hold a locally-made Kentish cast loop and tongue decorated with spaced triple grooves. This suggests that it was old and worn when repaired, implying a date of deposition no earlier than the middle and more probably within the second half of the seventh century. It is interesting to note the presence of two droplet amethyst beads also imported from the Mediterranean region and a gold pendant copy of a Roman coin in this female assemblage. There was also an iron triangular belt plate in this grave assemblage (see above).

Buckle with a raised box plate: 89:12

This copper-alloy buckle appears to have linear decoration on cast loop as well as its cast rectangular plate and seems to possess a square shield on its tongue. It can be assigned to Marzinzik's Type II.15a, implying a sixth to early seventh-century date range for this item.[221] Similar belt plates from Buckland I Grave 98 were assigned to Phase 3 (575–625) there and we can also compare it to the Bifrons Grave 22 buckle.[222] We can reasonably suggest a late sixth- or early seventh-century date for this burial.

Small buckles with attached squared plates: 76:2, 76:4, 76:10, 76:11 76:17, 76:18, 76:20, 76:21, 76:27, 76:35; 89:5, 89:12; 89:24 and 89:26

Small buckles with or without squared plates fastened through the belt leather by rivets are a typical dress fitting of the seventh century, particularly in the middle and later decades.[223] In terms of Marzinzik's scheme, these belong to her Type II. 24a.[224] They can be relatively plain, *e.g.* the iron buckles from graves 76:2, 76:10, 76:20, 76:21, 76.27 and 76:35, the iron buckle with a copper-alloy plate fastened by five rivets from Grave 76:4, the copper-alloy version fastened by two rivets from Grave 76:18 and those with three rivets from graves 76:11 and 89:5. Only the iron plate survives from Grave 76:17, with no trace of the loop or tongue. Others are relatively elaborate, *e.g.* that from 89:26 with its cast linear ornament and row of punchmarks along the plate.[225] The example from Grave 76:11 is associated with a cast triangular-plated buckle (see above), implying some overlap between the two types. Matches can be found from Finglesham from graves 33, 108, 125, 144 and 196 for the 76:2 simple buckle and from Grave 144 for a copper-alloy buckle with four rivets rather than the five from 76:4.[226]

Simple buckles: 76:14, 76:16 and 76:33

A simple buckle loop and tongue forms the most basic type of buckle. Several of these are made of iron (graves 76:14 and 76:33) and others of copper alloys (Grave 76:16). The forms of the loops appear to be more oval than D-shaped and so fit Marzinzik's scheme Type I.11.[227]

Fire-steel and purse-mount: 89:39

Iron fire-steels which acted as purse-mounts for a pouch containing the flint and tinder are considered by Geake.[228] The example from Updown resembles those from Shudy Camps (Cambridgeshire) Grave 19 and Buckland I Grave 157, the latter assigned to phase 5 (650–675).[229] They are found in both male and female burials and the Updown burial would appear to be a female assemblage.

Chatelaine: 76:10, 76:15, 76:21, 76:25, 76:26, 76:27 (?), 76:36; 89:5, 89:18, 89:26, 89:34, 89:35 (?), 89:45 and 89:46

Chatelaines have been defined as 'one or more chains or rings carrying from the waist and carrying a collection of objects', and the bulk of those represented at Updown consist of interlinked iron rods with keys, latch-lifters or other key-like objects suspended from them.[230] Such chatelaines have their origins in the sixth century, as at Buckland I, Dover Grave 28 assigned to phase 2 (AD 525–75) there.[231] It has been argued that they achieve their period of greatest popularity in the second half of the seventh century and in the early eighth century.[232] Associations with *thrymsa* coins have been noted for several burials: Finglesham Grave 7 (coin of *c.* 660–

65), Buckland I Grave 110 (*c.* 660–80) and Lechlade, Gloucestershire, Grave 179 (*c.* 665–80) and also with *sceatta* coins at Boss Hall, Ipswich Grave 93 (*c.* 690) and Harford Farm, Norfolk, Grave 18 (*c.* 690–700).

Just one burial from the 1989 excavation produced a copper-alloy chatelaine mount of Frankish type. This distributor has an openwork cross design ornamented with circlet punch-marks and with a single suspension opening at the top and four subsidiary openings to suspend other items at the bottom (89:45). This was misidentified as a 'probable wrist-clasp', though its position on the grave plan parallel to the left thigh and above a workbox should have provided sufficient grounds for questioning such an interpretation.[233]

There is some debate as to whether chatelaines are functional or symbolic, amuletic objects, but no question that they are primarily linked to adult female status.[234] They do also occur in the graves of children under the age of ten, however, as at Finglesham Grave 7 (2–5 years), Buckland I Grave 55 (about 5 years) and Polhill Grave 104 (about 7 years). In at least two cases chatelaines have been associated with spearheads, though at Shudy Camps, Cambridgeshire, Grave 76 the spear was interpreted as a weaving tool, whereas at Buckland I Grave 9 the skeleton was sexed as male and the spearhead occupies a conventional position. The distribution of chatelaines is weighted towards Kent in this period.[235] Iron chatelaines at Finglesham that include a double-hook key as in 76:21 occur in graves 21B, 174 and 180.[236]

Rings: 76:25, 76:35; 89:20, 89:23, 89:34 and 89:45

Rings have a wide range of uses but tend to feature in female assemblages, particularly as parts of purse or bag collections.[237] The ring from 76:25 is matched at Finglesham Grave 174, where it functions as a chatelaine suspension ring for a set of keys and a spoon.[238]

Shoe fittings: 76:12 and 76:15 (lace-tags)

The tiny iron objects from 76:12 were assigned a function linked to shoe fittings on the basis of their location associated with the ankles within the grave. The copper-alloy rolled-sheet lace-tags from 76:15 are a well-known artefact type; all the examples recorded from the Buckland I cemetery are assigned to dates after 650 (graves 113, 150, 156 and 160) and Finglesham Grave 145 tags were found in a bag collection with eight *sceatta* coins (*c.* 695–700). There is no strong gender link, with rolled types found with women, men and at least one younger child, while sites from east Kent feature in their overall distribution.[239]

Personal Equipment

Staff cap-end: 76:20

What appears to be a sheet copper-alloy mount shaped to fit around the knob-end of a wooden staff or baton, presumably fastened by rivets, is a unique item at present.

Antler comb: 89:45 and 89:47

Combs which in the past have been described as made of animal bone, frequently turn out to be fashioned from antler when subjected to analysis. Only one of these is illustrated and the fragment from 89:47 appears to represent a double-sided comb.[240] It can be assumed that the same is the case for 89:45. This is a long-lived comb type and cannot be used to date the burials in question, though it can be noted that grave 89:45 also contained a copper-alloy workbox associated with a young adult (16–24 years) whereas the other comb comes from a child burial. A majority of combs in the seventh century are buried with women or female children, but they can also occur in male graves. Their distribution occurs across the whole of Anglo-Saxon England in this period.[241]

Knives

The typology published for the Buckland, Dover cemetery by Evison has been adopted here.[242] The only versions which seem not to be represented are Type 3 (with an angled back and curved cutting edge) and Type 6 (with a straight back, incurved near the tip and a curved cutting edge), but it should be noted that there are a number of incomplete or damaged knives from the 1989 season whose radiographs might yet enable us to attribute them to one of these types. The range matches what we would expect to find in a seventh-century cemetery. The size of knives has been considered significant (small knives having a blade length of 45–99 mm, medium ones blades of 100–129 mm and large knives blades of 130–175 mm). The relationship of their tangs to the blade can also be recorded, but these additional factors have not been considered here.[243]

Type 1 with a curved back and a curved cutting edge: 76:4, 76:13, 76:15, 76:23, 76:31, 76:34, 76:36; 89:9, 89:21, 89:24, 89:26, 89:36, 89:39, 89:43 and 89:52.
Type 2 with a straight back and a curved cutting edge: 89:38 and 89:41 (razor/knife).
Type 4 with a curved back and straight cutting edge: 76:1, 76:5, 76:7, 76:10, 76:14, 76:16, 76:20, 76:24, 76:27, 76:28, 76:29, 76:33, 76:35, 76:36; 89:1, 89:18, 89:25, 89:28, 89:40, 89:45, 89:46, 89:48 and 89:51.
Type 5 with an angled back and straight cutting edge: 76: 11, 76:12, 76:17, 76:19, 76:20, 76:21, 76:25, 76:26, 76:27; 89:5, 89:34 and 89:41.

Uncertain: 76:18, 76:25 (x2), 76:36; 89:23, 89:26, 89:34 (x2), 89:47 and 89:49.

Shears: 76:26; 89:5 (G5e–g) and 89:34.

Shears of iron feature in seventh-century female graves, often in association with a chatelaine, and elsewhere the majority of datable examples appear to belong to the second half of the seventh and the early eighth century. Geake cites seven associated with copper-alloy workboxes and two coin-dated contexts from Buckland I Grave 110 with *thrymsa* coins (*c.* 660–80) and Harford Farm, Norfolk Grave 18 with a *sceatta* coin (*c.* 690–700). They are linked to adult female and child burials, with no recorded examples from a male grave context in England.[244] The shears from the Updown graves fit the established pattern of being associated with well-furnished female burials. There are several burials at Finglesham containing shears.[245]

Tools: 76:10, 76:14, 76:15, 76:20, 76:25, 76:27, 76:29 and 76:35.

A variety of iron tools are represented and seem to represent a characteristic element in seventh-century burial assemblages. Most of those from graves excavated in 1976 were spatulate tools with a rectangular or sub-rectangular blade section and a tang. These occur in graves 76:15, 76:20, 76:25, 76:27, 76:29 and 76:35. Dating evidence demonstrates these occur both in the first half of the seventh century, *e.g.* Finglesham Grave 25 associated with an imported silver-inlaid iron triangular belt set, and the later seventh or early eighth century as in Castledyke South (Humberside) Grave 183, Harford Farm, Norfolk Grave 28 and Uncleby (Humberside) Grave 31 with copper-alloy workboxes, etc.[246] These seem to occur with adults of either gender associated with weapons in some cases and with female items in others.[247] Other examples from Finglesham occur in graves 59, 67, 129B, 133, 163 and 202.[248]

Another iron tool type is pointed in form and occurs in 76:10. It is represented in east Kent at Buckland I Grave 149 and Finglesham, where 'awls' were identified in ten burials. Two Finglesham graves with such tools contain triangular buckles implying burial as early as the first half of the seventh century, one of which is an inlaid iron belt fitting in Grave 25. Examples are also found in late seventh or early eighth-century contexts as at Finglesham Grave 145 with *sceatta* coins (*c.* 695–700). A majority of such burials are male, but Burwell, Cambridgeshire Grave 121 was a well-furnished female assemblage with a copper-alloy workbox.[249]

An iron tanged object is described from the female assemblage of 89:26, but unfortunately it is not illustrated.[250] The interpretation as part of a box lock plate on the basis of a comparison with the Buckland I Grave 55 box fittings may be correct, but alternatively it could represent a socketed blade tool.[251]

Iron spoons: 89:45 and 89:47

Small iron spoons are a characteristic feature of some seventh-century burials in Kent. They are not strong enough to be used as tools (augers or gouges) and probably functioned for measuring or mixing materials (perhaps medicine or ointment). They are usually found in adult or adolescent female burials and datable examples seem to belong to the later seventh or early eighth century, *e.g.* Buckland I Grave 119 with *thrymsa* coins (*c.* 660–680) or Grave 129 assigned to Phase 5 (AD 650–75).[252] At Updown they occur in a child burial (89:47) and with a female aged 16–24 (89:45).

Vessels and containers (including coffins)

Stave iron-bound buckets: 76:7

The iron remains of two collapsed metal-bound wooden buckets were recorded from the north-east corner of Grave 76:7. The legs of the corpse may have been deliberately flexed to provide sufficient space, but one iron band fragment was found at pelvic level as if the bucket had 'exploded' inside the grave.[253] Reconstruction views were prepared in 2002 for this publication by Mr K. Singh based on this report (Fig. 28) and the author is grateful to Dr Martin Comey for commenting on these drawings and suggesting small modifications based on his own research into stave bound wooden vessels in the Early Medieval Period. Since then, one of the missing drawings of these buckets prepared for Sonia Hawkes by Mrs Cox has been relocated and is included here (Fig. 29).

Iron-bound wooden buckets first appear in Anglo-Saxon graves around the middle of the sixth century and come to replace copper-alloy bound stave buckets.[254] The appearance of these iron-bound vessels in a seventh-century grave here is not surprising, though the presence of just a single knife in the grave is unusual, as we would expect normally to find gender-related artefacts with a pair of these buckets. Such seventh-century buckets can be found in both male and female burials, but in the case of 76:7 accompanied an adult male in his thirties.[255]

Dr Carole Morris examined the bucket iron fittings and concluded in 1981 that 'there were two buckets because the (iron) fragments would not allow there to be only one, some being too small for the size of the largest one'. She noted that the first and largest bucket had a top band 20–24 cm diameter, probably 22–23 cm and a width of 1.9 cm, a middle or bottom band 23 cm diameter and with a width of 1.2 cm.; the second bucket has a top band *c.* 16–16.2 cm diameter, a handle diameter between ends (reconstructed) of *c.* 16 cm.; fragments of another band *c.* 21.4 cm diameter that could be part of one of the bands of the first bucket, *e.g.* part of a middle band of *c.* 22 or so cm, making the band of 23 cm the bottom of three bands (otherwise it could be the bottom band of the second bucket, but this is a little less likely);

lastly that there are other fragments that could be parts of any of the bands mentioned above of similar width, including part of a handle.

These reconstructions would make the first bucket almost parallel-sided and the second bucket, if the lowest band were 21.4 cm diameter, would be more of a sloping-sided vessel, wider at the bottom than the top. The first bucket should have a height of approximately 20–22 cm. and the second bucket should have a height of approximately 17–19 cm. Although Morris' thesis remains unpublished, her discussion of buckets and tubs from Anglo-Scandinavian York has appeared in print.[256]

Turned wooden vessels: 76:14; 89:5 and 89:24

Copper-alloy mounts for decorating or repairing splits on lathe-turned wooden vessels occur in three graves here. There may well have been other such vessels that did not require such repairs, but if so they were not visible to the excavators.[257]

It is particularly unfortunate that the pair of gilt copper-alloy rim-mounts from 89:5 is inadequately described and illustrated in the published report.[258] It is clear that the *repoussé* ornamentation consists of Salin Style II animal interlace, yet this is referred to misleadingly as 'interlocking "wavy-lines" (6 mm. wide) surmounted by pierced dots beneath another narrow band of "wavy-lines".' In fact these two vessels are important additions to a growing corpus of Style II ornamented rim-mounts from late sixth and seventh-century burial contexts. Such vessels are represented in high-status burials from Sutton Hoo in mounds 1 and 2, the recently excavated Prittlewell (Southend) Essex chamber grave, the Taplow (Buckinghamshire) barrow burial, and from the site at Farthingdown, Coulsdon (Surrey).[259] Kentish cemeteries at Old Park, Dover and Faversham have produced further examples. A copper-alloy die for making such *repoussé* mounts was recovered from a medieval rubbish pit in Rochester and is matched by dies from Salmonby (Lincolnshire) and from Mitchell's Hill, Icklingham (Suffolk). Circular dies for producing related *repoussé* metalwork have also been recorded from a grave at Castledyke South, Barton-on-Humber (formerly Lincolnshire) and from Lullingstone in west Kent. A review of this material was published by Hawkes in association with Speake.[260] The Updown rim mounts would benefit from a thorough first-hand assessment by a scholar with Speake's expertise and deserve proper publication in their own right. Assessment as to whether they were used on small stave-built or on lathe-turned containers would also be valuable.

The vessel mounts from Updown 89:5 were associated with a ? male sexed adult, which included a dress pin with a facetted head and a pair of shears. They seem likely to have been placed in a wooden box at the foot (east) end of the grave around the middle of the seventh century.

Rectangular repair plates made of sheet copper-alloy and wrapped around the rim of a cracked turned wooden vessel often provide the best evidence for the presence of such a vessel. A simple repair plate occurred in 89:24, but was misidentified as a belt plate; this was despite the fact that it was located above the skull area in a child's grave (age 4–5 years), which also contained a spiked spearhead and a buckle, implying a boy.[261]

In the case of 76:14, there is a copper-alloy band fastened by a rivet at either end, perhaps acting as a handle, two rim-edge plates with serrated decorative edges fastened by a pair of copper-alloy rivets and a copper-alloy clip. All these were associated at the foot (east) end of the coffin with a curved soil stain indicating the partial survival of the bowl itself. This was associated with one of the richest weapon assemblages with a tall-cone shield boss and spearhead with an adult aged between 25 and 45 years.

A useful summary of the published literature is provided by Geake and research into their construction and manufacture using a pole-lathe formed an important element of Carole Morris' research.[262]

Wooden casket or box: 76:21, 76:22 (possible bed); 89:5, 89:26

As we have already noted, the pair of turned wooden vessels with Style II rims were placed in a small wooden box or casket prior to burial at the foot end of the female assemblage of 89:5. Small wooden boxes with iron mounts start to appear in six burials in the later sixth century at Buckland I (phase 3, AD 575–625), but they also occur in one grave attributed to phase 4 (625–50), three in phase 6 (675–700) and one in phase 7 (700–750). This sequence is confirmed at Finglesham with a box associated with a triangular buckle of early to mid seventh-century date in the adult male assemblage of Grave 95 and another with a copper-alloy workbox in Grave 8 implying a probable date in the second half of the seventh century.[263] Other Finglesham burials (all female) containing box fittings are recorded in graves 59, 62B, 65, 157 and 163.[264] Only one burial is definitely male (Finglesham 95) and the vast majority are adult women together with a few childrens' graves.[265]

The hinged brackets of 76:22 probably belong to a box, but alternatively might relate to some other item of wooden furniture, and a bed was an initial suggestion. They are paralleled in Buckland I Grave 35 with other iron box fittings, attributed to phase 3 (AD 575–625).[266] Their association in 76:22 with two iron split pins and two angle brackets suggests that a box is the more probable interpretation and these can also be compared to the iron fittings from Finglesham boxes in graves 8 and 34.[267]

The iron lock-plate and two large split pins from 89:5 are described in the 1989 excavation report, together with two angle brackets from a female assemblage in 89:26, both being female assemblages.[268]

Pouches and purses: 76:28 and 76:36

Mounts and other fittings for leather or other organic purses and pouches are commonplace. A double-ended mount from 76:28 resembles those described as fasteners from pouches or small boxes in graves 57, 62B and 180 at Finglesham.[269] Again, the incomplete copper-alloy mount from 76:26 resembles a complete example from Finglesham Grave 138.[270]

Copper-alloy cylindrical workbox: 76:34; 89:45

Workboxes are one of the key type-fossils of seventh-century cemeteries. With the possible exception of one ornamented with Style II animal ornament from Burwell, Cambridgeshire Grave 42, none seem to belong earlier than the middle of the seventh century, and one from Harford Farm, Norfolk Grave 18 is associated with *sceatta* coins (*c.* 690–700).[271] If we include the Updown examples, well over fifty have been recorded now and both the Updown boxes belong to Gibson's Type I with a pull-push lid secured by a chain: this is by far the most common version. These are normally adult female items as in the case of Updown 89:45 (aged 16–24 years), but there are other child burials containing them to match 76:34. Examples are the assemblages with children at Marina Drive, Bedfordshire Graves E1/E2 and Didcot, Oxfordshire Grave 12. The Updown 76:36 workbox has been discussed in an article by Crowfoot, but this concentrated on the contents comparing them to those from six other sites.[272] Unfortunately this article wrongly attributes two of the workboxes to the sixth century (Kempston grave 46 and Uncleby), but otherwise it provides a reasonably sound discussion of these cylindrical lidded containers and their contents. Interpretations have included the suggestion that they might contain Christian relics, and the fragments of silk recovered from 76:34 represented the first time silk had been recognised in an early Anglo-Saxon archaeological context.[273] An alternative is that they might be linked symbolically to textile production, traditionally a female activity, though their presence in child burials argues against that suggestion.[274] Finglesham Grave 8 has produced the only example from that neighbouring cemetery.[275]

Wheel-thrown pottery: 76:29; 89:47, 89:49 and 89:50

The carinated biconical jar from 76:29 was attributed by Sonia Hawkes to the 'Beerlegem type', with its upper body divided by spaced horizontal corrugations into three zones filled by an incised wavy line. It is a blackware (grey-black) and can be compared to the dark brown, tall, carinated biconical jar with corrugated ornament restricted to its upper half from 89:50. In turn, both resemble a lost pot from Ozingell described as made of 'pale red clay', and Evison cites a continental buff-coloured vessel from Ecques.[276] Other biconical corrugated vessels are illustrated by Evison from cemeteries at Prittlewell, Essex, (opposite the Kent coastline) and from Breach Down Grave 5.[277] None of these is as tall as the Updown 89:50 vessel, but tall rounded biconical forms do occur at Valetta House, Broadstairs Grave 10 and Sibertswold Grave 176.[278] The jar from 89:50 represents the sole find from its burial, whereas the pot from 76:29 is associated with an imported silver-inlaid belt set and an E3 spearhead.

A biconical bowl from 89:47 with incised ornament on a red-brown and dark brown surface unusually has zones of decoration on both the upper and the lower surfaces of the vessel. It cannot be paralleled amongst the biconical bowls illustrated by Evison.[279] The associated finds from this child's grave are not particularly helpful. A more rounded biconical form is represented by the small plain red-brown bowl with a slightly everted rim from 89:49. It bears some resemblance to a grey-black squat biconical bowl from Breedon-on-the-Hill in Leicestershire, but this lacks the everted rim.[280] Much closer parallels are provided by three shouldered jars from St Peter's, Broadstairs graves 39, 55 and 194 with grey and black surfaces.[281] The Updown pot was found in a child-sized grave with a B1 spearhead and a knife.

Hand-made pottery: 89:25 and 89:36

Little can be said about the local hand-made pottery recovered near the head of a male burial with a spear and a knife (89:25) or the small rounded jar from the child-sized grave 89:36. A few sherds were noted from graves and associated features in the 1976 season and some of these appear to be of Anglo-Saxon manufacture, while others were identified by C. F. C. Hawkes in 1976 as dating to the Iron Age. All of these isolated sherds might represent residual material and are thus not particularly helpful. Research on pottery fabrics for the region developed to interpret the Canterbury excavation material would provide a basis for future assessment of the limited quantity of handmade pottery present here.

Glass palm cup: 89:35

The only recorded glass vessel is a plain palm cup (Harden Type Xb) datable no earlier than the seventh century. Other graves in east Kent containing single palm cups include the rich female assemblage in Kingston Down Grave 205, attributable within the first half of the century as well as Buckland I Grave 160 and Finglesham graves AA4/14 and 132.[282]

Coffin fittings: Nails: 76:1, 76:14 (?), 76:19, 76:28, 76:35; 89:5 and 89:49; cleats or brackets: 89:31

Wooden coffins do not necessarily require iron fittings

as they could have been fastened by jointing and/or the use of wooden pegs or trenails. Only one of the Updown graves produced iron cleats of the type recovered from the Sutton Hoo mound 1 ship-burial or Buckland I, Dover Grave 41.[283] These were used to fasten two adjacent planks together. Simple iron nails feature in at least a further seven burials here. The three with disc-shaped heads from 76:1 are matched in five sets of coffin nails from Finglesham graves 7, 56, 67, 145 and 204, the latter belonging within the sixth century.[284]

Amulets

Cowrie shell: 89:20 and 89:45

Complete cowrie shells (*Cypraea pantherina*) were imported ultimately from the Red Sea region and seem to be prized items buried with adult women and occasionally with children. Although they can be found in contexts dating as early as the later sixth century, more commonly they were buried in the seventh century and they are to be found associated with union pin sets or with copper-alloy workboxes.[285]

Oyster shell: 89:20

Alternative shells may have been used as substitutes for imported cowries, as seems to be the case in this burial, which also contains a cowrie.

Roman Coin: 89:18

Whereas in the fifth and sixth centuries Roman coins of third and fourth-century date are often pierced so that they can be strung with beads, in the seventh century such coins are often left undrilled or pierced. They are more commonly found in adult female assemblages, as is the case in this Updown grave.[286]

ANALYSIS AND INTERPRETATION

The analysis of the excavated sample of 78 burials will be conducted initially for the community as a whole as a single-phase site. Then a basic binary phasing will be proposed and its implications considered. This phasing is based on the available stratigraphic and topographic evidence combined with the relative chronology of artefact types from the grave assemblages.

Relationships between grave assemblages, age bands and sex/gender attributions

As expected within a sample of 78 burials, we find a full range of grave assemblages here. There were 12 individuals (15.4%) accompanied by no visible dress fasteners or other associated finds (76:8, 76:9, 76:32, 89:15, 89:16, 89:19, 89:22, 89:27, 89:29, 89:30, 89:33 and

89:44). A case can be made for two graves being robbed in antiquity, one being 76:18 and the other an unspecified grave from the 1989 season.[287] It might be 89:31 with coffin fittings, but no surviving bone or finds, or perhaps one of the six burials with no reported finds for which unfortunately no grave plan has been published (89:19, 89:22, 89:27, 89:29, 89:30 or 89:33). Other burials are accompanied by no more than a knife (76:23, 89:9, 89:28, and 89:48) or by a single bead (76:30 and 89:32). Not all of those found with a single object can be regarded as low-ranked individuals, however. There is a jewelled disc brooch in a child-sized grave (76:6), a seax in each of two adult burials (89:37 and 89:42) and an imported pot in another case (89:50). Moving up the scale from knife-only or single bead graves are those equipped with a buckle and knife. Some of these are also accompanied by one or more weapons. There are only two weapon assemblages of real note, however, these being 76:14 (shield and spear) and 76:19 (seax and spear), though perhaps the two seax-only burials (89:37 and 89:42) are of equivalent rank. While weapon and buckle sets are unambiguous male indicators, we cannot be equally certain that every one of the buckle and knife combinations belonged with males, though a majority certainly did. Turning to the female dress fittings, these range upwards from just a single bead on to a couple of beads with a chatelaine or a wooden box to much more impressive assemblages that can include at least one exotic object, as represented in 76:26, 76:36, 89:5 and 89:45.

These artefact-based gender patterns can be related in a majority of cases to the estimated biological age and sex indicators obtained from the human remains, including the teeth. In the following discussion the term 'sex' will be used to indicate a biologically-determined attribution and 'gender' to define a culturally-determined identity. Cross-reference will be made to the skeletal report in Appendix I and following standard practice no sex determinations have been made there for sub-adults. Nevertheless, gender identifications can be proposed for sub-adults based on artefact evidence. Both sex and gender attributions are provided for adult burials whenever the evidence is available. For a significant number of graves at Updown, however, the skeletal evidence is so inadequate we have to make use of grave and internal coffin dimensions. These suggest that we can separate child-sized from adult burials. Children's graves here could be as long as 2.30 m (76:17) and 2.27 m (76:15), whereas an adult grave could be as short as 1.75 m (76:5), so we have to allow for a significant degree of overlap. As a rule of thumb, it would seem that any grave shorter than 1.75 m might well have contained a child rather than an adult (*i.e.* 76:6 at 1.40 m, 76:22 at 1.10 m and 76:34 at 1.00 m long).

A total of twelve burials were identified as containing children (76:2, 76:9, 76:15, 76:20, 76:27, 89:21, 89:23, 89:24, 89:30, 89:38, 89:39 and 89:47) and a further nine were either attributed to children by the excavators or assigned on the basis of grave dimensions alone (76:6,

76:17, 76:22, 76:30, 76:34, 76:37, 89:36, 89:43 and 89:49). These 21 graves represent nearly 27% of the cemetery sample and almost a quarter of these are accompanied by a B1 type spiked spearhead (24%), implying a significant male presence (76:17, 76:20, 89:21, 89:24 and 89:49). One or more female-gendered items occurred in ten graves (76:6, 76:15, 76:22, 76:30, 76:34, 89:23, 89:36, 89:38, 89:39 and 89:43) representing 48% of the children. That leaves six (28%) with no finds or no securely gendered finds (or just inadequately recorded at 76:37). Ten of the twelve children have mean ages ranging from 4.9 to 11.1 years and the absence of any children below the age of three should be noted. Comparisons with the much larger sample from a cemetery on Thanet with similar bone condition are helpful. Over 400 graves were recorded at St Peter's Tip near Broadstairs and Duhig has established the identity of 328 individuals.[288] Her sample included only 2 neonates (0.6%) and 2 infants (0.6%), together with 47 children (14.3%) and 17 adolescents (5.2%), making a total of 68 sub-adults (20.7%). The absence of any babies or infants in the Updown sample seems less surprising in the light of these figures, though we might have anticipated one or more adolescents and they are missing here as well.

The presence of B1 spiked spearheads in five pre- or early teenage child burials suggests that this weapon was a significant indicator of inherited status at Updown. Two of these child burials with spears were additionally marked by a ring-ditch (76:17 and 89:49), emphasising inherited social standing. It is particularly unfortunate that neither grave produced any bone. The remaining three children with spears occupied standard grave cuts, which are unlikely to have had an associated mound. Only two of the five could be aged and both appear to be around five years old (76:20 and 89:24), well below the contemporary Anglo-Saxon age of majority at ten years.[289] Thus a guardian from the father's kin is required to protect a child whose father has died up to the age of ten according to cap.6 of the late seventh-century Kentish laws of Hlothere and Eadric, while a ten-year old can be an accessory to theft in Ine's West Saxon code cap.7.[290] We should note that the remaining Updown B1 spearhead came from an atypical adult grave context (76:31: age-band: Adult 2 of 25–35 years and sex possibly female). As the spearhead was not positioned in the normal head (or foot) areas, it seems more appropriate to discuss it with the other Adult 2 female burials (see below).

Female-gendered items from child burials were similarly associated with ring-ditch enclosed graves in two cases (76:15 and 89:39). The 7–12 year old in the coffined grave 76:15 wore items fully appropriate for an adult female burial (a silver-wire ring and glass bead necklace, an iron-rod chatelaine, a knife and shoe lace-tags), but the 9–12 year old in 89:39 was more modestly dressed (three monochrome glass beads, an iron fire-steel, a copper-alloy mount and a knife). Of the seven standard grave cuts with female-gendered children (76:6, 76:22,

76:30, 76:34, 89:23, 89:36 [coffined] and 89:43), only one could be aged: a five-year old in 89:23 with another modest assemblage (three monochrome glass beads, a copper-alloy disc pendant, an iron ring and a knife). Single items such as the jewelled disc brooch from 76:6 need not be reliable gender indicators, as they may represent heirlooms consigned with the child, and this may even be the case for the workbox and knife in 76:34. Workboxes are generally adult female items, however, and the other Updown workbox belongs to a probable female adult (89:45). So not all of these seven children were necessarily girls and it may have been appropriate to bury some young boys with female items. Nevertheless a majority of the child burials probably represent girls, particularly with so many children being accompanied by male-gendered spears. For all the furnished child graves it can be assumed that burial appropriate to the social position of the parents or foster parents is being signalled.

Turning to the adult burials, three individuals are categorised as adolescent/adult (76:19, 76:24 and 76:35). These represent individuals of fully adult size, who could either be late adolescents who had finished growing, or indeed adults of any age. Grave assemblages indicate at least two of them are male and the seax, spear and knife burial may well represent a full adult (76:19), while the same may be the case for the male with a spear and a *cloisonné* ornamented buckle (76:35). On the other hand, though the triangular iron buckle and knife in 76:24 is probably associated with a man, we cannot be certain here. A single tooth from 76:18 aged a fourth individual to between 6–20 years (child/adolescent/adult), but comes from an adult-sized grave that appears to have been robbed in antiquity. The surviving finds include an iron socket from a spearhead or a spear ferrule, suggesting an adult male identity. These four burials represent 6.1% of the skeletal material.

The Adult 1 band (17–25 years) is represented by just four males and four females amounting to 13.2% and comparable to the 16.5% for St Peter's Tip (24 males, 20 females and 10 unsexed individuals). A male gendered spear and ferrule is recorded for 76:3, but the knife in 89:28 and a wheel-thrown pot in 89:50 do nothing to confirm the sexing here. All three occupied standard graves, though there was probably sufficient space for a mound over 76:3. A ring-ditch enclosed 89:40 containing a spear and knife to contradict its 'probable female' sexing. A female gendered counterpart was also enclosed by a ring-ditch (76:26) with a particularly impressive assemblage (a necklet of amethyst and green glass beads, a gold coin-imitation pendant, a Byzantine bronze buckle, a pair of shears, a knife and a chatelaine). Unfortunately her skeleton could not be sexed. The three remaining burials are probable females occupying standard graves, though the assemblage from 89:45 (a cowrie shell, workbox, an openwork chatelaine mount, five monochrome glass beads and a copper-alloy buckle set) is almost as grand as that from 76:26. The buckle with a cast box plate from 89:12 is not helpful and no finds at all are reported from 89:29.

Thirteen males and seven females were assigned to the Adult 2 band (25–35 years) forming 32.7% of the skeletal sample compared to 22% in the Adult 2 band at St Peter's Tip (33 males, 30 females and 9 unsexed individuals). Spears are associated with three burials sexed as males (76:1, 76:11 and 76:29) and one of these was enclosed by a ring-ditch (76:11). Another sexed male in 76:7 is accompanied by two iron-bound stave buckets and a knife. There is no reason to change the sexing here, but buckets can also occur with women.[291] No finds at all are recorded with the three sexed males from 89:15, 89:16 (a prone burial) and 89:27, two of which had been dug into clay hollows (89:15 and 89:16) rather than into chalk bedrock. For the three probable males confirmation of the sexing is provided by the seax in the ring-ditched 89:37 and the spear, buckle and knife from 89:52, while the triangular copper-alloy buckle and knife from the ring-ditch enclosed 76:12 fits a man's grave. A clear case can be made for the possible male from the ring-ditched 76:4 (a large spearhead, buckle and knife). No diagnostic skeletal features occur in 76:28, but a triangular buckle and knife again probably implies a man. A possible female identity has been assigned to the skeleton accompanied by an ambiguous assemblage in 76:31 (mentioned above). This included a B1 spiked spearhead normally associated with sub-adult males at Updown, together with an inlaid iron triangular buckle and a knife. Sonia Hawkes attributed this burial to a boy, but did not have access to a reliable skeletal report.[292] The positioning of the spearhead close to the left hip, as if detached from a shaft and part of a pouch-bag collection, would support an adult female here. It is even possible that the spearhead had been converted into a weaving tool. On the other hand, a male gender identity cannot be ruled out definitively in view of the buckle and knife combination here.

Of the seven Adult 2 females, three were definitely or in one case possibly enclosed by ring-ditches (76:10, 76:21 and 89:46), but in a fourth case (89:44) this could be accidental, as the grave might pre-date the ring-ditch. This is appropriate as there were four ring-ditched male burials for the same age band (76:4, 76:11, 76:12 and 89:37). Firmly sexed females occurred in two graves with female-gendered items (89:18 and 89:20), but also with no recorded finds in 76:8. A probable female in 89:46 is associated with beads and a knife, but in 89:44 the contracted corpse is again unfurnished. A possible female from 76:10 perhaps set within a ring-ditch appropriately possesses gendered items including beads and a chatelaine, while the unsexed skeleton in a coffin from the ring-ditched 76:21 was accompanied by a bracelet, a chatelaine and a wooden box among other items. A more balanced sample in terms of sex distribution within this age band would have provided us with more examples of moderately-furnished female assemblages. Nevertheless, there is sufficient here to suggest that the overall status range of male and female burials is similar across this age band and might well have included heads of households and other married couples.

The last two adult age bands produce significantly fewer burials with just eight (13.2%) for Adult 3 (35–45) and three (4.9%) for Adult 4 (45+). These proportions are reasonably close to the 48 individuals (14.6%) at St Peter's Tip in the Adult 3 band (26 males, 14 females and 8 unsexed) and the 15 people (4.6%) in the Adult 4 band (8 males and 7 females). The one definite Updown Adult 3 male came from the ring-ditched 76:33 accompanied by a simple iron buckle and a knife, while the 'probable male' from the ring-ditched 89:51 has a spear, buckle and knife. The remaining two probable males either have no associated finds (89:22) or a clearly female-gendered assemblage (89:5) including a dress pin, a bead, a pair of shears and two wooden vessels from a wooden box by the feet. An unsexed skeleton from 76:14 is accompanied by a spear, a shield and a fine triangular buckle, so is clearly gendered male. Fortunately one of the two definite females possessed female dress fittings (89:34) including an amethyst and a monochrome glass bead, a copper-alloy cast ring and a pair of shears, though the other (89:32) produced just a single glass bead. A probable female in the ring-ditched 89:9 has just a knife. For each sex then there was a single grave marked by a ring-ditch in this age band, but in both cases the assemblage was distinctly basic, with its status indicated by the earthwork. Reassigning 89:5 to a gendered woman we find a balanced set of four males to four females for Adult 3. Moving on to the oldest individuals, a definite male in the coffined 76:13 is accompanied a spear, a triangular buckle set and a knife, but the coffined 'probable male' of sixty plus years in 76:5 has just a buckle and a knife. The possible female coffined in 76:25 seems to be a woman in gender terms, for though the iron fittings by the right shoulder need not represent a chatelaine, the tools and knives associated with an iron ring above the waist suggest a woman. It seems improbable that the relative rarity of such older individuals implies that some elderly people were buried elsewhere. Rather it seems to be the case that few lived into their forties or older. Some of them were buried with normal adult assemblages (*e.g.* 76:13 and 89:5), but others seem to have been assigned token items, though they could still be marked by a ditched earthwork (*e.g.* 76:33). This may reflect their former social roles having passed on to the next reproductive generation.

That leaves the few remaining adults who cannot be placed into an age band. There are those who might well be men. Two possible males in 76:23 (coffined) and 89:48 are each accompanied by a knife, while an unsexed individual in the ring-ditched and coffined 76:16 wore a fine silver-inlaid iron buckle and a knife. There are probable female equivalents in 76:32 and 89:25, the former with no visible finds, but the latter containing a spear, so a gendered man. We seem then to have four male and just one 'probable female' among this un-aged adult group. To these we can add the unsexed adults in 89:1, 89:19, 89:26 and 89:41, together with one further individual who could be neither sexed nor aged in the adult-sized grave 89:35. A female gender can be proposed from the beads and a knife in 89:1 and from the beads, cast bracelet and chatelaine fittings

in the coffined 89:26. Equally a male identity can be accepted for 89:41 with its spear and two knives, but there are no finds in 89:19. Grave 89:35 contains a glass palm cup implying relatively high status, but the assemblage is ambiguous in gender terms.[293] So we seem to have five male or probable male adults (76:16, 76:23, 89:25, 89:41 and 89:48), three female adults (76:32, 89:1 and 89:26), and one of uncertain gender (89:35). Altogether, these nine burials provide 13.8% of our sample to which we can add the four adolescent/adult burials (76:18, 76:19, 76:24 and 76:35) with male genders (6.2%) making 20% overall. For completeness we need also to consider the four adult-sized graves with no surviving bone (76:36, 89:31, 89:33 and 89:42) associated in turn with a female assemblage (76:36), with a seax (89:42), with just four coffin cleats (89:31) and with no finds at all (89:33). These added to the 17 unaged or unsexed adults form a total of 21.8% of the recorded burials. This 20% or 21.8% is matched at the St Peter's Tip by its total of 71 un-aged adult skeletons forming 21.6% (24 females, 23 males and 24 unsexed). Indeed overall the comparison with St Peter's Tip is remarkably close. Thus the total adult sample for St Peter's represents 79.3% (114 males, 95 females and 51 unsexed), while the 49 adults from Updown represent 78.4% (28 males, 19 females and 2 unsexed). As we have seen the sub-adult proportions are also comparable with 14.3% children at St Peter's compared to 19.7% children at Updown, providing we allow for the neonates and infants (1.2%) and the adolescents (5.2%) who are absent from the Updown sample.

To summarise: we can suggest genders for fourteen children (five male and seven female) out of a total of 21 graves, though no finds at all occurred in one child-sized grave (89:30) and possibly in another (76:37). For the 57 adult burials, 39 can be sexed from the skeleton (22 as male, 17 as female with 17 unassigned) and 36 gendered from associated finds (23 as male, 13 as female and 8 as questionable or unassigned). Adult male sex identification is supported by gendered object types in thirteen cases and adult female in eight cases (nine if we include 76:31 left unassigned above). Equally male sex identification is not actually contradicted by artefacts in six cases and for females in two cases. Also gender identifications can be used in twelve cases where the bones could not be sexed or there were no bones surviving at all: seven male and five female adults. Significant discrepancies between sex and gender identifications are limited to just four graves: the problematic 76:31 (a possible female adult, but with the presence of a typical boy's spearhead), 89:5 (probable male sex, but female gendered items), 89:25 and 89:40 (probable female sex, but a spear that indicates male gender). We have sex identifications, but no associated finds for four adult males and four adult females and there is no surviving bone, but clear gender indicators for one man and one woman respectively. Allowing that our sample consists of human remains from 65 burials out of 78 graves and that bone condition ranges from rather poor to non-existent, then this is not a bad outcome.

Social standing, gender identity and age bands related to chronological phasing and grave alignment

Most archaeologists would accept that burial practices in this period consist of symbolic statements designed to impress the community and those of its neighbours who attended its funerals. This symbolism was marked in terms of both above-ground and below-ground structures, as well as by the manner in which the deceased was laid in the grave, the costume in which the corpse was dressed and the placement of other non-dress items with the corpse. We also acknowledge that burials did not necessarily mirror the status of the individual in life, but rather reflected the image that the family or household organising the funeral wished to convey about the household as a whole through the public deposition of a member. Nevertheless, it is clear that most burials fall into defined bands and it seems reasonable to assume that the most important individuals, such as the heads of household, received special treatment. Others will have fallen into categories that probably reflected their social distance from the heads of household. Age was also an important factor here. As we have seen children are present, but are in some senses under-represented in this cemetery and there were no babies, infants or adolescents in the excavated sample. Older individuals, particularly women but also men, may have passed on their social role to their younger successors some years even decades before their death. Their mode of burial might reflect their dependency on their successors, the replacement heads of household, and the modification of their own value to the family or household unit. It may be that the wisdom of experience and memory they carried were especially valued in a society operating in an oral environment. A mature woman, often perhaps a widow, who was past her child-bearing years, no longer needed to be buried wearing the elaborate dress fittings appropriate to the young wife in her late teens or twenties of a farmer who was acting as the head of his household. She may well have worn a costume in later life that reflected her revised status, just as widows in some southern European countries still wear black even today. The older man, perhaps a widower, might retain the status of a free warrior, being buried symbolically with a weapon such as a spear, but could also be deposited without a weapon. This need not imply that he had never carried weapons or fought on behalf of his kin or his lord, but it might indicate that his role had changed to that of valued advisor and 'living memory' to the household and community at large.

We will begin by examining the significance of the above-ground external markers visible to the archaeologist as penannular ring-ditches. Their relationship to the dimensions of the grave-cuts they enclosed and the nature of the burial assemblages contained therein is considered. The key issue is whether the ring-ditched graves can be correlated with the richest artefact assemblages or whether there is no significant difference between the range of assemblages found in unenclosed graves and those marked by a ring-ditch structure. Alternatively, might the creation of earthwork structures be adopted as a substitute for an elaborate display of costume fittings and other items normally placed in a burial? We also need to establish whether there were gender or age correlations linked to the grave structures in this cemetery.

As we have observed, ring-ditches definitely enclose ten graves excavated in 1976 (76:4, 76:11, 76:12, 76:15, 76:16, 76:17, 76:21, 76:26 and 76:32 and 33) with possibly a further two (76:10 and 76:18), while eight were recorded enclosing nine graves in 1989 (89:9, 89:37, 89:38, 89:39 and 44, 89:40, 89:46, 89:49 and 89:51). In terms of grave-cut dimensions the ring-ditched graves are neither bigger nor deeper than the unenclosed graves. The largest of the ring-ditched graves, number 76:4, was 2.80 m long by 0.90 m wide and 0.68 m deep. Yet this is exceeded by the unenclosed 76:29 (2.86 × 1.13 × 0.85 m deep). The shallowest of the ring-ditched graves contained the skeletal remains of children or were child-sized, *e.g.* 89:49, a mere 0.34 m deep, but then 76:17 had a depth of 0.90 m, making it the deepest of the ring-ditched burial cuts. Adults enclosed by ring-ditches occupied graves that ranged in depth from 0.48 m (76:12) to 0.85 m (76:16). A similar picture emerges from the ordinary grave cuts. Here a child-sized 76:34 was only 0.16 m deep, yet the children of 76:20 and 76:30 were buried at a depth of 0.61 m, deeper than many ordinary adult graves. The deepest of the adults in standard graves was the weapon assemblage with a probable male in his thirties in 89:52 at over a metre (1.02 m) deep. So we cannot point to a simple division between larger, deep graves containing the leaders marked by ring-ditched mounds or berms and smaller, shallower coffined graves for the remainder. Such a phenomenon has been observed in the sixth-century 'Frankish' cemetery at Basel-Bernerring in Switzerland.[294] More locally in Kent there are the chamber graves dated within the first half of the seventh century at the central cemetery excavated near Saltwood.[295] None of the Updown graves achieved the outsize dimensions of a chamber-sized grave (*Kammergrab*) and equally there are no truly outstanding grave assemblages present here to match the very richest recorded in contemporary cemeteries elsewhere in east Kent.

In terms of age bands and assemblages, two of the ring-ditched graves belonged to children accompanied by spears in the coffined 76:17 and in 89:49. The child/adolescent/adult in a despoiled adult-sized coffin in 76:18 was also accompanied originally by a spear represented by a socket for a spearhead or its ferrule. This should probably be included in the single-spear grave category. The only Adult 1 male occurred in 89:40 gendered by its spear and knife despite the probable female sexing. In the Adult 2 age band a single weapon (seax) in 89:37 may signify a higher status than does the combination of a spear, triangular buckle, smaller buckle and knife in the coffined 76:11, or the spear, buckle and knife in the coffined 76:4. A weapon-free male with a triangular buckle and knife occurred in the coffined 76:12. For the Adult 3 band, there is 89:51 with its spear, buckle and knife, and 76:33 with a simple iron buckle and knife (10.5%). That only leaves the coffined 76:16 with a fine silver-inlaid iron buckle and knife accompanying an adult. It seems reasonable to suggest that these ten assemblages (eight with weapons and two without weapons, but with showy, decorated buckles) represent boys and men of similar standing in this community. Significantly, the simplest was associated with a mature man of around forty (76:33), perhaps an individual who had surrendered the position of head of household to the next generation. His seniority seems to be marked by the grave structure rather than the burial itself. In the other nine cases, however, the burial tableau at the funeral was of equal importance.

Similarly, female dress fittings occurred with three children in graves enclosed by ring-ditches. One was a child of seven to twelve years wearing a silver-wire ring and glass bead necklet, an iron-rod chatelaine, a knife and a pair of shoe lace-tags in the coffined 76:15: items more appropriate for a woman of marriageable age. The second was the nine to twelve year old in 89:39 accompanied by three glass beads, an iron fire-steel, a copper-alloy mount and a knife; and the third in 89:38 had a dress pin and knife. Again such items would more usually be found with adult women. There was only one Adult 1 female in grave 76:26: a particularly fine assemblage featuring a necklet of amethyst and green glass beads, a gold coin-imitation pendant, a Byzantine buckle, a pair of shears, a knife and a chatelaine. Three females belong in the Adult 2 band: one containing eight glass beads and a knife (89:46), the second two glass beads, a buckle, a knife and a chatelaine (the coffined 76:10) and the third produced a buckle, knife, chatelaine and a wooden box (the coffined 76:21). The Adult 3 woman of some 40 years in 89:9, however, has nothing more than a knife (5.25%) and seems to match the simplicity of her male counterpart in 76:33.

These burials are matched by others in ordinary grave cuts, such as the three weapon burials in 76:14 with its spear, shield and a fine triangular buckle; 76:19 with its spear and seax; and 89:42 with just a seax. Twelve graves contained a single spear (76:1, 76:3, 76:13, 76:20, 76:29, 76:31, 76:35, 89:21, 89:24, 89:25, 89:41 and 89:52) usually accompanied by a buckle or a knife, or even by both. In four cases the buckle involved was a well-made, showy item, as with the triangular buckle from 76:13, the fine imported inlaid belt set from 76:29, the inlaid and jewelled triangular buckle from 76:31 and the *cloisonné* ornamented buckle from 76:35, but it could also be a simple buckle with a rectangular plate as in 76:20 or 89:24. In just four cases a spear was accompanied by a knife, but no buckle (76:1, 89:21, 89:25 and 89:41). Male or probable male burials featuring a buckle and/or a knife without any associated weapons range from grave 76:28 with its fine Style II ornamented and jewelled triangular buckle and knife to grave 89:12 with just a buckle and grave 76:23 with only a knife. The man buried with two iron-bound stave buckets and a knife in 76:7 may well

have been as important as many of the other men buried without weapons in the cemetery.

Female dress fittings range equally widely amongst the unenclosed graves. They can again include assemblages as fine, if not superior to those buried under ring-ditched mounds. The clearest example is the coffined 76:36 with its silver dress pin, a small jewelled silver buckle, a pendant made from a copy of a contemporary Merovingian coin, three knives and an iron rod chatelaine. Another assemblage has a dress pin accompanying a wire ring and bead necklace, etc. in 89:20 and there is the cowrie shell, workbox and beads in grave 89:45. Further down the rankings would be the two beads, buckle, knife, tool and 'chatelaine' in the coffined 76:10, the chatelaine, knife and tool in the coffined 76:25 and five other adult assemblages featuring beads from graves 89:8, 89:23, 89:26, 89:32 and 89:34. A child can be accompanied by a jewelled cast disc brooch – probably an heirloom (76:6), or by a workbox and a knife (76:34), or by a pair of beads and iron box fittings (76:22), but can be limited to a single monochrome glass bead in one case (76:30). A single knife is recorded in four adult burials (89:9 with a ring-ditch, 76:23, 89:28 and 89:48) that can be sexed as belonging to men (76:23, 89:28 and 89:48), but the individual from a ring-ditched grave was a probable woman (89:9).

There are two unfurnished graves enclosed by ring-ditches, but certainly in the case of the probable woman in 76:32, it seems probable that her burial had been an ordinary one and its whereabouts forgotten when accidentally and only partially cut by its successor of 76:33. It is presumably for 76:33 that the ring-ditch was dug, which is reasonably well aligned with its eastern causeway. The situation for 89:44 is less clear-cut, though there is no doubting that its neighbour 89:39 is the one aligned on the eastern causeway. It is possible that the Adult 2 probable woman placed in an unusual contracted position in 89:44 represents a contemporary death to the furnished child of nine to twelve years accompanied by female gendered items in 89:39. She may even play a protective role for the girl here, but this could be another case of an earlier unfurnished burial being forgotten by the time the burial plot was used for the girl in 89:39. All the remaining ten unfurnished graves were in ordinary grave cuts (76:8, 76:9, 89:15, 89:16, 89:19, 8:22, 89:27, 89:29, 89:30 and 89:33), two of which were children (76:9 and 89:30) We will return to the pairing of 89:39 and 89:44 shortly.

So while ring-ditches are more likely to contain a well-furnished burial, there are exceptions, and in two cases these are linked to relatively old age. Nevertheless, ordinary grave cuts can also contain well-furnished burials, though it is possible that all the unfurnished individuals occurred in ordinary grave cuts that predated the ring-ditches on their plots.

Cemetery Phasing

Phasing can be approached initially by assessing stratigraphic relationships between inter-cutting features (a pair of graves and one case of inter-cutting ring-ditches, with each ditch enclosing a single central grave). The observations that emerge from this analysis will then be considered in relationship to the orientation relating to these inter-cutting features. This suggests that relatively subtle variations in grave orientations within the overall east to west alignment might bear some chronological significance. If this case is accepted, it permits the establishment of two successive and slightly overlapping phases. An alternative, but complementary approach will take the grave assemblages as its starting point. It will propose that many of these assemblages can be assigned to either an earlier or a later phase within the seventh century. Again the possibility of some overlap in a boundary zone between these successive relative artefact-based phases cannot be ruled out. In particular allowance must be made for the age at death of the deceased. Thus a child or young teenager wearing the latest fashions might be buried before an elderly adult accompanied by objects mostly acquired as a teenager or as a young adult.

Mention has already been made of the inter-cutting graves represented by 76:32 and 76:33 located within a single ring-ditch. There is also the set of inter-cutting ring-ditches enclosing 76:15 and 76:16. Although the scope for deriving a significant contribution through conventional stratigraphic relationships might seem to be limited, these relationships do provide a key to phasing based on orientation. In the case of the inter-cut graves, 76:32 contained a probable female adult accompanied by no visible finds. It was clear to the excavators that this burial had been cut towards its foot end by 76:33. The latter had been dug to take a mature (Adult 3) male accompanied by a simple iron buckle and a knife. It is quite possible that this was done in ignorance of the earlier burial here and it is rather unlikely that two successive burial episodes would have taken place after the mound or berm for this ring-ditch had been constructed. The secondary male occupied a grave aligned with the causeway entrance to the associated penannular ring-ditch, whereas the alignment of grave 76:32 bears no relationship to the alignment of the ring-ditch. It seems that it was the furnished male grave (76:33) that was signalled externally by a ring-ditch and its associated earthwork monument.

A number of other graves excavated in 1976 share a similar orientation to that for the primary burial of 76:32, notably the four of 76:13, 76:27, 76:26 and 76:34, and two of these were enclosed by ring-ditches (76:26 and 76:27). We can suggest tentatively that these five represent a compact sequence of funerary events. Four more graves excavated in 1989 also share a similar orientation to 76:32, being recorded as on an axis of around 100° (graves 89:24, 89:40, 89:43 and 89:51). Similarly the alignment of the secondary 76:33 is matched by the orientation of graves 76:25, 76:23, 76:24, 76:20, 76:19, 76:28, 76:31, 76:36, 76:35 and 76:37 to mention only those closest to the ring-ditch enclosing 76:32 and 76:33. Graves excavated in 1989 sharing a similar orientation seem to be among those with an axis in the range of 65° to 72° (89:1, 89:16, 89:20,

89:23, 89:31, 89:32, 89:33, 89:35, 89:41, 89:42, 89:44 and 89:47). Again a tentative case can be made for regarding this common orientation range as a new phase of burial activity. Obviously though, we will need to consider whether such variations in grave orientation really do represent separate burial episodes or whether variations of alignment were the norm throughout this cemetery's development.

Turning next to the inter-cutting ring-ditches 15 and 16, it has been argued on the basis of probability that the ring-ditch enclosing Grave 76:15 was constructed before that dug around Grave 76:16. If that is correct, then the earlier of the two burial episodes was for a child wearing classic Final-Phase female dress fittings in 76:15 that would be equally appropriate for an adult woman.[296] Yet the secondary ring-ditch for grave 76:16 enclosed an unsexed adult, probably gendered male with a silver-inlaid iron buckle, a second small buckle and a knife. On the basis of these finds, it would normally be argued that the adult in 76:16 would have been interred earlier than the child in 76:15. As the sections at the inter-cutting between the ring-ditches were not decisive, however, that might actually be the case. On the other hand, the man might have been wearing his decorated belt for several decades before his death and long before the young girl acquired her dress fittings.

Either way, it seems reasonable to suggest that only a limited time-gap may have separated the deaths of this girl and the man and the construction of their adjacent burial structures. It is also worth noting that the ring-ditch for the adult 76:16 enclosed a significantly greater area than any of the other eighteen (or twenty) ring-ditches recorded in 1976 and 1989. While it is possible that those digging the ditch for 76:16 felt no excessive respect for the pre-existing southern neighbour in 76:15, it is equally plausible that a shared family or household relationship was being signalled here. If the adult here died just a few months later than the female child, he might even have been a parent or foster parent to this girl. In the future DNA evidence from human bone may allow us to explore such relationships in cemeteries of this period. Unfortunately the epigenetic evidence derived from the skeletal evidence is relatively limited at Updown. There is some dental evidence to indicate that the well-dressed girl in 76:15 shared the characteristic of incisor shovelling with the adults in graves 76:7 (male), 76:31 (possibly female) and 89:20 (female). These four cases are scattered spatially across the southern half of the cemetery and chronologically as well (see the artefact phasing below). There are also two examples of another dental feature, Carabelli's cusp, in children from graves 76:20 and 89:39. Finally bowed femora are shared by two unfurnished adult males in 89:15 and 89:16. Exploring family relationships in any detail for this cemetery sample, however, remains problematic.

The presence of two further adjacent graves located side by side within a single ring-ditch enclosure excavated in 1989 (89:39 and 89:44) deserves more detailed consideration in the light of the interpretation offered here for the inter-cutting graves 76:32 and 76:33. The unfurnished and unusual contracted burial in 89:44 contained a probable female of 25 to 30 years and her grave was within the southern half of the ring-ditch enclosure. By contrast, the child of nine to twelve years in grave 89:39, already mentioned as possessing a Carabelli's cusp, was accompanied by modest female-gendered items including three glass beads. This assemblage contrasts with the much more elaborate dress assemblage worn by the girl of a similar age with incisor shovelling from 76:15. The girl's grave 89:39 was both more centrally located and also aligned with the causewayed entrance to the penannular ring-ditch. It is reasonable to suggest that the contracted adult female of 89:44 might represent an earlier and possibly lower-status burial. Whereas in the case of 76:32 (the unfurnished probable female adult), the grave was actually cut by the adult male in 76:33, there can be no certainty that 89:44 actually preceded the digging of 89:39 with its associated ring-ditch. Nevertheless, the available evidence presents this as an intriguing possibility. Equally the alternative that both 89:44 and 89:39 represent a contemporary burial event still cannot be ruled out. Burial position is a relevant issue here, as the adult in 89:44 is the only true contracted burial recorded to date from this cemetery. Supine burial within a single east-west grave-cut is the norm here, though three other burials (two adults and a child) do appear to have been placed lying on one side with or without the legs being flexed (76:5, 76:7 and 76:20). Additionally there are two other graves containing unfurnished adult males placed in unusual positions. One lay prone (*i.e.* face-down) with its legs crossed (89:16) and the other had its legs slightly flexed and crossed, though its upper body occupied a normal supine position (89:15). Interestingly these two individuals were linked by the skeletal feature of bowed femora. Not one of these five exceptional burials was enclosed by a ring-ditch, however, though all of them were located in the vicinity of ring-ditched burials (*e.g.* 76:4, 76:33, 76:11 and 76:17). All this seems to strengthen the suggestion that both graves 76:32 and 89:44 may have predated the ring-ditches that enclosed them and that quite possibly they belonged to a lower-ranked group of burials.

Contribution of the grave assemblages to the phasing of the cemetery

At this precise moment in time, we lack a refined dating sequence for the Anglo-Saxon cemeteries of the east Kent region in the seventh to eighth centuries. This will change in the near future and then we will have thirty-year (human-generation length) phases for furnished burials from the later sixth century to the early eighth century. For the sixth century such a thirty-year scheme already exists for east Kent, as established on the basis of seriated female grave assemblages. Brugmann's phases II-IV make use of imported continental dress fittings, including glass beads, to correlate each phase to an absolute date range, derived from coin-dated burials in the Frankish kingdoms.[297]

In the meantime, we can relate the Updown finds to those from the Buckland I (Dover) cemetery excavated in the 1950s and published in the 1980s.[298] Although there is no independent basis for checking the absolute date ranges assigned to the Buckland I seventh and eighth-century burials, we can accept the relative sequence of the graves in Buckland I phases 3 to 7, based on their eastward migration across the site. The principles of horizontal stratigraphy (or topochronology as some prefer to call it), first developed by Flinders Petrie in his analyses of prehistoric cemeteries in Egypt, produces a relative sequence. This in turn can be combined with the date ranges assigned by Evison to particular artefacts and grave assemblages to produce her series of twenty-five year phases (4–6) from AD 625–700. The rarity of closely-datable imports or of coins in closed-find grave contexts in these Buckland phases limits their application to other cemeteries, even within the region of east Kent. So we cannot apply information from the Buckland phases and their absolute date boundaries in a simplistic manner to the Updown assemblages.

Fortunately, within the next five years, we will be rather better informed, as we will be in a position to use radiocarbon dates to provide a verifiable chronology for this period. A national survey of seventh and eighth-century furnished graves, funded by English Heritage, is nearing completion. This will permit the presentation of a much more refined sequence than can be attempted in the present publication. The national project combines the seriation of selected finds assemblages, using correspondence analysis, with high-accuracy radiocarbon dates, derived from collagen samples taken from human bone in the same closed-find burial contexts.[299] Bayesian modelling of these two data sets permits the establishment of a detailed dating scheme, which will be applicable across the whole of Anglo-Saxon England for a date range extending in thirty-year phases from the last third of the sixth century into the early eighth century. For Kent, that will permit us to extend Brugmann's sixth-century phases on through the seventh century and right up to the last phase of furnished burial here in the early eighth century. Interestingly, the initial results (subject to revision) suggest that the traditional artefact-based chronology for the period centred on the seventh century will essentially be confirmed. Of course, there will be some clarification involving refinements and revisions of dating at a detailed level.

All that will be attempted in the present report is a very basic division between an earlier and a later period. Artefacts believed to typify burial within the first half of the seventh century are assigned here to Updown Phase 1. These include the jewelled disc brooch from Grave 76:6, the Kentish triangular buckles, sometimes decorated with animal ornament in Style II, the imported Frankish silver-inlaid belt set from 76:29 and the silver-inlaid iron buckle with a rectangular plate from 76:16 and the other related iron belt fittings.[300] The association of a triangular buckle decorated with confronted Style II boar heads and a tall-cone shield boss in 76:14 adds to evidence elsewhere that such shield bosses developed rather earlier than the classic tall curved cone 'sugar-loaf' shield boss type, making a first-half seventh-century date appropriate.

By contrast, finds typical of the 'Final Phase' as first defined by E. T. Leeds are assigned here to Updown Phase 2.[301] The copper-alloy cylindrical 'workboxes' from 76:34 and 89:45, the glass palm cup in 89:35, as well as classic female dress fittings help to define this phase. The dress items include single silver pins and necklaces made up of silver-wire slip-knot rings combined with amethyst beads and/or with monochrome opaque glass beads. These fittings are normally dated no earlier than the middle of the seventh century and the English Heritage project indicates that they are likely to have been deposited within the third quarter of the seventh century. Other items attributed to Updown Phase 2 include the numerous graves containing small buckles with rectangular plates, though the possibility that such buckles were being used earlier in the century should not be denied.

Eleven of the 1976 furnished burials (76:5, 76:6, 76:11, 76:12, 76:13, 76:14, 76:16, 76:24, 76:28, 76:29 and 76:31) can be assigned with some confidence to Updown Phase 1, but there seem to be only two Phase 1 graves amongst the burials recovered in 1989. These attributions are based on the type of polychrome glass beads from grave 89:18 and the buckle with a rectangular box plate from grave 89:12, both of which suggest dates no later than the early seventh century. This gives us only thirteen Phase 1 graves. Some fourteen 1976 burials (76:2, 76:10, 76:15, 76:18, 76:20, 76:21, 76:22, 76:25, 76: 26, 76:27, 76:30, 76:34, 76:35 and 76:36) can be attributed to Updown Phase 2 and a further fourteen burials from 1989 (89:1, 89:5, 89:20, 89:23, 89:26, 89:32, 89:34, 89:35, 89:36, 89:38, 89:39, 89:43, 89:45 and 89:46) giving a total of twenty-eight. If the Phase 1 adult in grave 76:16 was buried after the Phase 2 child wearing classic Final Phase female costume items in 76:15, should we reassign 76:16 to Phase 2 (thus giving a total of fifteen graves for Phase 2 in the 1976 sector)? Alternatively we could leave 76:16 in Phase 1 and recognise the existence of a period of overlap between the deposition of Phase 1 assemblages and the earliest Phase 2 assemblages. On the other hand, if it was instead ring-ditch 15 that cut ring-ditch 16, then the phased sequence can stand.

In terms of their distribution, most of the Phase 1 graves are to be found broadly spaced across the southern half of the cemetery as excavated. They are sometimes somewhat isolated, but also occur in pairs or even threes. Moving across the site from west to east, there is firstly the pair of graves 76:5 and 76:6, then 76:14 is located between the ring-ditched 76:11 and the ring-ditched 76:12, while 89:18 is sited part way between 76:14 and the ring-ditched 76:16 and to the south of 76:16 is 76:13. The isolated burial of 89:12 is some distance to the north of 76:16 and 76:29 is set to its east. Quite a way east of 76:13 is 76:24 and finally there is the pairing of 76:28 and 76:31. The Phase 2 graves are located both to the south of and in-between and to the north of the Phase 1 burials, but they also extend further to the west and east of the Phase 1 graves.

Not surprisingly, this artefact assemblage-based exercise in phasing still leaves a considerable number of furnished graves unassigned, because they lack any fine-dating indicators. This is particularly true of those weapon graves that are not accompanied by distinctive buckle fittings, dominated as they are by single spear finds. None of the spearhead forms can be dated very precisely and therefore none of them can provide a sound basis for assigning burials here to a specific phase within the seventh century. Nor can we phase the three graves that contained a single-bladed seax (graves 76:19, 89:37 and 89:42) with any confidence. To the extent that the seax seems to represent a substitute for the high-status double-edged sword (*spatha*), it is more probable they belong in Phase 2, but we cannot be dogmatic here. It is not particularly surprising that no find of a *spatha*-type sword has been recorded at Updown. Likewise the presence in the excavated sample of a single shield boss with a tall straight cone from grave 76:14 is typical of so many seventh-century cemeteries in Kent and elsewhere. The absence of shield boss forms fashionable in the early decades of the seventh century may again be significant.[302] It seems to suggest that few of the Updown weapon burials belong to those decades. Further excavation of other sectors at Updown might well rectify this situation however.

On balance, it seems best to attribute a more general seventh-century date to a total of ten 1976 burials (76:1, 76:3, 76:4, 76:7, 76:8, 76:9, 76:17, 76:19, 76:23 and 76:37). To these can be added two more, firstly 76:32 possibly attributable to Phase 1, as its construction precedes the ring-ditch for 76:33, and then 76:33, possibly, but by no means certainly in Phase 2. From the 1989 excavations there are a further seventeen graves (89:9, 89:12, 89:21, 89:24, 89:25, 89:28, 89:31 – possibly robbed?, 89:37, 89:40, 89:41, 89:42, 89:47, 89:48, 89:49, 89:50, 89:51 and 89:52). This gives us a total of twenty-nine burials with a general date.

Combining the alignment of the phased graves with artefact dating attributions and picking up on the relationship between graves 76:32 (primary) and 76:33 (secondary) unfortunately fails to produce a clear result. Of those graves that shared a similar orientation to 76:32, only one (76:13) can be assigned to Phase 1 on the basis of its assemblage, while three (76:26, 76:27 and 76:34) are attributed to Phase 2. There are also two general seventh-century grave assemblages (76:32 and 89:9) with this same alignment. Then of the thirty-one graves with orientations broadly similar to 76:33, seven (76:6, 76:11, 76:14, 76:24, 76:28, 76:29 and 76:31) are assigned to Phase 1, but twelve (76:10, 76:15, 76:18, 76:20, 76:21, 76:25, 76:30, 76:35, 76:36, 89:1, 89:35 and 89:46) to Phase 2. A further twelve share more general seventh-century date (76:1, 76:3, 76:4, 76:7, 76:17, 76:19, 76:23, 76:33, 76:37, 89:32, 89:41 and 89:42).

If we look just at the graves in the immediate vicinity of the ring-ditch enclosing 76:33, a similar orientation to the primary grave 76:32 can be found to the west in 76:26/89:53 (Phase 2). Alignments closer to that for the secondary 76:33 can be found with assemblages assignable to Phase 1 (*e.g.* 76:24 and 76:28) and Phase 2 (*e.g.* 76:20). Overall, this pattern suggests that both 76:32 and 76:33 are rather more likely to have been deposited within Phase 2 than in Phase 1, though we cannot rule out the possibility that either or both could have been buried within Phase 1. So the conclusion seems to be that variations of alignment were the norm throughout this cemetery's development.

Finally, perhaps we should not be surprised to find a lack of coherence resulting from this particular exercise. We have been using in the main male belt equipment to define burials to Phase 1 and female dress fittings to identify Phase 2 graves. What we have demonstrated is that this sector of the cemetery seems to contain burials that belong to the decades either side of 650, with a significantly greater emphasis on the second half of the seventh century.

Comparative studies with other cemeteries in East Kent and beyond

Surprisingly few cemeteries in use during the seventh century in east Kent have been published, which explains the reliance usually placed in modern studies on the Buckland I report.[303] Reference also can be made to comparative material from the Gilton sandpit cemetery and from barrow cemeteries of the later sixth and seventh centuries on the North Downs as recorded by Bryan Faussett in the eighteenth century and published in the mid nineteenth century.[304] Fortunately we can now refer to the long-awaited Finglesham report, though this publication lacks the analytical chapters its excavator intended to include.[305] Otherwise we tend to look at reports on partial site investigations, *e.g.* rescue excavations at Monkton or the re-excavation of known sites as at Sarre.[306] It is very important that another substantial cemetery excavated at St Peter's Tip, Broadstairs, now close to publication, appears soon.[307] This will help us put into context such smaller samples including the present report.

The Finglesham near-neighbour comparison of a cemetery with its origins early in the sixth century and continuity up to at least the end of the seventh century is particularly relevant here. It shares much in common with Updown, such as its grave orientations (east-west or north-east to south-west) and the use of penannular ring-ditches, normally with the entrance set to the east (though one unusual example from Finglesham has a southern entrance and encloses three graves). In terms of its artifact range, Finglesham provides virtually everything one would expect to find in a cemetery of this date, though one significant absence involves seventh-century jewelled disc brooches. Admittedly Updown has produced only one such disc brooch and that from a child's grave (76:6). Again there were no iron shield parts from Finglesham seventh-century contexts and Updown presents just one, a tall straight-cone boss with associated iron fittings (76:14). On the other hand, there was a fine imported Frankish inlaid iron belt set from Finglesham Grave 25 as well as twelve triangular buckle sets from Finglesham, all of which are contemporary with the *floruit* of the jewelled

cast disc or composite disc brooches.[308] Once again inlaid iron belt equipment and Kentish-made cast triangular buckles feature at Updown, two of the latter being closely matched at Finglesham. Indeed these are key artifacts for defining the Updown Phase I graves.

By contrast, triangular buckles are not particularly well represented at Buckland I. The finest example there, a silvered copper-alloy cast triangular belt set from Grave 56, almost certainly represents an import from Frankish Gaul rather than a Kentish product.[309] It was associated with a two-edged sword, seax, spear and shield.[310] There was also a sheet-metal triangular buckle plate from Buckland I Grave 158, a burial attributed to phase 6 and smaller iron triangular buckles from graves 135 and 149 assigned to phases 4 (625–650) and 6 (675–700) respectively.[311] It should be noted, however, that these phase attributions and the rather late dating implied by them have been questioned.[312] Nevertheless a small triangular buckle plate does occur at Updown in a mid to second half seventh-century woman's burial (76:26). If we wish to examine a range of published Kentish-made triangular buckles, then we need to look at those from Faussett's excavations at Gilton, Kingston Down and Sibertswold or at examples from the Ashmolean Museum's collection, notably from Faversham.[313]

Overall, the Updown grave assemblages seem to fit known patterns established from other known cemeteries within the east Kent region. Admittedly the absence of a two-edged sword (*spatha*) in a male assemblage or of a composite disc brooch from a female costume is surprising and certainly there are no shortage of swords in Buckland I phases 3 and 4 (575–650), but it may be that such graves remain to be excavated in another sector at Updown. So our 1976 and 1989 cemetery sample represents a community that is comfortably off, though not outstandingly wealthy. For example, none of the Updown female assemblages can match the coin and jewelled pendants from Sibertswold Grave 172, the nearest being two graves containing imitation coin pendants (76:26 and 76:36).[314] Probably a further social rank down is represented by the silver or copper-alloy wire rings on female necklets in 76:15, 89:20 and 89:45. The last of these is associated with a copper-alloy workbox, but even the discovery of silk thread in the workbox from a child's burial (76:34), though a first at the time of its discovery, is something that will be repeated as more such sites are excavated.

The fact that the rest of Anglo-Saxon England adopted fashions that were developed in east Kent from the late sixth century onwards means that we can find analogies for all the artifacts present at Updown in cemeteries outside Kent.[315] The only obvious exception is the imported wheel-thrown pottery primarily limited to Kent, a by-product of trade links across the Channel that appeared no earlier than the late sixth century.[316] This involved the acquisition of pottery manufactured for the most part in the hinterlands of such ports as the Quentovic *emporium* (near Étaples) and Boulogne. Even seemingly more exotic items, such as the cowrie shells imported from the Red Sea, the amethyst droplet beads traded via the East Mediterranean region, or a Byzantine copper-alloy buckle, are relatively common in Kent. For example, a different type of Byzantine buckle has been recognized recently amongst the assemblages recovered from a seventh-century double cemetery at Springhead near Gravesend in west Kent.[317] This was excavated in advance of the Channel Tunnel high-speed rail-link and the author is grateful to Wessex Archaeology for access to its grave finds.

To conclude, the graves and material from the 1976 excavations at Updown are now fully in the public domain and it would be helpful if the 1989 Updown assemblages and plans could be re-published to a higher standard. In the meantime the present publication should add to our overall appreciation of the seventh-century archaeology of Kent. Its graves and material have already been incorporated into a computer database (the Anglo-Saxon Kent Electronic Database or ASKED) which will become accessible through the Archaeology Data Service's HEIRNET Portal. This

database has facilitated innovative research by Dr Stuart Brookes in an assessment of the economic and social development of Kent, analyzing archaeological data in its geographic setting using GIS technology.[318] Data from ASKED has also provided the case-studies for research into textile production by Sue Harrington.[319] The Kent database will soon be updated beyond its original census date of 2000 and will be added to matching databases for all available sites dating between the fifth and eighth centuries across England south of the Thames, as far west as Dorset, Somerset and Gloucestershire. This enhanced resource will permit comparative research by Dr Harrington and the author into the archaeological evidence for the formation of the early kingdoms of the West Saxons (Wessex), the South Saxons (Sussex) and Kent, financed by the Leverhulme Trust. The Updown cemetery will make a modest contribution to our project and hopefully also to the research of many other scholars in the future.

Appendices

APPENDIX I:
The human skeletal material from Updown, Eastry, Kent

Corinne Duhig PhD MIFA and Elizabeth Rega MA PhD

Basic skeletal information is summarised in Tables 4 and 5, and in the main text, and the demography of the cemetery is shown in Table 3.

Material
The skeletons from the 1976 excavations were packed in newspaper bundles, tied with string and stored in insubstantial boxes, some of which had crumpled and broken the contents. The skeletons had a light sandy loam soil adherent to and filling the medullary cavities of long bones, foramina of the skull and so on. Bone condition was very poor, the material being light, crumbly and extremely friable with root-marked and heavily eroded cortices. The bone, therefore, was not washed, for this would have caused almost total destruction of the assemblage. The light soil was eased out of some medullary cavities with dental picks, to reduce weight, although in many cases only the soil held the flakes of bone in position and enabled them to be identified.

The skeletons excavated in 1989 had been brushed and carefully packed by the Kent Archaeological Rescue Unit, each in its own box with separate skull boxes where necessary. When necessary for observation, matrix was removed by washing and reconstruction was carried out using water-soluble white glue. For both excavations, teeth generally preserved well and dental attrition served as one of the primary determinants of age-at-death for adults. Some of the teeth were washed with tap water using a soft brush.

Sixty-five samples were recorded, the other graves having contained no bone or bone that could not be recovered due to fragility. Most of the skeletons are at preservation stage 2 (see below) or less. Repacking of the 1976 assemblage was in acid-free tissue (considerable amounts were needed to support the fragile bone) and plastic bags, in flat-pack boxes supplied by the Centre for Archaeology, English Heritage, to which the material will be returned. The 1989 assemblage was returned to original packing material, and currently resides at the Department of Archaeology and Prehistory in Sheffield.

Methods
Methods used are primarily those of, or referred to in, Cho *et al.*, Iscan and Kennedy, Steele and Bramblett, Stewart and Ubelaker with others referenced as appropriate.[320]

Sexing

The 'five sexes' classification (F, ? F, ?, ? M, M) is used in recording. Certain individuals had only one or two skeletal features which could be used for determination of sex. This is insufficient for any conclusion, but the sex suggested by these features has been noted as either ?? F or ?? M in Table 4, for comparison with sexing from the grave goods. Sex determination was not attempted for the immature individuals, for this is generally deemed to be unreliable.

Discrepancies between skeletal and grave good sexing were discussed with the Project Director. From this it was concluded that, due to unequivocally gender-specific grave goods, four skeletons (89:05, 89:25, 89:40 and 89:41, as shown in Table 4) should be reassigned to make the demographic reconstruction more accurate, and these corrections are included in Tables 3, 4 and 5.

Ageing

Immature individuals

Subadult age bands are defined as: foetal/neonate, up to one month after birth; infant, one month to one year of age; child, one year to puberty at a notional 13 years; adolescent, puberty to skeletal adulthood at a notional 18 years (when height has reached its maximum due to fusion of long-bone epiphyses). There are no foetal, neonate or infant remains but there are twelve children, their ages determined by dental formation/eruption or by long-bone size. The youngest child was nearly 5 and the oldest just over 11 years.

Three skeletons are 'adolescent/adult' because their long-bone lengths are within the adult range but the epiphyseal ends of the long bones are not present and growth might still have been continuing. If these three are adolescents, they go some way to representing a sector of the population which we would expect to be present. Skeleton 76:18 was represented by only one tooth. As this is a permanent first or second molar with wear at stage 1 or 2 the individual could be anywhere between just over 6 years – when the first molar erupts – to about 20 years when wear on the second molar advances beyond stage 2. These four are not, therefore, shown on Table 3. Skeleton 89:38 consists of only two unidentifiable fragments, but the grave is of child size (with female grave goods) so it has been included.

Overall, the percentage of immature individuals, 19.7% (12 definite children out of the 61 which can be determined as either 'immature' or 'adult'), is within the same range as many earlier and contemporary Anglo-Saxon cemeteries of good size (*e.g.* Castledyke, Melbourn, North Elmham, St. Peter's Tip). Size of grave appears to broadly correlate with size of body at this cemetery and nine graves without bone are small enough to suggest that they contained additional child skeletons, one a skeleton of adolescent or small adult size and three of adult size. The differential

preservation of immature skeletons in an Anglo-Saxon cemetery has been discussed elsewhere, but the findings for that cemetery, Barrington, do not transfer to Updown: Barrington had excellent bone preservation and there was no correlation between age and loss of skeletal elements.[321] By contrast, the poor preservation at Updown appears to have had a greater effect on the remains of the children, and particularly the younger children.

Taking this evidence from the graves as well as the skeletons, the percentage of immatures for the cemetery is at least 28.8% (21/73), a figure approaching that for modern under-developed or developing countries – which are thought to be likely parallels for such ancient societies.[322] If the four skeletons which are 'adolescent/adult' or 'child/adolescent/adult' are included, the figure is 34.2%, within the modern range. Other Anglo-Saxon cemeteries, and, indeed, cemeteries of most prehistoric time periods in Britain, have a 'child shortage' for which explanations of taphonomy and/or differential disposal may be offered. Updown is unusual in having close to the expected number of immature individuals.

The total absence of foetal/neonate and infant remains is clearly unreasonable, however, and needs to be accounted for. Poor preservaton and inadequate recovery can be discounted, because even one bone from a neonate skeleton can be enough to establish the presence of that individual (and, as said above, even an empty grave can be indicative). As Sally Crawford has noted: 'given the number of infants that must have died in the earlier period, and that in most cemeteries, one or two infant burials survive, the probability is that more would be discovered if they were normally buried in the adult cemetery'.[323]

Disposal of newborns in the domestic area, close to or in dwellings, is attested from some ancient and modern societies, and appears to indicate that children, who had different social personae to adults, also had burial locations apart from the adults; equally, there is some evidence of exposure of the body or disposal in water for those falling into certain social categories, albeit not commonly in Britain.[324]

Adults

For adults, all possible ageing methods should be applied to each skeleton and the most reasonable estimate made from them, but, as stated above, damage to bone has necessitated the majority of the adult age estimates being made from dental attrition.[325] Brothwell's system, used for the 1976 material, gives age bands of 17–25 years, 25–35 years, 35–45 years and over 45 years, which restricts the upper age limit severely. Apart from this problem, when used on late prehistoric/early historic material the system has been shown to correlate reasonably well with ages determined by other methods. The material from Updown is unusual, however, in that the wear is already high on the first molar when the second comes into occlusion, and similarly for the second and third, so that the Brothwell system has had to be modified by giving greater importance to the condition of the third molars.

The Miles system, used for the 1989 material, calibrates the wear on successively-erupted molars (*i.e.*, how much wear there is on the first molar when the second comes into occlusion six years later, and similarly for the second and third), therefore setting a standard for the population and correcting for dietary differences. It performed well when tested on a modern population and correlates well with other methods used on the same individual. To check comparability, the dental charts on the 1989 record sheets were assessed using the Brothwell system and there were no significant discrepancies, although the Miles system produced narrower age ranges.

In Table 3 the adults have been grouped into age bands following Brothwell, that is: 17–25, 25–35, 35–45 and 45+. This system has been used in several other reports on Anglo-Saxon cemeteries of the Migration Period and Final Phase, which are therefore easily comparable.[326] The age ranges, however, are notional in the absence of absolute ageing methods, and some authors prefer to use terms such as 'young adult', 'prime adult', 'mature adult' and 'older adult'. Underageing, due to intrinsic problems of the methods used, is a recognised problem in osteoarchaeology: the '45+' band contains three individuals who might have reached advanced age, including 76:05 who could be shown to be at least 60 years old at death. The mean ages of adults are presented in Table 4, with the unaged adults shown on the base line.

The peak, predominantly of males, in the 'adult 2' age band is similar to that found at St. Peter's Tip, Broadstairs, a site of similar date, and is dissimilar to modern mortality profiles.[327] Whilst St. Peter's has a sample size of over 300, however, the Updown sample is so small that the peak could well be just a statistical artefact; for example, only 20 individuals are to be found in the 'adult 2' age band. Again, although the numbers are small, the difficulty of determining ages for older adults does not entirely explain the shortage of the 'adult 4' group in the Updown population. Just as differential burial practice and locations have been invoked to explain the absence of foetuses, neonates and infants, we suggest that older adults might also have been differentially buried when they passed a particular social threshold.

Stature

Statures are calculated from the regression formulae of Trotter and Gleser and are shown in Tables 4 and 5.[328] Although skeleton 89:05 was estimated as '? M' on skeletal features, grave goods confirm it is that of a female and the stature has been calculated accordingly. We have not used upper limb bones due to the wide errors (leg length is more closely correlated with height than arm length). Four individuals had complete femora and tibiae: skeletons 76:08 and 89:18, women, and 76:11 and 89:15, men. The plus/minus ranges on the statures of these are therefore 3.55 cm and 2.99 cm respectively. The others had complete femora but no lower leg bones, so the plus/minus range on their statures is 3.72 cm for females and 3.27 cm for males.

Whilst it is not possible to draw conclusions from the small sample here, most of the heights fall within the usual range for Anglo-Saxons. Skeleton 76:05 was short for an Anglo-Saxon man at 1.61 m (5' 3.3"). There are, however, at least three males of similar height at the earlier cemeteries of Barrington and Castledyke, although contemporary Melbourn and St. Peter's have taller populations.[329] Skeleton 76:05 was of advanced age and would have been 1.8 cm (0.7") taller in his prime, thereby coming somewhat closer to the average. The female 89:34 was also short but paralleled by a Barrington female.

Pathological conditions

Identification of pathology is based mainly on Iscan and Kennedy, Ortner and Putschar and Steinbock.[330] Congenital/developmental and epigenetic (non-metric) variants of the axial skeleton are from Barnes and Hauser and De Stefano and of the teeth from Hillson.[331]

Dental disease and arthritis

Various types of dental disease are the most common disorders: 15:40 relevant dentitions have at least one disease change, that is, 37.5%. Ante-mortem tooth loss is the most frequent dental disorder (14 affected/40 observable dentitions/35.0% prevalence), as is usual in Anglo-Saxon material, for example contemporary Melbourn, Cambridgeshire has 46.9%, and St Peter's Tip, Broadstairs, Kent has 39.8%.[332] Carious dentitions are found at an average percentage (8/39/20.5). It should be borne in mind that the loss of teeth before death can be caused by dental caries, and the number of lost teeth decreases the apparent caries rate, so only general comparisons between populations are possible. This is compounded in our population by the damage to jaws: it is often not possible to determine whether ante- or post-mortem tooth loss accounts for the absence of particular teeth. Equally the absence of many tooth sockets reduces the number of abscess cavities which can be identified; three individuals had abscess cavities (3/40/7.5), all of whom also had another dental disorder.

The second most common pathological disorders in this population are arthritic changes in the spine (10 affected/28 adults with any appropriate vertebral joint preserved/35.7% prevalence). This is slightly higher than the prevalence at contemporary St Peter's Tip, although lower than Cambridgeshire sites of similar date and considerably lower than those of earlier date.[333] Limb joints are hardly affected at all, with only one case of arthritic changes in the cuboid/third cuneiform joint of the foot of skeleton 76:12 (1/21/4.8), which is discussed under '*Other conditions*' below.

Epigenetic traits

Epigenetic traits, small developmental variants in the skeleton of no clinical significance, can be indicators of relatedness of individuals, although the relative contribution of multiple-genetic and environmental components is unclear for many traits. Shovelled incisors have ridges on each edge of the inner face of the tooth, producing a spade-shaped tooth profile. They are present in 24–100% of individuals depending on population, most commonly in Native American and Oriental groups. They are found in four skeletons here, 79:07, 79:15, 79:31 and 89:20, although two show the trait in atypical form. Two individuals (79:02 and 89:39) have Carabelli's cusp, an additional cusp on the upper first molars which is found in 35–85% of individuals and most frequently in Europeans. Displaced or overcrowded anterior teeth are found in 89:20, 89:44 and 89:47 (the last with marked dental prognathism).

Skeletons 89:15 and 89:16 have bowed femora. We do not know whether this is a trait related to activity – it is not mentioned by Kennedy in his definitive study of skeletal markers of habitual activity – or is a heritable feature indicating the relatedness of these two men.[334]

Epigenetic traits found singly are: congenital absence of lower third molars; misshapen lower left second and third molars; spondylolysis of the second lumbar vertebra. The latter describes a break between vertebral body and arch, caused by activity stresses acting on a congenital thinning of the lamina which joins body and arch. Unless further severe stresses cause slipping of the arch, the condition is usually asymptomatic because the bone is held firmly in place by soft tissue.

Stress indicators

Three individuals have dental enamel hypoplasia, in which physiological stress such as dietary deficiency or severe feverish illness has damaged the developing tooth and produced stripes of inadequately mineralised enamel.[335] The prevalence in the population is 3/27/11.1, within the usual range for this period. One case, that of skeleton 76:33, is severe, with four bands of defective enamel on a lower canine, indicating at least four episodes of stress; the two carious teeth in this individual might have been more susceptible to caries attack because of faults in the enamel.

Another indicator of physiological stress is cribra orbitalia, a sieve-like formation of bone in the eye orbits caused by iron-deficiency anaemia.[336] Two cases from this cemetery gives a prevalence of 2/40/5.0, which is at the low end of the range for earlier Anglo-Saxon cemeteries.[337]

Infection and trauma

Infection/inflammation and trauma of bone are usually easy to observe on skeletonised material, although most infection only affects soft tissue and therefore some of the most common causes of death are unidentifiable in the skeleton. In this assemblage, there are two examples of disorganised new-bone development: on the outer surface of the distal ulna of skeleton 76:05, possibly caused by proximity to the site of an infection or inflammation of the soft tissue; in the spine of skeleton 76:29, which might be a response to local trauma to the back with ossification into a bleed (ossifying haematoma).

There are two clear examples of trauma. Skeleton 89:34 (female 40–50+ years) had a healed spiral fracture of the right distal tibia, well resolved although the evidence of a cloaca – a hole for the outlet of pus – indicates a compound fracture that had broken the skin and allowed pus-forming bacteria into the bone. Surprisingly, the injured tibia is the same length as the normal, even though it is clear that the fractured ends have slid past each other and overlapped to some extent, as shown in Plate 2. This recovery of symmetry may indicate that the fracture occurred whilst the individual was still young and growth could compensate; this type of injury in adulthood usually results in limb shortening in the absence of remedial traction.

Skeleton 89:16 (a male of 20–27 years) had a left ulna with a transverse 'parry' or 'nightstick' fracture, caused by the arm being thrown up to ward off a blow to the head from a weapon such as a staff. There is non-union – partial healing but without any reparative bone linking the broken ends – to which such fractures are prone even today.[338] The gross and radiographic appearance of the forearm bones is shown in Plates 3 and 4. The right ulna has a thick shell of bone covering the shaft in a similar location to that on the left, but no fracture line can be identified on the radiograph. Perhaps the bone was only struck hard enough to cause periostitis (new-bone production provoked by injury to the bone-covering membrane) or ossifying haematoma. The left clavicle is also fractured with non-union. Although we cannot determine the time when these injuries were suffered, it would not be unreasonable to suggest that all occurred at the same time, unless the man was an 'injury recidivist' who was either accident-prone or frequently injured in violent episodes.[339] Had he been a warrior, the non-union would have been handicapping.

Habitual activity ('occupational change')

Habitual activity, especially when strenuous, can cause changes to areas of muscle attachment on the bone. Skeleton 76:05 has heavily marked insertions of the deltoid muscle (which participates in many movements of the shoulder) on both humeri, but this does not necessarily indicate an unusually heavy workload, because individuals vary considerably in the extent to which activity alters bone. Skeleton 76:16 has 'squatting facets' – small flattened patches on the ankle joints which are thought to be due to habitual squatting posture.[340]

The left upper central incisor of the female skeleton 76:26 is marked by two grooves which pass over the occlusal edge on to the labial (front) face of the crown.

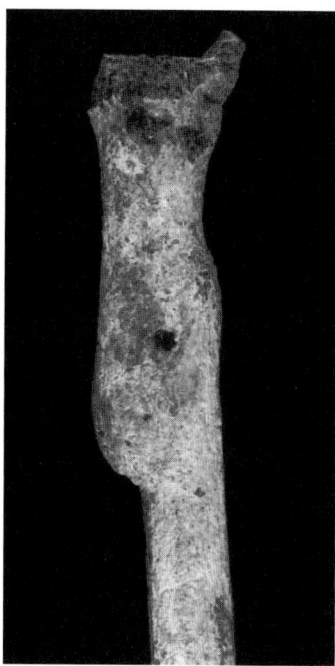

Plate 2. Skeleton 89:34 – healed spiral fracture of the tibia

Microscopic examination is needed to determine the form of the grooves, but they are likely to have been produced by parafunctional wear, the use of the teeth for 'third hand' activities such as pulling threads during spinning. Similar cases have been observed in other early Anglo-Saxon material and compare with ancient and ethnographic examples.[341] Skeletons 89:18, 89:20 and 89:46, all adult females, have severe bevelled wear on the inner surfaces of the upper anterior teeth (Plate 5). The opposing teeth in the lower jaws do not have severe wear, showing that the wear was probably not produced by normal mastication and is possibly parafunctional in cause. It does not resemble other cases related to textile production and the agent is inexplicable.

Other conditions

Certain pathological changes fall outside the general range of classifications, while others are impossible to diagnose. One left proximal hand phalanx (a small finger bone) of skeleton 76:08 has a normal base but narrowed mid-shaft and pointed distal end. This 'whittled' shape is found in leprosy, commencing with the distal phalanges (the fingertips) and tends to affect more than one digit. Unfortunately, diagnosis is hampered because only seven finger bones from both hands are present in this burial, of which only four can be identified to the left hand and none are more distal than the affected bone. Further, other signs of the disease on the skull must be identified before a diagnosis of leprosy can be made.[342] Psoriatic arthritis – a little-known complication of the skin disorder psoriasis

– also affects the finger joints, producing a whittled shape to phalanges, and is often mistaken for leprosy in archaeological material.[343] It tends, however, to be the middle rather than the proximal phalanx which is affected. Once again, the absence of most of the hand bones and the impossibility of accurately positioning the remainder is unfortunate, although psoriatic arthritis affects the spine and sacro-iliac joints and these are unaffected in this specimen, making the diagnosis unlikely.

Skeleton 76:12, in addition to an arthritic cuboid/third cuneiform joint, in which osteoarthritis is suggested by pitting and new bone around and on the joint surface, has a right foot with ankylosed calcaneum and talus (fusion of the two major heel/ankle bones). They are smoothly fused over part of their contact area with neither loss of joint space nor any changes suggestive of arthritis or infection. The changes have some resemblance to those of one of the sero-negative spondyloarthropathies (ankylosing spondylitis, psoriatic arthritis or Reiter's syndrome), but these must be excluded as there are no changes in the rest of the skeleton.[344] A congenital cause would probably have precluded normal growth to adult size and proportion, so the cause is, at present, inexplicable.

The second and third cervical vertebrae of skeleton 89:48 are also ankylosed, the cause unknown. The costal cartilage – cartilage which flexibly joins the ribs to the breastbone at the front of the thorax – was partly ossified in skeleton 76:29 and was found as loose fragments, as well as some ossification (which would have been into the costal cartilage) on the end of the first rib. This develops with age, indeed, it is used as a rough ageing method, but some individuals tend to develop more ossifications than average into soft tissue. Skeleton 76:29 is that of a 25–35 year-old man, so his ossification occurred at a relatively early age and suggests that he was one of these 'bone makers'.

APPENDIX II:

The Textiles from the graves excavated in 1976[345]

Elizabeth Crowfoot

The fibres of all the textiles but one from this cemetery were replaced by metal oxides; the exception, a fine fragment from a thread-box in child's grave (76:34), is of flax, but has scraps of silk thread adhering and loose with it, the only silk of this date recovered from an Anglo-Saxon cemetery at the time of writing.[346]

Apart from this flax fragment, there is only one other possible piece of selvedge (Grave 76:10); as in the majority of textiles woven on the warp-weighted loom the higher count is normally the warp, this has been placed first where counts are given in the catalogue. The direction of spinning twist in the yarns is indicated by the letters S and Z.

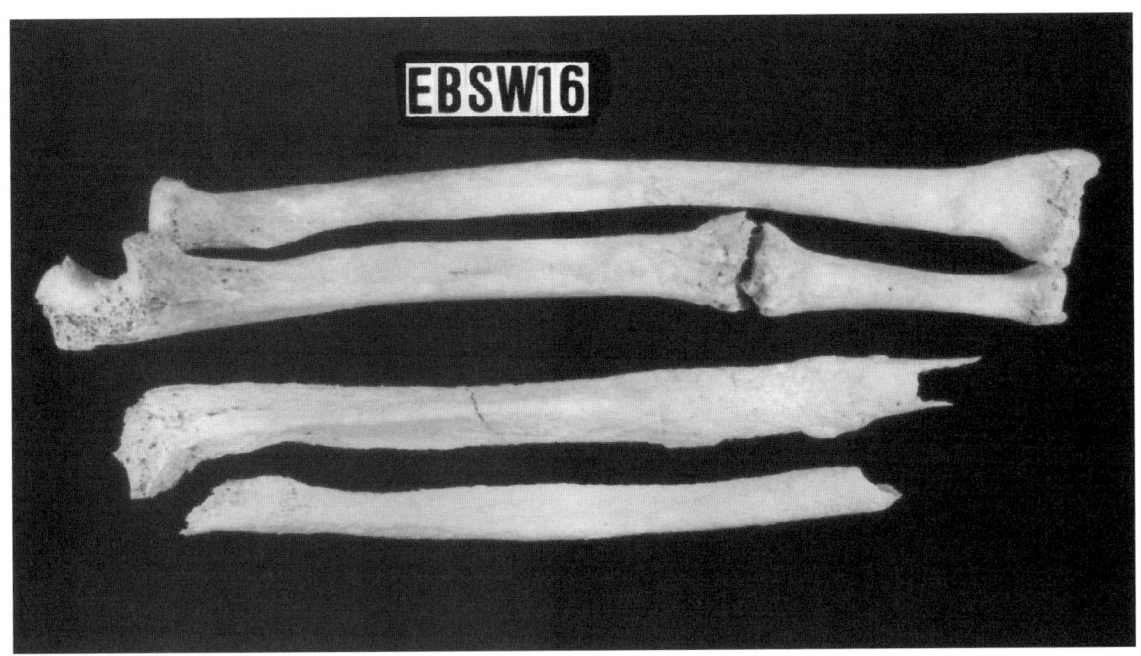

Plate 3. Skeleton 89:16 – parry fracture of left ulna

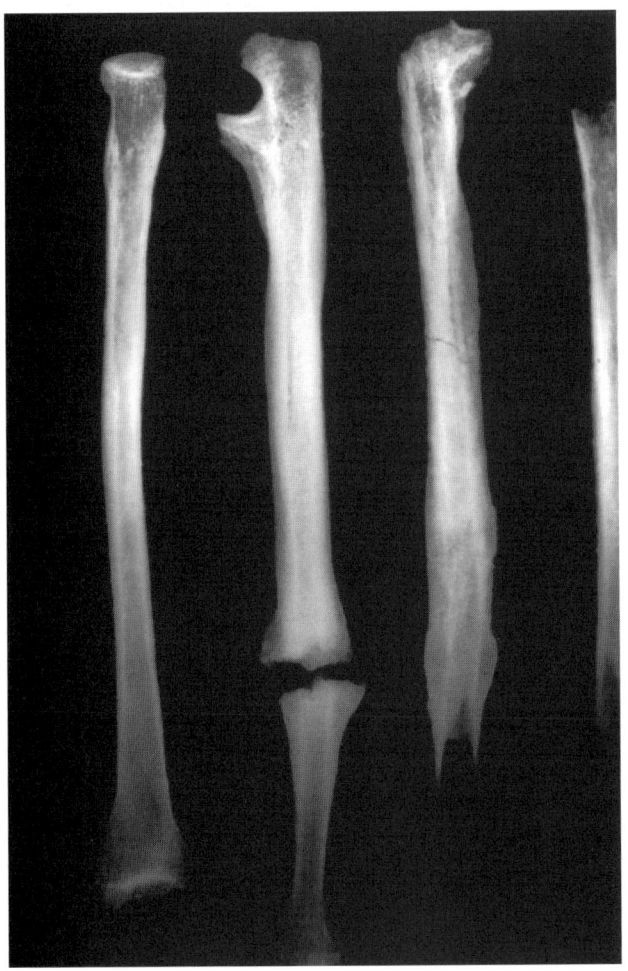

Plate 4. Skeleton 89:16 – parry fracture of left ulna

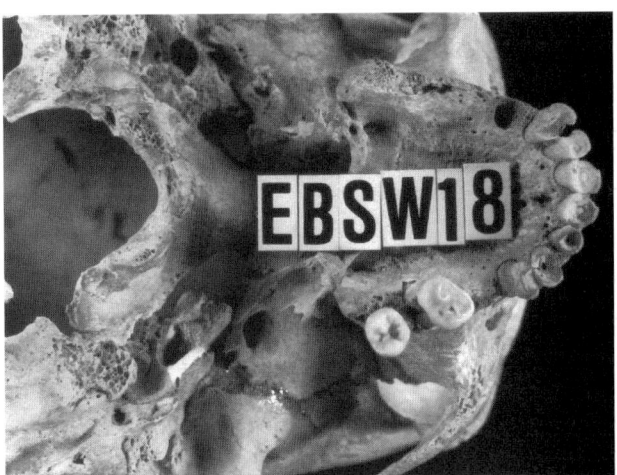

Plate 5. Skeleton 89:18 tooth wear

Textile Catalogue

Grave 76:2

1. Iron buckle and plate

On plate, remains of replaced leather, and under this area 2.0 × 1.3 cm replaced textile, Z,Z, tabby, count *c.* 12/12 per cm; yarns well spun but slightly uneven. On underside of buckle ring [*i.e.* loop], leather, and deteriorated patches similar tabby.

Grave 76:4

4. Iron buckle

Underneath, large area replaced textile in two layers, overall roughly 5.0 × 5.0 cm, Z,Z, tabby, count 17–18/14 per cm; the coarser system has alternate coarse and finer threads, *i.e.* probably woven with two wefts, pick and pick; cf. Graves 76:16.7 and 76:10.6. Replaced grass stems on surface.

3. Iron knife
All over one side, length 9.0 cm, and part of the other, lying in folds, fine replaced textile, Z,Z, tabby, count 16–17/14 per cm; probably the same as on the buckle, though the differences in the weft thread are not so marked in this piece; from the tight folds obviously a soft fabric, ?flax. On the other side, traces of twill, one system Z spun.

Grave 76:5
2. Iron buckle
Replaced textile in small fragments on both plate and buckle, the large 1.8 × 1.7 cm, lying in triple folds, all Z,S, twill, 2/2 (all showing same diagonal) count 11/10–11 per cm, regular spinning and weaving.

Grave 76:10
4,7. Iron links from chatelaine
On one piece, replaced grasses on top of fragment of fine replaced tabby (see no. 6 [from Grave 76:10] below) at one end, and at other fragment replaced Z,Z, twill count *c.* 8/7 on 5 mm, folding round the end of the link; lying across this a fragment 1.5 × 1.0 cm, solid twill, possibly the same, a selvedge or braid, surface deteriorated. Z threads on other links.

5. Iron buckle and plate
Deteriorated very small fragment twill, replaced, one system Z.

6. Wood and metal object
Round one end of metal, length *c.* 3.0 cm, fine replaced Z,Z, tabby, count 9/7 on 5mm (18/14 per cm), same ridged effect by use of coarse and fine threads in weft as in Graves 76:4.4 and 76:16.7, though not so marked; the textile lies in folds. Traces of coarser threads on wood.

Grave 76:12
1. Bronze buckle
On underside, replaced textile patches over most of the plate and under the ring [loop], fine Z,Z, tabby, count 20/19 per cm, ?flax. Loose, small scraps of leather from belt or strap.

Grave 76:13
2. Buckle
Underneath, against plate, replaced leather, then, over area *c.* 8.0 × 2.5 cm, replaced Z,Z, tabby, count 15/14 per cm, thread irregular in both systems. On top of this (*i.e.* nearer to body) small fragments replaced in deteriorated area *c.* 2.5 × 2.0 cm, and near buckle clear area *c.* 1.5 × 1.5 [cm], replaced Z,S, twill, count 13 (Z)/14 (S) per cm, weave rather open and pulled diagonally, regular 2/2 diagonal as far as preserved. Some detached scraps of the tabby weave, in folds.

Grave 76:14
11. Bronze buckle
Replaced area of textile, 0.8 × 1.4 cm, tabby, count 22 (11 on 5 mm)/17 per cm, checked, threads 1Z, 6S, 7Z/8Z, 10S, 5Z; very fine and even, (Fig. 73.3). Fragments against the buckle, mostly leather, some thread traces.

Grave 76:16
7. Small bronze buckle
Underside, two layers or folds fine replaced textile, area 0.8 × 1.5 cm, Z, Z, tabby, count 18 (9 on 5 mm)/11 per cm; here the closer count is noticeably variable as in Graves 76:4 and 76:10, so perhaps this should be the weft; appearance suggests flax.

3. Iron buckle, silver inlay
Mass of folds, all round back and most of front of buckle, all appear to be the same fine Z, Z, tabby, count 9/6 on 5 mm; variability of thread gives a slightly striped appearance in some parts, and tightness of folds suggest flax; probably same as on small buckle no. 7 [from Grave 76:16 above].

Grave 76:17
1. Miniature iron spear
Replaced area textile *c.* 8.0 × 2.0 cm on shaft, Z, Z, coarse 2/2 twill, count 7/4–5 per cm, the closer count thread being noticeably finer than the other, and the weave open.

3. Iron buckle
One side of plate, replaced leather; other side deteriorated replaced textile, Z, Z. probably tabby, finer than twill on [Grave 76:17] no. 1.

Grave 76:20
4. Iron buckle
Very deteriorated textile areas replaced on top of ring [loop] and tongue, Z, Z, tabby, surface poor; underneath textile remains and leather, replaced.

Grave 76:21
5. Iron buckle
Underneath, and to one side on top surface, area *c.* 5.0 × 4.0 cm of very deteriorated Z, Z twill, in tight folds; lying across this, on top of the buckle, very fine deteriorated tabby, surface too badly damaged by insects for spinning to be clear.

9. Iron fragment
Underneath, replaced leather. On top, all over area 5.0 × 2.8 cm, replaced textile (a), Z,Z, tabby, count 13/10 per cm, regular spinning and weaving, but fibres deteriorated leaving weave open; lying in folds.

11. Iron fragment
As no. 9 [Grave 76:21], leather one side, tabby (a) on other.

12, 13. Iron fragments
As nos.9, 11 [Grave 76:21]; the tabby lies in close folds.

14. Iron buckle with bronze plates
Between plates, replaced leather, and clear tongue of belt through buckle. On top, leather belt coming through, and on top of plate and ring [loop] folds textile (b), finer Z,Z, tabby, count 16/13 per cm, weave much closer and finer than (a) as nos.9 etc. [Grave 76:21]; best area, 1.5 × 1.0 cm.

19. Iron fragment
On back, coarser tabby, probably (a). On front, areas 3.0 × 1.3, 3.0 × 2.0 cm, textile (c), Z, S, very fine twill (Fig. 73.1), lozenge 2/2 twill.

20, 22, 23, 24. Iron fragments
Traces and folds of Z,Z, tabby, (a) as on no. 9 [Grave 76:21].

26. Iron disc
Replaced textile in folds all over both surfaces, tabby, Z,Z, count 18/13 per cm., *i.e.* (b) as on no. 14 [Grave 76:21].

27. Iron fragment
On one side, area 2.2 × 1.2 cm of Z,S, twill (c); underneath, a fragment of tabby (a).

28. Iron rod fragment
All over one surface, area 3.5 × 2.0 cm, folds of twill (c), replaced; on back, fragment of replaced tabby (a) and bunch of S-ply threads, possibly from a fringe.

29. Iron rod

Area 3.5 × 1.3 cm, deteriorated, fine Z,S, twill, surface damaged but must be (c).

Loose remains of leather, and two fragments of replaced textile, (a) Z,Z, tabby, count 9/7 on 5 mm, *i.e.* 18/14 per cm, and (b) Z,Z, tabby, count 13/10 per cm.

Grave 76:26

10. Strap tag

Underside, leather replaced. Other side, over area 4.0 × 2.0 cm, Z,Z, tabby, count 8/8 on 5 mm, thread rather uneven in both systems; a fragment of this shows from the underside beyond the bronze also.

Grave 76:27

1. Iron and wood object

Small fragments of two replaced textiles, one Z,S, twill, the other Z,Z, tabby, both too small for counts.

5. Iron buckle

Area all over top of plate and part of ring, *c.* 3.0 × 2.0 cm, surface very deteriorated, replaced fine Z,Z, textile, probably tabby, in which case count *c.* 7/7 on 5 mm, rather loose spinning and open weave, Cf. Grave 76:21, textile (a).

Grave 76:28

3. Bronze buckle

Inside buckle, replaced leather. On top surface, on pin [tongue], tiny replaced fragment 0.7 × 0.3 cm, (a) tabby, Z,Z, very fine and even, count estimated *c.* 24–26/16 per cm (12–13 on 5 mm/4 on 2.5 mm); probably flax. On under surface, area 1.5 × 2.0 [cm], (b) coarser tabby, Z,Z, count 11/10 per cm; some coarser threads, Z, and grass stems replaced on this. On earth from under buckle, all round under pin [tongue] impression and wider part of plate, the coarser tabby (b), surface confused by grass stems; at narrower end of plate, mass of grass, and under this deteriorated remains same, count 7/6 on 5 mm.

Grave 76:29

5. Iron buckle

On top surface, patches replaced textile (a), one clear fragment 1.2 × 0.8 cm, tabby, count 21/10 (taken as 8 on 8 mm) per cm, one thread system Z, the other Z4, S4; other less clear remains on top of pin [tongue] and ring [loop] of buckle (see [Grave 76:29] no. 11).

11. Iron belt plate

On largest piece, at back of body, patches of replaced textile, clearest 1.2 × 1.0 cm, (a) tabby, count 20/10 per cm, close system all Z spun, looser system 5Z, 5S, S thread slightly coarser, *i.e.* a fabric probably with coloured stripes (Fig. 73.2); the other fragments all come from the same weave, but are too deteriorated for more than the Z spinning of the close system to be seen.

7. Pair of bronze plates

Among debris preserved by bronze, fragments deteriorated Z,Z, tabby, count *c.* 14/15, probably (b), area *c.* 2.2 × 1.6 cm, surface poor; underneath, coarser threads. One fragment of (a), as on [76:29] nos.5, 11, 0.4 × 0.9 cm, one system close Z, the other 5Z, 3S, count estimated *c.* 20/12 per cm. (c) much coarser, replaced, Z,Z, as far as can be seen tabby, count 4/3 on 5 mm. On the plates, impressions, lines going lengthwise of plates (see below).

8. Double bronze belt plate

Front of one half-plate, replaced area 1.3 × 1.8 cm fairly clear, weave (b), Z,Z, tabby, count 14/12 per cm; slight frizzing of fibres here suggests this is wool. In debris under plates, replaced fragments (b). Back of other half-plate, similar parallel lines to those on [no.] 7, replaced, ?leather, lines run across plate; front, tiny fragment tabby, ?(a).

10. Double bronze belt plate

Front of one half-plate, replaced area 3.6 × 1.4 cm, (b) Z,Z, tabby, count 15/11 per cm, even spinning and weaving. Deteriorated fragments wood and leather and some coarser threads, cf. (c) on [Grave 76:29] no. 7.

Back of other half-plate, parallel lines going lengthwise on plate, over whole width, probably replaced leather; very thin detached fragments; fibres ?Z visible in lines. Probably tooling on leather, as a tablet-weave, which could leave similar lines, would not run in the other direction (crosswise) on [Grave 76:29] no. 8. See Textile Report Appendix II.2 below.

Grave 76:34

2. Bronze thread box

Tiny fragment, flax, woven area 0.7 × 0.3 cm, lying double, with longer ends of threads protruding in warp and weft. 6 threads in ?warp direction, soft, Z,S-ply, 7 in ?weft direction, fine Z flax, tabby weave; the appearance, and the plyed ?warps suggests this may be from a tubular selvedge; otherwise it is a tiny scrap folded down the middle. One S spun silk thread runs in the same shed as a flax one at one torn end of the piece; a small tangle of detached threads include some Z fine flax, others S fine silk; all fibres are near white.

See Textile Report Appendix II.1 below.

Grave 76:36

8. Links of chatelaine

One side, area *c.* 2.0 × 0.8 cm, replaced, very loosely lying Z threads with other Z threads interlacing here and there, possibly from tabby weave; plyed threads lying across, possibly fringe, possibly tablet twists unravelling, L.0.7 cm, W. area 0.5 cm; all threads seem to be replaced, but some areas are stained blue.

9, 10. Links of chatelaine

On 9, traces coarse Z threads as on [Grave 76:36 no.] 8, and fine Z threads. On 10, underneath, some coarse threads, Z; on other side replaced fine Z,Z, tabby patches, in layers, all along the piece, count 8/6 on 5 mm.

As mentioned above, in all the textiles from this cemetery but one the fibres have been replaced by metal oxides, but the exception – fine fragments from a thread box in an infant [child burial], Grave 76:34.2 – is of outstanding interest, as it includes the only silk threads so far identified from an early Anglo-Saxon site (Appendix II.1). The box contains only a fragment of flax tabby weave, possibly from its appearance and its plyed ?warps part of a tubular selvedge (Plate 7), and a small bunch of flax threads from the weave mixed with S spun silk threads. One of these is preserved in position in the weave, run into the same shed as a flax waft, and it seems likely the silk was a decoration on the original linen cloth or garment; both yarns are still nearly white, and show no signs of dyeing.

Fragments of fine material have been found in these thread-boxes from a number of other sites – tiny pieces of fine wool twill with embroidery in coloured wools, loose threads, and two linen fabrics, one a broken diamond, the other a tabby weave, from boxes at Kempston, Bedfordshire; a scrap of fine wool tablet-weave and loose plyed yarns in green and brown from Sibertswold, Kent; similar plyed woollen threads, blue, red, yellow and black, and a ball of flax yarn, from Uncleby, Yorkshire; linen and wool tabby weaves from Marina Drive, Dunstable; and possible flax threads from Polhill, Kent. It has been suggested that these scraps might have been hoarded for future use, but some of them are too small for any obvious purpose, and it seems more likely that they were kept for sentimental reasons, or, considering their general high quality, as indications of the owner's standing.[347] The inclusion of the silk scraps in the child's grave goods suggests that these were intended to indicate the high status of the child's family.

Apart from this find, the 1976 textile material from Updown cemetery is interesting for another reason. Of seventeen graves in which identifiable textile remains have been found, all but three contain male burials. The fabrics in all of these are replaced, but they are unusually clear for fibres preserved by contact with iron, with the result that here we have identifiable material from men's burials, which usually yield very little evidence.

Twill weaves

The fragments of twill are very small, all four-shed (2/2) constructions. Three (Graves 76:10, 76:21.5 and 76:17) have Z spinning in both thread systems, and four (Graves 76:5, 76:13, 76:21.19 and 76:27) Z spinning in one system (warp) and S in the other (weft). This combination often indicates a chevron or diamond design in the weave, but in only one grave is enough clearly preserved to show that this was the case here at Updown (Grave 76:21, fig 73.1); the pattern here is a broken lozenge, similar to finer examples from Sutton Hoo and Broomfield Barrow.[348] Fragments with the same centre to the lozenge, though repeating on different numbers of threads, have been found from other Anglo-Saxon cemeteries, and there are numerous earlier and later Scandinavian examples.[349] The weave is known in both flax and wool, though the use of the two spinning directions here indicates the latter. Recent tests on broken lozenge twills from Sutton Hoo, Broomfield and Ganton Wold suggest that these were sometimes woven with different colours in warp and weft, a practice which throws up the diamond pattern.

Tabby weaves

Fragments of tabby weave come from fifteen graves, three of which (Graves 76:21, 76:28 and 76:29) each include at least two different fabrics of this type. All are Z spun throughout, with the exception of two in which the combination of groups of S and Z spun threads produces striped or checked patterns. In Grave 76:14 just enough is preserved to show that here the weave had stripes of different numbers of threads in both systems, but insufficient to show if this was from a plaid pattern, or if the variation

was simply caused by the checks being measured by eye to correct the different spinning of the two threads (Fig. 73.3). The fragments from Grave 76:29 are all too small to show if in this case the weave was checked, or only striped (Fig. 73.2); their position suggests they may come from a cloak. A number of replaced textiles with similar stripes and checks indicated by Z and S threads have been found from Worthy Park, Hants. (Grave 75.1), Finglesham, Kent (Graves 8 and 169) and Mucking, Essex (Graves 448 and 975). The counts in the Updown pieces are fine, of similar quality to those at Finglesham, but not so fine as to suggest the S spun silk threads of Grave 76:34.

In three tabbies (Graves 76:4, 76:10 and 76:16) the unevenness of the probable weft thread, producing a ridged appearance, suggests that the weavers were working with two different wefts (pick and pick), of which one was slightly finer than the other. The width of the warp-weighted loom, on which two women often wove together, would have encouraged this practice.[350]

As in other Kentish cemeteries, Finglesham and Dover, the proportion of tabby weaves to twills is higher than in the Anglian [region] cemeteries. In the Updown graves, the appearance of many of the tabbies suggests flax (Graves 76:2, 76:4, 76:10, 76:12, 76:16, ?76:21(b) and 76:28), but since most of these are from from the underside of buckles in a belt position, it is likely they come from garments, not shrouds; very similar fine tabbies were noted in men's graves at Finglesham, again mostly on objects from the waist position.

Belts

Remains of belt fragments, wherever preserved, suggest leather; there is no evidence of woven [textile] belts. In Grave 76:29 traces of leather could be found in crystalline remains on bronze plates; these showed parallel lines, running lengthwise on some plates and across on others, suggesting perhaps that the surface of the belt or strap had a tooled pattern (Appendix II.2 below).

The spinning and weaving from this cemetery, as far as can be judged from replaced material, was of very good standard, and it is perhaps legitimate to suggest that the preponderance of light fabrics, and the all-important presence of silk, are due to the Frankish connections of the ruling family in this area [the 'eastern region' within east Kent], to whom the occupants of the cemetery were probably related.

APPENDIX II.1:
Fibre examinations

H. M. Appleyard, F. T. I.

1. Sample from loose threads, Grave 76:34 threadbox: these threads appear to be silk, in general they seem to be fairly well-preserved, even though there is quite a bit of deposit on them.

Plate 6 Grave 76:6 Jewelled disc brooch (scale 1:1)

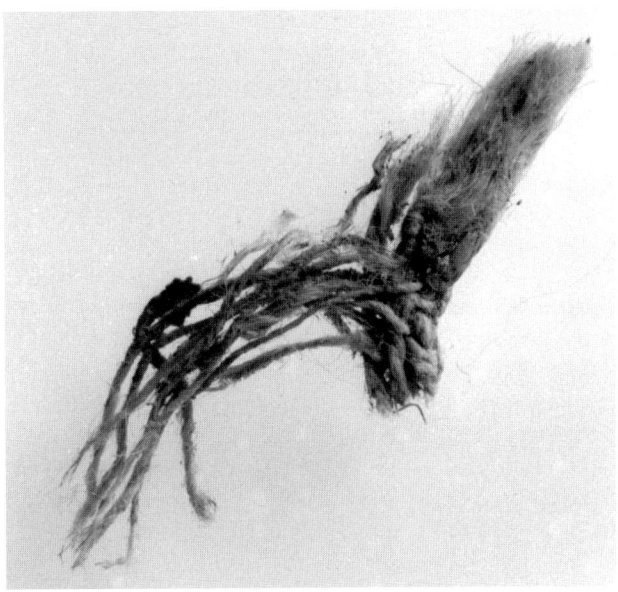

Plate 7 Grave 76:34 Textile from workbox

2. Sample of Z spun threads, warp and weft: these are both clearly vegetable, and have the characteristics of flax.
3. S threads, loose, and from that run into weave: these are both fine silk; they are very light in colour, some are badly degraded and there is a lot of mineral deposit.

APPENDIX II.2:
Examination of fragments from Grave 76:29, belt plate 10

by J. H. Thornton and G. Edwards

Mr. J. H. Thornton (Northampton College of Technology; consultant, Ancient Monuments Laboratory) examined these, and reported:

> 'There is a suspicion of leather on the green (bronze) side, but the crystalline deposits everywhere predominate.'

At his suggestion X-ray analysis was carried out by Miss Glynis Edwards (Ancient Monuments Laboratory); she reported that the piece was similar to other pieces of textile and leather sitting directly on top of bronze, where the corrosion products do not seem to replace the organic material, just to coat the fibres, and the bacteriostatic effect protects them. The piece has the appearance of ?wood, with a layer of textile or leather on top of this, and deposits of bronze corrosion on top of that.

APPENDIX III:
Statement on organic survival on metalwork finds

Glynis Edwards

A report on the mineral preserved textile from the Updown, Eastry site has been prepared, the material examined shortly after excavation. In 2000 the metal artefacts from the graves were examined to assess the potential of a detailed study of the other mineral preserved organic material. Unfortunately the interventive methods in use at the time the material was conserved mean that very little of the organic material survives and any report would present a very incomplete picture. Many of the copper-alloy buckles have been chemically stripped which would have removed any surviving leather. Iron artefacts have also been intensively cleaned removing any material and where it survives heavy coatings of lacquer make it impossible to see any details. The only way forward is to use the conservation notes which record presence of organic material, mentioning this source in the report. It must be remembered that in the 1970s the material of knife handles was often recorded as wood, but closer study in more recent years has shown that the most common material used for this purpose was horn, wood being rarely used.

APPENDIX IV:

Report on two coin-like pendants from the Updown Cemetery, Eastry, Kent (1976)

Gareth Williams

The two pendants represent two different types within a larger body of coin jewellery, typical of Anglo-Saxon England in the late sixth and seventh centuries. Gold coins and pseudo-coins with similar suspension loops are known, either singly or in groups, from a number of late sixth- and seventh-century graves, as well as from a rather smaller number of single finds. These span from Canterbury (St Martin's), part of which was probably deposited in the late sixth century through Faversham (deposited *c.* 600) to Finglesham (deposited *c.* 670).[351]

Grave 26, pseudo-coin pendant[352]

Gold uniface *repoussé* pseudo-coin, with ribbed suspension loop. The design shows a helmeted bust right, with the inscription IMP CONSTA[N]TINVS MAX AVG. Both the size of the design (diameter 17 mm) and the clarity of the impression on the reverse of the pendant suggest that the design was created by using a genuine coin of Constantine I to create the impression, probably a bronze *centennialis* of the '*Victoriae Laetae Princ Perp*' type from the mint of Ticinum in northern Italy, as this provides the best match for the form of the bust.[353] The diameter of the object as a whole is 21 mm, and the weight 1.186 g. The flan is extremely thin, and a small section has been folded over onto the reverse between 300 and 330° in order to even out the shape.

The use of a coin of Constantine I as a die does not imply that the pseudo-coin was made in the fourth century, although the coin appears still to have been in good condition at the point that it was so used, to judge from the clarity of the impression. However, coins of the house of Constantine are themselves common finds from early Anglo-Saxon graves, while coins of the same period also provided models for a number of Anglo-Saxon coin designs of the seventh century, including relatively early types such as the 'Licinius' type represented in the Crondall hoard (deposited *c.* 640) and some of the later transitional pale gold types attributed to the 670s.[354] The closest match that I have been able to trace for the suspension loop comes from a mounted Merovingian *tremissis* from grave 172 at the Sibertswold cemetery in Kent, one of two such *tremisses* from the grave, thought to have been deposited *c.* 650.[355] This shares the characteristic of having one end of the loop pointed, with the other end flat, with a slight projecting lip.

A parallel for the object as a whole can be found in a similar *repoussé* pseudo-coin pendant from the Breach Down cemetery, now in the British Museum, with the registration number 1853, 4–12, 94.[356] That carries the

inscription IMP MAXIMINUS PIVS AVG, and shows a diademed bust right, having apparently been been produced in the same way from a coin of the emperor Maximinus I (235–238). The Breach Down example has a slightly smaller diameter than the one from Updown, but a thicker flan, and the suspension loop is narrower than the Updown example, and flat at both ends. The style of the loop on the Barham Downs pendant is more akin to the earlier coin-dated deposits such as St Martin's and Faversham, but has been assigned a broad date-range of late sixth-seventh century.[357]

Thus, the object seems to be dateable to the late sixth or seventh century, with the style of the suspension loop possibly suggesting a date in the mid-seventh century. However, the date of deposition could be later still. The presence of a gold solidus of Sigebert III (634–56), mounted as a pendant, and found in the same grave at the Boss Hall cemetery as a Series B silver penny (*sceat*) of *c.* 690, provides a useful reminder that coin jewellery could remain in use for some time after the coin would normally have ceased to circulate as a coin.[358] It would therefore be rash to attempt to use the pseudo-coin to date the burial any more precisely than the seventh century.

Grave 36, imitation *tremissis*, mounted as pendant[359]

The object is an imitation of a Merovingian gold *tremissis*, which has been mounted for suspension, although most of the suspension loop has been lost. The object is gold-plated, over a base-metal core, but with the gold-plating worn or flaked away in places to reveal the core. The suspension loop was riveted to the pseudo-coin, but all that remains of the loop is a small area on each face of the pseudo-coin immediately surrounding the rivet, with nothing to indicate the shape or pattern of the loop itself. It is unclear whether the object should be interpreted as a contemporary forgery of a coin, which was subsequently mounted as a pendant, or whether it was intended to be used as jewellery from the start. The fact that it weighs only 0.93g, including what is left of the loop fitting, means that it would have been suspiciously light to circulate amongst genuine coins, but that is consistent both with its being withdrawn from circulation as an unsuccessful forgery, and with its being made for jewellery.

The obverse shows a diademed bust right, with a fragmentary inscription HΛOA___-S. The reverse shows a Byzantine-style cross-on-steps, with the letters C and A on either side, with the inscription RIS___IN. Both inscriptions appear to be blundered, and are difficult to link with known inscriptions, although the obverse inscription could perhaps represent a blundered version of the mint name CHOAE (Huy). The letters C and A on either side of the cross were originally a feature of coins from Chalon-sur-Saone (CABILONNVM), and the design is certainly consistent with having been copied from a Chalon *tremissis*, but the C and A of Chalon were copied on coins of other mints, and both the obverse and reverse designs were relatively commonplace. The best that one can realistically say is that the inspiration for the coin would appear to have been a Merovingian *tremissis* of the so-called mint and moneyer type, which was introduced in the late sixth century, arguably in 587, and survived in use until *c.* 670.[360] The imitation was probably produced in the same period, but the usual problem of estimating how long after the object was created it was deposited applies, and it would be unsafe to date its deposition more closely than the seventh century.

Conclusion

Neither pendant can be dated very precisely, either for production or deposition. As discussed above, even genuine and dateable coins used in such pendants may on occasion be deposited well after such coins would normally have ceased to circulate. However, a more general comparison of coin finds from England in this period shows a marked decline in coins and pseudo-coins being re-used in pendants from the second quarter of the seventh century. Although coin-jewellery certainly continued to be used beyond this point, few dateable coins appear to have been converted into pendants beyond the 630s, and the same probably applies to the pseudo-coins. This transition coincides with the increased production and circulation of Anglo-Saxon gold coins, and the increased availability of such coins is also an argument against the late production of pseudo-coins, especially in an area like Kent which was one of the main areas of coin production and circulation.[361] On balance, it seems unlikely that either pendant was produced later than the first quarter of the seventh century, although deposition may well have been somewhat later.

Acknowledgements

The air photographs that revealed this site were taken in June 1973 by Dr David Wilson of the University of Cambridge.[362] Excavation of a small sector of the cemetery in 1976 by Sonia Hawkes owed much to Mary James, the wife of the landowner Major Arthur James. Mary had dug on several early Anglo-Saxon sites in southern England and was a valued member of the excavation teams at Worthy Park, Kingsworthy and Finglesham.[363] She became seriously ill during the excavation, which began on 28 March and her death on 21 April cast a shadow over the last few days of the investigation, which ended on 24th April.[364] Subsequently Sonia Hawkes personally observed the laying of the water pipe in June 1976. This revealed one additional child's burial immediately to the east of the excavated area (76:37), but its entire contents had been removed before her visit.

Many of the excavators stayed as guests at Updown House, Betteshanger, Deal: Angela Calder, Alison Cook, Oliver and Tania Dickinson, Mark Horton, Gillian Preston, John Shephard, George and Birgitta Speake, Eric and Eleanor Stone and the author. A number of experienced and locally-resident archaeologists participated on a daily basis: Barbara Steed, Guy Grainger, David Mannering and Cecil Hogarth, who brought over four assistants including David Brook. If the names of other contributors have been omitted, the author hopes that they will forgive him after this time gap. Distinguished site visitors included Audrey Meaney and often such individuals assisted in digging or recording. Professor Christopher Hawkes joined towards the end of the season, recording his observations on potsherds from grave and post fills and contributing to the site notebooks. Professor E. T. Hall, University of Oxford Archaeology Research Laboratory, undertook remote sensing surveys using a magnetometer and a metal detector, though none of his results were available to the author. Mr Holyoak, East Kent Water and Drainage Division, provided for both the initial machine site clearance and its subsequent backfilling, following the pipe laying. Limited exploration within the area designated as a scheduled monument (no. 298) took place and required the consent of the Inspectorate of Ancient Monuments (then part of the Department of the Environment). Correspondence survives in the archive with Miss Gail Heath, Mrs J. K. Brown, Mr J. M. Meluish and Dr Geoffrey J. Wainwright. Some funding was provided in particular by the Kent Archaeological Society. [365]

The present report draws on the archive and the grave finds which Sonia Hawkes transferred to the author shortly before her death. It consists of notebooks, correspondence files, plans, grave plans, cross-sections of excavated features, together with a specialist report on the textiles by Elizabeth Crowfoot (Appendix II) and an assessment of two buckets (from 76:7) by Dr Carole Morris, site photographs, conservation notes and radiographs on treated artefacts, and drawings and photographs of selected grave finds. The finds conservation was undertaken by laboratory staff of the Institute of Archaeology, University of Oxford: Mrs Judi Startin and Sue Rouillard. Post-excavation photography was by R. L. Wilkins, FSA on the Institute's staff and plans and finds drawings were prepared by Mrs Marion Cox. The author's task was to draw this material into a report, together with information and other material subsequently made available by the Institute of Archaeology, University of Oxford, thanks to Professor Helena Hamerow. An assessment of the artifacts was provided by Glynis Edwards (Ancient Monuments Laboratory, English Heritage) to establish whether further research on the organic materials would be productive, concluding that this would not be worthwhile (Appendix III).

The whereabouts of the skeletal material from the 1976 excavation had been a mystery for two decades, but it was located in 1997 at an English Heritage store near Nottingham. Sonia Hawkes was notified of this shortly before she handed over the archive. Generously, English Heritage agreed to fund a full study and report on the human remains and obtained the services of Dr Corinne Duhig. Her prior experience of assessing over 400 burials from the seventh-century Anglo-Saxon cemetery at St Peter's Tip, Broadstairs, Thanet was invaluable, as both the geological conditions and levels of skeletal preservation were comparable to Updown.[366] Subsequently an opportunity arose to combine the 1976 skeletal analysis with an unpublished report by Beth Rega on the skeletons excavated in 1989 at the same Updown site. Construction of a road bypass around Eastry permitted the Kent Archaeological Rescue Unit (KARU) to mount a series of rescue excavations along its line. One of these involved an overlapping sector of the site investigated by Hawkes in 1976 and an abbreviated report on this excavation has been published in a short format A4 monograph.[367] Rega's study of the Updown 1989 skeletons formed part of a postgraduate project supervised by Dr Andrew Chamberlain in the Department of Archaeology, University of Sheffield. She had since returned to the USA, but generously agreed to work in partnership with Corinne Duhig, so that her full results could be integrated with the 1976 material and appear in the present report. English Heritage funded Duhig's analysis and joint reassessment of Rega's record sheets in order to provide a dataset comparable to that recorded from the 1976 skeletal sample. The combination of the 1976 and 1989 human material provides a viable sample of the total cemetery population, which would certainly not have been the case from either the 1976 or the 1989 material in isolation (Appendix I). One further specialist report was needed and the author is grateful to

Dr Gareth Williams, British Museum, for his observations on two coin-like pendants from two female burials: 76:26 and 76:36 (Appendix IV).

It is regrettable that Brian Philp of KARU would not consider a single integrated publication of the 1976 and 1989 investigations. As the KARU report is now in the public domain, the present report has drawn on its datasets to present an overview of this cemetery sector.[368] It has also offered alternative interpretations for particular identifications and observations and has pointed to key areas where there is insufficient information in the KARU report, which lacks a detailed catalogue of the 1989 grave assemblages and in which the finds illustrations are not presented in grave groups. Instead key data is summarized in an over-simplified table, including the skeletal information, hence the need to present Rega's results in full.

Returning to the present report, however, additional artwork by Kikar Singh was commissioned to fill a few gaps. In turn this artwork has been revised by Faith Vardy (Museum of London Archaeology Service), who has prepared all the artwork electronically mounted as figures for the present report. All the additional artwork was funded by English Heritage and the assistance of Dr Helen Keeley, the English Heritage project officer, in the preparation of three grant applications is gratefully acknowledged. Finally the award of a grant from the Marc Fitch Fund towards the cost of publishing this report is gratefully acknowledged here.

Notes

1. St Joseph 1974, pl. XXVIII
2. Philp and Keller 2002; Willson 1990
3. St Joseph 1974, pl. XXVIII
4. Chadwick 1958, Fig. 2; Hawkes and Grainger 2006, fig.1.1
5. Margary 1973: no. 100
6. Philp and Keller 2002, 2, fig. 2
7. Parfitt and Haith 1995
8. Sawyer 1968: S41
9. Sawyer 1968: S1264
10. Sawyer 1968: S1268
11. Smith 1956a, 196–7; 1956b, 82
12. Hawkes 1979, fig. 4.1; Smith 1956a, 197
13. Blair 2005, 57, 144 and 278; Rollason 1982 and 1989
14. Yorke 1990, 34–5
15. Hawkes 1979, 96–7, fig. 4.7
16. Hawkes 1979, 82–94, Figs 4.2–6
17. Richardson 2005, II, 31
18. Parfitt 1999, 51–2
19. Parfitt 1999, 45–9, Figs 2.1 and 2
20. Ager 1989
21. Böhme 1974, Taf.34.10 and Böhme 1986, Abb.61
22. Parfitt 1999, 49–50, fig. 2.3
23. Hawkes 1979, 95, fig. 4.7
24. Arnold 1982
25. Philp 2003
26. Millett and James 1983
27. Parfitt 1996; Welch 2007, 204–5
28. Chadwick 1958, 63–70, fig. 3
29. Hawkes and Grainger 2006, fig. 1.1
30. Parfitt and Brugmann 1997; Parfitt and Brugmann 1997, 1–11
31. Davidson and Webster 1967; Evison 1967
32. Hawkes 1979, 97
33. Parfitt and Needham 2007, 46
34. Brugmann 1999
35. Evison 1987
36. Welch 2007, 204–5
37. Margary 1973, no. 10
38. Faussett 1856; Geake 1997, 163; Parfitt pers.comm.
39. Hill 1981, 14–15, map 19
40. Chadwick 1958, fig. 3; Hawkes and Grainger 2006, fig. 1.1
41. Brookes 2007
42. Parfitt in Hawkes and Grainger 2006, 27–8
43. Brookes 2007; Richardson 2005; Welch 2007
44. Hawkes 1979
45. Hawkes 1981
46. As marked in Philp and Keller 2002, fig. 2
47. Philp and Keller 2002, fig. 2
48. Evison 1979b, Figs 6.1 and 6.2; Evison 1987
49. Philp and Keller 2002, 9
50. Härke 2000, 391–2, Table 5
51. Philp and Keller 2002, 8, fig. 2
52. Philp and Keller 2002, fig. 2
53. Welch 2007, 232–3; Hawkes and Grainger 2006
54. Hogarth 1973, 113, Figs 4 and 8
55. Philp and Keller 2002
56. Swanton 1973; Dickinson and Härke 1992; Evison 1987
57. Hawkes 1981; Werner 1984; van Bostraeten 1967; Evison 1979a; Ross 1991
58. Hawkes 1981, 60, fig. 3.4.1
59. Hawkes 1981, 62, fig. 3.5.2
60. Hawkes 1981, 60, fig. 3.4.2

61. Werner 1984
62. Van Bostraeten 1967, fig. 4.2; Evison 1979a, 40, pl. IIIB
63. Hawkes 1981, 54–56, fig. 3.3
64. Hawkes 1981, 60–1, fig. 3.5.1
65. Ross 1991, Type L
66. Philp and Keller 2002, 3, Table A and 4, fig. 3, not 'prime adult of 30–40 years', F, Table A; 15 [E.23] fig. 16.G1a; 9 [A.6], fig. 11.G1b
67. *Ibid.* 3, Table A and 4, fig. 3; not 'prime adult of 36–42 years, F, stature 1.73m (5ft 8⅛ins)', Table A; Ross 1991 Type LXXII; Philp and Keller 2002, 9 [A.7], fig. 12.G5a; *ibid.* 9 [A.6], fig. 11.G5b; 15 [E.23], fig. 16.G5d; 12 [A.8], fig. 13.G5c; 15 [E.24], fig. 18.G5e/f/g; 15 [E.27], not illustrated; 12 [C.15], no illustration; 15 [C.18], fig. 13.G5h; 20 [F.30], fig. 19.G5n; 20 [F.31] no illustration; 20 [F.34], fig. 19.G5q; 20 [G.38], not illustrated; 20 [G.38], fig. 20.G5s; 20 [F.31], not illustrated.
68. *Ibid.* 3, Table A and 4, fig. 3; not 'mature adult of 48–54 years, F', Table A; 2, fig. 2; 15 [E.23], fig. 16.G9a.
69. *Ibid.* 3, Table A and 4, fig. 3; reported as 'young adult of 20–30 years, F' in Table A; 15 [C.19], not illustrated; 10 [A.8], fig. 13.G12b
70. *Ibid.* 3, Table A and 4, fig. 4; not 'prime adult of 30–40 years, M, stature 1.65m (5ft 5ins)' Table A
71. *Ibid.* 3, Table A and 4, fig. 4; not 'young adult of 20–27 years, M, stature of 1.59m (5ft 2⅜ins)', Table A
72. *Ibid.* 3, Table A and 4, fig. 4; not 'mature adult of 35–45 years, F, stature 1.62m (5ft 3¾ins)', Table A; 20 [F.32], not illustrated; 12 [B.13], not illustrated; 15 [E.23], fig. 16.G18d; 15 [E.25], not illustrated; 15 [C.19], not illustrated; 20 [F.32], fig. 19.G18g; 9 [A.6], fig. 11.G18h; 12 [B.10], not illustrated
73. *Ibid.* 3, Table A: no grave plan published; reported as adult, sex unknown in, Table A
74. *Ibid.*, 3, Table A and 5, fig. 5; reported as prime adult of 30–36 years, F, stature 1.57m (5ft 1¾ins), Table A; 12 [B.11], fig. 13.G20a; 12 [B.11], not illustrated; 9 [A.6], fig. 16.G20c; 9 [A.1], fig. 11.G20d/e/f/g; Ross 1991, Type LXI; Philp and Keller 2002, 9 [A.7], fig. 12.G20h
75. *Ibid.* 3, Table A and 5, fig. 5; not 'an infant of 7–9 years, sex unknown', Table A; 15 [E.23], fig. 16.G21a; 12 [C.14], fig. 13.G21b; 15? not illustrated; 15 [C.19], not illustrated
76. *Ibid.* 3, Table A: no grave plan published; reported as 'mature adult of 40–44 years, M' in Table A
77. *Ibid.* 3, Table A and 5, fig. 5; reported as 'infant of 5–6 years, F, teeth only surviving', Table A; 9 [A.2], fig. 11.G23a; 9 [A.6], fig. 12.G23b; 15 [E.23], fig. 16.G23c; 20 [F.35], fig. 19.G23d
78. *Ibid.* 3, Table A and 5, fig. 5; reported as 'infant of 4–5 years, M', Table A; 15 [E.23], fig. 16.G24a; 12 [A.8], fig. 13.G24b; 12 [C.14], fig. 13.G24c; 9 [A.5], fig. 11.G24d
79. *Ibid.* 3, Table A and 5, fig. 5; reported as 'adult, M', Table A; 15 [E.23], fig. 16.G25a; 20 [G.37], not illustrated; 15 [D.20], fig. 14.G25c
80. *Ibid.*, 3, Table A and 5, fig. 6; reported as 'adult, F' Table A; 9 [A.6], fig. 12.G26a; 9 [A.3], fig. 11.G26b; 12 [A.8], fig. 13.G26c; 20 [F.36], fig. 19.G26d; 15 [C.19], not illustrated; 20 [F.36], fig. 19.G26f; *ibid.*, not illustrated; 15 [E.23], fig. 16.G26i/j; 15 [E.23], fig. 16.G26k; 15 [E.27], fig. 18.G26l; 15 [E.25], fig. 18.G26m; 15 [C.16], not illustrated
81. *Ibid.* 3, Table A: no grave plan published; reported as 'young adult of 24–30 years, M' in Table A
82. *Ibid.* 3, Table A and 5, fig. 6; and not 'young adult of 18–24 years, M, stature 1.75m (5ft 8⅞ins)', Table A; 15 [E.23], fig. 16.G28a
83. *Ibid.* 3, Table A: no plan published; reported as young adult of 20–25 years, F in Table A
84. *Ibid.* 3, Table A: no plan published; reported as infant of 4–6 years, sex unknown in Table A
85. *Ibid.* 3, Table A and 5, fig. 6; and not 'adult, sex unknown', Table A; 20 [F.29], fig. 19.G31a-d
86. *Ibid.* 3, Table A and 5, fig. 6; and not 'mature adult of 38–45 years, F', Table A; 9 [A.6], fig. 12.G32a

87. *Ibid.* 3, Table A; no plan published
88. *Ibid.* 3, Table A and 6, fig. 7; and not 'mature adult of 40–50 plus years, F, stature 1.52m (4ft 11⅞ins)' Table A; 9 [A.1], fig. 11.G34a; 20, [F.31], not illustrated; 15 [E.23], fig. 17.G34c; 9 [A.6], fig. 12.G34d; 9 [A.6], fig. 12.G34e; 15 [E.23], fig. 17.G34f; 15 [E.23], fig. 17.G34g; 15 [E.24], fig. 18.G34h; 15 [E.27], not illustrated
89. *Ibid.* 3, Table A and 6, fig. 7; and not 'adult, sex unknown' Table A; 9 [A.7], fig. 12.G35a; 12 [C.15], not illustrated; 15 [C.19], not illustrated; 23 [G.40], fig. 20.G35d
90. *Ibid.* 3, Table A and 6, fig. 7; and not 'infant, sex unknown' Table A; 9 [A.6], fig. 12.G36a; 15 [E.23], fig. 17.G36b; 20 [G.37], fig. 20.G36c
91. *Ibid.* 3, Table A and 6, fig. 7; reported as 'young adult of 25–35 years, M' in Table A; 15 [D.21], fig. 15.G37a
92. *Ibid.* 3, Table A and 6, fig. 7; and not 'infant of 9–10 years, sex unknown' Table A; 15 [E.23], fig. 17.G38a; Ross 1991, Type LXXII; Philp and Keller 2002, 12 [A.7], fig. 12.G38b
93. *Ibid.* 3, Table A and 6, fig. 8; and not 'adult, sex unknown' Table A; 15 [C.17], fig. 13.G39a; 9 [A.6], fig. 12.G39b; 15 [E.23], fig. 17.G39c; 15 [E.22], fig. 16.G39d
94. *Ibid.* 3, Table A and 6, fig. 8; and not 'young adult of 18–21 years, M' Table A; 15 [E.23], fig. 17.G40a; 15 [D.20], fig. 14.G40b
95. *Ibid.* 3, Table A and 6, fig. 8; and not 'adult, M', Table A; 15 [D.20], fig. 14.G41a; 15 [E.23], fig. 17.G41b; 20 [E.28], fig. 18.G41c; 20 [F.33], not illustrated
96. *Ibid.* 3, Table A and 6, fig. 8; and not 'adult, M', Table A; 15 [D.21], fig. 15.G42a
97. *Ibid.* 3, Table A and 6, fig. 8; and not 'infant, sex unknown', Table A; 15 [E.23], fig. 17.G43a; 15 [C.19], not illustrated; 9 [A.6], fig. 12.G43c
98. *Ibid.* 3, Table A and 7, fig. 9; 2, fig. 2; and not 'young adult of 25–30 years, F, stature 1.72m (5ft 7¾ins)', Table A
99. *Ibid.* 3, Table A and 7, fig. 9; reported as 'young adult of 16–24 years, F' in Table A; 12 [B.11], fig. 13.G45a; 23 [G.39], fig. 20.G45b; 9 [A.4], fig. 11.G45c; 15 [E.23], fig. 17.G45d; 12 [A.8], fig. 13.G45e; 15 [E.25], not illustrated; 15 [E.26], fig. 18.G45g; 9 [A.1], not illustrated; 9 [A.6], fig. 12.G45j; 12 [B.9], not illustrated; 12 [B.9], not illustrated
100. *Ibid.* 3, Table A and 7, fig. 9; 2, fig. 2; reported as 'young adult of 32–36 years, F' in Table A; 15 [E.27], not illustrated; 15 [E.23], fig. 17.G46b; 9 [A.6], fig. 12.G46c
101. *Ibid.* 3, Table A and 7, fig. 9; and not 'infant of 11–12 years, F', Table A; 22 [G.37], fig. 20.G47a; 15 [E.23], fig. 17.G47b; 15 [E.26], fig. 18.G47c; 12 [B.12], fig. 13.G47e; 12 [B.12], fig. 13.G.47e
102. *Ibid.* 3, Table A and 7, fig. 10; and not 'mature adult of 50 plus years, M' Table A; 15 [E.23], fig. 17.G48a
103. *Ibid.* 3, Table A and 7, fig. 10; and not 'infant, sex unknown', Table A; 22 [G.37], fig. 20.G49a; 20 [F.31], not illustrated; 15 [E.23], fig. 18.G49c; 12 [C.14], fig. 13.G49d
104. *Ibid.* 3, Table A and 7, fig. 10; reported as 'young adult of 22–28 years, M, stature 1.67m (5ft 5¾ins)', Table A; 22 [G.37], fig. 20.G50a
105. *Ibid.* 3, Table A and 7, fig. 10; 2, fig. 2; and not 'prime adult of 35–40 years, M', Table A; 12 [A.8], not illustrated; 15 [E.23], fig. 18.G51b; 15 [D.20], fig. 14.G51c
106. *Ibid.* 3, Table A and 7, fig. 10; reported as 'prime adult of 30–34 years, M', Table A; 15 [D.20], fig. 14.G52a; 12 [A.8], not illustrated; 15 [E.23], fig. 18.G52c/e; 20 [F.32], not illustrated; 15 [C.19], not illustrated
107. Crawford 1999, 53
108. Geake 1997, 72.
109. Gale 1989, Underwood 1999
110. *E.g.* Böhner 1958, 130–45, Taf.25–27
111. Hawkes in Philp 1973, 188–90, Figs 53 and 59; Hawkes and Grainger 2006, 51, 112–3, 116, Figs 2.84, 2.124, 2.126
112. Härke 1992; Geake 1997, 72–4, fig. 4.25, Tables 4.14 and 4.15; Gale 1989, 79–80

113. Evison 1963
114. Dickinson and Härke 1992, 24–6, fig. 17
115. Evison 1963, Figs 22 and 23
116. Evison 1963, Figs 17 and 19
117. Dickinson and Härke 1992; Evison 1963; Spain pers. com.
118. Evison 1963, 59–60, fig. 10
119. Dickinson and Härke 1992, 63, fig. 44 etc; Geake 1997, 67–8, fig. 4.23
120. Evison 1963, fig. 21; Swanton 1973, 179, fig. 70; Barfoot and Williams 1976, fig. 4; Evison 1963, fig. 26; Swanton 1973, 159, fig. 61; Musty 1969; Swanton 1973, 163, fig. 62
121. Philp 2002, Figs 3 and 13.1; Boyle *et al* 1998, 71–2, Figs 5.8 and 5.52
122. Spain 2000
123. Swanton 1973
124. Geake 1997, 68–70, Table 4.13
125. Geake 1997, 167, fig. 64e; Hawkes and Grainger 2006, fig. 2.115
126. Geake 1997, Table 4.13
127. Swanton 1974, 51–2
128. Swanton 1973, 37–9, 151–3, Figs 6, 57 and map fig. 8; Geake 1997, 68
129. Swanton 1973, 51–64, 157–69, Figs 11, 13, 15, 16, 61–64 and maps Figs 12, 14 and 17
130. Swanton 1973, 167, fig. 64
131. Swanton 1973, 67–71, 173–5, Figs 20, 66 and map fig. 33
132. Swanton 1973, 81–7, 177–81, Figs 25, 27, 69, 70 and maps figs 26 and 28
133. Swanton 1973, 91–3, 183–5, Figs 31, 72 and map fig. 19
134. Geake 1997, 163
135. Speake 1980, Figs 9 and 10
136. Avent 1975, pl. 77.190; Philp 1973, 190–1, fig. 53.486; Speake 1980, 60, pl. 10; Avent 1975, pl. 75.186; Meaney and Hawkes 1970, 14, 33–6, pl. II; Speake 1980, 47, 60, fig. 9j, pl. 10i
137. Boyle *et al* 1998, fig. 5.43 and pl. 5.18; Geake 1977, fig. 4.1
138. Brugmann 1999, 49–51
139. Geake 1997, 32–4, fig. 4.1; Webster and Backhouse 1991, 51–3, pl. 33a and b
140. *e.g.* Geake 1997, 66–7, fig. 4.22; Ross 1991
141. Cool 1990, 168, fig. 10.6, 7 and 11; the author thanks S. Youngs for this reference
142. Geake 1997, 35–6, fig. 4.3, 67; Evison 1987, 82–4
143. Ross 1991, 224–31, 557–62, fig. 5.22, map 5.11
144. Faussett 1856, 109, pl. XII.22: Grave 39
145. Evison 1987, 82–5, Figs 4, 8, 54 and 91 plan
146. Hawkes and Grainger 2006, 58, fig. 2.88
147. Lethbridge 1936, fig. 4c1
148. Ross 1991, 306–9, 637–9, fig. 5.43g, map 5.22; Faussett 1856, 81, figure; Hawkes and Grainger 2006, 115, fig. 2.125
149. Hawkes and Grainger 2006, 34, fig. 2.71
150. Evison 1987, 83, fig. 62.160.1
151. Faussett 1856, 173–4, pl. XII.18
152. Ross 1991, 245–9, 569–72, fig. 5.27, map 5.14, esp. see fig. 5.27g
153. Faussett 1856, 133–4, pl. XII.20
154. Hawkes and Grainger 2006, 43, fig. 2.77
155. Philp and Keller 2002, 20
156. Philp and Keller 2002, fig. 4 plan
157. Philp and Keller 2002, fig. 6
158. Philp and Keller 2002, fig. 10 plan
159. Guido 1999; Brugmann 2004
160. Philp and Keller 2002, 9, fig. 11
161. Philp and Keller 2002, 9, fig. 12
162. Philp and Keller 2002, 9, fig. 12
163. Philp and Keller 2002, 9, fig. 12
164. See Schretzheim colour plate 1 types 4.1 and 4.2: Koch 1977
165. Philp and Keller 2002, 9, fig. 12
166. Philp and Keller 2002, 9, fig. 12
167. Philp and Keller 2002, 9, fig. 12
168. Philp and Keller 2002, 9, fig. 11
169. Philp and Keller 2002, 9, fig. 12
170. Philp and Keller 2002, 9, fig. 11
171. Koch 1977
172. See Schretzheim nos.35.3 and 33.14 on colour plate 3: Koch 1977
173. See Schretzheim colour plate 1 nos.1.3–1.5: Koch 1977
174. Brugmann 2004, 70, 80, Figs 155, 157 and 158
175. Brugmann 2004, 70, 81, fig. 161
176. See Schretzheim no. R1 on colour plate 5: Koch 1977; Brugmann 2004, 70, 80, fig. 153; Hyslop 1963, 179, fig. 12g
177. Philp and Keller 2002, 9, fig. 12
178. Philp and Keller 2002, 9, fig. 12; Brugmann 2004, 70, 81, fig. 160
179. Philp and Keller 2002, 9, fig. 12
180. Geake 1997, 41–2, fig. 4.5, map 12; Huggett 1988, fig. 2; Brugmann 2004, 63, map fig. 66
181. Hawkes and Grainger 2006, Figs 2.77, 2.89, 2.91, 2.92, 2.105, 2.114, 2.122, 2.132, 2.133
182. Dickinson 1993, 50–2, fig. 6.4; Meaney 1981, 166–8, Figs V.t, V.u and V.v; Boyle *et al* 1998, 59, fig. 5.40: 3i.
183. Hines 1984, 13
184. Hyslop 1963, 190–1, Figs 8 and 9; Hawkes in Meaney and Hawkes 1970, 37–8, fig. 9; Geake 1997, 41–50, fig. 4.10, map 18
185. Welch 1983, 82, fig. 20
186. Hines 1984, 225–35; Geake 1997, 37–9 and 40–1, fig. 4.4–5
187. Meaney 1981, 159–62, Figs V.o-V.p
188. Faussett 1856, pl. I; Evison 1987, 55–6, Figs 19, 21, 22 and 37, colour pl. Id
189. Hawkes and Grainger 2006, 119, 98, Figs 2.129, 2.117
190. Faussett 1856, 130–2; Meaney and Hawkes 1970, 47–8, pl. VI; Geake 1997, 9
191. White 1988
192. Faussett 1856, 130–2; Meaney and Hawkes 1970, 47–8, pl. VI; Geake 1997, 9
193. Hawkes and Grainger 2006, 36, fig. 2.73
194. Hawkes and Grainger 2006, 104–5, fig. 2.120
195. Geake 1997, 55–6, fig. 4.14, Table 4.12
196. in Philp and Keller 2002, 9, fig. 11; Evison 1987, fig. 58
197. Evison 1987, fig. 37
198. Hawkes and Grainger 2006, figs 2.84, 2.149 and 2.130; Drinkall and Foreman 1998, fig. 98
199. Geake 1997, 76–7, fig. 4.26, map 40
200. Evison 1987
201. Brugmann in Hawkes and Grainger 2006, 21
202. Evison 1988, 18–20, fig. 27
203. Hawkes and Grainger 2006, 113, fig. 2.124; 84, fig. 2.106
204. Geake 1997, 76–7
205. Philp and Keller 2002, 12, fig. 13
206. Green *et al* 1987, fig. 310; Marzinzik 2003, 49–50, 218, pl. 130.2
207. Geake 1997, 76–7
208. Hawkes 1981, 62, fig. 3.5, 2
209. Hawkes 1981, 54–6 and 58, fig. 3.3
210. Hawkes 1981, 60–2, fig. 3.5, 1
211. Hawkes 1981; Hawkes and Grainger 2006, fig. 2.82
212. Hawkes 1981, 60, fig. 3.4, 2
213. Hawkes 1981, 60, fig. 3.4, 1
214. Nieveler and Siegmund 1999, fig. 1.4
215. Webster and Backhouse 1991, 24–5, pl. 6; 25, pl. 7; Detsicas and Hawkes 1973
216. Speake 1980, 58, fig. 6n, pl. 2a
217. Smith 1902, 253–4, colour pl. no. 1 (opposite p.233); Speake 1980, 64
218. Dickinson 2005, 154–7; Eleanor Lewis-Bale pers. comm.
219. Simon Burnell pers. comm.; Werner 1984
220. Kazanski and Sodini 1987, 78–80, fig. 11
221. Marzinzik 2003, 43–4, 201–2, pls.86–7
222. Evison 1987, fig. 47; Marzinzik 2003, pl. 86.2; Hawkes 2000, fig. 11

223. Geake 1997, 79, fig. 4.27
224. Marzinzik 2003, 51, 218–20, pls.130–7
225. Philp and Keller 2002, fig. 13
226. Hawkes and Grainger 2006, Figs 2.84, 2.108, 2.113, 2.119 and 2.135; fig 2.85
227. Marzinzik 2003, 32–4, *e.g.* pls.51.2 and 60.3
228. Geake 1997, 79–80, fig. 4.27, map 45
229. Lethbridge 1936; Evison 1987, fig. 62
230. Geake 1997, 57; fig. 4.16
231. Evison 1987, 117–8, fig. 16
232. Geake 1997, 58
233. Philp and Keller 2002, 9, fig. 11.G45c; fig. 9
234. Hawkes in Philp 1973, 195–6
235. Geake 1997, 57–8, Figs 4.16–18, map 23
236. Hawkes and Grainger 2006, Figs 2.79, 2.129 and 2.134
237. *e.g.* Evison 1987, 119
238. Hawkes and Grainger 2006, 120 fig. 2.129
239. Evison 1987, text fig. 27, Figs 50, 60–62; Geake 1997, 64–5, fig. 4.21, map 30
240. Philp and Keller 2002, 12, fig. 13
241. Geake 1997, 63–4, fig. 4.21, map 29
242. Evison 1987, 113–6, text fig. 23
243. Härke 1989
244. Geake 1997, 96–7, fig. 4.39, map 58
245. See graves 8, 57, 62B, 138, 150: Hawkes and Grainger 2006, 38, 62, 68, 101, 106, Figs 2.74, 2.88, 2.92, 2.116, 2.119
246. Hawkes and Grainger 2006, 48, fig. 2.81
247. Geake 1997, 93–4, Figs 4.37–38, map 54
248. Hawkes and Grainger 2006, Figs 2.90, 2.93, 2.113, 2.115, 2.125 and 2.137
249. Geake 1997, 93–4, fig. 4.36, map 55
250. Philp and Keller 2002, 15 (26g), fig. 13
251. Evison 1987, fig. 30.5; Geake 1997, 94–5, map 56
252. Geake 1997, 97–8, fig. 4.40–41, map 59
253. Cook 2004, 64
254. East 1983, 587
255. Geake 1997, 90–1, table 4.17, fig. 4.35, map 52
256. Morris 1984; Morris 2000, 2225–37
257. Morris 2000, 2188–92
258. Philp and Keller 2002, 22–3, fig. 20
259. Bruce-Mitford and East 1983; Carver 2005; Hirst *et al* 2005
260. Hawkes, Speake and Northover 1979
261. Philp and Keller 2002, 9, Figs 5 and 11
262. Geake 1997, 92, fig. 4.36, map 53; Morris 1984; Morris 2000, 2116–2220
263. Hawkes and Grainger 2006, Figs 2.103–4 and 2.75
264. Hawkes and Grainger 2006, Figs 2.90, 2.92, 2.93, 2.122 and 2.125
265. Geake 1997, 81–2, fig. 4.29–31, map 47
266. Evison 1987, fig. 21.8a
267. Hawkes and Grainger 2006, Figs 2.75 and 2.84
268. Philp and Keller 2002, 20, fig. 19; 20, fig. 19
269. Hawkes and Grainger 2006, 62, 68, 126, Figs 2.88, 2.92, 2.130
270. Hawkes and Grainger 2006, 101, fig. 2.116
271. Lethbridge 1931, 56
272. Crowfoot 1990, 51 and 54, fig. 6.1 2
273. Crowfoot 1990
274. Geake 1997, 34–5, fig. 4.2, map 5
275. Hawkes and Grainger 2006, 37–8, fig. 2.74
276. Evison 1979a, 40, pls.IIA and IIIB; fig. 31g
277. Evison 1979a, 40–1, 80, fig. 16a-c
278. Evison 1979a, 40, 80, fig. 16e; 40–1, 81, pl. IVA
279. Evison 1979a, Figs 14–16
280. Evison 1979a, 77–8, fig. 14g
281. Evison 1979a, 41–2, 83, Figs 17f,g and 18a
282. Faussett 1856, pl. XIX.1; Geake 1997, 88, fig. 4.33, map 49; Chadwick 1958, 27, 37, fig. 5t; Hawkes and Grainger 2006, 94, fig. 2.114
283. Evison 1979b, Figs 6.1–2; 1987, fig. 24
284. Hawkes and Grainger 2006, Figs 2.72, 2.87, 2.93, 2.120 and 2.145
285. Geake 1997, 62–3, fig. 4.20, map 28
286. Geake 1997, 32, fig. 4.1, map 3
287. Philp and Keller 2002, 9
288. Hogarth 1973; Duhig 1996
289. Crawford 1999, 47, 50–1, 53
290. Crawford 1999, 175
291. Geake 1997, 91
292. Hawkes 1981, 60, fig. 3.5
293. Geake 1997, 88–9
294. Martin 1976
295. Glass 1999; Canterbury Archaeological Trust and Wessex Archaeology 2000; Welch 2007, 221 and 224
296. Hyslop 1963; Meaney and Hawkes 1970
297. Parfitt and Brugmann 1997; Brugmann 1999
298. Evison 1987
299. Hines (ed.) forthcoming
300. Hawkes 1981
301. Leeds 1936
302. *e.g.* late forms of Dickinson Group 3 bosses with a convex cone or Group 6 low-cone bosses: Dickinson and Härke 1992; Spain 2000
303. Evison 1987
304. Faussett 1856; Hawkes 1990; Rhodes 1990; Richardson 2005 II, Map 3
305. Hawkes and Grainger 2006
306. Hawkes 1974; Hawkes and Hogarth 1974; Perkins and Hawkes 1984; Geake 1997, 164; Perkins 1991 and 1992
307. Hogarth 1973; Marzinzik forthcoming
308. Hawkes 1981, 53–4, fig. 3.2; Hawkes and Grainger 2006, fig. 2.82; Avent 1975; Faussett 1856, pls.I and II
309. Evison 1987, 87, text fig. 15
310. Evison 1987, fig. 31
311. Evison 1987, 89, fig. 62; 89–90, Figs 56 and 60
312. Geake 1997, 76
313. Faussett 1856, pls.VIII and IX; MacGregor and Bolick 1993, 193–8
314. Faussett 1856, pl. IV; Meaney and Hawkes 1970, pl. VI; Hawkes 1990, pl. 4
315. Geake 1997; Meaney and Hawkes 1970
316. Evison 1979a
317. Welch 2007, 234–5
318. Brookes 2007
319. Harrington 2002
320. Cho *et al.* 1996; Iscan and Kennedy 1994; Steele and Bramblett 1988; Stewart 1979; Ubelaker 1989
321. Duhig 1998: 156–7, Figure 4.3
322. Waldron 1994: 16–20, Figure 2.4
323. Crawford 1991: 21
324. discussed for different time periods in, for example, Crawford 1991; 1999; Molleson 1993; Parker-Pearson 1999: 102–9; Scott 1999; Taylor 2001
325. Brothwell 1981; Miles 1963
326. Duhig 1998; In prep a; b; Taylor *et al.* 1999
327. Waldron 1994
328. Trotter and Gleser 1952
329. Duhig 1998; Wiggins *et al.* 1999
330. Iscan and Kennedy 1994; Ortner and Putschar 1985; Steinbock 1976
331. Barnes 1994; Hauser and Stefano 1989; Hillson 1990
332. Duhig in prep-a; Duhig In prep b
333. Duhig 1998; In prep-a; b
334. Kennedy 1994
335. Dobney and Goodman 1991; Goodman and Armelagos 1985; Goodman *et al.* 1980; Hillson 1990; Karhu 1990; Sweeney *et al.* 1971; Van Gerven *et al.* 1990
336. Stuart-Macadam 1982; 1994
337. surveyed in Duhig in prep-a

338. Adams 1969: 145, 151–5
339. Judd 2002
340. Kennedy 1994
341. Duhig 1998, and refs.
342. Andersen 1991; Andersen and Manchester 1992
343. Rogers and Waldron 1995: 71; Rogers *et al.* 1987
344. Rogers and Waldron 1995, 69–77
345. Ancient Monuments Report no. 2194. This report was compiled shortly after the excavations in 1976, so the text does not take account of subsequent developments. The text has been edited with modification of grave numbers adding the 76: prefix, but other significant editorial changes are signified by placing the word(s) within squared brackets. The term bronze has been retained in the text where copper-alloy would normally appear nowadays in such a report.
346. Several finds of silk have been recorded subsequently at Buckland II grave 247: around the edge and on the back of a Frankish *cloisonné* disc brooch at the throat; Ozengell 168: attached to a seventh-century chatelaine; Tattershall Thorpe: smith's grave or hoard (Susan Harrington pers. comm.).
347. Crowfoot 1973, 202–3.
348. Crowfoot 1983, III, SH 1 and 12, B 2. The Broomfield assemblage was deposited in a chamber grave, but it is not certain (though it is probable) that it was covered by a barrow.
349. Op.cit., SH 9, B 1; Crowfoot 1967, fig. 7; Crowfoot 1969, 51; Mucking, Essex; Dover; Fonaby; Welbeck Hill, Irby; Sewerby; unpublished.
350. Hoffmann 1964, 44, fig. 130.
351. Haith in Webster and Backhouse 1991, 23–4, 53–4; Rigold 1975, 653–77 nos. 16, 46, 48–9, 51, 62, 65–6, 69, 73, 77–8, 115, 132; Hawkes, Merrick and Metcalf 1966, 115–16; Abdy and Williams 2006, 11–74; Williams 2006, 145–92.
352. Abdy and Williams 2006, 273
353. Bruck 1961, 75.
354. J. P. C. Kent, 'From Roman Britain to Anglo-Saxon England' in R. H. M. Dolley, (ed.), Anglo-Saxon Coins: Studies presented to F. M. Stenton on the occasion of his 80th birthday, 17 May 1960, London 1961, pp. 1–22; M. D. King, 'Roman coins from Anglo-Saxon contexts' in J. Casey and R. Reece (eds), Coins and the archaeologist (2nd edn), London 1988, pp. 224–9; R. H. White, Roman and Celtic Objects from Anglo-Saxon Graves: A catalogue and an interpretation of their use, BAR British Series 191, Oxford 1988, 62–101; T. S. N. Moorhead, 'Roman bronze coinage in sub-Roman and early Anglo-Saxon England', in B. Cook and G. Williams (eds), Coinage and History in the North Sea World, *c.* AD 500–1250 (Leiden 2006), 99–110: D. M. Metcalf, Thrymsas and Sceattas in the Ashmolean Museum, Oxford, vol 1 (London 1993); Williams, G. 'Early Anglo-Saxon Gold Coinage', BNJ 78 (forthcoming).
355. Hawkes, Merrick, and Metcalf, 'X-ray fluorescent analysis', pp. 111–13; Rigold, 'Sutton Hoo coins', nos. 85, 98; M. Warhurst, Sylloge of Coins of the British Isles, 29, Merseyside County Museums, London 1982, nos. 17–18; Abdy and Williams, 'Catalogue', Hoards, no. 12.
356. Abdy and Williams, 'Catalogue', no. 272.
357. Abdy and Williams, 'Catalogue', Hoards, nos. 5 and 6.
358. A.C. Evans, in Webster and Backhouse, The Making of England, pp. 51–3, no. 33; Abdy and Williams, 'Catalogue', no. 35.
359. Abdy and Williams, 'Catalogue', no. 47.
360. P. Grierson and M.A.S. Blackburn, Medieval European Coinage, vol. I, The Early Middle Ages (5th to 10th centuries), Cambridge 1986, pp. 90–94, 117–28.
361. Williams, 'Circulation and Function', pp. 161–9; Williams, 'Early Anglo-Saxon Gold Coinage'
362. St Joseph 1974; the former Aerial Photography Unit is now the Unit for Landscape Modelling
363. Hawkes and Grainger 2003, xii; Hawkes and Grainger 2006
364. Detsicas 1976
365. Detsicas 1976
366. Duhig 1996
367. Philp and Keller 2002
368. Philp and Keller 2002

Bibliography

Abdy, R. and Williams, G. 2006. 'A catalogue of hoards and single finds from the British Isles, *c.* AD 410–675' in B. Cook and G. Williams (eds), *Coinage and History in the North Sea World, c AD 500–1250*, 11–74, Leiden.

Adams, J. C. 1969. *Outline of fractures*, Edinburgh and London: E. and S. Livingstone.

Ager, B. M. 1989. 'An Anglo-Saxon supporting-arm brooch from Eastry, Kent', *Medieval Archaeology* **13**, 148–51

Andersen, J. G. 1991. 'The medieval diagnosis of leprosy,' in D. J. Ortner and A. C. Aufderheide (eds), *Human paleopathology: current synthesis and future options*, 205–10, Washington, D.C.: Smithsonian Institution Press.

Andersen, J. G. and Manchester, K. 1992. 'The rhinomaxillary syndrome in leprosy: a clinical, radiological and palaeopathological study', *International Journal of Osteoarchaeology* **2** (2): 121–30.

Arnold, C. J. 1982. 'Excavations at Eastry Court Farm, Eastry', *Archaeologia Cantiana*, **98**, 121–35

Avent, R. 1975. *Anglo-Saxon Garnet Inlaid Disc and Composite Brooches*, BAR British Series 11: Oxford.

Barfoot, J. F. and Price Williams, D. 1976. 'The Saxon barrow at Gally Hills, Banstead Down, Surrey', *Research Volume of the Surrey Archaeological Society* **3**, 59–76

Barnes, E. 1994. *Developmental defects of the axial skeleton in paleopathology*, Niwot, Colorado: University Press of Colorado.

Blair, J. 2005. *The Church in Anglo-Saxon Society*, Oxford: Oxford University Press.

Van Boestraeten, H. C. 1967. 'Merovingisch aardewerk van het type 'Beerlegem'', *Helinium* **7**, 229–52

Böhme, H. W. 1974. *Germanische Grabfunde des 4. bis 5. Jahrhunderts zwischen unterer Elbe und Loire: Studien zur Chronologie und Bevölkerungsgeschichte*, Munich.

Böhme, H. W. 1986. 'Das Ende der Römerherrschaft in Britannien und die angelsächsische Besiedlung Englands im 5. Jahrhundert', *Jahrbuch des Römisch-Germanisches Zentralmuseum Mainz* **33.2**, 469–574

Böhner, K. 1958. *Die fränkischen Altertümer des Trierer Landes*, Berlin.

Boyle, A., Jennings, D., Miles, D. and Palmer, S. 1998. *The Anglo-Saxon Cemetery at Butler's Field, Lechlade, Gloucestershire*, vol.1, Oxford.

Brookes, S. 2007. *Economics and Social Change in Anglo-Saxon Kent AD 400–900. Landscape, communities and exchange*, BAR British Series 431, Oxford.

Brothwell, D. R. 1981. *Digging up bones*. 3rd edition. Oxford: Oxford University Press and British Museum (Natural History).

Bruce-Mitford, R. 1983. *The Sutton Hoo ship-burial Vol 3*, London.

Bruce-Mitford, R. and East, K. 1983. 'Drinking-horns, maplewood bottles and burr-wood cups', in R. Bruce-Mitford, *The Sutton Hoo Ship-Burial* Vol.3, 316–408, London.

Bruck, G. 1961. *Die Spätrömische Kupferprägung: Ein Bestimmungsbuch für Schlecht Erhaltene Münzen*, Graz.

Brugmann, B. 1999. 'The role of continental artefact-types in sixth-century Kentish Chronology', in J. Hines, K. Høilund Nielsen and F. Siegmund (eds), *The Pace of Change. Studies in Early-Medieval*

Chronology, 37–64, Oxford.

Brugmann, B. 2004. *Glass Beads from Early Anglo-Saxon Graves. A study of the provenance and chronology of glass beads from Early Anglo-Saxon graves, based on visual examination,* Oxford.

Canterbury Archaeological Trust and Wessex Archaeology 2000. 'Saltwood', *Current Archaeology* 168 (XIV.12), 462–3

Carver, M. 2005. *Sutton Hoo: a seventh-century princely burial ground and its context,* London.

Chadwick, S. E. 1958. 'The Anglo-Saxon cemetery at Finglesham: a reconsideration', *Medieval Archaeology* 2, 1–71

Cho, H., Falsetti, A. B. McIlwaine, J. Roberts, C. Sledzik P. S. and Willcox A. W. (eds), 1996. *Handbook of the Forensic Anthropology Course of the Department of Archaeological Sciences, University of Bradford and the NMHM/AFIP, Washington, D.C*

Cook, J. M. 2004. *Early Anglo-Saxon Buckets. A corpus of copper alloy and iron-bound stave-built vessels,* Oxford.

Cool, H. E. M. 1990. 'Roman metal hair pins from southern England', *Archaeological Journal* 147, 147–82

Crawford, S. 1991. 'When do Anglo-Saxon children count?' *Journal of Theoretical Archaeology* 2, 17–24.

Crawford, S. 1999. *Childhood in Anglo-Saxon England,* Stroud

Crowfoot, E. 1967. 'Appendix I: The Textiles', *Medieval Archaeology,* 11, 37–39.

Crowfoot, E. 1973. 'Textile fragments from Polhill', in B. Philp (ed.), *Excavations in West Kent 1960–1970,* 202–3.

Crowfoot, E. 1983 'The Textiles' in R. Bruce-Mitford, *The Sutton Hoo ship-burial Vol 3,* 409–79, London.

Crowfoot, E. 1990. 'Textile fragments from 'relic-boxes' in Anglo-Saxon graves', in P. Walton and J-P. Wild (eds), *Textiles in Northern Archaeology, NESAT III: Textile Symposium in York 6–9 May 1987,* 47–56, London.

Crowfoot E. 1969. In P. J. Tester, 'Excavations at Fordcroft, Orpington', *Archaeologia Cantiana,* 84, 51

Davidson, H. R. E. and Webster, L. E. 1967. 'The Anglo-Saxon burial at Coombe (Woodensborough), Kent', *Medieval Archaeology* 11, 1–41

Detsicas, A. P. 1976. 'Obituaries: The Hon. Mrs. Mary James', *Archaeologia Cantiana* 92, 273

Detsicas, A. P. and Hawkes, S. C. 1973. 'Finds from the Anglo-Saxon Cemetery at Eccles, Kent (Ballot Notes)', *Antiquaries Journal* 53, 281–6

Dickinson, T. M. 1993. 'An Anglo-Saxon 'cunning woman' from Bidford-on-Avon', in M. Carver (ed.), *In Search of Cult. Archaeological investigations in honour of Philip Rahtz,* 45–54, Woodbridge.

Dickinson, T. M. 2005. 'Symbols of Protection: the significance of animal-ornamented shields in Early Anglo-Saxon England', *Medieval Archaeology* 49, 109–63

Dickinson, T. M. and Härke, H. 1992. *Early Anglo-Saxon Shields,* Archaeologia 110, London.

Dobney, K. and Goodman, A. H. 1991. 'Epidemiological studies of dental enamel hypoplasias in Mexico and Bradford: their relevance to archaeological skeletal studies,' in H. Bush and M. Zvelebil (eds), *Health in past societies,* BAR Int. Series 567, Oxford: Tempus Reparatum.

Drinkall, G. and Foreman, M. 1998. *The Anglo-Saxon Cemetery at Castledyke South, Barton-on-Humber,* Sheffield.

Duhig, C. 1996. *St Peter's Tip, Broadstairs, Kent. The Human Skeletal Remains* (unpublished report commissioned by the British Museum and English Heritage): see Duhig in prep. b, below.

Duhig, C. 1998. 'The Anglo-Saxon skeletal remains,' in T. Malim and J. Hines (eds), *The Anglo-Saxon cemetery at Edix Hill (Barrington A), Cambridgeshire,* CBA Research Report 112., 154–99, York: Council for British Archaeology.

Duhig, C. in prep. a. 'The human remains,' in H. Duncan, (ed.) *The Anglo-Saxon cemetery at Water Lane, Melbourn, Cambridgeshire.*

Duhig, C. in prep. b. 'The human skeletal remains,' in S. Marzinzik (ed.) *The Anglo-Saxon cemetery at St. Peter's Tip, Broadstairs, Kent,* London: British Museum Publications: see Duhig 1996 above.

East, K. 1983. 'The tub and buckets, in R. Bruce-Mitford, (ed.), *The Sutton Hoo Ship-Burial* Vol.3 (part 2), 554–96, London.

Evison, V. I. 1963. 'Sugar-loaf shield bosses', *Antiquaries Journal,* 43, 38–96

Evison, V. I. 1967. 'The Dover Ring-Sword and other sword-rings and beads', *Archaeologia* 101, 63–118

Evison, V. I. 1979a. *Wheel-thrown Pottery in Anglo-Saxon Graves,* London.

Evison, V. I. 1979b. 'The body in the ship at Sutton Hoo', *Anglo-Saxon Studies in Archaeology and History,* 1, 121–138, BAR British Series 72: Oxford.

Evison, V. I. 1987. *Dover: The Buckland Anglo-Saxon Cemetery,* London.

Evison, V. I. 1988. *An Anglo-Saxon Cemetery at Alton, Hampshire,* Winchester.

Faussett, B. 1856. *Inventorium Sepulchrale* C. Roach Smith (ed.), London

Gale, D. A. 1989. 'The Seax', in S. C. Hawkes (ed.), *Weapons and Warfare in Anglo-Saxon England,* 71–83, Oxford.

Geake, H. 1997. *The Use of Grave-Goods in Conversion-Period England, c.600–c.850,* BAR British Series 261: Oxford.

Glass, H. J. 1999. 'Archaeology of the Channel Tunnel Rail Link', *Archaeologia Cantiana* 119, 189–220

Goodman, A. H. and Armelagos, G. J. 1985. 'Factors affecting the distribution of enamel hypoplasias within the human permanent dentition', *American Journal of Physical Anthropology* 68, 479–93.

Goodman, A. H., Armelagos, G. J. and Rose, J. C. 1980. 'Enamel hypoplasias as indicators of stress in three prehistoric populations from Illinois', *Human Biology* 52, 515–28.

Green, B., Rogerson, A. and White, S. G. 1987. *The Anglo-Saxon Cemetery at Morning Thorpe, Norfolk,* East Anglian Archaeology Report 36: Dereham.

Grierson, P. and Blackburn, M. A. S. 1986. *Medieval European coinage, Vol 1, The early Middle Ages (5th to 10th centuries),* Cambridge.

Guido, M. 1999. *The Glass Beads of Anglo-Saxon England, c. AD 400–700. A preliminary visual classification of the more definitive and diagnostic types,* Woodbridge.

Härke, H. 1989. 'Knives in early Anglo-Saxon burials: blade length and age at death', *Medieval Archaeology* 33, 144–8

Härke, H. 1992. *Angelsächsische Waffengräber des 5. bis 7. Jahrhunderts,* Cologne.

Härke, H. 2000. 'The circulation of weapons in Anglo-Saxon society', in F. Theuws and J. L. Nelson (eds), *Rituals of Power. From Late Antiquity to the Early Middle Ages,* 377–99. Leiden.

Harrington, S. 2002. *Aspects of Gender and Craft Production in Early Anglo-Saxon England with reference to the Kingdom of Kent,* University College London, unpublished PhD thesis.

Hauser, G. and Stefano, G. F. D. 1989. *Epigenetic variants of the human skull,* Stuttgart: Schweizerbart.

Hawkes, S. C. 1974. 'The Monkton brooch', *Antiquaries Journal* 54, 245–56

Hawkes, S. C. 1979. 'Eastry in Anglo-Saxon Kent: its importance and a newly found grave', *Anglo-Saxon Studies in Archaeology and History,* 1, 81–113, BAR British Series 72: Oxford.

Hawkes, S. C. 1981. 'Recent finds of inlaid iron buckles and belt-plates from seventh century Kent', *Anglo-Saxon Studies in Archaeology and History,* 2, 49–70, BAR British Series 92: Oxford.

Hawkes, S. C. 1982. 'Finglesham: a cemetery in East Kent', in J. Campbell (ed.), *The Anglo-Saxons,* 24–5, London.

Hawkes, S. C. 1990. 'Bryan Faussett and the Faussett Collection: an assessment', in E. Southworth (ed.), *Anglo-Saxon Cemeteries a Reappraisal,* 1–24, Stroud.

Hawkes, S. C. 2000. 'The Anglo-Saxon cemetery of Bifrons, in the parish of Patrixbourne, Kent', *Anglo-Saxon Studies in Archaeology and History* 11, 1–94.

Hawkes, S. C. and Grainger, G. 2003. *The Anglo-Saxon Cemetery at*

Worthy Park, Kingsworthy near Winchester, Hampshire, Oxford.

Hawkes, S. C. and Grainger, G. 2006. *The Anglo-Saxon Cemetery at Finglesham, Kent,* Oxford.

Hawkes, S. C. and Hogarth, A. C. 1974. 'The Anglo-Saxon cemetery at Monkton, Thanet', *Archaeologia Cantiana* **89**, 49–89

Hawkes, S. C., Merrick, J. M., and Metcalf, D. M., 1966. 'X-ray fluorescent analysis of some Dark Age coins and jewellery', *Archaeometry* **9**, 98–138.

Hawkes, S. C., Speake, G. and Northover, P. 1979. 'A seventh-century bronze metalworker's die from Rochester, Kent', *Frühmittelalterliche Studien* **13**, 382–92

Hill, D. 1981. *An Atlas of Anglo-Saxon England 700–1066,* Oxford.

Hillson, S. 1990. *Teeth.* (Cambridge Manuals in Archaeology). Cambridge: Cambridge University Press.

Hines, J. 1984. *The Scandinavian Character of Anglian England in the pre-Viking Period,* BAR British Series 124: Oxford.

Hines, J. (ed.) forthcoming, *Anglo-Saxon England c.570–720: the chronological basis,* Society for Medieval Archaeology Monograph Series: London.

Hirst, S., Nixon, T., Rowsome, P. and Wright, S. 2004. *The Prittlewell Prince: the discovery of a rich Anglo-Saxon burial in Essex,* London.

Hoffmann, M. 1964. *The Warp-weighted Loom.*

Hogarth, A. C. 1973. 'Structural features in Anglo-Saxon graves', *Archaeological Journal* **130**, 104–19

Huggett, J. W. 1988. 'Imported grave goods and the Anglo-Saxon economy', *Medieval Archaeology* **32**, 63–96

Hyslop, M. 1963. 'Two Anglo-Saxon cemeteries at Chamberlain's Barn, Leighton Buzzard, Bedfordshire', *Archaeological Journal* **120**, 161–200

Iscan, M. Y. and Kennedy, K. A. R. (eds) 1994. *Reconstruction of life from the skeleton,* 2nd edition, New York: Wiley-Liss.

Judd, M. 2002. 'Ancient injury recidivism: an example for the Kerma period of ancient Nubia'. *International Journal of Osteoarchaeology* **12**(2): 89–106.

Karhu, S. L. 1990. 'Inter-tooth distribution of dental enamel hypoplasias among Medieval Christian Nubians from Kulubnarti'. *American Journal of Physical Anthropology* **81**: 247.

Kazanski, M. and Sodini, J-P 1987. 'Byzance et l'art ‹nomade›: remarques à propos de l'essai de J. Werner sur le dépôt de Malaja Pereščepina (Pereščepino), *Revue Archéologique,* Fascicule **1**, 71–83

Kennedy, K. A. R. 1994. 'Skeletal markers of occupational stress,' in M. Y. Iscan and K. A. R. Kennedy (eds), *Reconstruction of life from the skeleton,* 2nd edition, New York: Wiley-Liss.

Kent, J. P. C. 1961. 'From Roman Britain to Saxon England' in R. H. M. Dolley (ed.) *Anglo-Saxon coins: studies presented to F. M. Stenton,* 1–22, London.

King, M. D. 1988. 'Roman Coins from Anglo-Saxon contexts' in J. Casey and R. Reece (eds) *Coins and the Archaeologist,* 224–9, 2nd edition, London.

Koch, U. 1977. *Das Reihengräberfeld bei Schretzheim,* Berlin.

Leeds, E. T. 1936. *Early Anglo-Saxon Art and Archaeology,* Oxford

Lethbridge, T. C. 1931. *Recent excavations in Anglo-Saxon cemeteries in Cambridgeshire and Suffolk,* Cambridge.

Lethbridge, T. C.1936. *A Cemetery at Shudy Camps, Cambridgeshire,* Cambridge.

MacGregor, A. and Bolick, E. 1993. *A Summary Catalogue of the Anglo-Saxon Collections (Non-Ferrous Metals),* BAR British Series 230: Oxford.

Margary, I. D. 1973. *Roman Roads in Britain,* London.

Martin, M. 1976. *Das fränkische Gräberfeld von Basel-Bernerring,* Basel.

Marzinzik, S. 2003. *Early Anglo-Saxon Belt Buckles (late 5th to early 8th centuries A.D.),* BAR British Series 357: Oxford.

Marzinzik, S. forthcoming, *The Anglo-Saxon Cemetery at St Peter's Tip, Broadstairs, Kent.*

Meaney, A. L. 1981. *Anglo-Saxon Amulets and Curing Stones,* BAR British Series 96: Oxford.

Meaney, A. L. and Hawkes, S.C. 1970. *Two Anglo-Saxon Cemeteries at Winnall, Winchester, Hampshire,* Society for Medieval Archaeology Monograph Series, 4: London.

Metcalf, D. M. 1993. Thrymsas *and* sceattas *in the Ashmolean Museum, Oxford,* Vol. 1, Oxford.

Miles, A. E. W. 1963. 'Molar attrition ageing scheme,' in D. R. Brothwell (ed.) *Dental Anthropology,* 191–209, Oxford: Pergamon Press.

Millett, M. and James, S. 1983. 'Excavations at Cowdery's Down, Basingstoke, Hampshire 1978–81', *Archaeological Journal* **140**, 151–279

MoLAS 2000. 'Cuxton Anglo-Saxon cemetery', *Current Archaeology,* **168** (XIV.12), 460–1

Molleson, T. L. 1993. 'The human remains,' in D. Farwell and T. L. Molleson (eds) *Excavations at Poundbury 1966–80. Volume II: the cemeteries,* Dorchester: Dorset Natural History and Archaeological Society.

Moorhead, T. S. N. 2006. 'Roman bronze coinage in sub-Roman and early Anglo-Saxon England', in B. Cook and G. Williams (eds), *Coinage and history in the North Sea World, c. AD 500–1250,* 99–110, Leiden.

Morris, C. A. 1984. *Anglo-Saxon and Medieval Woodworking Crafts: the manufacture and use of domestic and utilitarian wooden artefacts in the British Isles, 400–1500 AD,* University of Cambridge unpublished Ph.D thesis.

Morris, C. A. 2000. *Wood and Woodworking in Anglo-Scandinavian and Medieval York.* The Archaeology of York: The Small Finds 17/13, London.

Musty, J. 1969. 'The excavation of two barrows, one of Saxon date, at Ford, Laverstock, near Salisbury', *Antiquaries Journal* **49**, 98–117

Nieveler, E. and Siegmund, F. 1999. 'The Merovingian chronology of the Lower Rhine area: results and problems', in J. Hines, K. Høilund Nielsen and F.Siegmund (eds), *The Pace of Change. Studies in Early-Medieval Chronology,* 3–22, Oxford.

Ortner, D. J. and Putschar, W. G. J. 1985. *Identification of pathological conditions in human skeletal remains.* Vol. 28, Smithsonian Contributions to Anthropology: Washington and London: Smithsonian Institution Press.

Parfitt, K.1996. 'Whitfield-Eastry Bypass', *Archaeologia Cantiana* **116**, 319

Parfitt, K. 1999. 'Anglo-Saxon Eastry: some recent discoveries and excavations', *Archaeologia Cantiana,* **119**, 45–53

Parfitt, K. and Brugmann, B. 1997. *The Anglo-Saxon Cemetery on Mill Hill, Deal, Kent,* Society for Medieval Archaeology Monograph Series, 14: London.

Parfitt, K. and Haith, C. 1995. 'Buckland Saxon Cemetery', *Current Archaeology* **144** (XII.2), 459–64

Parfitt, K. and Needham, S. 2007. 'Ringelmere. Amber, gold and a Bronze Age barrow', *Current Archaeology* **208** (XVIII.4), 41–6

Parker-Pearson, M. 1999. *The archaeology of death and burial.* Stroud: Sutton Publishing.

Perkins, D. R. J. 1991. 'The Jutish cemetery at Sarre revisited: a rescue evaluation', *Archaeologia Cantiana* **109**, 139–68

Perkins, D. R. J. 1992. 'The Jutish cemetery at Sarre revisited: part II', *Archaeologia Cantiana* **110**, 83–120

Perkins, D. R. J. and Hawkes, S. C. 1984. The Thanet Gas Pipeline Phase I and II (Monkton Parish), 1982', *Archaeologia Cantiana* **101**, 83–114

Philp, B. 1973. *Excavations in West Kent 1960–1970,* Dover.

Philp, B. 2002. *The Anglo-Saxon Cemetery at Polhill near Sevenoaks, Kent 1964–1986,* Dover.

Philp, B. 2003. *The Discovery and Excavation of Anglo-Saxon Dover,* Dover.

Philp, B. and Keller, P. 2002. *The Anglo-Saxon Cemetery on the Eastry Bypass,* Dover.

Reaney, P. H. 1961. 'Place-names and early settlement in Kent', *Archaeologia Cantiana* **76**, 58–74

Rega, E. 1994. *Osteological analysis of the human skeletal material recovered from the Early Saxon cemeteries at Eastry and*

Polhill. University of Sheffield, Department of Prehistory and Archaeology.

Renner, D. 1970. *Die durchbrochenen Zierscheiben der Merowingerzeit*, Mainz.

Rhodes, M. 1990. 'Faussett rediscovered: Charles Roach Smith, Joseph Mayer, and the publication of *Inventorium Sepulchrale'*, in E. Southworth (ed.), *Anglo-Saxon Cemeteries a Reappraisal*, 25–64, Stroud.

Richardson, A. 2005. *The Anglo-Saxon Cemeteries of Kent*, BAR British Series 391:Oxford vols.I and II.

Rigold, S. E. 1975. 'The Sutton Hoo coins in the light of the contemporary background of coinage in England', in R. Bruce-Mitford, *The Sutton Hoo Ship Burial*, vol. 1, 653–77, London.

Rogers, J. and Waldron, T. 1995. *A field guide to joint disease in archaeology*. New York: John Wiley and Sons.

Rogers, J., Waldron, T., Dieppe, P. and Watt, I. 1987. 'Arthropathies in palaeopathology: the basis of classification according to most probable cause', *Journal of Archaeological Science* **14**, 179–93.

Rollason, D. W. 1982. *The Mildrith Legend: a study in early medieval hagiography*, Leicester.

Rollason, D. W. 1989. *Saints and Relics in Anglo-Saxon England*, Oxford.

Ross, S. 1991. *Dress Pins from Anglo-Saxon England: their production and typo-chronological production*, University of Oxford unpublished D.Phil thesis.

St Joseph, J. K. 1974. 'Air reconnaissance: recent results', *Antiquity* **48**, 213–5, pl. XXVIII

Sawyer, P. H. 1968. *Anglo-Saxon Charters: an annotated list and bibliography*, London.

Scott, E. 1999. *The archaeology of infancy and infant death*, Oxford: Archaeopress.

Smith, A. H. 1956a. *English Place-Name Elements Part I*, English Place-Name Society 25. Cambridge.

Smith, A. H. 1956b. 'Place-names and the Anglo-Saxon settlement', *Proceedings of the British Academy* **42**, 67–88

Smith, R. A. 1902. 'Anglo-Saxons Remains', *The Victoria History of the Counties of England: Northamptonshire* Vol. I, 223–56, Westminster.

Spain, S. 2000. *The Shield in Early Anglo-Saxon Kent*, University of York unpublished MA dissertation.

Speake, G. 1980. *Anglo-Saxon Animal Art and its Germanic Background*, Oxford.

Steele, D. G. and Bramblett, C. A. 1988. *The anatomy and biology of the human skeleton*. College Station: Texas A and M University Press.

Steinbock, R. T. 1976. *Paleopathological diagnosis and identification*. Springfield, Ill.: Charles C. Thomas.

Stewart, T. D. 1979. *Essentials of forensic anthropology*. Springfield, Ill.: Charles C. Thomas.

Stuart-Macadam, P. 1982. *A correlative study of a palaeopathology of the skull*. University of Cambridge, Ph.D. dissertation.

Stuart-Macadam, P. 1994. 'Nutritional deficiency diseases: a survey of scurvy, rickets and iron-deficiency anemia,' in M. Y. Iscan and

K. A. R. Kennedy (eds), *Reconstruction of life from the skeleton*, 2nd edition, 201–22, New York: A.R. Liss.

Swanton, M. J. 1973. *The Spearheads of the Anglo-Saxon Settlements*, London.

Swanton, M. J. 1974. *A Corpus of Pagan Anglo-Saxon Spear-Types*, BAR British Series 7: Oxford.

Sweeney, E. A., Saffir, A. J. and de Leon, R. 1971. 'Linear hypoplasia of deciduous incisor teeth in malnourished children', *American Journal of Clinical Nutrition* **24**, 29–31.

Taylor, A. 2001. *Burial practice in early England*. Stroud: Tempus.

Taylor, A., Duhig, C. and Hines, J. 1999. 'An Anglo-Saxon cemetery at Oakington, Cambridgeshire', *Proceedings of the Cambridge Antiquarian Society* **86**, 57–90.

Trotter, M. and Gleser, G. 1952. 'Estimation of stature from the long bones of American whites and negroes', *American Journal of Physical Anthropology* **10**(4), 463–514.

Ubelaker, D. H. 1989. *Human skeletal remains: excavation, analysis, interpretation*. (Manuals on Archaeology 2). Washington: Taraxacum for Smithsonian Institution.

Underwood, R. 1999. *Anglo-Saxon Weapons and Warfare*, Stroud.

Van Boestraeten 1967: see under Boestraeten (van) 1967 above.

Van Gerven, D. P., Beck, R. and Hummert, J. R.. 1990. 'Enamel hypoplasia in two Medieval populations from Nubia's Batn el Hajar', *American Journal of Physical Anthropology* **82**, 413–20.

Waldron, T. 1994. *Counting the dead. The epidemiology of skeletal populations*. Chichester: John Wiley.

Warhurst, M. 1982. *Sylloge of coins of the British Isles*, 29, Merseyside County Museums, London.

Webster, L. and Backhouse, J. 1991. *The Making of England. Anglo-Saxon Art and Culture AD 600–900*, London

Welch, M. 1983. *Early Anglo-Saxon Sussex*, BAR British Series 112: Oxford.

Welch, M. 2007. 'Anglo-Saxon Kent to AD 800 (chapter 6)', in J. H. Williams (ed.), *The Archaeology of Kent to AD 800*, 187–248, Woodbridge and Maidstone.

Werner, J. 1984. *Der Grabfund von Malaja Pereščepina und Kuvrat, Kagan der Bulgaren*, Bayerische Akademie der Wissenschaften, Phil. Hist. Kl. Abhand., NF Heft 91, Munich.

White, R. H. 1988. *Roman and Celtic Objects from Anglo-Saxon Graves*, BAR British Series 191: Oxford.

Wiggins, R., Boylston, A. and Roberts, C. 1999. 'Human skeletal remains,' in Drinkall and Foreman 1999, 221–36.

Williams, G., 2006. 'The Circulation And Function Of Coinage In Conversion-Period England, *c.* AD 580–680', in B. Cook and G. Williams (eds), *Coinage and History in the North Sea World, c. AD 500–1250*, 145–92, Leiden.

Williams, G. forthcoming. 'Early Anglo-Saxon gold coinage', *British Numismatic Journal* **78**.

Willson, J. 1990. 'Rescue excavations on the Anglo-Saxon cemetery at Eastry, 1989', *Kent Archaeological Review*, 100, 229–31

Yorke, B. 1990. *Kings and Kingdoms of Early Anglo-Saxon England*, London.

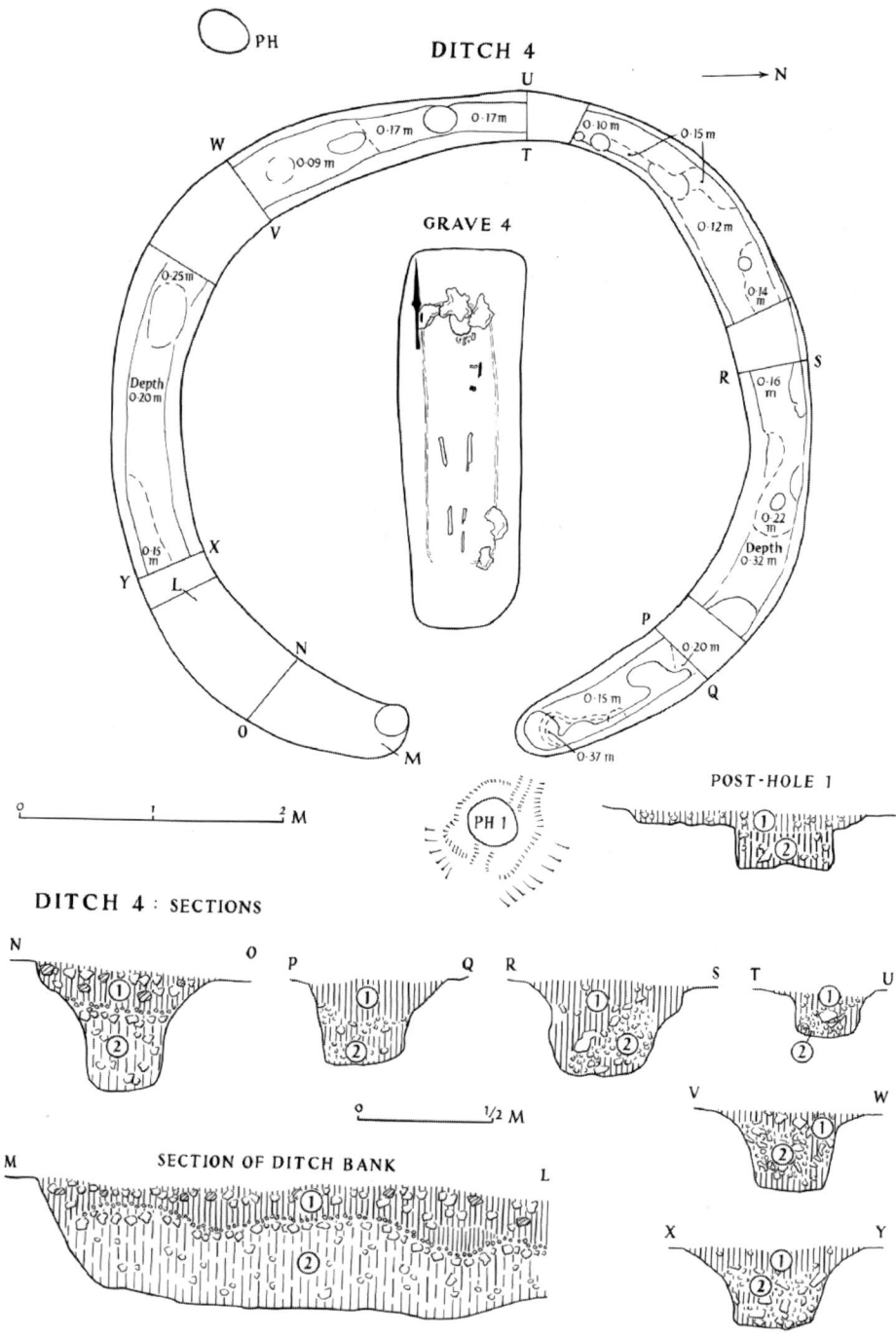

Figure 5. Plan and sections of the ring-ditch and the grave plan: 76:4 (M. Cox)

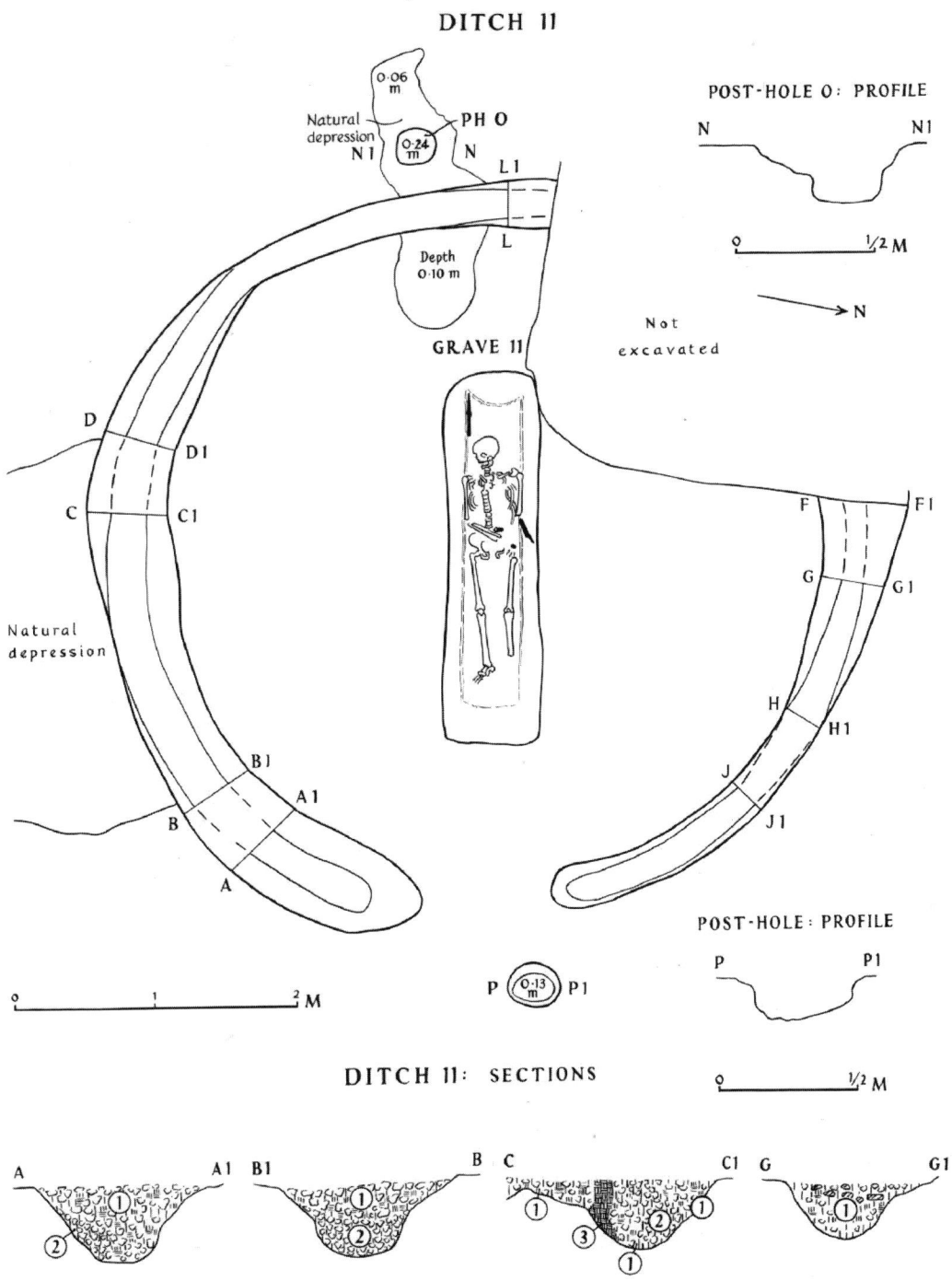

Figure 6. Plan and sections of the ring-ditch and the grave plan: 76:11 (M. Cox)

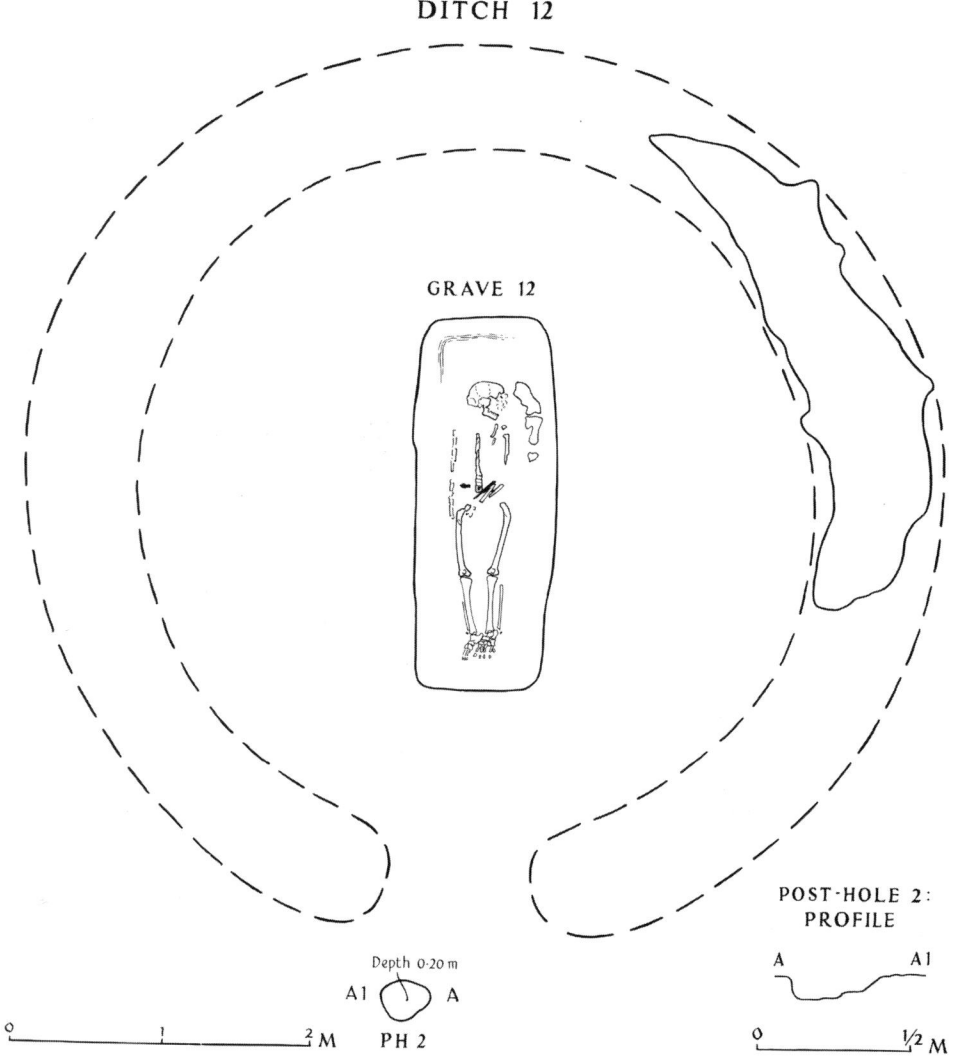

DITCH 12

GRAVE 12

POST-HOLE 2:
PROFILE

A   A1

0   ½ M

Depth 0·20 m
A1   A
PH 2

0   1   2 M

Figure 7. Plan and sections of the ring-ditch and the grave plan: 76:12 (M. Cox)

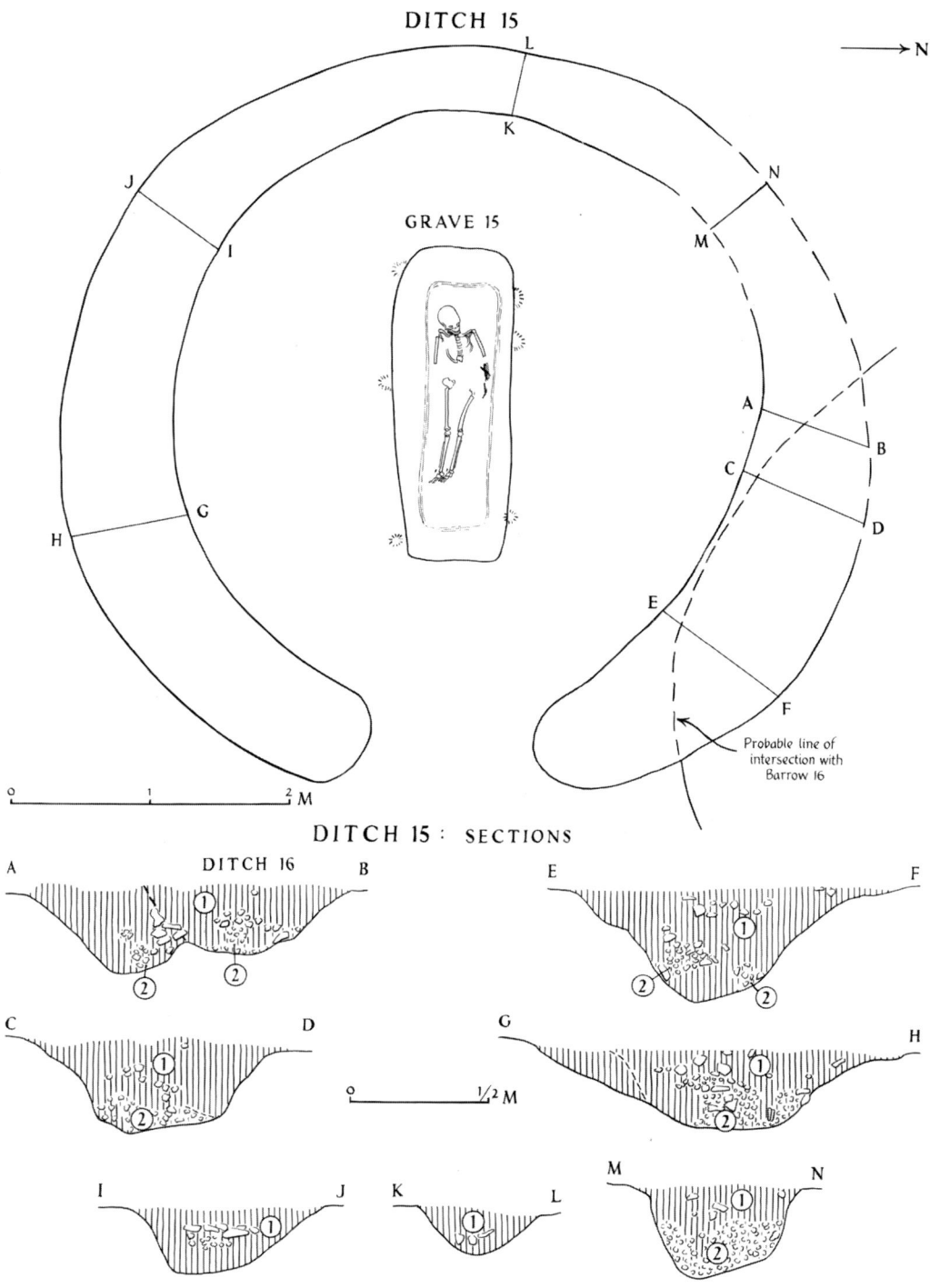

Figure 8. Plan and sections of the ring-ditch and the grave plan: 76:15 (M. Cox)

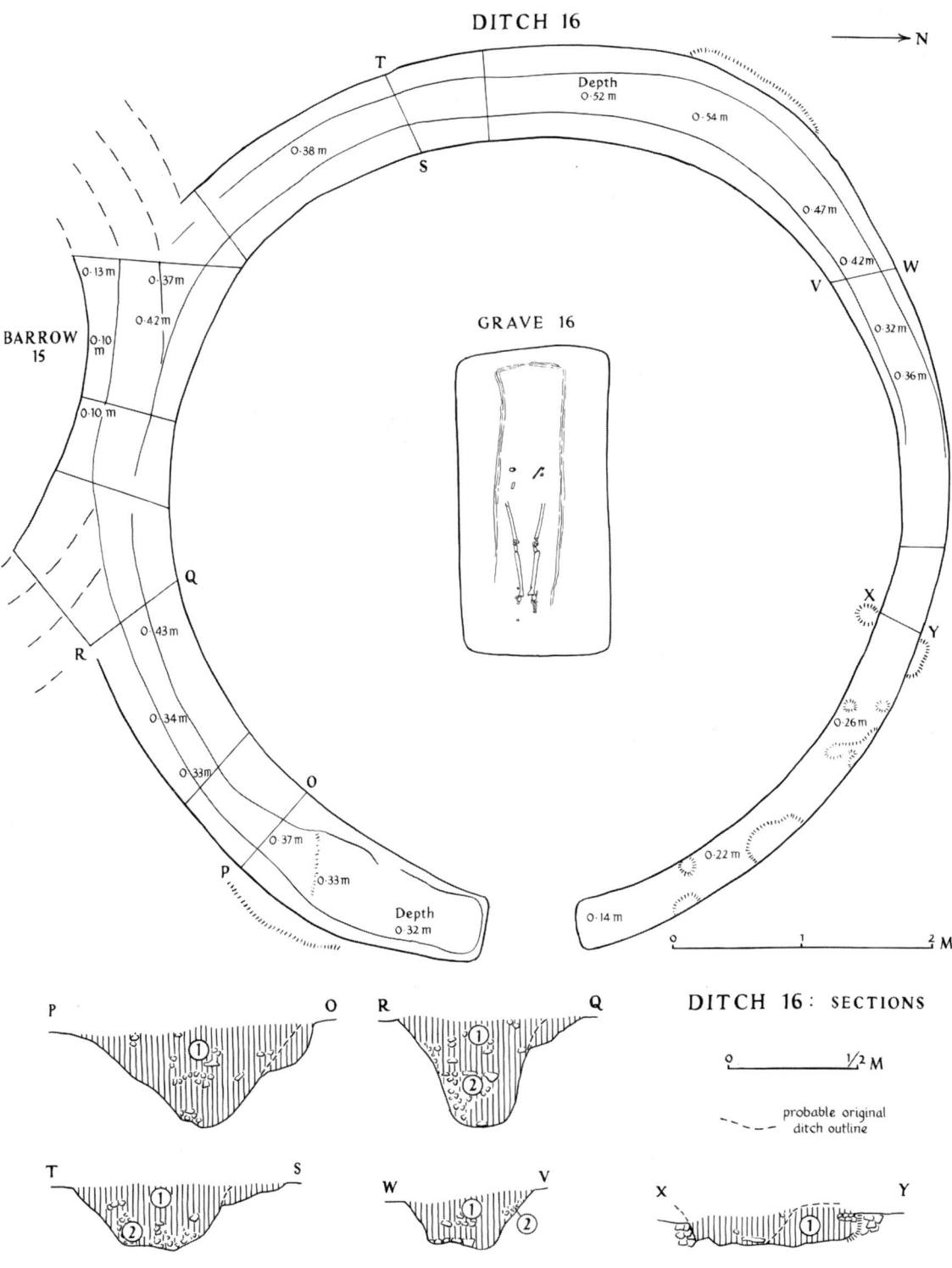

DITCH 16

BARROW 15

GRAVE 16

DITCH 16: SECTIONS

P   O   R   Q

T   S   W   V   X   Y

probable original
ditch outline

Figure 9. Plan and sections of the ring-ditch and the grave plan: 76:16 (M. Cox)

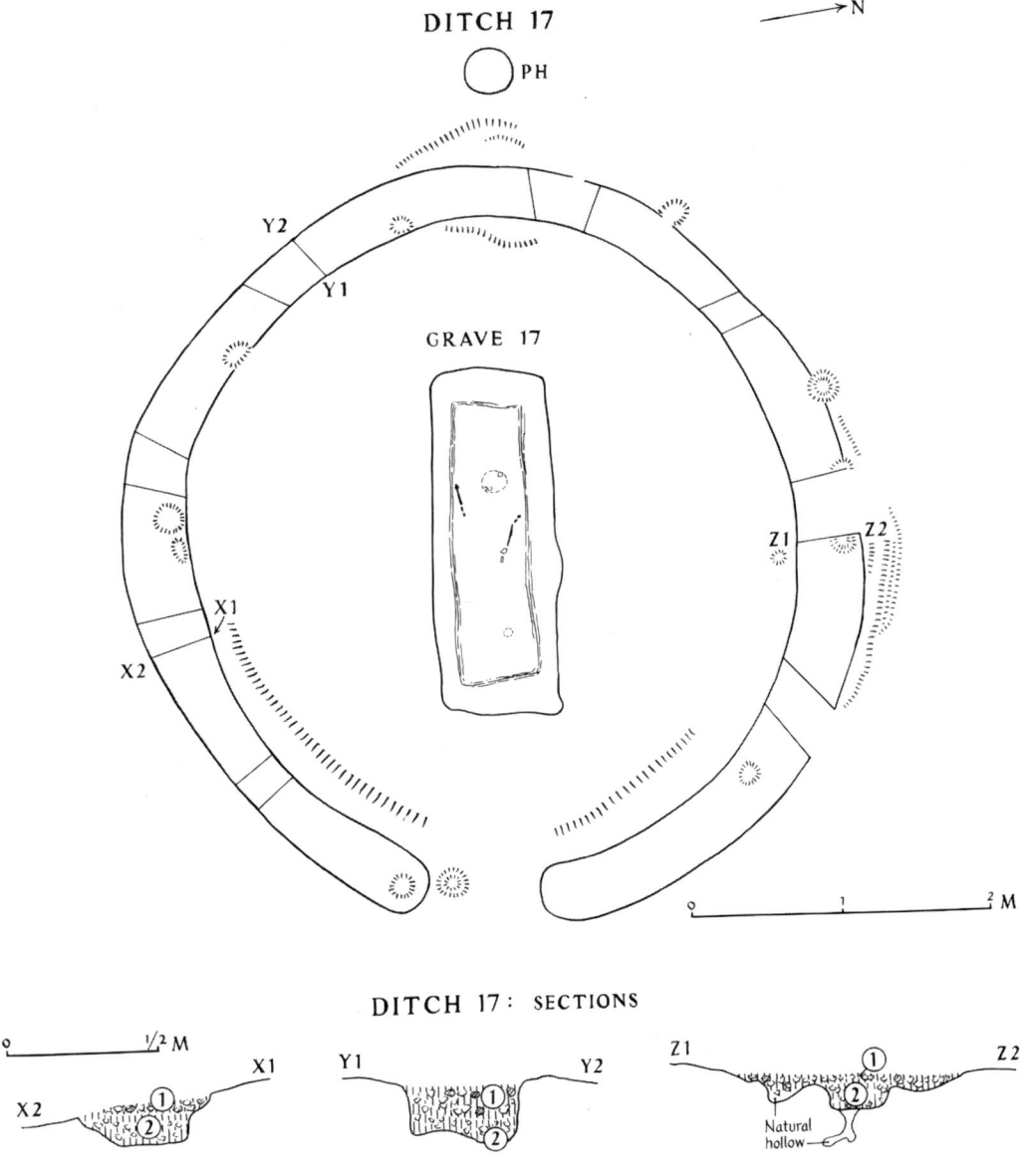

Figure 10. Plan and sections of the ring-ditch and the grave plan: 76:17 (M. Cox)

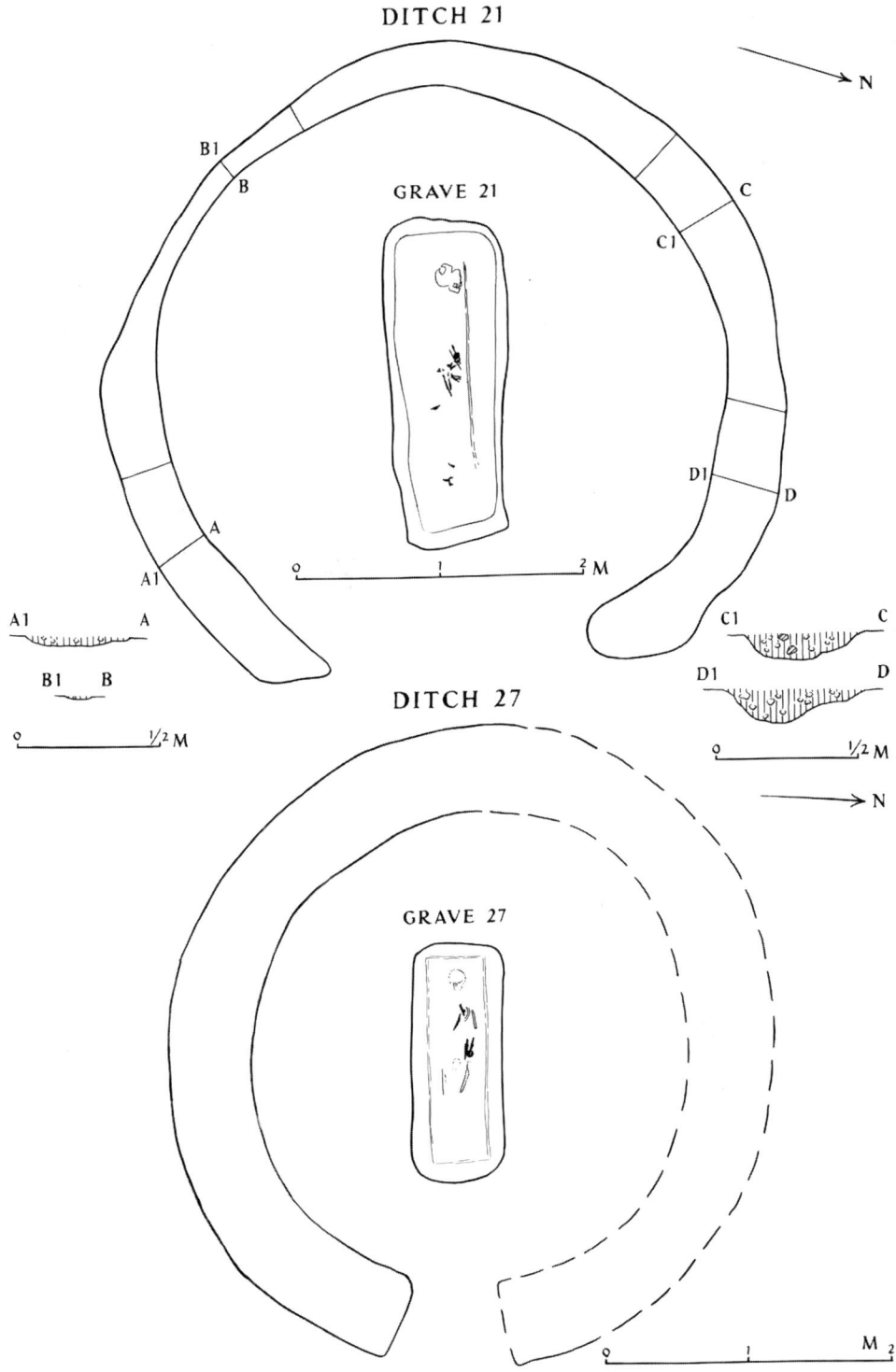

Figure 11. Plan and sections of the ring-ditches and the grave plans: 76:21 and 76:27 (M. Cox)

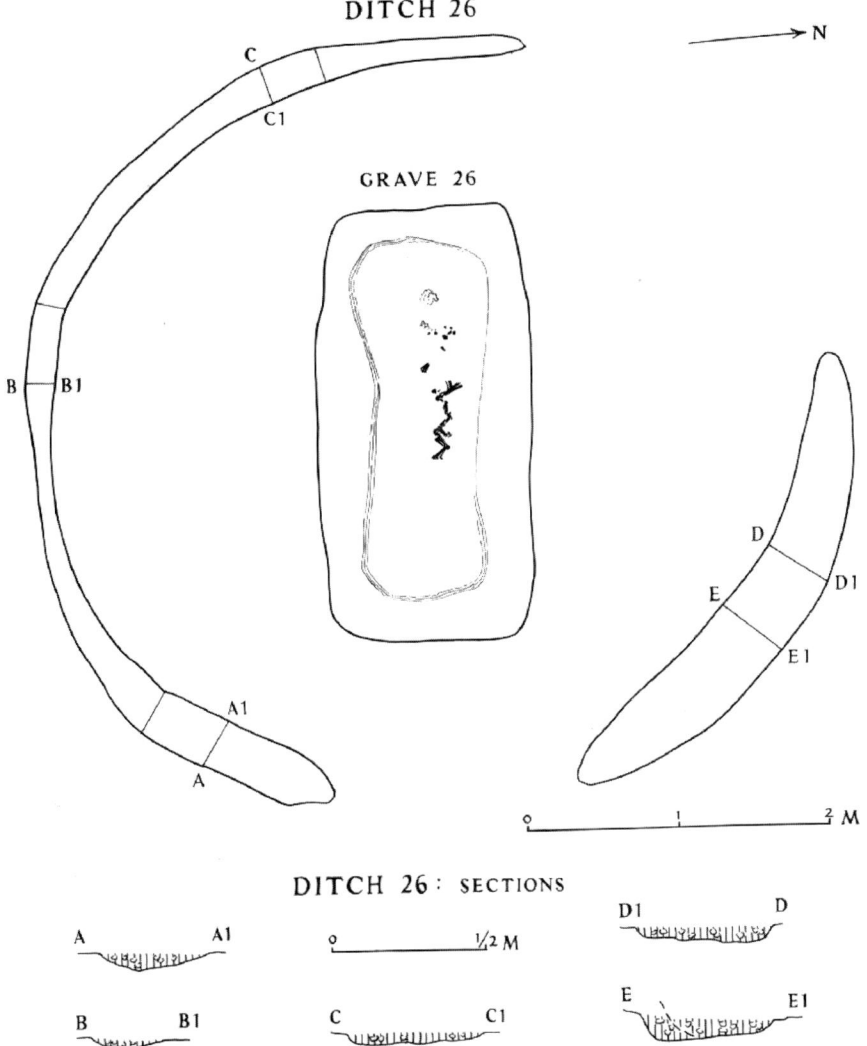

Figure 12. Plan and sections of the ring-ditch and the grave plan: 76:26 (M. Cox)

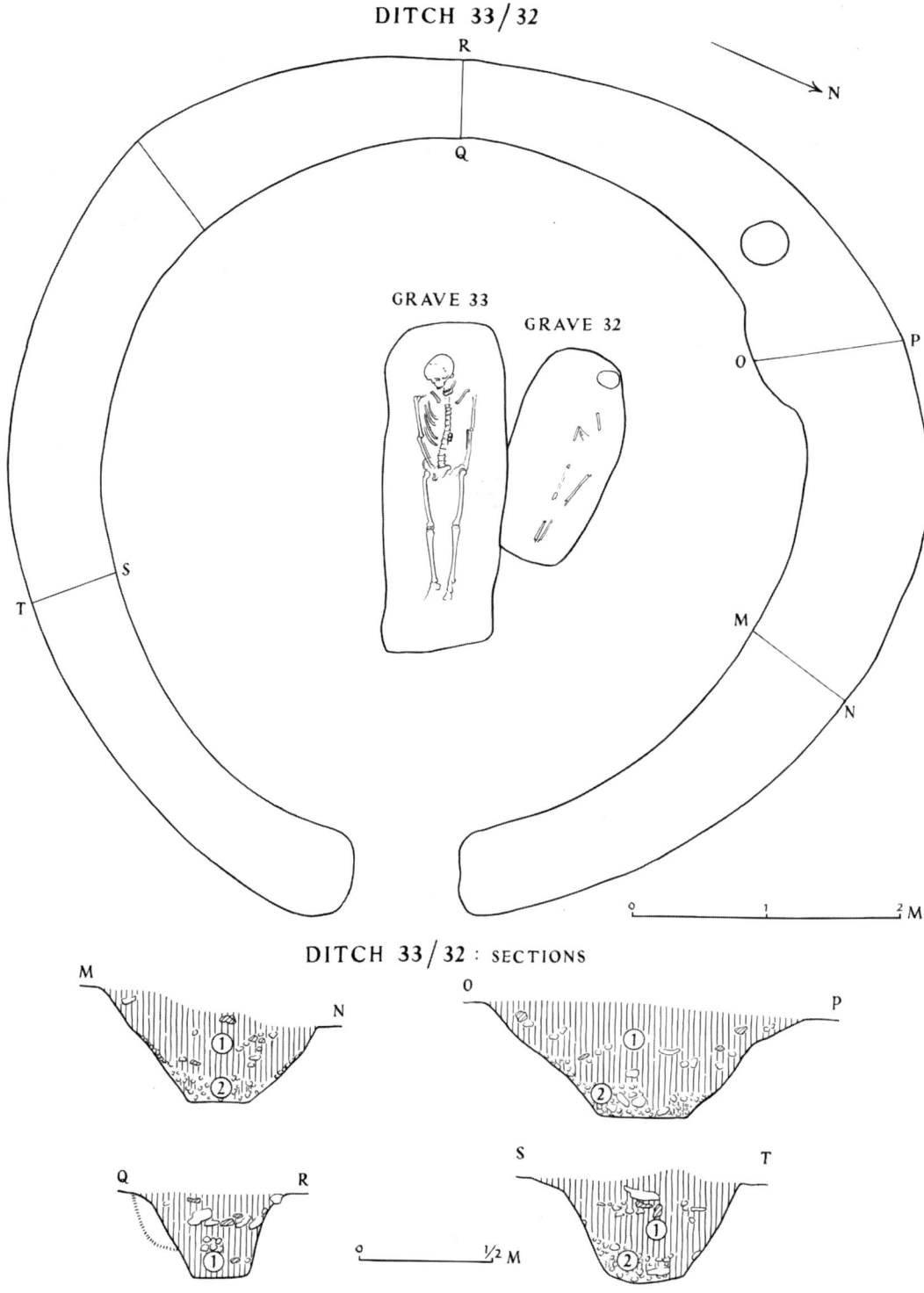

Figure 13. Plan and sections of the ring-ditch and the grave plans: 76:33 and 76:32 (M. Cox)

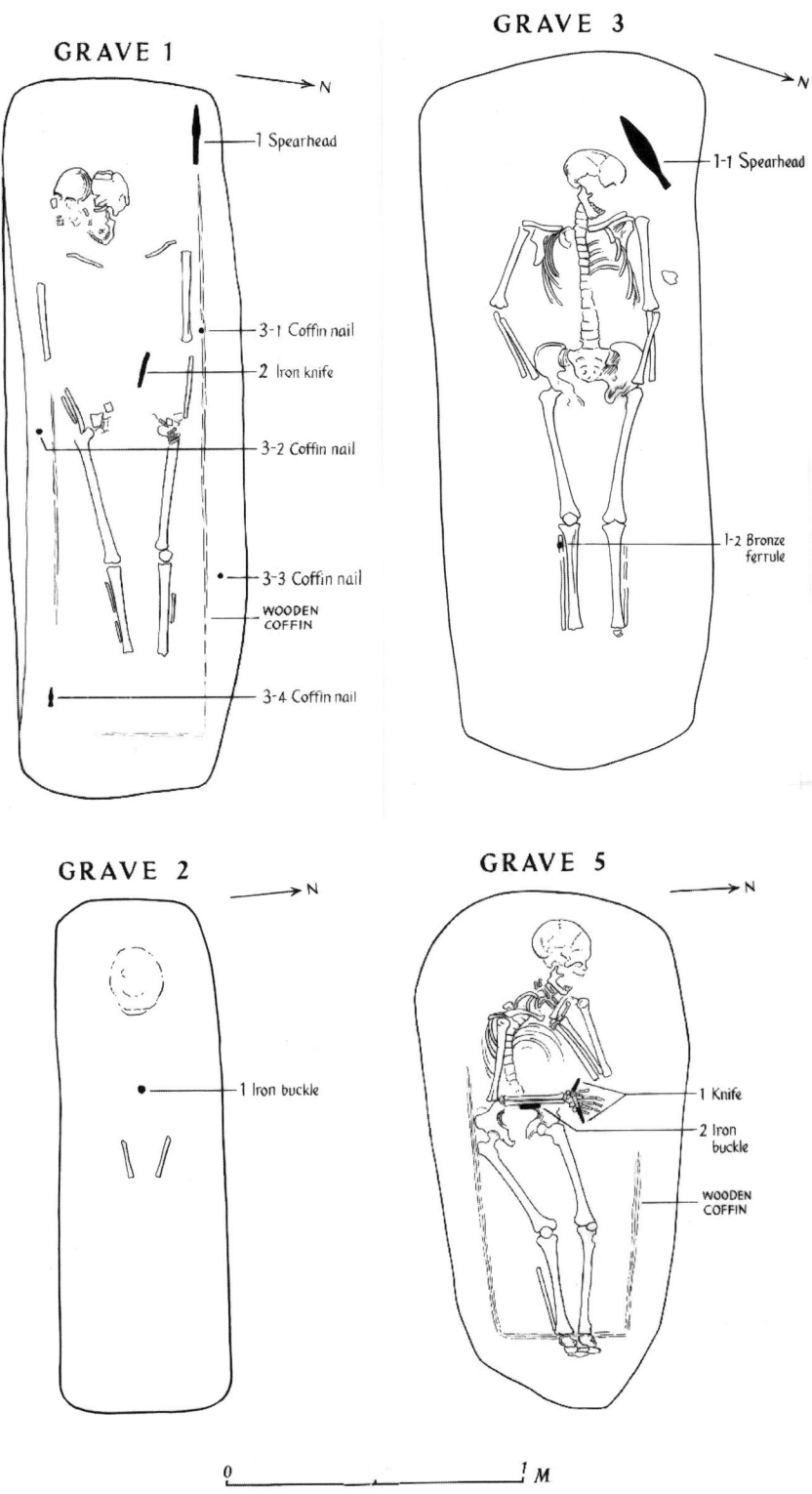

Figure 14. Grave plans: 76:1, 76:2, 76:3 and 76:5 (M. Cox)

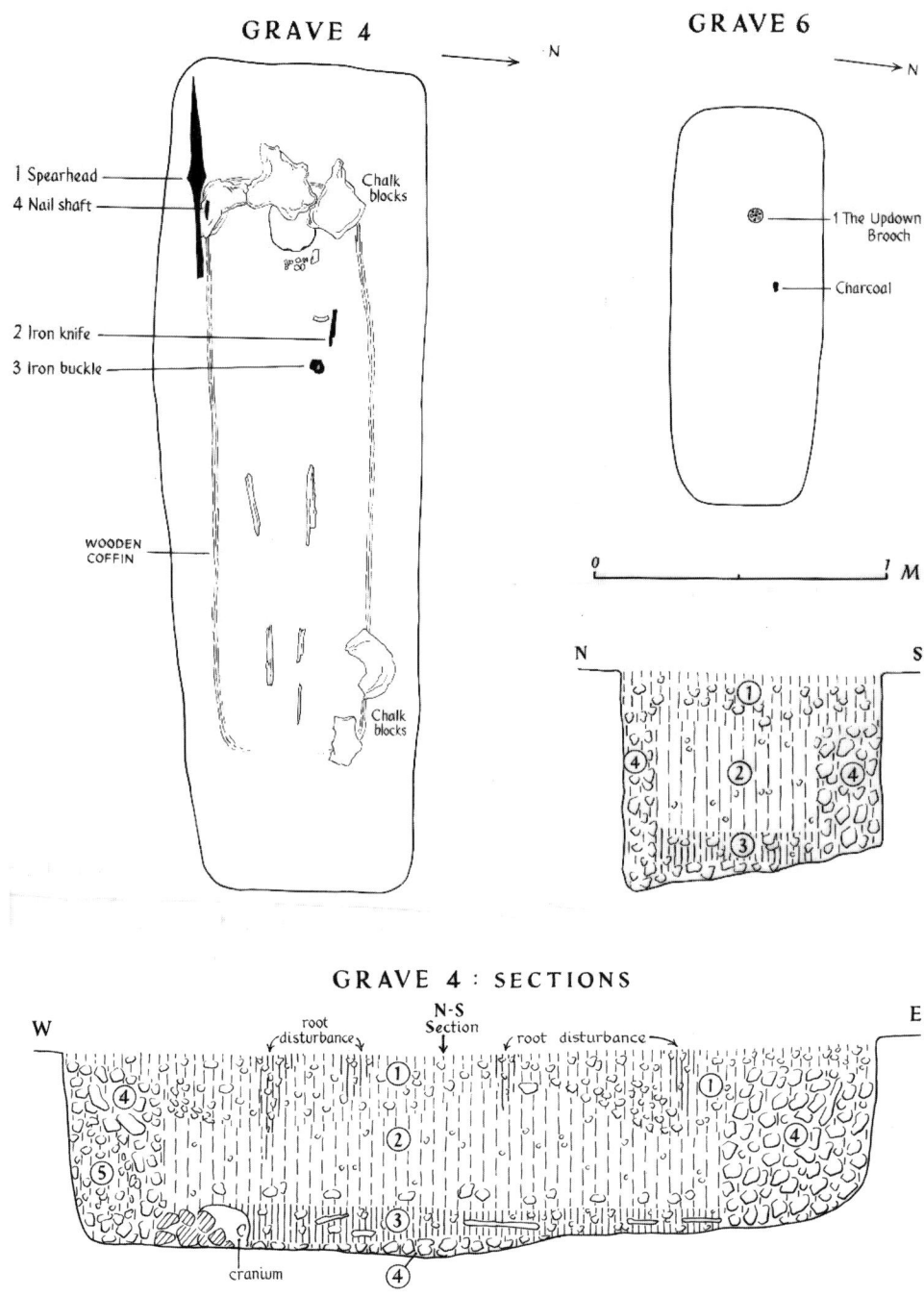

Figure 15. Grave plan and sections: 76:4 and grave plan: 76:6 (M. Cox)

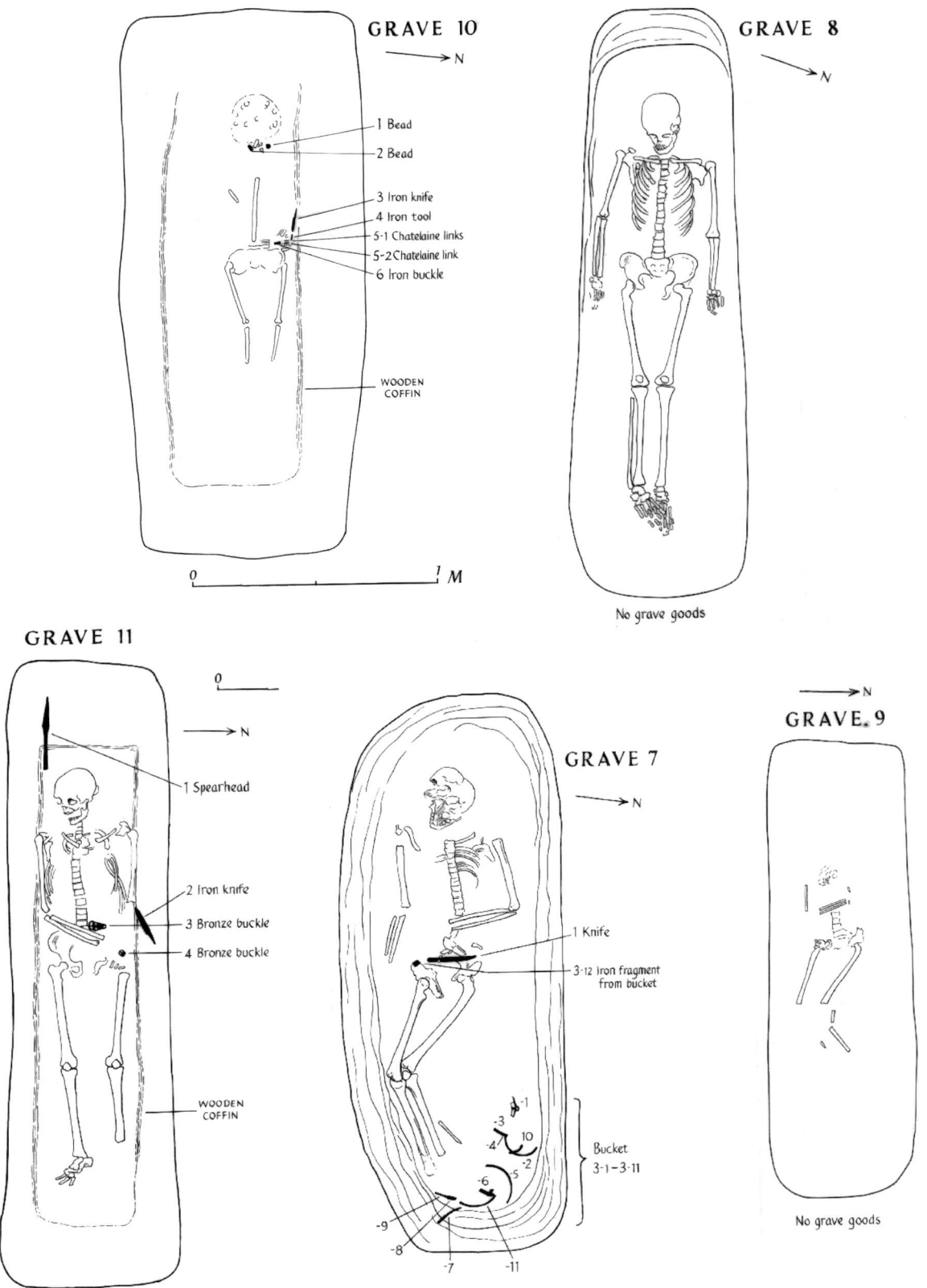

Figure 16. Grave plans: 76:7, 76:8, 76:9, 76:10 and 76:11 (M. Cox)

Martin Welch

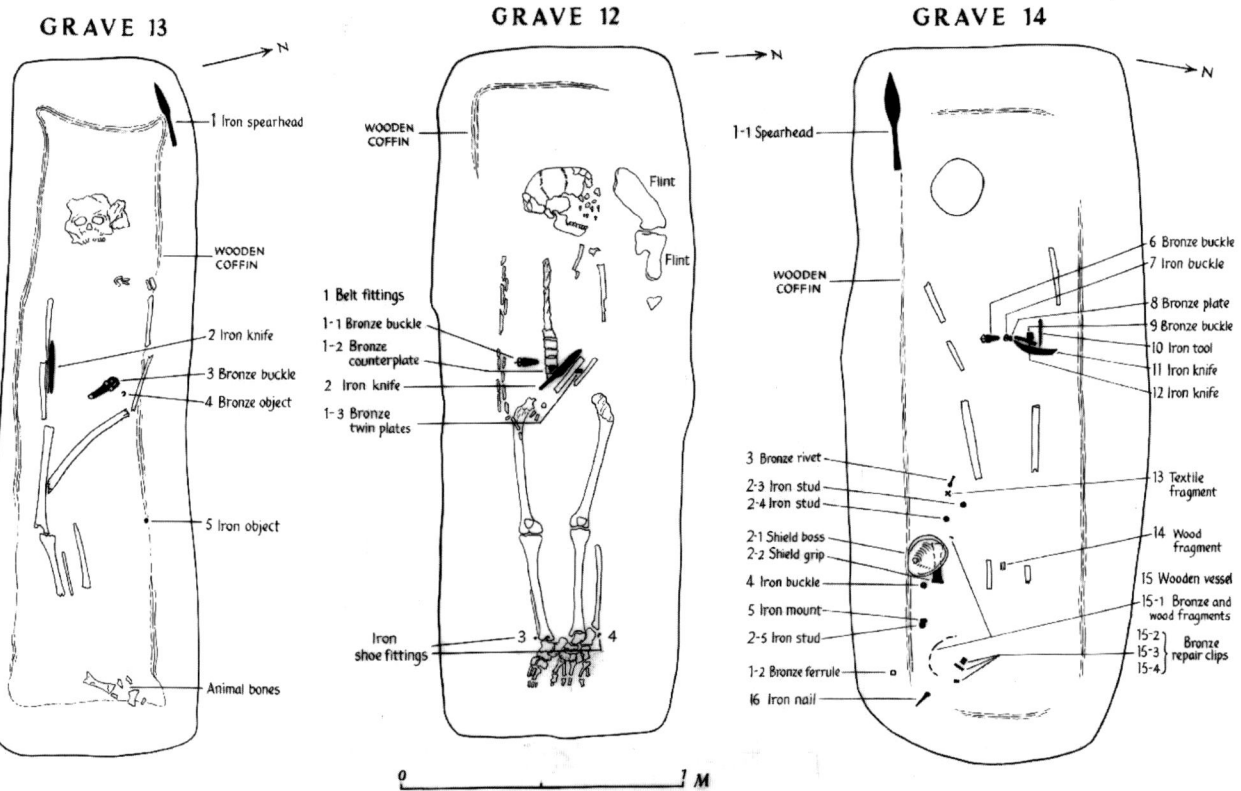

GRAVE 13

GRAVE 12

GRAVE 14

1 Iron spearhead

WOODEN COFFIN

2 Iron knife

3 Bronze buckle

4 Bronze object

5 Iron object

Animal bones

WOODEN COFFIN

Flint

Lozenge

Flint

1 Belt fittings

1·1 Bronze buckle

1·2 Bronze counterplate

2 Iron knife

1·3 Bronze twin plates

Iron shoe fittings

3   4

1·1 Spearhead

WOODEN COFFIN

6 Bronze buckle

7 Iron buckle

8 Bronze plate

9 Bronze buckle

10 Iron tool

11 Iron knife

12 Iron knife

3 Bronze rivet

2·3 Iron stud

2·4 Iron stud

2·1 Shield boss

2·2 Shield grip

4 Iron buckle

5 Iron mount

2·5 Iron stud

1·2 Bronze ferrule

16 Iron nail

13 Textile fragment

14 Wood fragment

15 Wooden vessel

15·1 Bronze and wood fragments

15·2
15·3 Bronze repair clips
15·4

0   1 M

Figure 17. Grave plans: 76:12, 76:13 and 76:14 (M. Cox)

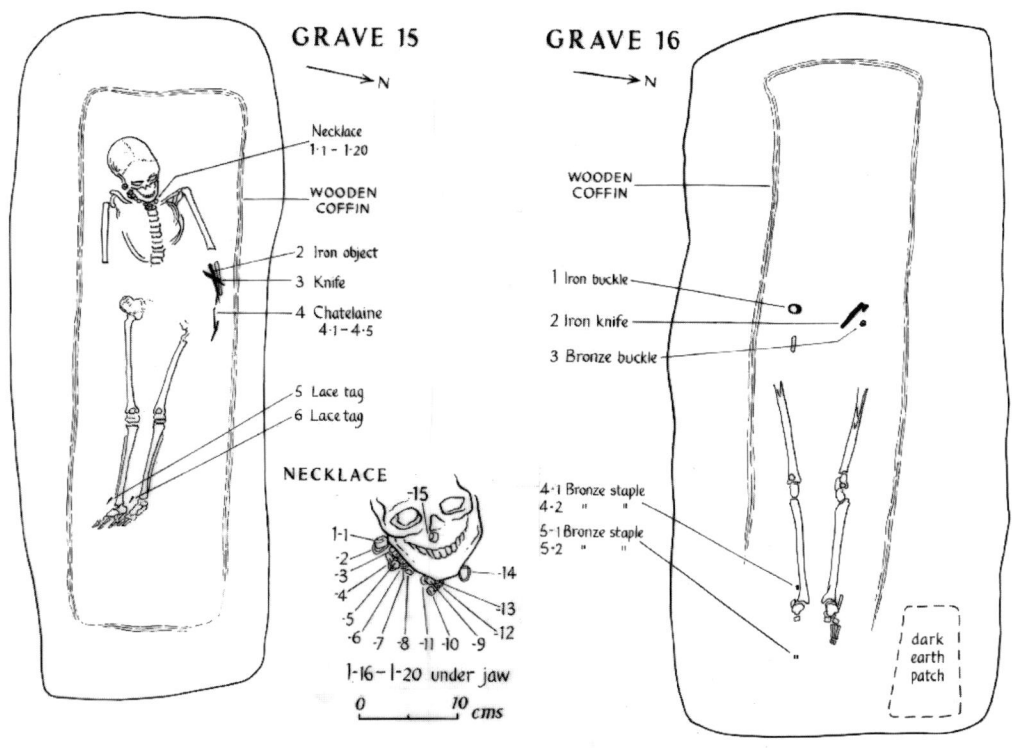

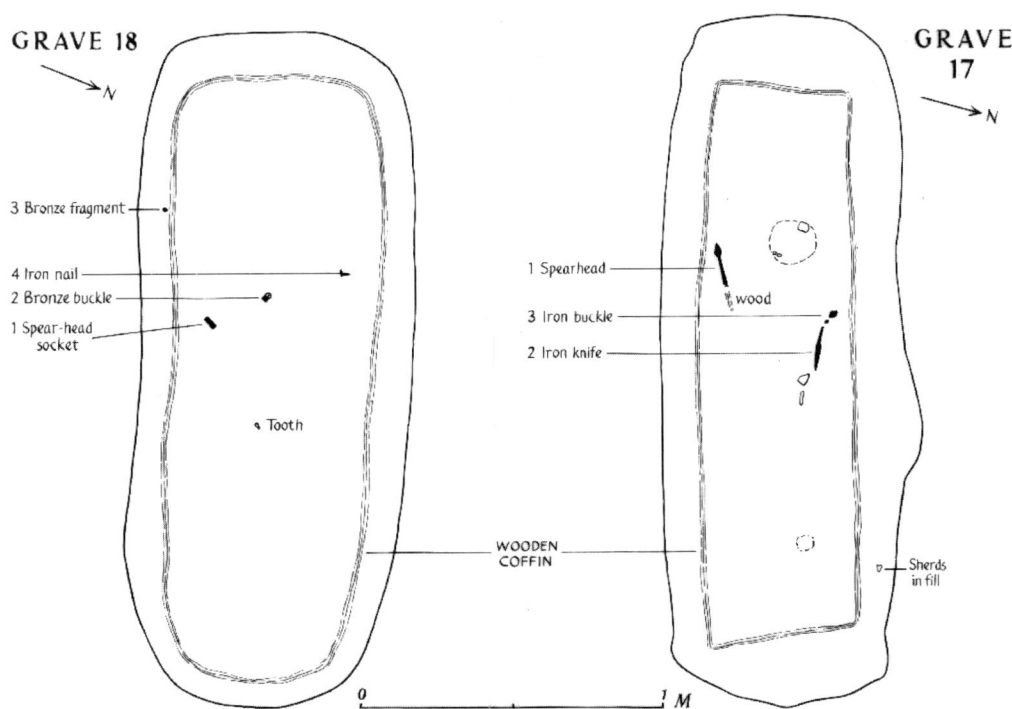

Figure 18. Grave plans: 76:15, 76:16, 76:17 and 76:18 (M. Cox)

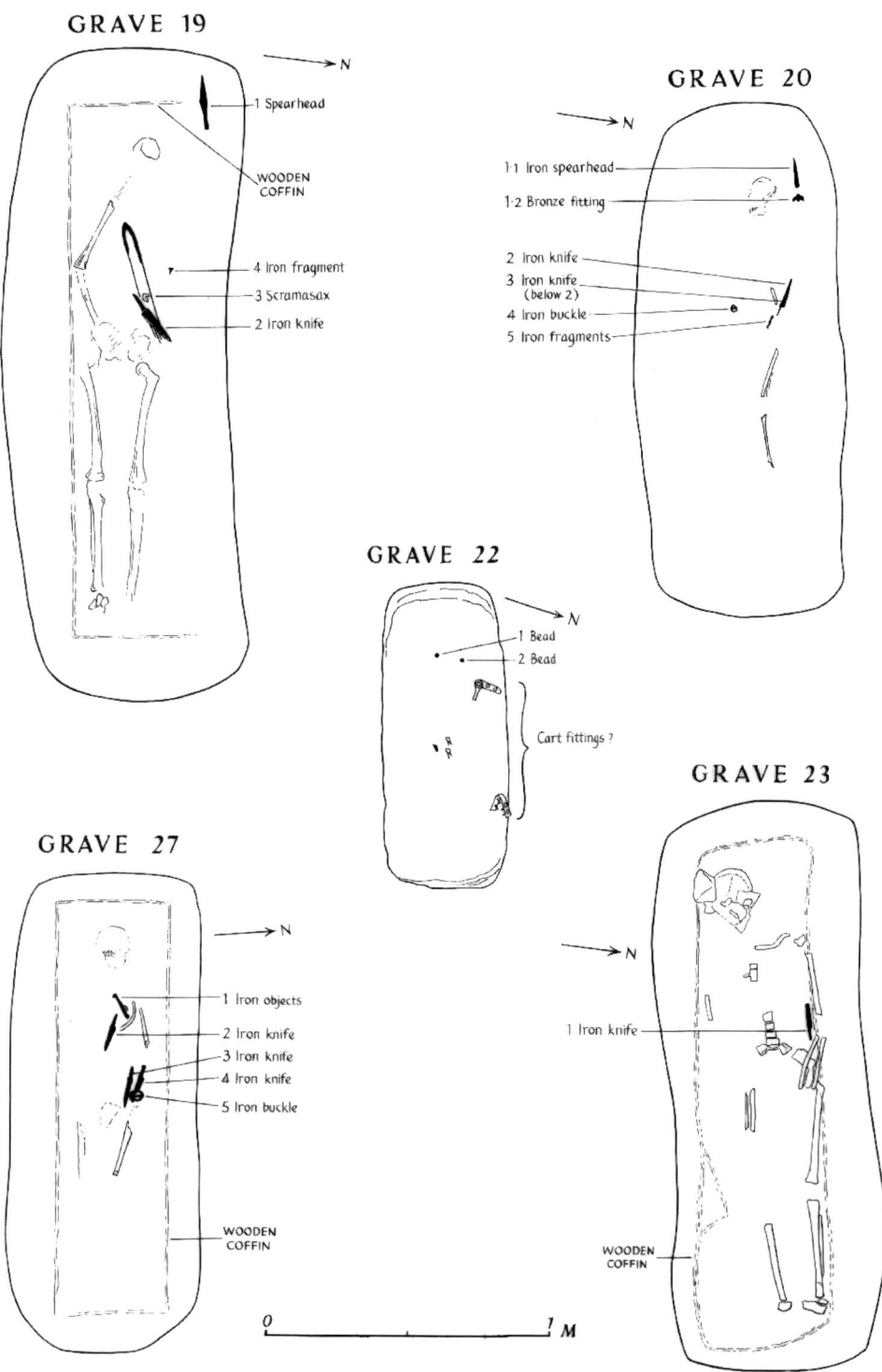

Figure 19. Grave plans: 76:19, 76:20, 76:22, 76:23 and 76:27 (M. Cox)

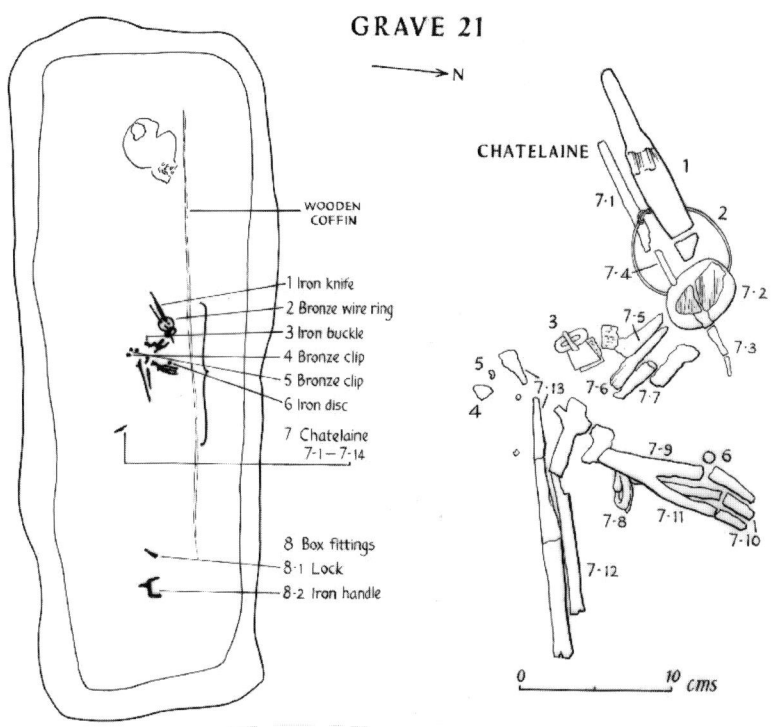

GRAVE 21

WOODEN COFFIN

1 Iron knife
2 Bronze wire ring
3 Iron buckle
4 Bronze clip
5 Bronze clip
6 Iron disc
7 Chatelaine 7·1 – 7·14

8 Box fittings
8·1 Lock
8·2 Iron handle

CHATELAINE

0   10 cms

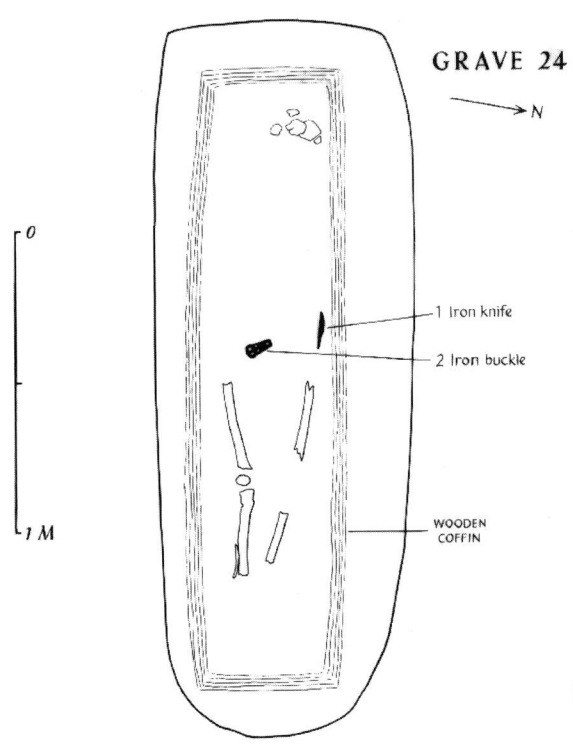

GRAVE 24

1 Iron knife
2 Iron buckle

WOODEN COFFIN

Figure 20. Grave plans: 76:21 and 76:24 (M. Cox)

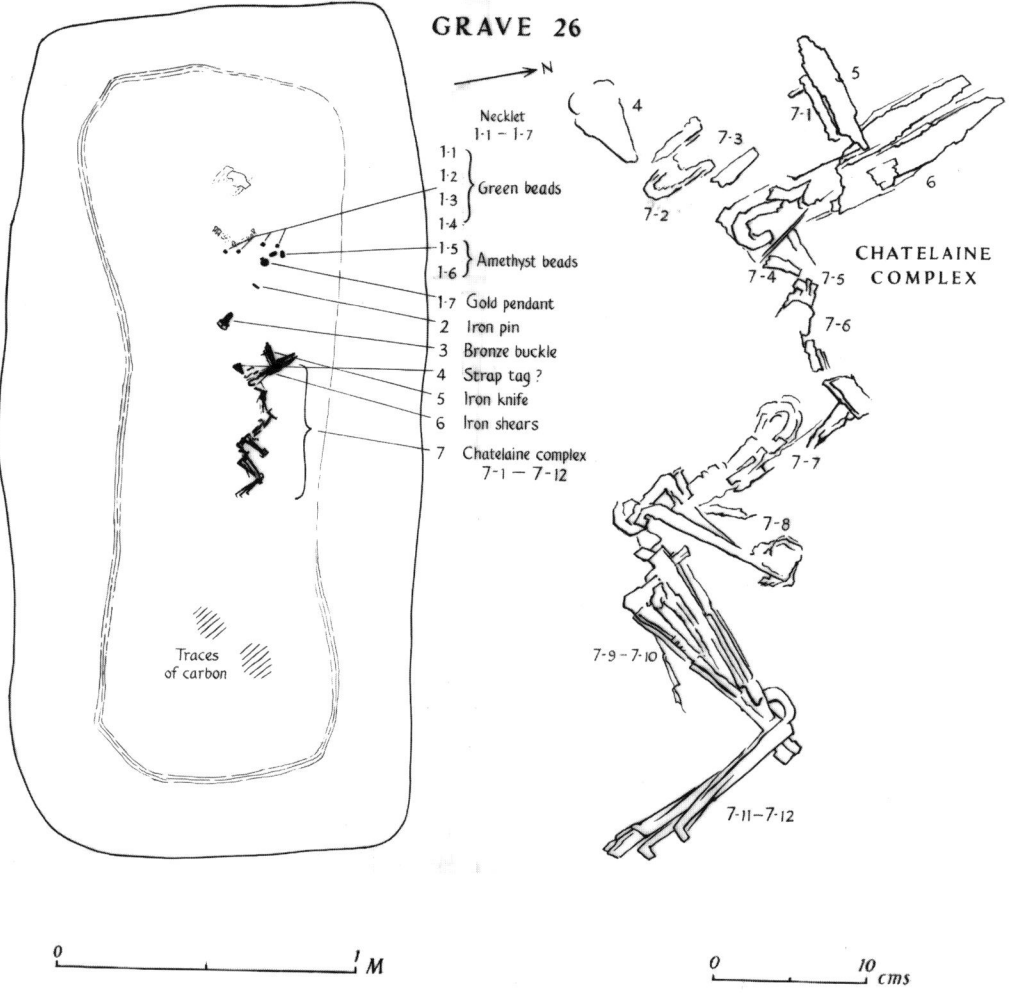

Figure 21. Grave plan: 76:26 (M. Cox)

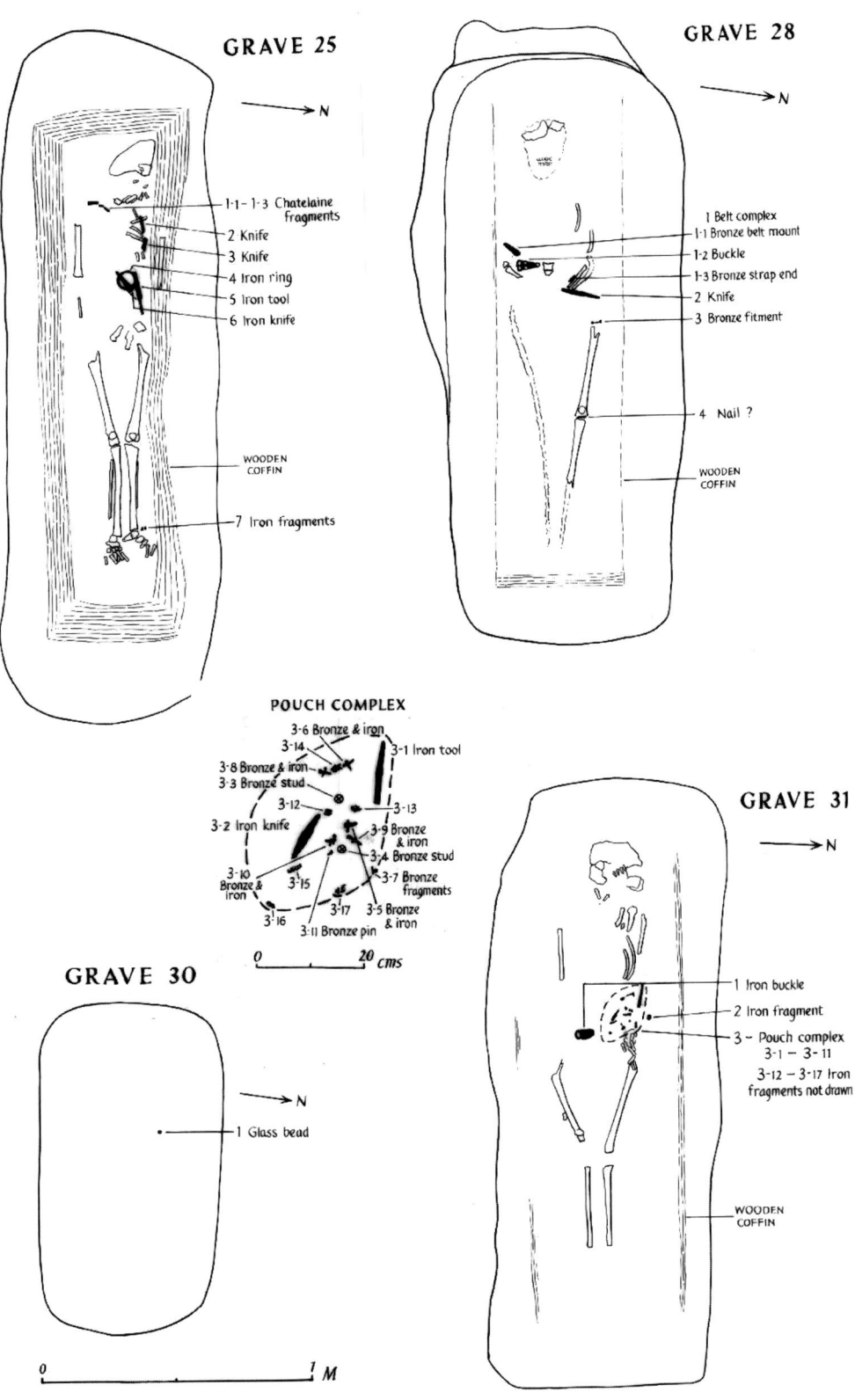

Figure 22. Grave plans: 76:25, 76:28, 76:30 and 76:31 (M. Cox)

Martin Welch

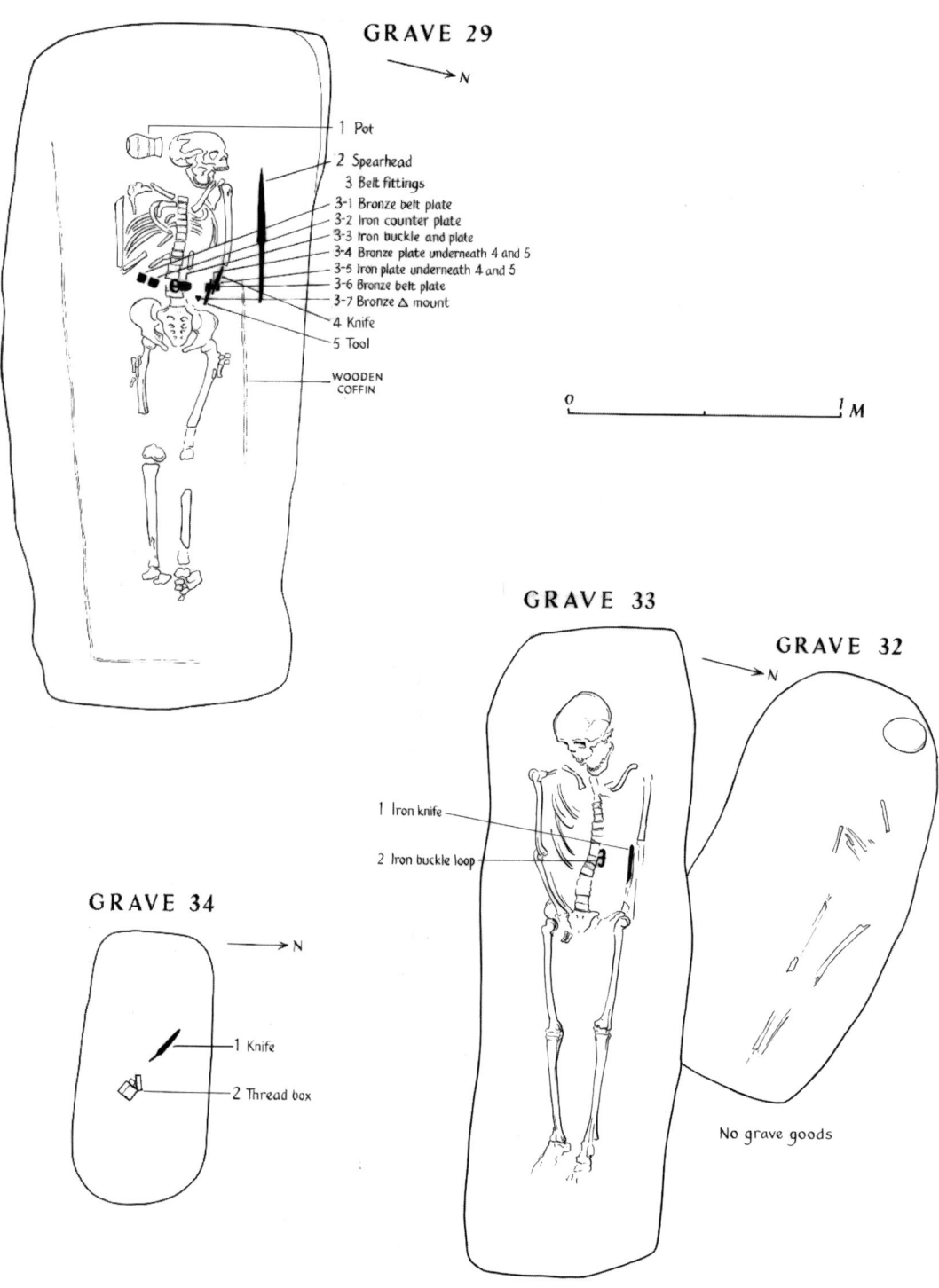

Figure 23. Grave plans: 76:29, 76:32, 76:33 and 76:34 (M. Cox)

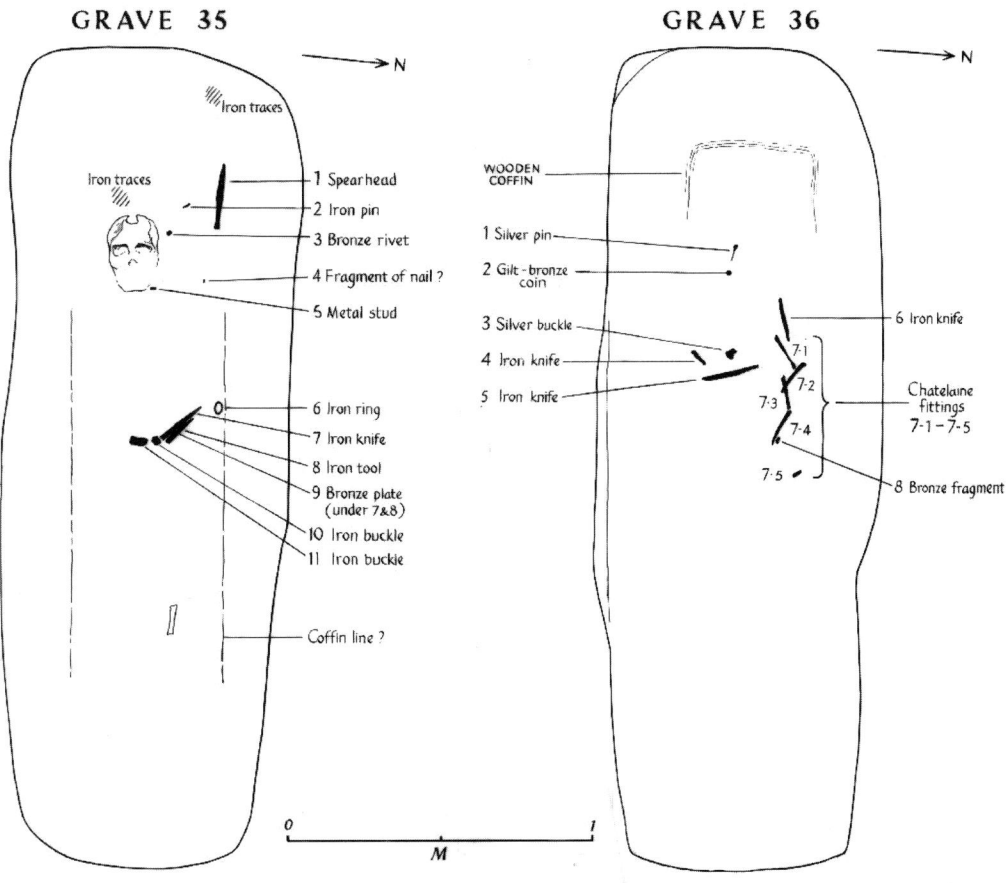

Figure 24. Grave plans: 76:35 and 76:36 (M. Cox)

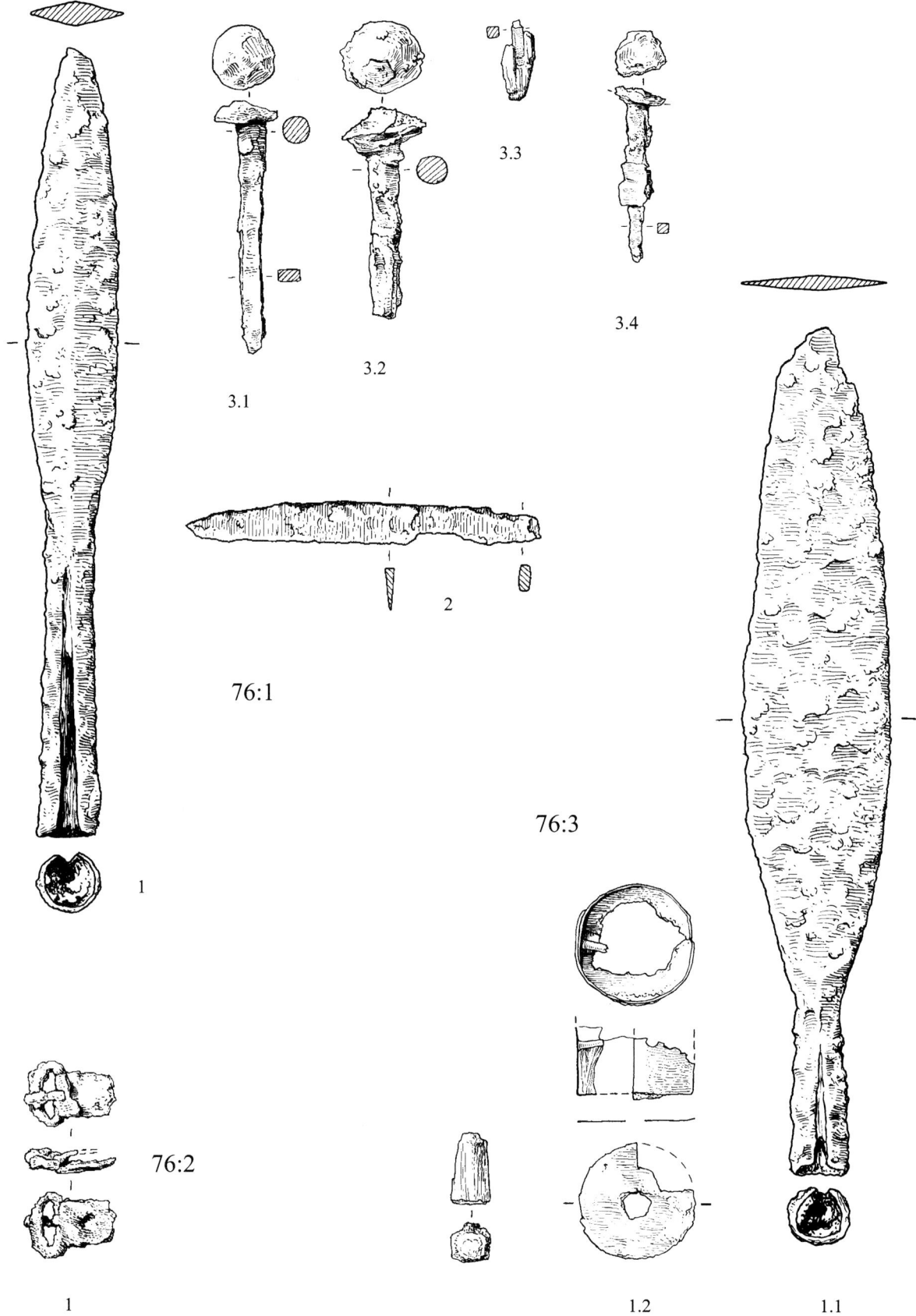

Figure 25. Grave finds: 76:1, 76:2 and 76:3 (M. Cox)

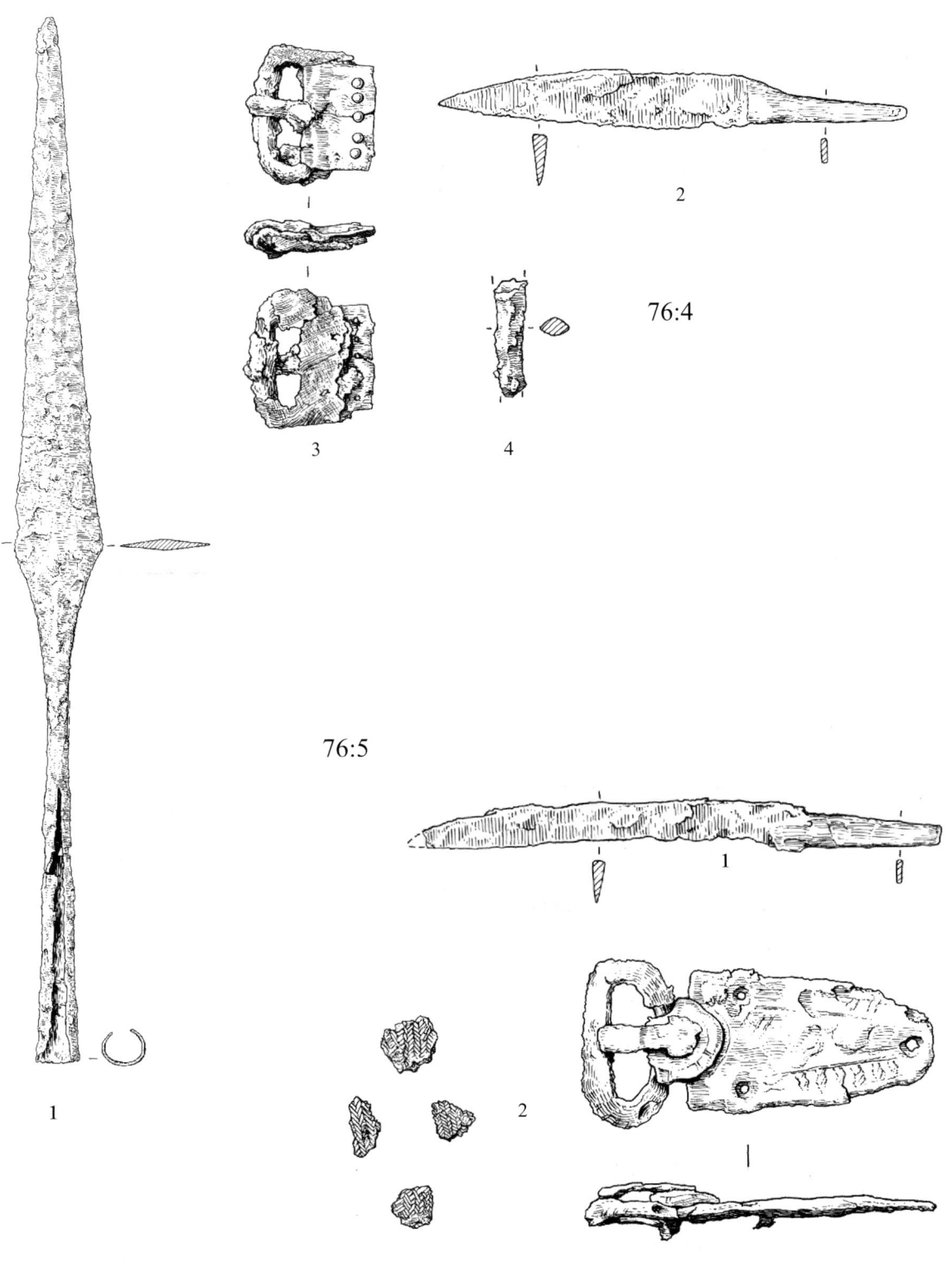

Figure 26. Grave finds: 76:4 and 76:5 (M. Cox)

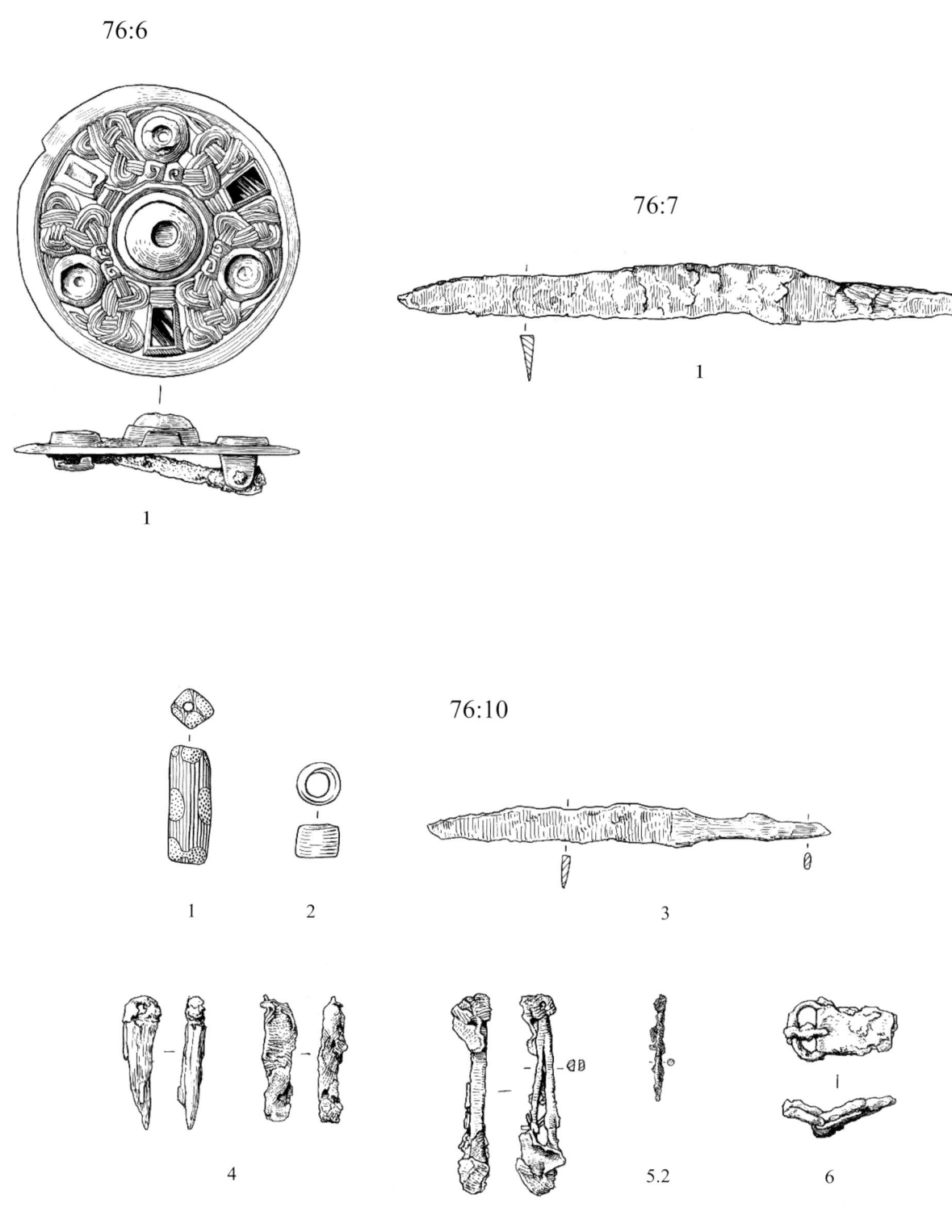

Figure 27. Grave finds: 76:6, 76:7 [no. 1] and 76:10 (M. Cox)

76:7

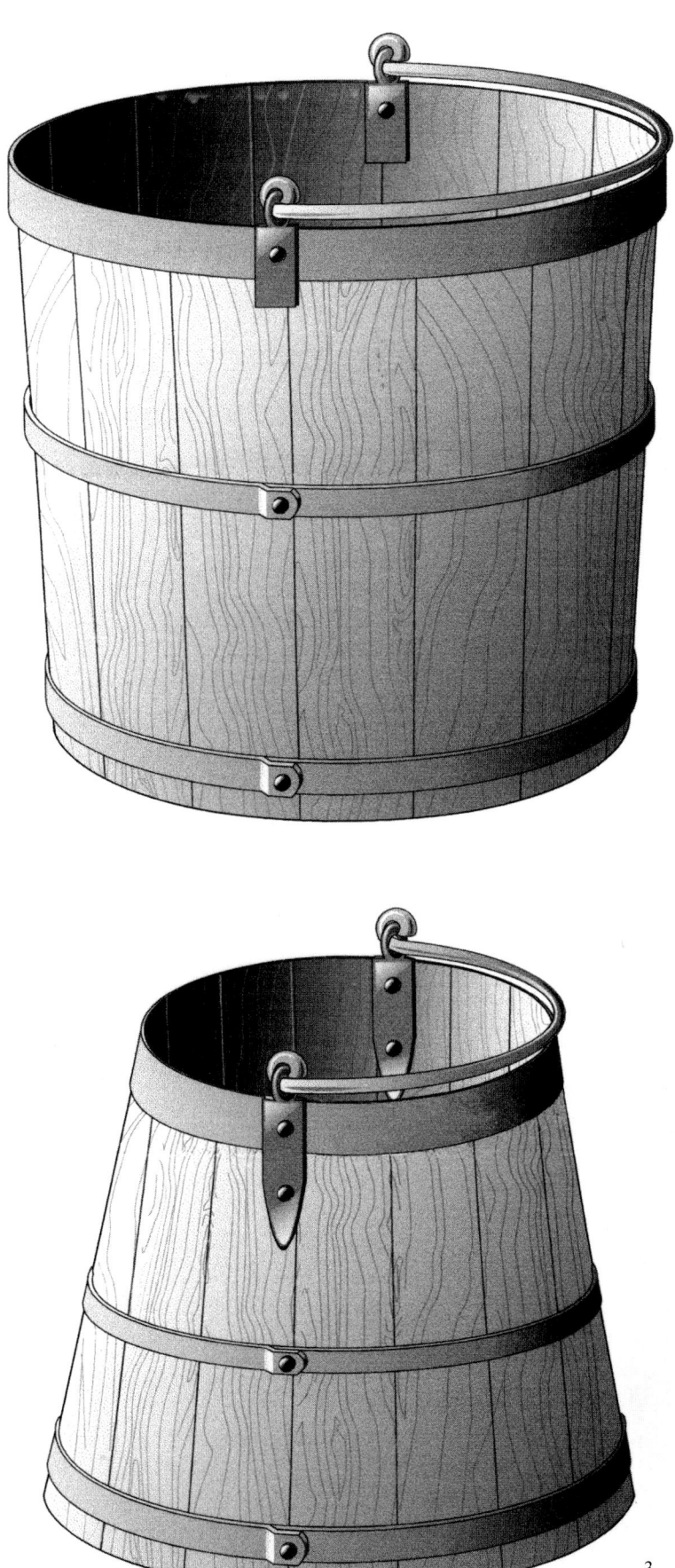

3

Figure 28. Reconstruction of two buckets from 76:7 [no. 3] (K. Singh)

Martin Welch

76:7

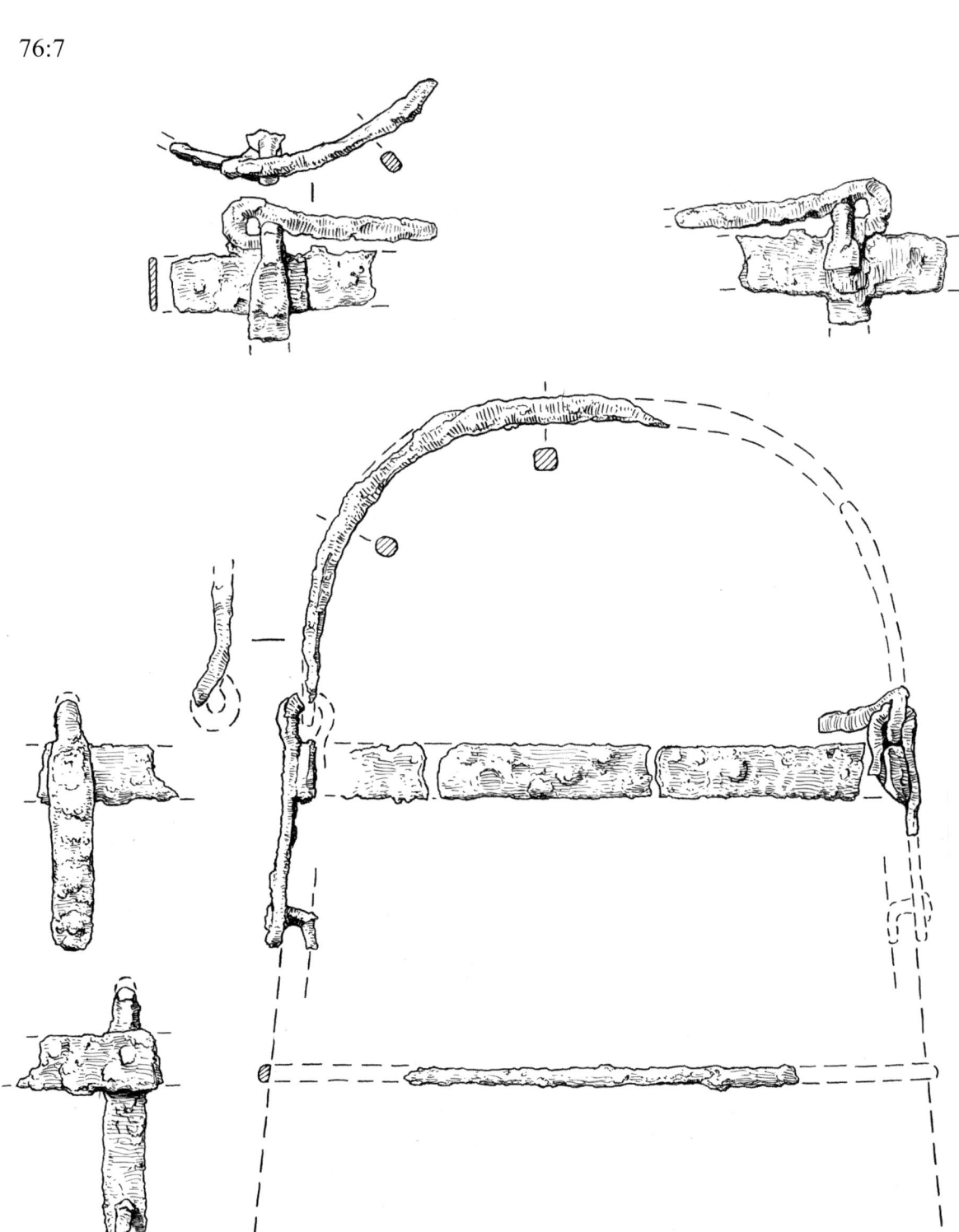

3

Figure 29. The fittings from one reconstituted bucket from 76:7 [no. 3] (M. Cox)

76:7

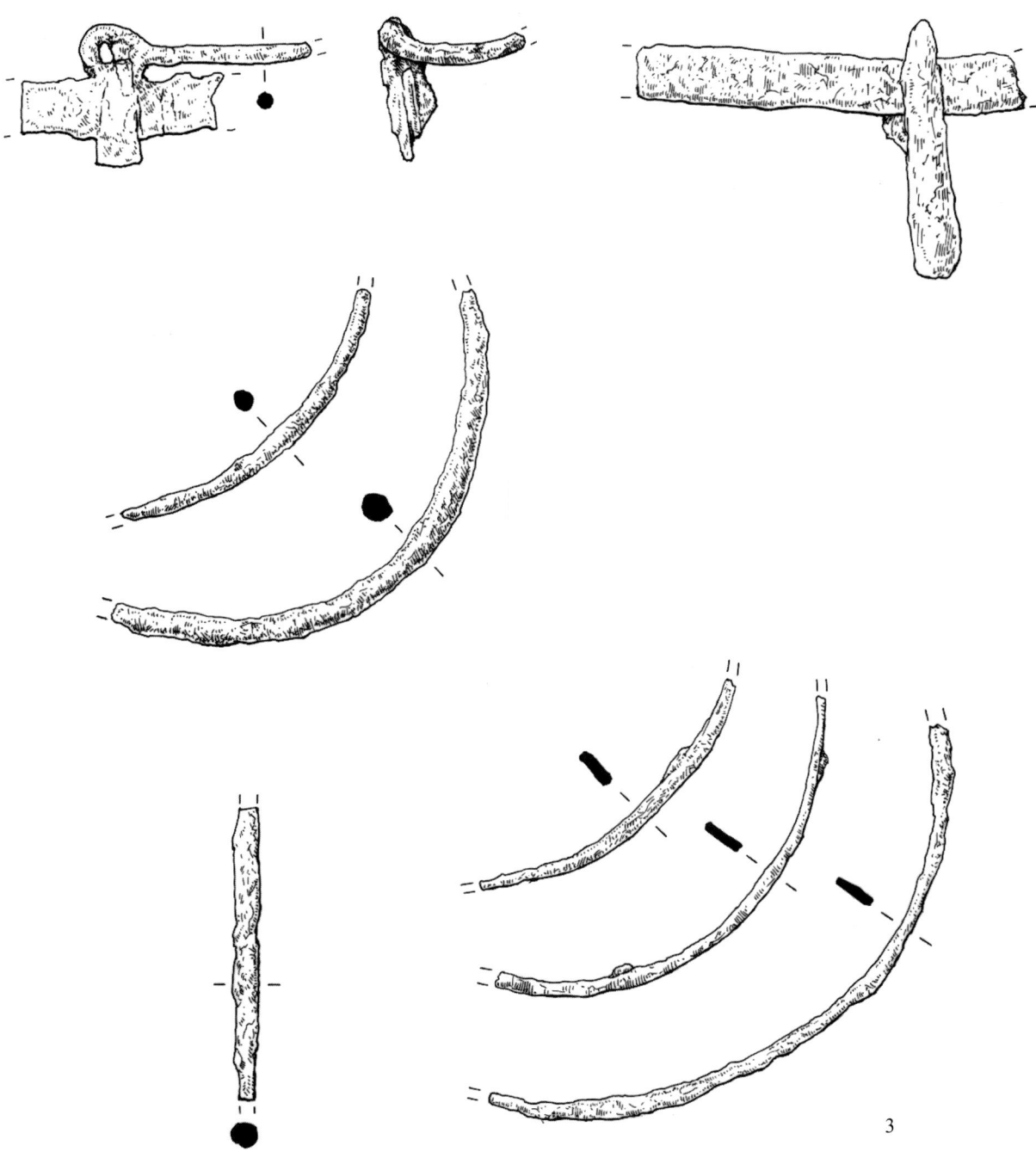

Figure 30. Bucket fittings from 76:7 [no. 3] (K. Singh)

Martin Welch

76:11

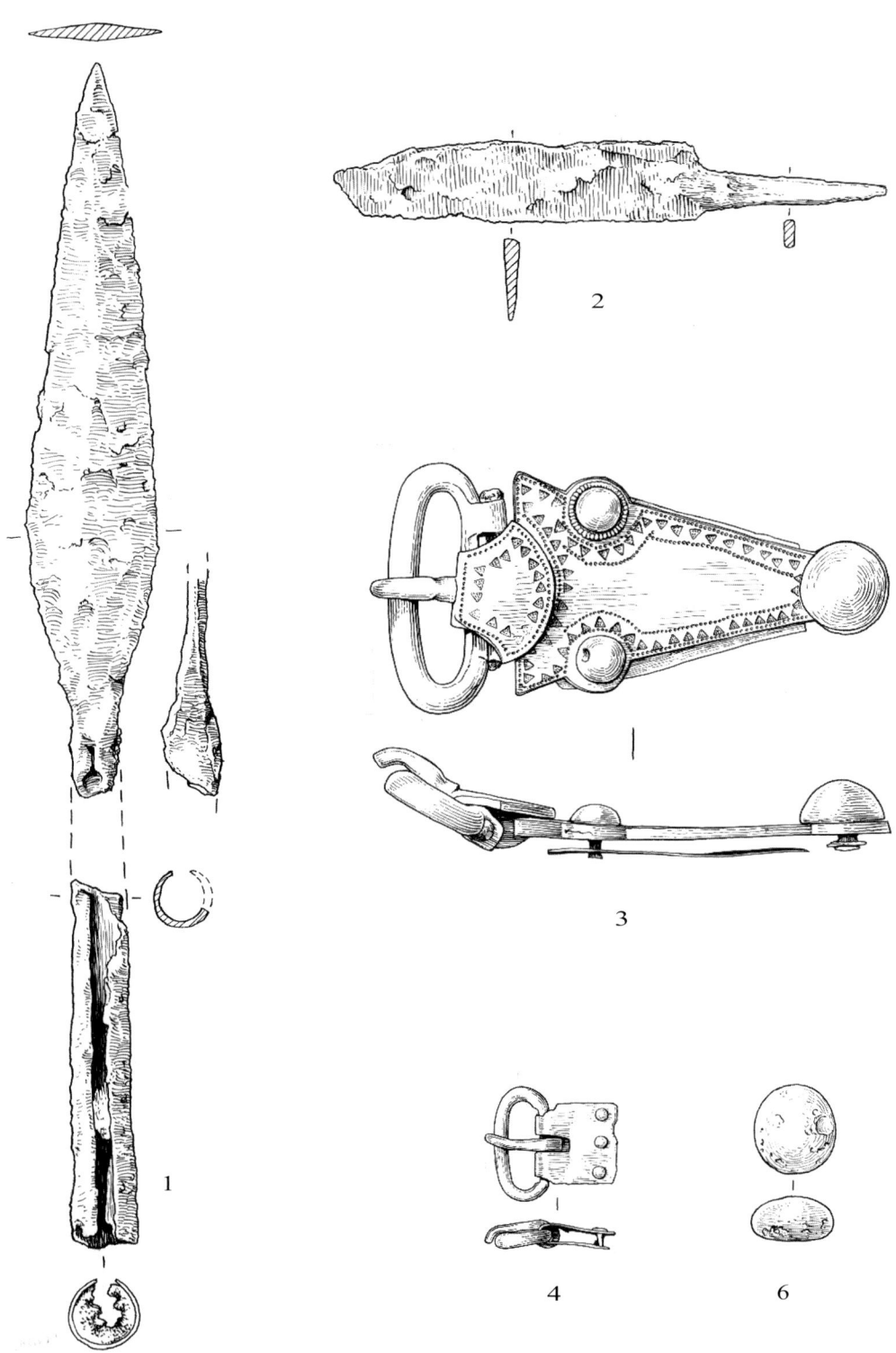

Figure 31. Grave finds: 76:11 (M. Cox)

76:12

76:13

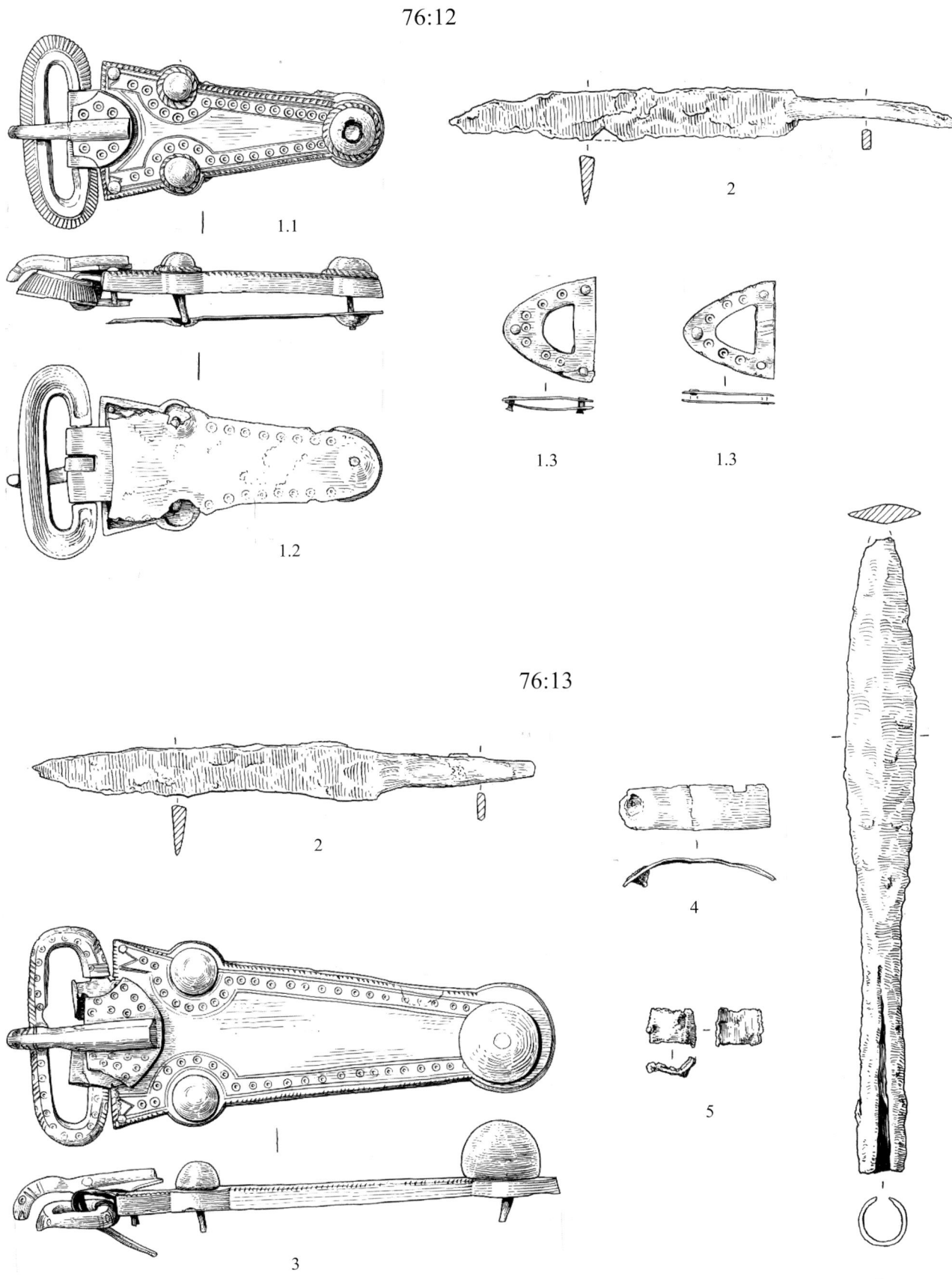

Figure 32. Grave finds: 76:12 and 76:13 (M. Cox)

98

Martin Welch

76:14

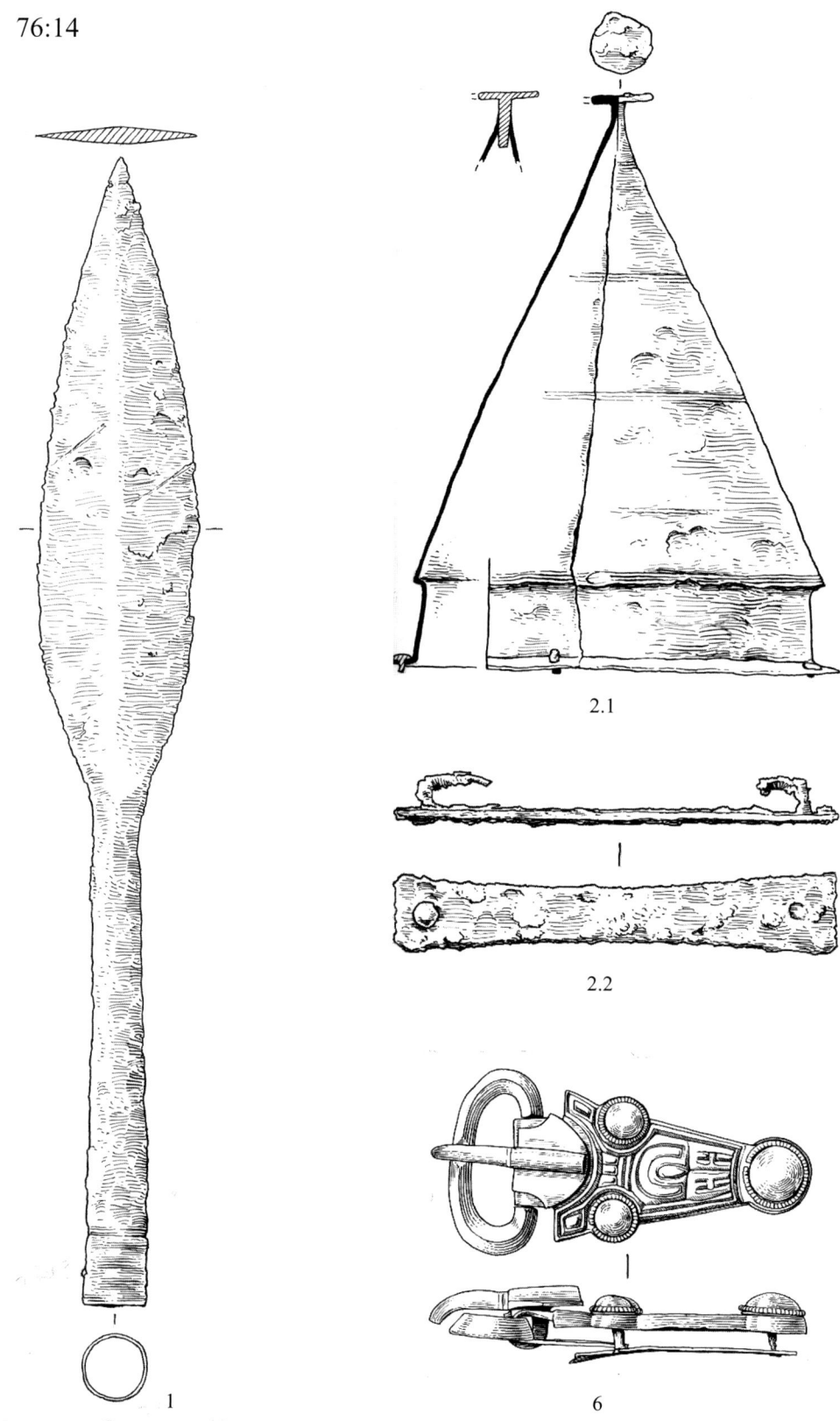

Figure 33. Grave finds: 76:14 [nos.1.1, 2.1, 2.2 and 6] (M. Cox)

76:14 continued

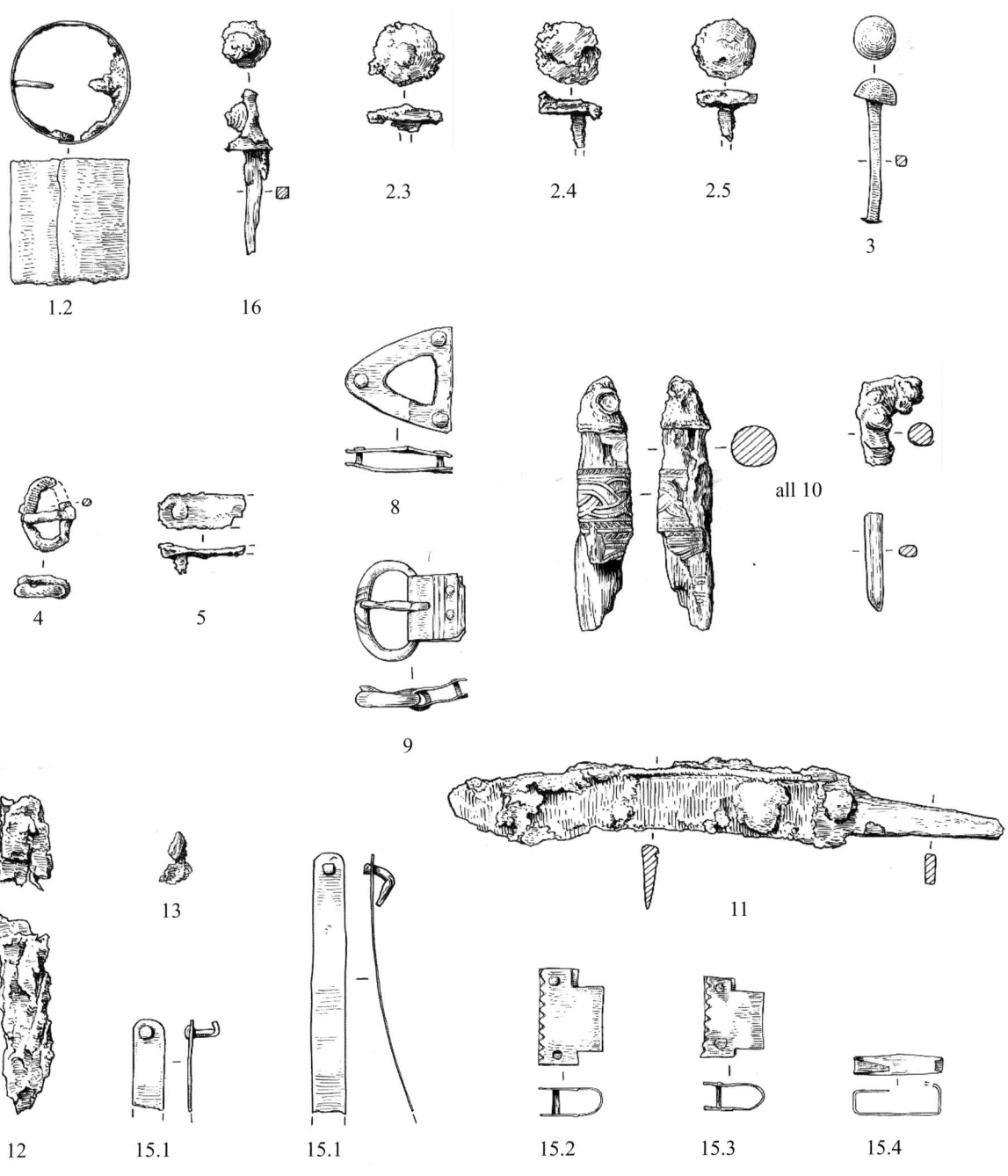

Figure 34. Grave finds: 76:14 continued [nos.1.2–5, 8–13 and 15–16] (M. Cox)

76:15

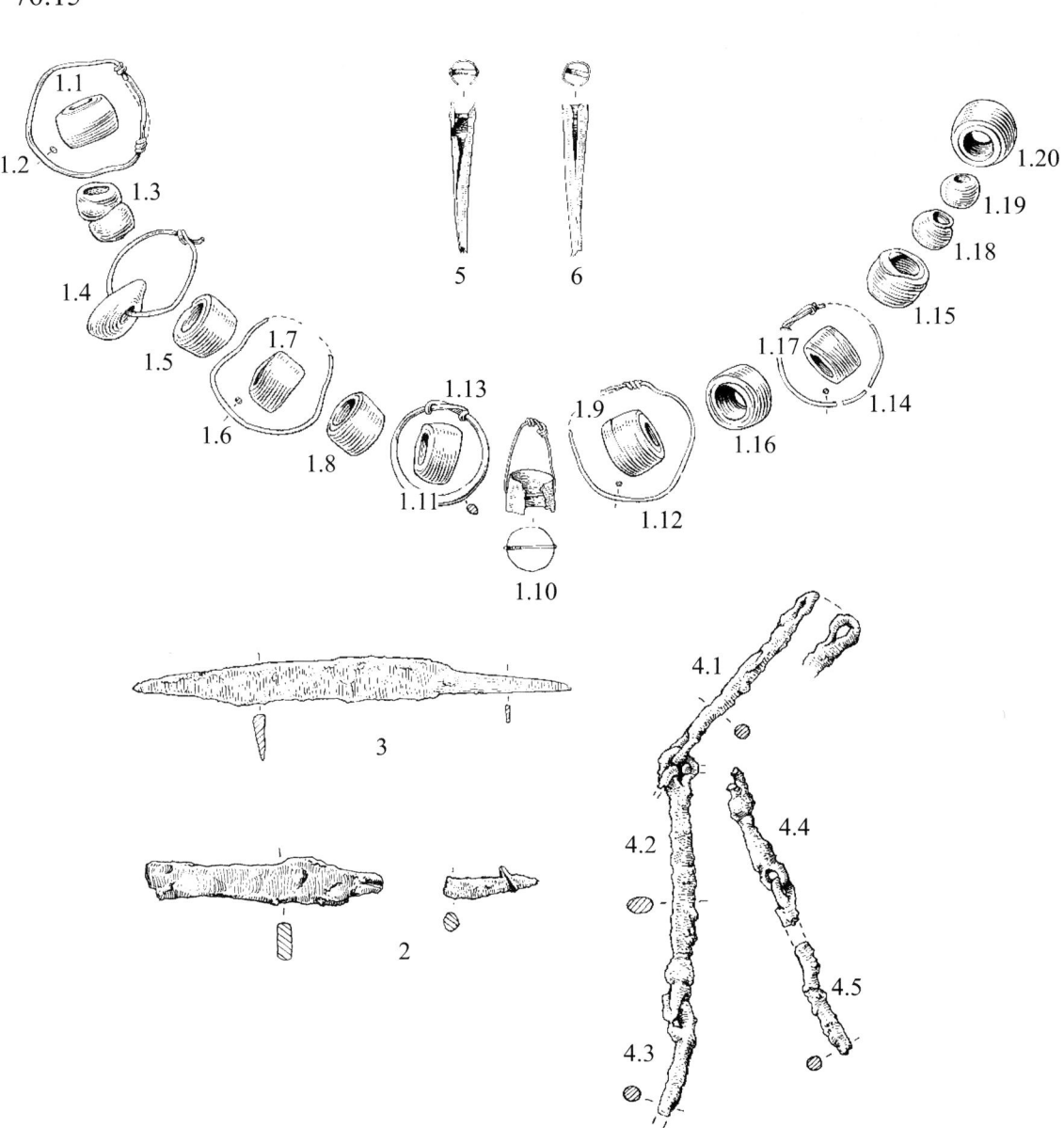

Figure 35. Grave finds: 76:15 (M. Cox)

76:16

76:17

76:18

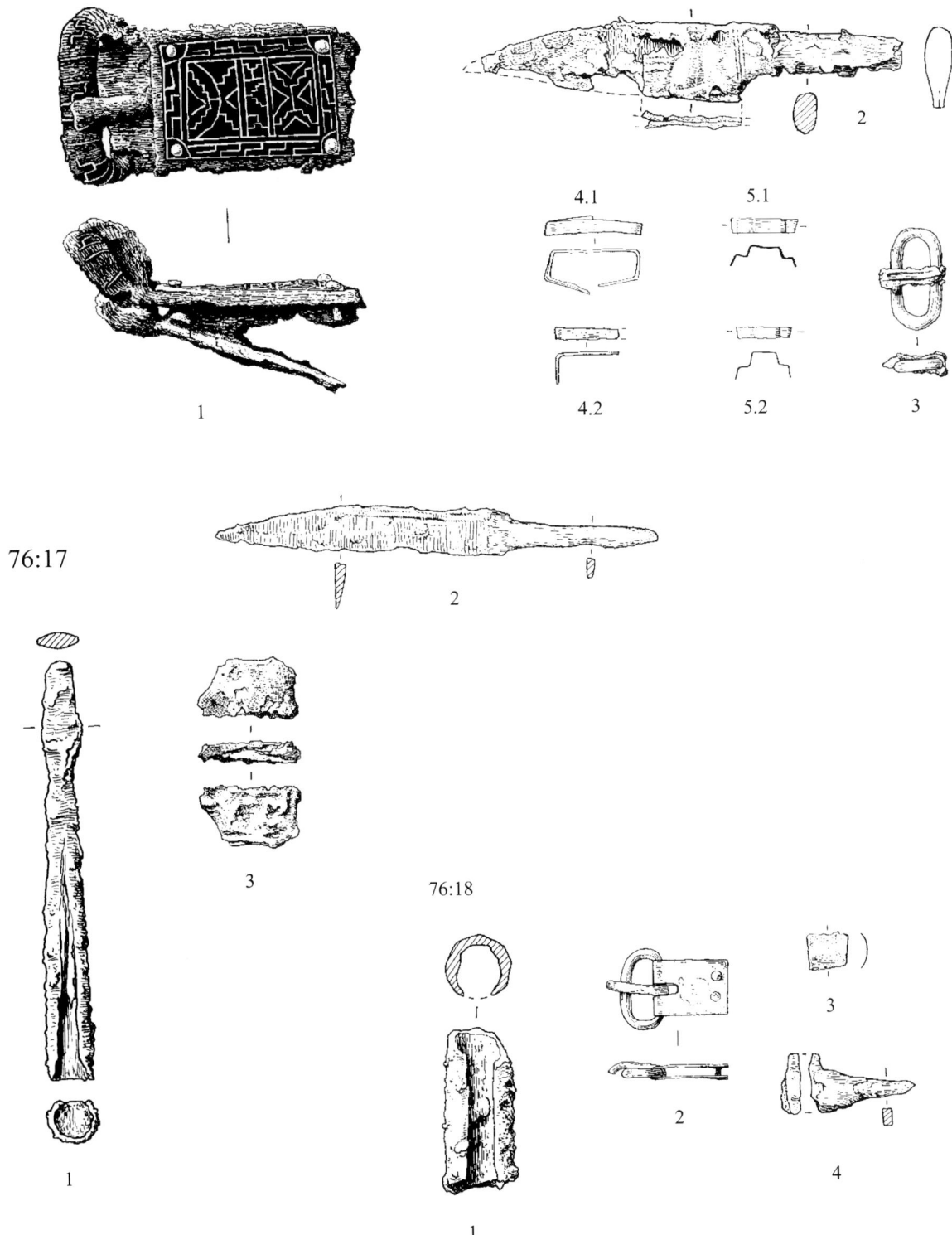

Figure 36. Grave finds: 76:16, 76:17 and 76:18 (M. Cox)

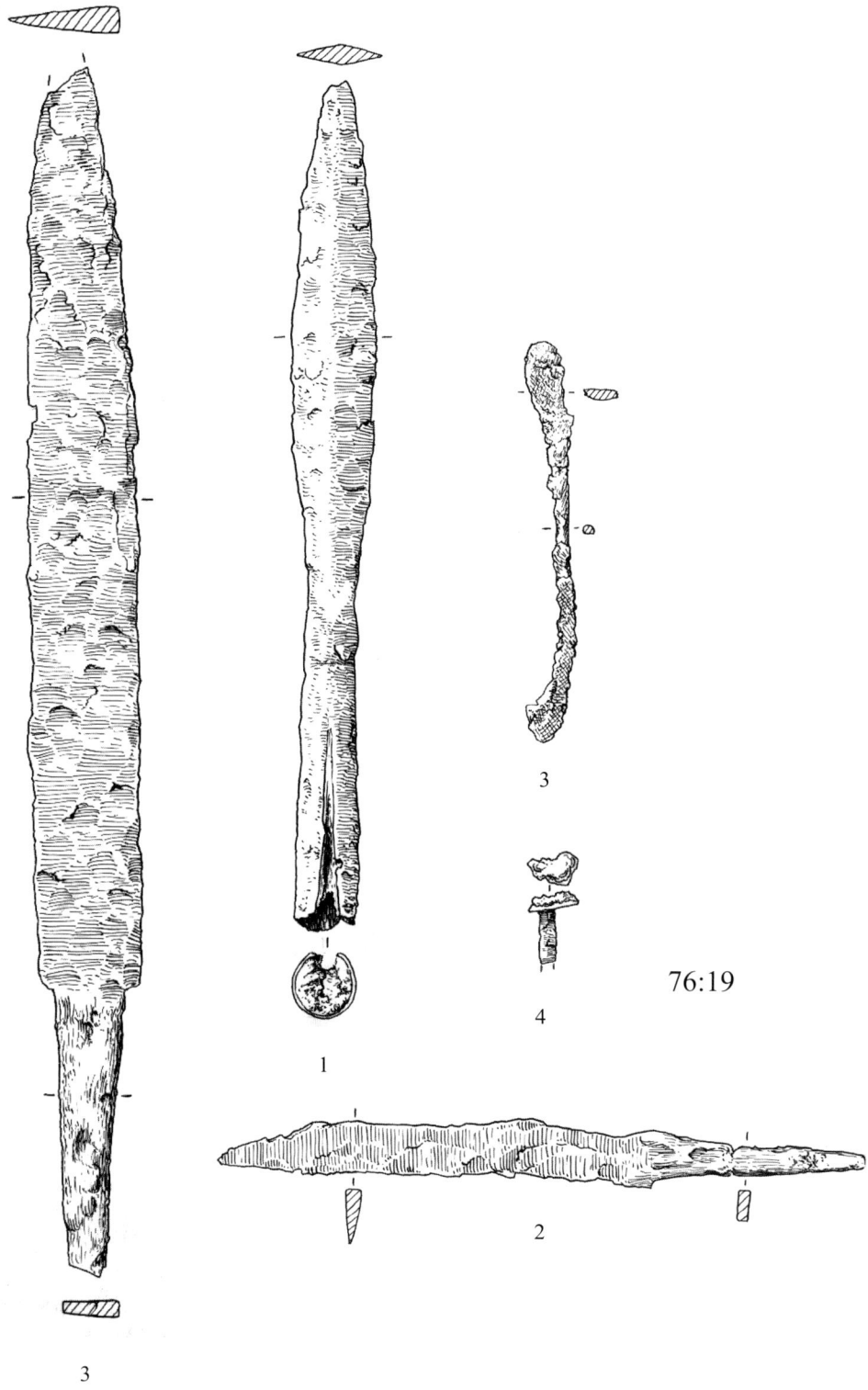

76:19

Figure 37. Grave finds: 76:19 (M. Cox)

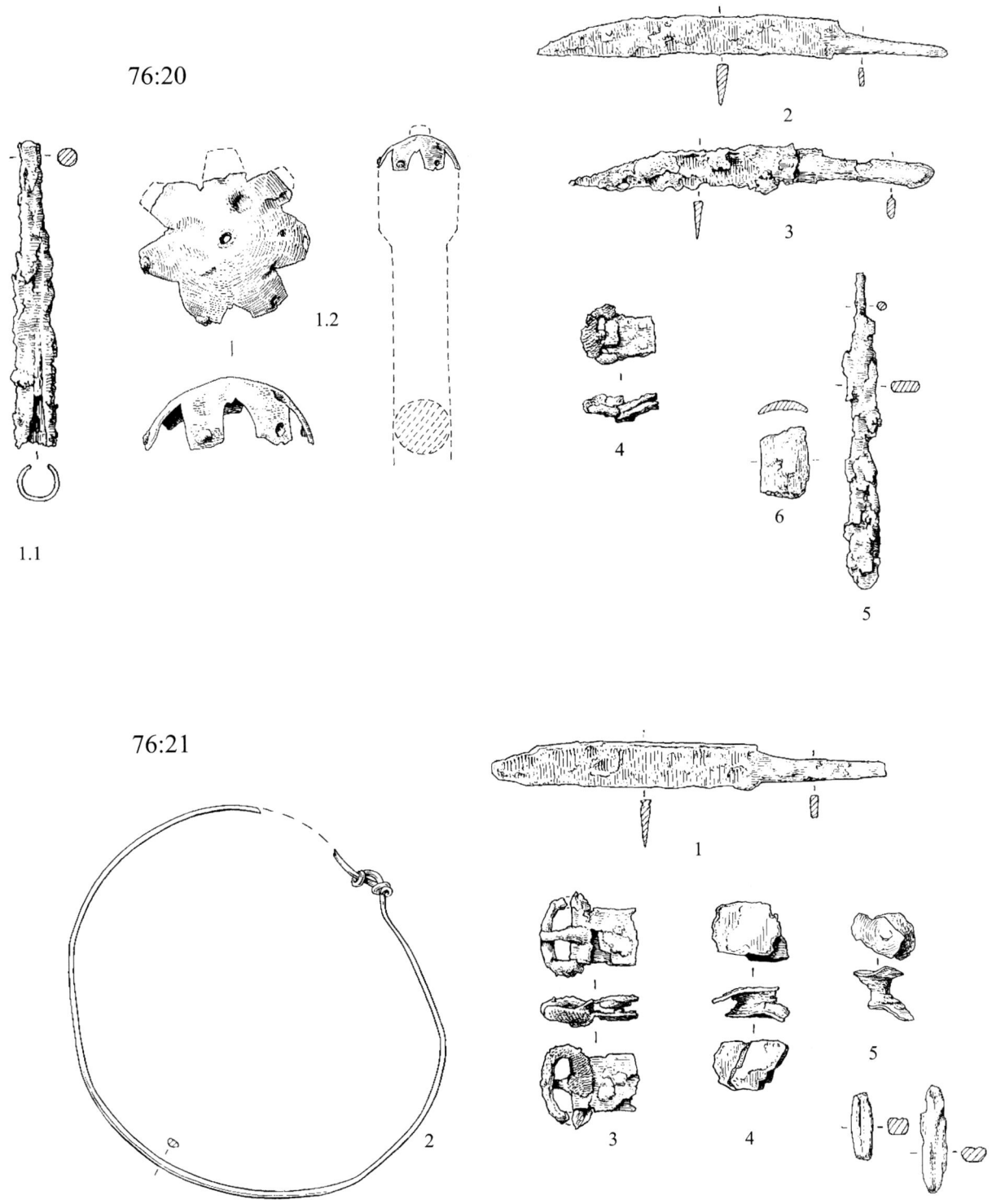

Figure 38. Grave finds: 76:20 and 76:21 [nos.1–5] (M. Cox)

76:21 continued

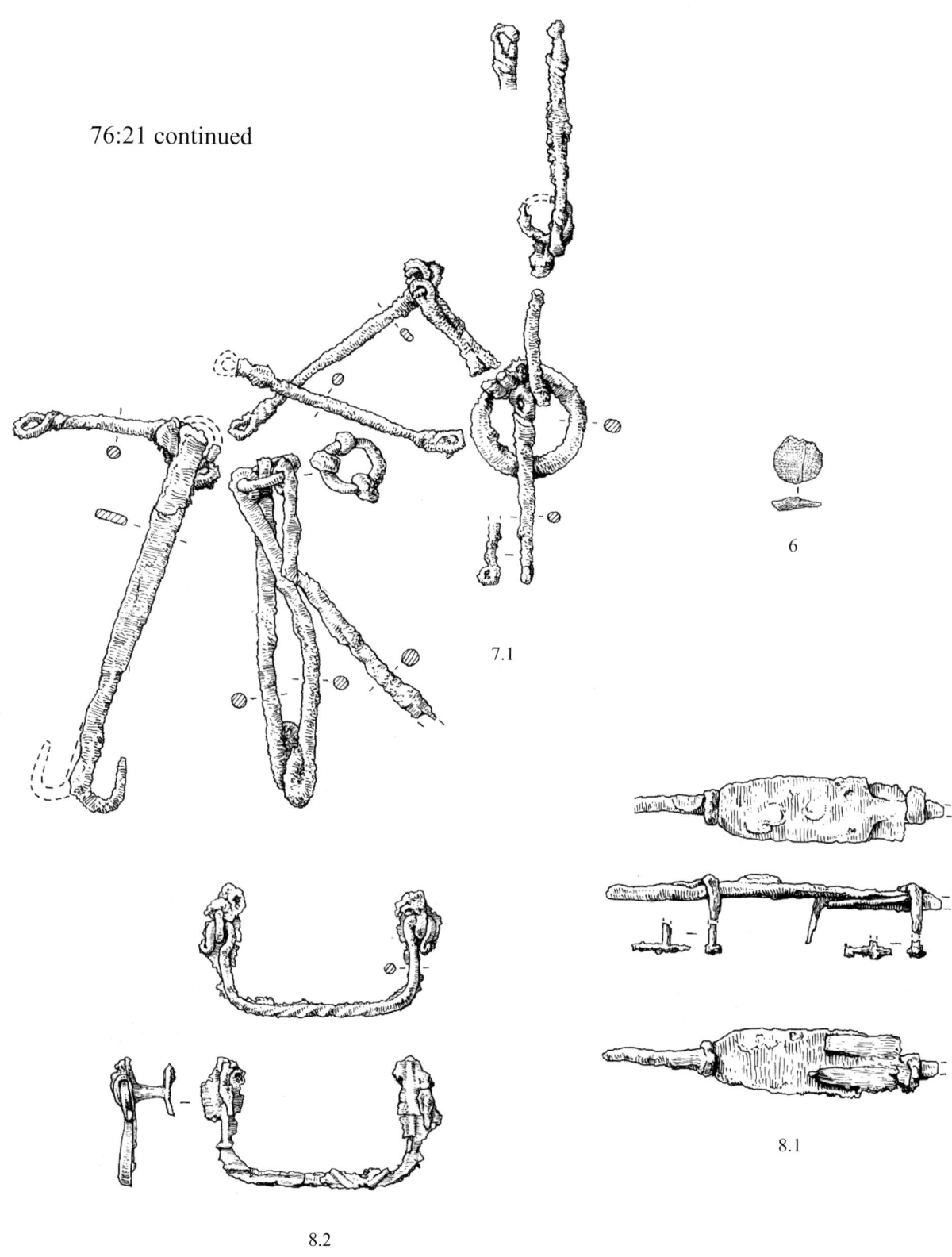

Figure 39. Grave finds: 76:21 continued [nos.6–8] (M. Cox)

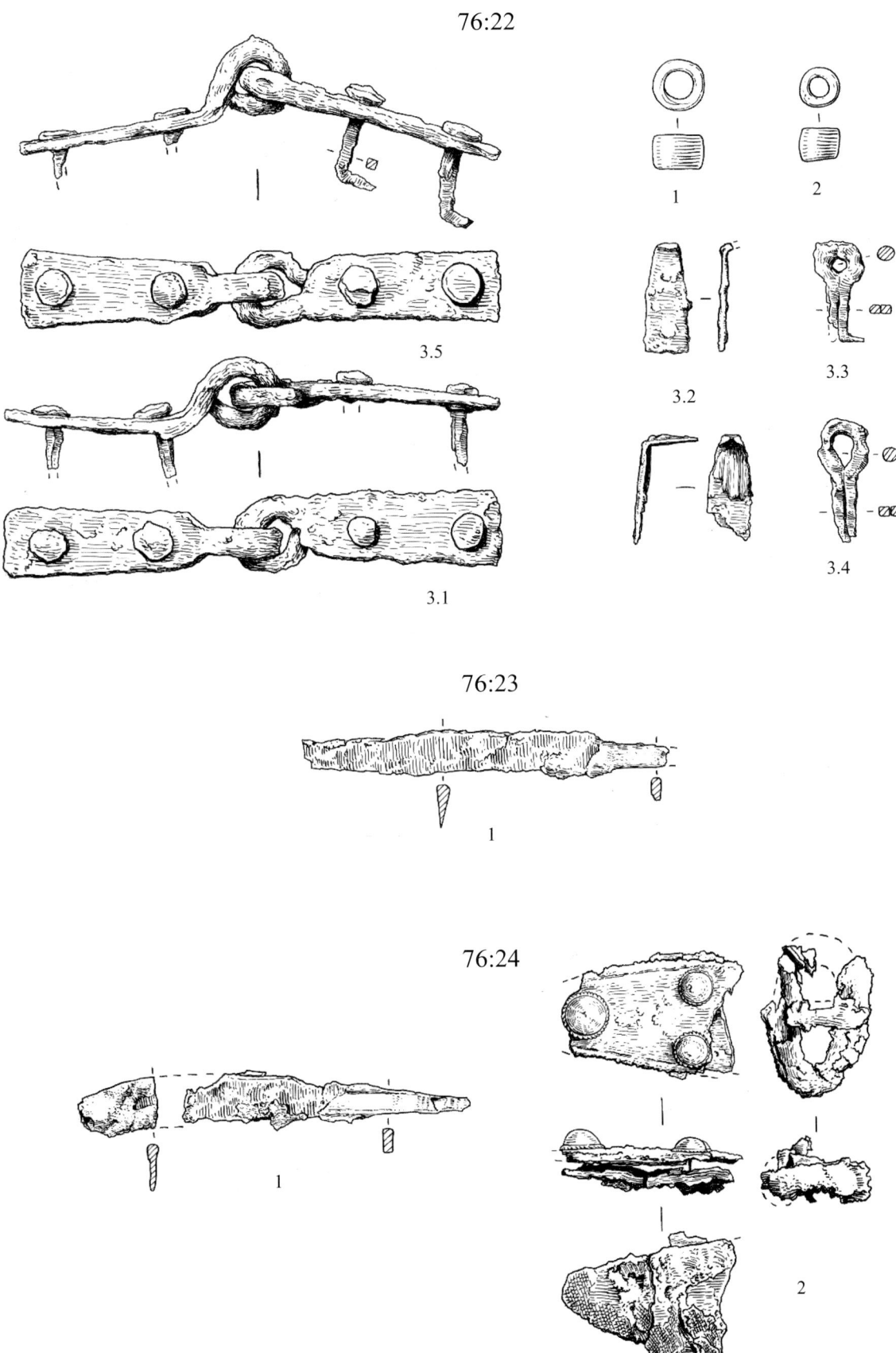

Figure 40. Grave finds: 76:22, 76:23 and 76:24 (M. Cox)

Martin Welch

76:25

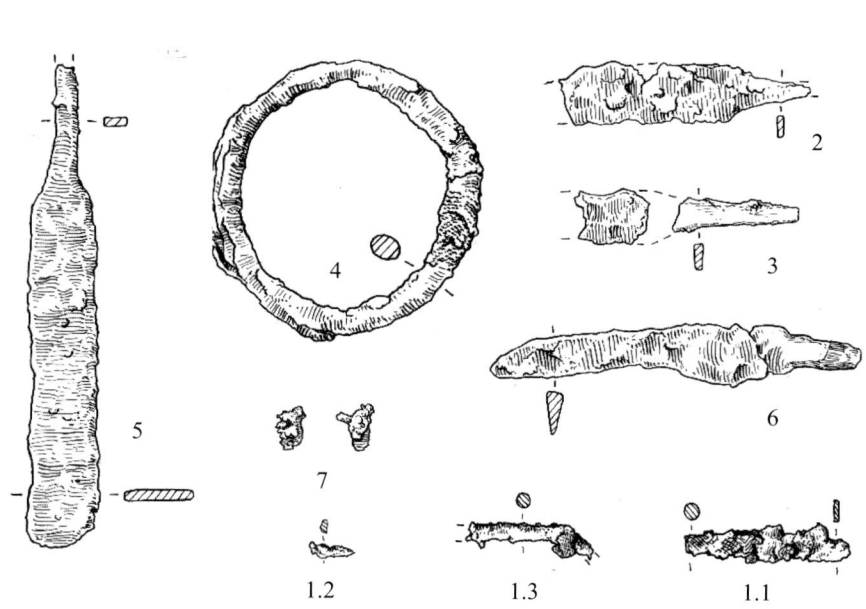

76:26

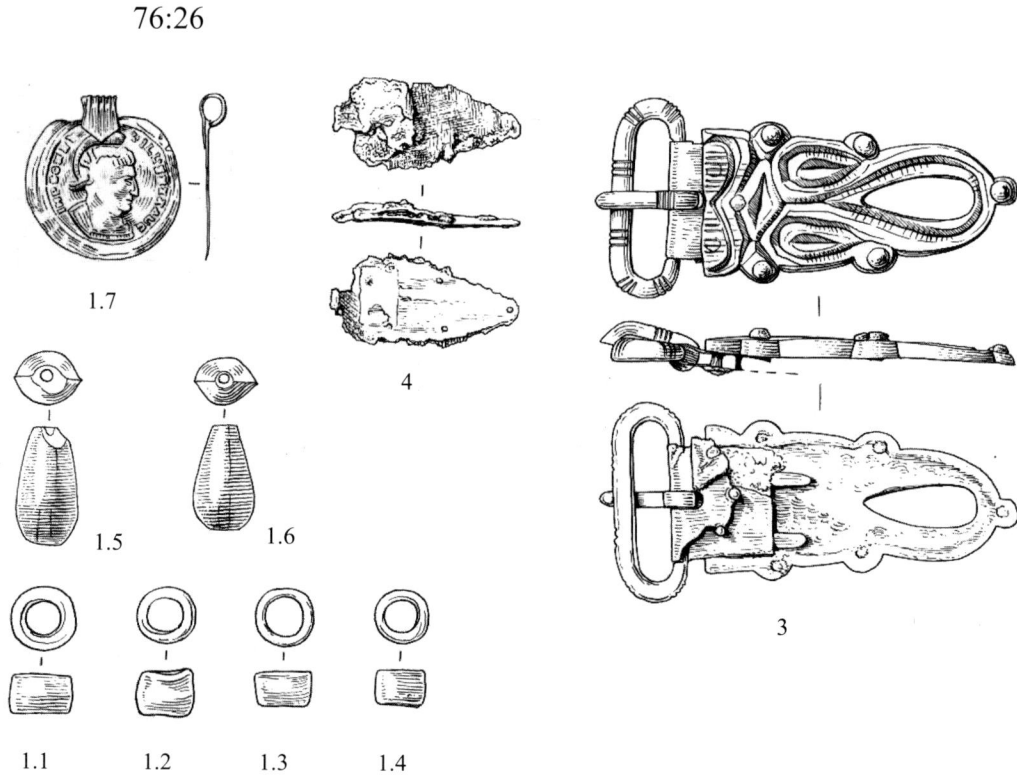

Figure 41. Grave finds: 76:25 and 76:26 [nos 1, 3 and 4] (M. Cox)

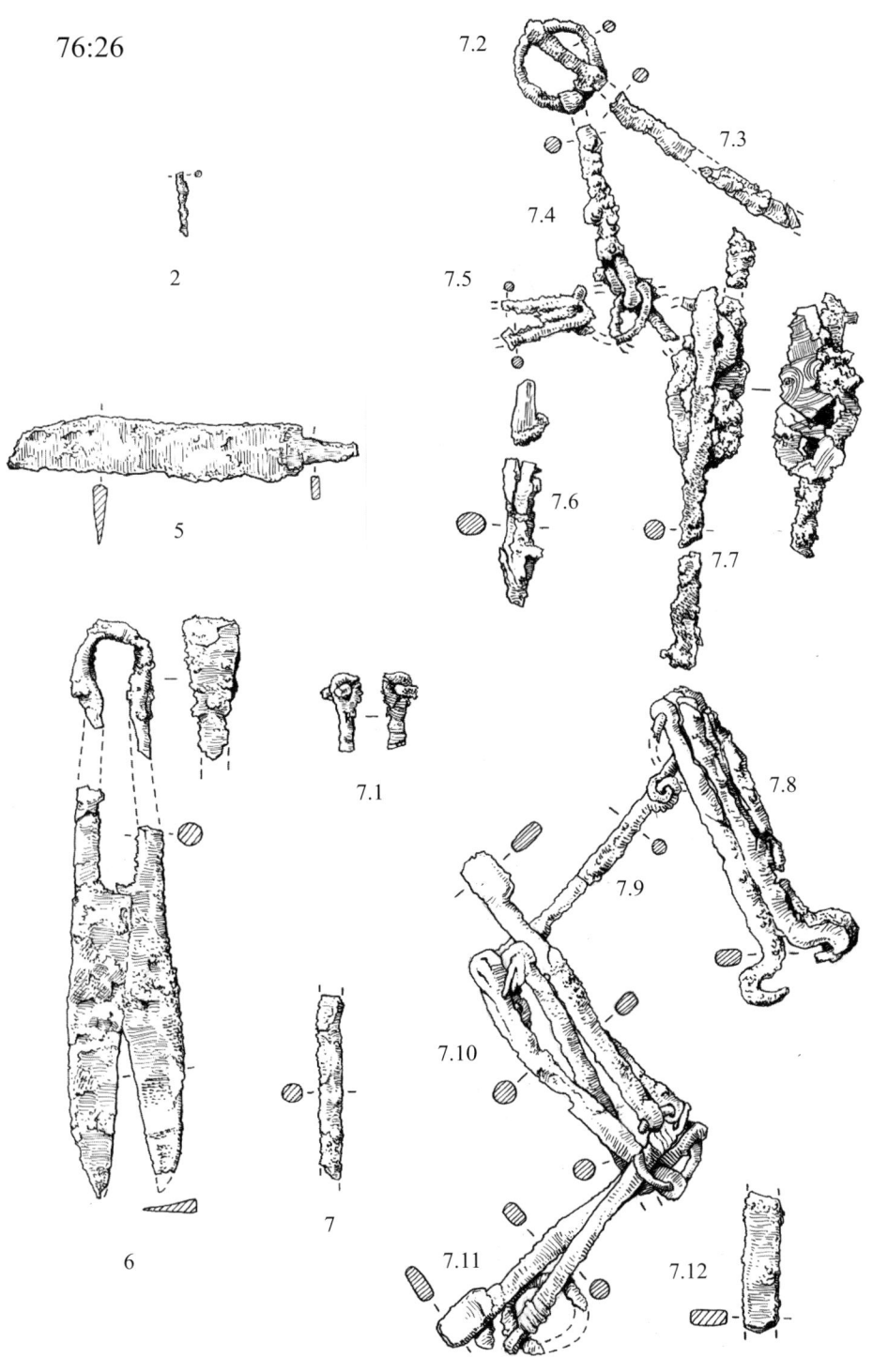

Figure 42. Grave finds: 76:26 continued [nos 2, 5–7] (M. Cox)

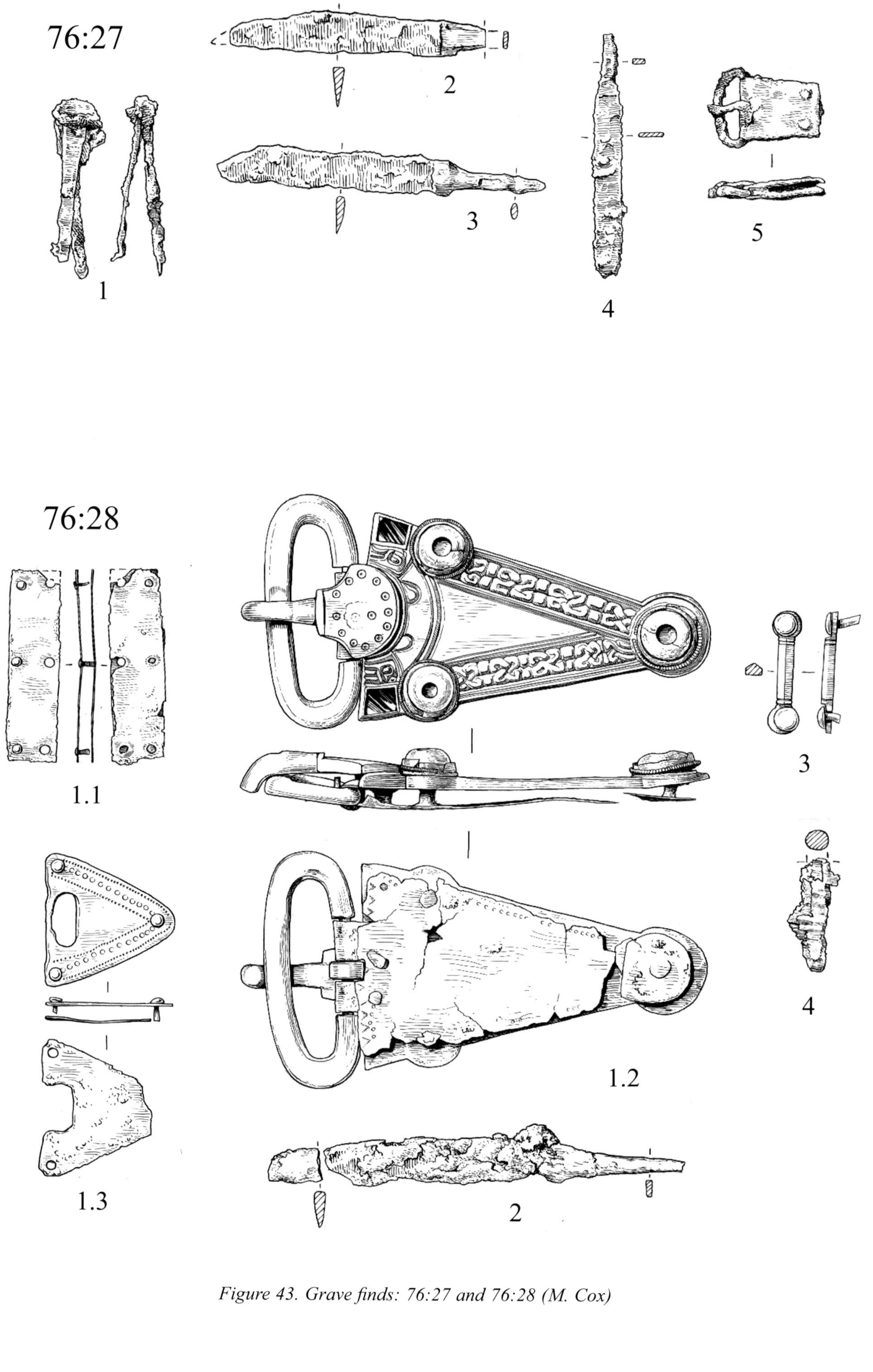

76:27

76:28

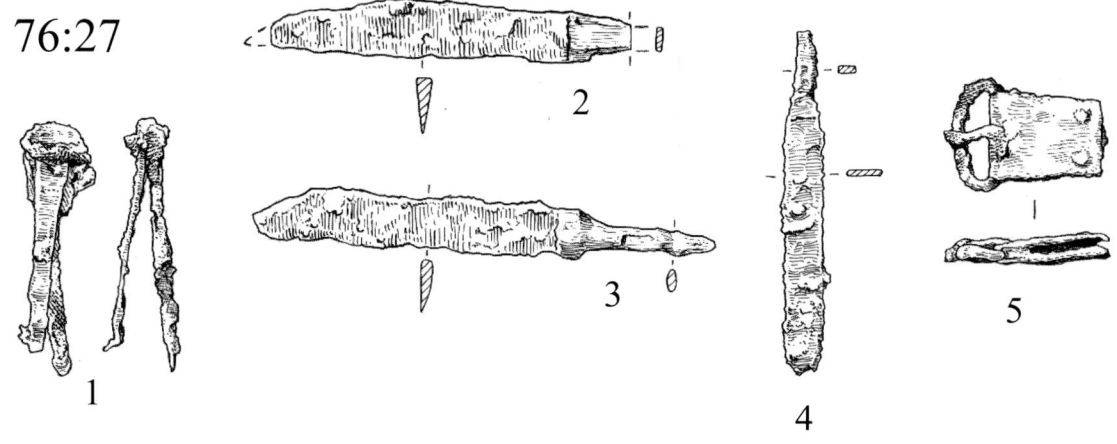

Figure 43. Grave finds: 76:27 and 76:28 (M. Cox)

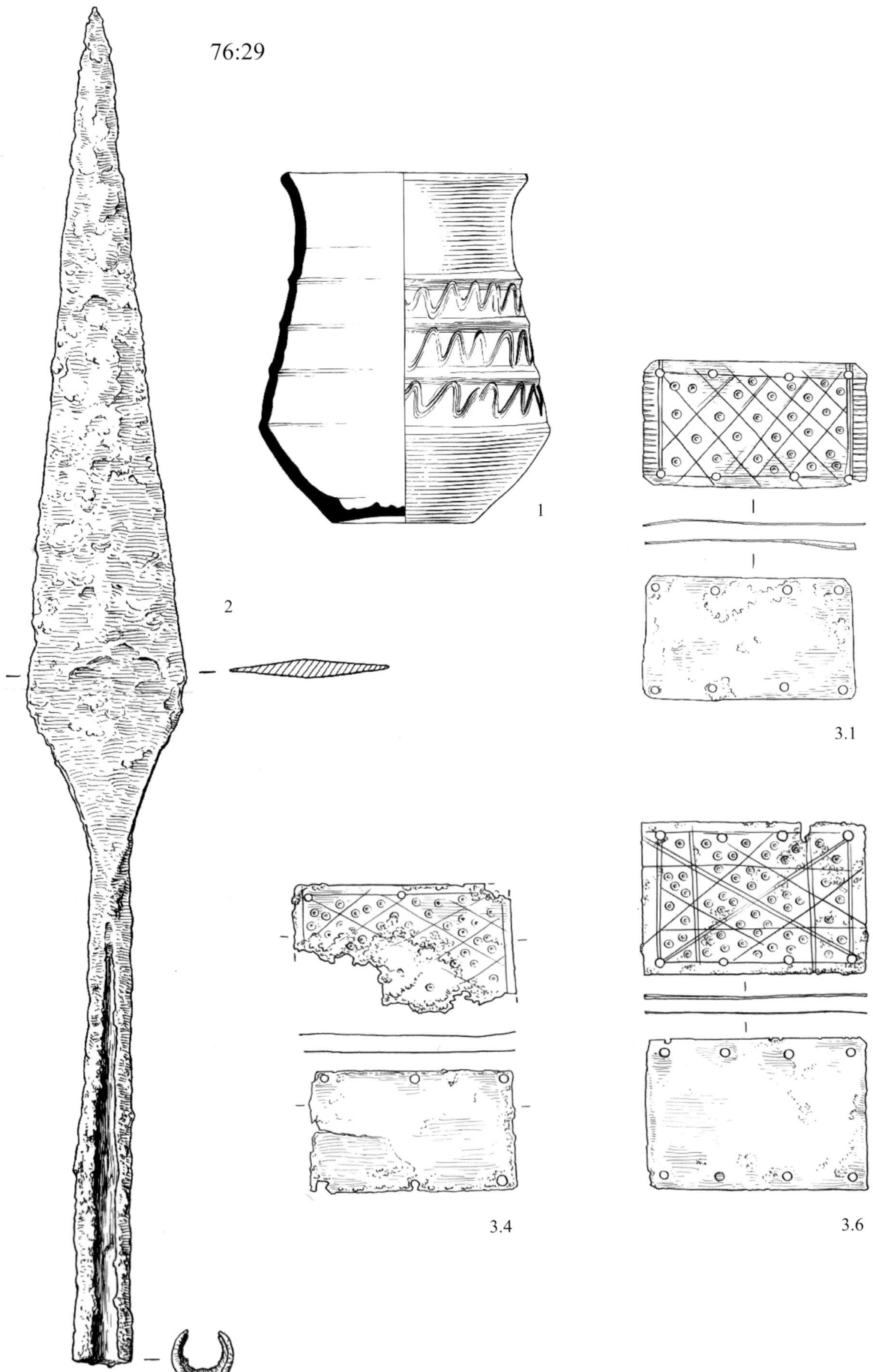

Figure 44. Grave finds: 76:29 [nos 1, 2 and 3.1, 3.4, 3.6] (M. Cox)

Martin Welch

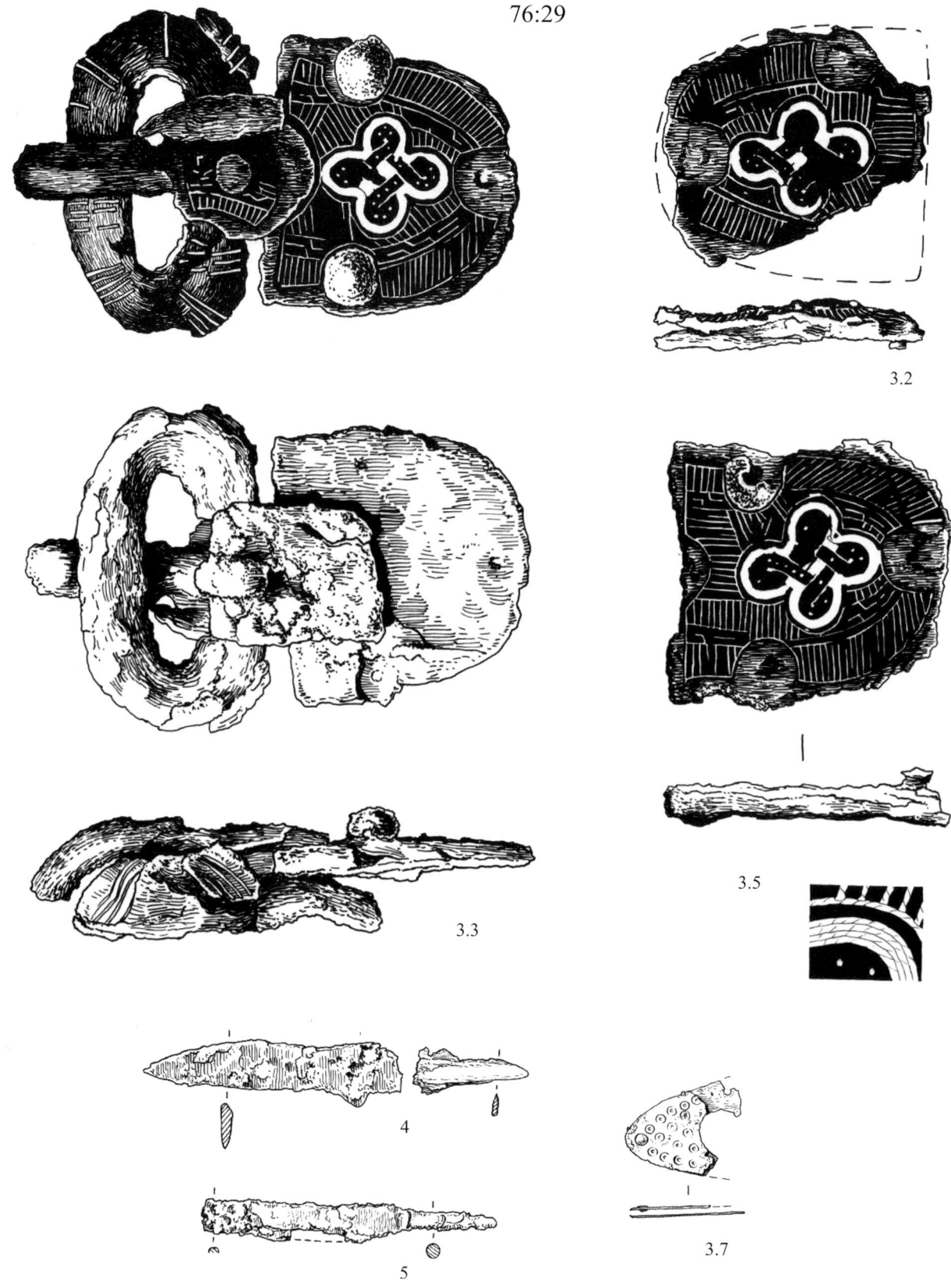

76:29

3.2

3.3

3.5

4

5

3.7

Figure 45. Grave finds: 76:29 continued [nos 3.2, 3.3, 3.5, 3.7 and 4–5] (M. Cox)

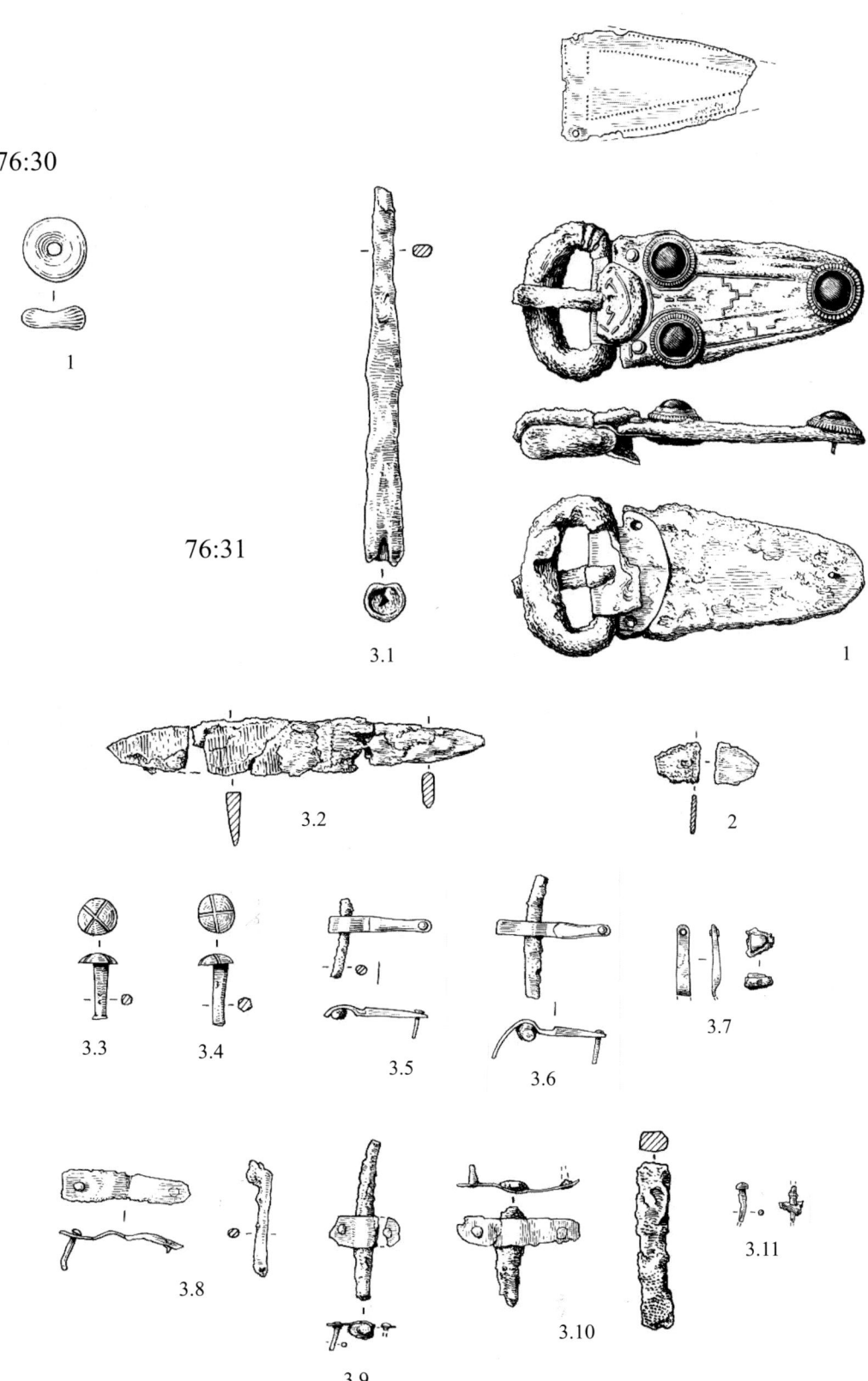

Figure 46. Grave finds: 76:30 and 76:31 (M. Cox)

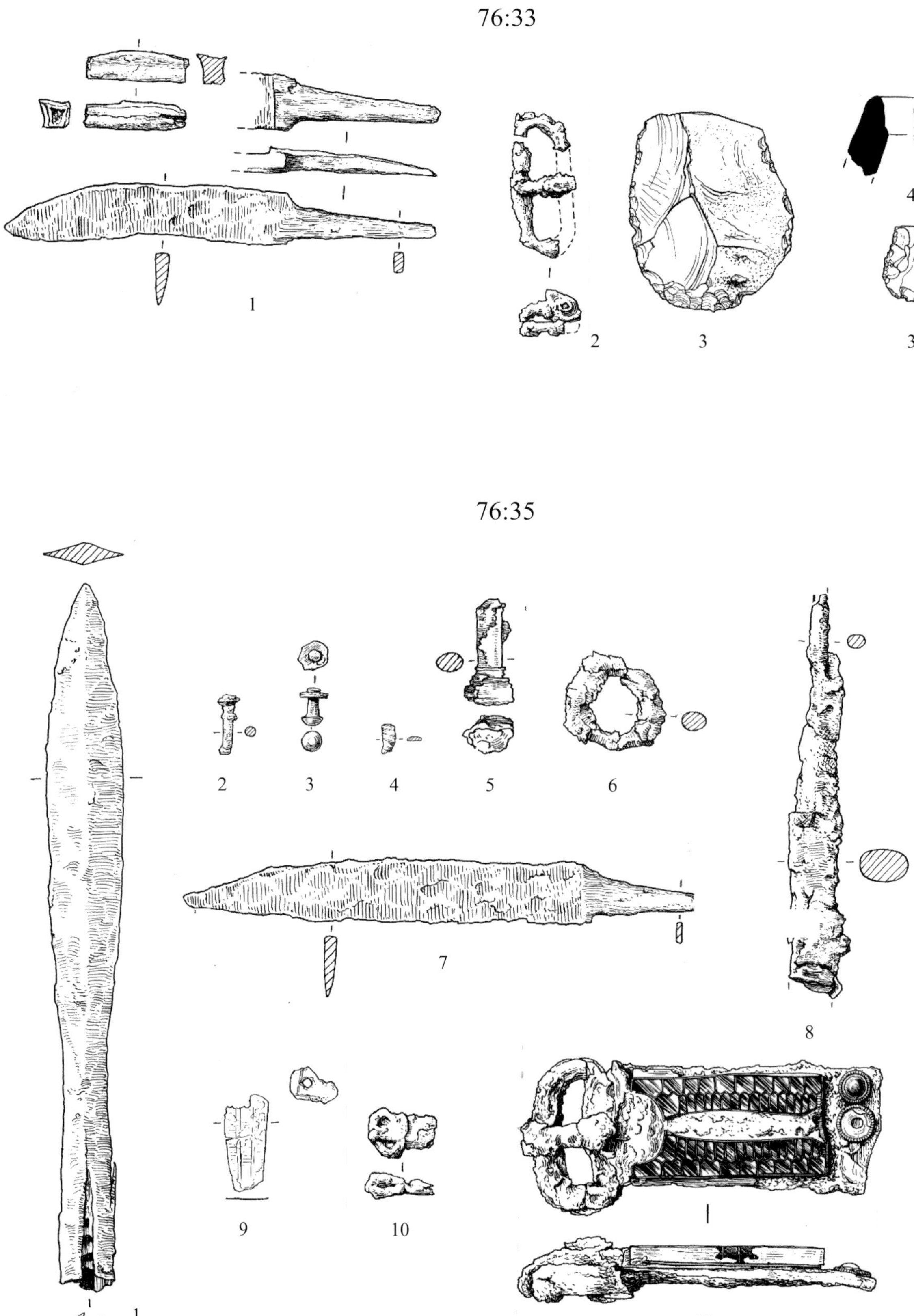

Martin Welch

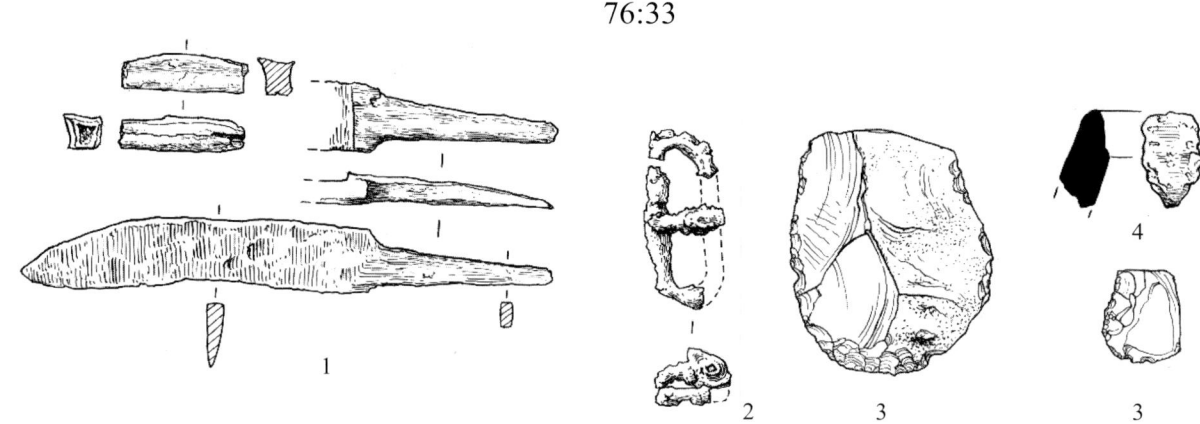

Figure 47. Grave finds: 76:33 and 76:35 (M. Cox)

76:34

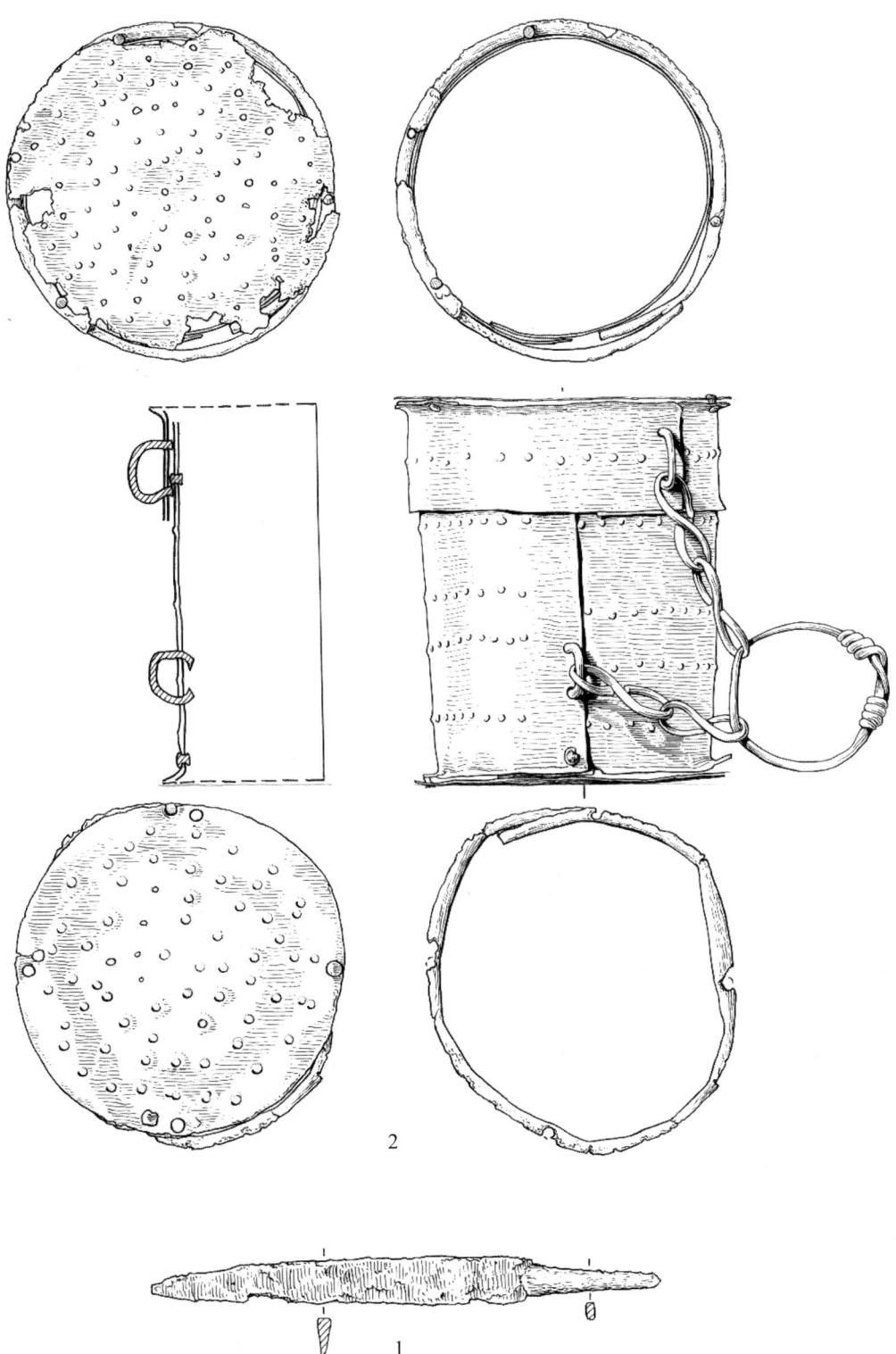

Figure 48. Grave finds: 76:34 (M. Cox)

76:36

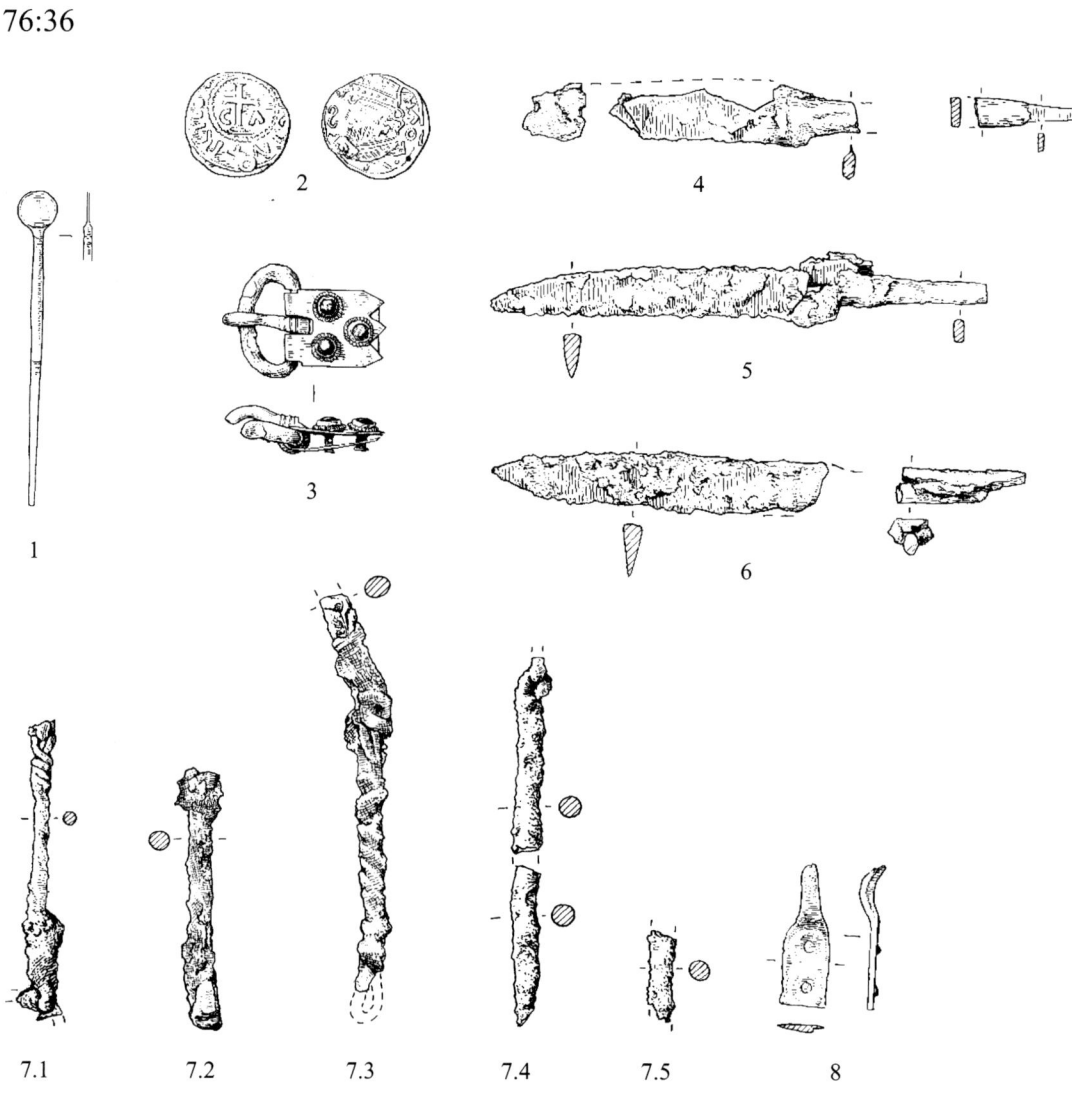

Figure 49. Grave finds: 76:36 (M. Cox)

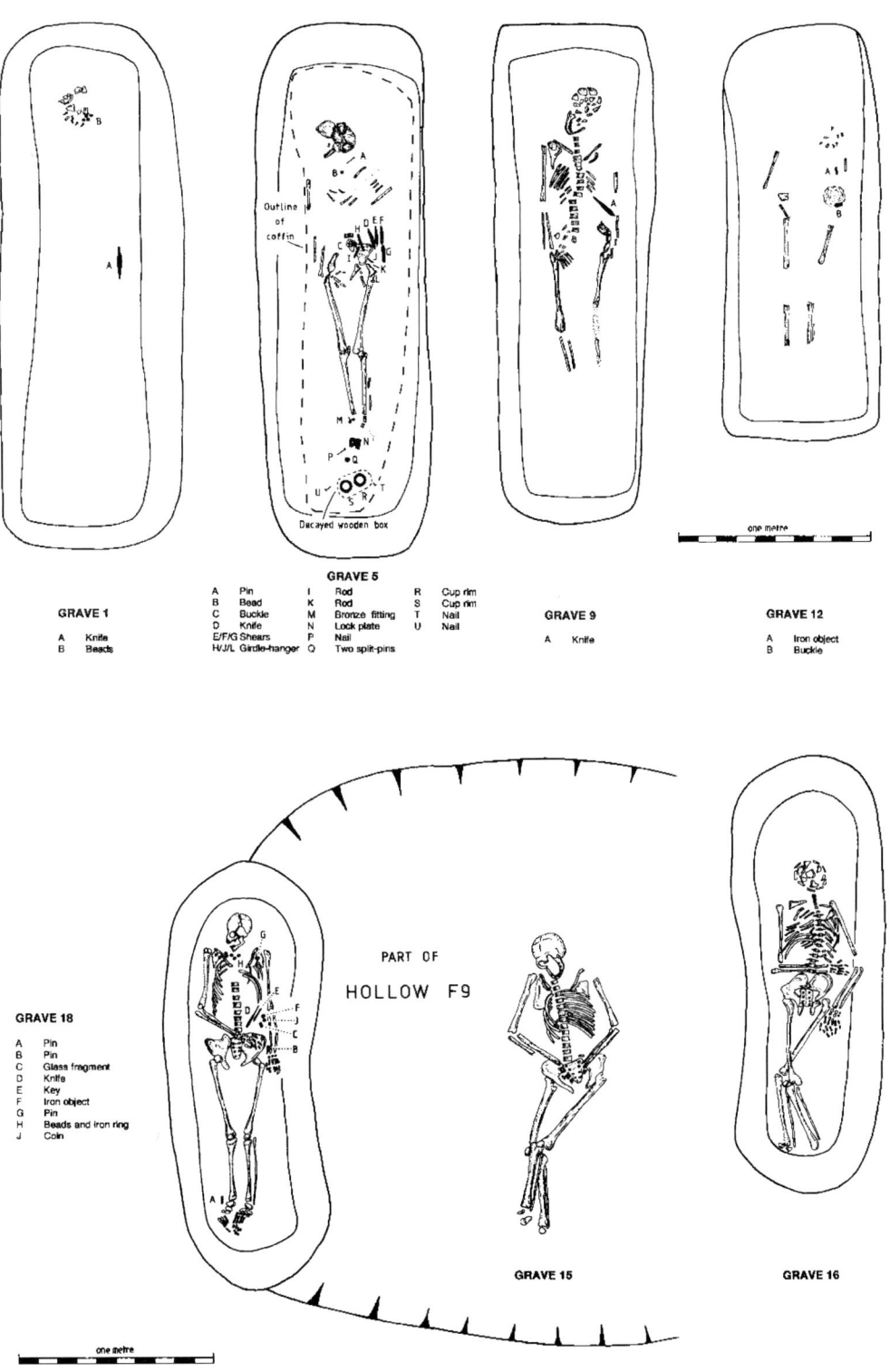

Figure 50. Grave plans: 89:1, 89:5, 89:9, 89:12, 89:15, 89:16 and 89:18 (after Philp and Keller 2002)

Martin Welch

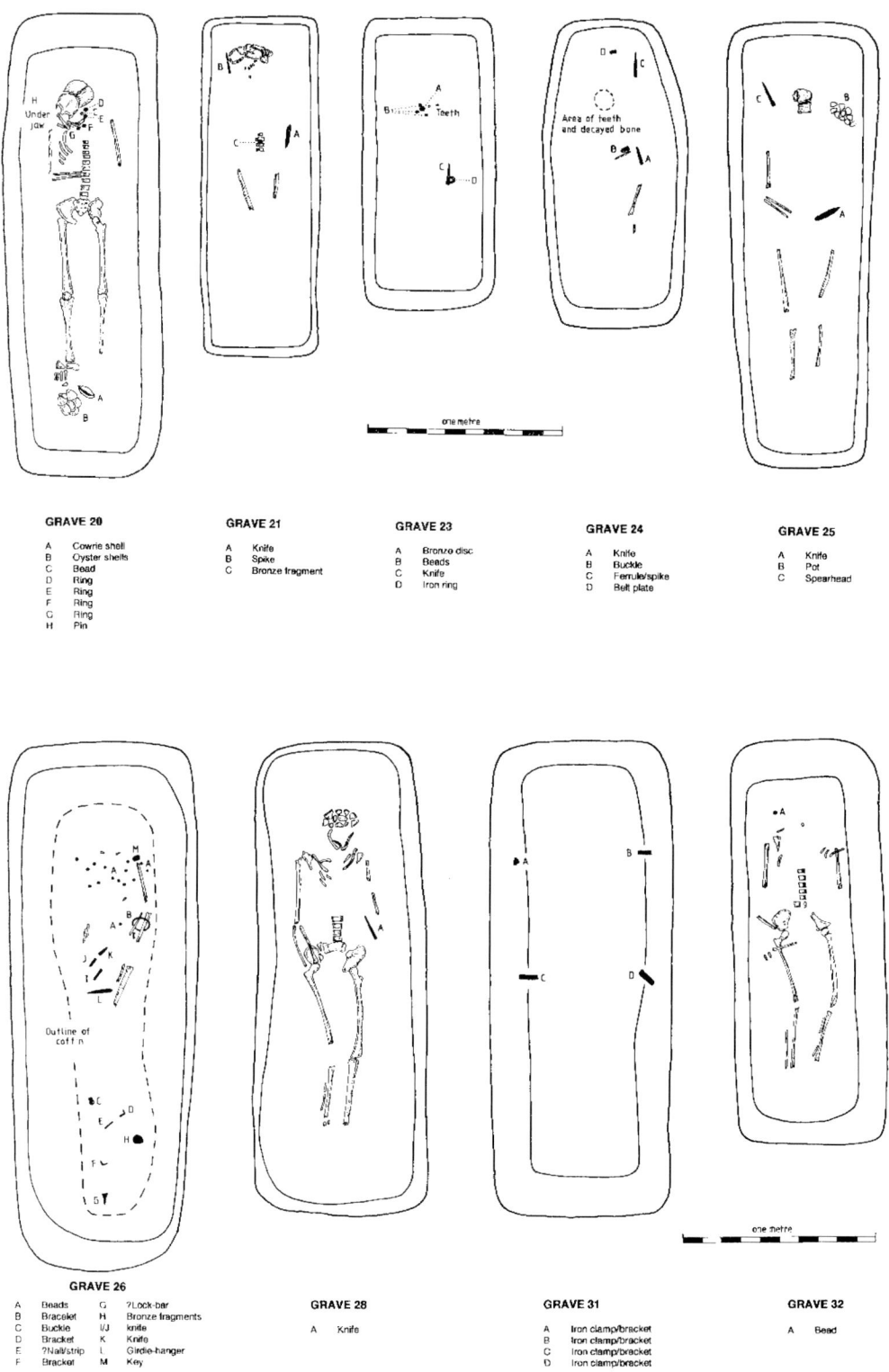

GRAVE 20

A   Cowrie shell
B   Oyster shells
C   Bead
D   Ring
E   Ring
F   Ring
G   Ring
H   Pin

GRAVE 21

A   Knife
B   Spike
C   Bronze fragment

GRAVE 23

A   Bronze disc
B   Beads
C   Knife
D   Iron ring

GRAVE 24

A   Knife
B   Buckle
C   Ferrule/spike
D   Belt plate

GRAVE 25

A   Knife
B   Pot
C   Spearhead

GRAVE 26

A   Beads   G   ?Lock-bar
B   Bracelet   H   Bronze fragments
C   Buckle   I/J   knife
D   Bracket   K   Knife
E   ?Nail/strip   L   Girdle-hanger
F   Bracket   M   Key

GRAVE 28

A   Knife

GRAVE 31

A   Iron clamp/bracket
B   Iron clamp/bracket
C   Iron clamp/bracket
D   Iron clamp/bracket

GRAVE 32

A   Bead

Figure 51. Grave plans: 89:20–21, 89:23–26, 89:28 and 89:31–32 (after Philp and Keller 2002)

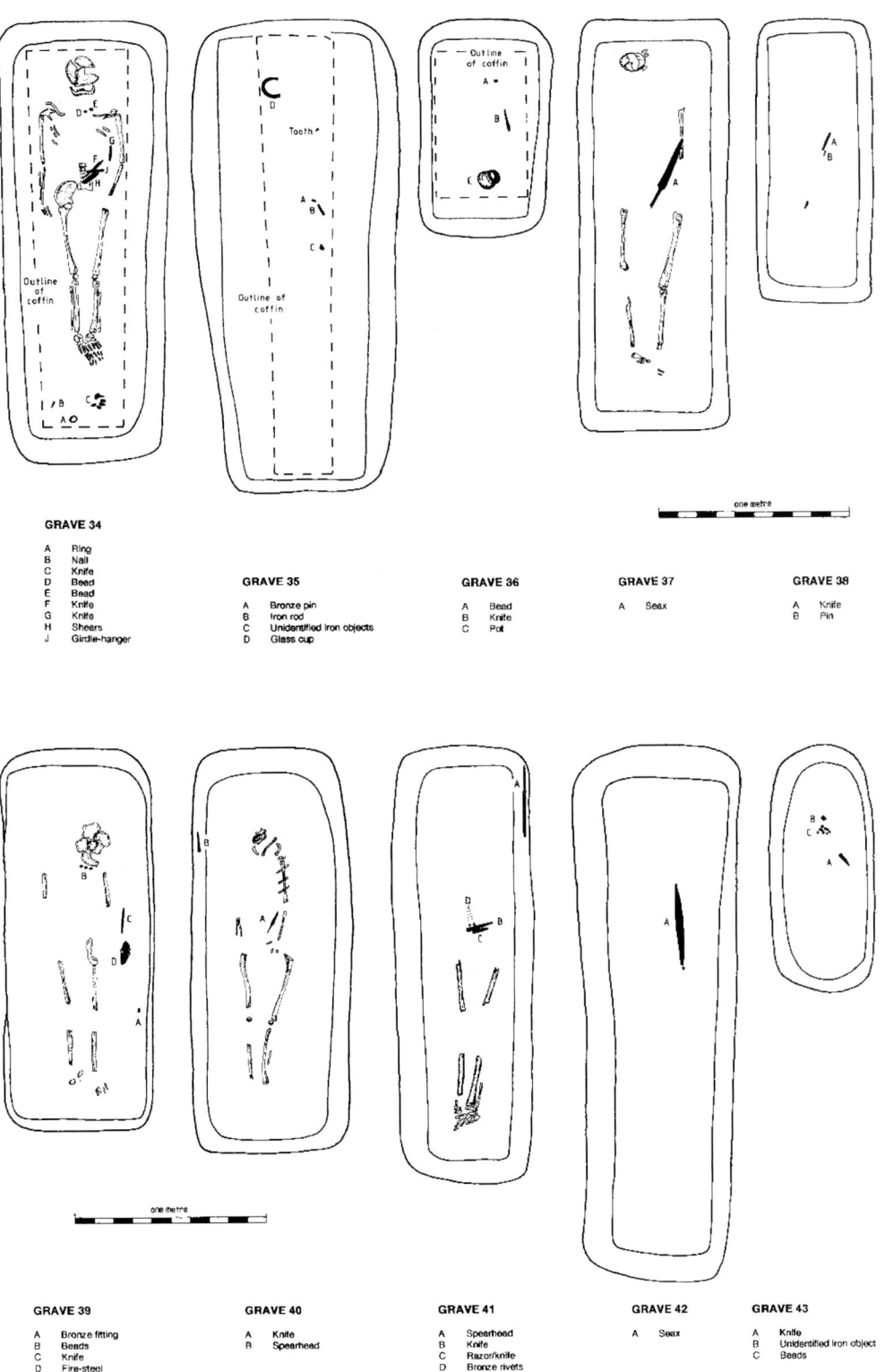

GRAVE 34

A	Ring
B	Nail
C	Knife
D	Bead
E	Bead
F	Knife
G	Knife
H	Shears
J	Girdle-hanger

GRAVE 35

A	Bronze pin
B	Iron rod
C	Unidentified iron objects
D	Glass cup

GRAVE 36

A	Bead
B	Knife
C	Pot

GRAVE 37

A	Seax

GRAVE 38

A	Knife
B	Pin

GRAVE 39

A	Bronze fitting
B	Beads
C	Knife
D	Fire-steel

GRAVE 40

A	Knife
B	Spearhead

GRAVE 41

A	Spearhead
B	Knife
C	Razor/knife
D	Bronze rivets

GRAVE 42

A	Seax

GRAVE 43

A	Knife
B	Unidentified iron object
C	Beads

Figure 52. Grave plans: 89:34–43 (after Philp and Keller 2002)

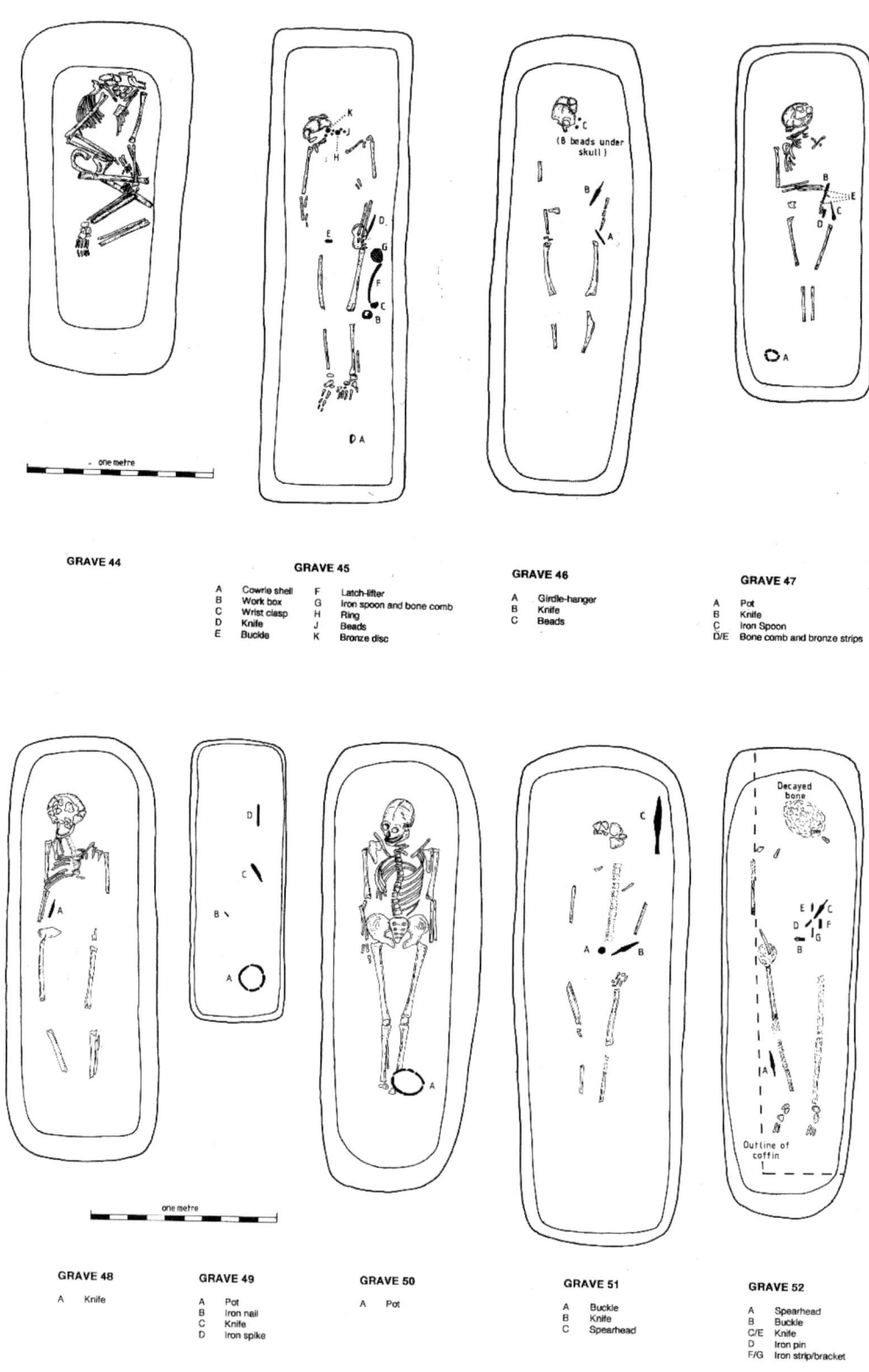

Figure 53. Grave plans: 89:44–52 (after Philp and Keller 2002)

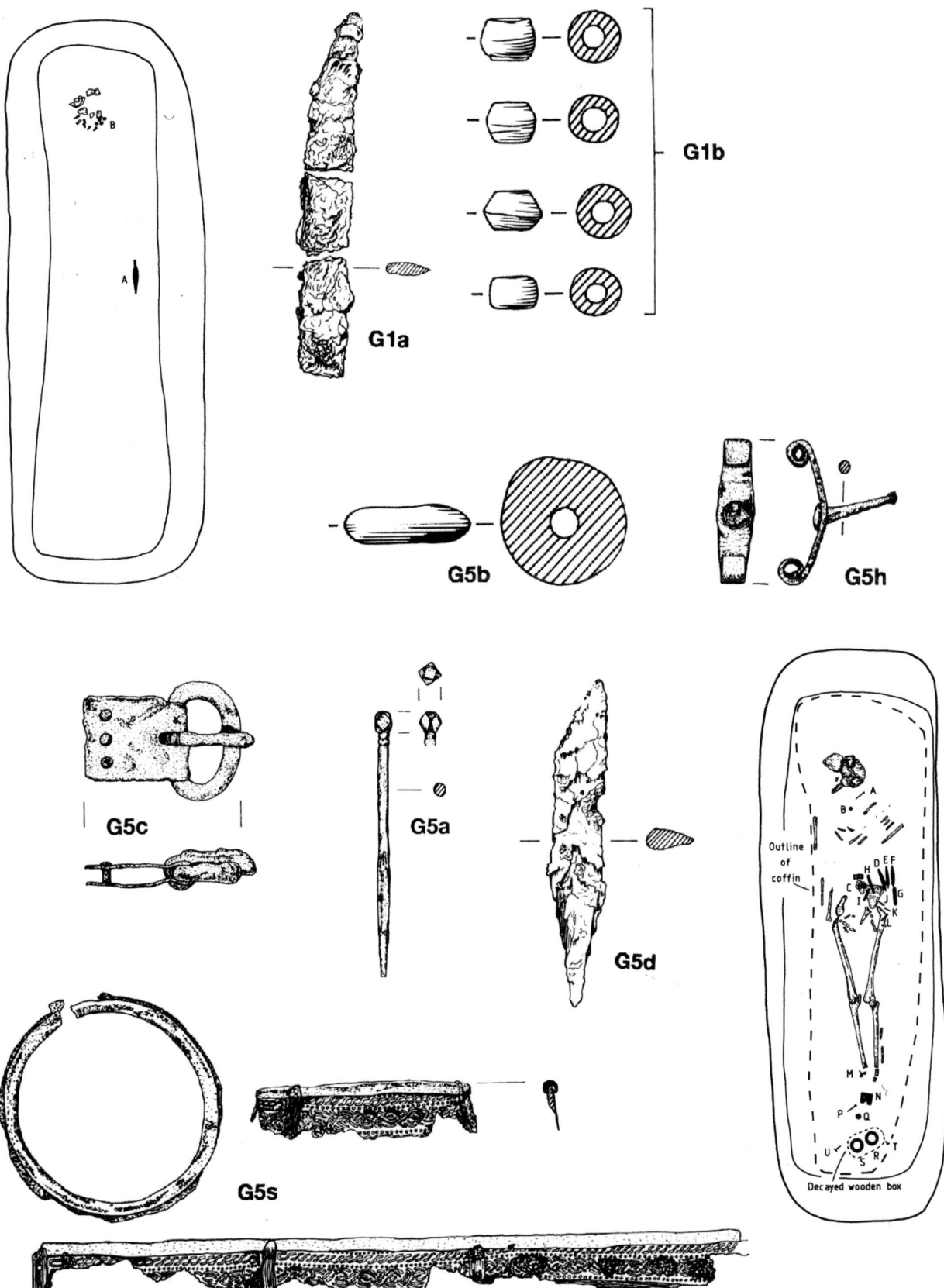

Figure 54. Grave plans and grave finds: 89:1 and 89:5 (after Philp and Keller 2002)

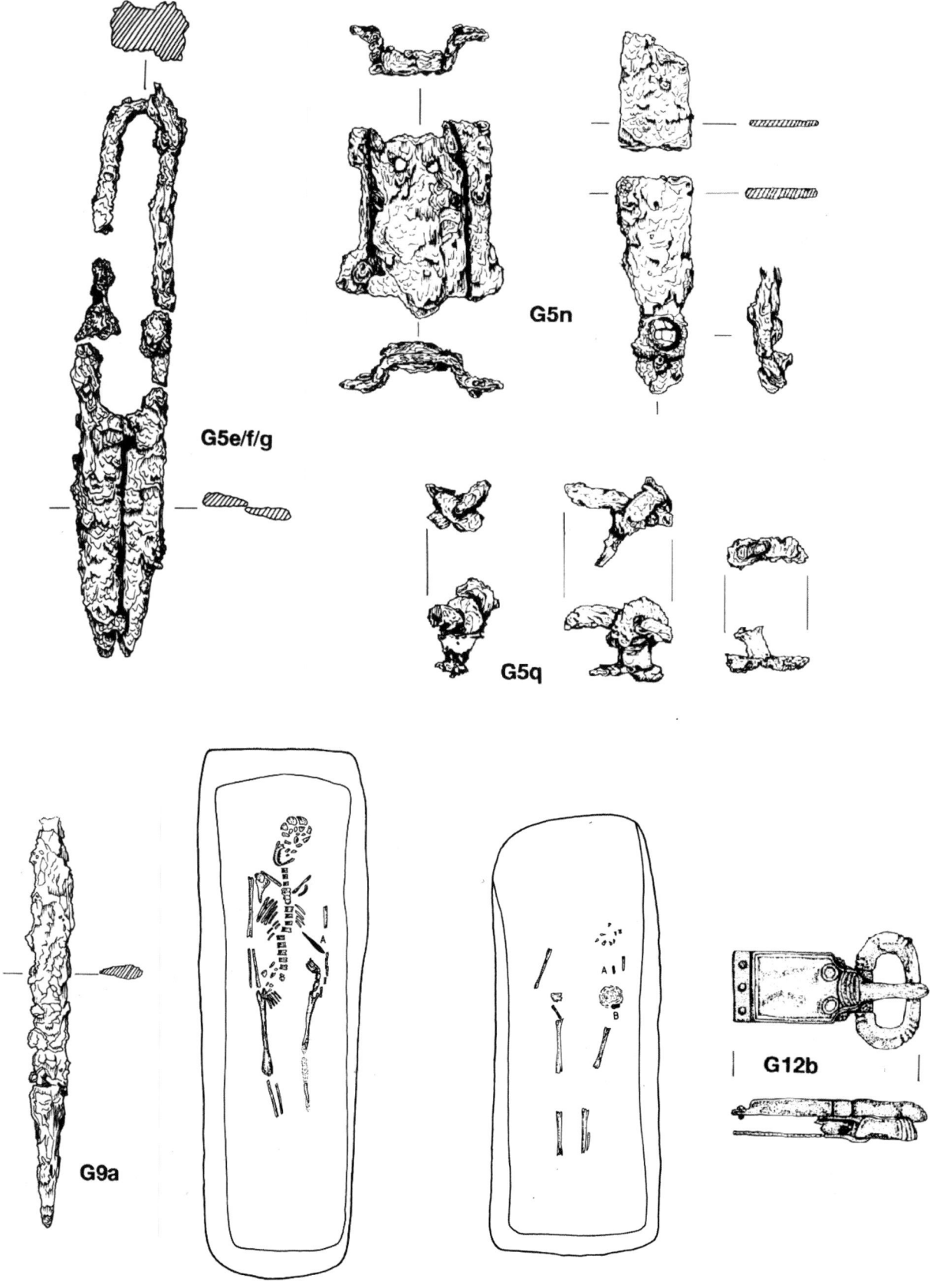

Figure 55. Grave plans and grave finds: 89:5 continued [e–g, n and q], 89:9 and 89:12 (after Philp and Keller 2002)

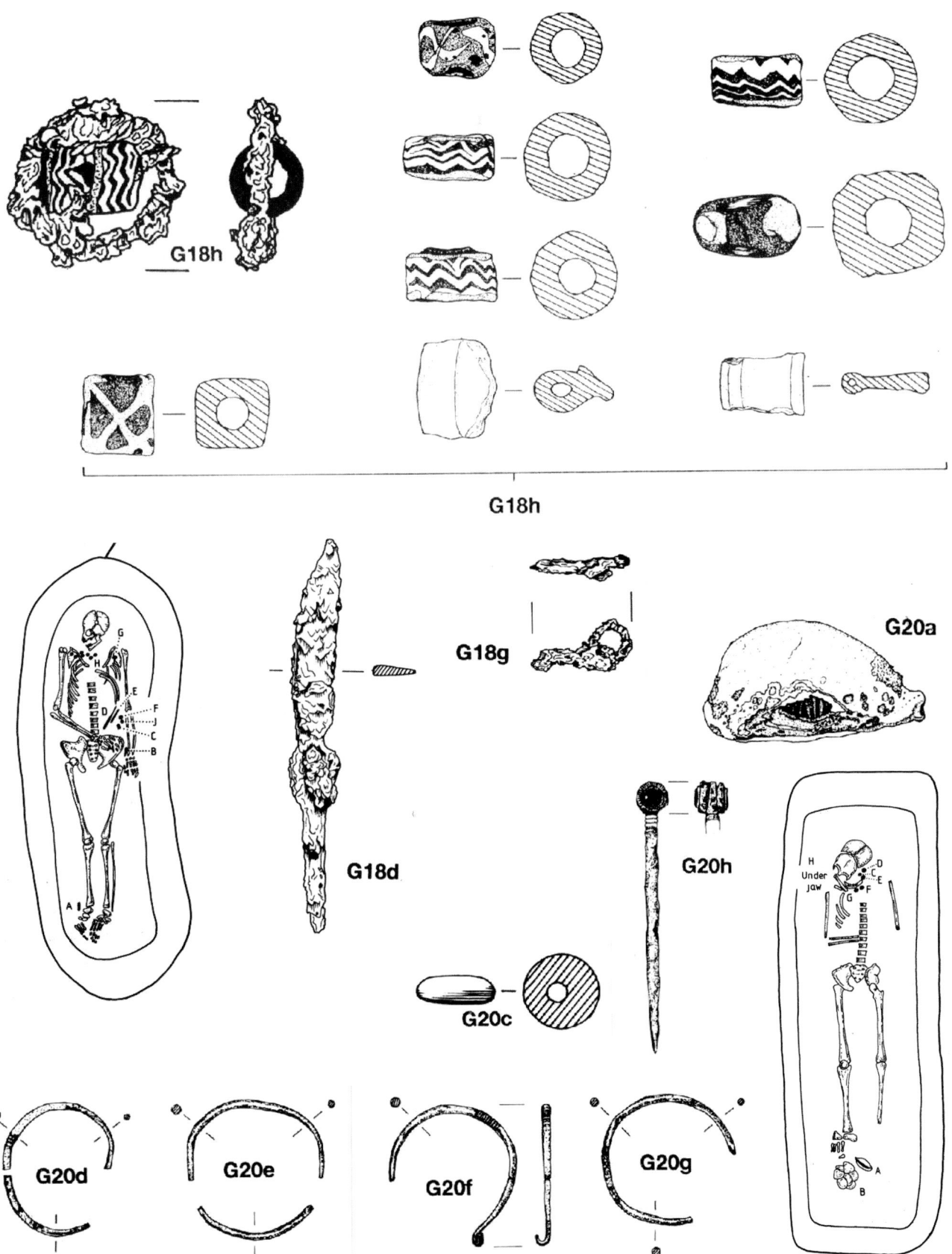

Figure 56. Grave plans and grave finds: 89:18 and 89:20 (after Philp and Keller 2002)

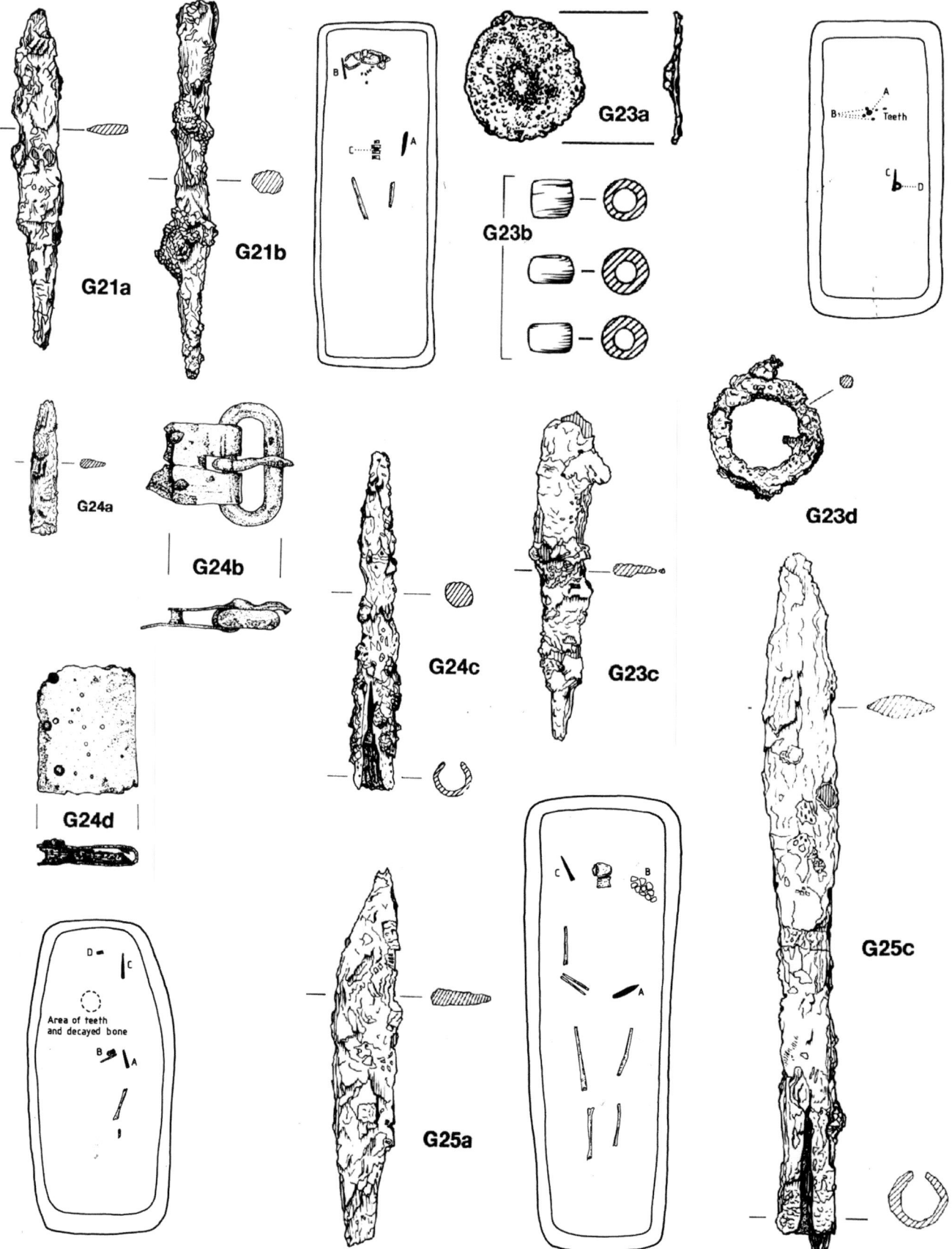

Figure 57. Grave plans and grave finds: 89:21, 89:23, 89:24 and 89:25 (after Philp and Keller 2002)

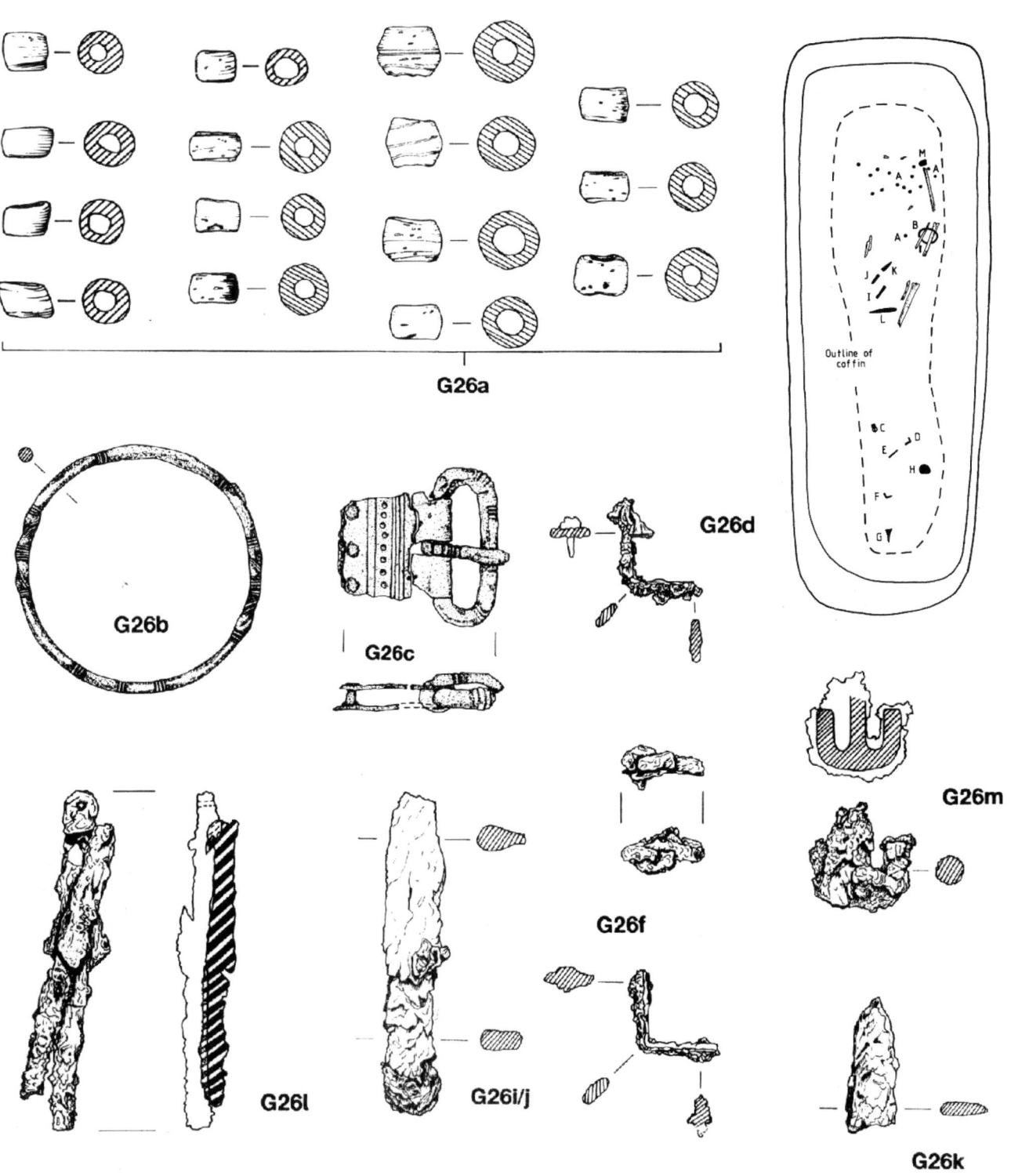

Figure 58. Grave plan and grave finds: 89:26 (after Philp and Keller, 2002)

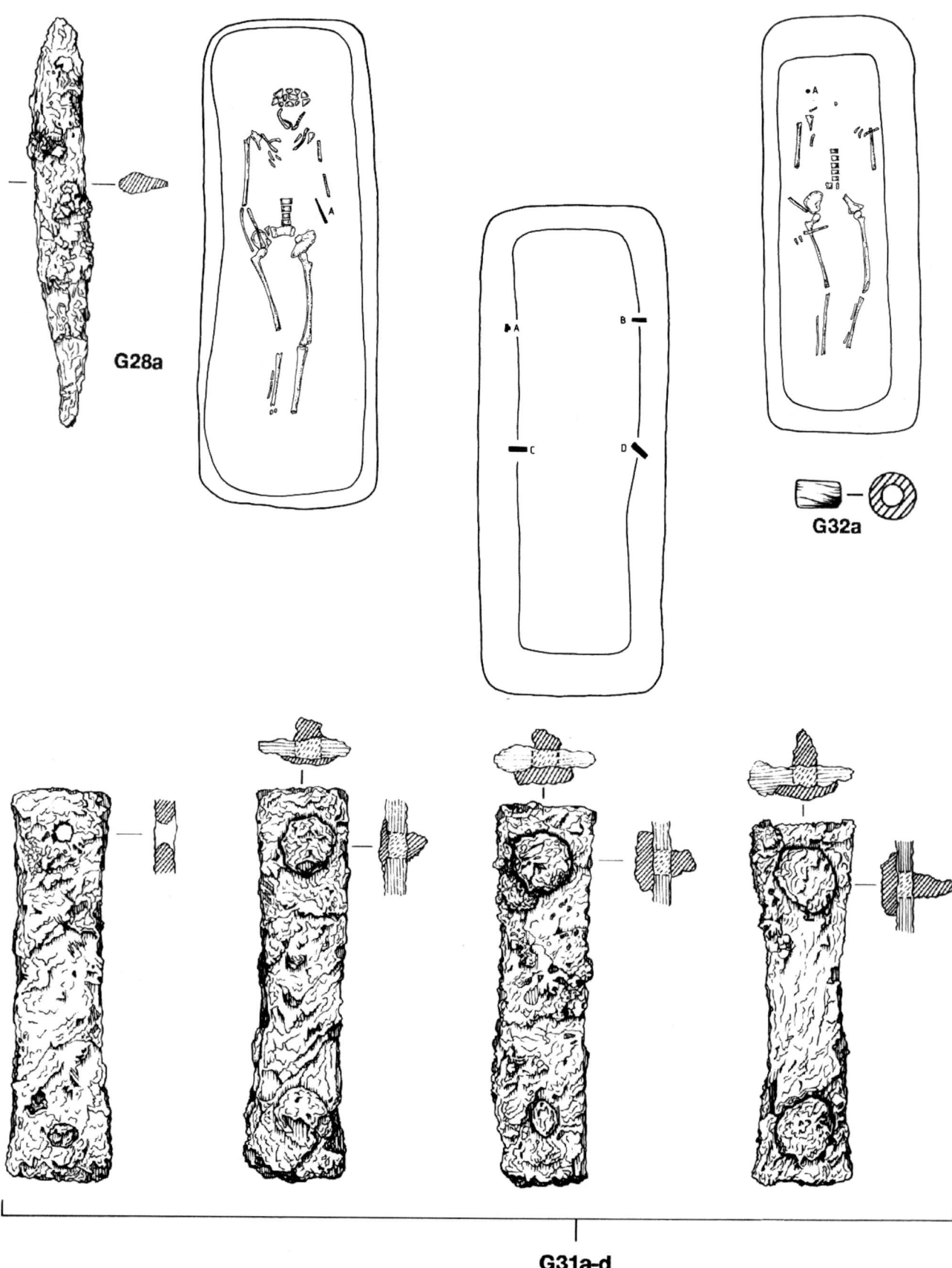

Figure 59. Grave plans and grave finds: 89:28, 89:31 and 89:32 (after Philp and Keller 2002)

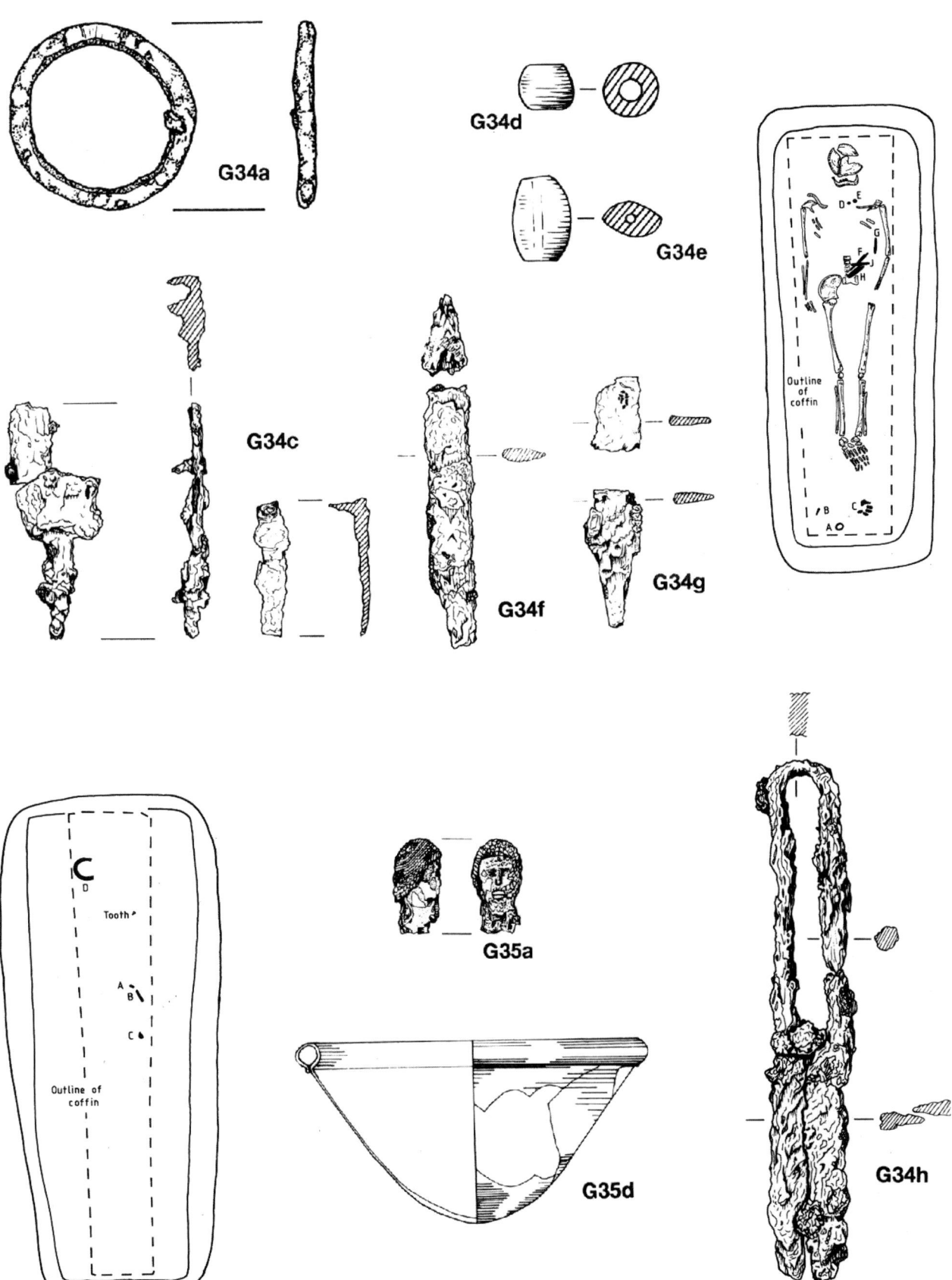

Figure 60. Grave plans and grave finds: 89:34 and 89:35 (after Philp and Keller 2002)

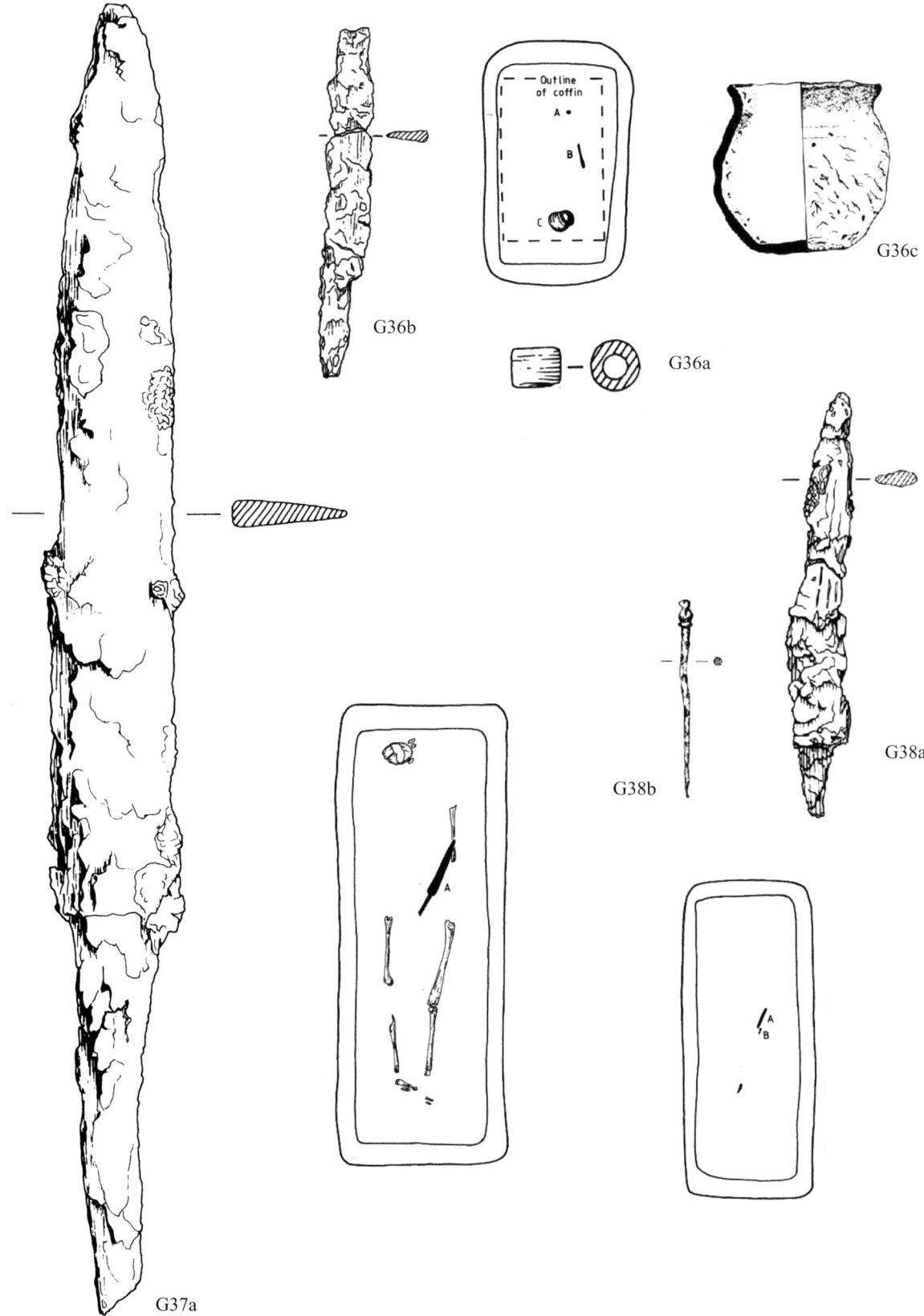

G36b

G36c

G36a

G38a

G38b

G37a

Figure 61. Grave plans and grave finds: 89:36, 89:37 and 89:38 (after Philp and Keller 2002)

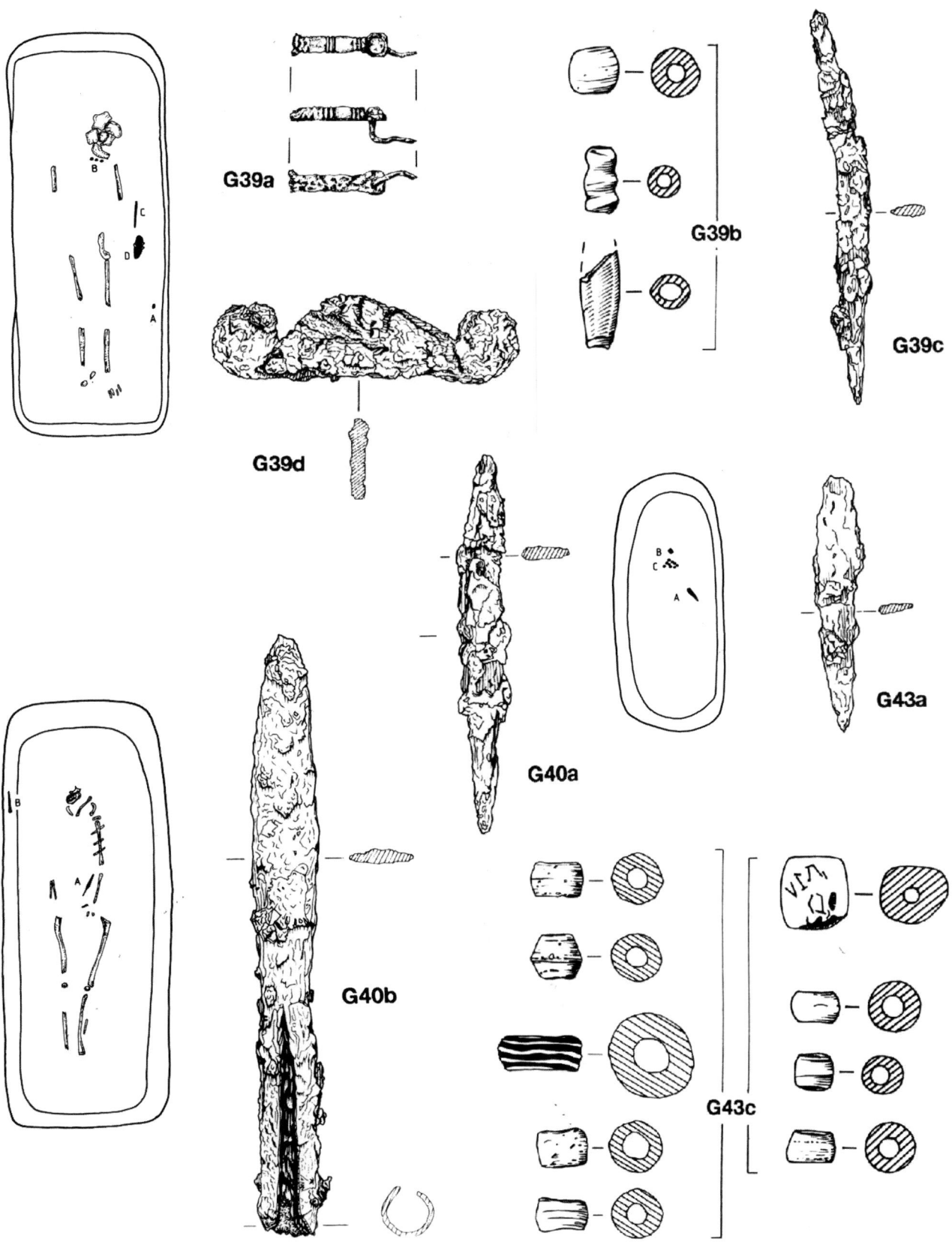

Figure 62. Grave plans and grave finds: 89:39, 89:40 and 89:43 (after Philp and Keller 2002)

Martin Welch

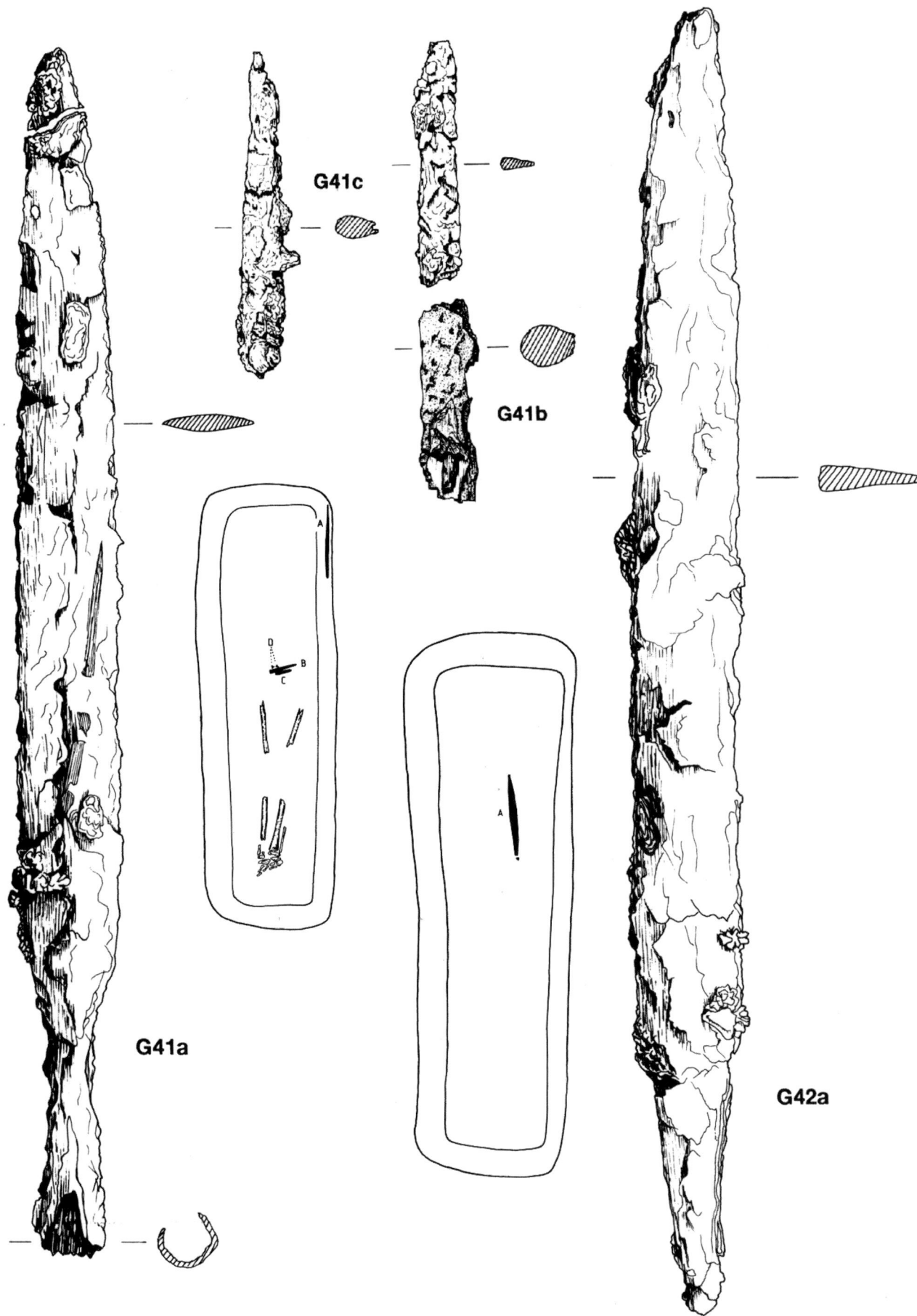

Figure 63. Grave plans and grave finds: 89:41 and 89:42 (after Philp and Keller 2002)

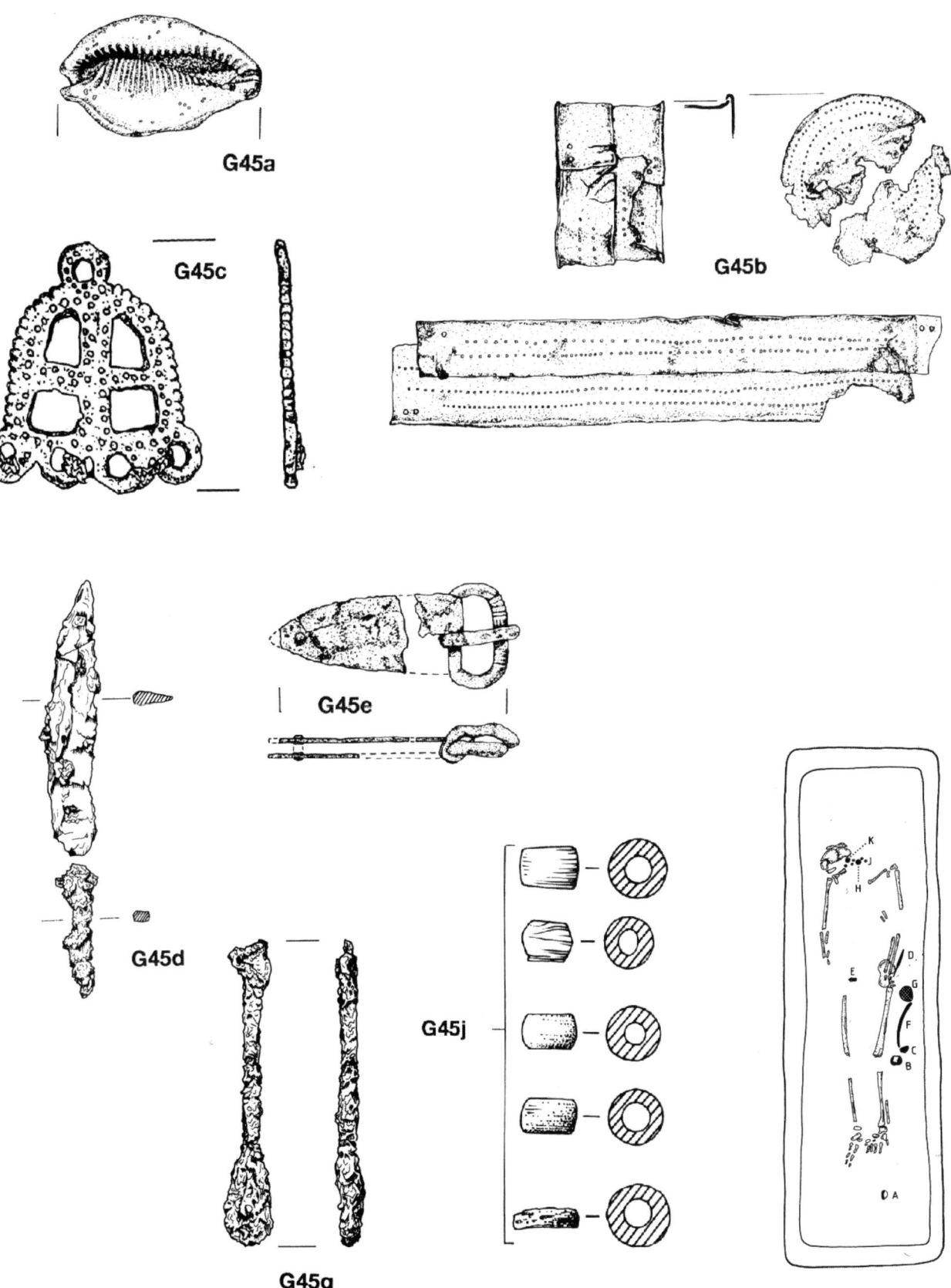

Figure 64. Grave plan and grave finds: 89:45 (after Philp and Keller 2002)

Martin Welch

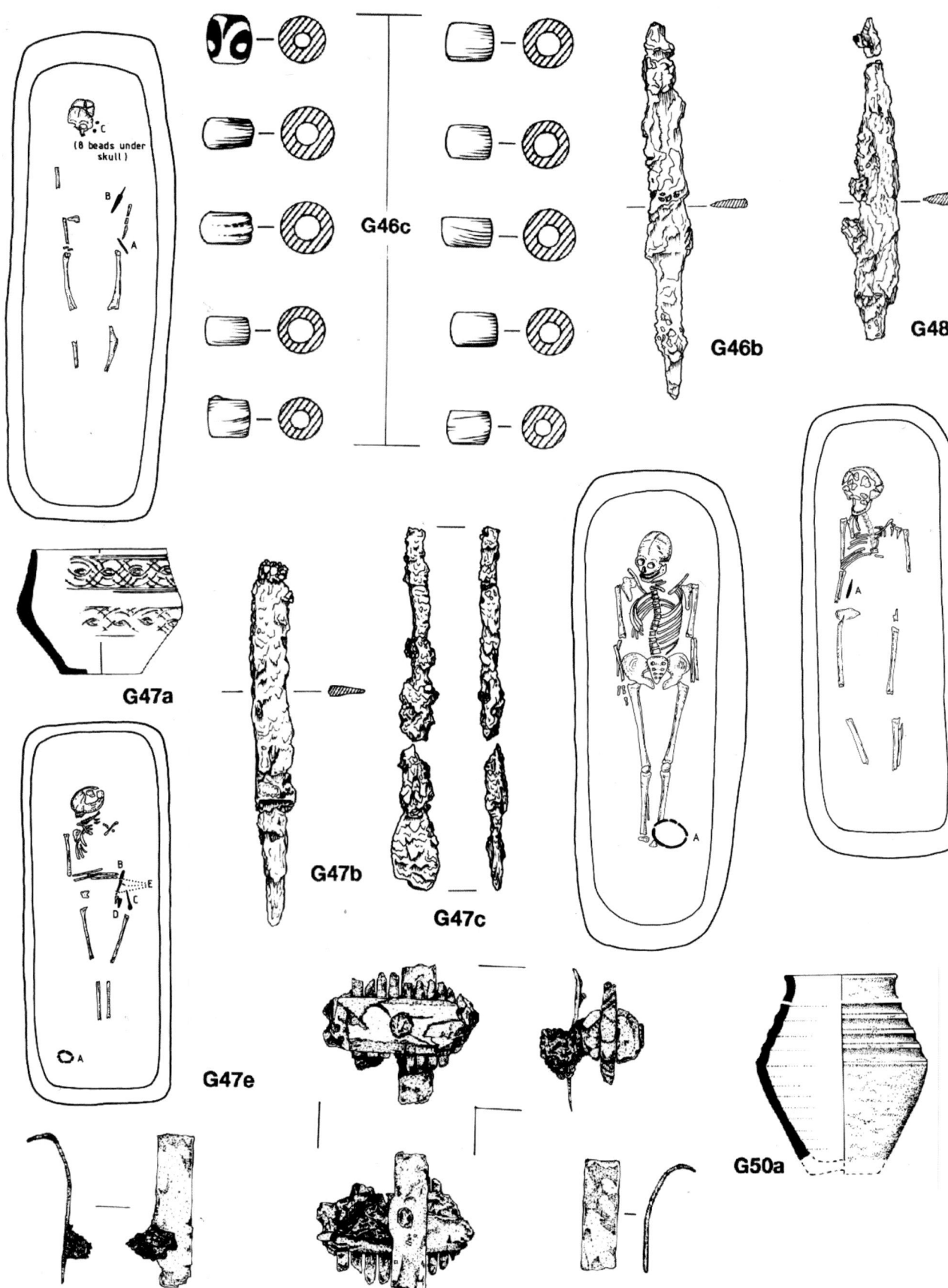

Figure 65. Grave plans and grave finds: 89:46, 89:47 and 89:50 (after Philp and Keller 2002)

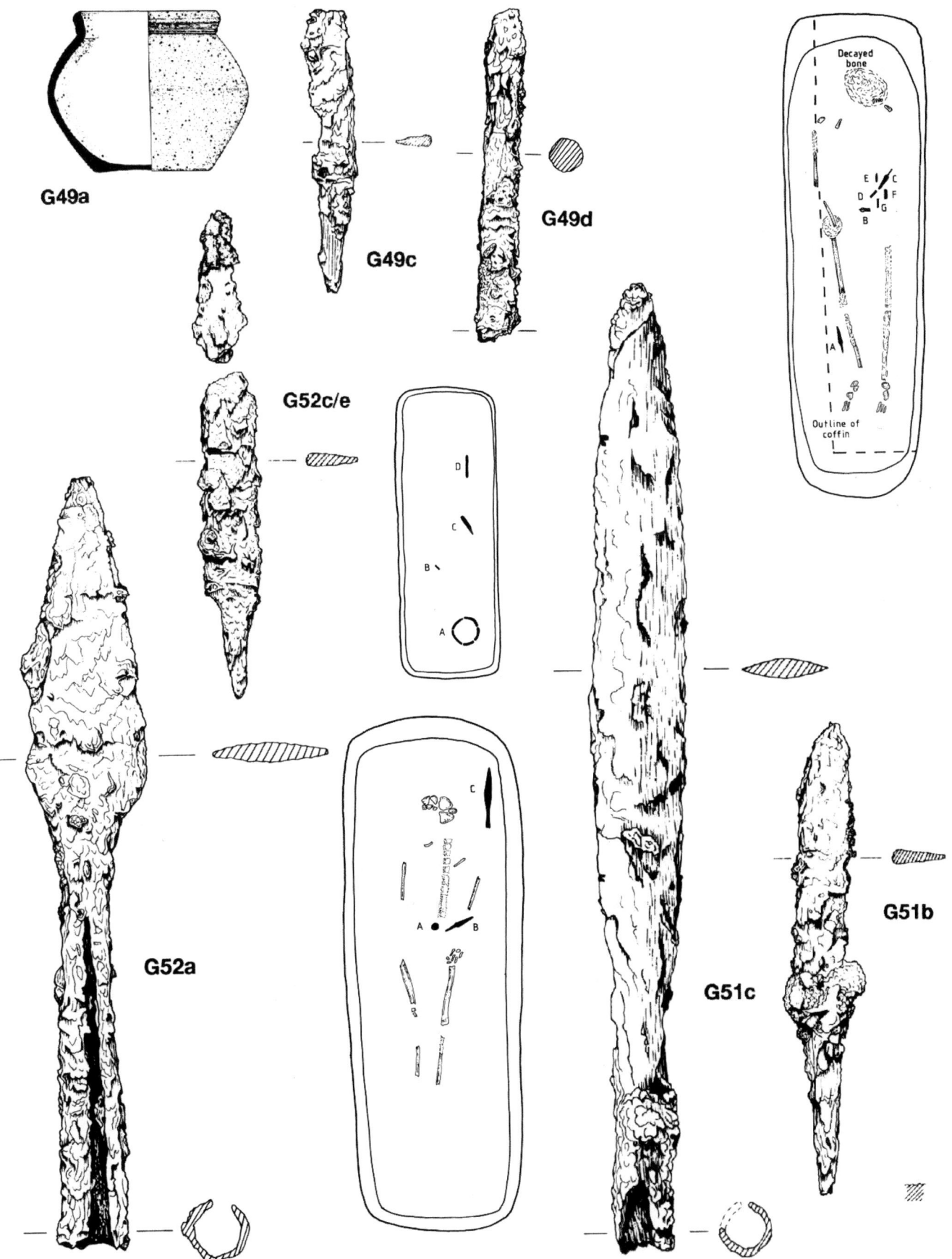

Figure 66. Grave plans and grave finds: 89:49, 89:51 and 89:52 (after Philp and Keller 2002)

Martin Welch

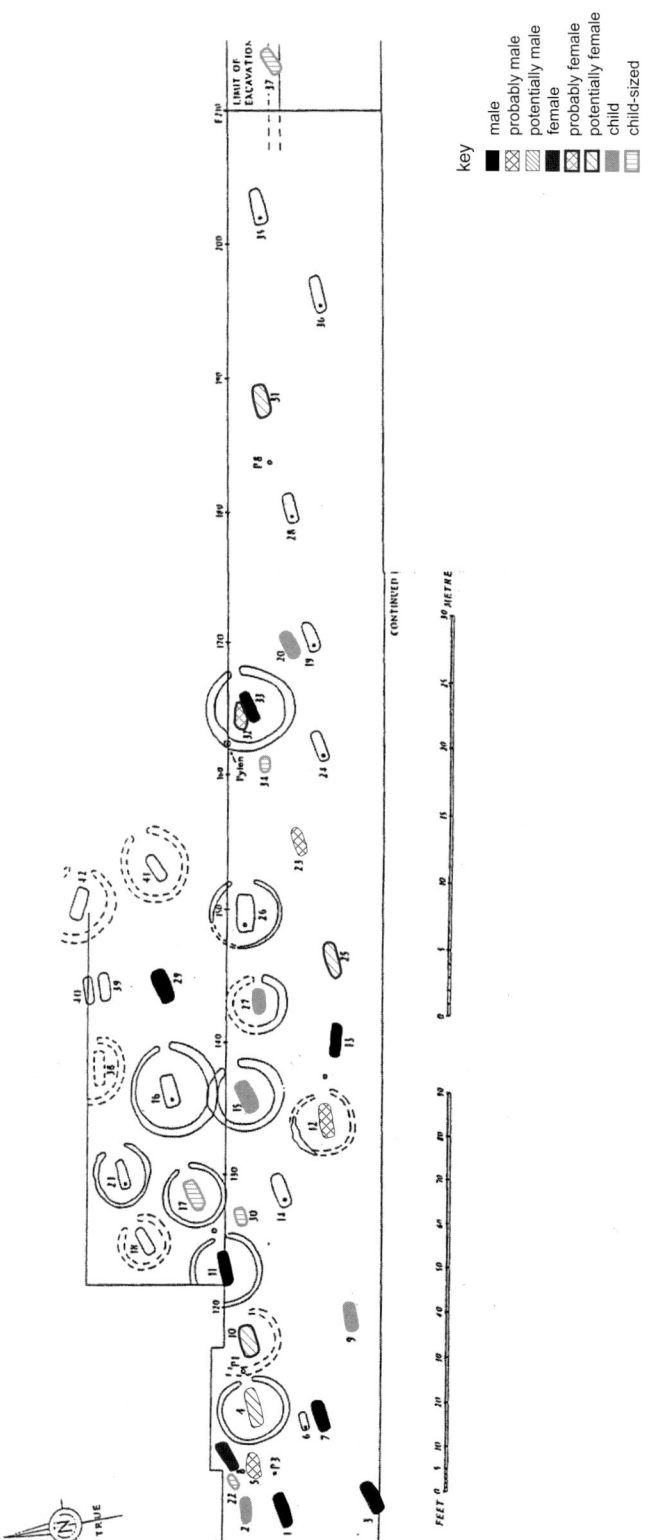

Figure 67. Distribution of biologically sexed burials excavated in 1976 (see Appendix 1 and section 5)

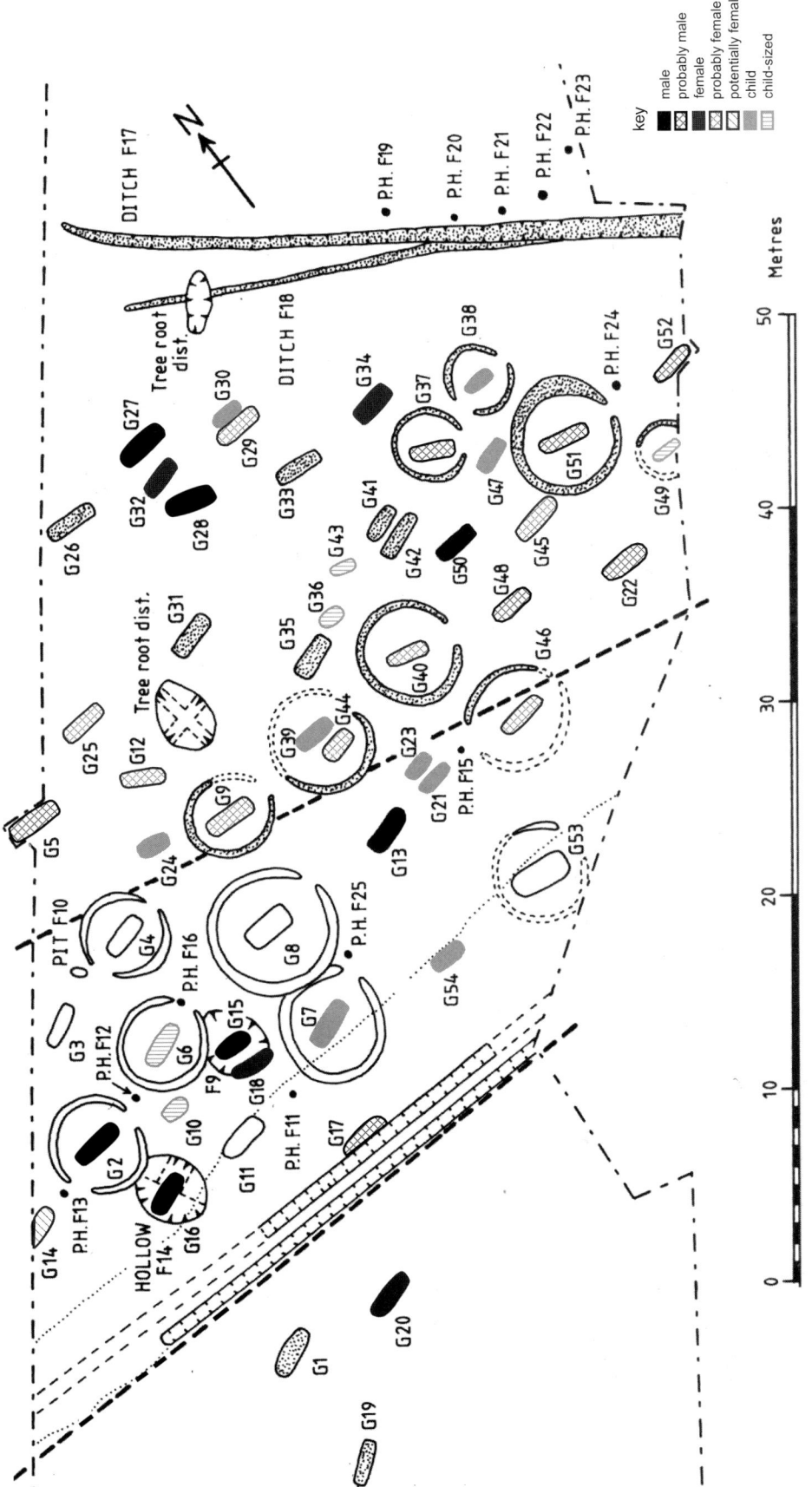

Figure 68. Distribution of biologically sexed burials excavated in 1989 (see Appendix I and section 5)

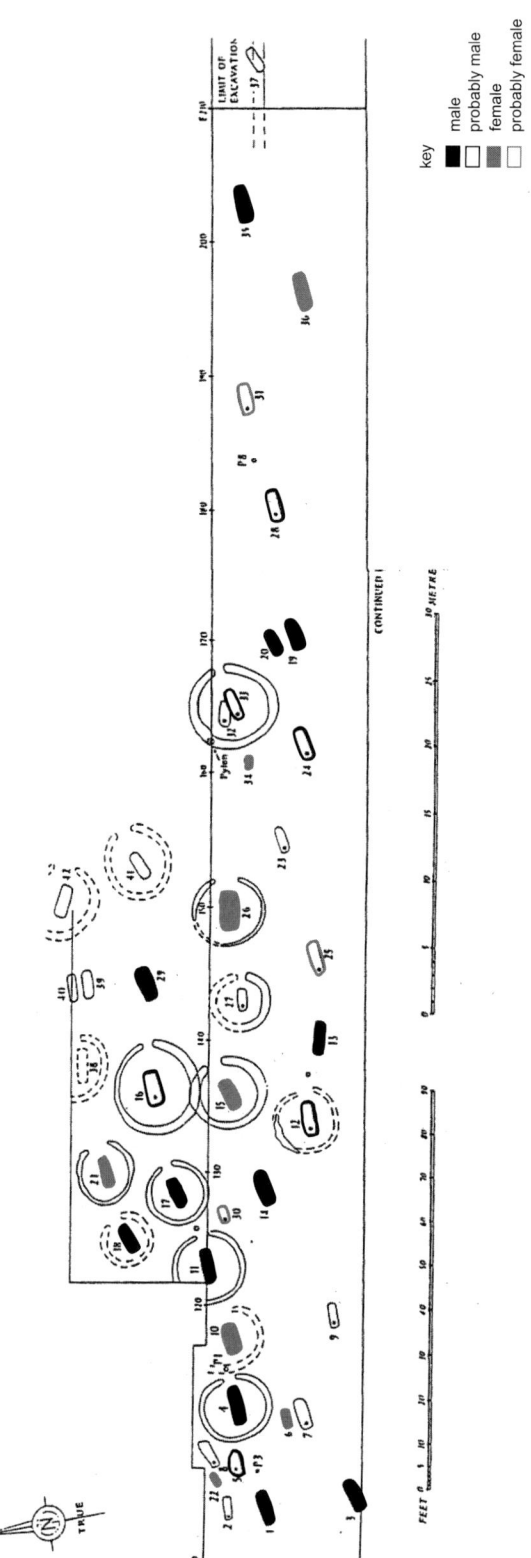

Figure 69. Distribution of culturally gendered burials excavated in 1976 (see Appendix 1 and section 5)

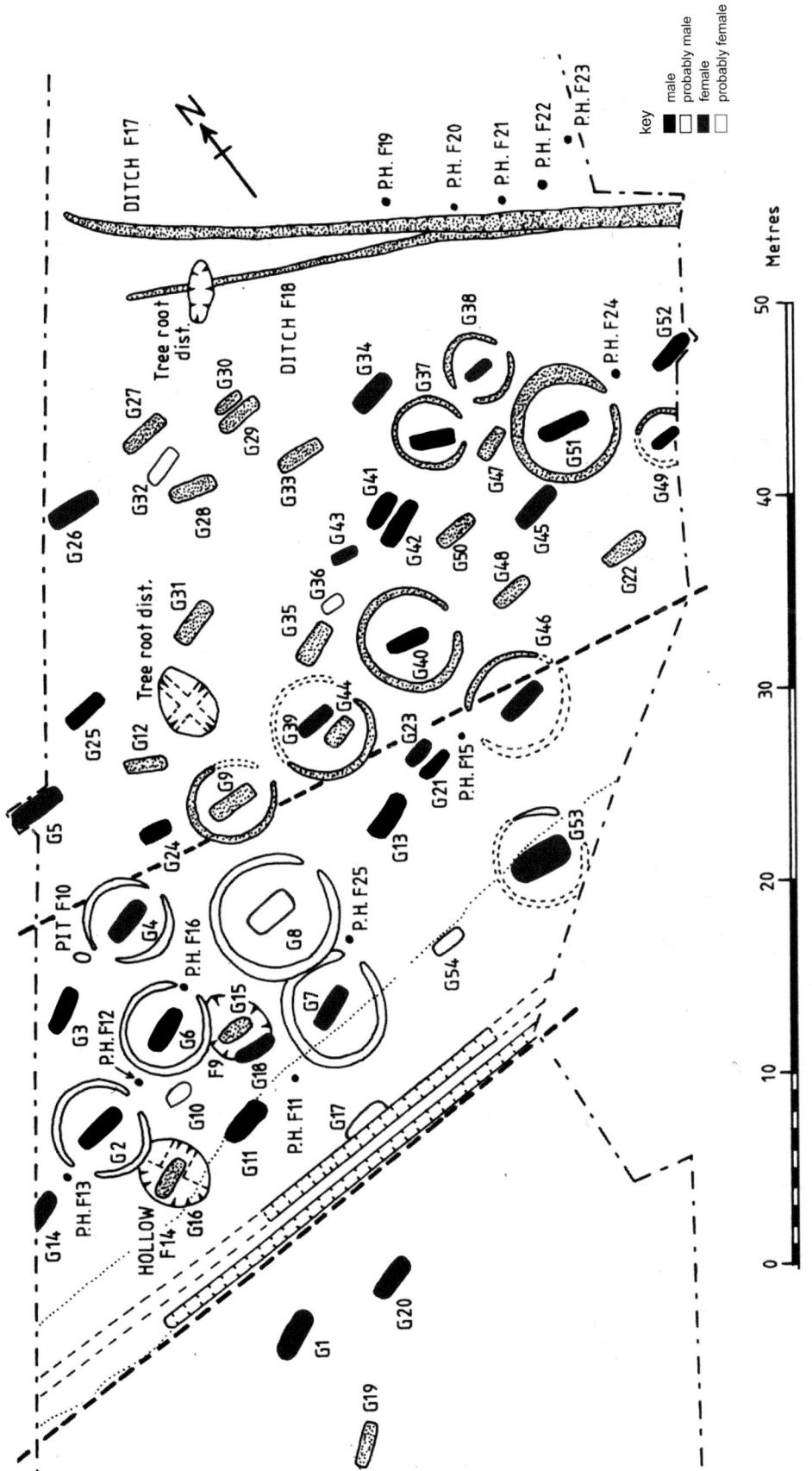

Figure 70. Distribution of culturally gendered burials excavated in 1989 (see Appendix I and section 5)

Martin Welch

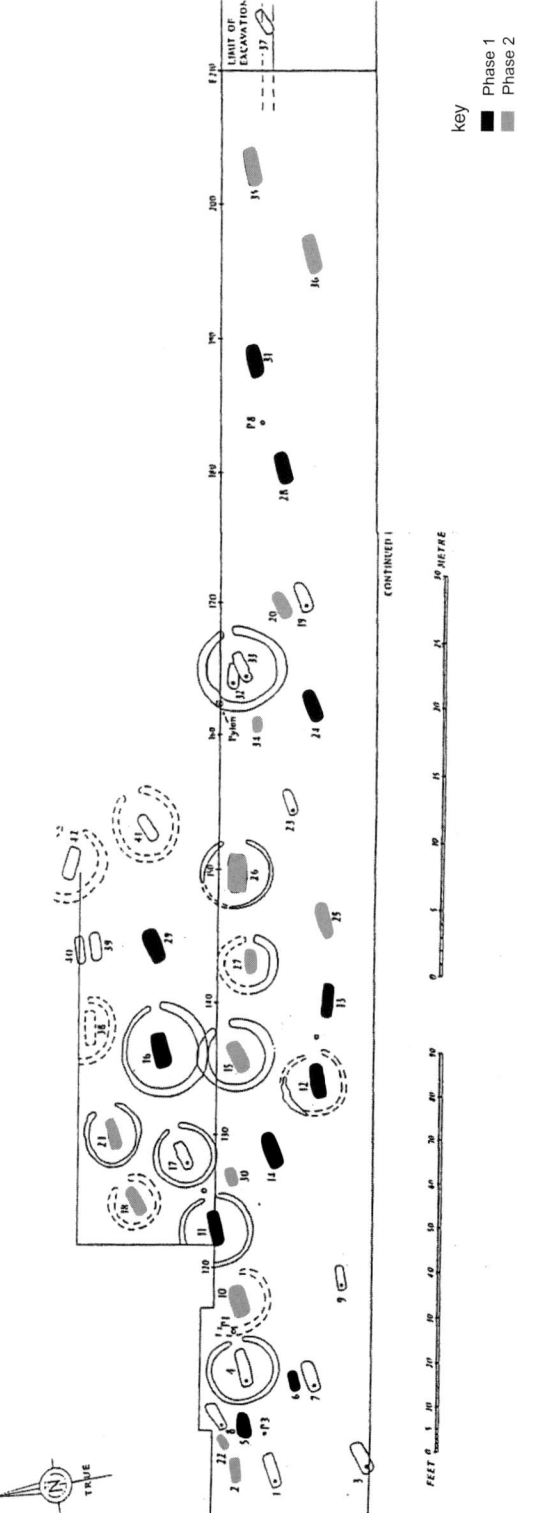

Figure 71. Distribution of burials excavated in 1976 and attributed to phase 1 or phase 2 (see section 5)

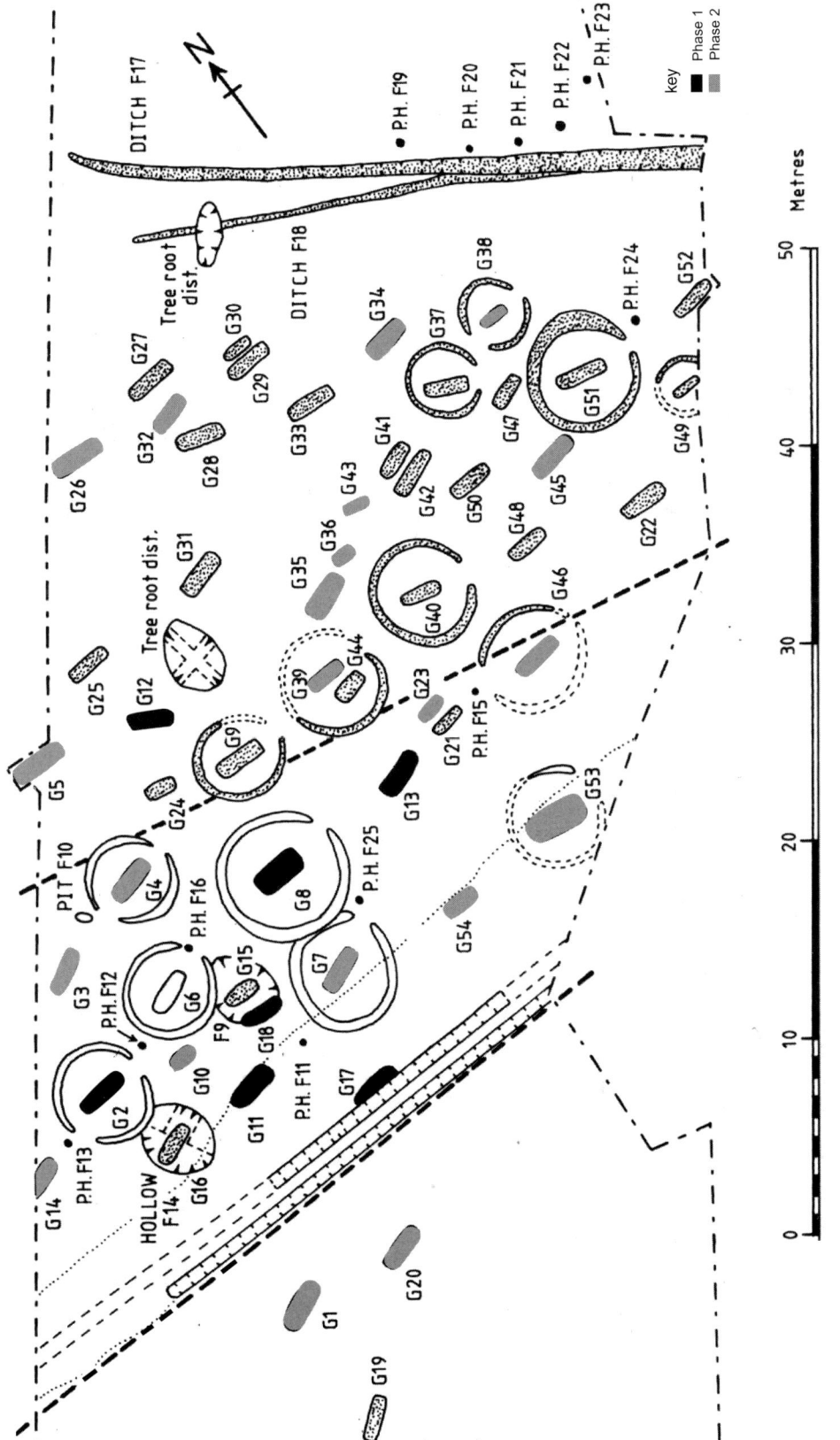

Figure 72. Distribution of burials excavated in 1989 and attributed to phase 1 or phase 2 (see section 5)

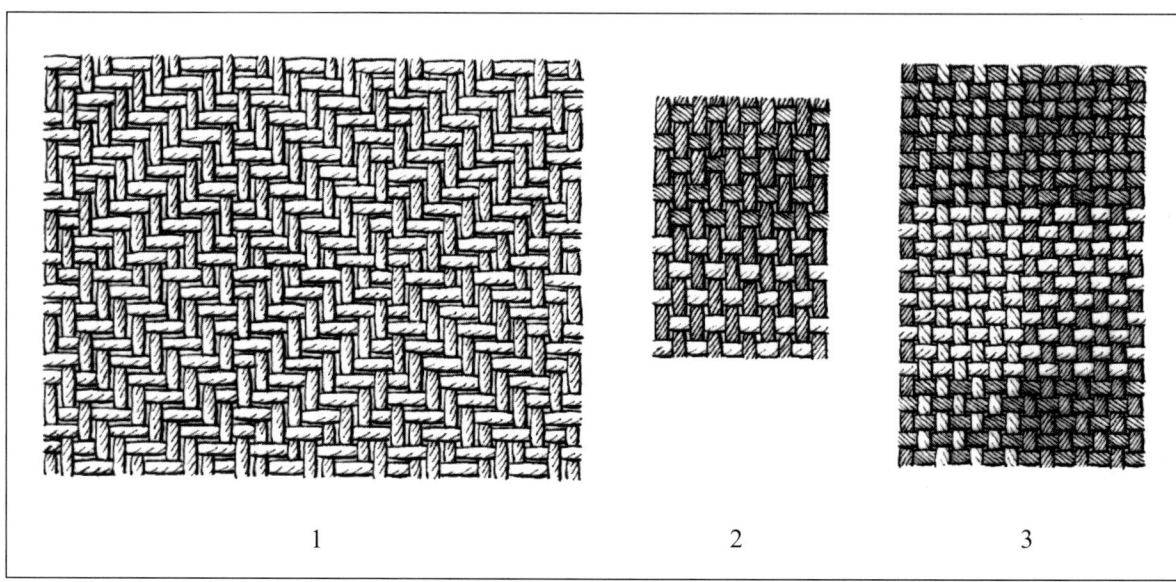

Figure 73. 1: Broken Lozenge Twill: Grave 76:21 (d), 2: Striped Tabby: Grave 76:29 (a); 3: Checked Tabby: Grave 76:14

Table 1. Concordance of graves excavated and numbered in 1976 and 1989

1976	1989	1976	1989	1976	1989	1976	1989	1976	1989
76:1	-	76:23	-	76:16	89.8	-	89:30	-	89:52
76:2	-	76:24	-	76:38	89:9	-	89:31	76:26	89:53
76:3	-	76:25	-	76:30	89:10	-	89:32	76:27	89:54
76:4	-	76:26	89:53	76:14	89:11	-	89:33		
76:5	-	76:27	89:54	-	89:12	-	89:34		
76:6	-	76:28	-	76:29	89:13	-	89:35		
76:7	-	76:29	89:13	76:10	89:14	-	89:36		
76:8	-	76:30	89:10	-	89:15	-	89:37		
76:9	-	76:31	-	-	89:16	-	89:38		
76:10	89:14	76:32	-	76:12	89:17	-	89:39		
76:11	89:2	76:33	-	-	89:18	-	89:40		
76:12	89:17	76:34	-	-	89:19	-	89:41		
76:13	-	76:35	-	-	89:20	-	89:42		
76:14	89:11	76:36	-	-	89:21	-	89:43		
76:15	89:7	76:37	-	-	89:22	-	89:44		
76:16	89:8	-	89:1	-	89:23	-	89:45		
76:17	89:6	76:11	89:2	-	89:24	-	89:46		
76:18	89:3	76:18	89:3	-	89:25	76:42	89:47		
76:19	-	76:21	89:4	-	89:26	-	89:48		
76:20	-	-	89:5	-	89:27	-	89:49		
76:21	89:4	76:17	89:6	-	89:28	-	89:50		
76:22	-	76:15	89:7	-	89:29	-	89:51		

Table 2. Weapon grave combinations correlated with age bands

Adults	Late adolescence to young adult	Sub-adults	Robbed
76:1 (spear) 76:3 (spear) 76:4 (spear) 76:11 (spear) 76:13 (spear) 76:14 (spear and shield) 76:29 (spear) 76:31 (spear) 89:25 (spear) 89:37 (seax) 89:40 (spear) 89:41 (spear) 89:42 (seax) 89:51 (spear) 89:52 (spear)	76:19 (seax and spear) 76:35 (spear)	76:17 (child-sized grave – spear) 76:20 (child 3–6 years – spear) 89:21 (child – spear) 89:24 (child 4–5 years – spear) 89:49 (child-sized grave – spear)	76:18 (spear or ferrule socket)

Table 3 . Demography of the cemetery

	sex n/a	%	male	%	female	%	sex n/d	%
foetal/neonate								
infant								
child	12	19.7						
adolescent								
adult 1			4	6.6	4	6.6		
adult 2			13	21.2	7	11.5		
adult 3			4	6.6	4	6.6		
adult 4			2	3.3	1	1.6		
adult age n/d			5	8.2	3	4.9	2	3.3
all immature	12	19.7						
all adult			28	45.9	19	31.2	2	3.3

plus adolescent/adult 3, child/adolescent/adult 1

Table 4. skeleton inventory arranged by skeleton number

Skeleton	Pres	Assoc with	Bio sex	G/g sex	Mean age	Age range	Stature	Pathologies etc	Comments
76.01	3		M	M	27.5	25.0–30.0	n/d	DE (Carabelli's cusp), S (hypoplasia)	vault and teeth only
76.02	1		n/a	n/d	6.0	child 4.0–8.0	n/a	A (verts), DE (congenital absence)	
76.03	5		M	M	21.0	17.0–25.0	176.8		
76.04	2		??M	M	27.5	25.0–30.0	n/d		extra maxilla: does not fit adjacent skels
76.05	5		?M	?M	60.0+	60.0+	160.8	A (verts), D (2), H, I	
76.06	0			?F (imm)					no bone
76.07	4		M	M	35.0	30.0–40.0	173.2	A (verts), D (2), DE (shovelling)	
76.08	5		F	n/d	30.0	25.0–35.0	162.7	A (verts), D (2), O	
76.09	2		n/a	n/d	9.0	child 7.0–11.0	n/a		
76.10	1		??F	F	30.0	25.0–35.0	n/d		skull and legs only
76.11	4		M	M	30.0	25.0–35.0	170.7	A (verts), D (2)	
76.12	3		?M	?M	30.0	25.0–35.0		A (foot), S (hypoplasia), O	
76.13	2		M	M	45+	45+	n/d	D (1)	
76.14	2		n/d	M	35.0	25.0–45.0			
76.15	4		n/a	F	10.0	child 7.5–12.5	n/a	DE (shovelling), S (cribra)	
76.16	2		n/d	?M	adult	adult	n/d	H	
76.17	0			M (imm)					no bone
76.18	1		n/d	M	n/d	child/adol/adult c. 6.0–c. 20.0	n/d		one tooth only
76.19	3		n/d	M	adol/adult	adolescent/adult	n/d		skull and legs only
76.20	1		n/a	M	5.0	child 3.9–6.3	n/a		
76.21	2		n/d	F	27.5	25.0–30.0	n/d		no bone
76.22	0			F (imm)					
76.23	2		?M	n/d	adult	adult	n/d	D (1)	legs only
76.24	1		n/d	?M	adol/adult	adolescent/adult	n/d		
76.25	2		??F	F	45+	45+	n/d	DE (misshapen molars)	
76.26	1		n/d	F	21.0	17.0–25.0	n/d	H (p/f wear)	vault frags only
76.27	1		n/a	n/d	6.0	child 4.0–8.0	n/a		two frags and teeth only
76.28	1		n/d	?M	27.5	25.0–30.0	n/d		also ossified cartilage
76.29	4		M	M	30.0	25.0–35.0	n/d	A (verts), D (1), E (s/lysis), T	
76.30	0			F (imm)					no bone
76.31	2		??F	?M	35.0	30.0–40.0	n/d	DE (shovelling)	
76.32	2	33	?F	n/d	adult	adult	n/d	D (1)	
76.33	4	32	M	n/d	40.0	35.0–45.0	n/d	A (verts, enth), D (2), S (hypoplasia)	
76.34	0			F (imm)					
76.35	1		n/d	M	adol/adult	adolescent/adult	n/d		skull and leg frags only
76.36	0			F					no bone
76.37	0			n/d (imm)					no bone
89.01	1		n/d	F	adult	adult	n/d		vault frag and teeth only
89.05	2		?M	F	37.0	36.0–38.0	170.9	A (vert)	
89.09	2		?F	n/d	40.0	35.0–45.0	n/d	D (1)	
89.12	2		?F	n/d	25.0	20.0–30.0	n/d	D (1)	

Grave	No.	Sex	Sex	Age	Age range	Stature	Pathology	Notes
89.15	3	M	n/d	33.5	21.0–46.0	169.0	A (verts), D (1), O (bowed femora)	bilateral parry fractures
89.16	3	M	n/d	26.5	19.0–34.0	n/d	A (verts), D (2), O (bowed femora), T	
89.18	4	F	F	35.0	25.0–45.0	161.3	D (2), O (p/f wear)	tibia frags only
89.19	1	n/d	n/d	adult	adult	n/d		
89.20	3	F	F	33.0	30.0–36.0	157.6	DE (shovelling), O x 2 (tooth crowding, p/f wear)	
89.21	1	n/a	M	child	child	n/a		vault, leg and vert frags only
89.22	1	?M	n/d	42.0	40.0–44.0	n/d		face and humerus frags only
89.23	1	n/a	F	5.5	child 5.5	n/a		two teeth only
89.24	1	n/a	M	4.9	child 4.5–5.3	n/a		limb frags and teeth only
89.25	2	?F	M	adult	adult	n/d		
89.26	1	n/d	F	adult	adult	n/d		humerus and femur frags only
89.27	3	M	n/d	27.0	24.0–30.0	n/d		
89.28	3	M	n/d	21.0	18.0–24.0	n/d		
89.29	2	?F	n/d	22.5	20.0–25.0	n/d		
89.30	1	n/a	n/d	5.5	child 4.5–6.5	n/a		vault frags and teeth only
89.31	0	n/d	n/d			n/d		no bone
89.32	3	F	F	40.0	38.0–42.0	n/d		
89.33	0	n/d	n/d					no bone
89.34	3	F	F	35.0	25.0–45.0	152.0	D (1), T	
89.35	1	n/d	n/d	n/d	n/d	n/d		tooth frag only
89.36	0	imm	imm					no bone
89.37	2	?M	M	30.0	25.0–35.0	n/d		
89.38	1	n/d	F (imm)	n/d	n/d	n/d		two unid frags only
89.39	2	n/a	F	10.75	child 9.2–12.3	n/a	DE (Carabelli's cusp)	
89.40	2	?F	?F	19.5	18.0–21.0	n/d		
89.41	2	n/d	M	adult	adult	n/d		
89.42	0		M					no bone
89.43	0		F (imm)					no bone
89.44	3	?F	n/d	27.5	25.0–30.0	n/d	D (1), O (malocclusion)	
89.45	2	?F	F	20.0	16.0–24.0	n/d	D (1)	
89.46	2	?F	F	34.0	32.0–36.0	n/d	O (p/f wear)	
89.47	3	n/a	n/d (imm)	11.1	child 10.9–11.3	n/a	O (tooth crowding; prognathism), S (cribra)	
89.48	3	?M	M	adult	adult	n/d	D (1), O (vertebral ankylosis)	
89.49	0		M (imm)					no bone
89.50	4	M	M	25.0	22.0–28.0	167.1		
89.51	2	?M	M	36.0	35.0–37.0	n/d		
89.52	1	?M	M	32.0	30.0–34.0	n/d		limb frags only

Notes:
1. ??F or ??M means that sex is not determined but that the few sexing characteristics present suggest the given sex
2. Mean age is not the most likely age, but is merely the central point for graphing purposes

Martin Welch

Table 5. skeleton inventory arranged by demographic groups

Skeleton	Pres	Assoc with	Bio sex	G/g sex	Mean age	Age range	Stature	Pathologies etc	Comments
76.01	3		M	M	27.5	25.0–30.0	n/d	DE (Carabelli's cusp), S (hypoplasia)	vault and teeth only
76.02	1		n/a	n/d	6.0	child 4.0–8.0	n/a	A (verts), DE (congenital absence)	
76.03	5		M	M	21.0	17.0–25.0	176.8		
76.04	2		??M	M	27.5	25.0–30.0	n/d		extra maxilla: does not fit adjacent skels
76.05	5		?M	?M	60.0+	60.0+	160.8	A (verts), D (2), H, I	
76.06	0			?F (imm)					no bone
76.07	4		M	M	35.0	30.0–40.0	173.2	A (verts), D (2), DE (shovelling)	
76.08	5		F	n/d	30.0	25.0–35.0	162.7	A (verts), D (2), O	
76.09	2		n/a	n/d	9.0	child 7.0–11.0	n/a		
76.10	1		??F	F	30.0	25.0–35.0	n/d		skull and legs only
76.11	4		M	M	30.0	25.0–35.0	170.7	A (verts), D (2)	
76.12	3		?M	?M	30.0	25.0–35.0	n/d	A (foot, S (hypoplasia), O	
76.13	2		M	M	45+	45+	n/d	D (1)	
76.14	2		n/d	M	35.0	25.0–45.0	n/a		
76.15	4		n/a	F	10.0	child 7.5–12.5	n/a	DE (shovelling), S (cribra)	
76.16	2		n/d	?M	adult	adult	n/d	H	
76.17	0			M (imm)					no bone
76.18	1		n/d	M	n/d	child/adol/adult c. 6.0–c. 20.0	n/d		one tooth only
76.19	3		n/d	M	adol/adult	adolescent/adult	n/d		
76.20	1		n/a	M	5.0	child 3.9–6.3	n/a		skull and legs only
76.21	2		n/d	F	27.5	25.0–30.0	n/d		
76.22	0			F (imm)					no bone
76.23	2		?M	n/d	adult	adult	n/d	D (1)	legs only
76.24	1		n/d	?M	adol/adult	adolescent/adult	n/d		
76.25	2		??F	F	45+	45+	n/d	DE (misshapen molars)	
76.26	1		n/d	F	21.0	17.0–25.0	n/d	H (p/f wear)	vault frags only
76.27	1		n/a	n/d	6.0	child 4.0–8.0	n/a		two frags and teeth only
76.28	1		n/d	?M	27.5	25.0–30.0	n/d		
76.29	4		M	M	30.0	25.0–35.0	n/d	A (verts), D (1), E (s/lysis), T	also ossified cartilage
76.30	0			F (imm)					no bone
76.31	2		??F	?M	35.0	30.0–40.0	n/d	DE (shovelling)	
76.32	2	33	?F	n/d	adult	adult	n/d	D (1)	
76.33	4	32	M	n/d	40.0	35.0–45.0	n/d	A (verts, enth), D (2), S (hypoplasia)	
76.34	0			F (imm)					no bone
76.35	1		n/d	M	adol/adult	adolescent/adult	n/d		skull and leg frags only
76.36	0			F					no bone
76.37	0			n/d (imm)					no bone
89.01	1		n/d	F	adult	adult	n/d		vault frag and teeth only
89.05	2		?M	F	37.0	36.0–38.0	170.9	A (vert)	
89.09	2		?F	n/d	40.0	35.0–45.0	n/d	D (1)	

89.15	3	M	M	33.5	21.0–46.0	169.0	A (verts), D (1), O (bowed femora)	bilateral parry fractures
89.16	3	M	M	26.5	19.0–34.0	n/d	A (verts), D (2), O (bowed femora), T	
89.18	4	F	F	35.0	25.0–45.0	161.3	D (2), O (p/f wear)	tibia frags only
89.19	1	n/d	n/d	adult	adult	n/d		
89.20	3	F	F	33.0	30.0–36.0	157.6	DE (shovelling), O x 2 (tooth crowding, p/f wear)	
89.21	1	n/a	M	child	child	n/a		vault, leg and vert frags only
89.22	1	?M	n/d	42.0	40.0–44.0	n/d		face and humerus frags only
89.23	1	n/a	F	5.5	child 5.5	n/a		two teeth only
89.24	1	n/a	M	4.9	child 4.5–5.3	n/a		limb frags and teeth only
89.25	2	?F	M	adult	adult	n/d		
89.26	1	n/d	F	adult	adult	n/d		humerus and femur frags only
89.27	3	M	n/d	27.0	24.0–30.0	n/d		
89.28	3	M	n/d	21.0	18.0–24.0	n/d		
89.29	2	?F	n/d	22.5	20.0–25.0	n/d		
89.30	1	n/a	n/d	5.5	child 4.5–6.5	n/a		vault frags and teeth only
89.31	0	n/d	n/d			n/d		no bone
89.32	3	F	F	40.0	38.0–42.0	n/d		
89.33	0	n/d	n/d					no bone
89.34	3	F	F	35.0	25.0–45.0	152.0	D (1), T	
89.35	1	n/d	n/d	n/d	n/d	n/d		tooth frag only
89.36	0		imm					no bone
89.37	2	?M	M	30.0	25.0–35.0	n/d		
89.38	1	n/d	F (imm)	n/d		n/d		
89.39	2	n/a	F	10.75	child 9.2–12.3	n/a	DE (Carabelli's cusp)	two unid frags only
89.40	2	?F	M	19.5	18.0–21.0	n/d		
89.41	2	n/d	M	adult	adult	n/d		
89.42	0		M					no bone
89.43	0		F (imm)					no bone
89.44	3	?F	n/d	27.5	25.0–30.0	n/d	D (1), O (malocclusion)	
89.45	2	?F	F	20.0	16.0–24.0	n/d	D (1)	
89.46	2	?F	F	34.0	32.0–36.0	n/d	O (p/f wear)	
89.47	3	n/a	n/d (imm)	11.1	child 10.9–11.3	n/a	O (tooth crowding; prognathism), S (cribra)	
89.48	3	?M	M	adult	adult	n/d	D (1), O (vertebral ankylosis)	
89.49	0		M (imm)					no bone
89.50	4	M	M	25.0	22.0–28.0	167.1		
89.51	2	?M	M	36.0	35.0–37.0	n/d		
89.52	1	?M	M	32.0	30.0–34.0	n/d		limb frags only

Notes:

1. ??F or ??M means that sex is not determined but that the few sexing characteristics present suggest the given sex

2. Mean age is not the most likely age, but is merely the central point for graphing purposes

Table 6 . textile inventory

Grave	Object	Position Textile	Fibre	Spin	Weave	Count	Measurement	Comments
76:2	1. Iron buckle	on plate & ring [loop]	replaced	Z/Z	tabby	c.12/12	2.0 x 1.3	under replaced leather, ?belt
76:4	4. Iron buckle	underneath	(a) replaced	Z/Z	tabby	17–18/14	c.5.0 x 5.0	2 layers; ?weft alternate coarse & fine, ?pick & pick (Cf. Graves 76:16, 76:10) probably (a), tight folds, ?flax; difference in ?weft not so marked
	3. Iron knife	one side, to other	(a) replaced	Z/Z	tabby	16–17/14	L. 9.0	traces
76:5	2. Iron buckle	other side	(b) replaced	Z/?	twill	n/a	n/a	triple folds; regular spin & weave
		plate & ring [loop]	replaced	Z/S	2/2 twill	11/10–11	1.8 x 1.7	
76:10	4, 7. Iron links, chatelaine	on top	(a) replaced	Z/Z	tabby	n/a	n/a	very solid fragment, ?selvedge of twill or braid, surface deteriorated
		round end link	(b) replaced	Z/Z	2/2 twill	8/7 on 5mm	1.5 x 1.0	deteriorated
76:12	5. Iron buckle		?(b) replaced	Z/?	twill	n/a	n/a	
	6. Wood & metal	metal end	(a) replaced	Z/Z	tabby	9/7 on 5mm	L.c.3.0cm	ridged pick & pick as in Grave 76:4, folds; coarser Z threads on wood
	1. Bronze buckle	underside	replaced	Z/Z	tabby	20/19	n/a	small patches; appearance ?flax
76:13	2. Buckle	under plate	(a) replaced	Z/Z	tabby	15/14	c.8.0 x 2.5	scraps, folds, thread irregular; lying over replaced leather
		on top	(b) replaced	Z/S	2/2 twill	13/14	c.2.5 x 2, 1.5 x 1.5	weave open, pulled
76:14	11. Bronze buckle	on metal	replaced	Z,S/Z,S	tabby	22 (11/17 on 5mm)	0.8 x 1.4	fine, even; check 1Z, 6S, 7Z/8Z, 10S, 5Z **fig.73.3**
76:16	7. Bronze buckle	underside	(a) replaced	Z/Z	tabby	11/18 (9 on 5mm)	1.5 x 0.8	2 layers or folds; close count thread varies, ?pick & pick (Graves 76:4, 76:10)
	3. Inlaid buckle	round back & front	? (a) replaced	Z/Z	tabby	6/9 on 5mm	n/a	many folds, appearance suggests flax
76:17	1. Miniature spear	on shaft	(a) replaced	Z/Z	2/2 twill	7/4–5	c.8.0 x 2.0	close ?warp finer, weave open
	3. Iron buckle	side of plate	(b) replaced	Z/Z	?tabby	n/a	n/a	traces, finer than (a)
76:20	4. Iron buckle	top of ring [loop]	replaced	Z/Z	tabby	n/a	n/a	deteriorated; leather underneath
76:21	5. Iron buckle	under & side	?(a) deteriorated	Z/Z	twill	n/a	c.5.0 x 4.0	tight folds, surface damaged
		on top	?(b) deteriorated	n/a	tabby	n/a	n/a	surface covered insect pupae
	9, 11, 12, 13. Iron fragments	on top underneath	(b) replaced	Z/Z	tabby	13/10	5.0 x 2.8	folds, weave open, damaged; leather replaced on 9, 11
	14. Iron buckle & bronze plates	top of plate & ring [loop]	(c) replaced	Z/Z	tabby	16/13	1.5 x 1.0	much closer than (b); replaced leather between plates

Fig	Object	Position	Status	Spin	Weave	Count	Measurement	Remarks
	19. Iron fragment	back	?(b)replaced	Z/Z	tabby	n/a	n/a	fig. 73.1
		front	(d) replaced	Z/S	2/2 broken diamond twill	n/a	3.0 x 1.3, 3.0 x 2.0	
	20, 22, 23, 24. Iron fragments		(b) replaced	Z/Z	tabby	n/a	n/a	traces, as on 9 etc.
	26. Iron disc 27. Iron fragment	both surfaces	(c) replaced	Z/Z	tabby	18/13	n/a	in folds all over
		one side	(d) replaced	Z/S	broken diamond twill	n/a	2.2 x 1.2	
	28. Iron rod	one surface	(b) replaced	Z/Z	tabby	n/a	n/a	
			(d) replaced	Z/S	broken diamond twill	n/a	3.5 x 2.0	folds
	29. Iron rod	other side	(b) replaced	Z/Z	tabby	n/a	n/a	with bunch S-ply threads, ?fringe
			(d) replaced	Z/S	broken diamond twill	n/a	3.5 x 1.3	surface deteriorated
		detached	(c) replaced	Z/Z	tabby	(18/14) 9/7 on 5mm 13/10	n/a	loose scraps with leather
76:26	10. Strap tag	top side	(b) replaced	Z/Z	tabby	8/8 on 5mm	n/a	thread uneven both systems
		underside	replaced	Z/Z	tabby	n/a	4.0 x 2.0	fragment same tabby under leather
76:27	1. Iron & wood		(a) replaced	Z/S	2/2 twill	n/a	n/a	tiny scraps
			(b) replaced	Z/Z	tabby	n/a	n/a	tiny scraps
	5. Iron buckle	top of plate & ring [loop]	?(b) replaced	Z/Z	?tabby	c.7/7 on 5mm	c.3.0 x 2.0	fine, loose spin, open weave, cf. Grave 76:21 (b)
76:28	3. Bronze buckle	top surface, pin [tongue]	a) replaced	Z/Z	tabby	(24–26/16) 12–13 taken on 5mm/ 4 on 2.5mm	0.7 x 0.3	very fine even weave, ?flax
		under surface, & on earth under	b) replaced	Z/Z	tabby	11/10	1.5 x 2.0	clear area; coarser Z threads, & deteriorated remains
76:29	5. Iron buckle	top	a) replaced	Z/Z, S	tabby	21/10 (8 on 8mm)	1.2 x 0.8	stripes ?weft, Z4, S4
	11. Iron belt plate	back of body	a) replaced	Z/Z, S	tabby	20/10	1.2 x 1.0	?weft Z5, S5, S coarser (**fig.73.2**)
	7. Bronze plates	in debris round	?b) replaced	Z/Z	tabby	c.14/15	c.2.2 x 1.6	surface poor; coarser threads below
			a) replaced	Z/Z, S	tabby	est. 20/12	0.4 x 0.9	?weft 5Z, 3S
			c) replaced	Z/Z	?tabby	4/3 on 5mm	n/a	much coarser threads; lines on plates see 10
	8. Double bronze plate	half front	b) replaced	Z/Z	tabby	14/12	1.3 x 1.8	fibres raised, i.e. wool; tiny scrap (a); raised lines on plate

146   *Martin Welch*

Table 6, contd.

	Item	Position	Fibre	Spin	Weave	Count	Measurement	Remarks
	10. Double bronze plate	half, front / other half, front	b) replaced / replaced	Z/Z / ?Z	tabby / n/a	15/11 / n/a	3.6 x 1.4 / n/a	deteriorated leather, coarser threads parallel lines in leather, Z fibres visible See Textile Report Appendix II.1 pp. 58–5[9]
76:34	2. Bronze threadbox, miniature	inside box	flax/flax, silk	Z,S-ply / Z,S	tabby	c.9–10/23 (6/7 threads)	0.7 x 0.3	tiny scrap, folded or perhaps from tubular selvedge; 1 silk thread in same shed as 1 flax near torn end, or sewing (p. 58) tangle detached Z flax, S silk threads (Textile Report Appendix II.1, pp. 58–59)
76:36	8, 9. Chatelaine links	one side	replaced	Z/Z / Z, S-ply	?tabby / n/a	n/a / n/a	c.2.0 x 0.8 / n/a	very loose threads, ?weave threads lying across, ?fringe
	10. Chatelaine links	one side	replaced	Z/Z	tabby	8/6 on 5mm	n/a	patches in layers, all along
	10. Chatelaine links	underside	replaced	Z	n/a	n/a	n/a	coarse threads

Note: the abbreviation "replaced" is used for "fibres replaced by metal oxides"

Note: the spinning direction of yarns is indicated by the letters Z and S, the probable warp thread being placed first

Note: weave counts are given in threads per 1cm, except where otherwise stated

Note: overall measurements of best fragments are given in centimetres

Revised August 1983

The Date and Nature of Wat's Dyke:
A reassessment in the light of recent investigations at Gobowen, Shropshire

Tim Malim and Laurence Hayes

Wat's Dyke is a linear monument consisting of a bank and ditch which ran along the western edge of the Midlands plain. It has been interpreted as a defensive earthwork for the Mercian frontier, but definitive dating has never been established. Excavation in 2006 of a 40 m length of the bank and two trenches through the ditch has revealed a V-shaped ditch up to 8 m in width and 2.7 m deep with an ankle-breaker slot in the base, and an earth and stone bank on its eastern side surviving to over 5 m in width and 0.5 m in height. No timber was used in its construction, although evidence for a marker bank and a well-laid cobbled foundation show that it was carefully planned. A series of optically stimulated luminescence (OSL) dates has provided scientific dating for the infill sequence and buried soil, showing construction and use occurred in the early ninth century, a possible episode of slighting occurring in the mid ninth century, and a deliberate major episode of infill associated with medieval ploughing in the fourteenth century. It is postulated that these dates can be related to historical events to suggest a construction for Wat's Dyke during either the reigns of Cenwulf and Ceolwulf (AD 796–723), or for that of Wiglaf during the 830s.

Introduction

During the summer of 2006 an excavation funded by Fletcher Homes (Shropshire) Limited was undertaken by Gifford on a section of Wat's Dyke immediately to the south of the settlement of Gobowen, near Oswestry in Shropshire (Fig. 1). The excavation took place in advance of the construction of an access road and roundabout for a scheme of residential housing, focussing on a 40 m stretch of the monument which would be directly affected by the construction works.

Although the bank of Wat's Dyke is clearly visible as a low, raised linear earthwork in the field immediately to the south of the development area, only faint surface features were recognisable within the line of the proposed access road. However, an evaluation undertaken in January 2006 located the line of both the ditch and bank in three trial trenches.[1] The infilled ditch was *c.* 8 m wide, and situated to the west of a robbed-out but still partially surviving bank up to 5 m wide. A total of six phases of activity were identified including the original buried land surface, construction of the ditch and bank and episodes of erosion and in-filling. The condition of preservation revealed by this evaluation identified the need for a larger-scale and more detailed excavation to

be undertaken prior to construction of the access road, a programme of archaeological work which was made a condition of planning permission.

Previous work elsewhere on Wat's Dyke has failed to establish a conclusive date for the monument, so one of the key research aims of the present investigation was to obtain samples for scientific dating. Three techniques were attempted: Optically Stimulated Luminescence (OSL) of the sediments within the ditch, radiocarbon determination of carbonised material, and earthworm casts, an experimental method being trialled by Matt Canti of English Heritage.

Background

The monument of Wat's Dyke is a linear earthwork which runs from the River Morda at Maesbury (the important Mercian estate of *Meresbyrig* to the south of Oswestry)[2] to Basingwerk on the Dee Estuary (Fig. 1), a distance of approximately 65 km, passing Oswestry and Yr Hên Dinas (Old Oswestry hillfort), Gobowen, Ruabon and Wrexham.[3] At its southern end the dyke meets the River Morda which has been straightened over a distance of *c.* 4 km, perhaps representing one of the earliest examples

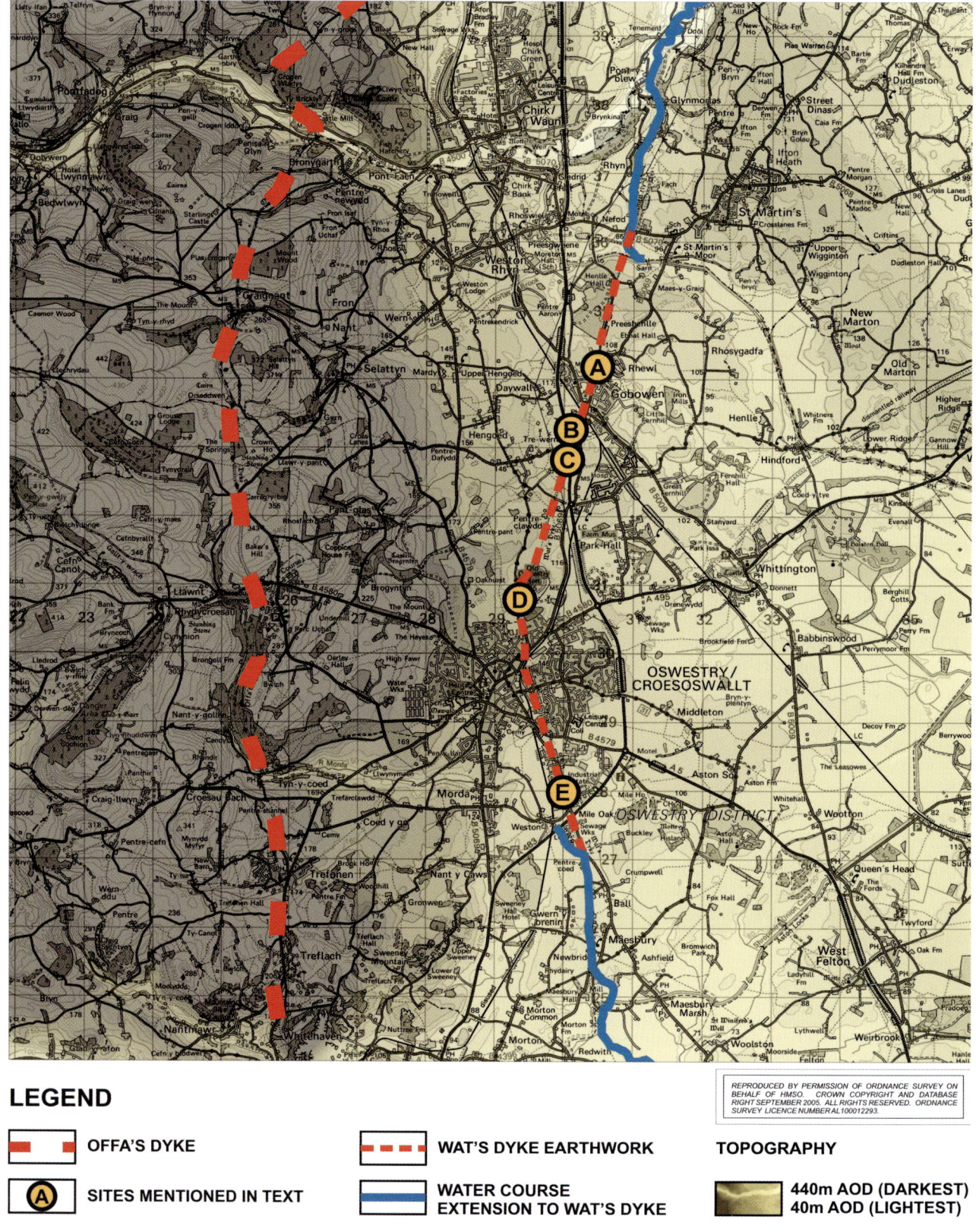

LEGEND

▬ ▬ ▬ OFFA'S DYKE

Ⓐ SITES MENTIONED IN TEXT

‑ ‑ ‑ ‑ WAT'S DYKE EARTHWORK

▬▬▬ WATER COURSE
EXTENSION TO WAT'S DYKE

TOPOGRAPHY

■ 440m AOD (DARKEST)
40m AOD (LIGHTEST)

Figure 1. Map showing the location of Wat's Dyke on the western edge of the Midland plain (light tone) and its relationship to Offa's Dyke on west-facing slopes of the Welsh hills (dark tone). Sites shown include: A: Bryn y Castell; B: Gobowen excavation 2006; c: Pentrewern excavation 1984–5; D: Old Oswestry excavation 1992; E: Mile Oak excavation 1997

of post-Roman hydraulic engineering in Britain,[4] and in keeping with examples of contemporary continental defensive canals instigated by strong kingship such as Kanhave in Denmark.[5] Wat's Dyke has been subjected to numerous archaeological investigations along its length which have demonstrated that it comprises a ditch of between 6 and 8 m wide and up to 4 m deep, flanked by a bank on its eastern side up to 1.5 m in height and 8 m wide.[6]

Wat's Dyke forms part of a series of earthworks, including Offa's Dyke and the Whitford Dyke, which were generally considered to be an eighth century AD boundary between Wales and Mercia. These have been attributed to Offa by Bishop Asser, writing in the ninth century, though differences in the constructional techniques employed on Wat's Dyke, and its more easterly location, have led to the suggestion that it is earlier than the other dykes, perhaps attributable to Æthelbald (AD 716–57).[7]

Despite the work that has been carried out on Wat's Dyke, it has remained inconclusively dated, whether through historical study, artefactual assessment or scientific dating methods. The controversy surrounding the age of Wat's Dyke is clearly demonstrated by the variety of hypotheses and date ranges put forward by various authors, and the vehemence with which new hypotheses are denounced. For example, Steve Blake and Scott Lloyd attempted to demonstrate from a variety of historical sources that Offa's and Wat's dykes were in fact built during the reign of Septimius Severus (AD 197–211), which is vigorously disputed by Keith Matthews.[8] Hugh Hannaford obtained a single radiocarbon date from a hearth or cooking fire on the buried ground surface immediately below the bank of Wat's Dyke following an excavation at Mile Oak, Oswestry in 1997.[9] This gave calibrated date ranges of AD 411–561 (1 sigma) and AD 268–630 (2 sigma). Hannaford considers a fifth century date for construction to be the most likely, probably carried out by a small British kingdom centred on Wroxeter – the former *civitas* of the Cornovii. It is dangerous, however, to place too much weight on a date obtained from a single radiocarbon sample, given the huge margin of error that is implicit in both the recovery of the sample and the dating method itself. Furthermore, the sample was recovered from below the bank, and therefore predates the construction of the dyke by an unknown period of time.

The only artefactual evidence to have been recovered from the ditch itself was found during an excavation at Mynydd Isa, Flintshire. Here a broken annular loom weight of middle Anglo-Saxon date (AD 650–800) was recovered from what appeared to be a clay hearth above the lower 0.05 m of primary fill of the ditch, suggested to be no later than thirty years older than the construction of the dyke itself (assuming that the ditch had never been cleaned and that the primary fill began to accumulate immediately following construction).[10] Frustratingly, although this is the best dating tool recovered from the ditch thus far, the age-range of the loom weight covers the majority of the

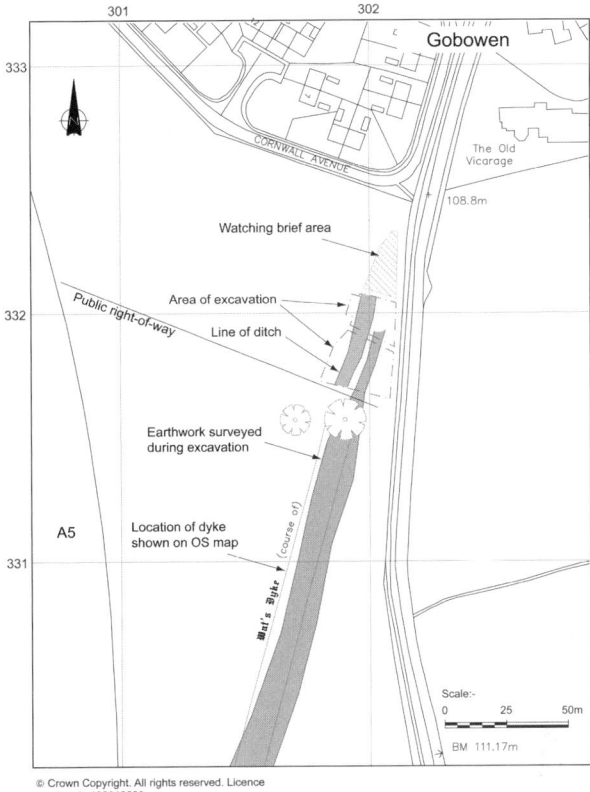

Figure 2. Detailed location plan of excavation area at Gobowen. Grey stipple shows surviving earthwork bank as surveyed in 2006

suggested dates for the monument's construction, and brings us no closer to a definitive conclusion.

Keith Matthews has considered at length the existing evidence surrounding Wat's Dyke and has explored the potential political situations under which it may have come to be built.[11] He dismissed outright the earlier dates for the dyke postulated by Blake and Lloyd and Hannaford, and suggested that the dyke should be viewed in terms of the relationship between two adjoining states, rather than the relationship between Angle and Briton. As the political situation within Wales was in a state of almost perpetual flux during the post-Roman period, and the expansion of Mercia was gradual and complex, Matthews suggested that, in the absence of absolute dating for the monument, an assessment of the political history of Powys and northwest Mercia from the fifth century onwards may help to determine the context in which it was built. He concluded that it is unlikely Wat's Dyke was built to defend Wroxeter or Chester, as neither option would have made strategic sense, but considered it a more attractive proposition that the dyke was built to defend the newly acquired Mercian territory of Cheshire in the mid to late seventh century, under the rule of Æthelræd I (AD 675–704), though his suggestion that the dyke could have been built in one year by one hundred men seems wildly optimistic.

Figure 3. Photographs of the site in its landscape context: top looking south across evaluation trenches (earthwork bank can be seen between two trees); base looking north from Pentrewern (the excavation is between two trees)

Figure 4. John Evans' 1795 map of North Wales showing place names, topographic detail, water-courses, and line of Offa's and Wat's dykes

EXCAVATION AT GOBOWEN 2006

Location, geology and topography

The site was located on agricultural land immediately to the south of Gobowen, to the west of the B5069 Oswestry Road and centred on NGR SJ 3019 3318 (Figs 2 and 3). The land use immediately prior to the development was pasture, although the excavation demonstrated that the land had also been ploughed in the past. A public right of way crossed the open field from east to west, marked by a line of mature oaks. This path delineated the southernmost extent of the development area.

The local drift geology comprises thick glacial and periglacial sands, gravels and boulder clays of the Pleistocene period described as undifferentiated fluvio-glacial deposits within the British Geological Survey map for the area. These extend southward into northeast Shropshire from the Cheshire basin, producing a gently rolling landscape. The underlying solid geology comprises Triassic soft red sandstones and pebble beds.

The topography of the site was generally flat at around 110 m AOD (Above Ordnance Datum), with a raised linear earthwork marking the course of Wat's Dyke visible in the field to the south running in a south-southwesterly direction from the public right of way towards the southern end of the field. In the northeast corner of the field there was a slight depression, possibly marking the location either of a former

pond or of a borrow pit for the adjacent Oswestry Road.

One of the earliest maps of the area, John Evans' 1795 map of North Wales (Fig. 4), shows Wat's and Offa's Dykes in relation to settlements, watercourses, roads and relief, and thus gives a very good impression of the wider landscape and topographical setting for the course of the monument and its specific setting at Gobowen. In common with the normal location of Wat's Dyke, this section runs along the western edge of the plain, on a slight ridge or eminence providing good views westwards towards the mountains. The excavated area lay between Gobowen (an ancient cross-roads) and the farmstead of Pentrewern to the south, in a field known as Big Meadow from the north-eastern corner of the 1840 Selattyn parish Tithe map. Further south the dyke crosses three streams that drain eastwards to join the River Perry as it flows towards the Severn from its origin to the northwest of Gobowen. Old Oswestry hillfort was the focus of this southward alignment, and the dyke can be seen exiting the fort on the south side to head into Oswestry itself. To the north of the excavated area higher land is shown between Gobowen and St Martins, and this ridge forms the watershed between two river valleys, with those streams on the north side flowing northwards to join the Dee. The focus of the alignment here might have been another hillfort at Bryn y Castell, the name of an existing farm, as suggested by Thomas Pennant.[12] The site therefore lies at

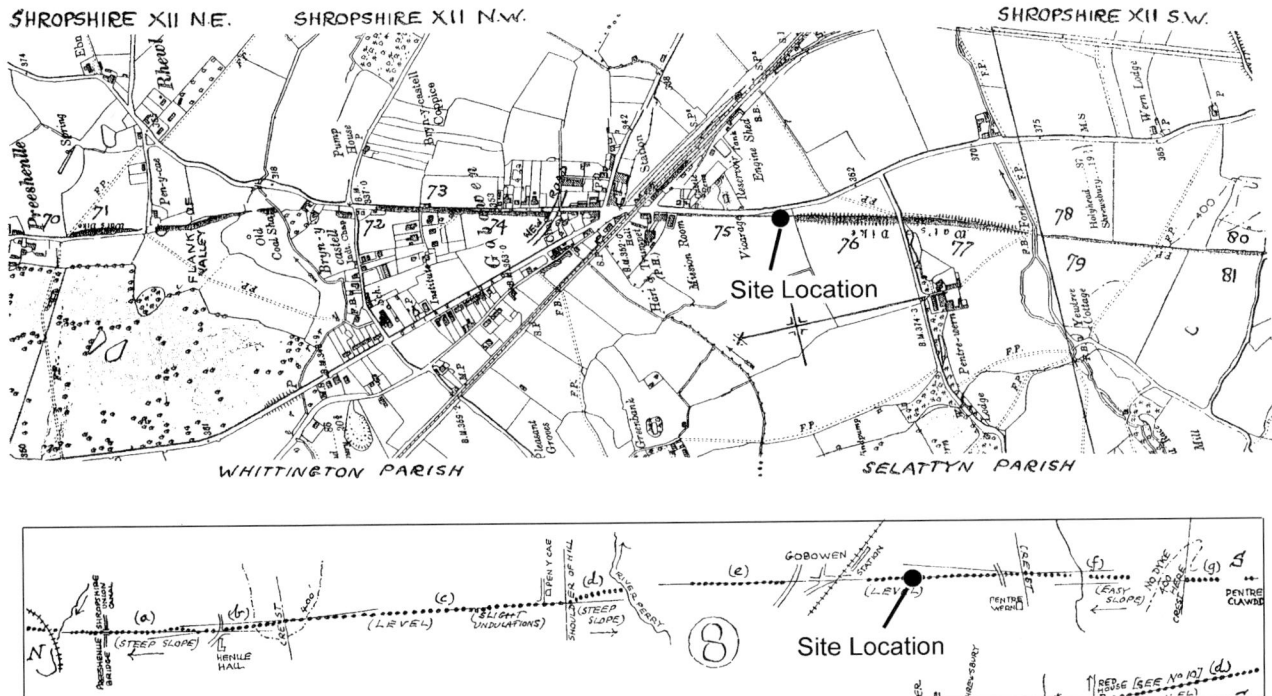

Figure 5. Reproduction of Cyril Fox's field survey for the Presshenlle to Pentrewern section of Wat's Dyke (Fox 1955: Figures 109 and 119). Note slight change in alignment in area of Pentrewern in area excavated in 1984–5 (Cane 1996)

an important juncture, just within the valley of the River Perry opening up to the east and south, and just south of the watershed from which drainage runs northwards to follow the River Dee to the sea at Chester. The detailed alignment of Wat's Dyke and its topographical setting in this area is described by Fox, in which the location for the present excavation is summarised under Field 75, with the better preserved section in Field 76 immediately to the south: "The Dyke forms a broad ploughed-down ridge in field 76. It is straightly aligned, and its line when projected exactly coincides with the visible Dyke in field 74: moreover there are traces on the same line in field 75. Since the ground is level we can deduce its course through Gobowen village with certainty…" *i.e.* following the line of the main road. His figure 109: "Presshenlle to Pentre-Wern" is reproduced here (Fig. 5) together with Figure 119 area 8,e and 8,f.[13] Note the substantial earthwork shown in Fields 76 and 77 but not in Field 75, and also the slight change in alignment of the Dyke in Field 77, the location for the 1980s investigations reported by Cane.

Aims, objectives and strategy

Research aims for the excavation were devised by Tim Malim with paramount importance given to the need for establishing a firm date for the monument. A secondary aim was to record the physical morphology of the bank and to study any evidence for structural elements within it, such as timber lacing or a revetment. In addition, sample excavation of the ditch was important, in order to test the accuracy of the contrasting published profiles, especially from the two most recent investigations.[14]

The specific objectives were: to retrieve samples for absolute dating techniques in order to help establish a chronological framework for the construction and use of the monument; to reveal the method and phases of construction, use and abandonment of the structure including any evidence for timber elements (revetment, boxed rampart etc) or artefacts; to record the morphology, profile and character of the monument; to retrieve samples for palaeoenvironmental analysis; and to further understand the historical context of the monument.

In order to best achieve these aims and objectives, a strategy of open area excavation was implemented to study a length of the bank, rather than just a section through it, as post-holes and constructional episodes need to be seen over a reasonable area in order for a pattern to be discerned. For the ditch, however, an excavation strategy of trenching in two locations was designed so as to obtain representative samples of the profile and infill sequence. As part of the overall strategy, extensive sampling for scientific analyses of the contemporary environment and chronological sequence was undertaken, to gain a fuller understanding of the dyke's origin and development.

Figure 6. Photograph of excavation area looking southeast, with stepped sections in Slot 2. Rise of bank and white stone foundation of bank core can be seen running between archaeologists and tree

Methodology

The main excavation area (*c.* 800 m²) was set out and the topsoil removed by machine under archaeological supervision. A contingency area was also marked and stripped to the north. Although this was not excavated, a watching brief was carried out here on the 24 October 2006 during the construction of the access road.

Two deep sections of 5 m basal width were excavated across the ditch of Wat's Dyke, corresponding to the locations of Trenches 1 and 2 from the evaluation of the site in January 2006. The upper fills were removed by machine, and the sides stepped to ensure safe working (Fig. 6). The lower fills were excavated by hand allowing the original profile of the ditch to be accurately recorded. Palaeoenvironmental samples were taken from the lower (primary) fills of the ditch, and samples for OSL dating were collected by Dr Jean-Luc Schwenninger and David Peat (Research Laboratory for Archaeology and the History of Art, University of Oxford) from six fills within the ditch. The southernmost section was labelled Slot 1, the northernmost Slot 2 (Fig. 7).

A 25 m length of the surviving bank to the east of the ditch was cleaned by hand, planned and examined for evidence regarding its method of construction, maintenance and work-gangs. This was then removed by hand in lengths to recover any potential dating material and palaeoenvironmental

evidence (Fig. 8). Following removal of the bank, the buried soil beneath was cleaned by hand and examined for features, dating evidence and palaeoenvironmental evidence, and then this in turn was removed to the top of the underlying drift geology. All features cut below the level of the buried soil were hand-excavated. The fills of discrete features were manually sieved for small finds, and a metal detector was used to locate any coherent signals which could then be hand-excavated. The spoil heaps were also scanned with a metal detector.

The sampling strategy employed on-site was developed during the works in consultation with the English Heritage Regional Science Advisor, Palaeoecology Research Services Limited and the Research Laboratory for Archaeology and the History of Art at Oxford. Bulk samples were taken from the ditch fills, buried soil and fills of discrete features, and column samples were taken from the buried soil for pollen analysis. Samples were also taken in a column from the buried soil, bank material and overlying earth to inspect for calcium carbonate granules produced by earthworms as part of an ongoing research project into experimental dating techniques by English Heritage.

The excavation was carried out between 24 July and 5 September 2006 during a particularly hot and sunny period, although the weather became increasingly unsettled towards the end of the excavation with some very heavy

Figure 7. Detailed plan of excavated area showing stone foundation of bank and location of trench excavations through ditch Slots 1 and 2

Figure 8. Photograph of bank looking north showing sections excavated through stone foundation; note band of larger stones along eastern edge and slope down to east

rain. A Watching Brief was conducted in October to observe the topsoil strip of the area north of the excavation, and record features that showed beneath the overburden.

Results

The underlying drift geology, comprising glacial and periglacial gravels, was encountered across the site at a depth of 109.6 m above Ordnance Datum (AOD), 0.5 m below the existing ground surface. In the south-eastern corner of the trench there was a natural slope to the east of Wat's Dyke falling gradually to a level of 109 m AOD. A control sample for luminescence dating (OSL 8) was taken from the natural gravel in Slot 2 which resulted in a date of 58,900 ± 5800 BP.

Phase 1: Mesolithic pits

During the excavation, four sub-oval pits were observed cut into the natural gravel within the line of the bank of Wat's Dyke (Figs. 9 and 10). Pit [1038] at the southern end of the excavated area was oval and oriented east-west. This was 1.85 m long and 0. 54 m deep. Pits [2022] and [2025] were located 15 m further to the north, measuring 1.95 x 1.8 m and 2 x 1.25 m respectively. Finally pit [2027] was identified at the northern end of the stripped area. Only a quadrant of this feature was seen as it ran beneath the trench edge, but it appeared to be oval in plan and the

excavated depth was 0.55 m. The fills of these pits were all well-humified mid-brown silty clay, which was easily defined against the underlying natural gravel. Pits [2025] (filled by context 2024) and [2027] (filled by contexts 2026–9) contained traces of burnt bone and charcoal, with fill (2024) also yielding a fragment of hazelnut shell and three worked stone fragments including two bifacial bladelets and a section of a polished stone axe. Pit [2027] contained a worked flake of dark grey flint and charred hazelnut shell in fill (2026). Pit [2022] yielded a single charred roundwood twig fragment from fill (2021).

All of the worked implements suggest a late Mesolithic or early Neolithic date for the backfilling of the pits (roughly BC 4500–3750). The hazelnut and twig fragments from pits [2022], [2025] and [2027] were sent to the Scottish Universities Environmental Research Centre for ^{14}C AMS (Accelerator Mass Spectrometry) and the results achieved are presented in Table 1.

Two additional pits were recorded during the watching brief in the northern contingency area. Although no artefacts were recovered, these can tentatively be ascribed to this phase on the basis of their form and stratigraphic location.

Phase 2: Buried Soil 1

The pits were sealed by a layer of brown clay loam (1040=2030) which contained a high proportion of small

Figure 9. Aerial view of excavation after removal of bank material and buried soil with Mesolithic pits cut into underlying geology. The line of the bank can be seen continuing under the tree (© Aerial Cam 2006)

pebbles, suggesting erosion between a buried soil and the underlying natural gravel. This layer was 0.15 m thick and can be interpreted as representing a period of soil formation extending from the Mesolithic through to the post-Roman period.

Phase 3: Buried Soil 2

Sealing the earlier buried soil was a second deposit 0.12 m thick. This was most easily recognised beneath the stone bank of Wat's Dyke where increased throughflow of water from the overlying stone had caused much of the mineral content of the soil to leach out. The resultant soil was ashen-grey in colour, with layers of iron-panning up to 10 mm thick on the top and bottom (1028). This process had not occurred to the west of the bank, and so here the soil remained in its original state as reddish-brown silty

clay (1010)=(2020) (Figs. 13 and 14). This buried soil was identified in the evaluation and recorded as layers (114) and (116) (Fig. 15).

The buried soil followed the natural slope down to the east of the bank, most clearly visible at the southern end of the excavation area (context 1030). Stone from the underlying natural gravel had been worked into the buried soil here through erosion or possibly ploughing. Attempts were made to date the buried soil where it had been sealed by the bank. As with the prehistoric pit fills, organic preservation within this soil was extremely poor. Two column samples taken from layers (1010) and (1028) were almost entirely inorganic, containing no pollen or microfossil remains, and a bulk sample taken from (1028) yielded only tiny fragments of charcoal which were unsuitable for ^{14}C AMS dating. Samples taken from the soil were assessed for suitability for an experimental

Table 1. ^{14}C AMS results for materials from pits [2022], [2025] and [2027] Phase 1.

Sample type	Context	SUERC No.	Radiocarbon Age BP	Calibrated date 1σ	Calibrated date 2σ
Hazelnut charred	Pit fill 2024	12827 (GU-14867)	6130±35	5210–4990 BC	5210–4980 BC
Hazelnut charred	Pit fill 2026	12828 (GU-14868)	6060±35	5020–4910 BC	5060–4840 BC
Twig	Pit fill 2021	GU-14869	Insufficient carbon		

dating method using earthworm calcite granules, but none were found. In addition there was only a single artefact recovered from (1028); a single late-Mesolithic bi-facial blade which is in keeping with the date of the underlying pits. A sample for dating (OSL 7) was taken from context (2020) in Slot 2 (equivalent to (1028) in Slot 1) which resulted in a date of 1110 ± 130 BP (AD 767–1027) (see Fig. 14).

Phase 4: Pre-Dyke activity (Fig. 10)

A linear gully aligned northeast-southwest was cut into the surface of the buried soil beneath the bank of Wat's Dyke, situated 17 m to the north of the southern edge of excavation. The cut [1031] was 0.2–0.3 m wide and less than 50 mm deep, and was 4 m long, its orientation suggesting it had no association with Wat's Dyke. The fill of the gully (1032) was a dark brown silty loam containing occasional pebbles. This context was sieved for artefacts but none were recovered and no burnt material suitable for dating was found.

During the evaluation another possible gully 2 m wide and 0.38m deep had been found beneath the bank in Trench 2 (210). It had a flat base 0.85 m wide and was filled with yellow clay. The fill was also undated, but can be attributed to pre-dyke activities. A third feature cut into the Phase 3 buried soil was seen in the north facing section of Slot 2 (Fig. 14). Initially interpreted as a step in the side of the ditch marking an anomaly in the otherwise uniform construction of the dyke, the stratigraphy suggests that this was in fact an earlier pit, situated slightly to the east of the ditch, which had been heavily truncated during the ditch's construction. The shape of the pit is unknown – the feature was not identified in plan due to plough damage – but the section indicates that it was at least 2.2 m in diameter and 2 m deep with gradually sloping sides and a flat base. The primary fill (2019) was a clean grey to mottled-brown silt up to 0.4 m thick. This was sealed by a second fill (2007) of mid brown gritty silt containing up to twenty per cent small to medium sub-angular pebbles. This single deposit was 1.6 m deep. Neither of the fills contained any organic remains or artefactual material.

The age and function of the pit is unclear, but it perhaps represents the location of a tree removed prior to the construction of the dyke. Its fills were very similar to those seen in the ditch of Wat's Dyke, the earliest deposit suggesting that the pit had been left open for enough time to partially silt up. The later fill was almost identical in appearance to some of the bank-collapse deposits in the ditch (see Phase 6).

Phase 5: Construction of the bank and ditch

The earliest phase (sub-phase 5a) in the construction of Wat's Dyke was the creation of a 'marker' bank (Fig. 10), apparently formed from the upcast earth generated while de-turfing the line of the ditch and bank area. This was seen as an earthen bank at the southern end of the excavation area (Figs. 11 and 12) extending 9.5 m northwards (1035). It was 5 m wide and 0.6 m high (although partially truncated) and ran along the eastern side of the ditch sealed by the main stone bank to the east. There was no berm (a shallow ledge) between this bank and the edge of the ditch.

Context (1035) was a clean, mid brown silty clay which overlay buried soil (1010). This is equivalent to (106) in the evaluation (Trench 1). Since the earthen bank was effectively formed by redeposition of soil (1010), there was no discernable boundary between the two deposits. Again, no datable material was recovered from this deposit. The bank did not extend as far to the north as Slot 1, and so was only seen in section at the southern end of the trench. This may have been due to the fact that the ditch was de-turfed in sections, with the excavated spoil heaped in separate locations, or possibly that the earthen bank had been truncated further to the north by a much later shallow cut, possibly excavated to reinforce the boundary formed by the main bank after the infilling of the dyke.

Sub-phase 5b was marked by the ditch cut. The profile of the ditch (context [1009]/[2009]) was between 7 m and 8 m wide and varied in depth from 2.16 m to 2.7 m. In Slot 1 at the southern end of the excavation area the profile of the ditch had uniform, steeply sloping sides of between 35° to 45°. It was 7.4 m wide and 2.16 m deep with an 'ankle breaker' in the base up to 1 m wide (Fig. 13). In Slot 2 the ditch was between 6 – 6.8 m wide and was 2.7 m deep with an ankle breaker in the base 0.7 m wide. Again the ditch had steeply sloping sides (around 40°) giving the ditch a 'V'-shaped profile (Fig. 14). In both Slots 1 and 2 the profile of the ditch was easily identified as the fills were excavated by hand onto the underlying natural gravel. Manganese and iron minerals had accreted at the interface between the natural gravel and ditch fills, giving the ditch sides a distinctive black/orange mottled appearance.

The upcast gravel from the excavation of the ditch had been piled to the east to form a bank (sub-phase 5c) which was *c*. 5m wide (1034), corresponding to contexts (101) and (113) from the evaluation (Figs. 7 and 15). With the exception of the earthen marker bank (1035) (Fig. 11), this feature directly overlay buried soil 1028. There was a notable concentration of large stones (rounded cobbles up to 0.25 m in diameter) along the eastern edge of the bank, with smaller pebbles and gravel in the centre (Figs. 8 and 16). This may reflect the way that the stones were tipped during its construction, the larger stones naturally rolling towards the back of the bank, or may have been a deliberate measure to increase the stability of the eastern side of the bank. Large white stones were observed along the eastern edge of the bank, apparently spaced at uniform intervals of around 1.6 m, which may have been used as markers to delineate the limits of the bank during construction (Fig. 17). Along the western edge there also appeared to be a spread of large stones,

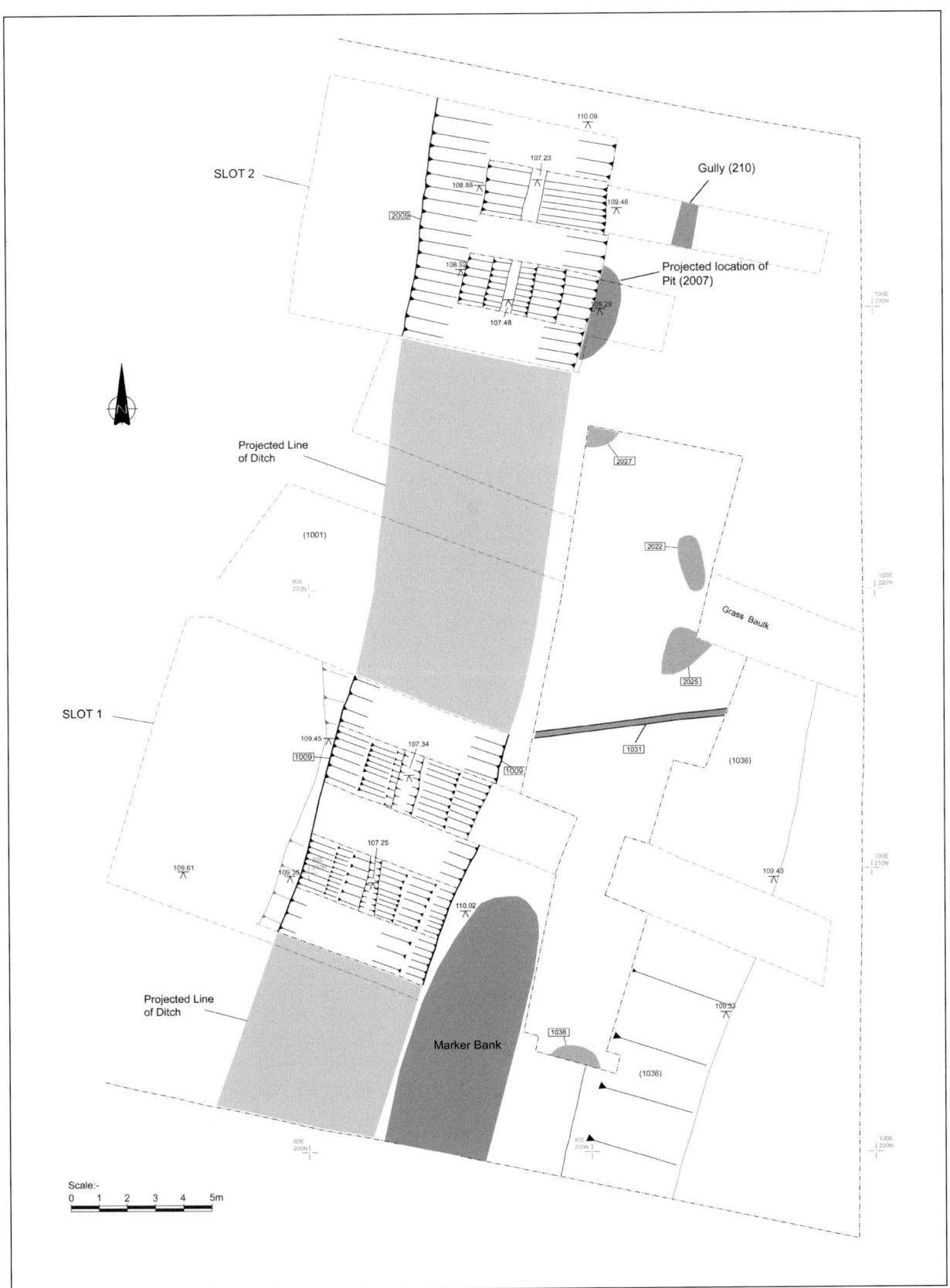

SLOT 2

110.09

107.23

108.88

109.46

2009

Gully (210)

108.92

Projected location of
Pit (2007)

107.48

109.29

Projected Line
of Ditch

2027

(1001)

80E
220N

2022

Grass Baulk

2025

SLOT 1

109.45

107.34

1009

1009

1031

(1036)

109.61

107.25

109.35

109.43

110.02

Projected Line
of Ditch

Marker Bank

1038

109.33

(1036)

50E
200N

90E
200N

100E
200N

Scale:-
0   1   2   3   4   5m

Figure 10. Plan of pre-bank features and marker bank

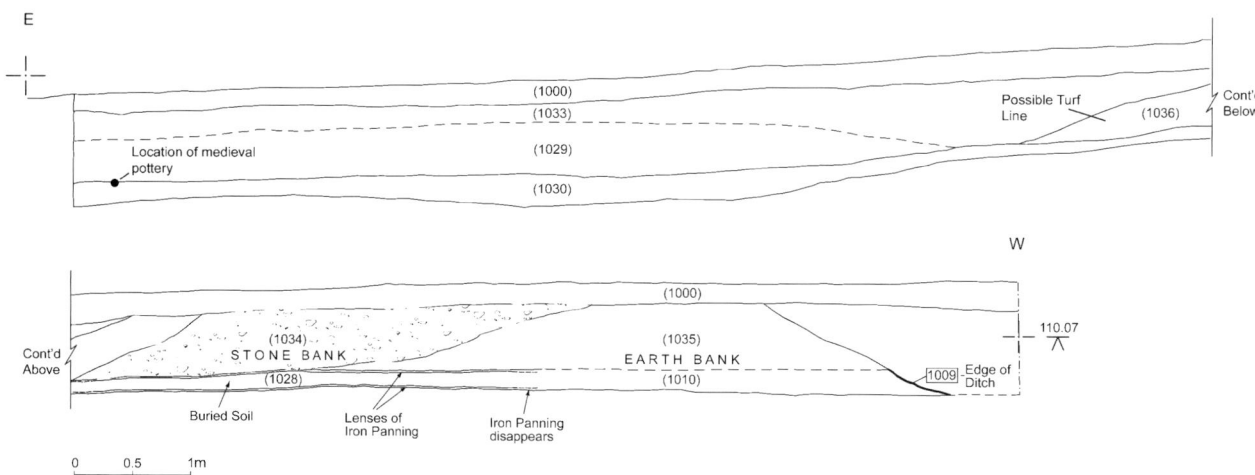

Figure 11. North-facing section along southern edge of excavation area showing marker bank and stone core sealed by "turf" growth and ploughsoils

Figure 12. Photograph of section along southern edge of excavation (see Figure 11)

although of much less uniform character than those to the east. The survival of the bank was better at the southern end of the excavation area, standing to a height of 0.5 m. This continued *c*. 25 m to the north before the feature was completely truncated by plough damage just to the south of Slot 2. It is also of note that in the location of Slot 1 the stone bank (corresponding with context 118 from the evaluation) appeared to have been cut away along its western edge, possibly during a phase of ditch cutting, perhaps to reinforce a field boundary in relatively recent times. This may also have truncated the northward extent of the earthen marker bank (1035).

The eastern edge of the bank was sealed by a layer of silty clay and small stones (1036) 0.3 m thick which may represent the remains of a turf covering for the stone bank, and replicates the evidence from the evaluation (111) (Figs. 11, 12, 15 and 16). The excavated evidence suggests a single phase of construction for the bank implying that in this location the construction was not only simple, but seemingly structurally sound requiring no maintenance or rebuilding. As the top of the feature had been lost through ploughing, it has not been possible to determine whether or not there was a structure or hedge-line along the top of the bank.

To the east of the bank a probable stabilisation episode

(sub-phase 5d) is represented by (1036=111); a reddish-brown silty clay with small pebble inclusions which is interpreted as a possible turf layer covering the bank. This had been truncated along with the stone bank in the post-medieval period (Figs. 11, 12 and 13) and partly sealed by plough deposits dating to the thirteenth to fourteenth centuries (see sub-phase 6.5 below).

Phase 6: Erosion of bank, infilling of ditch and medieval cultivation

In both of the excavated ditch sections it was clear that the erosion of the bank and infilling of the ditch was characterised by episodic collapse or destruction of the bank's stonework interspersed with gradual accumulations of silt and fine sands. The sequence of these deposits in each section varied, indicating that the rate of erosion had differed along the length of the bank. The sequences observed in Slots 1 and 2, broadly divided into five sub-phases, are presented below. No finds were recovered from any of the ditch fills.

In Slot 1, the primary fill of the ditch (sub-phase 6.1) comprised coarse stony material filling the ankle breaker to a depth of 0.34 m (1022) (Figs 13 and 18). The stones measured up to 0.15 m in diameter, and were mixed

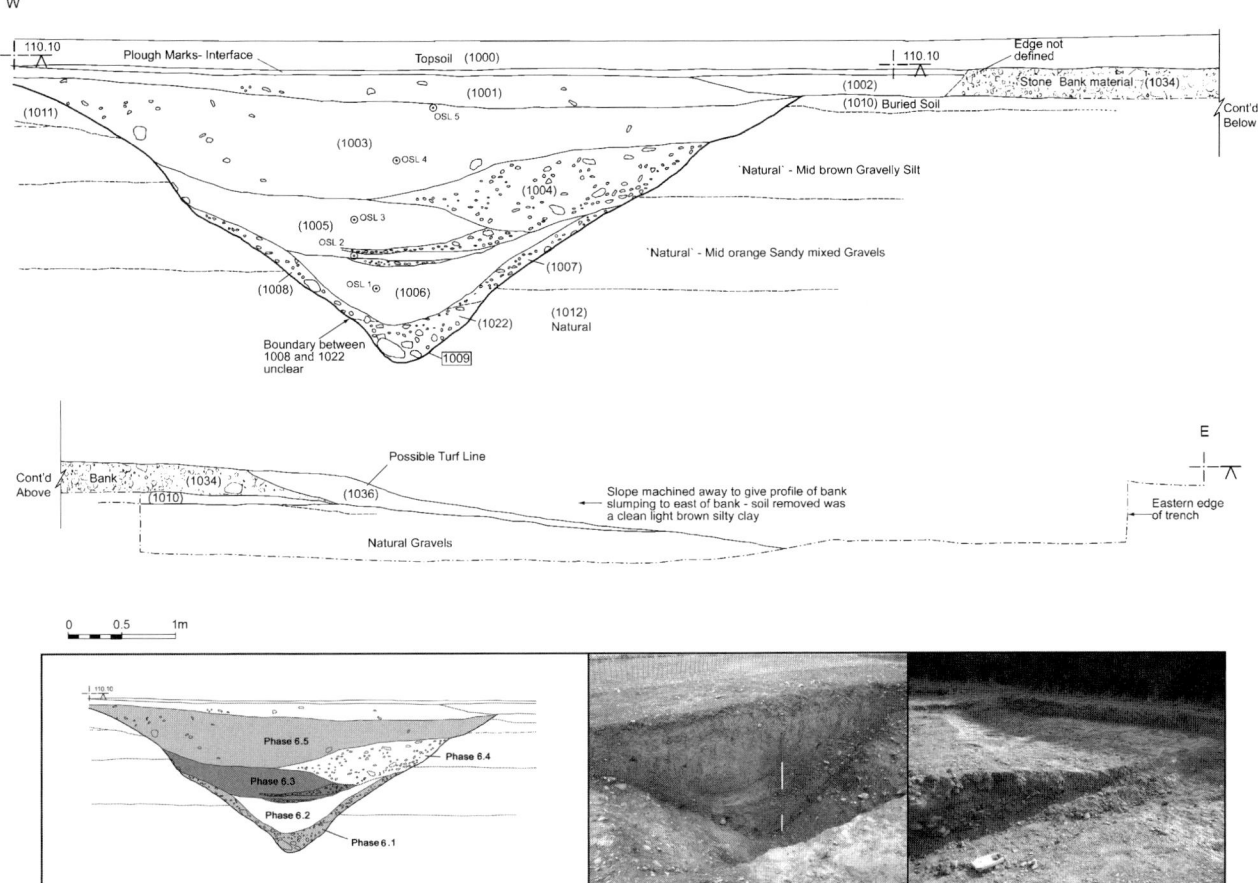

Figure 13. South-facing section through bank and ditch in Slot 1, with phase diagram and photograph

with dark brown silty clay. On each side of the ditch the primary fill (1022) merged into thin coverings of loosely compacted sandy gravel (1007=1008). The primary fill was sealed by a deposit of clean blue-grey silt containing very fine lenses of coarser sands and fine gravels (sub-phase 6.2) (1006). OSL sample 1 was recovered from this deposit, and an environmental sample (3/T) yielded a single charred twig suitable for AMS dating. The date calculated is presented in Table 2.

This deposit was 0.52 m thick suggesting that no significant episodes of bank collapse had occurred for some time. The OSL date for sample 1 is 1110 ± 105 BP (AD 792–1002).

A deposit of clean grey silt (sub-phase 6.3) (1005) overlay (1006). This had a fine lens of gravel at the base

overlying the top of (1006) and a second larger lens of coarse stones and gravel within the lower quarter of the deposit. The orientation of these lenses indicate that the coarser material was eroding from the bank to the east, while finer silts were being washed in from the land surface to both the east and west. OSL samples 2 and 3 were taken from (1005); OSL 2 from between the two lenses at the base of the context and OSL 3 from the middle. OSL dates for sample 2 and 3 were 1170 ± 90 BP (AD 747–927), and 1160 ± 105 BP (AD 742–952). A large slump of pea grit and larger sub-angular stones (1004) up to 0.14 m in diameter overlay (1005), tipped into the ditch from the east (sub-phase 6.4). This was 0.68 m deep, and spread up to 3 m across the lower fills of the ditch. Finally (1004) was sealed by an extensive

Table 2. ^{14}C AMS results for material from Ditch Fill 1006: Phase 6.2

Sample type	Context	SUERC No.	Radiocarbon Age BP	Calibrated date 1σ	Calibrated date 2σ
Twig (species unknown)	Ditch fill 1006	12826 (GU-14866)	2825±40	1030–910 BC	1120–890 BC

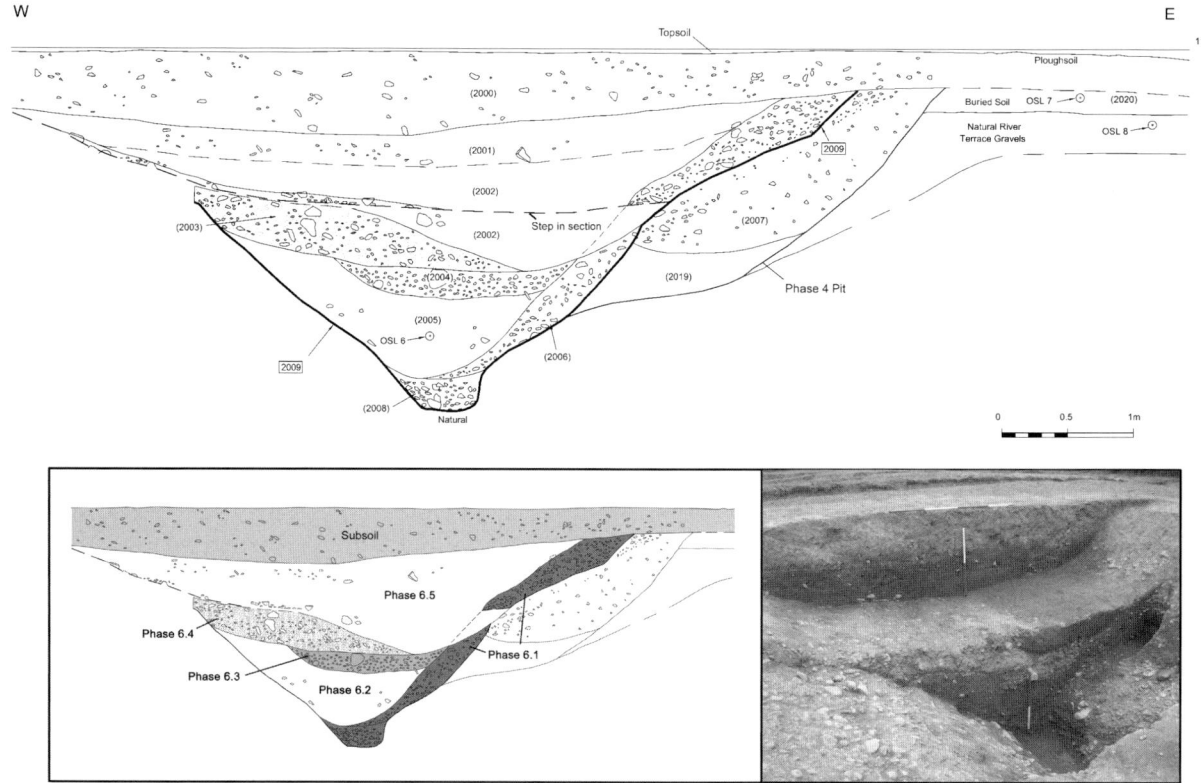

Figure 14. North-facing section (reversed) through ditch in Slot 2, with phase diagram and photograph (reversed)

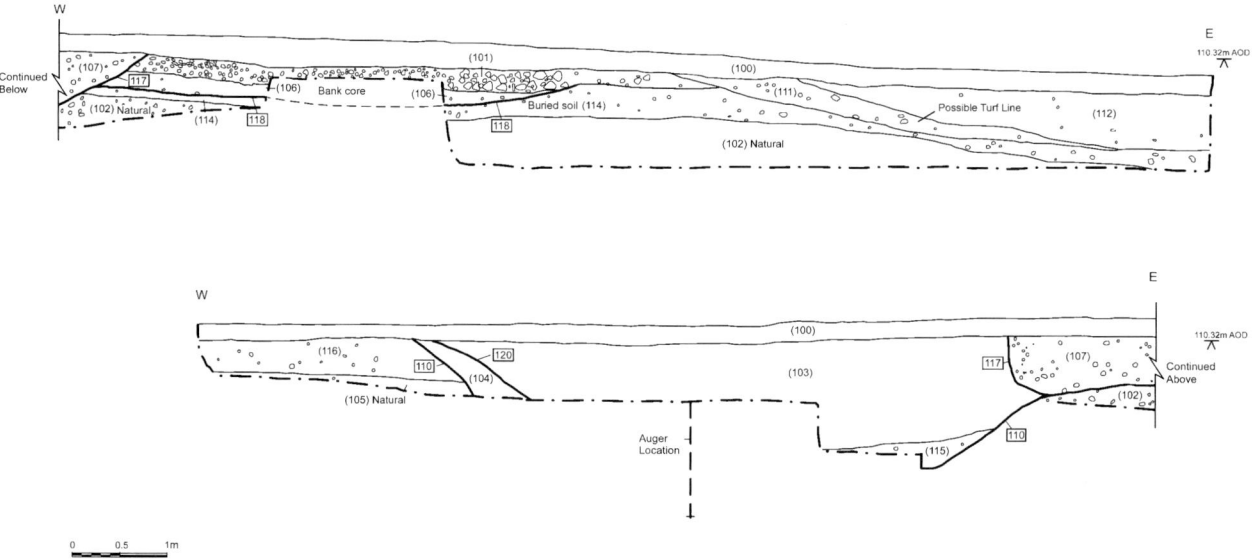

Figure 15. South-facing section through Trench 1 from the evaluation showing top of ditch and bank deposits (compare to Figure 13)

deposit of pale brown silty clay (1003) which sealed all earlier fills across the width of the ditch (sub-phase 6.5). This contained very few stones, and was 0.9 thick x 7.15 m wide, representing the final silting of the ditch and providing clear evidence that no further erosion of the stone bank had occurred after this point.

Two further OSL samples were taken from (1003); OSL 4 was taken from the middle of the deposit, and OSL 5 from the upper surface, in the centre of the ditch. OSL dates for samples 4 and 5 were 680±60 BP (AD 1267–1387) and 610±70 BP (AD 1327–1467).

In Slot 1, although there was no definitive indication

Figure 16. Photograph of stone core to bank looking south showing band of larger stones to east and marker bank on western side

Figure 17. Stone bank: detailed photograph looking south showing possible white marker stones along eastern edge, band of large stones on eastern side, smaller pebbles in centre and slightly larger stones on west side

Figure 18. Photograph of south-facing ditch section in Slot 1 showing detail of infill sequence and ankle-breaker slot (filled with large stones) at base

Figure 19. Photograph of south-facing section of ditch in Slot 2 showing complex infill and narrow slot at base

that the ditch had been recut at any point after the feature had fallen into disrepair, and the sequence of fills appear to suggest that they were washed in or collapsed due to natural events, there is, however, a possibility from the stony deposit in sub-phase 6.4 that this derived from deliberate dismantling of the upper part of the bank, and of it being thrown down into the ditch.

In Slot 2 (Figs. 14 and 19) the primary fill of the ditch (sub-phase 6.1) was similar to that seen in Slot 1. Context (2008=2018) filled the ankle breaker in the bottom of the ditch to a depth of 0.24 m and comprised an unsorted mixture of large rounded pebbles, mixed gravels and finer sands which would almost certainly have eroded into the base of the ditch from the sides. This was sealed from the east by a slump of grey clayey silt containing around ten per cent small pebbles up to 0.06 m in diameter (2006=2017). The primary fills were sealed by a deposit of clean pale grey silt (2005=2015, 2016) 0.6 m deep which had accumulated in the base of the ditch (sub-phase 6.2). A sample was taken from the centre of (2005) for OSL dating (sample 6) which resulted in a date of 1240 ± 85 BP (AD 682–852). Context (2005) was in turn sealed by two deposits of coarse pale brown sandy gravel containing occasional larger gravel and stones up to 140 mm in diameter (sub-phase 6.3 and 6.4). The

earlier of these contexts (2004=2013) was 0.21 m deep, centred above the mid-line of the ditch. It appeared to sit within a possible recut into context (2005). The later deposit (2003=2011) was up to 0.42 m thick and tipped into the ditch from the west, suggesting that part of the western edge of the ditch had collapsed, or alternatively had been deliberately slighted to reduce the steepness of the western ditch-side and level up the ditch.

The final in-filling of the ditch (sub-phase 6.5) was represented by two final deposits of silty clay. The lower context (2002=2012) was up to 0.86 m deep in the centre of the ditch and 4.8 m wide, comprising clean pale grey sandy silt with very few visible inclusions. This was sealed by context (2001), very similar in appearance to (2002), but containing around five per cent small angular stones up to 0.05 m in diameter.

As part of sub-phase 6.5 (which represented medieval ploughing, erosion of bank and deposition of ploughsoil), to the east of the bank a layer of clean mid-brown silty clay 0.4 m thick and containing very few inclusions (1029) overlay the stony buried soil (1030=1028/1010) which was seen in the southeast corner of the excavation area (Figs. 11 and 12). This deposit partly overlay the possible turf covering of the bank and appears to represent a gradual process of erosion on the eastern side of the dyke as finer particles in the soil were washed down slope. Abraded sherds of thirteen to fourteen century pottery from a single vessel were recovered at the interface between (1029) and (1030), as well as iron objects including hob nails and a possible strap fitting. This would suggest that the bulk of the erosion from the bank occurred during or after the medieval period, and that by this time the activity responsible for the formation of (1030) had ceased. Such a date conforms well with the OSL dates obtained from the upper fills of the ditch, which also suggest that they are derived from a major episode of deposition during the late medieval period.

Phase 7: Subsoil

A stony subsoil was observed across the site, which can be seen as a by-product of more intensive ploughing in the post-medieval period. Represented by contexts (1001), (1033=112) and (2010), the layer varied in depth from 0.2 m to 0.5 m. Small to medium sized stones (<0.05 m diameter) occurred frequently in this layer and are presumably derived from ploughing across the bank and mixing them into the upper soil layers to either side of the feature. Where the layer was exposed in plan, darker plough marks were clearly visible in its surface running in a north/north-westerly direction parallel with the western field boundary. The stone bank can be seen to have been dragged eastwards (Fig. 7) as it thins out and disappears in the northern part of the excavation area.

Phase 8: Field boundary ditch

Visible in the section of Slot 1, and apparently truncating the northward extension of the earthen marker bank, was a shallow ditch (1002) the fill of which was a friable silt containing unsorted gravels. This feature was situated along the eastern edge of the ditch and to the west of the stone bank, suggesting that it had been excavated in the post-medieval period to emphasise a field boundary.[15]

Phase 9: Topsoil and turf

The topsoil which was removed during the initial machining of the trench was 0.07 m – 0.1 m thick and comprised dark brown humic loam. Finds recovered from this layer were all nineteenth or twentieth century in date.

ARTEFACT AND SOIL SAMPLING ANALYSES

Pottery analysis

Alan Vince

A small collection of medieval pottery was recovered from the buried soil (context 1030) in the southeastern corner of the excavation. The sherds are all small and abraded but appear to come from the same vessel. The sherds, ten in total with a weight of 20 g, probably come from a wheel-thrown jug with an external plain lead glaze and widely-spaced grooves which give the profile a corrugated appearance. The fabric is oxidized and soft. At x20 magnification, moderate rounded quartz grains, mainly up to 0.5mm across with rare grains up to 1.5mm across, are present together with sparse sub-angular dark brown siltstone and sandstone fragments. The quartz grains include clear and milky grains, all of which have a matt surface typical of quartz from Permo-Triassic sands. Moderate brown clay pellets of similar texture and hardness to the groundmass, up to 0.3mm across, were also present. The groundmass consists of a silty micaceous clay in which the inclusions are less than 0.1mm across.

The fabric characteristics suggest that the vessel was made from a borderlands clay of Silurian or Devonian age, or a boulder clay derived from such a clay, and that it was tempered with a mixed sand which includes Silurian/Devonian and Permo-Triassic material. This combination of rounded quartz and a silty micaceous groundmass is not found on pottery in central or southern Shropshire and Herefordshire,[16] nor is it common at Hen Domen or Montgomery.[17] It does occur in Cheshire, however, as at Ashton[18] and Audlem (which is about 26 miles to the east of Gobowen.)[19] Such a source is near the limit for overland distribution of pottery in medieval England (except where sea- or river-transport was used or long-distant trade routes could be utilized) and a source closer to Gobowen is quite possible. Boulder clays containing redeposited Palaeozoic strata from the west outcrop over much of the lower-lying land of northern Shropshire, whilst Bunter sandstone outcrops in the north-eastern part of the county and, because of its relative durability, quartz from this source is a major component of cover sands in the area.[20] Wheelthrown lead-glazed jugs were produced in the Welsh borderland from the early to mid thirteenth century onwards but became much more common in the second half of the thirteenth century (as demonstrated at Hereford).[21] The likelihood is that this example is of late thirteenth to fourteenth century date.

Figure 20. Sampling for OSL dating in Slot 1; narrow slot (ankle-breaker) is clearly visible at base filled with large stones

Palaeoenvironmental analysis

John Carrott

Seven bulk sediment samples[22] and two kubiena tin samples were recovered by Palaeoecology Research Services Limited (PRS), County Durham, for an assessment of their bioarchaeological potential. Ancient biological remains recovered from the bulk sediment samples were restricted to small quantities of unidentified charcoal (present in all samples) and other charred plant macrofossils (hazelnut shell in Contexts 2024 and 2026 and occasional charred and possibly ancient seeds, *e.g.* Context 1037 – all Mesolithic pit fills) and a trace of unidentified tooth fragments (Context 1006 – primary fill of Wat's Dyke). The charcoal presumably represents fuel remnants and the hazelnut fragments discarded waste from gathered food.

No identifiable microfossils were recorded from the buried soils sampled using kubiena tins (samples CS1 and CS2) and, other than unidentified fine charcoal, no ancient macrofossils from the corresponding bulk samples (Samples 1 and 2 from Contexts 1028 and 1010, respectively). There was, therefore, no evidence from the biological remains to support the stratigraphic interpretation of these layers as buried soils or provide additional information for ecological or depositional reconstruction.

SCIENTIFIC DATING RESULTS

Optically Stimulated Luminescence dating

Jean-Luc Schwenninger

A series of five samples [X2833, X2834, X2835, X2836 and X2837] were collected from the sedimentary fill of the ditch in the south facing section of Slot 1 (Fig. 20) and three further samples [X2838, X2839 and X2840] were obtained from the north-facing section of Slot 2 for optically stimulated luminescence. [23] This included one sample [X2840] from the river deposit which was processed in order to compare the luminescence signal from the natural fluvial sediment to the signal measured from the archaeological sediments associated with the ditch fill. In-situ radioactivity measurements were obtained using a calibrated portable gamma-ray spectrometer in order to calculate the external gamma dose rate received by the sample. The beta dose rate was derived from laboratory based geochemical analyses of the concentrations of potassium, uranium and thorium by ICP-MS using a fusion sample preparation method.

For each sample, sand sized grains of quartz (180–250μm) were extracted from the sediment and luminescence measurements were carried out on twelve replicate multigrain aliquots using standard measurement procedures. [24] The results of the OSL dating are summarized in the table below. Further details regarding individual samples may be found in the site archive and specialist technical information on the luminescence dating will be provided in a forthcoming publication. The overall luminescence characteristics of the samples were considered to be very satisfactory for OSL dating, providing good recycling ratios and low inter-aliquot variability. As expected, a substantially higher palaeodose was obtained for sample X2840 and resulted in a Pleistocene date for the deposition of the gravel. All seven samples from the ditch sequence are of Late Holocene age and are in overall good stratigraphic order. The OSL age estimates suggest that the formation of the ditch dates from the eighth to ninth centuries AD (Table 3).

Accelerator Mass Spectrometry

Although sieving and flotation of soil samples was undertaken in order to retrieve carbonised remains for radiocarbon dating, this approach only produced four potential samples (see table below). Three radiocarbon dates were obtained from the Scottish Universities Environmental Research Centre. Two were for hazelnuts from pits sealed by the buried soil and these date to the Mesolithic period. The third date was for a twig recovered from the primary ditch-fill of Wat's Dyke and this derives from the Bronze Age. The significance of this single date is discussed in comparison to the OSL results in the general discussion and conclusions section below (Table 4).

Table 3. Optically Stimulated Luminescence samples, measurements, and estimated age ranges

Field code	Lab. code	Depth (cm)	Palaeodose (Gy)	Dose rate (Gy/ka)	Age (years before 2007)
GOB06–01	X2833	210	2.73±0.19	2.47±0.15	1110±105
GOB06–02	X2834	190	2.79±0.10	2.37±0.15	1170±90
GOB06–03	X2835	155	2.72±0.16	2.34±0.15	1160±105
GOB06–04	X2836	95	1.58±0.06	2.32±0.17	680±60
GOB06–05	X2837	46	1.50±0.06	2.44±0.26	610±70
GOB06–06	X2838	230	2.89±0.06	2.33±0.14	1240±85
GOB06–07	X2839	40	2.88±0.08	2.59±0.29	1110±130
GOB06–08	X2840	60	185.5±10.8	3.15±0.24	58900±5800

Table 4. Accelerator Mass Spectometry samples and date ranges

Sample type	Context	SUERC No.	Radiocarbon Age BP	Calibrated date 1σ	Calibrated date 2σ
Hazelnut charred	Pit fill 2024	12827 (GU-14867)	6130±35	5210–4990 BC	5210–4980 BC
Hazelnut charred	Pit fill 2026	12828 (GU-14868)	6060±35	5020–4910 BC	5060–4840 BC
Twig	Pit fill 2021	GU-14869	Insufficient carbon		
Twig (species unknown)	Ditch fill 1006	12826 (GU-14866)	2825±40	1030–910 BC	1120–890 BC

Interpretation of the excavation results

The buried soil has an OSL date that is broadly in keeping with the dates from the ditch infill. This suggests that it was exposed to daylight as part of the construction activities for Wat's Dyke, presumably de-turfed as a preliminary exercise in marking out the line of the bank. This buried soil was found not only beneath the mound of the bank but also extended over the eastern area of the excavation, to the rear of the bank (but whether it extends to the west was not tested during the investigation). Although disturbed on the northern side by ploughing, the fact that the buried soil was preserved beyond the sealed context beneath the bank suggests that the ground behind was not quarried to help form the earthwork, and that the bank was composed primarily of the ditch arisings. This also confirms the microtopography contemporary with construction which shows that the bank was aligned along a slight natural rise that falls off to west and east.

Construction of the monument appears to have been relatively simple, in that no timber structure was used to act as a framework for the bank or revetment. An earthen mound was recorded in the south of the excavation area, and this formed an initial stage in the bank's formation, although not a continuous feature; it was not aligned in exactly the same orientation as the main bank, and petered out 9.5 m into the excavated area. A continuous spread of cobblestones had been laid against this and placed over the buried soil to the east of it to form a foundation for the main core of the bank (Figs. 23.6-23.8). Careful planning of this feature showed that larger boulders were used to the rear (eastern edge) including marker stones every 1.6 m, and slightly larger stones than in the centre were also used along the western edge. Although a detailed examination was undertaken to look for post-holes or beam slots, there was no indication of timber lacework within the cobblestones or the underlying layers. Thus the foundation of the bank consisted of a carefully-laid 5 m wide stone core, on the eastern side of which a thick soil layer, or turfline, accumulated (this presumably covered the entire bank until it was ploughed down).

Hill and Worthington's study of how Offa's Dyke might have been constructed includes a calculation for how many men would be needed.[25] This is based on information within the burghal hidage that gives twelve furlongs of burh wall requiring 1,920 hides for its upkeep and defence, and at one man per hide this equates to 160 men for each furlong, or one man for every 4 ft 1½ in. (1.25 m) of rampart. This approximate estimate of length is reasonably close to the distance between the marker stones found at Wat's Dyke (*c.* 1.6 m apart), perhaps providing evidence for a similarly planned and organized process.

The ditch was steep-sided and V-shaped, with a narrow slot at the base; a type of feature known as an "ankle-breaker".[26] Some erosion of the top of the ditch is to be expected, but this is certainly exaggerated on the western side of Slot 2, and suggests that the ditch may have been modified and re-cut to form a shallower gradient at some point after initial infill had already occurred.

The infilling of the ditch can be divided into five sub-phases which are broadly consistent between the

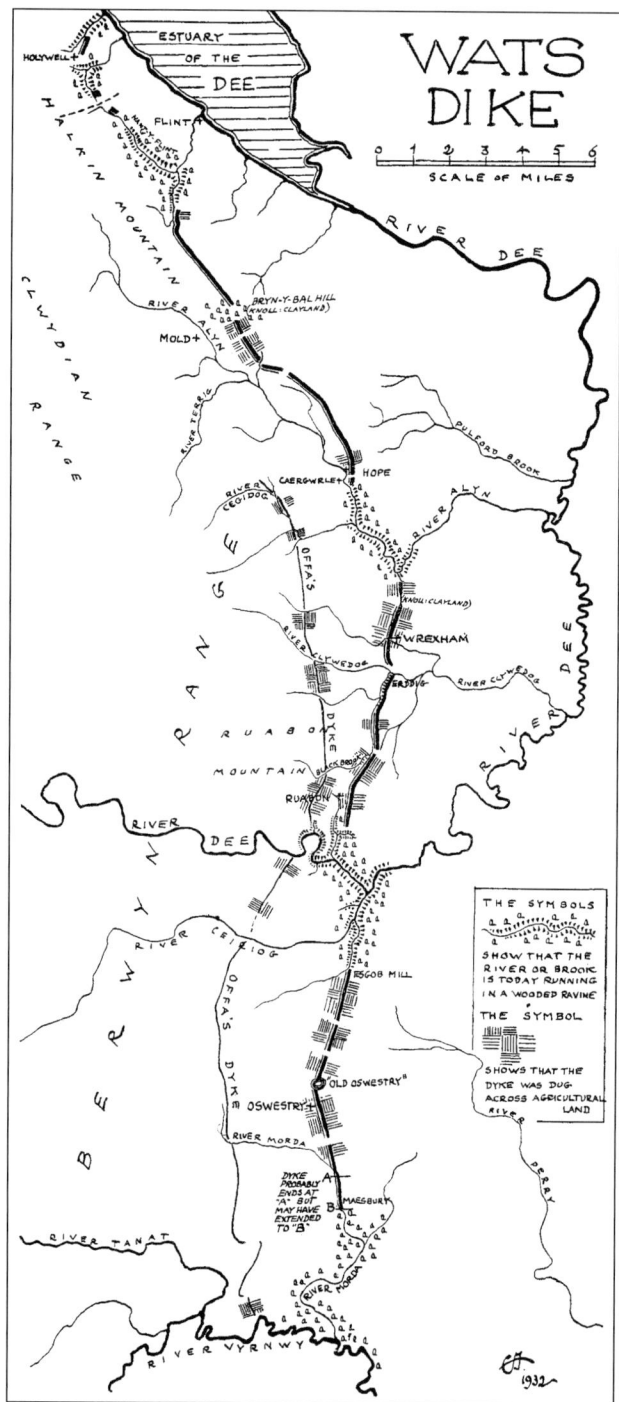

Figure 21. Reproduction of Cyril Fox's plan showing full extent of Wat's Dyke, steep valleys and drainage pattern (Fox 1955; Figure 117)

The second sub-phase, 6.2, includes a period of stagnation, with deep silts (possibly derived from wind blown sediment and/or eroded soil material into standing water, or gradual erosion from the sides of the feature) interspersed with lenses of fine gravels, perhaps representing episodes of heavier rainfall and in-wash into the ditch. The depth of the clean silt deposits suggests that there was a long period of gradual infilling. The third/fourth sub-phases (6.3 and 6.4) comprise continued periods of sporadic in-wash, including some deep fills of stone and gravel, potentially indicating key points in the collapse of the bank and ditch sides. These deposits in particular varied along the length of the ditch, in Slot 1 appearing to have occurred more frequently and with less intensity than Slot 2. This is to be expected, as the rate of erosion of the bank and ditch sides would have depended both on factors of local topography and the variations in the structural integrity of the bank along its length. The possibility of a recut within Slot 2 between sub-phases 6.2 and 6.3 would also indicate that sections of the feature were singled out for piecemeal maintenance, perhaps targeting areas where collapse of the bank or ditch sides had been particularly bad. An alternative hypothesis, however, would suggest a more dramatic interpretation, with the large dumps of stony material evident in sub-phase 6.3 as being deliberate infill, an indication for slighting of the defences. In Slot 1 the deposit is hard against the east side of the ditch and its shape would support a suggestion that this originated from the top of the bank. In Slot 2 the deposit is on the west side, but the original steep-sided profile of the ditch on this side has been flattened out and could have been pushed into the ditch to partially level it.

Finally, the erosion/slighting of the bank and ditch ceased, and the remaining fills of the fifth sub-phase (6.5) comprise deep, clean silty clay containing very few inclusions, interpreted as a deliberate major episode of infill associated with cultivation.

Comparative analysis and previous archaeological work

Wat's Dyke has been the subject of much research over the past century, much of it conducted as part of wider investigations into Offa's Dyke and the group of linear earthworks within the Welsh Marches which have been variously interpreted as boundaries between communities, at a local and a national level. Sir Cyril Fox established a baseline hypothesis on the origin and extent of Wat's Dyke in his publication on what he termed the 'frontier works of Mercia', and although the detail of this has been altered and added to by later workers, it has remained an immensely useful survey to help in understanding the monument in its topographic landscape (Fig. 21).[27] With its ditch towards the west and defensive bank on the east, he saw it as a discontinuous boundary and probable Mercian precursor to Offa's Dyke. Fox's field survey shows how it was laid out in a series of straight sections between

excavated sections (Figs. 23.7 and 23.9). Initial erosion of the ditch sides into the base produced a layer of stony material filling the ankle breaker and loosely covering the lower ditch sides. If the ankle breaker in the base was re-cleaned after its construction there would have been a period of time before maintenance ceased and the feature was allowed to begin filling up.

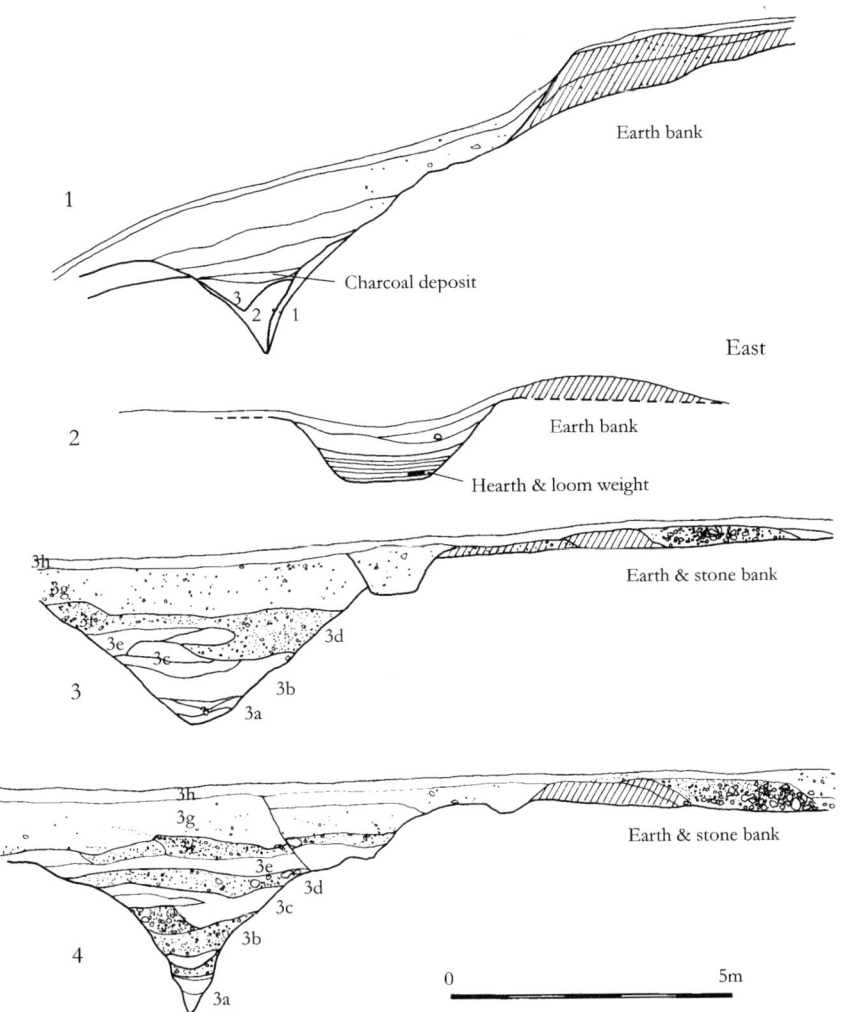

Figure 22. Comparative sections through Wat's Dyke from various excavations (Large numbers = code for site (see below), small numbers = phases): 1: Nant valley, Flintshire 1995 (Earthworks Archaeology); 2: Mynydd Isa, Flintshire 1957 (Varley); 3: Pentrewern 1985 field 77 (main area) (Cane) ; 4: Pentrewern 1985 field 76 (northern area) (Cane)

prominent points in the landscape, and that its alignment, situated in the lowlands east of the Welsh hills, followed ridges and hillocks and joined with hillforts to give it strategic views to the west, whilst he also concluded that it made use of deeply cut topographical features which would have emphasised or replaced the need for construction of the dyke as a continuous rampart.

David Hill and Margaret Worthington have dominated the physical surveying and investigation of the monument during the latter half of the twentieth century by undertaking over sixty excavations through Wat's Dyke and demonstrating the continuity of the monument into areas where Fox supposed there were gaps.[28] Their survey has also traced the full extent of Wat's Dyke extending from its northern terminal at Basingwerk (SJ195775), near Holywell on the Flintshire coast, to Lower Morton (SJ305233), at the confluence of the rivers Vyrnwy and

Morda south of Oswestry; a distance of 38.6 miles. In spite of all this research, definitive dates for its construction and use have eluded archaeologists, and the debate has largely centred on historical context and spatial relationships with Offa's Dyke and the other linear earthworks in the Marches region, to construct a chronology and appropriate story for shifting frontiers within this politically volatile zone during the fifth to the ninth centuries AD.[29]

Other individuals and organizations have, however, also undertaken discrete investigations into Wat's Dyke, and these add substantially to the detail and complexity of the monument. The most significant results are synthesized below with a summary presented in Table 5, and comparative sections in Figures 22 and 23. Within 4 km of its northern end, Earthworks Archaeology excavated a complete section through bank and ditch at Nant Farm (Pentre Halkyn) (SJ21537279) in 1995 (Figs. 22.1 and

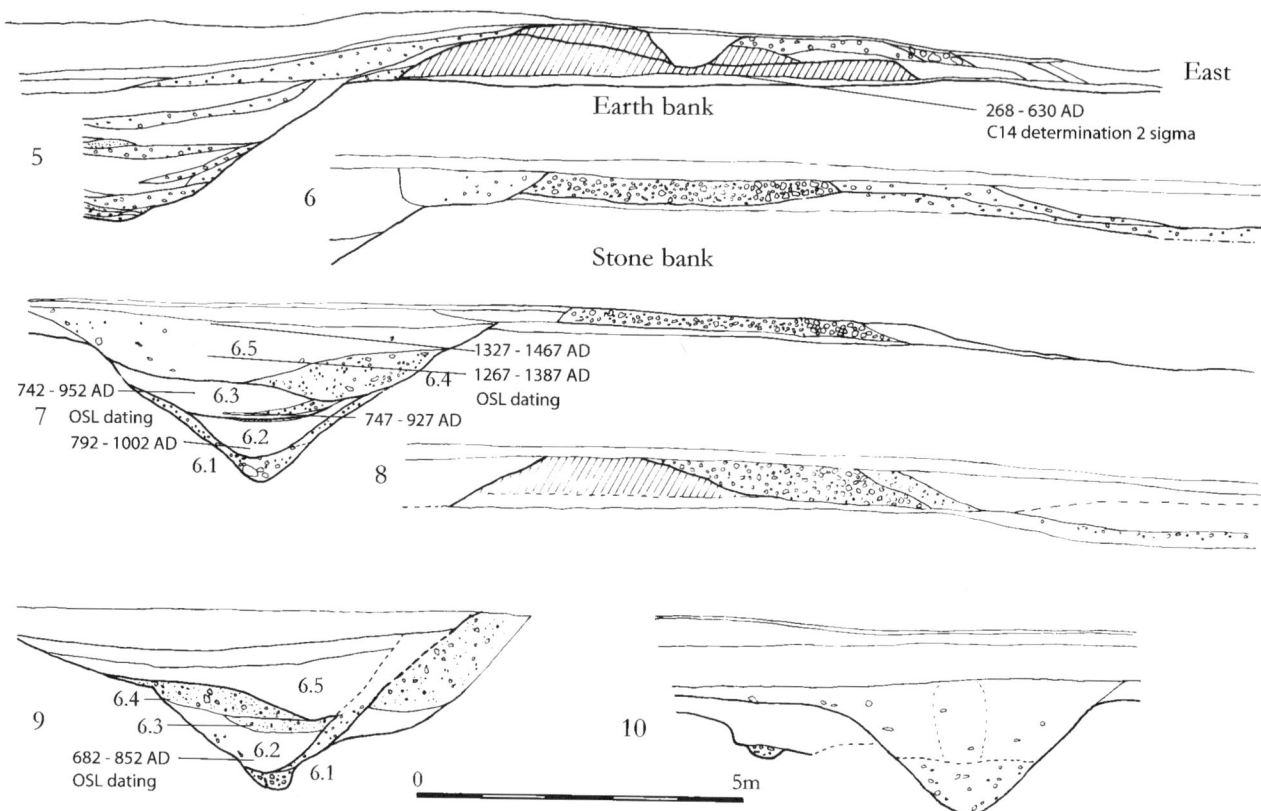

Figure 23. Comparative sections through Wat's Dyke from various excavations (Large numbers = code for site (see below), small numbers = phases); 5: Mile Oak, Oswestry 1997 (Hannaford); 6: Gobowen 2006 trench 1 evaluation (Webster and Malim); 7: Gobowen 2006 Slot 1 (Malim and Hayes); 8: Gobowen 2006 south end of excavation (reversed) (Malim and Hayes); 9: Gobowen 2006 Slot 2 (reversed) (Malim and Hayes); 10: Old Oswestry 1992 (Rogers). n.b. comparison shows profiles of 1 and 4 are identical, as are 3, 7, 9 and 10

24), as part of a programme of archaeological monitoring along a petroleum pipeline.[30] The V-shaped ditch was 4 m wide and 2 m deep; the bank was 7 m wide and 1m high, with a height of 5 m from base of ditch to top of surviving bank (Fig. 25); three phases of ditch construction were identified, as well as a possible stone revetment for the bank. As this has not been published previously a fuller account, section drawing and photographs are included below by kind permission of Will Walker:

Prior to the topsoil stripping of the pipe corridor across the line of Wat's Dyke, a trial excavation was undertaken to locate any surviving sub-surface remains, and to assess the damage which would result as a consequence of pipeline construction. The uppermost layer, context (1). consisted of a dark grey sandy silt with < 5% sub-rounded stones. This was a topsoil which covered most of the area of the trial excavation. Below this lay a compact mid-grey silty clay, context (2), with up to 10% small to medium sub-rounded coins. In extent context (2) was restricted to the top end of the excavation trench where it immediately overlay context (3), a compact mid-grey silty clay with up to 20% inclusions of sub-rounded stone and sub angular shale fragments. Context

(3) extended across the entire width of the trench and was c.450mm thick. Below context (3) lay a mid-orange brown silty clay, context (4), again compact and covering the entire width of the trench. Layer (4) was approximately 6 m wide and 0.5 m thick. Below (4) was a compact mid-orange clay, context (5), which overlay a thin band of dark grey clay (6) with up to 30% fragments of slate. Context (7) lay below (6) and took the form of a compact mid-grey shale/mudstone laid in bands. Below context (I) and above context (3) was a friable mid-brown silty clay, context (10), containing 2% small sub-rounded stone and 1% charcoal flecks; this layer was up to 0.75 m thick and produced glass, pottery and clay tobacco pipe fragments of nineteenth century date. Below (10) lay a light brown silty clay, context (11), existing up to a depth of 0.4 m and again with 1% charcoal flecks and up to 2% sub-rounded stone. Context (11) overlay a light brown silty clay (12) with 2% inclusions of small sub-rounded stone. Context (12) may represent the uppermost fill of cut (17), a linear feature running roughly north-south and approximately 3 m wide and 1.40 m deep; the eastern edge of cut (17) was irregular and convex whilst the western edge was a straight slope at a c.45 degree angle. Both edges tapered to a point at the base. Context (17) was filled by two other contexts:

Figure 24. Photograph showing location of Earthworks Archaeological Services' (EAS) excavation on the east side of the Nant Valley, Flintshire (© EAS)

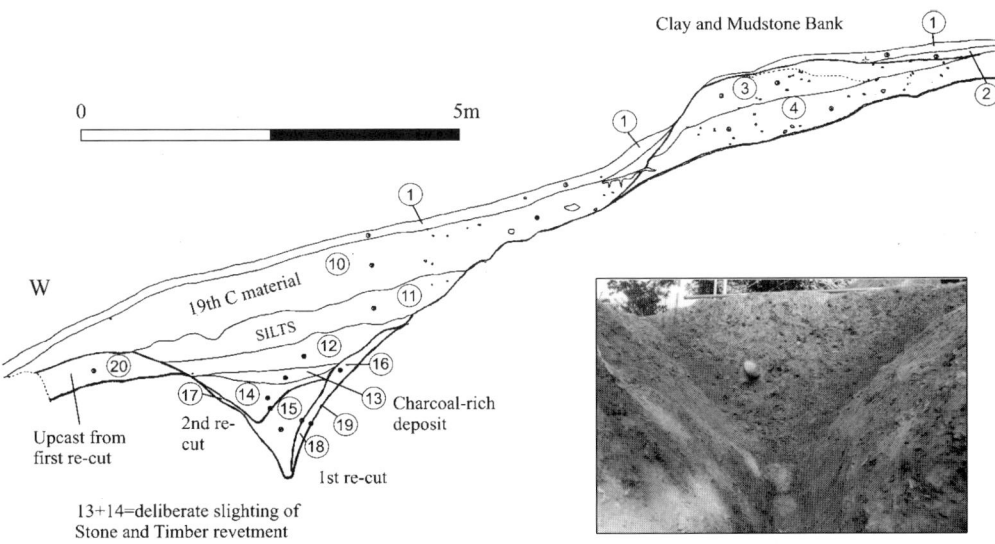

Figure 25. South-facing section through bank and ditch at Nant Farm (after EAS)

context (13), a light brown friable clayey silt with 2% small rounded stone and 5% charcoal flecks, lay directly beneath (12). Below (13) was a mid-brown silty clay, context (14), with c.30% angular to sub-rounded stone up to 250mm in diameter, c.10% mudstone/shale fragments and 1% charcoal flecks.

Feature (17) was cut through two contexts. Firstly, a compact light brown silty clay, context (15), which had 25% sub-rounded stone and angular shale/mudstone fragments. Context (15) was the only discernible fill of a deeper linear feature (18). Feature (17) also appeared to cut a light orange brown silty clay, context (20), with < 5% angular shale/mudstone fragments. Context (20) lay directly above context (7) at the western end of the trench; it covered the

Table 5. Wat's Dyke: Index of comparative excavations (from north–south)

Ditch

Excavator	Date of excavation	Location	width Top	width Base	depth	Profile	Angle of ditch sides West	Angle of ditch sides East	1st Phase primary silt	2nd phase recut infill	3rd phase recut infill	Early ditch
Garner D. & Turner Flynn B.	1995	Nant valley SJ21537279	4m		2m	V-shaped	50°	40°	primary silt	recut silty clay	recut charcoal, stones & clay	
Grenter S.	1984	Northop Middle Hill SJ23286895										
Varley W. J.	1957	Mynydd Isa SJ262639	3.66m	1.8	1.44m	flat base	40°	40°	turf growth	hearth/occupation accumulation	gradual accumulation	
Hill D.	1974	Sychdyn Site 25 SJ252659	5.6m		1.95m	V-shaped with cleaning slot	25°	30°	homogeneous clayey silt (single fill)			
Kenney J.	2003	PEN Y Bryn SJ31603864	2.1m		1.1m	V-shaped with slot	50°	40°				
Malim T. & Hayes L.	2006	Gobowen SJ30193318	8m		2.7m	V-shaped with cleaning slot	40°	40°	gravel cobbles	silt	possible recut gravel stone	possible
Cane J.	1984–5	Pentrewern SJ302329	8m		4m	V-shaped with cleaning slot	40°	40°	silt	gravel stone	silt	
Rogers I.	1992	Old Oswestry SJ294307	6m – 8m		2 – 4m	V-shaped	40°	40°	large stones silty clay	silty clay cobbles	charcoal	yes
Hannaford H.	1997	Mile Oak SJ300280	c.7		2.3m	uncertain		30°	silt			

Bank

Excavator	Date of excavation	Location	BERM	width	height	1st phase Marker	2nd phase	Revetment	Environmental evidence	Dating
Garner D. & Turner Flynn B.	1995	Nant valley SJ21537279	possible	7m	1m	clay & mudstone platform & clay		yes	none	none
Grenter S.	1984	Northop Middle Hill SJ23286895		c.6m	c.0.5m		stone rubble		none	none
Varley W. J.	1957	Mynydd Isa SJ262639	none	6.09m	0.76m	platform & clay	stone rubble	no	none	Middle Saxon loom weight
Hill D.	1974	Sychdyn Site 25 SJ252659		c.5.5m	1.5m	turf	earth		pollen	
Kenny J.	2003	Pen y Bryn SJ31603864	possible	c.3.8m	0.4m	silty sand		no	buried soil	none
Malim T. & Hayes L.	2006	Gobowen SJ30193318	none	5m	0.5m	earth	stone core	no	buried soil	C14, OSL, medieval pot
Cane J.	1984–5	Pentrewern SJ302329	none	6m (2 + 4)		earth sandy-clay and stone line	stone core	no	none	none
Rogers I.	1992	Old Oswestry SJ294307		c.8m					none	none
Hannaford H.	1997	Mile Oak SJ300280	0.7m	7.5m	0.75m	clay core	sands, gravels, cobbles	no	buried soil, hearth charcoal	C14 & Roman pot in buried soil 13th C pot in mid ditch fill

entire width of the trench, was approximately 2 m wide and up to 0.4 m deep.

Linear feature (18), orientated north-south, was at least 3 m long, 2 m wide and 1.50 m deep. The top of the cut had been destroyed by context (17), both edges were slightly irregular, convex and tapered to a blunt point at the base. Feature (18) cut through context (16), a light greyish brown silty clay with 50% inclusions of small angular shale/mudstone fragments: context (16) was the only fill of linear feature (19), which again was linear and ran north-south cutting through context (7). Cut (19) was at least 3 m long, approximately 4 m wide and c.3 m deep on its eastern side.

Interpretation

Contexts (5), (6) and (7) were natural boulder clays and mudstone/shales; context (6) may represent a buried turf deposit but, if so, it is of inter-glacial date. The earliest archaeological activity detected during the evaluation consisted of the cutting of linear feature (19) through the naturally occurring deposits, contexts (5), (6) and (7). Context (19) has been interpreted as a ditch which was sited to exploit the defensive capabilities of a natural scarp slope. The material excavated for cut (19) was redeposited on the crest of the escarpment and has been recorded as contexts (3) and (4). This redeposited clay and mudstone was used to construct a bank with a base c. 6–7 m wide and surviving to a height of approximately 1 m. This bank and ditch are considered to be the surviving, original features of Wat's Dyke earthwork and on the assumed line of the monument. Ditch (19) would have originally been approximately 4 m wide and c. 2 m deep on its eastern edge, as opposed to 1.40 m deep on its western edge. The vertical distance between the base of (19) and the top of the bank is approximately 5.20 m, presenting a considerable barrier.

Subsequent to the cutting of the primary ditch (19), a substantial degree of silting appears to have taken place; this silt (context 16) had a clay content and a high percentage of mudstone fragments, suggesting that it had been caused by wash from up-slope. Although the duration of time involved in the silting process is hard to estimate, the thickness of context (16), where not disturbed by later cut(s), indicates that it resulted in the almost total infilling of ditch cut (19).

After context (19) had completely silted up a slightly narrower re-cut was made; ditch (18), which was of the same depth and profile as the original ditch (19). The upcast from this secondary ditch appears to have been tipped on the western edge of the cut, and survived in the archaeological record as context (20). Deposit (20) was again a silty clay with inclusions of mudstone fragments, and would have taken the appearance of a low bank at least 2 m wide and 0.4 m high on the western edge of ditch (18). Whether intentional or not, this low westerly bank would have made ditch (18) c. 0.5 m wider and deeper on its west side than the primary ditch cut (19).

As before, ditch (18) appears to have been almost completely infilled with a silty clay containing mudstone fragments (15), again suggesting downslope wash. The next activity on the site was the cutting of a third linear feature, ditch (17). which followed the same line as the previous two ditches. Context (17) seems to have cut the edge of deposit (20) and the upper limits of silty clay fill context (15). This third ditch was considerably shallower, at c. 0.75 m, than

the previous two and had a noticeably different profile. The western edge of (17), c. 1.30 m deep, maintained the character of the earlier cuts, but the eastern edge was much shallower and gave the impression of being stepped. Ditch (17) again subsequently became infilled, but in a very different manner from the previous two ditches. The lowest fill (14), a clayey silt, contained a high percentage of angular to sub-rounded stone up to 0.25 m in diameter, and a few lumps of charcoal. The stony nature of context (14) implies deliberate infilling of ditch (17); it is totally different from the earlier ditch fills (15) and (16). The fill above (14) was a thin context in comparison and was characterised by a higher occurrence of charcoal lumps. This charcoal rich layer, context (13), was overlain by context (12) a fairly pure silty clay, more in keeping with the fills of ditches (18) and (19).

Subsequent to the accumulation of context (12), over one metre of soil had accumulated, represented by contexts (1), (10) and (11). The upper limits of contexts (11) merged into the lower limits of context (10) making the horizon difficult to distinguish: context (10) was rich in nineteenth century material. It would seem likely that contexts (10) and (11) represent levelling layers associated with the brick two-roomed dwelling and associated garden plot which later occupied the site.

The primary ditch (19) and bank, represented by contexts (3) and (4), are the result of initial construction of the dyke. The subsequent series of silting, re-cutting and further silting in the area of the ditch shows that the frontier established by the dyke must have been intermittently maintained, though not frequently enough to prevent the almost complete silting of ditches (18) and (19). Alternatively, the silt accumulations and re-cuts may represent periods of abandonment and refortification. Whatever the circumstances, it remains hard to estimate the length of time each ditch remained functional, or for that matter the length of time between each ditch cut.

In comparison to the recutting of the ditch, the bank shows little evidence for maintenance, with the possible exception of context (21) which may represent an attempt to consolidate the earthen rampart. The inherent problem with earthen banks is their tendency to erode; this factor, coupled with damage caused by many established trees along this section of the dyke, has led to any evidence regarding the rampart top being completely lost. However, if the earthen bank was surmounted by a timber palisade then this could have been maintained by the periodic replacement of rotten/damaged timbers without the need for large-scale earth moving for bank reconstruction. Unfortunately, the evidence for this timber structure was lacking within the area of the bank, though its original existence may still be implied.

The last re-cut of the ditch (17) showed evidence for having been deliberately infilled. The fill, containing stones up to 0.25 m across, is completely different from earlier ditch fills and certainly suggests importation of material for the purposes of infilling. One possible source for this stone is a stone revetted rampart, a possible constituent element of the bank. The charcoal rich layer (13) implies burnt timbers, and this deposit may represent the remains of a timber palisade that once crowned the earthen bank.

In conclusion, the evaluation showed strong evidence for a prolonged period of ditch maintenance and/or re-use, and confirmed the line of Wat's Dyke as plotted through this area.

Excavations at Middle Hill, Northop (SJ23286895), in 1955 and 1984 revealed a scarped bank with a 2.4 m wide stone platform, similar to the bank construction recorded in 1990 at Hope, Wrexham (SJ30955875).[31] At Sychdyn near Mold, excavation of the bank and ditch during construction of the Soughton oil pipeline (SJ252659) in 1974 uncovered a 5.6 m wide V-shaped ditch, 1.95–2.4 m deep, with a cleaning slot in the base, and a turf and earth bank 5.5 m wide on the east.[32] An earlier flat-based ditch might have preceded the V-shaped final phase. Professor Varley excavated a section through the bank and ditch at Mynydd Isa (between Buckley and Mold *c.* SJ258646), in 1957.[33] This revealed a complete section of the bank and ditch, the former 6 m wide and 0.75 m high and the latter a flat-bottomed feature 3.6 m wide and 1.2 m deep (Figure 22.2), as well as some dating evidence in the form of a Middle Saxon annular clay loom-weight found within a hearth near the base of the ditch. In comparison to most other excavated sections Varley's results seem anomalous, and it is conceivable that his use of workmen to dig the ditch, unskilled in the task of identifying archaeological deposits, may have failed to reveal the complete depth and profile of the ditch.

Birmingham University Archaeological Field Unit excavated two areas through the monument in 1984–5 prior to construction of the A5 around Gobowen, at Pentre Wern, Shropshire (SJ302329).[34] This excavation, which investigated an 80 m and a 30 m length of the bank and ditch, has provided the most extensive record for the monument at a single location, with a bank consisting of a 2 m wide clay core next to the ditch, and a 4 m wide stone rubble foundation behind (0.35 m high). The northern-most of the ditch sections was a steep V-shape with a 'cleaning slot' at the base, 8 m wide and 4 m deep, whilst the southern area revealed a less acutely angled profile (Fig. 22.3; 22.4). The variations in these ditch sections within a short distance of one another can be accounted for by Fox's observation that two sections of Wat's Dyke on slightly different alignments meet just east of Pentre Wern, and it is therefore probable that these sections reflect the product of different work gangs, or possibly alternative designs for different geological and topographical situations.[35] Cane's interpretation identifies six phases of ditch infill, alternating bands of silts and stony rampart slippage, before the final sealing of the ditch deposits by 'two successive turf lines' and ploughsoil; in contrast he phases the bank construction as a single episode consisting of a clay core at the front, with larger stones at the rear (eastern side), and the whole of this bank capped with a layer of stones, interpreted as a reversal of the natural stratigraphy as it was thrown up during excavation of the ditch.

Approximately 3 km south of this excavation, a small investigation for a water pipeline was conducted by Gifford in 1992 which produced a useful section through the ditch at a location immediately south of Oswestry Hillfort (SJ294307).[36] This suggested a possible earlier flat-based ditch or large pit with posts set in it (Fig. 23.10), before excavation of the more typical V-shaped ditch profile; the latter 6-8 m wide by 2.4-4 m deep. This had been filled with silty clays containing pebbles and cobbles, with the larger stones in the basal fills. A sandy-clay bank was observed during the subsequent watching brief, approximately 8 m wide with a line of boulders on its eastern edge.

Further south, Shropshire County Council Archaeology Service partially excavated the ditch in 1997, and obtained a complete profile of the bank, at Mile Oak (Maes-y-Clawdd), Oswestry (SJ300280).[37] Sealed beneath the bank (7.5 m wide and 0.75 m high), and lying on top of a buried soil, Hannaford found a hearth and from a substantial charcoal sample obtained a single radiocarbon date ranging between AD 268-630 at 2 sigma (UB-4158 1571 ± 69; AD 411–561 at 1 sigma). The bank and ditch were separated by a slight berm (0.7 m wide) and the bank consisted of a clay core with sands, gravels and cobbles spread over and behind (east) of it. The ditch was partially excavated to give a profile 2.3 m deep and one that could be extrapolated to suggest a width of 7.4 m (Fig. 23.5); thirteenth-century pottery was recovered from the middle fills.

Chronological and historical synthesis from previous studies

In spite of this considerable corpus of evidence for the physical characteristics of the monument, the date of construction, use and abandonment of Wat's Dyke is a matter of much conjecture, with little substance to support historical arguments of one persuasion or another. Its geographic location, in close proximity but east of Offa's Dyke, has been used to suggest a model of frontier defence during Mercian times, with Wat's Dyke as a precursor for Offa's Dyke, the latter having been generally attributed to King Offa (AD 757–796) because of its name and a passage from Bishop Asser's *Life* of King Alfred, written in AD 893, which refers to King Offa as having built a dyke between Wales and Mercia from sea to sea. Fox discusses the literary and heroic origins for the names, with Wat's Dyke first recorded in English in 1587 but with Welsh sources as early as 1431.[38] Even earlier than this, Anglo-Saxon poetry referred to the hero Gado (Wade), a prince of the vandals, helping Offa I in his wars with the Romans, a connection between two heroes which Offa of Mercia may have evoked as he emulated the achievements of his ancestral namesake in creating a secure frontier for his kingdom.[39] Wat's Dyke has also been variously attributed to Penda (632–655)[40] within a historical context that sees Penda acquiring the eastern part of Powys, with its royal centre at Pengwern (Shrewsbury and Wroxeter) in 642, and thus the authority and need to establish a formal boundary with western Powys; and Aethelbald (716–757)[41] when the political context is a resurgence of Powys under Eliseg. The spatial relationship of Wat's Dyke to English place-names on its eastern side and predominantly Welsh ones on its west, plus the fact that the hidated parts of Cheshire at Domesday (the hundreds of Atiscross and Exestan) ran up to Wat's Dyke, strongly suggests that it formed an important boundary from early Saxon times, as this form of land valuation was established from the seventh century onwards.[42]

There have also been suggestions, however, that Wat's Dyke was built after Offa's Dyke, and to understand the context for this hypothesis we need to review the shifting political fortunes of Mercia in the ninth century. Offa's successor, Cenwulf (796–821), campaigned in north Wales as far as Snowdonia, before his death at Basingwerk. In 822 Mercian attacks continued under Ceolwulf, who captured Powys and sacked Deganwy, a royal stronghold of Gwynedd.[43] Several years of instability then ensued with rival Mercian dynasties seizing power in a series of coups and insurrections; during this period Cyngen managed to recover Powys from the Mercians, which he ruled until 854. On his death, Rhodri Mawr, King of Gwynedd, took over Powys and became supreme ruler in Wales until his death in 878.[44] In 830 the Welsh Princes accepted King Egbert of Wessex as their overlord, as had Mercia and Northumbria, and from 841 Danish attacks began to exert an increasingly heavy toll on the Mercians, culminating in the viking seizure of power in Mercia in 874. But before this point, Welsh attacks had forced King Burgred of Mercia to appeal to Wessex for aid in 854. So a logical argument could be made for Wat's Dyke to have been a defensive barrier or definitive political boundary established during the second quarter of the ninth century, during a period of Mercian weakness

Direct archaeological dating evidence is limited, although abraded sherds of Roman pottery have been found within and beneath the bank at more than one location, suggesting a post-Roman date for its construction.[45] A single radiocarbon sample from Mile Oak (Maes-y-Clawdd), Oswestry, from charcoal recovered as part of a hearth sealed by the bank, has given a date range of AD 268–630 at two sigma. Hannaford discusses two historical options within this range, and he suggests that a fifth century date is more plausible, with Wat's Dyke being the product of a small British kingdom centred on Wroxeter and extending to Chester (*i.e.* the *civitas* of the Cornovii), whose western frontier was demarcated by this great earthwork. He cites Wansdyke as a contemporary and similar monument. The only other secure dating comes from Varley's excavation near the northern end, at Mynydd Isa, where he found a clay loom weight located on an occupation surface within the ditch of Wat's Dyke. The type is unmistakably Anglo-Saxon, of probable seventh-eighth century date within this region, and was found in association with a hearth, lying on top of a turf horizon. Varley suggested that this turf over the primary fill of the ditch could have developed over a generation, *c.* 30 years, and therefore provided a valuable indication of the period of construction for the monument. Implausible

as Varley's interpretation may seem with occupation, and thus a building, located within the ditch fill, it is not unique, as a parallel is given by Tom Lethbridge, who found Anglo-Saxon pottery associated with a grubenhaus within the fill of Car Dyke, a Roman canal at Waterbeach, Cambridgeshire.[46] Weaving was conducted in such sunken featured buildings and it would possibly make sense, therefore, to construct one over a ready-made basement provided by a ditch.

Recent work by the Clywd Powys Archaeological Trust into the Short Dykes in Powys has included a programme of radiocarbon dating from peat and charred material sealed beneath the banks, which has produced five dates that all cluster within the period AD 340–780.[47] Although these dates do not provide a definitive date on construction of the Short Dykes, they do provide a period during or after which the earthworks were constructed. The interpretation placed on these dykes is that of possible boundaries for administrative units, cantrefs, defined in the post-Roman period to help clarify territorial divisions on the ground. The construction of Wat's Dyke would therefore sit comfortably within this tradition as a well-established type of socio-political marker. In contrast to these closely attuned dates, however, is one from Devils Mouth Cross Dyke in Shropshire which came up with a Middle Bronze Age date through radiocarbon assay of a single sample.[48]

General Discussion and Conclusions

The results of the scientific dating for ditch deposits from the present investigation requires discussion and interpretation. The failure of the experimental worm-cast method leaves a single radiocarbon determination for the primary fill of the ditch, and seven OSL dates for the buried soil and ditch infill sequence. The former method produced a Bronze Age date, whilst the latter has resulted in a closely dated group centred on the ninth century AD. It is reasonable to suggest that an isolated C14 date does not accurately represent the date of construction of the ditch, and can probably be attributed to a residual carbonised twig that became incorporated into the ditch fill when Wat's Dyke was in use. In contrast the seven OSL dates, however, would reasonably offer a compact and persuasive group of dates that provide a solid basis for the date of use and infill of the monument. The age ranges for the four individual samples within Phases 6.2 and 6.3 (primary and secondary fill episodes) all overlap within the period 792–852 (Fig.26), whereas the two samples from Phase 6.5, an episode interpreted as deliberate and extensive infill connected with agricultural activity, fall mostly within the fourteenth century (Figs 13, 14 and 27). This date is in agreement with the date of the pottery found within the agricultural deposits behind the bank, a valuable correspondence between two very different dating techniques. Such correlation between techniques for this later episode would also suggest the

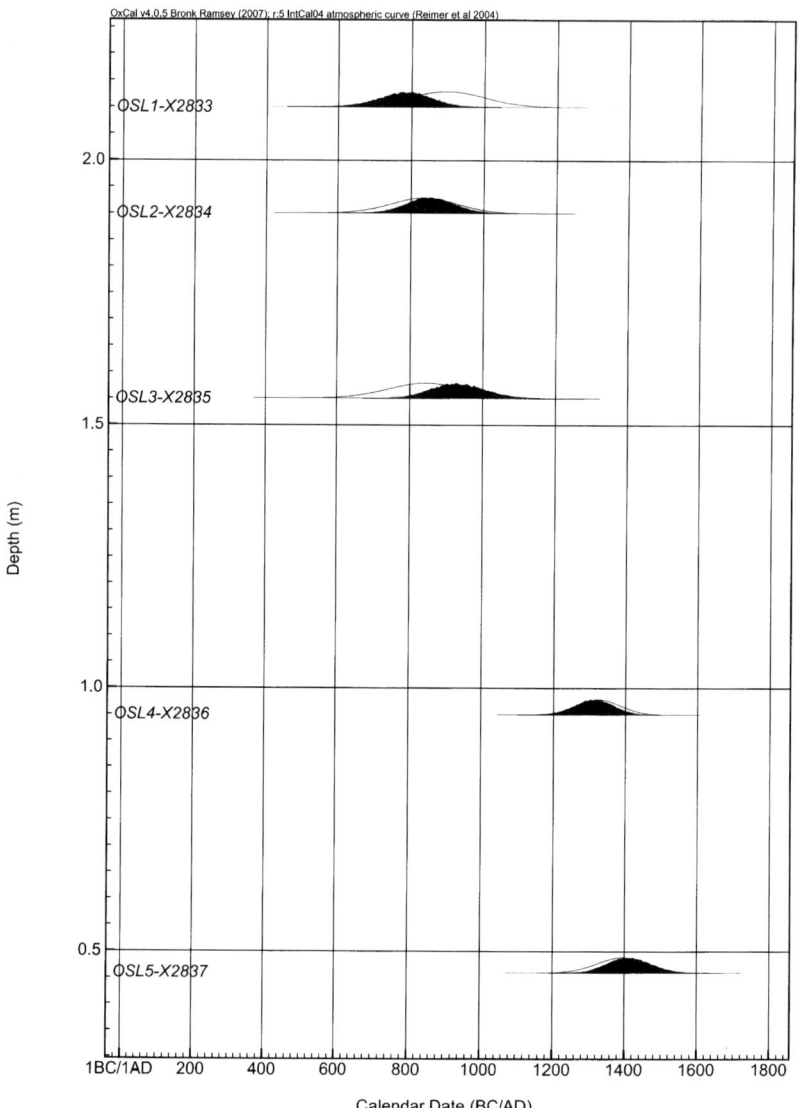

Figure 26. Baysian model of five OSL dates from one ditch section at Gobowen (Jean-Luc Schwenninger)

degree of reliance that can be attributed to the OSL dating for the earlier episodes. The seventh OSL date relates to the buried soil, which begins within the eighth century, and, although also overlapping with the general ninth century consensus, its date range does not extend to the later medieval phase of cultivation.

Such definitive results strongly suggest that this part of Wat's Dyke can be attributed to an historical interpretation of post-Offa Mercian frontier defences, and certainly is not from an earlier epoch such as Penda, or the sub-Roman kingdom of Powys. The overlapping range between the relevant five OSL dates also suggests that the monument is best ascribed to the ninth century fluctuations in the fortunes between Mercia and Powys, and it might be speculated that the defensive nature of the earthwork would perhaps best fit following the Mercian military successes of Cenwulf, when a resurgent kingdom of Powys under Cyngen and his successor

Rhodri Mawr (who was king of Gwynedd, Powys and Ceredigion threatened Anglo-Saxon settlements along a wide frontier.[49] The stratigraphic relationship between the dates would tend to suggest that the infill comes later within the range of 792–852, because OSL 1 from sub-phase 6.2 has a range that starts (at AD 792) and ends later than OSL 2 and 3 from sub-phase 6.3 (with ranges that start in the 840s), whilst OSL 6 (also from sub-phase 6.2) has a range that terminates at AD 852. The buried soil (OSL 7) shows contemporaneity with the other dates and would therefore suggest disturbance and exposure to light during construction of the monument; thus the OSL dating can be seen as establishing the period of construction as well as of use for Wat's Dyke. On this basis, we would suggest that the balance of probability makes either King Cenwulf (at the beginning of his reign *c.* 798 when he defeated Caradog, King of Gwynedd, after the Welsh took advantage of instability following Offa's and his

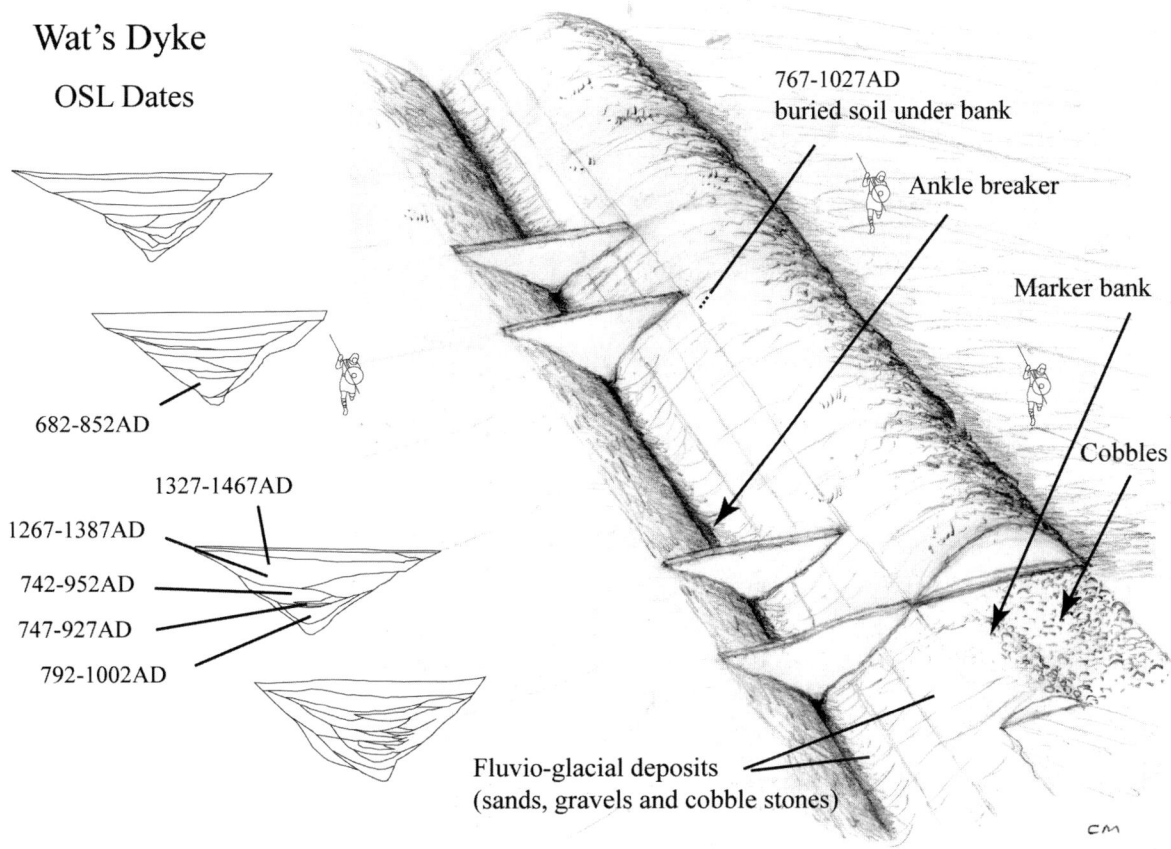

Wat's Dyke

OSL Dates

682-852AD

1327-1467AD

1267-1387AD

742-952AD

747-927AD

792-1002AD

767-1027AD
buried soil under bank

Ankle breaker

Marker bank

Cobbles

Fluvio-glacial deposits
(sands, gravels and cobble stones)

CM

Figure 27. Bird's-eye view of ditch and bank with sections superimposed, OSL dates shown in sequence, and impression of original bank (© Caroline Malim)

son King Ecgfrith's deaths in quick succession in 796); Ceolwulf in *c.* 822 as part of his Welsh campaigning; or the relatively more stable decade of Wiglaf's reign in the 830s [50] for the building of Wat's Dyke.

Cenwulf's death at Basingwerk may also be more than a mere co-incidence, as this forms the northern end of Wat's Dyke and perhaps this was one of the military strongpoints integral to ensuring the dyke's effective function. It could suggest that Wat's Dyke was the product of a long-term strategy by this relatively successful and long-lived king, and implies either a withdrawal from the line of Offa's Dyke, or a secondary defence for the better land of the Mercian plain to also include an area west of the Dee at the expense of Gwynedd. Ceolwulf's campaign could be seen as a direct continuation of this policy.

An alternative hypothesis would be for Wat's Dyke to have been constructed in response to Welsh attacks that took advantage of Mercian in-fighting from 823–830, to a time after Wiglaf's seizure of power in 827 and subsequent defeat and exile in 829 by King Egbert of Wessex with his Welsh allies, to a period when Wiglaf retook Mercia and the country once again had a king of sufficient longevity and prestige to have the authority and resources to build a defence against any future Welsh incursions, *i.e.* the

period AD 830–839.[51] If we assume the initial infill of Wat's Dyke was relatively rapid within the first few years, but that secondary silting represented by sub-phase 6.2 took place over a longer timespan, then conceivably a period of some 10-20 years might have passed before a more deliberate slighting of the defences suggested by the stony deposits of sub-phases 6.3 and 64 . These latter have a date range that starts in the 740s.

The nine investigations of Wat's Dyke (excluding Kenney), summarized above and in Table 5 (and Figs. 22 and 23), show a considerable degree of consistency in the design and construction method employed throughout the length of the monument, confirming its creation as a single action and in response to a single concept. The bank ranges from 5.5–8 m in width, with evidence for a stone foundation 2.4–5m in width at four of the nine sections. Marker banks and marker stones are present at three of the investigations, those grouped between Gobowen and Oswestry. With the exception of Varley's excavation (possibly incomplete: see comment above), the ditch at Wat's Dyke seems to have been of a distinctive design, V-shaped and with a 'cleaning trench' or 'ankle-breaker' type of narrow gully at the base, a design that perhaps owes its origin to knowledge of Roman military

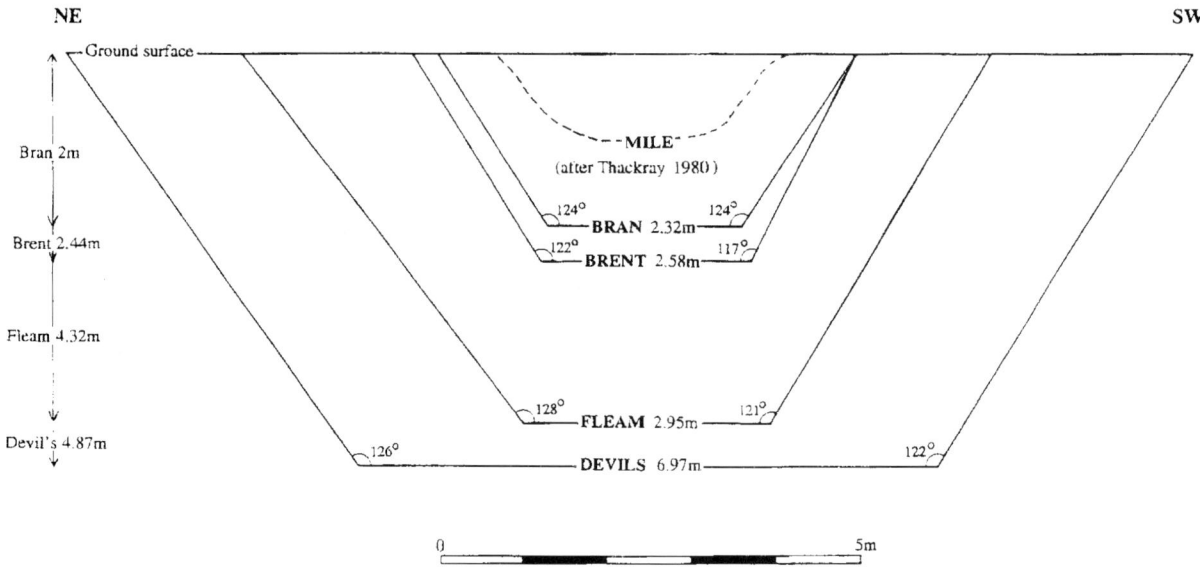

Figure 28. Average comparative profiles through the Cambridgeshire Dykes showing template design

engineering.[52] The ditch ranged from 4 m wide on a steep hillside at Nant Farm, to 8 m wide, and 2–4 m in depth. All four of the investigations along the southern part of the monument (Gobowen and Oswestry) fall within the widest and deepest dimensions, presumably as they are located in more vulnerable, lowland situations. The 'cleaning slot' or ankle-breaker feature is found at Nant Farm, Sychdyn (Mold), Gobowen, and Pentre Wern. A flat-based earlier ditch is tentatively suggested at Sychdyn, and it is worth noting that a feature in the present excavation (pit 2009; Fig. 14), as well as one at Gifford's south of Old Oswestry (Fig. 23.10), could also be interpreted from a single section as an earlier flat-based ditch: if this feature actually existed it might also be used to explain Varley's uncharacteristic findings, but its presence has been sufficiently inconsistent as to suggest other causes such as occasional quarry pits or anomalies in the natural geology. Phasing the monument is more difficult, but most excavators have agreed that the surviving bank consists of a single episode of construction, with no evidence for subsequent maintenance. The ditch infill sequence has a broadly similar correlation between different excavated sections, within which, however, considerable minor variability exists: this sequence has been interpreted as having three phases at Nant Farm, six phases at Pentre Wern, and five phases in the present excavation, and all have some evidence to suggest recuts.

Apart from comparative information along Wat's Dyke itself, it is also instructive to consider some other parallels from similar types of contemporary monument. David Hill and Margaret Worthington have distinguished that Offa's Dyke was a single earthwork feature that ran for 64 miles along the boundary between Mercia and Powys, from Treuddyn near Mold in the north to the hills above the

River Wye near Hereford, which should not be confused with other linear earthworks such as Wat's Dyke, the Whitford Dyke, or the Short Dykes.[53] A series of short dykes in the Herefordshire Plain and West Gloucestershire might have formed a continuation of Offa's Dyke between heavily wooded areas.[54] Offa's Dyke was carefully sited to give strategic advantage by maintaining views to the west at all times, and the structure consisted of a V- or U-shaped ditch up to 2 m deep and 6 m wide, with a 12 m wide bank to the east; sometimes a smaller ditch with counter-scarp bank was constructed, and evidence for a marker bank of turves, or a line marked by a furrow or posts, has been found beneath the bank. Stones were laid as a foundation in some parts and possibly used as a wall or facing in others, with a berm of 0.8 m found between bank and ditch at, for example, Chirk Castle Home Farm.[55] In essence, Offa's Dyke has been previously interpreted as a political boundary and a physical barrier to keep the Welsh out of Mercia, but an alternative argument is that Offa's and the other dykes were built instead to allow controlled access to and from Mercia as a means for facilitating secure trade and taxation for the Mercian state.[56] The similarity between the general concept and design of Offa's and Wat's Dykes is evident, but there are also differences and it is worth outlining what these are and what the reasons might be for such changes.

Firstly the area that Wat's Dyke defends overlaps with the northern end of Offa's Dyke, but continues to the Flintshire coast. This suggests a new danger coming from not only Powys but also Gwynedd. The historical connections of the death of Cenwulf at Basingwerk (the northern end of Wat's Dyke) and the sacking of Deganwy by Ceolwulf, fit comfortably with the Dyke being constructed as a military response for an enemy along the

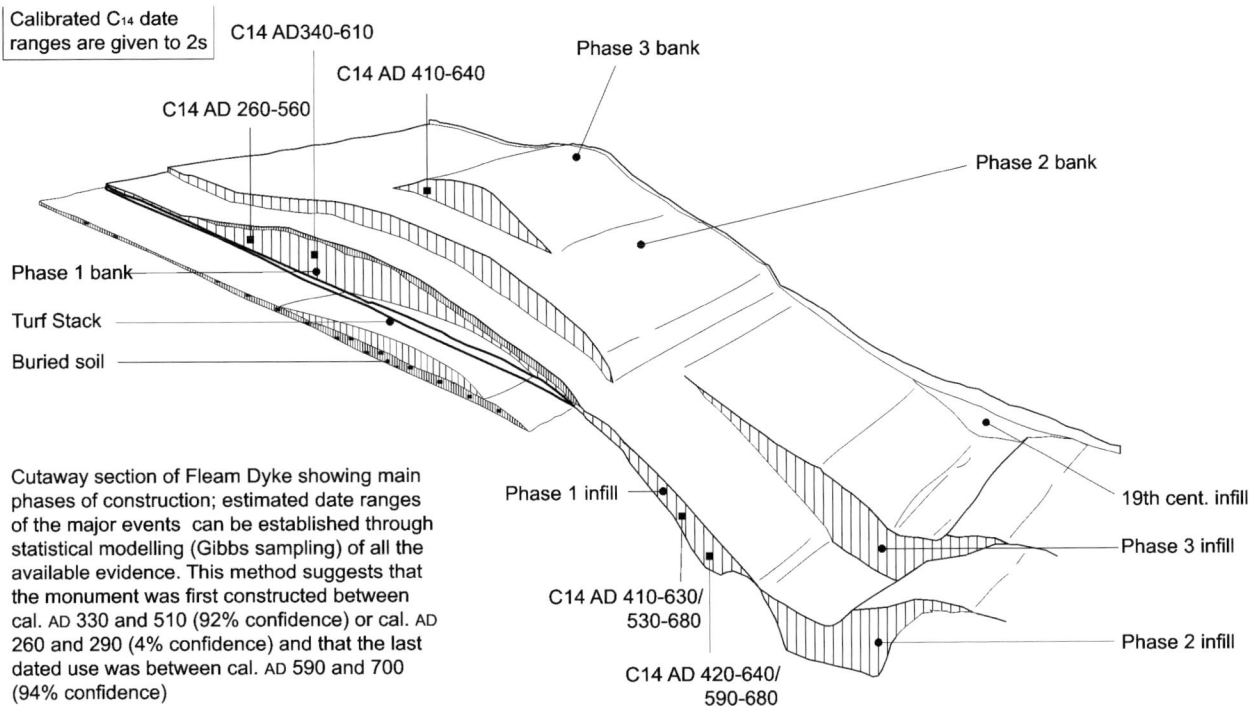

Figure 29. 3-D view of Fleam Dyke, Cambridgeshire, showing bank and ditch phases as a series of cutaways, together with sequence of C14 dates(drawn by John Cane[60])

north Wales coastal zone as well as inland further south, a threat posed by Rhodri Mawr in Gwynedd, and Cyngen in Powys (and after 854 by Rhodri Mawr). Second, the strategic location for Wat's Dyke is not always as obvious as that for Offa's; it was designed as a series of straight lines between prominent survey points whilst Offa's Dyke, in contrast, ran through sparsely populated countryside and was designed to carefully follow topographical features and contours. Although Wat's Dyke is set back several miles into Mercian territory on the edge of the Midland Plain, it actually links a number of pre-existing forts from the Mercian estate centre at Maesbury, through Old Oswestry and Alyn Fort for example, to the Welsh royal residence at Bagillt and fortification at Basingwerk on the Dee estuary. This suggests the possibility of a tactical retreat from Offa's carefully planned frontier, which must have become untenable as a defence against new threats, to a new line at Wat's Dyke, which nonetheless still maintained some strategic advantage through its use of local topography to maximise views to the west. Third, the ditch is generally deeper and of a more uniform shape than Offa's Dyke, and a comparison of excavated profiles is shown in Figures 22 and 23: the V-shape and dimensions of the ditch from one site, if superimposed over that from another, match almost identically. The bank is also more solid and consistent in its technique of construction than has been revealed by the investigations of Offa's Dyke, with a carefully laid cobblestone core topped by a clay and gravel rampart. Such an increase

in the defensive qualities and better engineered structure argues for a definite military purpose rather than a political boundary.

Fourth, evidence for a berm has only been found once from Wat's Dyke, at the section excavated at Mile Oak, Oswestry. This absence of a berm is similar to a group of monuments from Cambridgeshire, which achieved an angle of ditch and bank that resulted in minimal erosion without the need for berm or revetments. In fact, the Cambridgeshire Dykes have demonstrated a template that was probably followed in their construction, with banks and ditches increasing in scale as the earthworks were located closer to the heartland of the Anglo-Saxon migrants (Fig. 28).[57] These ditches ranged from 5 m-14 m in width and 2 m-5 m in depth, with the largest bank at Devils Dyke surviving to over 5 m in height and 22 m in width. Although Devils Dyke was a single phase monument, the next largest was Fleam Dyke which had been re-modelled on more than one occasion and provided a complex stratigraphic sequence with a series of seven radiocarbon dates which have established a solid chronological framework for its construction and use (Fig. 29). The major difference in design between these earlier monuments and Wat's Dyke is that the Cambridgeshire Dykes have flat bases, whereas Wat's Dyke generally has a pronounced V-shape with a 'cleaning slot' in the base.[58] This type of feature has parallels in the ankle-breaker design that the Roman army used, for example, in construction of ditches surrounding temporary camps, a design that would have made crossing the ditch considerably more difficult than with a flat-based design. Such a design also emphasises the military nature of Wat's Dyke, and it would seem reasonable to assume Wat's Dyke functioned as a very real barrier between Mercia and its enemies, operating in much the same way that Hill and Worthington suggest for Offa's Dyke; as a patrolled rampart with strongpoints from which rapid armed response could be deployed if a warning was raised of impending attack, or of a raid over the boundary.[59] The location of the Gobowen section of Wat's Dyke lies between the low-lying Old Oswestry hillfort to the south and Bryn-y-Castell to the north, both likely locations for such strongpoints, and thus would provide a good fit for this hypothetical model. Even without this sort of patrolled defence and rapid response, Wat's Dyke would still have constituted a particularly effective barrier to cavalry and wheeled transport, and if a thorn hedge was planted on the bank or thorn branch obstacle was laid in the ditch, then this would have acted as a contemporary form of barbed-wire to impede the movement of attackers on foot.

In conclusion, the investigations at Gobowen have been extremely useful in providing for the first time substantive evidence for the date of construction and initial infill of Wat's Dyke, which in turn has helped in reassessing its historical context. The nature of the surviving monument has confirmed previous excavations and testified to the skill and scale of the bank and ditch as a carefully planned piece of military engineering and a massive undertaking. The present article is offered here as a spark to re-ignite debate over this major monument, as well as the date and function of the other linear earthworks within the Welsh Marches.

Acknowledgements

The authors[61] would like to thank Fletcher Homes (Shropshire) for funding the works and Matt Wason, Land Manager, Keith Sudlow (Contracts Manager), Richard Hilditch (Site Manager) and Jonathan Westwood (Managing Director) for their support throughout. Many people have helped during the project including: Matt Canti, John Carrott, Rob Davies, Brian Dix, James Griffiths, Hugh Hannaford, Mark Jones, Caroline Malim, Lisa Moffat, George Nash, Dave Peat, Gill Reaney, Des Roberts, Jean-Luc Schwenninger, Jeff Spencer, Adam Stanford, Andy Towle, Alan Vince, Will Walker, Penny Ward, Mike Watson, Tam Webster, and Steve Witham.

This article has been published with the aid of funding from Fletcher Homes (Shropshire) Ltd. The authors thank their employers, SLR Consulting Ltd, for support in production of this article.

Notes

1. Webster and Malim 2006
2. Gelling 1990, 229–230
3. Hill and Worthington 2003
4. Fox 1955, 253
5. Blair 2007, 3–4
6. Hannaford 1998; Hill 1991
7. Cane 1996
8. Blake and Lloyd 2000: Matthews 2001a
9. Hannaford 1998, 6
10. Varley 1976
11. Matthews 2001b
12. Fox 1955, 226
13. Fox 1955, 247–248
14. Cane 1966; Hannaford 1997
15. Cane 1996, similar feature Figures. 22.3 and 22.4
16. Vince 1984
17. Barker and Higham 1982; Barker and Higham 1988; Vince 1982
18. Rutter in Davey. 1977, 70–85
19. Webster and Dunning 1960
20. Earp and Hains 1971, 87 and 97–8
21. Vince 1985; Vince 2002
22. 'GBA'/'BS' sensu Dobney *et al.* 1992
23. Aitken 1998
24. Murray and Wintle 2000
25. Hill and Worthington 2003, 116–118
26. see for example Webster 1969, 174
27. Fox 1955
28. Hill and Worthington 2003, 163 and Appendix 3; Kenney 2004
29. see for example Matthews 2001
30. Dan Garner unpublished ms
31. Grenter 1984; Jones and Brassil 1990

32. Hill 1980, 34–5
33. Varley 1976
34. Cane 1996
35. Fox 1955, 248
36. Rogers 1992
37. Hannaford 1998
38. Fox 1955, 226
39. *ibid.*. 287–90
40. Higham 1993, 101; Hannaford 1998
41. Fox 1955, 273; Bu'lock 1972, 37–9
42. Bu'lock 1972, 38; Higham. 1993, 100–01; Matthews 2001
43. Bu'lock 1972, 41
44. Bartrum 1993, 558
45. *e.g.* Hannaford 1998
46. Lethbridge 1935
47. Hankinson and Caseldine 2006
48. Dinn, Greig, Limbrey, Miln, and de Rouffignac 2004
49. Bartrum 1993, 558
50. Walker 2000, 22–37
51. Walker 2000, 34–7
52. Webster 1969, 174
53. Hill and Worthington 2003, 108–14; Hooke 1989
54. Fox 1955, 207–11; see also Hooke 1989, 114–5 for supporting data on woodland in Anglo-Saxon boundary zones
55. Fox 1955, 48, 75–6, 122, 125–6
56. Malim 2007
57. Malim, Penn, Robinson, Wait and Welsh 1996
58. Cane 1996; Kenney 2004
59. Hill and Worthington 2003, 126
60. Malim 2003
61. SLR Consulting, Mytton Mill, Forton Heath, Montford Bridge, Shrewsbury SY4 1HA

Bibliography

Aitken, M. 1998. *An Introduction to Optical Dating: The dating of Quaternary sediments by the use of photon-stimulated luminescence*. Oxford University Press.

Barker, P. A. and Higham, R. A. 1982. *Hen Domen, Montgomery: a timber castle on the Welsh Border*, Royal Archaeological Institute: Monograph.

Barker, P. A. and Higham, R. A. 1988. *Hen Domen, Montgomery: a timber castle on the English-Welsh border. Excavations 1960–1988: a summary report*, Hen Domen Archaeological Project 1988.

Bartrum, P. 1993. *A Welsh Classical Dictionary: People in History and Legend up to about A.D. 1000*, The National Library of Wales.

Blair, J. 2007. *Waterways and Canal-Building in Medieval England, Medieval History and Archaeology*: Oxford University Press.

Blake, S. and Lloyd, S. 2000. *The Keys to Avalon: The True Location of Arthur's Kingdom Revealed*, Shaftsbury.

Bu'lock, J. D. 1972. *Pre-Conquest Cheshire 383–1066*, Cheshire Community Council: Chester .

Cane, J. 1996. 'Excavations on Wat's Dyke at Pentre Wern, Shropshire in 1984–85' in *Trans. of the Shropshire Arch. and Hist. Soc.*,**71**,

Davey, P. J. 1977. *Medieval pottery from excavations in the north west*, Liverpool: University of Liverpool.

Dinn, J., Greig, J., Limbrey, S., Miln, J. and de Rouffignac, C. 2004. 'Three Long Mynd Earthworks: excavation and assessment of environmental potential', *Transactions of the Shropshire Archaeological Society*, **79**, 77.

Earp, J. R. and Hains, B. A. 1971. *British Regional Geology: The Welsh Borderland*, HMSO: London.

Fox, C. 1955. *A Field Survey of the Western Frontier Works of Mercia in the Seventh and Eighth Centuries AD*, London, British Academy: Oxford University Press.

Garner, D. 1997. *Archaeological Excavation at Wat's Dyke Crossing, Flintshire BHP Petroleum Pipeline from Point of Ayr to Connah's Quay, Flintshire* Unpublished Earthworks Archaeology project No. E67.

Gelling, M. and Foxall, H. D. G. 1990. *The Place Names of Shropshire: Part One*, EPNS Vols. 63/63.

Grenter, S. 1984. 'Wat's Dyke, Middle Hill, Northop', *Archaeology in Wales CBA Group 2*, **24**, 66–7.

Hankinson, R. and Caseldine, A. 2006. 'Short Dykes in Powys and their Origins' *Archaeological Journal*, **163**, 264–69.

Hannaford, H. 1998. An Excavation on Wat's Dyke at Mile Oak, Oswestry, Shropshire in *Transactions of the Shropshire Archaeological and Historical Society* Vol LXXIII.

Higham, N. J. 1993. *The Origins of Cheshire*, Manchester University Press.

Hill, D. 1980. *Recent work on Offa's and Wat's Dykes* University of Manchester unpublished manuscript.

Hill, D. 1991. 'Offa's and Wat's Dykes', in *The Archaeology of Clwyd*, (Manley *et al.* eds).

Hill, D. and Worthington, M. 2003. *Offa's Dyke History and Guide*, Stroud: Tempus Publishing.

Hooke, D. 1989. 'Pre-Conquest woodland: its distribution and usage', *Agricultural History Review*, **37:2**, 113–29.

Jones, N. and Brassil, K. 1990. 'Wat's Dyke, Hope', *Archaeology in Wales CBA Group 2*, **30**, 65–6.

Kenney, J. 2004. 'A trench dug through Wat's Dyke at Pen y Bryn, demonstrating its presence along the eastern side of the Ceirog Valley'. *Shropshire History and Archaeology*, **77**, 10–14.

Lethbridge, T. 1935. 'The Car Dyke, the Cambridgeshire Ditches and the Anglo-Saxons', *Proc. of the Cambridge Antiquarian Soc.* **35**, 90–6.

Malim, T., Penn, K., Robinson, B., Wait, G., and Welsh, K. 1996. 'New evidence on the Cambridgeshire Dykes and Worsted Street Roman Road', *Proc. of the Cambridge Antiquarian Soc.*, **85**, 27–122.

Malim, T. 2003. *The Anglo-Saxons in South Cambridgeshire*. Cambridgeshire County Council.

Malim, T. 2006. *Wat's Dyke, Gobowen – Project Design for an Archaeological Excavation*, Gifford Unpublished Report No 13159.R03revA.

Malim, T. 2007. 'The origins and design of linear earthworks in the Welsh Marches', *Landscape Enquiries: Proceedings of the Clifton Antiquarian Club*, 8.

Matthews, K. 2001a. The 'Wall of Severus' www.wansdyke21.org.uk

Matthews, K. 2001b. *Wat's Dyke: a North Welsh linear boundary* www.wansdyke21.org.uk

Murray and Wintle 2000. 'Luminescence dating of quartz using an improved single aliquot of quartz', *Radiation Measurements* **32**, 57–73.

Rogers, I. 1992. *Report on an Archaeological Investigation and Monitoring at the Whittington-Oswestry Low-Level Water Main Installation*, Gifford unpublished client report for Severn Trent Water.

Varley, W. J. 1976. 'Wat's Dyke at Mynydd Isa, Flintshire', *Flintshire Historical Society Publications*, **27**, 129–37.

Vince, A. G. 1985. 'Part 2: the ceramic finds.', in R. Shoesmith (ed.), *Hereford City Excavations: Volume 3. The Finds, CBA Research Report 56*, The Council for British Archaeology: London.

Vince, A. 2002. 'The Pottery', in A. Thomas and A. Boucher (eds), *Hereford City Excavations Volume 4: Further Sites and Evolving Interpretations*, 65–92, Logaston Press: Logaston,

Walker, I. W. 2000. *Mercia and the Making of England*, Sutton Publishing: Stroud.

Webster, G. and Dunning, G. C. 1960. 'A Medieval pottery kiln at Audlem, Cheshire', *Medieval Archaeology*, **4**, 109–126.

Webster, G. 1969. *The Roman Imperial Army*, A. and C. Black: London.

Webster, T. and Malim, T. 2006. *Wat's Dyke, Gobowen – Report on An Archaeological Evaluation*, Gifford Unpublished Report No 13159.R02.

The Middle and Late Anglo-Saxon Defences of Western Mercian Towns

Steven Bassett

Elaborate defences, which are commonly assumed to have been built by the Mercian ruler Æthelred and/or his wife Æthelflæd and therefore to be of late ninth-/early tenth-century date, have been located and investigated at Hereford (two major sites and nine other sightings), Tamworth (eleven sites), Winchcombe (two or three sites), and Worcester (two sites). However, this assumption has a fragile basis, being based mainly on sparse documentary references and 'identification by association', not on primary archaeological data. Sealed directly beneath them at Hereford, Tamworth and Winchcombe were other, earlier defences, of which there has been little systematic discussion. The paper re-examines the relevant archaeological evidence, published and unpublished, and reaches two important conclusions: (1) that the defences in question at Hereford, Tamworth and Winchcombe can be safely regarded as being of late ninth-/early tenth-century date, but that those at Worcester may need reappraisal; and (2) that the defences sealed below them at the first-named three places were much more substantial than has previously been presumed, that enough survives for their form and function to be reliably characterised, and that they were probably built in the eighth century or very early in the ninth century.

Introduction

We still know surprisingly little about the defences by which some of the more important settlements of western Mercia were surrounded by 918 (Fig. 1).[1] According to the short set of annals preserved in the B manuscript of the Anglo-Saxon Chronicle and collectively known as the Mercian Register, Alfred's daughter Æthelflæd built defences at *Bremesburh*, *Scergeat*, *Bricg* (?Quatford), Tamworth, Stafford, Eddisbury, Warwick, Chirbury, *Weardburh* and Runcorn between 910 and 915.[2] Another contemporary source shows that prior to his death in 911 she and her husband Æthelred, the ruler of western Mercia from *c.* 881 to 909, had also done so at Worcester (by *c.* 889x899); and, although the evidence is only circumstantial, they had probably built them at Hereford, Winchcombe and Shrewsbury too.[3] It is also probable that they had repaired the Roman walls at Gloucester and Chester.[4] Yet despite many excavations in seemingly appropriate locations, only at Tamworth, Hereford, Winchcombe and, most recently, Worcester have Æthelred's and Æthelflæd's defences been said to have been identified on the ground;[5] and it is on the evidence for them and for any earlier defences there that this paper is focused. Even at these four places, however, the widely held belief that the excavated ramparts and

ditches are of late ninth- or early tenth-century origin rests on a worryingly flimsy evidential basis. There is more than a whiff of circularity in some of the identifications which have been made of 'Æthelflædan' defences, and consequently there is an active danger of our perpetuating, and even extending, a myth about the date of origin and even the very appearance of the western Mercian fortifications of the 'reconquest' period.

The same excavations have thrown up other significant uncertainties. At Tamworth, Hereford and Winchcombe two other phases of defensive work of potentially Anglo-Saxon date have been identified. One represents the subsequent refurbishment of the allegedly late ninth-/early tenth-century defences, with the rampart's timber revetment being replaced in stone at all three places. This activity is often said to have occurred at the end of the tenth century or early in the eleventh, when a renewed and far better organised Danish assault on England occurred in the reign of Æthelred II;[6] but the dating evidence is not straightforward, and it has never been adequately scrutinised. Both phases of fortification – the initial one with its timber-revetted rampart and the succeeding masonry phase – were found to be well preserved at Hereford and Winchcombe and had left

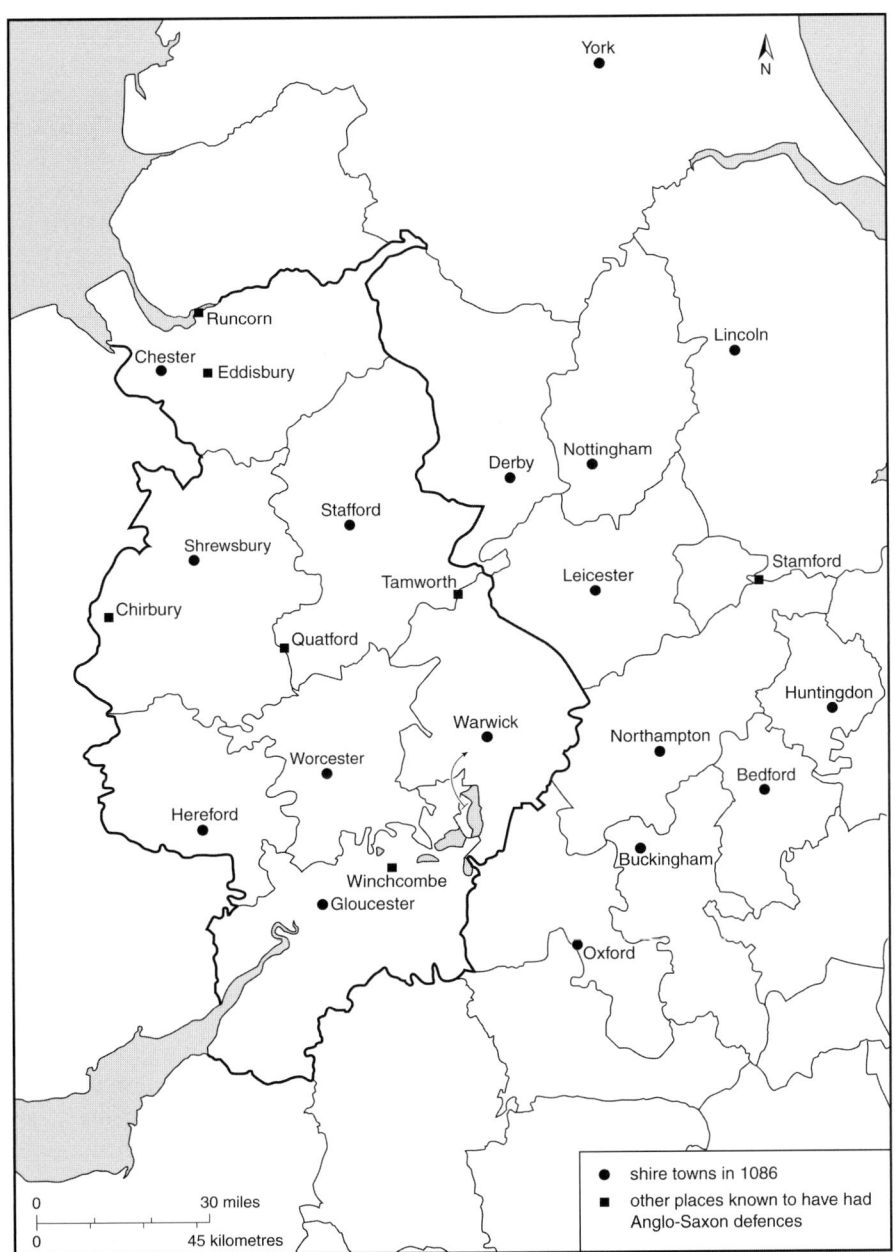

Figure 1. Shires and shire towns in midland England in 1086, as mapped from the evidence of Domesday Book, with small detached portions of Worcestershire shown shaded. The area referred to in this paper as 'western Mercia' is outlined.

sufficiently strong traces at Tamworth too for a confident statement to be made about their appearance. Sealed beneath them, however, at all three places was a yet earlier set of defences, of which the remains were far less substantial but were nonetheless distinct. Their first excavator at Tamworth merely identified them as 'pre-rampart features', *i.e.* pre-Æthelflædan ones, and surmised that they were 'concerned with the building of the palace complex' and might be of pre-ninth-century origin.[7] At Hereford and Winchcombe the evidence was better preserved and the discussion of them correspondingly

fuller, but opinions varied significantly about both their function and their date of origin.

However, in a seminal paper Nicholas Brooks pointed up their significance in respect of the references to obligatory military renders which Mercian land charters were beginning to make by the 740s.[8] These include the requirement to contribute a labour force for '*burh* work', *i.e.* 'work on a fortified place', which plainly implies that such places existed by the middle of the eighth century.[9] The geographical distribution of the lands on which charters show that this burden was levied is very uneven;

but it reflects the pattern of their survival and cannot be taken to mean that only some parts of the Mercian kingdom had fortified places.

As has been argued elsewhere, it is likely that during the long period in which the Mercian kings regularly had overlordship over most, and sometimes all, of the rest of England south of the River Humber, they oversaw the establishment of a network of fortified settlements across the whole area over which they had direct rule. Hereford, Winchcombe and Tamworth were all major royal centres under the Mercian kings,[10] and it is likely that they accurately epitomise the sort of place which was chosen to be fortified. No defences of this period have yet been identified elsewhere in the midlands, but that may reflect a paucity of appropriate excavations rather than a scarcity of Mercian fortified places of the middle Anglo-Saxon period. Our persistent failure to identify most of the defensive circuits which Æthelred and Æthelflæd built in the west midlands underlines how much we rely on written sources for our knowledge of the programme of fortification which they undertook between *c.* 881 and 918. Only four such circuits may have been located (and only at Tamworth has the likely full extent of one been determined), and below three of them were found the shredded remains of earlier defences of which the existence had previously been unsuspected.

Yet, wholly dependent as we still are on written sources for our knowledge of the locations of the Mercian fortified places of the 'reconquest' period, we get nothing from them beyond a bare record of place-names (some of which remain unidentified). It is essential, then, that when instances of these defences are found and excavated, as much information as possible should be wrung from them, and the reliability of the conclusions about their dates of creation and modification should be of the highest order. With so few of them yet known to us the burden which they bear as presumed representatives of a much more numerous group is very considerable; and the understandable tendency to make more of their excavators' often tentative explanations and legitimate speculations can lead to a significantly distorted understanding of what was actually found and of what it means. And so it will be salutary to re-examine the evidence from the excavations at Hereford, Tamworth, Winchcombe and Worcester and the published interpretations of them.

Hereford

Hereford's defences

In many respects the sections excavated across the pre-Conquest defences of Hereford are the most satisfactory ones undertaken in the west midlands, but they have left some key questions unanswered. There have been two major excavations – by P. Rahtz on a site on Victoria Street and by R. Shoesmith at 5 Cantilupe Street; and the chance to gain further information came from observation of contractors' trenches.[11] As a result it is known that Hereford had three main stages of medieval defences. The first comprised a gravel rampart enclosing an apparently rectangular area, the west and north sides of which have been proved archaeologically (Fig. 2).[12] The second stage made use of the same line to the west and north, but ignored the east side of the first-stage defences so as to enclose a larger area. At both stages the River Wye formed the south side, along which there is no evidence of man-made defences.[13] By and large the third stage followed its immediate predecessor's west and east sides but ran on beyond them both so as to enclose a substantial northern suburb. It is almost certain that the first two stages are of pre-Conquest date, with the second one arguably created in the period of rule in western Mercia of Æthelred and his wife, then widow, Æthelflæd[14] and refurbished later in the tenth century or in the early eleventh, and that the third stage is of the late twelfth century and later.[15]

The most valuable aspect of the Hereford excavations is the opportunity which they afford for a reliable understanding of the defensive sequence, with much information having been recovered about the structure and make-up of the second- and third-stage ramparts. Something useful is also known of the make-up of the first rampart; but on no site could its front be properly examined. Nor was a section of the first- or second-stage ditch ever excavated, either mechanically or by hand, although both were seen in contractors' trenches.[16] This increases the difficulty of making reliable comparisons between Hereford's defensive sequence and those excavated at Tamworth, Winchcombe and Worcester. Nonetheless the high quality of the evidence from Hereford and of its publication makes it the obvious starting-point for any discussion of the region's pre-Conquest defences.

Although only the tail of the first-stage rampart has been excavated, it is widely considered to have been substantial enough to be defensive (Figs 3–4).[17] It overlay a boundary bank and ditch (F64) and, to the east of them, a probably contemporary timber building of posthole construction which may have been taken down to allow the rampart to be built, and which itself overlay one of a pair of grain-drying ovens.[18] Shoesmith comments that the rampart may have had a revetted face. Although there is no secure evidence of this, a timber slot which was seen when subways were being built at the north-west corner of the circuit, and which was sealed by material associated with the second-stage rampart, 'could have been an emplacement for [frontal] timberwork and may belong to this stage of the defensive works.'[19] Its ditch, seen in the same contractors' works, was over 10 m. wide and at least *c.* 1.5 m. deep.[20]

It was superseded after an unknown period of time by a turf-and-clay rampart which was laced with branches and had a stout timber face. The rampart is estimated to have been *c.* 2.5 m. high at the front, with a wide flat top which may have had a low timber fence along its rear edge, either for protection against erosion or as part of

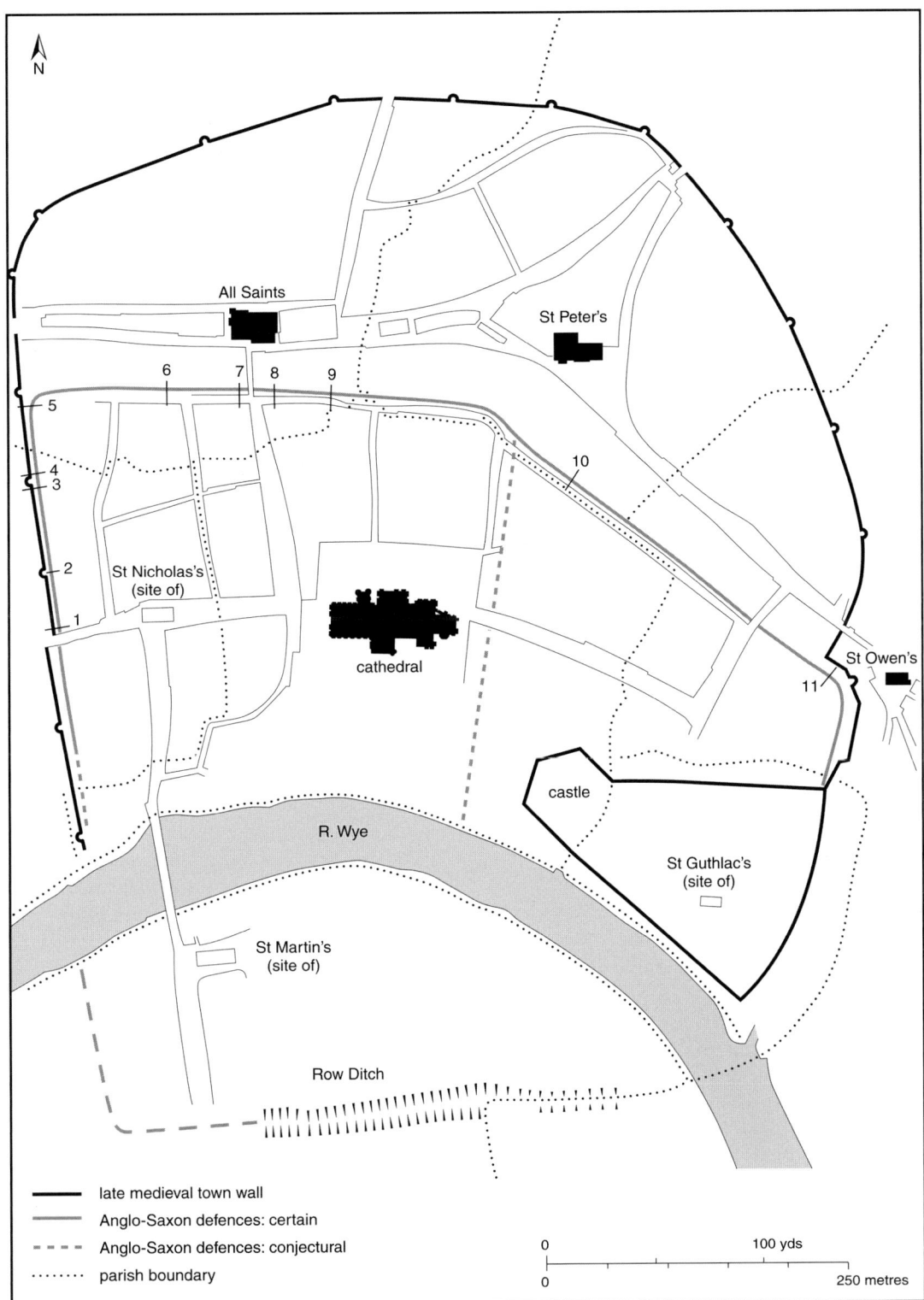

Figure 2. Medieval Hereford, showing the sites of excavations on and adjacent to the Anglo-Saxon and later medieval defences: 1. Friar's Gate. 2. Berrington Street. 3. 'Western rampart' site. 4. Victoria Street. 5. Subway sections. 6. 'Inner northern defences' site C. 7. King's Head. 8. City Arms Hotel. 9. 'Inner northern defences' site D. 10. Town Hall. 11. Cantilupe Street.

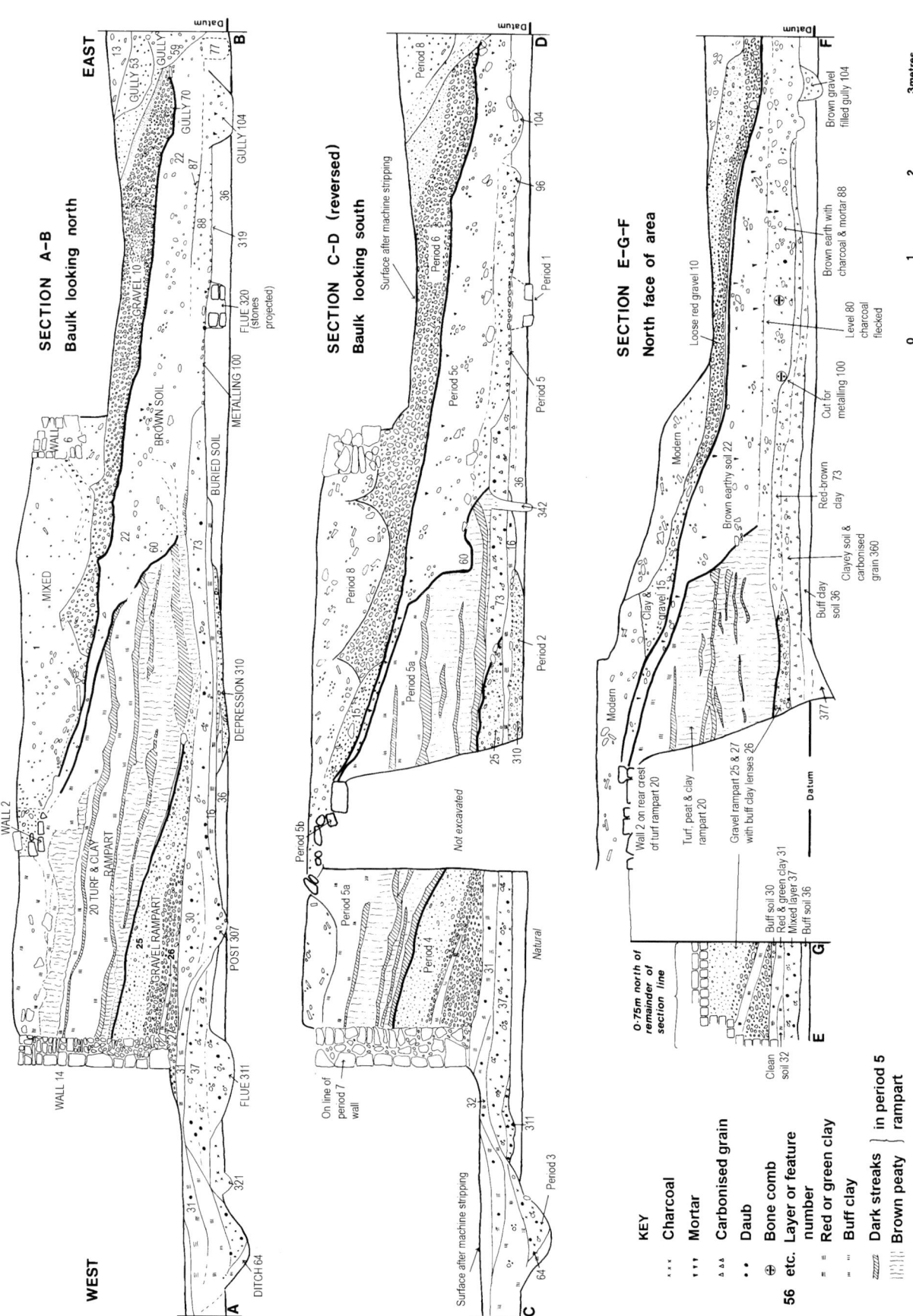

Figure 3. Victoria Street, Hereford: the Anglo-Saxon and later defences, as drawn in sectional view by P. Rahtz. (Originally published as R. Shoesmith, Hereford City Excavations Volume 2. Excavations on and close to the Defences (Council for British Archaeology; Research Report 46, 1982), fig. 22, on 33: 'Victoria Street. The main sections A–B, C–D and E–G–F across the defences', and reproduced with the excavator's, author's and publisher's permission.)

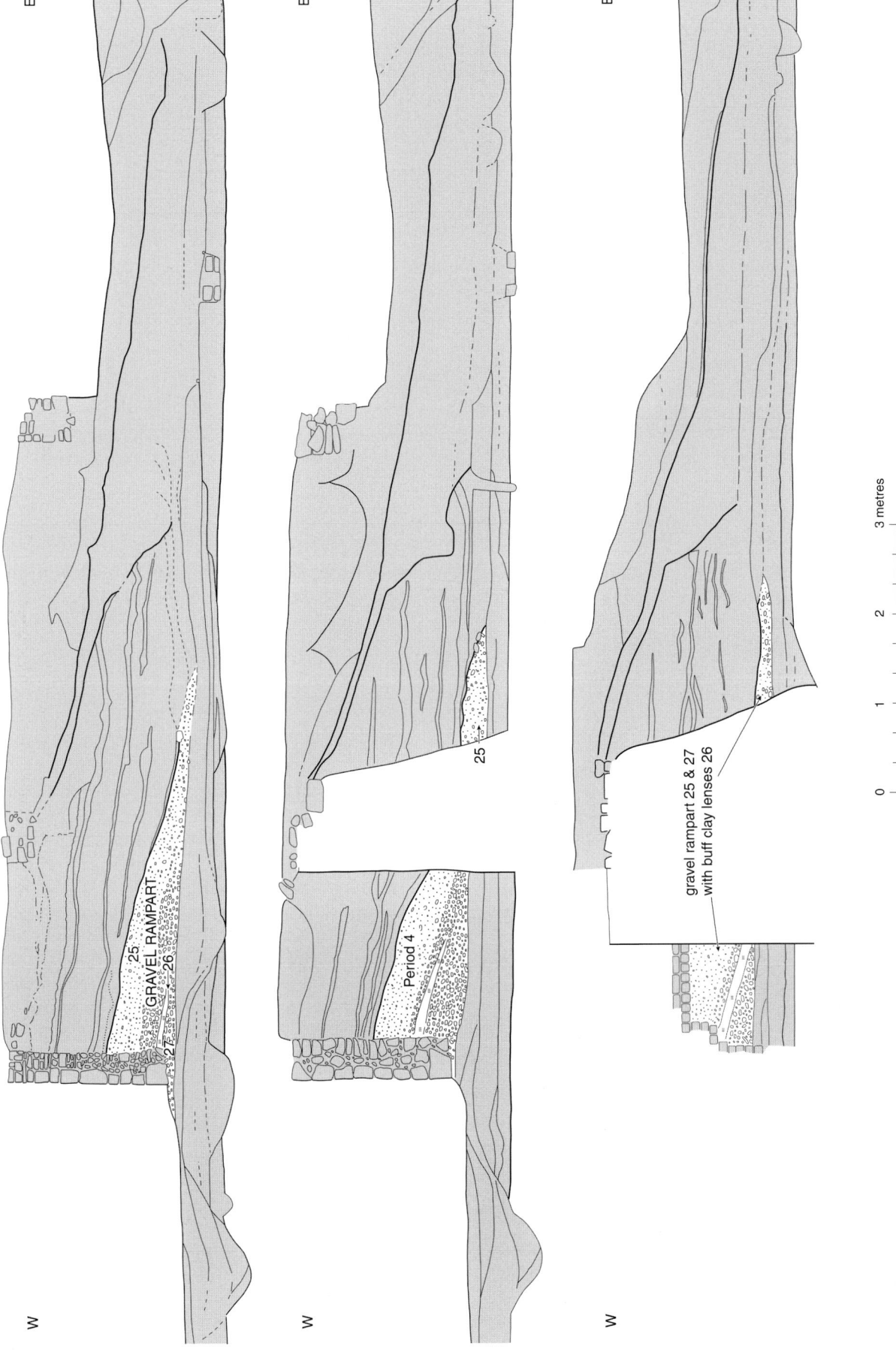

Figure 4. An analysis of P. Rahtz's Victoria Street, Hereford, section drawing (Fig. 3): suggested components of the middle Anglo-Saxon defences. (Those of other periods are shown grey-tinted.)

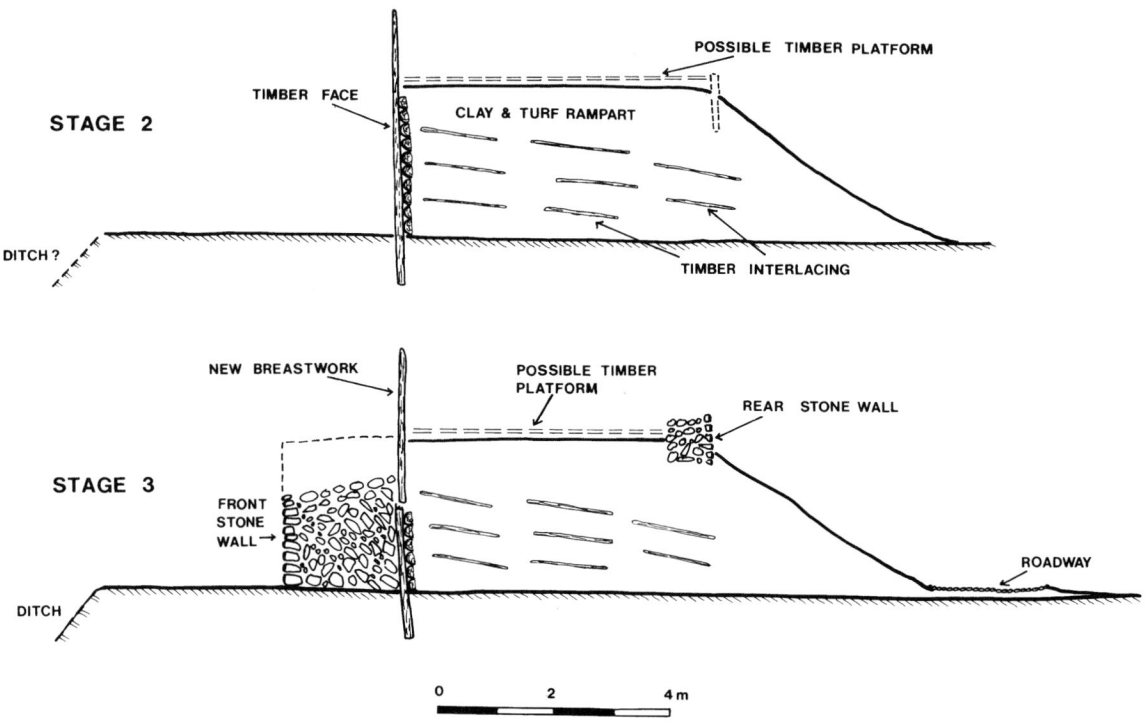

Figure 5. Hereford: idealised reconstructions of the late Anglo-Saxon defences, as drawn by R. Shoesmith. (Originally published as R. Shoesmith, Hereford City Excavations Volume 2. Excavations on and close to the Defences *(Council for British Archaeology, Research Report 46, 1982), fig. 133, on 79, and reproduced with the author's and publisher's permission.)*

the substructure of a timber floor (Fig. 5).[21] It should be noted that if the rampart's width had been the same on the Victoria Street site as it was at 5 Cantilupe Street, its front would have been directly on the line of the 'Period 3' boundary ditch 64 (Fig. 3).[22] This apparently early feature may, then, have established, or reinforced, a line which was subsequently respected by both pre-Conquest ramparts. Alternatively, in view of the only very slight evidence of its stratigraphical relationship to the gravel rampart, as recorded in two of the published sections, it may itself originally have contained vertical timbers which formed the first-stage rampart's frontal revetment. At length the front of the second-stage (turf-and-clay) rampart was reinforced by the construction of a substantial stone wall of almost 2 m. width, and of a small one at the rear edge of its top.[23]

A lengthy period of disuse and deterioration ensued, with some sporadic robbing of stone from the walls, until the rampart had weathered to a smooth profile.[24] This was brought to an end on the west side of the defences, and perhaps on the north side too, by the dumping of thick deposits of clean gravel onto the rampart. Because the immediately underlying layers were found to contain late tenth- and eleventh-century sherds, but nothing later, it was considered likely that the gravel was deposited in the mid or late eleventh century.[25] On the east side no

similar heightening is thought to have been made, but evidence was found that 'a flimsy defensive feature such as a brushwood and thorn paling fence' had been erected along the crest of the rampart.[26]

At some time in the early to mid thirteenth century a substantial stone wall was built in front of the second-stage rampart on the latter's west and east sides, the lines of which had by then been extended to the north so as to enclose the previously suburban market-place which had been laid out in High Town by, it seems, 1086. On the west side its construction trench cut away the front part of the pre-existing rampart, but at 5 Cantilupe Street it stood further forward, using the latter's ditch as part of its construction trench.[27] The north extension consisted of a substantial gravel rampart, and some parts of the pre-existing ramparts (*e.g.* at Cantilupe Street) were strengthened with a thick deposit of gravel.[28]

Hereford: dating evidence

The excavations on Hereford's defences have produced very little dating evidence for their first two stages; but before this sparse material is reviewed it is important to note that the second-stage rampart has analogues in southern England which have been widely assumed to point to its being of late ninth- or early tenth-century origin. Being composed of turf and clay reinforced with timber lacing and frontally revetted with timber, then stone, it is broadly similar to the defences, normally attributed to Alfred, at sites such as Cricklade, Lydford and Wareham.[29] It is reliably recorded that Alfred's son-in-law Æthelred and his wife Æthelflæd built defences at Worcester, and that after his death she built many more, so that by the time of her own death in 918 it appears that all of the future west midland shire towns were fortified.[30] However, our main source for this activity, the so-called Mercian Register, fails to mention the building of defences at the most important western Mercian centres which lacked Roman walls, such as Hereford, Shrewsbury, Winchcombe and Worcester, so that with a single exception (Worcester) the evidence for their being fortified by the second decade of the tenth century is only circumstantial. (It is from charter evidence preserved at Worcester itself that we know that Æthelred and Æthelflæd had fortified the place by *c.* 889–899; and since no comparable contemporary material survives from the other western Mercian sees, it is unsurprising that this is a solitary record.)

This general silence can also be explained by noting that the earliest surviving annal in the Mercian Register is for 902, and that most of the places recorded in it as being fortified (all in annals for the period 910–915) were not of the first rank. It is probable, then, that Hereford, like Worcester, had been fortified before 903, and that the general similarity of its second-stage rampart to those of the defences being constructed by Alfred in Wessex is no mere coincidence but is evidence of their general contemporaneity.[31] Hereford almost certainly had defences by 914, when the Anglo-Saxon Chronicle reports that, 'Then the men from Hereford and Gloucester and the nearest fortified places met them [*sc.* a Danish army] and fought against them.'[32] If so, the fact that the Mercian Register does not refer to their construction may well mean that they had already been built by 902.

Even though it cannot be proved beyond doubt that Hereford was given new defences in the period *c.* 881–918 (since the case that it was rests on circumstantial documentary evidence alone), it is nonetheless a reasonable working hypothesis. This does not mean that the turf-and-clay rampart can be automatically dated to that period, however; the substantive dating evidence produced by the excavations of Hereford's defences also needs to be considered, so that the rampart's identification as the one which is likely, on *a priori* grounds, to have been built at Hereford by Æthelred and/or Æthelflæd will be archaeologically secure.

It is possible that a subsequent phase in the second-stage defences' development can also be linked to a reliably recorded event. The Anglo-Saxon Chronicle records that Earl Harold 'had a ditch made about the town [*sc.* Hereford]' in 1055. Glossing this, the source known as the Worcester *Chronicon ex chronicis* says that 'On returning to Hereford with the rest of the host, he encircled it with a broad and deep ditch, and fortified it with gates and bars.'[33] Despite Shoesmith's misgivings this activity may well be represented by the dumped deposits of clean gravel found on, for example, the Victoria Street site on top of the second-stage rampart and the layers overlying it which derived from its disuse and decay (and which contained 'a reasonable quantity of late tenth and eleventh century pottery'), since the likeliest source of the gravel is from a recutting of the second-stage ditch.[34] If so, the Worcester source would provide a documentary *terminus ante quem* for the addition of stone walls to the turf and clay rampart (unless, of course, it is that actual activity to which the source is referring).

To turn now to the archaeological dating evidence, five samples from the excavations on Victoria Street and Cantilupe Street were submitted for a radiocarbon determination, and one from the Berrington Street sites was also thought relevant to establishing a chronology for the defensive sequence. However, only four of the samples produced a result which Shoesmith thought sound enough to be used (after recalibration).[35] Although these have been newly recalibrated in 2007 (Fig. 6; Table 1), the measurements were made so long ago that none of the resulting date ranges can be considered wholly reliable.[36] Shoesmith's appropriately cautious conclusions about their significance have often been repeated, but not all of them are incontestable and they need to be reviewed.

The sample found in the earliest context was a piece of carbonised timber from one of the grain-drying ovens (F309) at Victoria Street, identified by Shoesmith as 'presumably either charcoal used as fuel or the carbonized remains of a small stake used in the construction of the grain-drying oven', but usually referred to by him simply as a 'carbonized stake' or 'burnt stake'. As one of only two apparently reliable pieces of dating evidence for the Anglo-Saxon contexts on the site the item's chronological importance is very considerable. It came from low down in the fill of the oven (309D), which almost certainly had a working life of no more than several years.[37] The sample (BIRM 111) yielded an uncalibrated date of 760±85 and a calibrated one of AD 725±85. The new recalibration gives a 1σ range of AD 714–950 and a 2σ one of AD 668–992, which are much later than the equivalent ranges of AD 640–810 (1σ) and AD 555–895 (2σ) which Shoesmith published.[38] If the piece of timber was freshly cut, either for fuel or to be made into a stake for use in building the oven, the date range, if reliable, would give a tight *terminus post quem* for the oven's final use, making it almost certain (95.4%) that it was last used in or after 668 and that it was twice as likely as not (68.2%) to have been last used in or after 714. If the piece of timber had not been cut for either of these specific uses, however, it could have been old already when burnt in the oven, making the *terminus* correspondingly less tight.

This would threaten to turn an already constricted chronological model for the Victoria Street site into one which was so abbreviated as to be arguably impossible. The ovens were succeeded by a posthole building, which was repaired at least once, and which was in turn overlain by the gravel rampart. While not wholly ruling out the possibility that the posthole building had been in contemporary use with oven F309, Shoesmith argued that it had not been built until both ovens had been destroyed.[39] In that case, and given that the building was apparently refurbished at least once, there may have been an interval of up to half a century between the burning of the 'burnt stake' and the construction of the gravel rampart. A date for the latter, therefore, in or after the late eighth century looks likelier than one in the early eighth century; but there is no good reason why it need be assigned a construction date as late as the mid ninth-century one favoured by Shoesmith.[40]

His preference for that date seems to have been

significantly influenced by the result obtained from a sample (HAR 1375) of charcoal and daub from excavations on a number of adjoining sites between the rear of the west arm of the defences and Berrington Street, and known collectively as the Berrington Street sites. The material came from a series of 'patches' (layer L111) of what was interpreted as the burnt remains of timber buildings which had fronted onto the east side of a north-south roadway. The posthole building on the Victoria Street site was considered by Shoesmith to belong to the same constructional phase of Hereford's development, and therefore he saw the radiocarbon determination as a possible *terminus post quem* for the gravel rampart (which partly overlay the posthole building).[41] The newly recalibrated date ranges are AD 986–1154 at 1σ

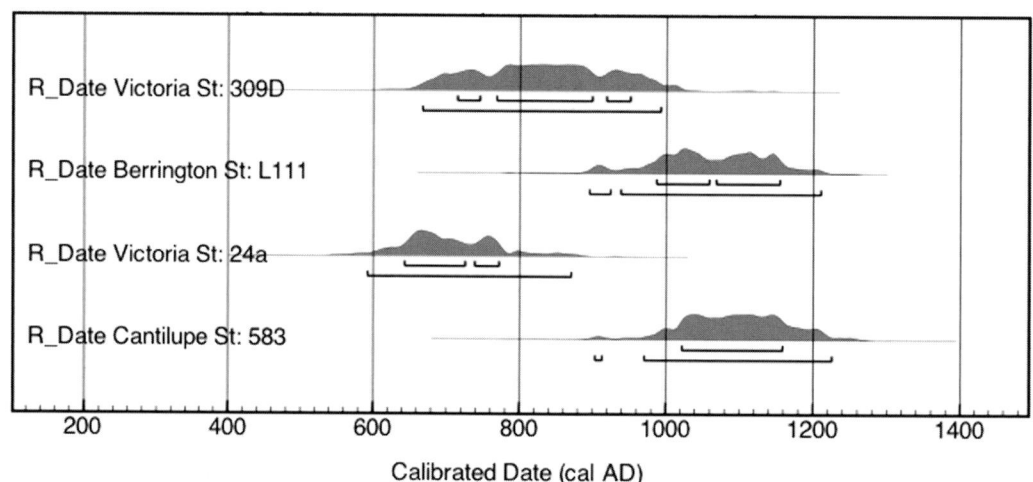

Figure 6. A plot of the recalibration (2007) results for four radiocarbon dates from Hereford (undertaken by Christopher Bronk Ramsey and reproduced with his permission). Also see Table 1.

Table 1. Radiocarbon determinations from excavation sites in Hereford. Two pairs of recalibrated dates are shown for each sample: those published in 1982 by R. Shoesmith and those supplied in 2007 by Bronk Ramsey.

				original (1982) recalibration		*new (2007) recalibration*	
site	*material*	*reference*	*BP–1950*	*1σ*	*2σ*	*1σ*	*2σ*
Victoria St: context 309D	burnt stake	BIRM 111	AD 760±85	AD 640–810	AD 555–895	AD 714–950	AD 668–992
Berrington St: context L111	charcoal and daub	HAR 1375	AD 960±70	AD 860–1000	AD 790–1070	AD 986–1154	AD 896–1210
Victoria St: context 24a	large piece of timber lacing	BIRM 110	AD 615±67	AD 508–642	AD 441–709	AD 643–771	AD 592–870
Cantilupe St: context 583	animal bones	HAR 1620	AD 1000±70	AD 900–1040	AD 830–1110	AD 1022–1158	AD 904–1225

and AD 896–1210 at 2σ. If they are reliable, and if the sample was indeed derived from a layer representing their destruction, the new 2σ date range shows that the Berrington Street buildings had almost certainly (95.4%) not been built – or perhaps had not been renovated for the last time – prior to 896, and that it is twice as likely as not (68.2%) that they had not been built or last renovated prior to 986.[42] To use these date ranges as *termini post quos* for the first-stage (gravel) rampart, as Shoesmith did with the results of the 1982 recalibration, would involve accepting that it, not its turf-and-clay successor, had been built by Æthelred and Æthelflæd or, more probably, that Hereford was still undefended when Æthelflæd died in 918. The latter, however, is almost certainly ruled out by the Anglo-Saxon Chronicle's reference to 'the men from Hereford and Gloucester and the nearest fortified places' acting together in 914.[43] But this is an unnecessary dilemma: there is no need for the posthole building on the Victoria Street site to be umbilically linked to the Berrington Street buildings in respect of the time of its construction, let alone of its destruction. Even if they did all originate in a single structural campaign, the building on Victoria Street (for which there is no independent dating evidence, except for the radiocarbon date provided by the 'burnt stake') could have gone out of use long before the buildings on Berrington Street did – something which would certainly have happened if its site had been needed for the construction of the gravel rampart.

Thirdly, another sample from Victoria Street for which Shoesmith thought that a reliable radiocarbon date had been obtained was from a substantial branch which had been used as lacing in the turf-and-clay (*i.e.* second-stage) rampart. The composite sample (BIRM 110) contained pieces of timber from the branch's inner and outer sections.[44] The new recalibration gives a 1σ range of AD 643–771 and a 2σ one of AD 592–870. Although the new date ranges are considerably later than those published by Shoesmith (AD 508–642 and AD 441–709 respectively), they are still earlier than the ones for the 'burnt stake' from grain-drying oven F309 and so add nothing useful to the dating of either of the overlying ramparts.[45]

The fourth and final radiocarbon date to be discussed comes from a group of bones of several animals found in layer 583 on the Cantilupe Street site (HAR 1620). The layer abutted the external face of the stone wall built at the front of the second-stage rampart, and directly underlay a later, *i.e.* secondary, stone face, 629, which was added *c.* 0.7 m. further forward and from a higher level (Fig.7).[46] Shoesmith argued that the date obtained (Table 1) showed that 'there is an 84% probability that the [stone] wall was built before the mid eleventh century.'[47] His argument rests on an assumption that the bones were deposited in layer 583 (described as a 'thick humic layer' which 'was presumably gradually deposited...while the defences were in use')[48] soon after each animal's death, and that if there is an 84% probability of the bones having been deposited in layer 583 before 1040, there can be no less a probability

that the stone wall, which is stratigraphically earlier than 583,[49] had been built by then. However, date of death is not the same as date of deposition. The radiocarbon date undoubtedly gives a *terminus post quem* for the latter event, which may not, however, have occurred until long after the animals' deaths. It would need to be proved that they had died only shortly before a few of their bones reached 583 for Shoesmith's argument to work, but this cannot be done. Alternatively, the date of death of the animals concerned may have occurred a long time after the wall was built – and perhaps even after the secondary stone face, 629, was built, since the published section suggests that 583 continued to accumulate even after its construction.[50] All that Shoesmith could have safely deduced from this sample is, then, that if the bones had been deposited before the secondary wall-face was built, the latter's construction almost certainly (95%) postdated AD 830. Their radiocarbon date can tell us nothing reliable about when the main stone wall was added to the turf-and-clay rampart.

The new recalibration of this date has produced a range of AD 1022–1158 at 1σ and of AD 904–1225 at 2σ. If the bones were deposited before the secondary stone face, 629, was built, these ranges give probable *termini post quos* for its construction.[51] The date ranges are also relevant to another of Shoesmith's arguments about these bones' value for dating purposes, for he also claimed that their radiocarbon date 'can be used to show that there is a reasonable probability that the Saxon defensive stone wall was built after the beginning of the ninth century.'[52] If his argument is adapted to conform to the new recalibration, it becomes one to the effect that there is a 68.2% probability that the stone wall which was added to the front of the second-stage rampart was built after 1022 and a 95.4% probability that it was built after 904. However, as was noted earlier, the bones' radiocarbon date cannot be reliably applied to earlier features and layers,[53] and therefore this line of argument is also an unsafe one.

Among other artefacts of pre-Conquest date found in the excavations were a coin of Alfred and a small amount of pottery. The coin came from a cultivated soil layer (60) which developed above the remains of the burnt timber buildings on the Berrington Street sites, but the context is one which cannot be reliably related to the defensive sequence. It is thought that by and large pottery was not used at Hereford until after *c.* 950;[54] and very few sherds were found on any of the excavation sites in layers earlier than those formed after stone walls had been added to the second-stage rampart. Moreover, some or all of these sherds 'may have been associated with unseen later features.'[55]

Shoesmith suggested that 'The pottery found in the decay levels on the rear of the stage 3 defensive works', *i.e.* the masonry phase of the turf and clay rampart, 'indicates that the defences were in a state of disuse by the late tenth century.'[56] This is misleading and ought to be rephrased

Steven Bassett

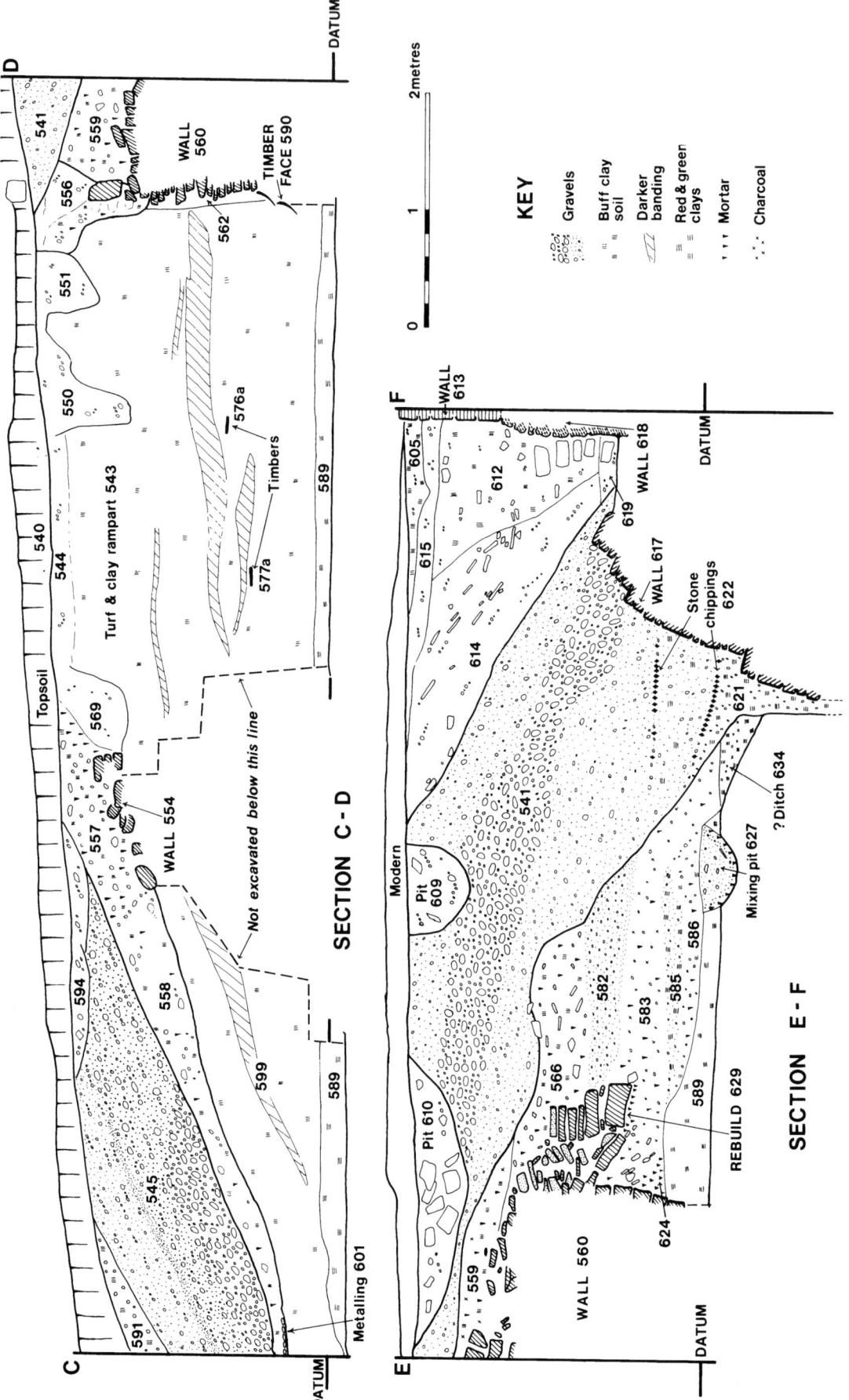

KEY

	Gravels		Buff clay soil
	Darker banding		Red & green clays
	Mortar		Charcoal

SECTION C - D

SECTION E - F

Figure 7. Cantilupe Street, Hereford: the Anglo-Saxon and later defences, as drawn in sectional view by R. Shoesmith. (Originally published as R. Shoesmith, Hereford City Excavations Volume 2. Excavations on and close to the Defences (Council for British Archaeology, Research Report 46, 1982), fig. 37, on 39: 'Cantilupe Street. Sections C–D and E–F', and reproduced with the author's and publisher's permission.)

as 'by no earlier than the late tenth century', since the length of time which elapsed between manufacture and deposition is unknown. Equally questionable is his statement that 'The decay levels containing this pottery were all apparently later than the construction of the stage 3 stone walls, and it can therefore be assumed that the stage 3 improvements to the stage 2 turf-and-clay rampart took place before the mid tenth century... A construction date in the early part of the tenth century is the most likely.'[57] For this to be inescapably true, proof would be needed that the sherds concerned had been both made and lost in the mid to late tenth century, but there is no evidence in support of either proposition. All that can be reliably said is that the decay levels on the rear of the second-stage rampart were almost certainly not deposited until in *or after* the mid to late tenth century.[58] That, of course, does not mean that the stone wall cannot have been added before then. It may have been added as early as Shoesmith argued that it was, *i.e.* 'early to mid tenth century',[59] but it need not have been. The sherds from the 'decay levels' can contribute nothing, then, to our assessment of the date at which walls were added to the second-stage rampart. This will remain so, even if the red-painted pitcher of which sherds were found in layers 22 and 87 on the Victoria Street site could ever be shown conclusively to have been a late ninth-/early tenth-century product of Stamford.[60]

Hereford: discussion

It must be admitted that the archaeological dating evidence for the successive stages of Hereford's defences offers very little concrete help. The single potentially useful item for dating the construction of the gravel and turf-and-clay ramparts is the 'burnt stake' from one of the two grain-drying ovens on the Victoria Street site. The new recalibration suggests that the oven was almost certainly (95.4%) not last used until in or after the mid to late seventh century, which provides what is very likely to be an accurate *terminus post quem* for the construction of the gravel rampart.

All that the archaeological evidence reveals about the construction of its turf-and-clay successor is that it came at the end of a period of unknown duration during which the gravel rampart was in decay. Shoesmith suggested that, at most, the rampart 'lasted for perhaps 50 years', but this must be seen as a minimum.[61] He preferred a date for its construction in the mid ninth century, but conceded that it could have originated in the late eighth century.[62] There is clear evidence of a spread of weathered material beyond the rampart's tail and of a turf-line which subsequently stabilised it (Figs 3–4). It is plain that Shoesmith's tentative assignment of no more than half a century to its life was predicated more on what he saw as the significance of the radiocarbon dates from the Victoria Street and Berrington Street sites than on the rampart's stratigraphic history.

There is no other archaeological evidence which bears

directly on the date at which the turf-and-clay rampart was built or stone walls were added to its front and its upper rear. After an unknown length of time, during which there was a considerable build-up of material in front of the frontal stone wall on the Cantilupe Street site (Fig. 7), a limited repair of it was made. If the animal bones found in the top layer of this build-up (583) were already present when the repair was done, the secondary wall-face was 'almost certainly' (95.4%) not built before 904 and 'very probably' (94.8%) not before 970 – *termini post quos* which are in line with the likely date of the single sherd of 'West Midlands early medieval ware' from the same layer.[63]

Therefore, while the archaeological dating evidence is not especially informative, it does nothing to disallow a chronological model for Hereford's defences which is informed by the evidence of reliable written sources. A *terminus ante quem* for the entire three-stage defensive sequence may be provided by Hereford's first murage grant in 1224.[64] By then all the earthwork components of the later medieval circuit must have been in place, and it is safe to assume that the building of the new stone wall was in progress or was about to begin. It had certainly been begun by 1251,[65] although it was not yet complete then. The rest of the model, however, lacks precision and allows multiple interpretations. The defences indicated by the Anglo-Saxon Chronicle's annal for 914 could, for instance, have been based on the gravel rampart, not on its turf-and-clay successor; the failure of our available sources to report on any fortifying of Hereford by Æthelred and/or Æthelflæd may reflect reality. Similarly, Harold's recorded refurbishment of its defences[66] might have left no recognisable trace in the excavated archaeology, or it could have produced either the turf-and-clay rampart or its later stone walls. However, these are unduly pessimistic hypotheses. The archaeological evidence does nothing to rule out the possibility that the turf and clay rampart had already been built by 903 and that it was refurbished with stone walls in response to the new Scandinavian military incursions of Æthelred II's reign;[67] and the dating evidence from the Cantilupe Street site comfortably allows the succeeding refurbishment to be identified as Harold's work.

Tamworth

Tamworth's defences

At least eleven sections have been excavated across the Anglo-Saxon defences at Tamworth (Fig. 8).[68] Something has been published about each one but in some cases it was no more than a few sentences. Very few plans have been published, and some of the section-drawings lack essential information. A mechanical digger was used on every site, sometimes for almost the whole investigation. Consequently, very few diagnostic finds were recovered; and much of what is depicted in the published section-drawings was never seen in plan view.

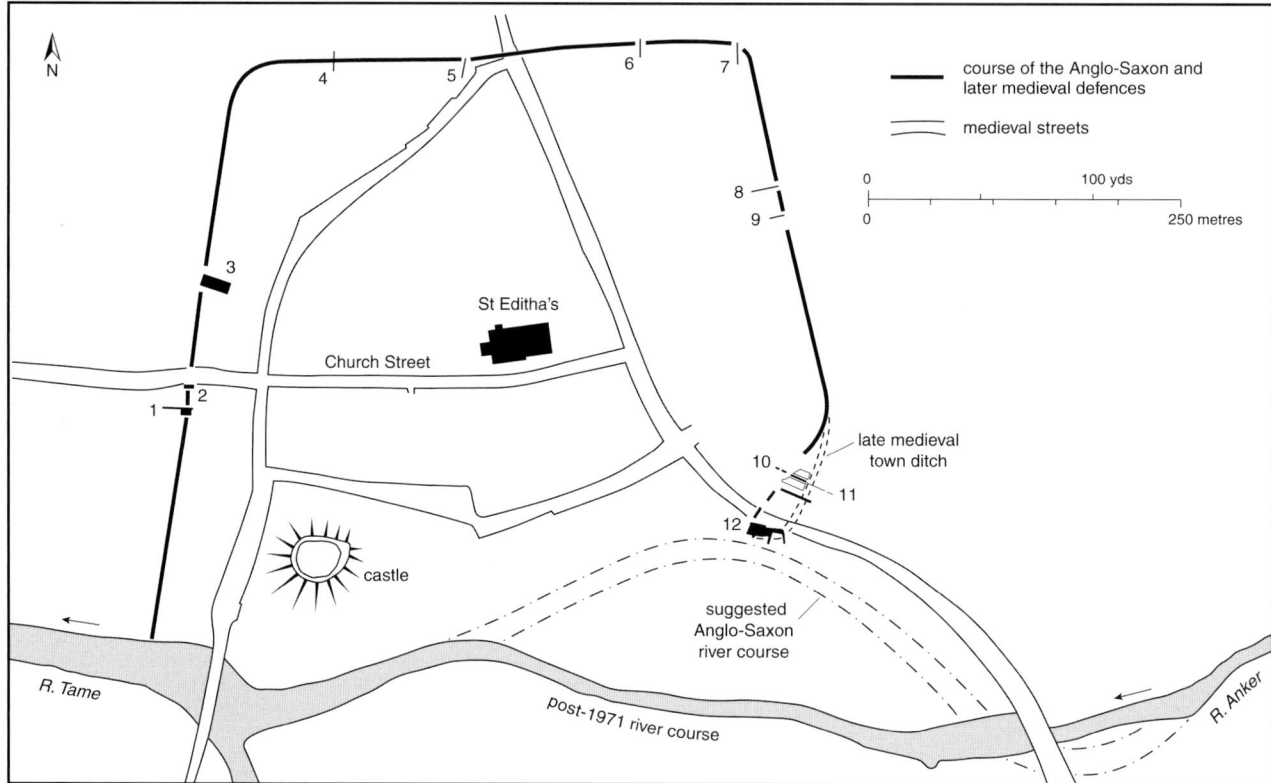

Figure 8. Medieval Tamworth, showing the sites of excavations on and adjacent to the Anglo-Saxon and later medieval defences: 1. Brewery Lane. 2. Lichfield Street. 3. Orchard Street. 4. Tamworth Hospital. 5. Bell Inn Corner. 6. Albert Road (1960). 7. Albert Road (1971). 8. Marmion Street (1964). 9. Marmion Street (1977). 10. Bolebridge Street (1978). 11. Bolebridge Street (1968). 12. Bolebridge (Anglo-Saxon water-mill).

It is hardly surprising, therefore, that significant differences of interpretation occur among the excavators about the appearance, the construction date, and even the number, of the successive defences uncovered. A review of the evidence shows that very little survived of the latest ones (referred to here as the third-stage defences), to which various dates have been given from the eleventh century onwards. The second-stage defences, unanimously accepted by their excavators as the ones which Æthelflæd created in 913, were better preserved; but on only one site did more than the base of the rampart survive, and only one complete section of the accompanying ditch has been published. Sealed beneath the second-stage rampart on many of the sites there was evidence of one or more substantial features. J. Gould proposed that the largest of these, which he variously described as a palisade trench and a ditch, had enclosed the Mercian 'royal palace' referred to in a charter of 781; but after finally deciding that it was a ditch, he subsequently argued that it was too slight 'to have been built as defence against an armed band'.[69] When other excavators found it, they labelled it 'Gould's pre-rampart ditch' but did not discuss its function.

It is unfortunate that on many sites little attention was paid to these earliest elements of the stratification, and

so the quality of the information available about them varies a lot but is mainly very poor. Nonetheless enough exists to reveal their common characteristics from site to site and to allow a useful reappraisal of their probable functions.

Brewery Lane

J. Gould's investigation of the defences on the Brewery Lane site was made partly by machine, partly by hand. Unfortunately, it is impossible to tell how much of what the drawn section shows (Figs 9–10) was revealed by the former method and how much by the latter.

'A trench 5 ft wide, 4 ft deep and 132 ft long was cut across the site... This located the Saxon and medieval ditches, which were later emptied by hand, and enabled the position of the rampart to be established. An area 20 ft by 41 ft adjacent to the trench was then opened to examine this. It was intended to clear only the top two feet mechanically but modern foundations were such that this could not be adhered to, and four feet had to be taken off in the south-west corner.'[70]

This may mean that only the lowest parts of the pre-modern features were excavated by hand.

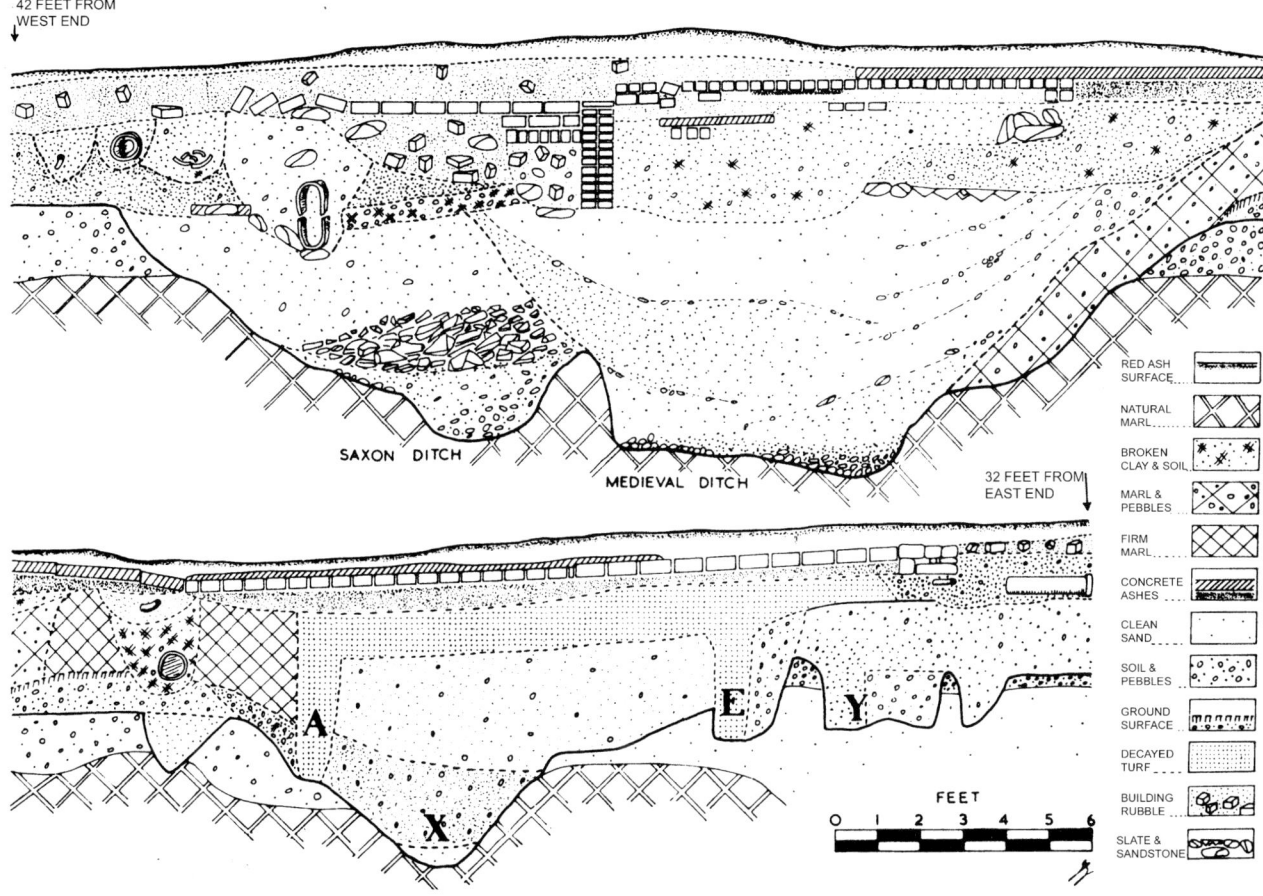

42 FEET FROM WEST END

SAXON DITCH

MEDIEVAL DITCH

32 FEET FROM EAST END

A

E

Y

X

FEET
0 1 2 3 4 5 6

RED ASH SURFACE

NATURAL MARL

BROKEN CLAY & SOIL

MARL & PEBBLES

FIRM MARL

CONCRETE ASHES

CLEAN SAND

SOIL & PEBBLES

GROUND SURFACE

DECAYED TURF

BUILDING RUBBLE

SLATE & SANDSTONE

Figure 9. Brewery Lane, Tamworth: the Anglo-Saxon and later defences, as drawn in sectional view by J. Gould. (Originally published as Transactions of the Lichfield and South Staffordshire Archaeological and Historical Society, *9 (1967–68), Fig. 2, on 19: 'Part of section C–D', and reproduced with the author's and editor's permission.)*

Gould evidently found it hard to make up his mind about what he entitled the pre-rampart features (*i.e.* those referred to here as the first-stage defences). He initially referred to feature X as a small ditch, but then said that it was 'possibly an early palisade trench' because of 'the impression of upright posts' in the clean loose wet sand in its bottom.[71] But in the bone report, which he himself wrote, the feature is unequivocally referred to as a palisade trench, as it also is in a brief interim report which he had written soon after the excavation: 'Below the Saxon rampart and sealed by it was a palisade trench and beam slot.'[72] When in the following year he found the same feature on the Lichfield Street site he reverted to calling it a ditch, commenting that 'It was cut partly through soft sand, had post- or stake-holes in the bottom and contained ox bones in the primary silt.'[73]

Gould also mentioned a wide slot and a posthole, referred to together as Y.[74] The posthole is part of the feature labelled Y on Fig. 9 and presumably held one of a series of posts set up in a continuous slot. The fact that

only one posthole is referred to in the report may well mean that most of the feature had been removed during the mechanical stage of the excavation. Gould reported that, 'The course of these pre-rampart features could not be traced in the time available', but he did not elaborate on this.[75] In his earlier interim report he had been a little more informative when reporting the discovery of a 'palisade trench and beam slot' sealed below the rampart, stating that 'time did not allow these earliest features to be examined except in section'.[76] The 'beam slot' must be feature Y. No posthole was mentioned in this earlier report, but there can be no doubt that Gould believed the feature to be continuous and to have had a structural role. Regrettably, he had nothing more to say about these pre-rampart features, ignoring them even in the section entitled 'Discussion' at the end of his report.[77]

In Fig. 9 feature X is shown with a west side which slopes more gently than its east side. The upper part of the latter was apparently removed by a wide, shallow cut (Fig. 10: V)[78] which may represent dismantlement of a row of vertical posts. The fill of the latter (5) is likely to

Steven Bassett

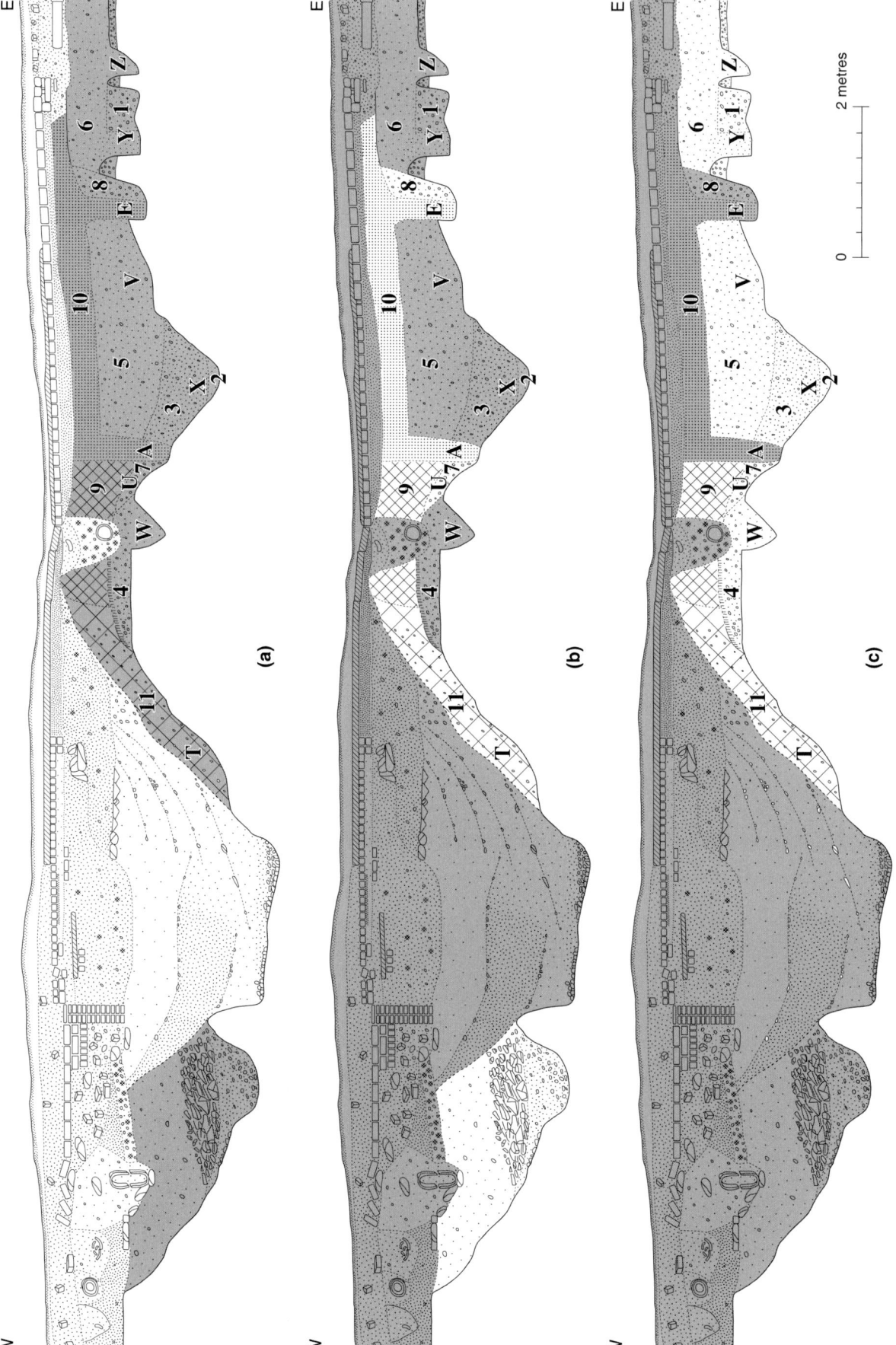

Figure 10. A phased analysis of J. Gould's Brewery Lane, Tamworth, section drawing (Fig. 9): (a) suggested late medieval and modern features and layers; (b) suggested late Anglo-Saxon ones; (c) suggested middle Anglo-Saxon ones. (In each case those of other periods are shown grey-tinted.)

Figure 11. Brewery Lane, Tamworth: J. Gould's feature X (Figs. 9–10), interpreted by him as, at first, a palisade trench and, subsequently, a ditch. The plate shows 'the impression of upright posts' found along its bottom (see note 85). It is not known if the viewpoint is from the north or the south, but the latter seems likelier (in which case 'A', a posthole associated with the frontal revetment of the second-stage rampart, is the feature which is clearly visible close to the left-hand side of the plate). The plate has been made from a colour print, supplied to the author by R. Meeson and made from one of a series of colour transparencies which he took during the excavation.

be the same as the infill (6) of features Y and Z. Beneath this apparently secondary feature V, X had two fills: a small amount of clean loose wet sand in the bottom (2, in which were seen the impressions of upright posts), and above it a layer of what the key to Fig. 9 describes as soil and pebbles (3). It is unclear how far this continued to the west, but a similar material (4) is shown infilling feature W to the west of X, which may have held a raking timber. The rather more pebbly soil between these two similar deposits (7) may have been a continuation of them; or else it may have been specifically associated with the construction of the overlying rampart.

If the marl layer (9) which lay immediately west of the second-stage rampart was laid, as Gould suggested,[79] to bolster or protect the base of its frontal revetment, the surface which it overlies (4) should represent the contemporary ground surface. In that case it is very probable that the post in feature E was set up from the surface of 4, as a result of the cut made through it (Fig. 10: feature U, filled with 7), which is clearly illustrated on Figs 9 and 12. Feature E's depiction on Fig. 9 indicates that it was cut from the surface of pebbly sand 5/6 (8 being the exact equivalent of 7). Layers 5 and 6 therefore very

probably consisted of make-up of the first-stage rampart, which must have slumped considerably after the removal of the vertical posts from X and Y and from any similar feature at its rear. Once the second-stage timber framework was in place, marl layer 9 was laid against its front face, and the rampart was heightened with the turf and soil (10) which Gould identified as its chief constituent. This interpretation is supported by Fig. 12, which shows the frontal revetment with, on its west side, an insertion cut sealed by the marl layer, and the intermediate one with a similar cut made from what he depicts as the contemporary ground surface.[80]

This new interpretation also has important implications for the area to the west of marl 9. Fig. 12 gives the marl a gently rounded west edge, but this is seriously at odds with how it is shown in Fig. 9, where it has a near vertical west edge. The latter is shown being abutted by a layer of marl and pebbles (11), which is said to have 'faced the inner side of the [later] medieval ditch' and been capable of being distinguished from 9 because it 'contained pebbles and was of a slightly different colour.'[81] However, the east end of 9 overlies the same layer (4) as marl 9 does, and, crucially, the smooth profile of 4's surface is continuous

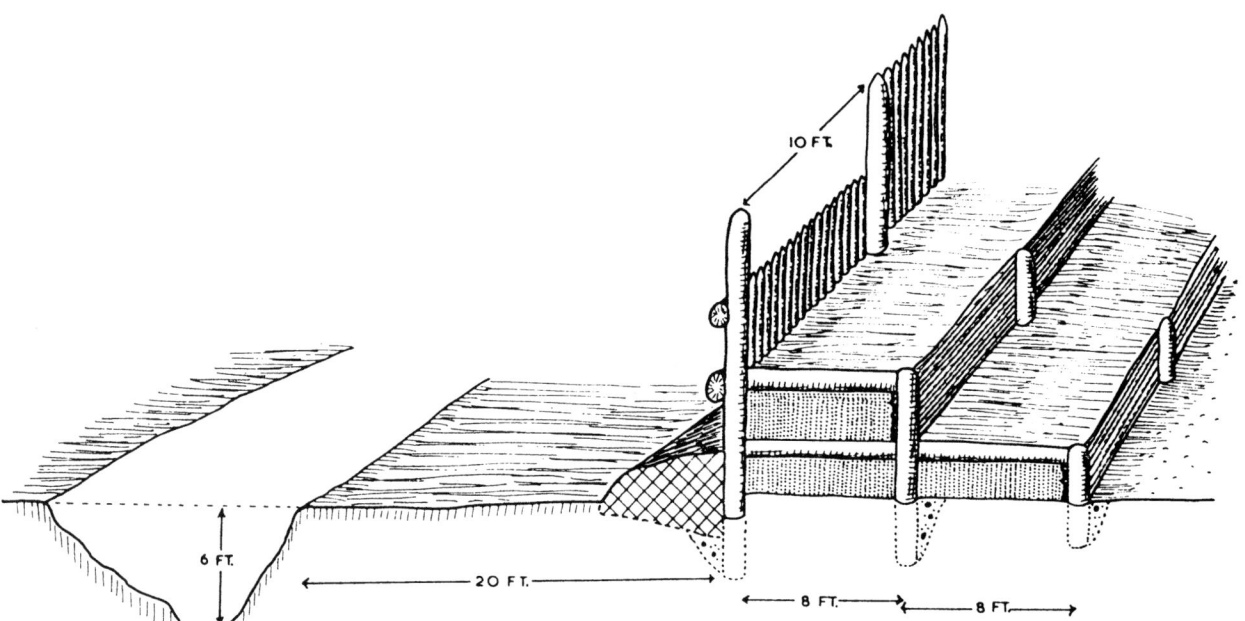

Figure 12. Brewery Lane, Tamworth: an idealised reconstruction of the late Anglo-Saxon defences, as drawn by J. Gould. (Originally published as Transactions of the Lichfield and South Staffordshire Archaeological and Historical Society, *9 (1967–68), fig. 4, on 22, and reproduced with the author's and editor's permission.)*

below both layers. This is far more likely to mean that 11 filled a feature which was at length largely cut away by the later medieval ditch than that it was one of the latter's fills.

Gould says nothing else about layer 11, nor does he discuss the awkwardly shaped profile of what he interpreted as the later medieval ditch's east edge. All the latter's main fills have their east edge against 11, and it is striking how this edge smoothly carries upwards the line of the lowest part of the ditch's east side. This strongly suggests either that they are the fills of a recut of the ditch and that pebbly marl 11 represents the only part of its first cut to survive,[82] or else that 11 infills a feature, T, which was unconnected with the later medieval ditch. The latter is much the better explanation because it removes the need to explain 11's function.

However, neither of these explanations addresses the question of why the feature which has 11 as its only known fill had so strange a profile up against 9. This problem would be resolved if marls 9 and 11 were one and the same deposit, used to infill a redundant linear feature and at the same time to protect the base of the new second-stage rampart. The differences between 9 and 11 which Gould noted[83] could easily occur within the site's natural marl subsoil, which was presumably the source of both of them. Fig. 9 shows that the ditch which he labelled as 'Saxon ditch', and which can be safely identified as the one contemporary with the second-stage rampart, cuts far down into the marl subsoil. This material would therefore have been readily available for infilling a superseded ditch and protecting the front of the new rampart.

It is likely, then, that the 'pre-rampart features' on the Brewery Lane site (*i.e.* the first-stage defences) included a rampart built with a timber framework and a substantial ditch. It does little violence to Gould's section-drawing to re-interpret it in this way. The rampart appears to have been frontally revetted by vertical timbers set in X, with others of 12 in. (0.30 m.) diameter standing about 9½ ft (2.90 m.) to the east in slot Y, and perhaps with a third line of posts at the rear of the rampart (Fig. 13). Although there is no archaeological evidence for them, horizontal timbers too may have been used in order to create a framework for a rampart which had a lot of sand and pebbles in its make-up. There may also have been raking timbers, perhaps set against a basal timber in W, to support the frontal revetment.[84]

Prior to the construction of the second-stage rampart this frontal revetment seems to have been dismantled by means of a cut, V, which allowed the timbers to be rocked out or else to be cut off well below the contemporary ground level. Layer 3 presumably represents disturbed original packing. If the timbers had been removed by rocking, it is unlikely that clear ghost impressions would be seen during excavation, but 'the impression of upright posts' was found in the clean loose wet sand (2) in the bottom of X (Fig. 11).[85] At the same time the timbers were evidently removed from W and Y, and, if it contained any, also from Z.

As already suggested, pebbly sand layers 5 and 6 probably formed part of the rampart's make-up, slumping (or pushed) forward into V once the supporting timbers had been dismantled. If so, it may seem strange that no similar

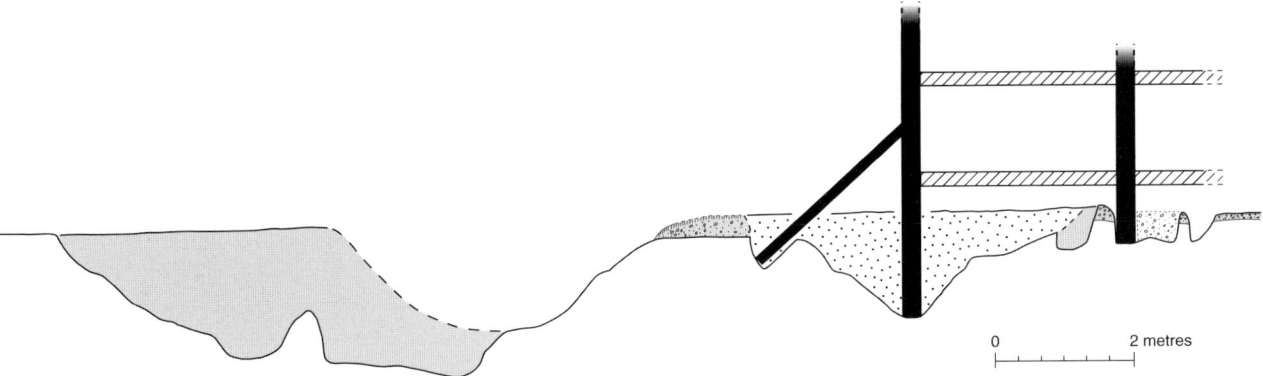

0   2 metres

Figure 13. A speculative reconstruction of elements of the middle Anglo-Saxon defences which were excavated by J. Gould at Brewery Lane, Tamworth.

material was found under marl 9. However, it would have been partly dug away when the frontal revetment of the new rampart was erected; and if W was filled in at the same time as Y and Z, its sandy fill is probably the same material as 5.

Little needs to be said about Gould's interpretation of the layers and features associated with the second-stage rampart and ditch and his discussion of their probable form on this site. His 'imaginative reconstruction' of the rampart's timber phase (Fig. 12) is still convincing. Although nothing was found of its rear, the evidence from other Tamworth excavations generally bears out his view of it.

His 'Saxon ditch' is stratigraphically divorced from the rampart by the later medieval ditch and modern disturbance, but there is no reason to disagree with his identification of it as the ditch of the second-stage defences. It held 'a quantity of sandstone' which he saw as 'suggesting the destruction of some near-by stone feature';[86] but he did not speculate that it might have come from a major refurbishment of the rampart, presumably because with all but the latter's base having been destroyed by later activity there was no direct evidence of its having had a masonry phase.

Lichfield Street

The linear feature sealed below the second-stage rampart was also found on Gould's Lichfield Street site, which was only *c.* 25 m. north of the Brewery Lane site (Figs 14–15). It lay 'in the same position relative to the Æthelflædan rampart' but seemed, unlike the latter, to run on under the modern road.[87] It was cut through soft sandstone and marl, was V-shaped, and had a rounded bottom, being 8 ft (2.44 m.) wide at the top and 5 ft (1.52 m.) deep. Gould reported that its sides were 'pitted with many stake-holes inclined at various angles as if for stakes pointing across the ditch or perhaps for the securing of thorns.'[88] However, these are likely to be root-holes, as are most or all of the

smaller 'postholes' which he believed to be part of the second-stage rampart. It was their presence which seems to have led him to think that the feature was after all a ditch, not a palisade trench: 'The sloping stake-holes in the side of the ditch and the vertical ones on the inner lip suggest defence against animals...or the occasional robber, rather than an army who could have fired the ditch obstacles with ease.'[89] He reported that no trace was found of a rampart, nor of postholes which could be associated with one; but he also noted that 'there were some postholes which did not appear to be certainly related to the later defences', which are presumably those shown as solid features on Fig. 16, including a slot-like feature.[90]

This so-called 'ditch' had a primary silt, which is not described in the report but is identified as 'clean sand' on Gould's section-drawing (Fig. 14). Its only other fill was 'a brown turfy soil containing few pebbles'.[91] To judge from the section-drawing and from colour transparencies taken by Philip Rahtz the feature had a profile on this site too which was much more in keeping with a palisade trench than a ditch. Except against the north edge of the excavation site (*i.e.* the one depicted in Fig. 16), it had a flat bottom, which was a little over 1 ft (30 cm.) wide, and near-vertical sides up to the level at which Fig. 14 shows the top of the primary fill; but from there upwards it broadened considerably. This marked change of angle of the feature's sides, which is clearly depicted on Fig. 16, arguably coincides with the base of a secondary cut made to remove the vertical posts which it had originally held. Since Gould himself thought that it was probably a palisade trench when he encountered it on the Brewery Lane site, and since it was, as it seems, his finding of many small holes in its sides (probably root-holes) on the present site which made him change his mind, it is reasonable to conclude that the feature was in reality a palisade trench. The close similarity of its upper fill to the material which forms a general spread to the east of the feature is best explained by the slumping forward of

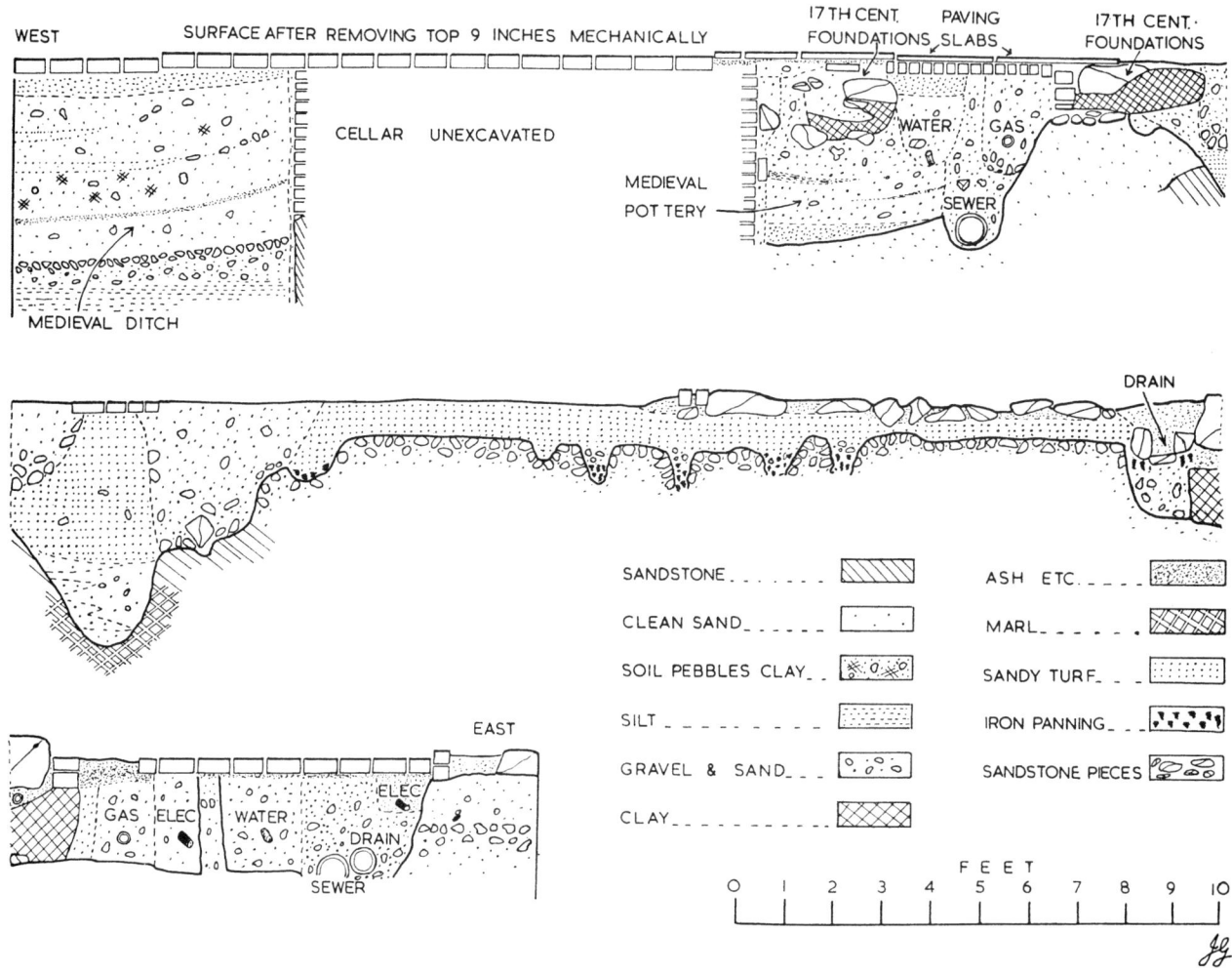

Figure 14. Lichfield Street, Tamworth: the Anglo-Saxon and later defences, as drawn in sectional view by J. Gould. (Originally published as Transactions of the South Staffordshire Archaeological and Historical Society, *10 (1968–69), fig. 2, on 34: 'Section of the northern side of the area excavated', and reproduced with the author's and editor's permission.)*

rampart make-up, once the posts which it contained had been removed.

The area to the west of it was too disturbed by the later medieval ditch (which ran closer to the palisade trench than on the Brewery Lane site) and by modern disturbance for evidence of a contemporary ditch to have survived, let alone any small feature such as W was on the Brewery Lane site. To the east were features which Gould thought unlikely to be related to the second-stage defences (Fig. 16). None of them coincided with the north edge of excavation and therefore none is shown in his section-drawing. Four of them were associated with a slot-like feature (which is not, however, referred to in the report), and two more continued its line northwards. Six others are shown lying in a line roughly parallel to them and a short distance to the east. It is unclear how many of these were archaeological features; since similar small features shown in the section-drawing (Fig. 14)

inspire little confidence, it would be sensible to assume that only the slot and the large posthole at its north end are certainly of human origin.[92] It is also unclear why Gould concluded that these features were unrelated to the second-stage defences. He offered no reason, stratigraphical or otherwise, for their exclusion but may simply have regarded them as superfluous to the plan of what he saw as one side of an imposing gateway.[93]

It is important to note, however, that the slot and the posthole situated at its north end lay at precisely the same distance to the east of the palisade trench as feature Y did on the Brewery Lane site. It is therefore likely that they were parts of the same slot – one which was well preserved on the latter site, but of which only the lowest part was found here.[94] It is not inconceivable that the line of posts originally continued northwards, but that the next ones had left so slight an impression (or even none at all) at the level to which modern development had reduced

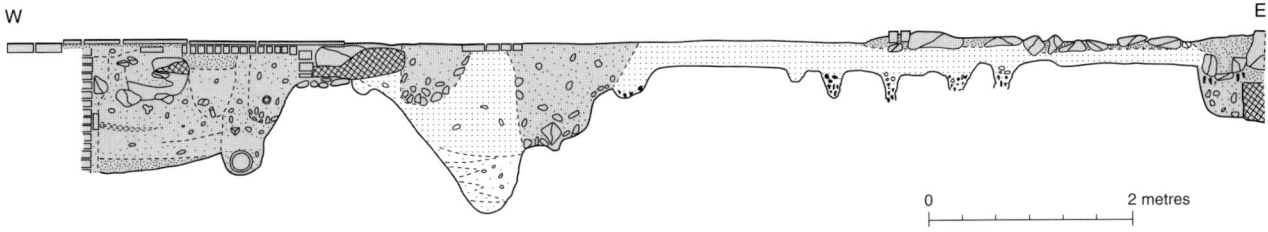

Figure 15. An analysis of part of J. Gould's Lichfield Street, Tamworth, section drawing (Fig. 14): suggested components of the middle Anglo-Saxon defences. (Those of other periods are shown grey-tinted.)

the pre-Conquest archaeology that nothing was seen of them during the excavation. However, since a road on the general line of Lichfield Street can be safely assumed to have existed by then, the rampart is likely to have ended within the site or only just to the north of it, in which case it would not be surprising if its structural features altered in appearance there.

There is no reliable evidence of yet another setting for vertical posts by which the rear of the first-stage rampart could have been revetted; but the part of the excavation site in which it might be expected to have lain had been badly disturbed by a large modern pit and was also littered with the small features which Gould identified as postholes associated with the second-stage rampart (shown in outline on Fig. 16). As a result, identifying genuine archaeological features is impossible, let alone distinguishing between those of the first- and the second-stage defences.

It is clear from this examination of Gould's excavation reports that a number of linear features, some of them substantial ones, predate what have been consistently referred to here as the second-stage defences. Not all of them were recognised by Gould as being what he called 'pre-rampart' (*i.e.* first-stage) features; in particular the ditch, T, excavated on the Brewery Lane site was not. Nor did he assign a defensive role to those which he did recognise. However, a case has been made here for identifying his 'pre-rampart ditch' as a trench which originally held the frontal revetment of a rampart. The latter seems also to have been strengthened by a line of intermediate posts, but modern disturbance had apparently removed any evidence which there might have been of a third line at the rear. At most no more than a depth of *c.* 21 in. (0.53 m.) of this rampart's make-up survived, but it is clear that the second-stage rampart had taken advantage of its existence. The ditch, however, was a new one, set well in front of the first-stage ditch so as to create a *c.* 20 ft (6.10 m.) wide berm.[95] Even, therefore, with a suitably conservative interpretation of the evidence the first-stage defences may have been far stronger than was previously supposed.

Orchard Street

In 1972 less than 100 m. north of Gould's two sites K.

Sheridan found a rampart which was 'of turf construction with three rows of posts, the main structural posts being 4 m. from the front of the rampart'.[96] He reported that it was 'immediately fronted by a ditch 2.2 m. wide by 0.8 m. deep', and that 'A close setting of postholes towards the front of the rampart may represent a tower set into it.'[97] The other notable feature of the site was that the rampart 'was succeeded by a possible later bank of clay further to the west.'[98] However, none of his interim statements refers to evidence of a refurbishment of the rampart in stone or to the finding of anything equivalent to Gould's 'pre-rampart ditch'.

Sheridan estimated the rampart to be 10 m. wide (almost 33 ft), which is twice the width (*c.* 16 ft) of the second-stage rampart on Gould's Brewery Lane site,[99] for which the evidence is particularly clear and convincing. It is possible, therefore, that the material/s which he identified as the rampart's make-up included some which had slumped when it, or perhaps a predecessor, had fallen into disrepair or been dismantled (as evidently happened at Hereford and Winchcombe).[100] This is a much more credible explanation of the rampart's suggested, but intrinsically improbable, doubling in width over so short a distance.

Another possible re-interpretation concerns the clay which lay to the west of the rampart. It directly sealed the ditch and was red.[101] Its colour and its position immediately in front of the rampart make it very probable that it was the same clay as Gould found at the Brewery Lane site (9), in which case the underlying ditch was an earlier, *i.e.* pre-rampart, feature and so is very likely to have been the palisade trench of the first-stage defences. It was V-shaped, with a flattish bottom *c.* 0.24–0.27 m. wide.[102] Its overall dimensions, 2.2 m. wide by 0.8 m. deep, show that much less of it had survived here than on Gould's two sites. It is interesting to note that feature X on the Brewery Lane site had an almost identical width at a height of 0.8 m. above its bottom (Fig. 9), and that its bottom was of a similar width.[103] It follows, then, that if this feature was not the ditch of the second-stage defences, the latter cannot have lain within the excavated area, in which case it may have been separated from the rampart by a berm of similar width to the one found on the Lichfield Street site.[104]

A final possible re-interpretation concerns the many

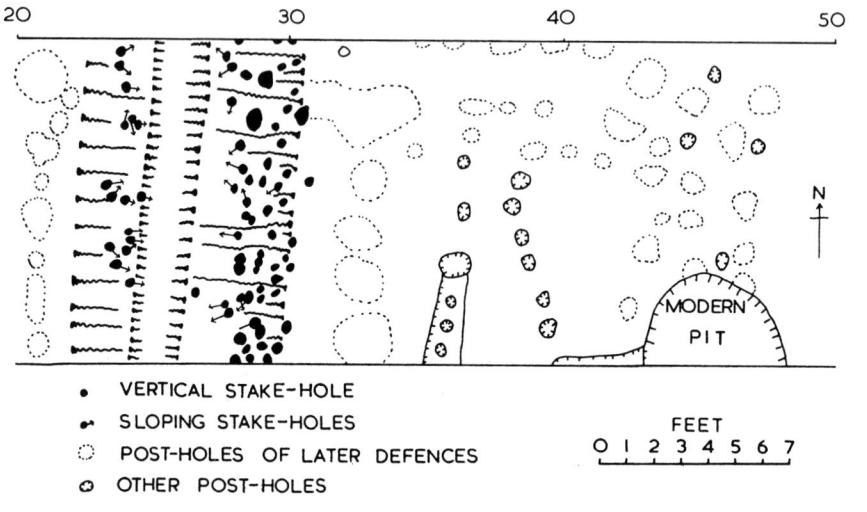

Figure 16. Lichfield Street, Tamworth: plan of the middle Anglo-Saxon defences, as drawn by J. Gould. (Originally published as Transactions of the South Staffordshire Archaeological and Historical Society, *10 (1968–69), fig. 3, on 36: 'Plan showing the pre-rampart ditch', and reproduced with the author's and editor's permission.)*

postholes identified as having held structural elements of the second-stage rampart. Sheridan stated that they were found beneath its make-up,[105] which, if taken at face value, seems to mean that they predated the second-stage defences. However, it may have been only the post-pits which were sealed by the rampart's make-up, whereas the post-pipes, *alias* the 'ghost' impressions of the posts, passed up through the make-up but were not seen during its removal. If so, and in view of the absence of any mention of post-pipes in the interim statements, some of the postholes may have belonged to the first-stage rampart.

Four sites on the north arm of Tamworth's defences have been excavated and published, two by K. Sheridan, one by F. T. Wainwright (published by Sheridan), and one by A. Richmond. All four can be seen, if with a considerable measure of licence and imagination in some cases, as having contained a defensive sequence which closely resembles the one found by Gould on the west side of the town.

Tamworth General Hospital

In 1996 Tempus Reparatum carried out an archaeological evaluation on the site of the former Tamworth General Hospital on Hospital Street (Fig. 17). Unlike the other excavations being discussed here this one's aim was limited to discovering what archaeological deposits lay on the site and assessing their extent and quality of preservation. In Trench A the south lip of the later medieval ditch (015) was located, as well as, to the south of it, a rampart which was identified as belonging to the defences built by Æthelflæd in 913. Once soilmarks had

been defined, an area *c.* 18 m. long by 1 m. wide was excavated to a general depth of no more than *c.* 1 m., but more deeply in a few places.

Only the lowest 0.5–0.6 m. of the rampart's make-up (027) was found to have survived. It had vertical edges to front and rear, with evidence of stakeholes along the front edge which were interpreted as 'a timber-laced line along the palisade front' comparable to what Gould had found on his Brewery Lane site.[106] A single posthole was found in the middle of the rampart, 2.5 m. to the rear of its front edge, in which the post had had a diameter of 20 cm. – dimensions which are closely similar to those of the intermediate posts of which Gould found evidence at Brewery Lane. In front of the rampart there was a thick, apparently deep deposit of homogeneous pink clay (016), which the excavator considered analogous to the red marl which fronted the rampart on the three western sites. About 0.6 m. in front of the rampart the clay began to deepen as it filled the upper part of a large linear feature. The report does not comment on it, but this too is reminiscent of the Brewery Lane site, where the red marl which abutted the front of the rampart also filled the putative ditch of the first-stage defences.

There are other suggestive features which this deliberately limited excavation found but could not investigate. Firstly, Fig. 17 shows the rampart's make-up as being *c.* 30 cm. deeper for a distance of *c.* 1 m. behind its front edge. The least forced explanation of this may be that the make-up was infilling the top of an earlier feature. If so, the latter would have been in an identical position to that of the palisade trench of the first-stage defences on Gould's sites. Secondly, immediately behind the rampart, layers 025 and 026 were 'slumping horizons...

perhaps pertaining to the fills of a ditch',[107] but they are not otherwise remarked on. Nothing similar appears to have been seen on any other Tamworth site.

This excavation made two particularly valuable contributions to our knowledge and understanding of Tamworth's defences. Firstly, it corroborated the conclusions which Gould drew from his Brewery Lane excavation about the size of the second-stage rampart and the method of its construction, by showing that its make-up had a vertical edge at both front and rear, and by uncovering an intermediate posthole which was very similar in its position and dimensions to those which Gould found. Secondly, it showed that the marl, which here as on the three western sites had been set against the front of the rampart, was also the fill of a large linear feature of some depth which lay a short distance beyond it. The feature's stratigraphical position proves that it predated the rampart, and therefore it is very likely to have been the ditch of the first-stage defences. It is most regrettable that no investigation of the depressed area immediately behind the rampart's front edge could be made, since to have confirmed the existence of an earlier linear feature and clarified its form and function would have been invaluable.[108]

Bell Inn Corner

In 1971–2 K. Sheridan cut two sections by machine across the north side of the defences (Figs 18–19). One of them was on a site at Bell Inn Corner, a little to the west of the presumed north gateway. Regrettably, only the lower layers of a 'shallow ditch' at the north end of the trench were excavated manually, and no artefacts were recovered. Sheridan tentatively concluded that the ditch (Fig. 19: 'e') was unlikely to have belonged to the second-stage defences and that 'the assignment of a pre-tenth date to it [is] more probable.'[109] It was 'possibly of two phases', with the earlier one having had a more gently sloping south side than the later one's.[110] A comparison of his section-drawing with Gould's and with others yet to be discussed suggests that his conclusion is sound. Cut into the top of the only partly filled feature, at the east edge of the trench, was the lowest 0.7 m. of a 20 cm. wide vertical post ('c') which was packed around with clay (5).[111] The clay lay across the full width of the trench, but no other posts were found. Sheridan identified this, no doubt correctly, as part of the frontal revetment of the second-stage rampart.

There was a posthole ('a') some way behind the frontal revetment.[112] This probably marks the rear of the rampart, which would therefore have been *c.* 5.1 m. wide, as compared to *c.* 4.8 m. on the Brewery Lane site and 4.9 m. at the Tamworth Hospital site. Adjacent to it to the south was a spread of broken sandstone (12), *c.* 3.5 m. wide, which was overlain by a layer of sandy clay (7). The clay extended to the south of the sandstone spread for up to 2 m., but not to the north. The latter may have belonged to an intervallum road; but, if so, it ran behind the

second-stage rampart rather than, as Sheridan suggested, behind the later medieval one.[113]

His belief that the sandstone spread had to be of post-Conquest date derived from the stratigraphical relationship of layer 6 to its neighbour 11. The latter, 'sandy soil', overlay the clay packing (5) and the stump of the post which he interpreted as part of the frontal revetment of the second-stage rampart. He stated that, to the south, 11 was 'cut away by a layer of sandy soils' (6), which itself underlay the sandstone spread.[114] (Although the trench was only 1.5 m. wide, the junction of 6 and 11 is shown to lie 1.5 m. further to the south in the east section than in the west one.[115]) The way in which these two layers met resembles what can be seen at the front of the second-stage rampart elsewhere. The idea that 6 lay in a cut made through 11 is unconvincing; their relationship is much better explained in terms of the frontal revetment's slow decay, as a result of which it started to lean forward under the weight of the rampart's make-up. According to this interpretation 6 represents make-up still *in situ*, while 11 looks like the equivalent of the marl which had been piled against the frontal revetment on the other sites discussed so far. This begs the question, however, of why 'sandy soil', not clay, was used here (except where a layer of clay (5) was put around the feet of the timbers).

Because so little of the rampart and the build-up in front of it survived, it is impossible to offer a fully satisfactory explanation of the sequence on this site. However, some firm conclusions can be drawn. Firstly, the stratigraphical sequence proves that, here as elsewhere, a substantial linear feature predates the second-stage rampart. The two phases of use which Sheridan suggested arguably represent the erection and the eventual removal of a timber revetment at the front of the first-stage rampart, of which layer 4, and perhaps 3 too, formed part of the make-up. Secondly, the site produced useful information about the second-stage rampart, including confirmation of its width and of aspects of its construction. (No evidence of a refurbishment in stone was found, but the subsequent removal of all but the very bottom of the rampart and the lack of any opportunity to examine the associated ditch mean that no significance should be attached to this.) Finally, a possible intervallum road was uncovered, but it is unclear if it had been laid when the second-stage rampart was built on the remains of its predecessor or if it was a later feature.[116]

Albert Road (site 1)

The earliest known examination of Tamworth's pre-Conquest defences was made by F. T. Wainwright in 1960 on a site on Albert Road which lay *c.* 65 m. east of Sheridan's Bell Inn Corner site. As a result of his death not long afterwards it remained unpublished until 1973.[117] So it is unsurprising that despite the valiant effort which Sheridan made to understand Wainwright's site notebook and incomplete section-drawing, the published account of the excavation leaves a number of important questions

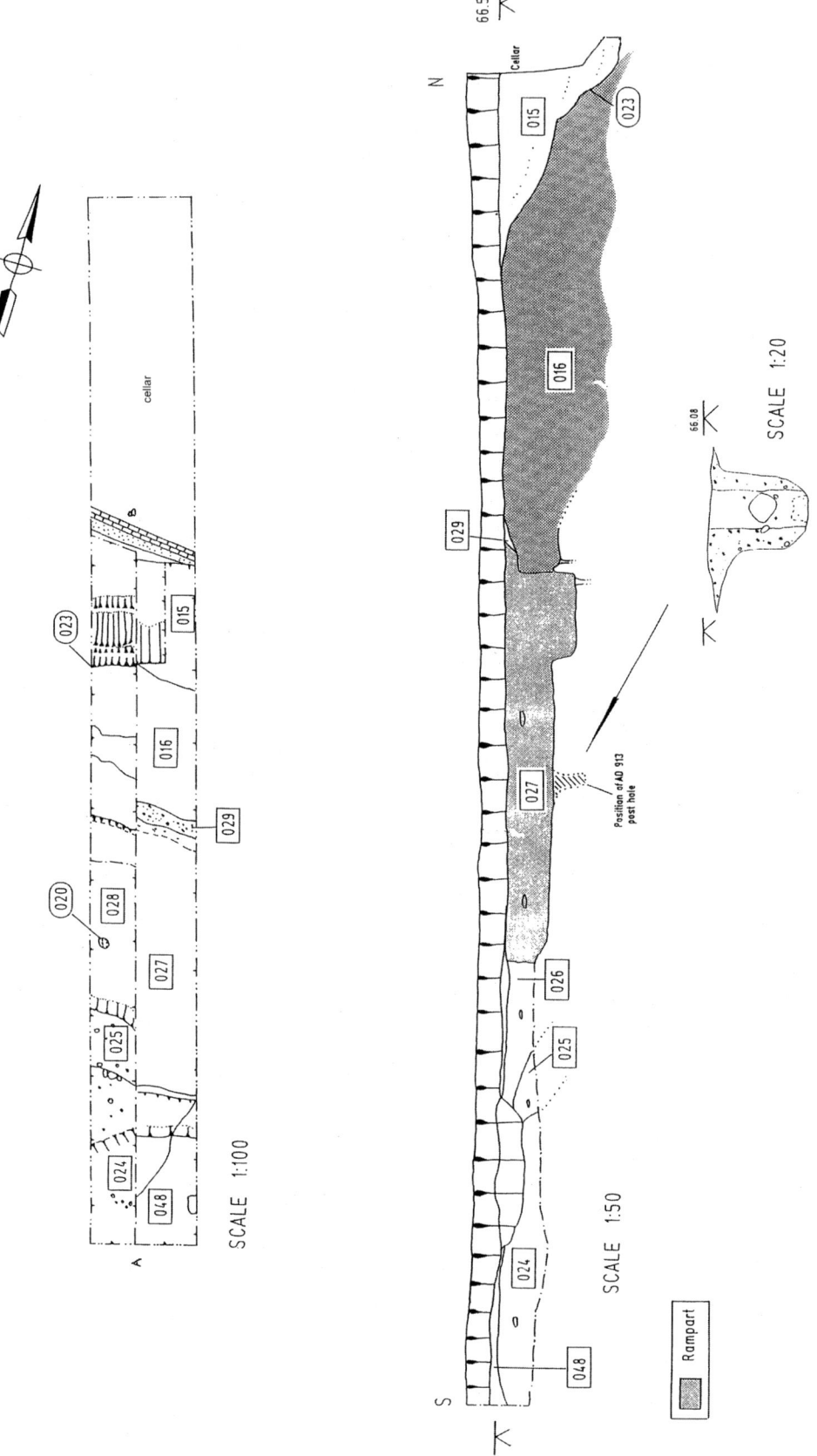

Figure 17. Tamworth General Hospital, Tamworth: the Anglo-Saxon and later medieval defences. (Originally published as A. D. W. Richmond, 'An archaeological evaluation of the former Tamworth Hospital site' (unpublished report, Tempus Reparatum Field Services Department, Oxford, 1996), fig. 4: 'Trench A, plan and section detail', and reproduced with the author's and developer's permission.)

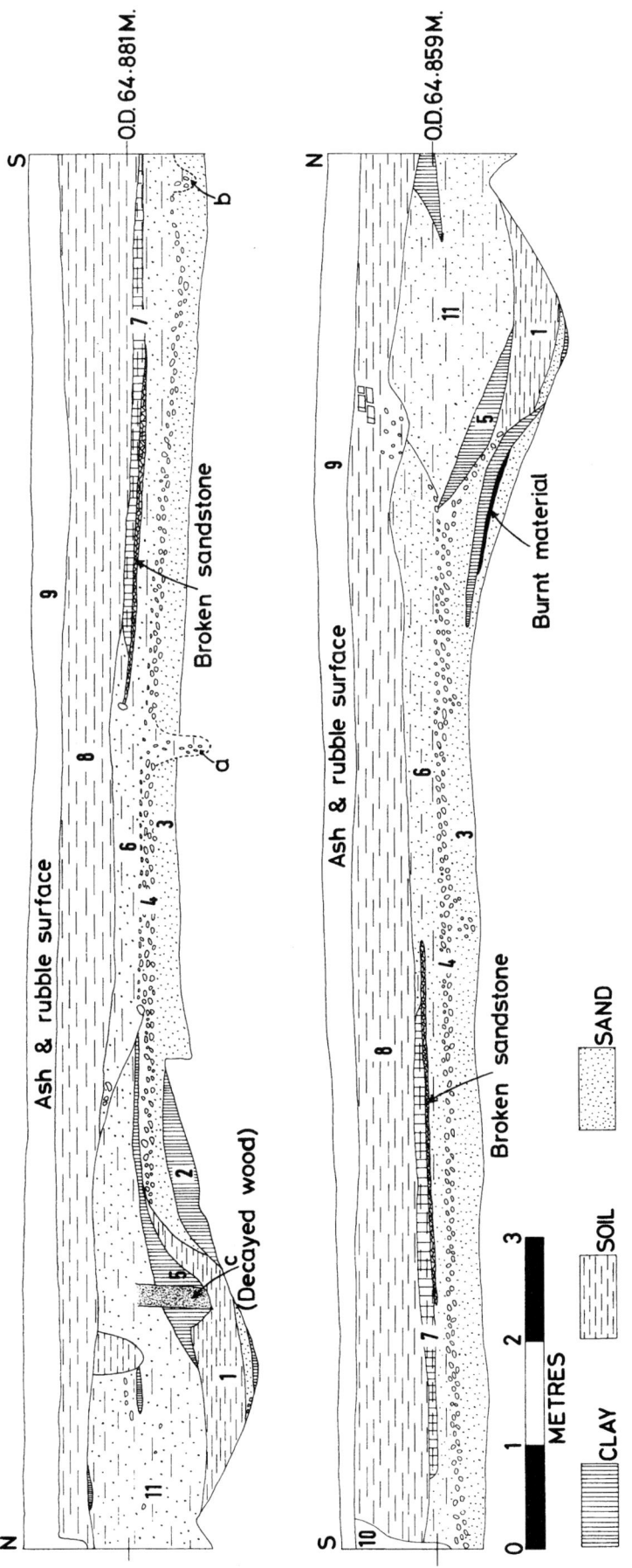

Figure 18. Bell Inn Corner, Tamworth: the Anglo-Saxon and later medieval defences, as drawn in sectional view by K. Sheridan. (Originally published as Transactions of the South Staffordshire Archaeological and Historical Society, 15 (1974), fig. 2, on 56: 'The section', and reproduced with the editor's permission.)

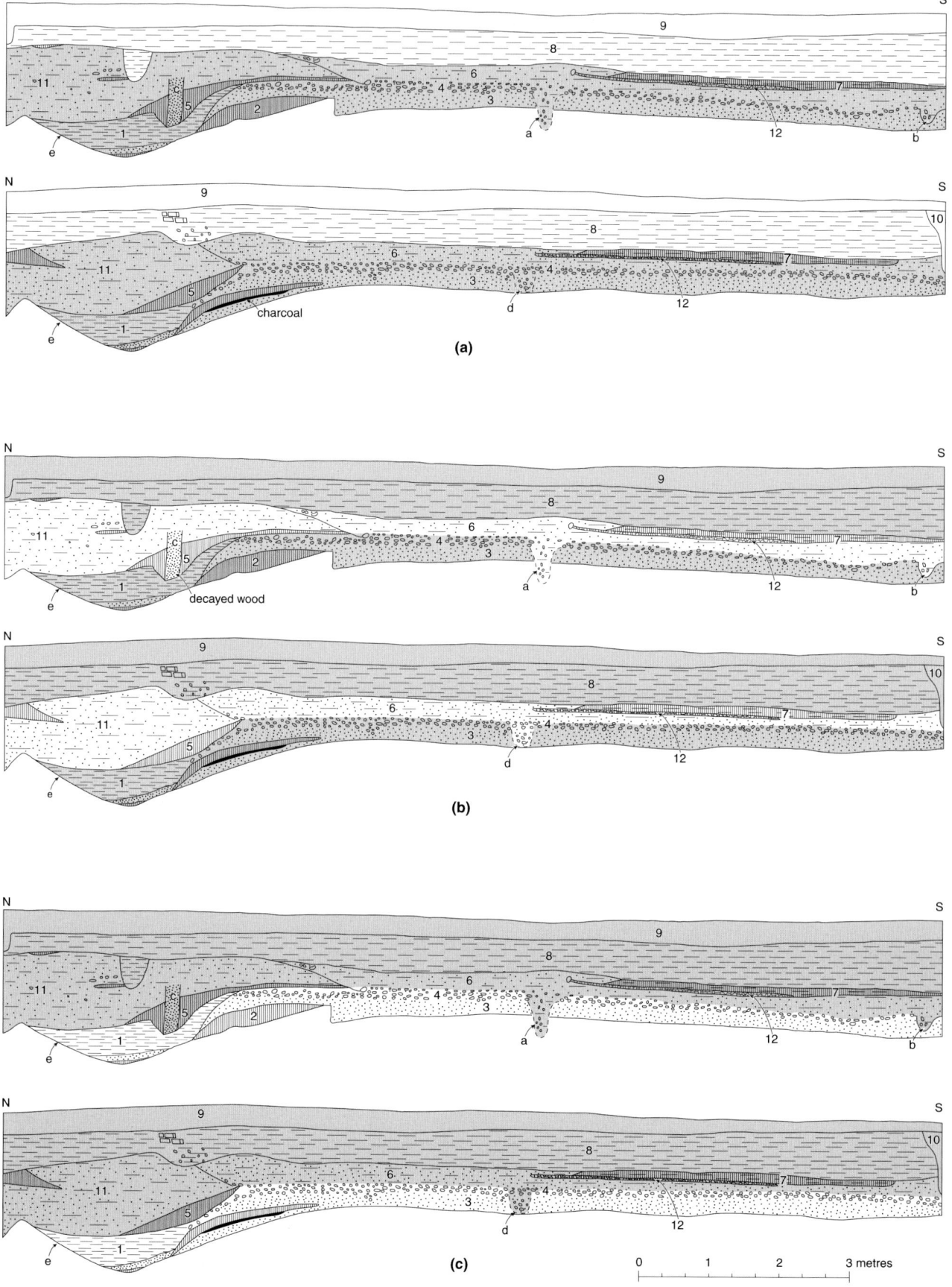

Figure 19. A phased analysis of K. Sheridan's Bell Inn Corner, Tamworth, section drawing (Fig. 18): (a) suggested late medieval and modern features and layers; (b) suggested late Anglo-Saxon ones; (c) suggested middle Anglo-Saxon ones. (In each case those of other periods are shown grey-tinted.) The section drawing of the trench's western side as shown in Fig. 18 has been reversed for ease of comparison with that of its eastern side.

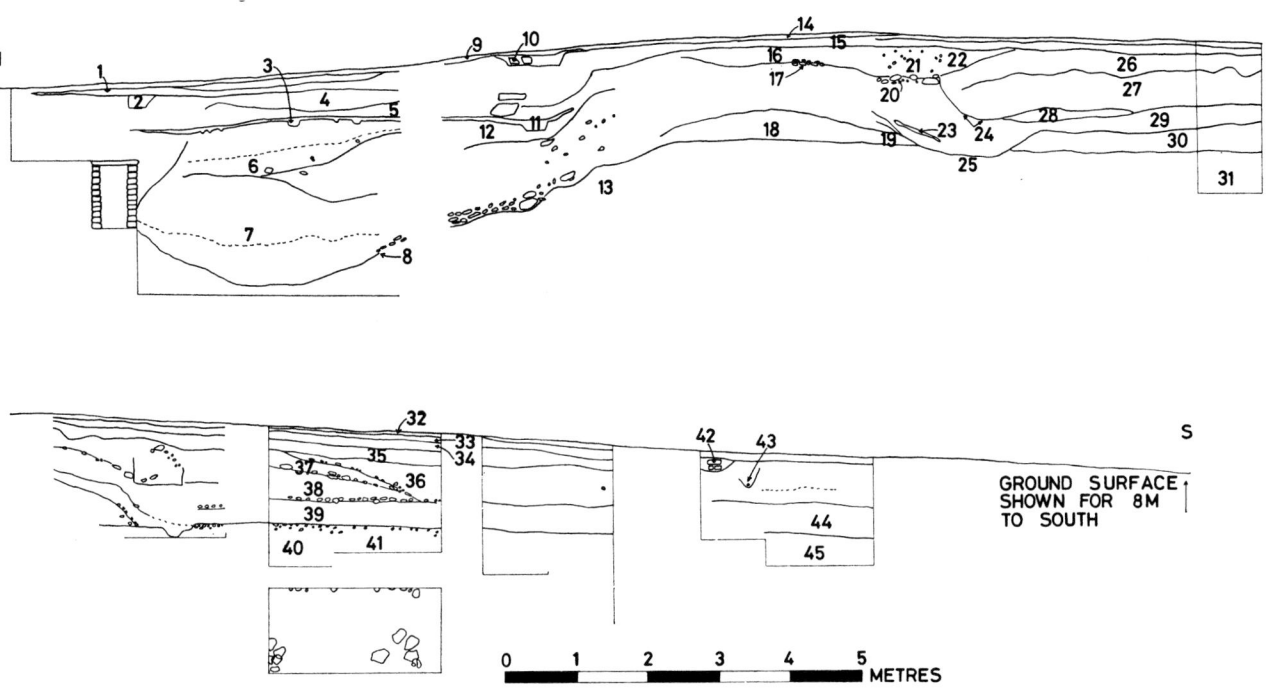

Figure 20. Albert Road, Tamworth: the Anglo-Saxon and later medieval defences, as drawn by F. T. Wainwright. (Originally published as Transactions of the South Staffordshire Archaeological and Historical Society, *14 (1973), fig. 1 on 40: 'Section of the north defences', and reproduced with the editor's permission.)*

unresolved. Nevertheless, despite many *lacunae* the broad outlines of the stratigraphical sequence look reassuringly familiar (Figs 20–21), and it is probably safe to interpret it in terms of what has already been seen elsewhere. Indeed, in some respects it provides evidence which is clearer than the evidence recovered from other more recent excavations of Tamworth's defences.

Layers 26–28 plainly formed the core of the second-stage rampart. As on the Bell Inn Corner site, they run north to form a north edge (24) with material which, although not adequately described, is said to be red and so was probably the same clay as was piled against the base of the rampart's frontal revetment on all but one of the other sites discussed so far. The rear of the rampart is marked by a feature, not mentioned in the report but apparently a posthole (46), which lay at the point where 26–27 seemed to be dying out to the south. There was a break here in the otherwise general spread which was variously called 'humus' and 'old turf and topsoil' (30, 39, 44); this was wide enough to allow there to have been a more deeply set post than the section-drawing suggests was the case. This produces a rampart which was *c.* 4.9 m. wide, which compares very well with its width elsewhere.

The front edge of the rampart's make-up shows that the same decay and bulging forward of the revetment must have occurred as was seen at Bell Inn Corner. Here, however, the evidence is better because the section-drawing also records a distinct downward trend in 26 and 27, the two most substantial layers of make-up. Even though no posthole or slot is recorded in that area, there can be very little doubt that these layers' steeply curving north edge equates to the vertical one at the front of the rampart on the Tamworth General Hospital site.

At both the front and the rear of the rampart there is evidence of what were almost certainly stone revetments built to replace the timber ones. At its front, at *c.* 0.7 m. above the base, there is a layer of stones (20) which Wainwright described as 'stones set in red bank'. These formed a layer *c.* 0.90 m. wide. The mortar-flecked soil directly above them (21) lies in a cut made into the front of the rampart (22), which Wainwright interpreted as a possible robber trench (*i.e.* a wall-removal trench).[118] The evidence clearly points to there having been a stone wall at that level, of which all but the lowest course was subsequently robbed. About 1 m. to the north there was another, narrower patch of stones (17), described as 'stones, ?wall' and overlain by a mortary clay (16). This presumably represents either another piece of the same wall's lowest course (which would then have been at least 2 m. wide at its base), or else an isolated lump of fallen masonry from a narrower version of the wall. At the rear of the rampart, almost directly above the posthole, Fig. 20 shows a slot-like feature (Fig. 21: 47), which is *c.* 0.65 m. wide. It looks like the removal trench of another, smaller wall.

Behind the rampart and overlying a dark humic soil

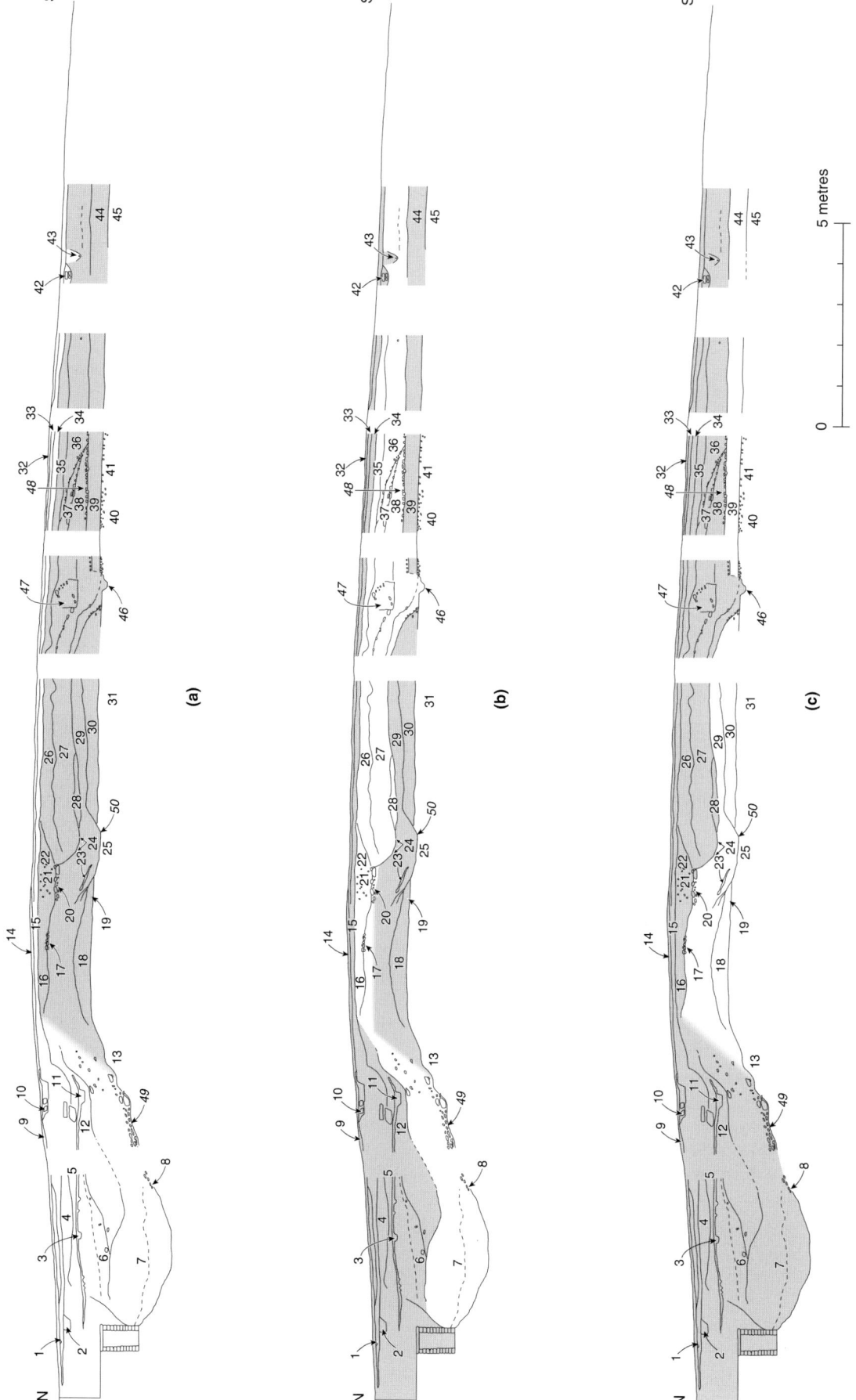

Figure 21. A phased analysis of F. T. Wainwright's Albert Road, Tamworth, section drawing (Fig. 20): (a) suggested late medieval and modern features and layers; (b) suggested late Anglo-Saxon ones; (c) suggested middle Anglo-Saxon ones. (In each case those of other periods are shown grey-tinted.)

(39) was a layer of stones which Wainwright interpreted as a road (48). Sheridan reported that a silver cut halfpenny of Edward the Martyr (975–8) had been found 'in the layer of stones immediately below layer 38';[119] while Wainwright himself said that it had been 'found in the tail of the bank', by which his site notebook plainly shows that he meant layer 39.[120] Layers 37 ('clayey humus') and 38 were very probably deposited as a result of the failure of the rampart's rear revetment and the consequent slumping of a large amount of its make-up. The rear wall must have been robbed from no lower in the stratigraphical sequence than the surface of 26 and of 38 or 37;[121] and if it had a foundation trench, it must have been built too from that level or higher up. It seems, then, that the layer of stones lay immediately to the rear of the timber-revetted second-stage rampart and was probably an exposed surface until the latter's collapse buried it. This would make its identification as a road a sound one. It would also contribute significantly to maximising the coin's use as dating evidence, since it would indicate that the latest time at which the coin could have reached its eventual findspot was when the back of the timber-revetted rampart collapsed.

Layers 35 and 36, the latest ones to be uncontaminated by bricks and other modern debris, may represent an enlargement of the rampart once the revetting walls had been robbed, so as to form the bank of the later medieval defences. The location of the latter's ditch is, however, unclear. Sheridan believed that it was the one found at the north end of the trench,[122] but the stratification suggests otherwise. The section-drawing looks particularly sketchy in its treatment of the lower fills of the ditch and of the area between it and the front of the second-stage rampart; nor is it certain that the natural subsoil was reached throughout the excavated area.[123] The stones lying down the ditch's south side (49) are reminiscent of those which Gould found at Brewery Lane sealing the primary silts of the second-stage ditch, and which were probably derived from the decay or demolition of a wall built to reinforce the front of the contemporary rampart. Moreover, if the wall on the present site had been robbed before the third-stage (*i.e.* later medieval) defences were built, as is likely, it would be hard to imagine how this layer of stones could be stratigraphically later than the feature which Wainwright identified as the robbing cut (22, with its mortary fills 16 and 21). On balance, then, it is at least as likely as not that some of the second-stage ditch was found and excavated. If there had been a berm of *c.* 5.5 m. width, as there was elsewhere, most or all of the ditch would have lain within the trench. However, that is not to say that much of what Fig. 20 shows at its north end does not belong to the later medieval ditch. The section-drawing is too imprecise to allow any firm interpretation to be made.

Finally, sealed below the front of the second-stage rampart there was an unnumbered feature cut into the old ground surface (50). It occupies the same position, both stratigraphically and physically, as the putative first-stage palisade trench found on all but one of the sites discussed so far. Wainwright's recording of it was minimal. Its fills were not described, nor were they adequately distinguished from each other in the section-drawing; and it must be suspected that the feature was not fully excavated.[124] Layer 29, 'Red upcast',[125] probably represents the only surviving *in situ* make-up of the rampart with which it was associated and is therefore equivalent to 5 and 6 at Brewery Lane (Figs 9–10). The section-drawing appears to show 29 as also forming part of the feature's fill but gives far too little detail to allow a secure sequence to be established. However, the upper fill was almost certainly the same clay as had been placed against the frontal revetment of the second-stage rampart elsewhere and been used to infill pre-existing features.[126] The clay, described as a 'red bank', underlay the single surviving course of the masonry wall built to strengthen the front of the rampart (20),[127] and was apparently a thick deposit which carried on northwards under layers 16 and 17 and over the top of 18.[128]

Albert Road (site 2)

The second section which K. Sheridan cut across the north side of the defences was also on Albert Road, close to their north-east corner.[129] His section-drawing shows many of the features which are illustrated in other published sections (Figs 22–3). He reported that the second-stage rampart had been represented by a *c.* 5 m. wide layer of heavy grey-brown earth, 'possibly decayed turf' (3, labelled 'Turf?'), and, overlying it, a layer of brown earth containing closely packed large stones (11).[130] However, it is far likelier that the rampart lay further north, where a deep accumulation of sandy soil (9, 10) is shown on Sheridan's section-drawing but is not referred to in his report. This overlay a layer of 'soft grey earth containing a few small pebbles' (8), which he convincingly interpreted as a horizontal timber (labelled 'Timber staining' on Fig. 22) but assumed to be lying on the berm. It was 4.7 m. long, which is almost exactly the width of the rampart on the Brewery Lane site.[131]

Immediately south of it is a feature which is labelled 'a' on his section-drawing but is not mentioned in the text. Arguably a posthole, this may mark the rear of the rampart. Although it looks insubstantial, it would have been *c.* 0.5 m. deep, and so of an adequate size, if in reality it was cut through the 'Buried soil' which is shown as its fill (Fig. 23:1). This suggests that the closely packed large stones (11), which should now be seen as having lain to the rear of the rampart, can be re-interpreted as a road. Its width, *c.* 5.2 m., is the same as that of the putative road on the Bell Inn Corner site.

The front of the rampart has the now familiar bulging appearance seen on other sites. No plan of the excavation trench was published, and in view of Sheridan's belief that the rampart lay further south it is unsurprising that his report says nothing about postholes or other structural

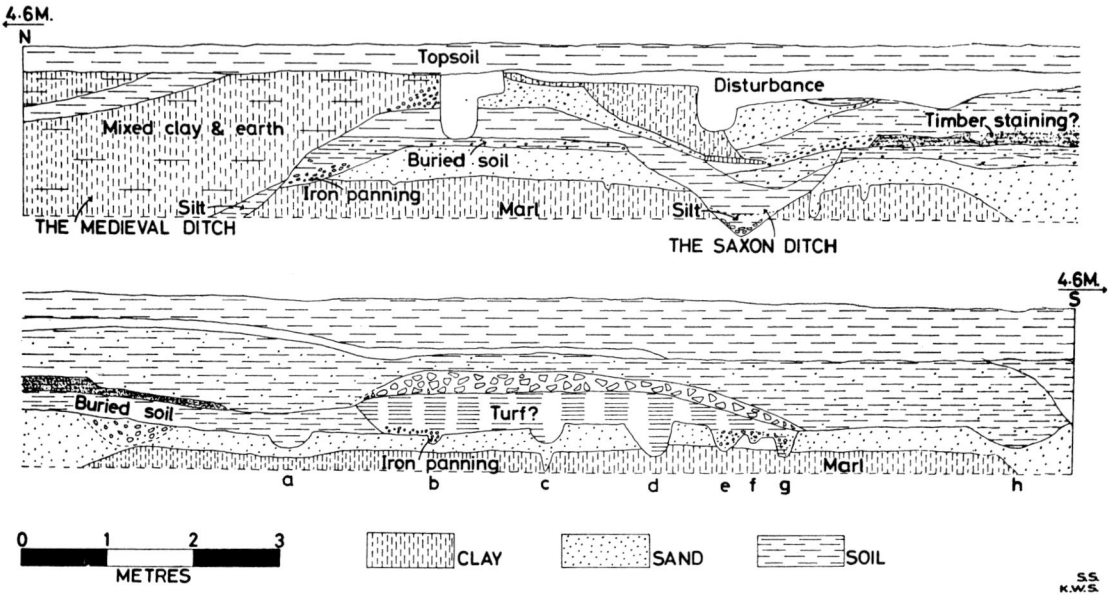

Figure 22. Albert Road, Tamworth: the Anglo-Saxon and later medieval defences, as drawn in sectional view by K. Sheridan. (Originally published as Transactions of the South Staffordshire Archaeological and Historical Society, *14 (1973), fig. 2, on 34: 'Part of the east section through the defences', and reproduced with the editor's permission.)*

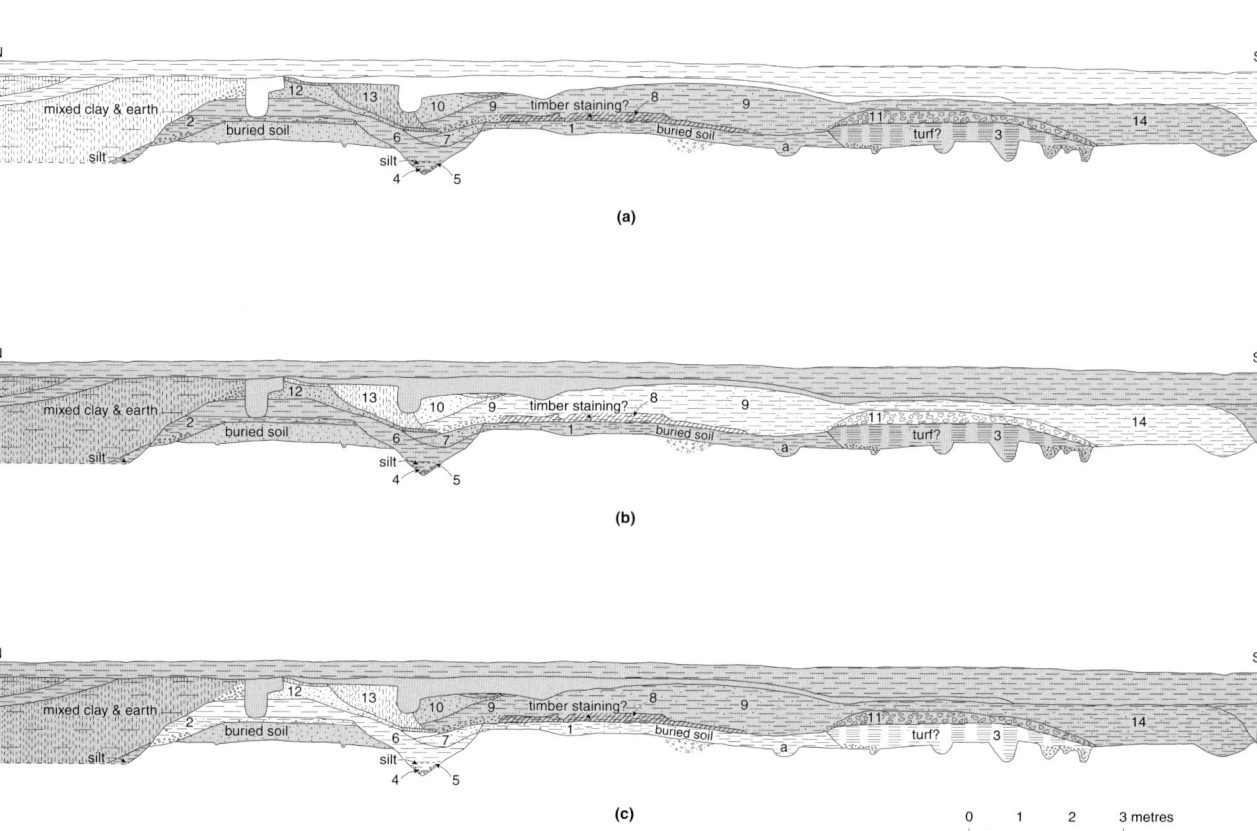

Figure 23. A phased analysis of K. Sheridan's Albert Road, Tamworth, section drawing (Fig. 22): (a) suggested late medieval and modern features and layers; (b) suggested late Anglo-Saxon ones; (c) suggested middle Anglo-Saxon ones. (In each case those of other periods are shown grey-tinted.)

features at its base,[132] apart from the N-S aligned timber (8) which provides the only evidence known from Tamworth of a structural element set at right-angles to the rampart's course. The usual marl, described as 'sandy clay' (13), was found against the front of the rampart.[133] As at Brewery Lane it had been used to infill the depressed area which remained at the front of the revetment after the latter's construction, and a thin spread of it (all that had survived a major lowering of the rampart) ran on northwards until cut away by later features. What Fig. 22 shows at this point closely resembles what Wainwright found, much better preserved, *c.* 75 m. to the west. There is the same evidence too that decay or removal of the rear revetment had led to the rampart's make-up being spread over the road and the area beyond (14), but it is unclear if this occurred when the second-stage stone walls were being built (of which no evidence survived on this site), or when the third-stage defences were put up.[134]

Directly below the front of the second-stage rampart was a linear feature, *c.* 1 m. deep. Although identified by Sheridan as 'the Saxon ditch',[135] *i.e.* that of the second-stage defences, there can be no doubt that it is earlier. Its profile is very similar to that of Gould's pre-rampart 'ditch' at the Brewery Lane site, re-interpreted here as a palisade trench. As elsewhere, the feature had a small amount of primary fill, described as 'fine silt and smooth round pebbles' (5) and labelled 'Silt' on the section-drawing, and a substantial secondary fill of 'light-brown soil' (6, 7).[136] Unlike what was found on other sites, the feature's bottom is shown V-shaped, but there are too many other close similarities for it not to be securely identified as the same one. The pebbles which were a notable element of its lowest fill (4) are most unlikely to represent a weathering product here and so may have been deliberately deposited to form a suitable base for posts.[137]

The feature's main fill, 'light brown soil' (6), continued beyond its north edge and may also have filled another linear feature to the north (2, not referred to in the report), of which an unknown amount had been cut away by the large ditch at the end of the trench. This feature lay at approximately the same distance in front of Sheridan's 'Saxon ditch' as the putative first-stage ditch at Brewery Lane did in relation to Gould's 'pre-rampart ditch', but too little of it survived for its function to be identified.[138] Its position in the stratigraphy shows, however, that it cannot have been the second-stage ditch. The latter might have been the one found at the north end of the trench and said to be filled with 'mixed clay and earth'; but, if so, the berm was much narrower here than elsewhere. It is likely that Sheridan was correct in his identification of this extensive feature as the [later] medieval ditch, an identification which he made on the grounds that it was too big to be anything else.[139]

Marmion Street

There have been three separate investigations of the east side of the defences. Two trenches were excavated by machine by R. Sherlock on a site on Marmion Street. The only publication of the results was a brief note in a regional news-letter, but the site drawings and photographs are still accessible.[140] A truncated bank was found which was reported as being *c.* 20 ft (6.1 m.) wide and which 'seemed to have been revetted with stones on the external face.'[141] A photograph of the excavation (Fig. 24) shows the stones lying on the ditch's inner slope in a position equivalent to that of the ones which Wainwright found in the ditch of the second-stage defences on his Albert Street site. It is very probable that they were derived from the collapse of a stone wall which had been added to the front of the second-stage rampart; however, in the absence of adequately detailed section-drawings and other relevant photographs it is impossible to be sure.[142] The published note says nothing about evidence of a timber revetment or about pre-rampart features.

Bolebridge Street (site 1)

C. Young excavated by machine near to the south-east corner of the defences on a site to the north of Bolebridge Street. The high water-table, running sand, and inadequate time and resources prevented him from making the thorough investigation which the site merited.[143] Two notes have been published but no line-drawings. He found a defensive sequence of three phases which may mirror what was found elsewhere but does not do so for certain. The first phase was 'possibly Saxon or earlier', comprising 'a small ditch which may have been a boundary', and which is reported as having 'completely silted' before the second-phase ditch was cut immediately to the east-south-east of it and on a parallel course.[144] The latter was wide and deep and apparently had been deliberately filled in. Part of it was waterlogged, and 'large preserved timbers' were found in it, as well as 'Roman-type building material', all being described as 'destruction material'.[145] No features or layers were certainly associated with it, but some horizontal timber features found *c.* 6.1 m. to the rear may have been 'the strapping of a rampart'.[146] Young suggested on the basis of what he had seen of the ditch that it was the same as the second-stage one which Gould had excavated the year before at Brewery Lane.[147]

It was succeeded by a large ditch situated *c.* 50 ft (*c.* 15 m.) to the south-east on an almost parallel course. Its fills apparently consisted in part of collapsed rampart make-up, but no other evidence was uncovered of an associated bank. The ditch was said to have been entirely filled by the late thirteenth century, and was identified as the third-stage, *i.e.* later medieval, ditch which had been sectioned elsewhere.[148]

Bolebridge Street (site 2)

R. Meeson excavated a section of the first- and second-stage defences on a site near to Young's. In a brief

Figure 24. Marmion Street, Tamworth: stone debris lying down the inner slope of the ditch of the second-stage defences, as excavated by R. Sherlock. The stones are presumed to be derived from a wall which had been added to the front of the timber-revetted rampart. Reproduced by permission of Staffordshire County Council and the National Monuments Record (negative reference: AA66/01629). Copyright: Staffordshire County Council.

published note he modified the latter's account of the fill of the first-stage 'ditch', noting that it 'had been largely silted before the top was deliberately filled'.[149] Immediately beyond it (*i.e.* south-east of it) Meeson found the second-stage ditch, which was 5 m. wide and 1.3 m. deep. Its lowest fills were black peaty silts. Two postholes and a narrow slot uncovered *c.* 6.8 m. behind its inner lip 'may together represent the front of a rampart.'[150]

Tamworth: dating evidence

The short set of annals preserved in the B manuscript of the Anglo-Saxon Chronicle and known as the Mercian Register records that in 913 'Æthelflæd...went with all the Mercians to Tamworth and built the *burh* there in the early summer.'[151] This, then, provides us with an unequivocal date for the construction of the place's defensive circuit.

There is, it seems, only one radiocarbon determination from the many excavations across the defences at Tamworth. This relates to one of the preserved timbers found in the bottom of the second-stage ditch on C. Young's Bolebridge Street site. It is said to have produced

a date centred on the early fifth century,[152] but being uncalibrated it is plainly unreliable and in any case would have no real value as a *terminus post quem*.

A small amount of probably Anglo-Saxon pottery was recovered from significant contexts, but none of it could be closely dated. On the Brewery Lane site three pieces of grass-tempered pottery were found in the make-up of the second-stage rampart.[153] There were no datable finds in the accompanying ditch. The lowest fill of the first-stage 'ditch' on the Lichfield Street site yielded 'a few crumbs of black, very friable pottery', but no date was suggested for them.[154] Another sherd, also undated, came from one of the post-pits associated with the second-stage rampart.[155] On the Orchard Street site the layers and features identified by Sheridan as being associated with the second-stage defences produced 'the largest number of sherds of Saxon coarse pottery...recovered from any single excavation in Tamworth', although none of them came from the ditch's primary silt. As a group they were said to 'fit a tenth century context'.[156] However, Sheridan's report is regrettably silent about the specific provenance of any of the sherds, and none of them has been published. Their whereabouts are now unknown.

At the Tamworth General Hospital and Bell Inn Corner sites nothing datable was found in the layers associated with the second-stage defences;[157] and the same is true of Sheridan's two sites on Albert Road and Marmion Street.[158] The two excavations on Bolebridge Street produced very little pottery which was useful for dating purposes; however, 'a final silting' in the second-stage ditch included what the excavator identified as twelfth-century pottery.[159] In this area the course of the third-stage defences diverged from that of its predecessors; and therefore the fact that the second-stage ditch was still open in the twelfth century has less significance for dating the third-stage defences than it would have had elsewhere on the circuit.

Finally, no pottery was found in significant layers on Wainwright's site on Albert Road; but a silver cut halfpenny of Edward the Martyr (975–8), minted at Torksey, came from earth lying between the stones of the putative road which lay immediately behind the rear timber revetment of the second-stage rampart. Sheridan noted that it 'came from the layer of stones immediately below layer 38',[160] 38 having been very probably derived from a collapse of rampart make-up caused by a failure of the revetment (Figs 20–21). Wainwright's records make it plain that he thought that the soil which surrounded the coin belonged to the top of the underlying layer (39), on which the stones had been laid and into which they are likely to have been pressed while in use as a road. However, a second possible origin of the soil in which the coin lay cannot be ignored – that it was dirt which had slowly accumulated in gaps between the stones during that time. Wainwright did not record the finding of any such dirt, but it must have existed originally. Being clayey, 39's surface is likely to have become a quagmire in wet weather, and so it is inconceivable that dirt and small objects alike which dropped into the gaps between the stones would not have been liable to end up being mixed into the top of 39. It is a strong possibility, then, that the coin was indeed surrounded by the soil of layer 39, as Wainwright recorded, but that it had arrived there by being pressed down into 39 after the stones' deposition.

The use to which the coin's date of minting can be reliably put as a *terminus post quem* depends, then, on the precise circumstances in which it reached its findspot. Since these can never be known, the only responsible course of action is to assume for dating purposes that the coin reached its findspot in circumstances which would dictate that the *terminus* which it provided was the least far-reaching in its implications – or, to put this another way, which affected no layer which was earlier in the stratigraphical sequence than the earliest one which it had to affect in all conceivable circumstances. The alternatives are as follows.

1. The coin had formerly been contained within one of the layers of rampart make-up, as a result of its originally being contained in the soil which had been heaped up to form this make-up, or of its having been lost while this soil was being heaped up. It reached its findspot as a result of a collapse of the rampart make-up; this created layer 38, which filled the interstices between the stones, depositing the coin onto the surface of the underlying layer 39. This would give a *terminus post quem* to the building of the second-stage rampart.

2. The coin had formerly been contained in the soil which, when deposited to the rear of the rampart, became layer 39. This would give a *terminus post quem* to the stones of the putative road and to the layers overlying them. If 39 was derived from weathering of the rear of the rampart itself, or from a limited collapse of its make-up, and if the coin had been contained in the soil ever since it had been heaped up to form this make-up, it would also give a *terminus post quem* to the building of the second-stage rampart.

3. The coin reached its findspot after 39 had been deposited but before the stones were laid on top of it. This would give a *terminus post quem* to the deposition of the stones and to the layers overlying them.

4. Layer 38 was derived from a collapse of some of the make-up of the second-stage rampart, and the coin, which had been introduced into 38 (*e.g.* by trample) while the soil concerned was part of the rampart make-up, tumbled into one of the interstices between the stones and ended up on the surface of 39. This would give a reliable *terminus post quem* only to the layers above 38 (since it would have to be assumed that it had not been introduced into 38 until after the stones had been laid).

5. The coin was lost while the stones were exposed (*e.g.* by someone walking on them). This would give a *terminus post quem* only to 38 and the layers above it.

Of these alternative hypothetical explanations of the arrival of the coin on the surface of layer 39 the fourth and fifth ones would be the least far-reaching in their chronological implications, since they affect no layer lower in the stratigraphical sequence than 38. Of all five the fourth seems the least likely to have occurred and the fifth one (*i.e.* that the coin had been lost by someone walking on the stones) the most likely; but in any event limiting the application of the *terminus post quem* to layer 38 and above has to be the most responsible course of action. This means that the coin can be reliably used to provide a *terminus post quem* for the deposition of 38 and, if 38 was part of the timber-revetted second-stage rampart's make-up, for this rampart's collapse.

The coin was struck between 975 and 978.[161] The normal conventions of archaeological dating require us to accept that it might not have been lost until long afterwards; but Michael Dolley proposed that in this instance an exception could be made. He argued that the issue to which the coin belonged had been continued for a short time under Æthelred II with his name being substituted for Edward the Martyr's, but that it had then been demonetarised, probably in late 979. In his view, 'all the evidence is that at this period demonetarization of a particular issue was virtually one hundred per cent effective', and so 'loss of the coin may be assumed to have occurred before the autumn of 979', or at the latest by mid 980.[162]

Dolley's opinion is still broadly in line with current views on tenth-century English recoinage. Dr Mark Blackburn comments that if the coin represents a casual loss from circulation, there is in his view a 95% probability that it had been lost 'by say 981'.[163] If it could have been proved, therefore, that the coin's original resting-place had been in 39 and that 39 was the same layer as 30, its date of manufacture (975–8) would have been, at least potentially,[164] the *terminus post quem* for the timber-revetted rampart's construction. However, this cannot be proved. It is at least as likely that the coin was 'introduced' into 39 after the stones had been laid on top of it and were being used as a road surface, or alternatively that it had been lying in the dirt which had accumulated between them and which therefore overlay 39. Nothing, then, can be safely deduced from the coin's discovery about the date at which the rampart was built, unduly uncompromising as some people may consider this judgement.

This conclusion needs to be stressed, if at the cost of some repetition. Firstly, if the coin's findspot was indeed within layer 39, its use for giving a *terminus post quem* to the rampart's construction would be fatally undermined by the possibility that it had arrived there through being pressed down into 39 long after the latter's deposition (either while 39 was still part of the rampart or after its collapse). Alternatively, if the coin's findspot was 'in', *i.e.* among, the stones, owing to its having been lost, for example, while they were a road surface, its use for giving a reliable *terminus ante quem* of *c.* 981 to the rampart – an alternative hypothesis which, if shown to be sound, would have equally important implications – would rely on two unsafe assumptions, the first being that the stones had not been laid until the rampart already existed, which is a reasonable but unprovable hypothesis; and the second one being that the coin had been lost by *c.* 981 (since after that date it would no longer have been in circulation), which ignores the possibility, authoritatively estimated as being 5%, that the coin was still in circulation, in the broadest sense of the term, after 981. Finally, if the coin's findspot was in reality in 38, the question must arise of whether this layer was collapsed rampart make-up, as argued here (in which case the coin would potentially give a *terminus post quem* of 975–8 for the rampart's construction),[165] or represented material brought in from elsewhere (in which case the coin could be used only for dating layers and features which were stratigraphically later than 38).

There is, however, one use to which the coin may be reliably put as dating evidence. There can be no reasonable doubt that the construction of the stone wall at the rear of the second-stage rampart's top occurred after the deposition of 38. This event is therefore given a secure *terminus post quem* of 975–8, and arguably, by association, so too is the construction of the stone wall at the front of the rampart.

Tamworth: discussion

No conclusion which is both useful and unassailably true can be reached, from the archaeological evidence alone, about the date at which the second-stage defences at Tamworth were constructed. Even the statement that they must predate the large ditch containing twelfth-century and later pottery which was found on several sites depends on one particular reading of the published sections, although to argue that they did not do so would need a very forced and ultimately self-defeating interpretation of key aspects of the results of the excavations concerned. There is, for instance, no direct stratigraphical evidence to prove that Gould's 'Saxon ditch' (Figs 9–10), excavated on the Brewery Lane site, belonged to the second-stage defences; and a different understanding of the *raison d'être* and inter-relationship of marls 9 and 11 on the same site would remove the basis for regarding his 'Medieval ditch' as being stratigraphically later than the timber-revetted rampart which was based on features A and E. Similarly, on the Tamworth General Hospital site one particular interpretation of the role of pink clay 016 is needed to establish that there was a direct relationship between the features identified as, respectively, the later medieval ditch (015) and the second-stage rampart (027). The section-drawing published for Sheridan's site on Albert Road (Figs 22–3) shows no credible stratigraphical relationship between the later medieval ditch and what has been interpreted in this paper (but not by Sheridan himself) as the timber-revetted rampart; and the one which Wainwright drew for his adjacent site is a seriously incomplete record.

Little direct dating evidence is available for the second-stage defences, and what there is is mainly unhelpful. The (uncalibrated) radiocarbon determination from one of the timbers found near the bottom of Young's section of the second-stage ditch on his Bolebridge Street site does no more than suggest that the ditch was very probably (95%) open in or after the second century AD. None of the few sherds of allegedly Anglo-Saxon date which were found in diagnostic contexts can now be located,[166] and in most cases the published statements about their dates of manufacture are too imprecise to be of use. The potential exception are those of 'Saxon coarse pottery', found by Sheridan in the ditch's fill on his Orchard Street site and said as a group to 'fit a tenth century context'.[167] If these represented sherds of contemporary pottery which were lost while the ditch was being allowed to fill up, and if they were correctly dated in 1972, they would point to the second-stage defences as being the work of Æthelflæd in 913. However, neither of these presuppositions can be confirmed: some or all of the sherds may have been residual; and a re-examination of the sherds today might well put a significantly different date on some or all of them.

Only the silver cut halfpenny of Edward the Martyr makes a fully reliable and immediately useful contribution to dating the second-stage defences. Whatever its precise findspot was, and whatever interpretation is put on the origins of 39 (the layer which sealed the stones among which, or conceivably under which, the coin was found), it gives an indisputable *terminus post quem* of 975–8 to the creation of the linear feature which has been identified here as having contained a wall put up at the rear edge of the rampart's top surface. If the coin had been lost by *c.* 981, as is very probable, it would allow for the putative wall to have been built in the reign of Æthelred II (978–1016), the period to which some have attributed the construction of other, similar walls,[168] and in which the undertaking of a major refurbishment of this sort would have made excellent sense, given what we know about the sustained Scandinavian assaults on England which occurred then. It may, however, have been built after that reign, belonging to a military context about which we know far less.

Despite the detailed reconsideration of the evidence undertaken here, therefore, very little progress has been made towards firmly establishing the date of the second-stage circuit at Tamworth. The Anglo-Saxon Chronicle unequivocally reports that Æthelflæd built defences there in 913, and so it was reasonable for those excavating in Tamworth to assume, as they all did, that if a distinct set of defences was found which was stratigraphically earlier than the town's later medieval ones, it must have originated in her work. This conclusion received general corroboration from the similarity of these earlier defences to the ones excavated in Wessex, where in the second phase of their use masonry had been added at the front and rear of the ramparts, at it had been at Tamworth.[169] This still seems sound. Although the identification of the second-stage defences as being those built by Æthelflæd gains no unequivocal support from the archaeological dating evidence, the latter does not contradict it and indeed can be seen to give the interpretation some useful circumstantial support.

To approach this problem from a different angle, establishing the date at which Tamworth's later medieval defences were created would give an unmistakable *terminus ante quem* to the second-stage ones. Not surprisingly, there is no known documentary reference to their creation. In its absence Gould argued that the third-stage ditch was of twelfth-century origin, on the grounds that its surviving fills contained many small sherds of twelfth- to fourteenth-century pottery but only twelfth-century ones in the lowest fills.[170] Since many English boroughs were given large earthwork defences in that century his proposal was both historically and archaeologically reasonable, and it is a matter of very considerable regret that no subsequent excavator was able to test it.

Winchcombe

Winchcombe's defences

Winchcombe differs from Hereford, Tamworth and Worcester in one very important respect: much of the north-west arm of its pre-Conquest defences survives as a substantial earthwork along the south side of Back Lane, a road which runs along the line of the later medieval ditch (Fig. 25). The course of the generally south/south-east arm of the circuit is unknown; it is possible that there were two courses – one of them, arguably the earlier one, along the north side of Langley Brook (which joins the River Isbourne within the town), and the other one to the south of the brook, where there may be visible remains of it in a large field, part of the former Almsbury Farm, to the west of Vineyard Street.

The less extensive of these two possible circuits, which is entirely hypothetical where its course diverges from that of the more extensive one, may have had a south/south-east side just above the steep north edge which Langley Brook has cut into the south slope of the Lias spur on which the medieval core of Winchcombe sits. The other, more extensive, one has been reconstructed from road lines and field boundaries, the majority of them surviving in the modern landscape and the rest being depicted on reliable late eighteenth- and early nineteenth-century maps.[171] Back Lane itself and the roads which project its line further to the north-east and east very probably mirror the full extent of the north-east arm of the defences; and Malthouse Lane and a major property boundary which continues its line to the south of Gloucester Street suggest the line of the south-west arm. The course of the south/south-east arm of this putative circuit is primarily indicated by the surviving earthworks in the field to the west of Vineyard Street, the line of which is continued to the north-east and north by narrow strips of land which are strongly suggestive of the course of a major bank and ditch and, beyond them, by a well established road, which makes a sharp turn so as to follow a closely similar course.[172]

There may have been an excavation in the 1940s on the possible rampart which crosses the field west of Vineyard Street; but, if so, no records of it appear to have survived.[173] In 1999 a substantial archaeological evaluation of the features in this field and adjacent ones was made by John Samuels Archaeological Consultants. It included the cutting of a trench across the same rampart and the large ditch-like feature on its south side.[174]

There have been at least five excavations on the north-west arm, of which the earliest known was undertaken in 1893, when the rampart was sectioned twice.[175] Those of 1939 and 1947 were never published and have left very few records.[176] In 1963 B. Davison sectioned the rampart in the field named Convent Close, and in 1972 J. Hinchliffe did so on a site, *c.* 150 m. to the south-east of Davison's, at Winchcombe County Junior School. Both excavations were published by P. Ellis,[177] who distinguished two main

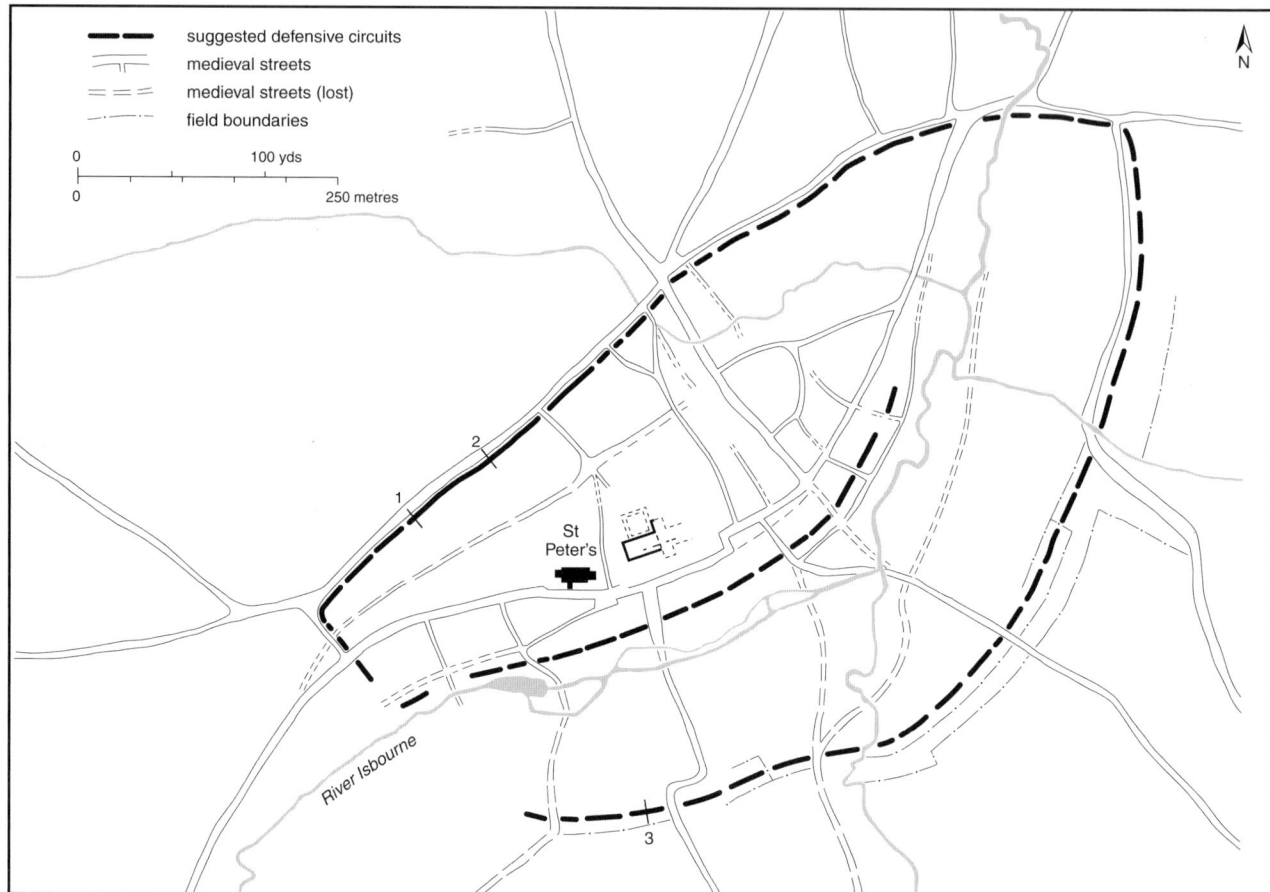

Figure 25. Medieval Winchcombe, showing the sites of excavations on the Anglo-Saxon and later medieval defences: 1. Junior School. 2. Convent Close. 3. Almsbury Farm.

periods of defences, the second of which he divided into two phases. He tentatively suggested that the Period 2 defences had been built in the early tenth century by Æthelflæd, and that the rampart's timber elements had been replaced in stone in the late tenth or early eleventh century (his Period 2, Phase 2). He dated their predecessor, those of his Period 1, to 'some time before the early tenth century'.[178] This simple periodisation is unexceptionable: the stratigraphical evidence which the excavators recorded leaves no room for doubt that there were two distinct stages/periods of defences. Moreover, dividing the second of these into two phases is fully justified on internal evidence – as it also is by analogy, since it is certainly the case that his Period 1 and Period 2 defences are closely similar to those found at Hereford and Tamworth which have been referred to here as first-stage and second-stages ones respectively. However, there is room to disagree with Ellis over his periodisation of certain key layers and features, and the dating of his periods will also need to be reviewed.

Because the two excavations were on closely adjacent sites and were published in a single report, their results are best discussed together.

Convent Close and the Junior School site: Period 1

In Ellis's opinion very little of the Period 1 rampart survived on either site. He identified layer 45 at Convent Close as '? Period 1 bank' and said that it 'appears to conform with the rampart above', *i.e.* that of Period 2, and to represent a possible primary bank' (Figs 26–7).[179] He went on to note that it could represent 'a turf dump placed on an area stripped of turf between layers 47 and 46' (to the north and south respectively).[180] As he himself acknowledged, then, this layer was far too small to be, by itself, the Period 1 (*i.e.* first-stage) rampart. It is very likely to have been either a local marking-out bank for the rampart material above it or merely an isolated dump of turf and topsoil. By contrast at the Junior School site, 'There was no evidence of an accompanying bank, though one may have been present as a lower part of the Period 2 rampart and was not recognized.'[181] Since Fig. 28 shows the great majority of rampart F87A as being made up of a single deposit (10), to accept this suggestion of his would effectively mean identifying all of 10, or even all of 10 and 8, as the Period 1 rampart. This is indeed best done,

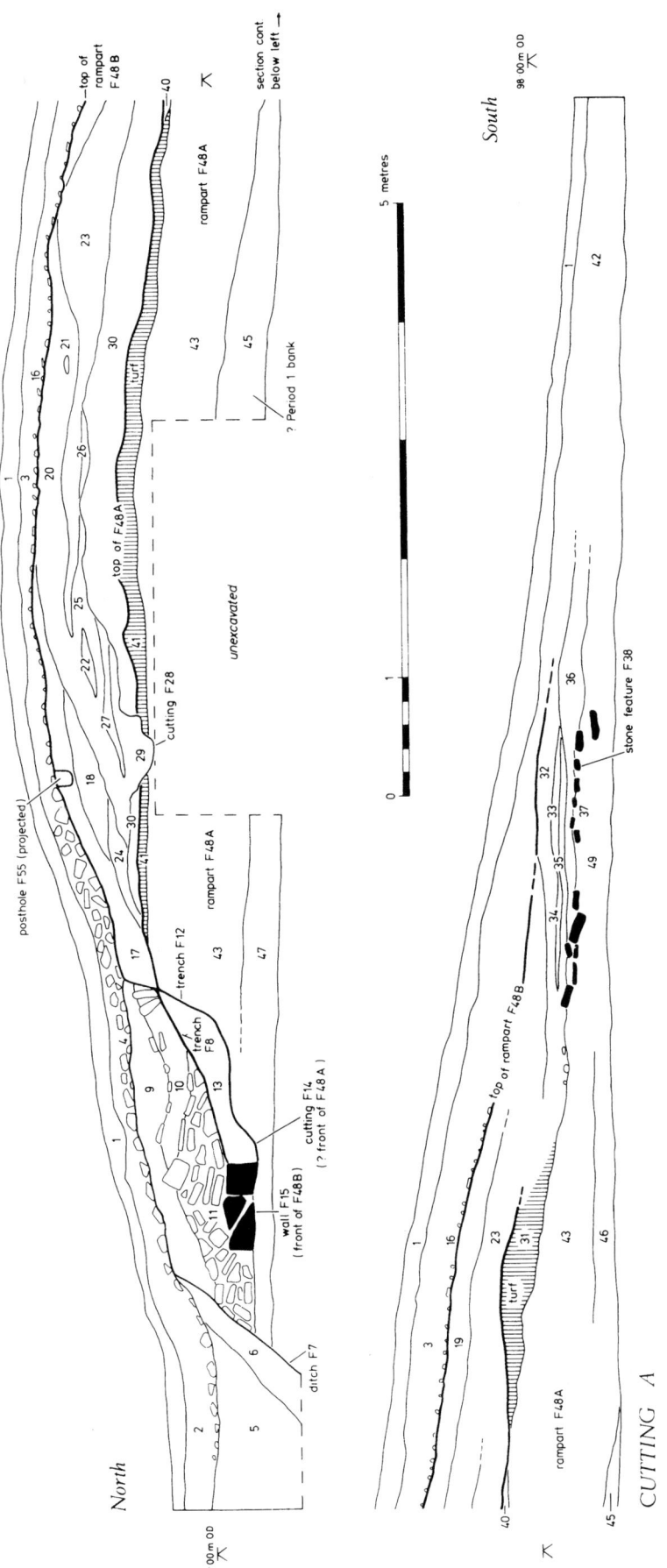

26. *Convent Close, Winchcombe: the Anglo-Saxon and later defences, as drawn in sectional view by B. Davison. (Originally published as Transactions of the Bristol and Gloucestershire Archaeological Society, 104 (1986), fig. 6, on 109: 'Convent Close 1963. Sections', and reproduced with P. Ellis's and the editor's permission.)*

Steven Bassett

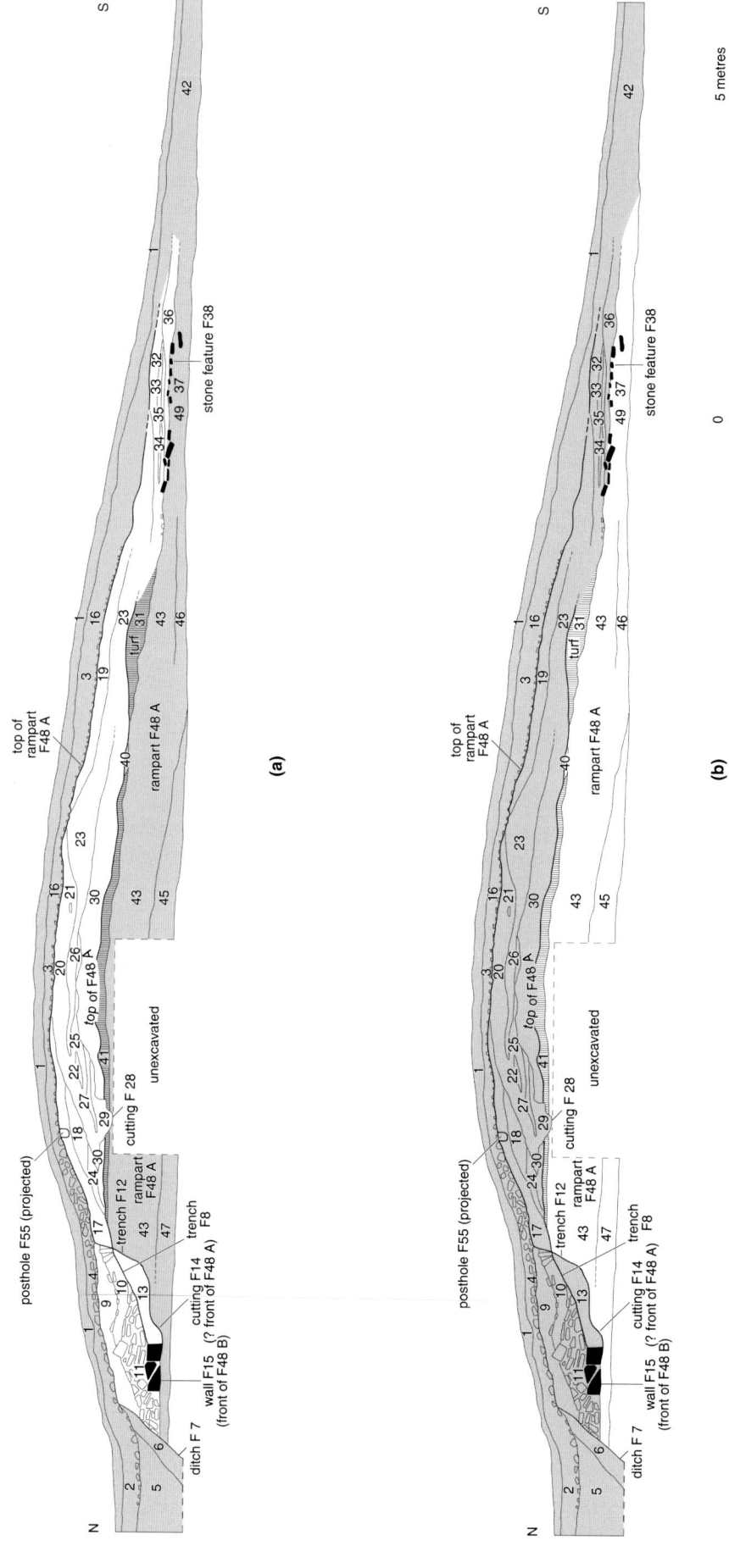

Figure 27. *A phased analysis of B. Davison's Convent Close, Winchcombe, section drawing (Fig. 26): (a) suggested components of the late Anglo-Saxon defences; (b) suggested components of the middle Anglo-Saxon defences. (In each case those of other periods are shown grey-tinted.)*

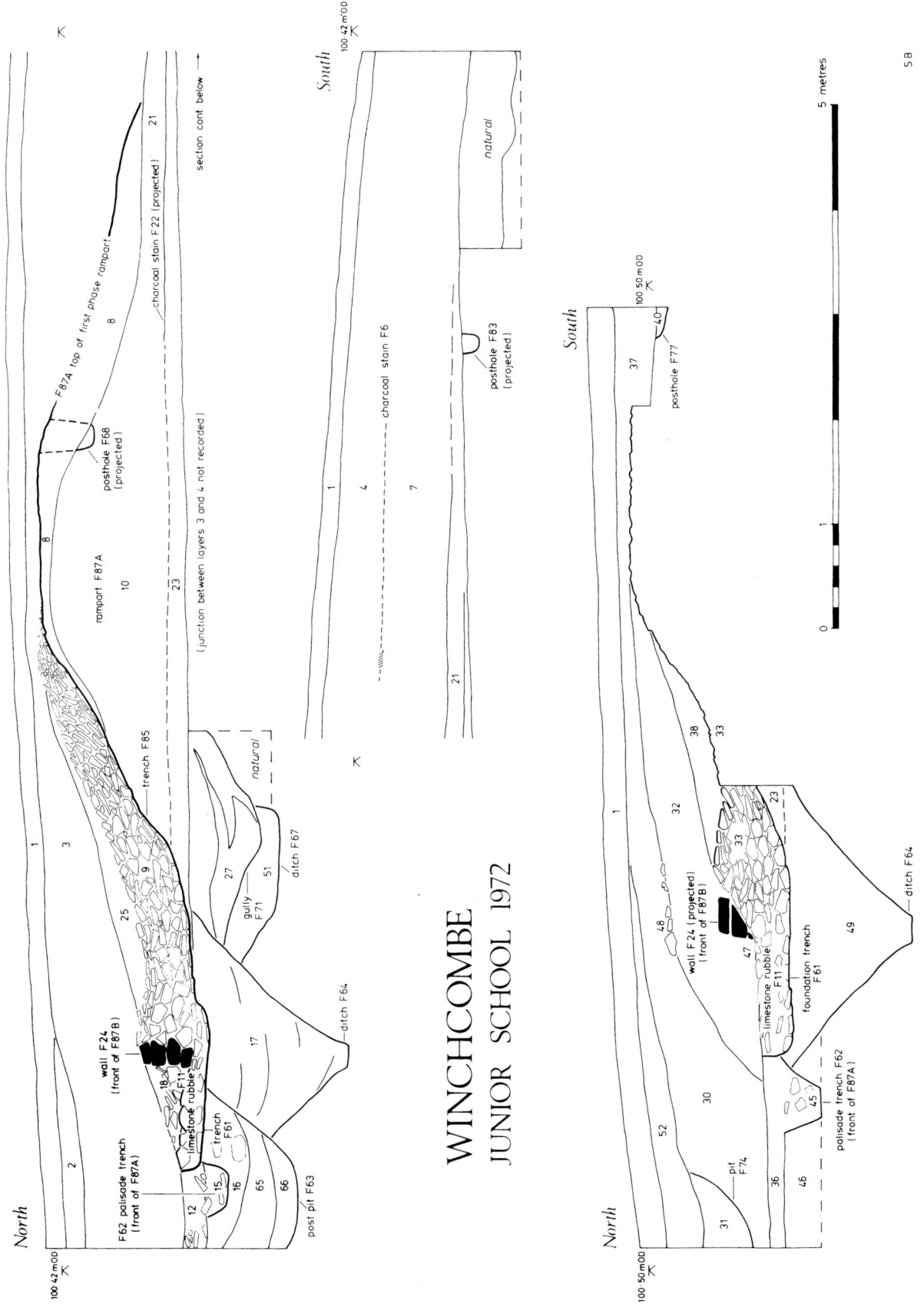

WINCHCOMBE
JUNIOR SCHOOL 1972

Figure 28. Junior School, Winchcombe: the Anglo-Saxon and later defences, as drawn in sectional view by J. Hinchliffe. (Originally published as Transactions of the Bristol and Gloucestershire Archaeological Society, *104 (1986), fig. 12, on 119: 'Junior School 1972. Sections', and reproduced with P. Ellis's and the editor's permission.)*

for if Ellis was correct in his claim that Winchcombe had two successive Anglo-Saxon defensive circuits, it is very hard to conceive of almost all of the earlier one's presumed rampart as having been removed before its successor was constructed.

Therefore, it is probable that what Ellis identified as the 'Æthelflædan' (*i.e.* Period 2, Phase 1) rampart actually belongs to his Period 1 (Figs 29–31). If so, it survived well on the Junior School site but seems to have collapsed or been much reduced at Convent Close. On the former site the relationship between its north edge and the Period 1 feature F64 is such as to allow the two of them to be contemporary. Fig. 28 shows a tiny amount of rampart material overriding the south edge of F64. If this was correctly drawn on site (which plainly is doubtful, since it creates a serious stratigraphical difficulty), it may have been a weathering deposit; if so, the section-drawing purports to show that it accumulated only after 'ditch' F64 had been fully infilled.

The latter feature, excavated on the Junior School site, was not found at Convent Close. This was probably because the excavation was not completed. Ellis stated that it had run out of time, with the result that some rampart features had never been examined.[182] It is evident that the lowest archaeological levels were left unexcavated. Although he passed no comment on the non-discovery at Convent Close of the Junior School site's 'ditch' F64, Ellis did say that what he accepted as being the Period 1 rampart on the former site 'may be associated with the ditch excavated in 1972 beneath the later rampart.'[183] If it originally crossed the area of the Convent Close site, it may have lain unrecognised below trench F12 and wall F15; or else it may have lain further to the north and been destroyed by ditch F7. It is important to note that despite what Fig. 30 shows, there is nothing in the original site drawings to indicate that layer 47 extended as a distinct layer under wall F15. Fig. 26 is much truer to these drawings, since it shows that the excavators were unable to distinguish between layers 47 and 43 in the vicinity of trench F12.

Since the Convent Close excavation was incomplete, a continuation of the Junior School site's F64 may well have been missed – especially if it was filled with redeposited rampart material, as Ellis thought that it was on the latter site.[184] However, on balance (and in view of further discussion below) it seems just as likely that the 'ditch' did not underlie the wall at Convent Close but lay a little to the north of it. But *was* F64 a ditch? or was it, as its stratigraphical equivalent at Tamworth is argued to have been, a palisade trench? It was steep-sided, especially on the south side, and had a flat bottom. Its depth (at least 1.5 m.) might seem too great for such a feature, but the putative palisade trench at Tamworth was also at least 1.5 m. deep.[185]

Convent Close and the Junior School site: Period 2

There are fewer problems attached to what Ellis said about the Period 2 (*i.e.* second-stage) defences. On the Convent Close site there is no evidence of a timber revetment in front of the Period 2, Phase 1 rampart; but any evidence of one which there may at first have been was entirely removed by ditch F7 which, Ellis argued, 'may represent the southern side of a later medieval ditch along Back Lane relating either to the town or to the abbey or to both.'[186]

However, Ellis believed that the feature labelled 'cutting F14' was a trench containing the timber revetment for the front of the Period 2, Phase 1 rampart. What is depicted in the section-drawing (Fig. 26) makes that seem most unlikely, since its fill (13) is also the fill of trench F12, which is best seen as a cut made into the front face of the Period 2, Phase 1 rampart for the erection of the Period 2, Phase 2 masonry revetment. Ellis thought that the same cut might have removed the timber frontal revetment and formed a trench for the wall. That is not impossible, but the setting for the former would surely have needed to be much deeper. Whereas on the Junior School site F63 penetrated the natural subsoil for *c.* 1 m., at Convent Close the bottom of the allegedly equivalent feature, trench F12, lay at least 0.15 cm. above the top of it. Ellis may have interpreted this feature as he did because the limestone rubble (11) did not itself fill it but overlay its fill (13); but if that were so, it would not have been logical to do so. Whether F12 had a single or a dual role, once it existed it was presumably available to be filled with limestone rubble if that was thought necessary (as is suggested by the fact that 13 appears to abut the south side of the wall, which, therefore, it presumably postdated). The fact that it was *not* thought necessary may mean that the Period 1 'ditch' does not underlie the wall here, unlike on the Junior School site. This suggestion is strengthened by the fact that at Convent Close the limestone rubble (11) did not underlie the wall, let alone protrude well forward of it.

On the Junior School site the Period 2, Phase 1 rampart seems to have had a frontal revetment.[187] No post 'ghosts' were mentioned in the report in respect of ?postpits F63 and F90, both of which are shown on Ellis's Figure 11 as being cut by the so-called palisade trench F62; but F90 was not excavated, or at any rate was not recorded, and F63 lay in the very corner of the trench.[188]

The masonry phase – Period 2, Phase 2 – has left a broadly similar sequence on both sites. Creating it was plainly a very substantial undertaking on the Junior School site, with limestone rubble running to the top of the rampart in the east trench and perhaps also doing so in the west one. On the Convent Close site it is reasonable to see the layers which overlie the turf line as belonging to the Period 2, Phase 1 rampart. If so, trench F12 cut all the way through them, notwithstanding the misleading impression given by Fig. 30. The north edge of rampart layer 17 was directly above the edge of F12 and continued its curvature (Fig.

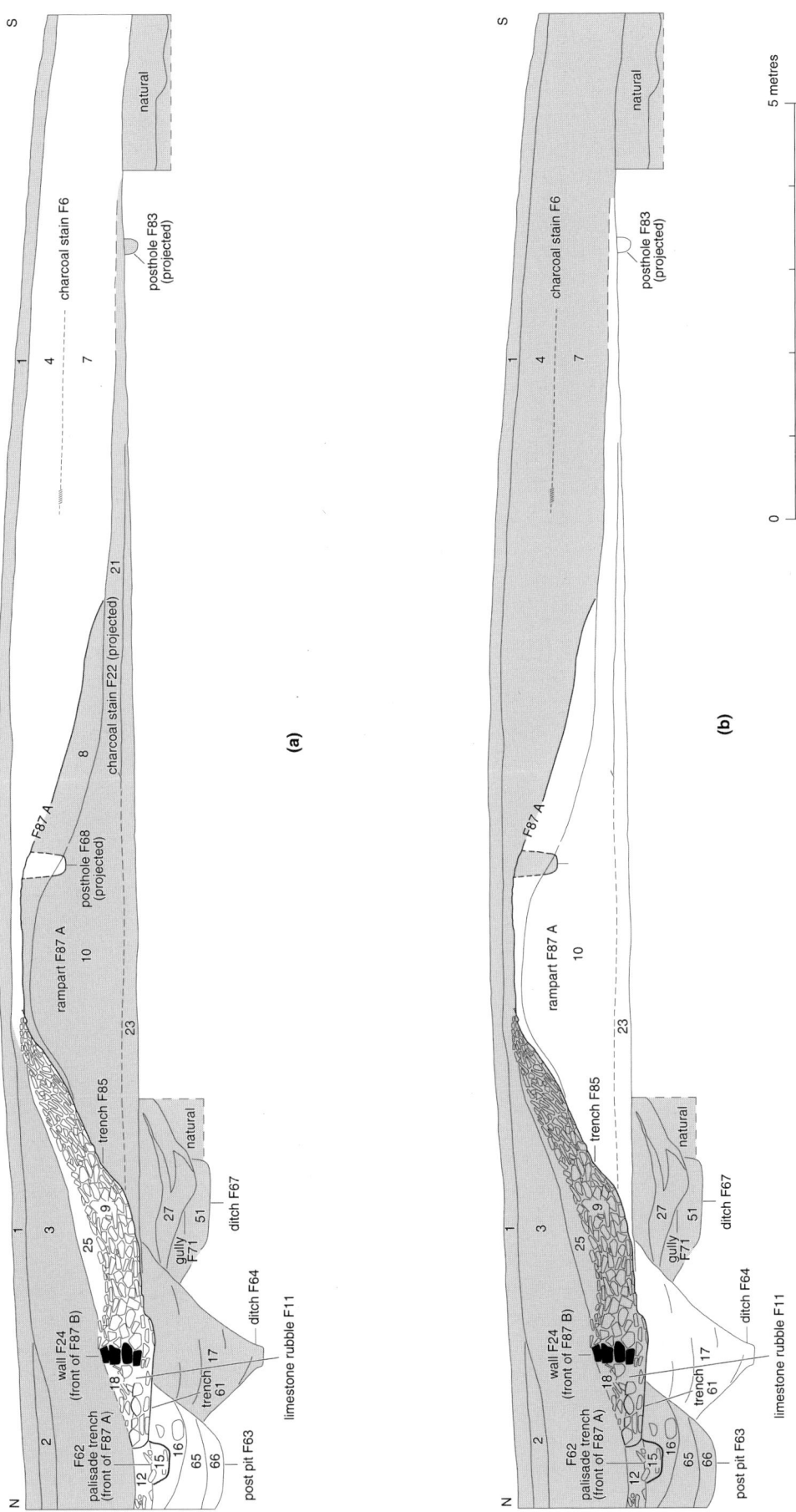

Figure 29. A phased analysis of J. Hinchliffe's Junior School, Winchcombe, section drawing (Fig. 28): (a) suggested components of the late Anglo-Saxon defences; (b) suggested components of the middle Anglo-Saxon defences. (In each case those of other periods are shown grey-tinted.)

220   *Steven Bassett*

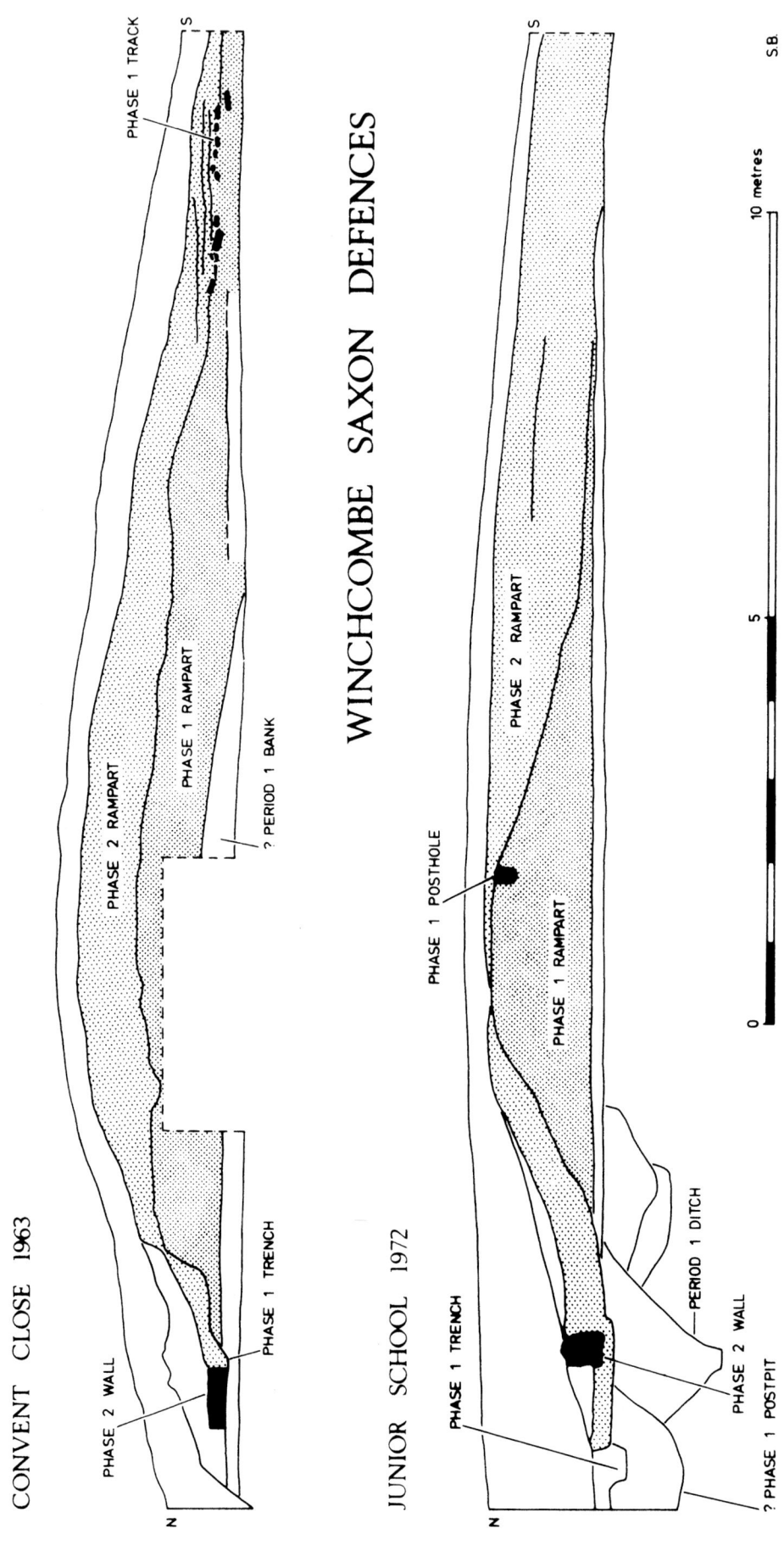

Figure 30. Winchcombe: comparative sections of the Anglo-Saxon defences excavated at Convent Close and Junior School. (Originally published as Transactions of the Bristol and Gloucestershire Archaeological Society, 104 (1986), fig. 17, on 132: 'Comparative sections through the Winchcombe Saxon defences', and reproduced with P. Ellis's and the editor's permission.)

26), and it is unhelpful to view them as separate features. The limestone rubble looks (as Ellis noted) like the result of the collapse forward of material which had been held in place by the wall.

To re-interpret the results of these two excavations in the way being suggested here produces two obvious anomalies. The first concerns a row of postholes found along the rear upper edge of the rampart F87A on the Junior School site (which Ellis interpreted as the Period 2, Phase 1 rampart, but which, it is being suggested here, should be assigned to Period 1). They were not seen in excavation above the level of layer 10, as Fig. 28 shows, but were assumed by him to have been cut through layer 8. This is a very reasonable assumption, given how little they penetrated layer 10; but there is nothing to prevent their being seen as features which had been cut from an even higher level. Since nothing similar was found on the Convent Close site in an equivalent position, despite the greater surviving depth there of rampart make-up,[189] it is probably best to treat these postholes as features which were not an integral part of the Period 2 rampart, in either of its phases, or of the Period 1 rampart.

The second anomaly concerns a spread of flat-bedded stones (F38) in a clay matrix (37) found immediately to the rear of rampart F48A on the Convent Close site (Figs 26–7). It was identified by Ellis as a possible stone-based track of Period 2 which may have continued in use even after the stones had been covered up;[190] but no evidence of it was recorded on the Junior School site, even though one of the trenches extended well beyond the rear of the rampart, and therefore Ellis's interpretation of it as 'an extra-mural street' may be unreliable. However, the trench concerned did not extend far enough to meet any continuation of a second possible west-east trackway found at Convent Close (F332), which was formed of a thin spread of gravel with fairly regular edges, and which, like F38, Ellis assigned to Period 2.[191] It lay directly on top of layer 49, which, according to the re-interpretation being offered here, either formed part of the Period 1 rampart or, more probably, was derived from its collapse, and it was sealed by a series of layers (32–36) which arguably were part of the make-up, still *in situ*, of its Period 2, Phase 1 successor. Ellis suggested that if F38 was not a track, it should be interpreted as being derived from the collapse of a retaining wall at the rear of the Period 2, Phase 2 rampart;[192] but even if it had been so derived, it would be the only evidence found on either site of there having been such a feature.

Almsbury Farm

The investigation made by John Samuels Archaeological Consultants comprised the mechanical cutting of 25 trenches of differing length in several fields belonging to Almsbury Farm (Fig. 25), with some archaeological features being excavated by hand. One of these, Trench 1 (28 m. long by 1.5 m. wide), was laid out north-south across what seemed to be a wide, low bank and, to the south of it, an equally wide ditch (Figs 32–3). The excavators concluded that the impression of a bank was chiefly created by a limestone ridge which produced 'a natural ripple in the ground surface', and which had been accentuated by agriculture and associated activity; and that the 'ditch', which was thought to have a flat-bottomed profile, was actually a sunken way.[193] There were a number of datable finds, of which some were Romano-British and the rest post-medieval. The latter all came from stratigraphically late contexts – a sherd of undated pottery from layer 120, and '3 house bricks of eighteenth/nineteenth century date' from 124.[194]

It is difficult to make a balanced reassessment of what was uncovered in Trench 1. This is for two reasons. Firstly, it must be suspected that the 'ditch' (125) was not bottomed. The excavators reported that almost as soon as mechanical removal of its contents had begun, it had filled up with water and the trench's sides had started to collapse. Its south edge was never located, since it lay outside the area available for excavation. The steepness of its north edge and the fact that the feature was permanently water-logged to within only a few centimetres of the modern ground surface both suggest that it was a very large, deep linear feature, very probably a ditch, of which only the highest part of the fill was removed. (Since neither hand excavation nor proper recording was possible,[195] the almost horizontal line by which the bases of its lowest illustrated fills are shown on Fig. 32 should be seen as an unreliable guide to the true profile of its bottom.)

The other reason why it is difficult to assess the stated results of Trench 1's excavation is that the report does not provide enough information about what was discovered. For instance, two potentially very early postholes were found, one of which (107, with a fill of 106) was less than 4 m. from the north edge of the ditch; but they are not shown on the plan; and many of the layers are not described in the text, nor are some of the features.

Despite these difficulties for the report's readers some general comments may be made. First, the excavators were clearly right to say that until recently the apparent bank has had a long history as a boundary. There is map evidence in support of this.[196] Moreover, ditch 113 and its recut, or enlargement, 130 are stratigraphically late features, and the latest fill of this probable field boundary ditch included a (regrettably undated) sherd of post-medieval pottery. The ditch had been cut through a series of layers, not all of them described in the report, which to the north lay with successively steeper angles of slope (127–9, 135–6). It is possible that they had been truncated almost horizontally, perhaps prior to the digging of ditch 130. If so, the top of the feature to which they belonged may originally have been at a much higher level. Moreover, the excavators pointed out that the layers through which the south side of ditch 113/130 had been cut (116, 131) might be the same as two of the lowest layers (129, 136) cut by its north side.

Much, then, of the supposed 'natural ripple in the

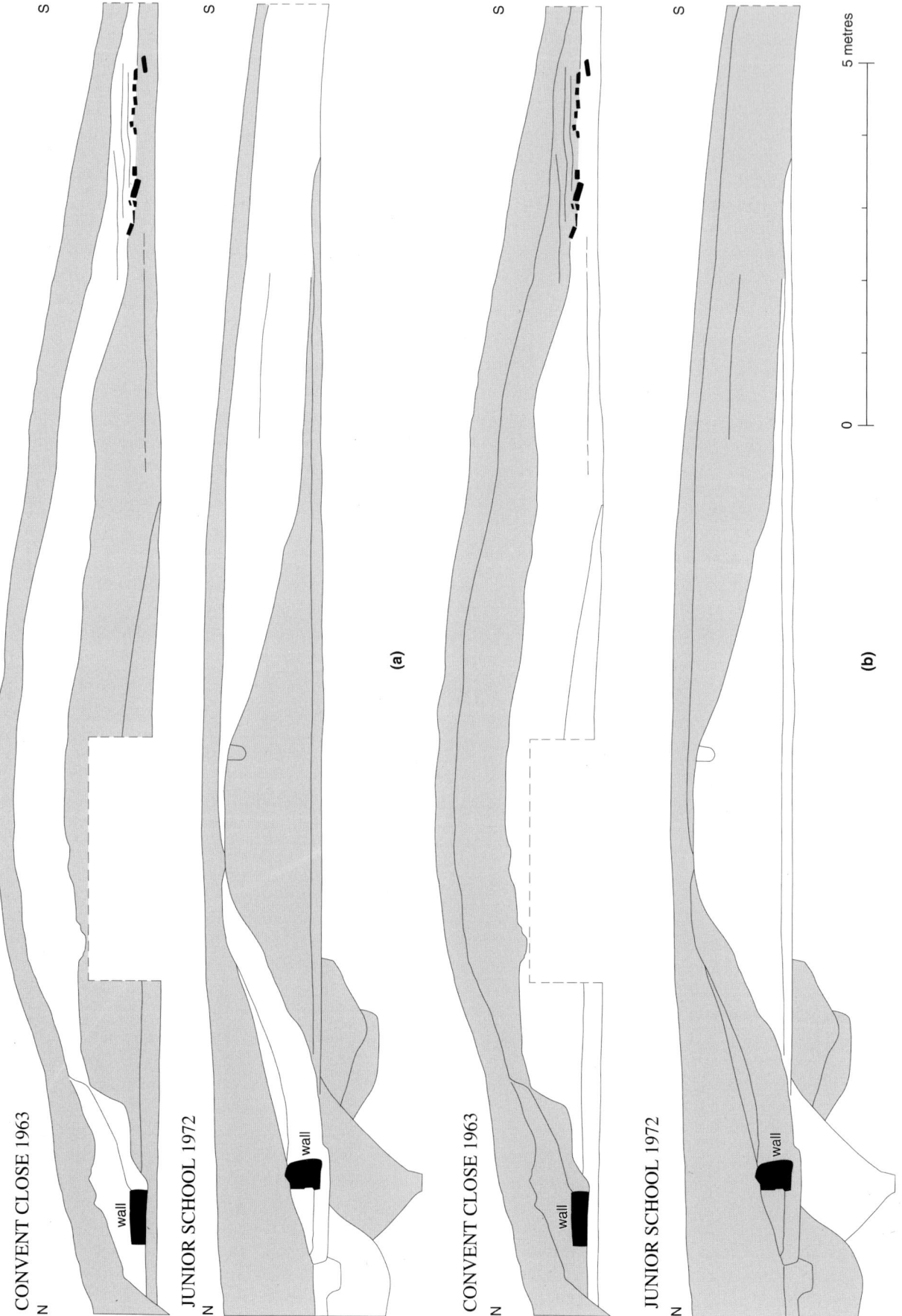

Figure 31. Winchcombe: a phased analysis of the Anglo-Saxon defences excavated at Convent Close and Junior School (Fig. 30): (a) suggested components of the late Anglo-Saxon defences; (b) suggested components of the middle Anglo-Saxon defences. (In each case those of other periods are shown grey-tinted.)

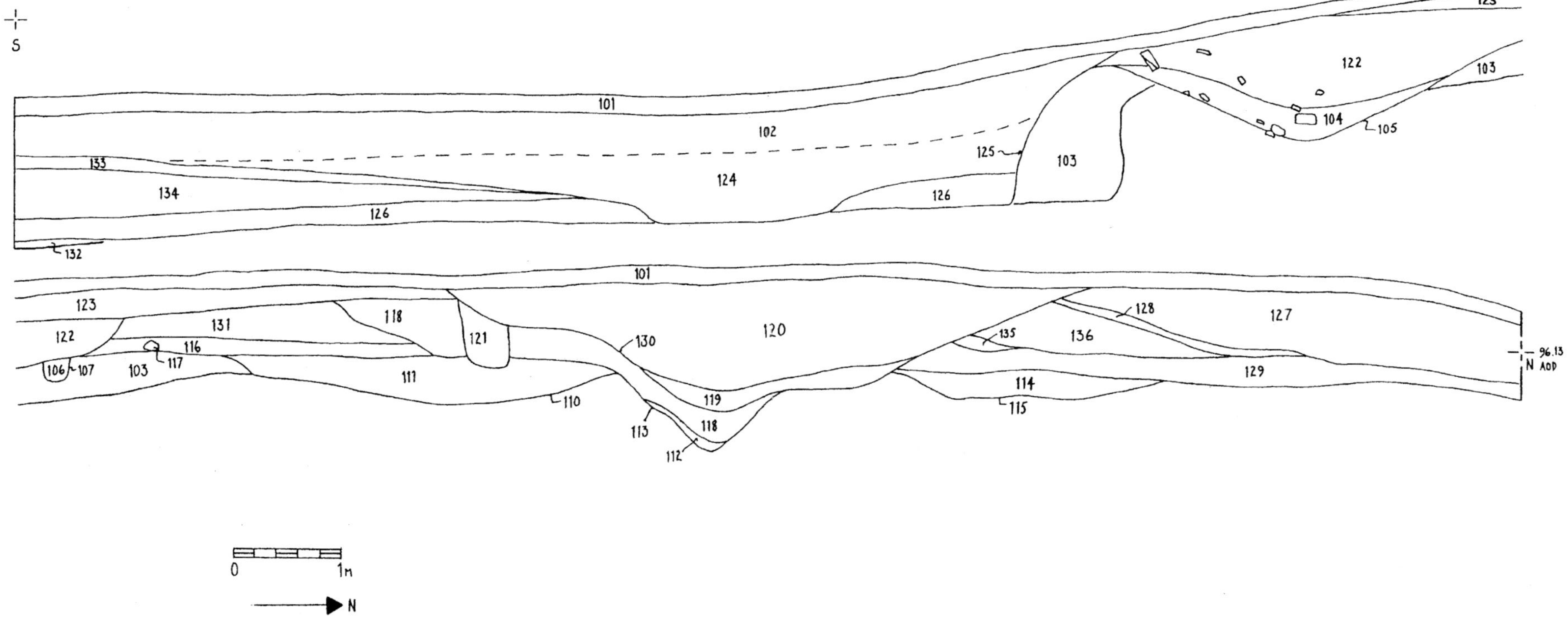

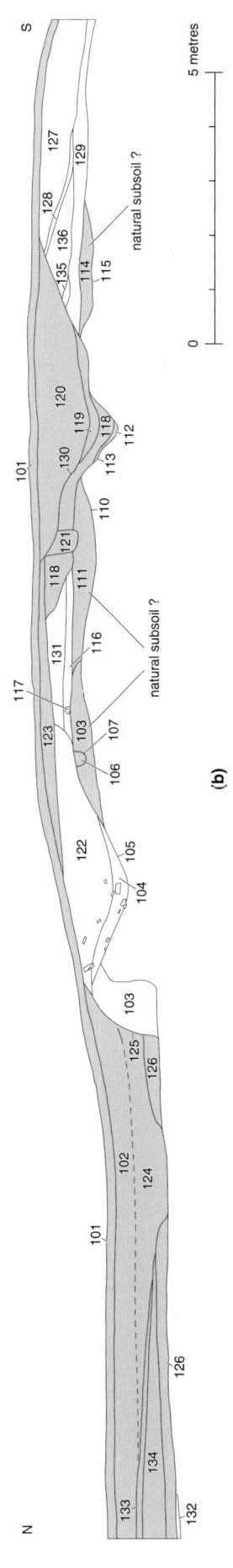

Figure 32. Almsbury Farm, Winchcombe: Trench 1 section drawing. (Originally published as J. Samuels and D. Slatcher, 'An archaeological evaluation at Almsbury Farm, Winchcombe, Gloucestershire', unpublished report JSAC 543c/2000/04, John Samuels Archaeological Consultants, Normanton-on-Trent, 2000, fig. 6: 'Trench 1 section', and reproduced with the authors' and developer's permission.) This sectional view of the trench's western side, although reproduced in two parts, is continuous.

Figure 33. A phased analysis of the features and layers excavated at Almsbury Farm, Winchcombe (Fig. 32): (a) suggested late medieval and modern features and layers; (b) suggested components of the putative late Anglo-Saxon defences. (In each case those of other periods are shown grey-tinted.)

ground surface' may be occupied by a truncated build-up of layers of clean clays and gravels which represent all that survives of a once substantial bank flanked to the south by a major ditch. The only dating evidence for these possible defences are the Romano-British sherds, which give a *terminus post quem* for the bank's construction, and the eighteenth- or ninteenth-century bricks found in layer 124, almost the highest of the ditch's fills. In view of the ditch's great width it is likely to be of later medieval date, which would make the presence of modern brick in its latest fills unsurprising.

One other important aspect of Trench 1 is linear feature 105. This 'has a maximum width of 5.00m and a depth of 1.20m with a U-shaped profile',[197] with two fills (104, 122) which are not described. Examination, however, of the report's plan, section-drawing and plates shows a concentration of limestone rubble in the feature's fill, mainly lying within the lower layer (104) down its south side.[198] Since there are no other pieces of limestone of a comparable size visible in the plates and none shown on the plan and section-drawing, this is plainly a significant spread. As illustrated in the site drawings, feature 105 does not look like a wall removal trench; but its place in the stratigraphical sequence, cutting as it does into what may be the front of a rampart and, in the process, removing the upper part of postholes 107 and 109,[199] is appropriate for a feature by which the footings of a stone revetment might have been removed.

Trenches 13, 18, 24 and 25 were machine-cut elsewhere in the same field with a view to locating parts of the same earthwork, but only Trench 18 has a plan and section-drawing included in the report. The other three trenches, which were short ones (8.3 m., 4.3 m. and 7.5 m. long respectively), positioned so as to coincide with a part of the supposed bank, are reported as having contained nothing archaeological, apart from late twentieth-century dumped material in Trench 25.[200] Trench 18, which was much longer (19.6 m.), was laid out down the rear slope of the bank (which here is on a south-west to north-east alignment) and at right-angles to it. It contained three features, one of which was identified as possibly being an earlier excavation trench, while another 'may have been a ditch or more likely [been] of geological origin'.[201] The third one ('ditch 1808') was a shallow U-shaped linear feature with two fills, the lower of which contained a sherd of Romano-British pottery. Below the topsoil were two layers which, increasing in depth from north-east to south-west, appear to be bank make-up, or possibly material derived from the rear of it. The upper one (1802) produced '7 sherds of medieval pottery', ranging in date from the late twelfth century to the fifteenth.[202] These layers' relationship to the U-shaped linear feature is unclear: the section-drawing shows them sealed by the upper one and cutting through the lower (1803); however, the report's Photo 45, which provides a close-up view of 'Trench 18, ditch 1808', suggests that 1803 and the lower fill of the 'ditch' (1810) are the same layer.

No entirely reliable conclusions can be drawn from this discussion of the report of the Almsbury Farm archaeological evaluation, except that a reasoned interpretation of the origins and *raison d'être* of the low but prominent earthwork lying west of Vineyard Street can be made which is significantly different from the excavators' own. Their conclusion, that 'neither the Saxon nor medieval defences of Winchcombe extended as far as the area of Almsbury Farm',[203] must be considered not proven until a further, appropriately funded, excavation can be carried out. In the meanwhile, it seems as likely as not that a major medieval bank and ditch ran across the Almsbury Farm area. The absence of any specifically early medieval, ie pre-Conquest, artefacts should not be held to rule out the possibility that its earliest use was in that period.

Winchcombe: dating evidence

There is no direct documentary evidence that Winchcombe was among the places which were fortified in the late ninth or early tenth century; but its possession of a mint by 973–5 indicates that it had defences by then, and in view of its importance under the Hwiccian kings and their Mercian successors it is almost certain to have gained them when Hereford and Worcester gained theirs.[204]

One piece of potentially very significant dating evidence for Winchcombe's Anglo-Saxon defences is to be found in the *vita* of Cynhelm (Kenelm), a son of the Mercian king Coenwulf who was allegedly murdered and buried at Winchcombe, and who was already being venerated as a child-martyr by between 969 and 978 when his name appears in monastic calendars.[205] The *vita*, which appears to have been composed in the period 1066–75, claims that Coenwulf founded a minster at Winchcombe 'when he had enclosed the town with a wall'.[206] It is impossible to say if this represents a genuine and reliable local tradition that Coenwulf (796–821) had been responsible for the Period 1 work, or if it merely reflects an understandable but spurious tendency on the part of local people to attribute any major element of Winchcombe's topography which was known to be old to an illustrious king with close, historically authenticated associations with the place.[207] However, we are on much safer ground in claiming that the statement affords a *terminus ante quem* of 1066–75 for the construction of the stone wall with which the Period 2, Phase 2 rampart is frontally revetted. While we cannot be certain that in this context *murus* can be safely taken to mean 'stone wall' as such rather than merely 'defences', the choice of word – in preference, for instance, to *vallum* – makes it very likely that at the time of the *vita*'s composition Winchcombe's defences already had a masonry component; while the attribution of the *murus* to Coenwulf may mean that the stonework had been added several generations or more before the writer's own day.

To turn to the archaeological dating evidence, on the Convent Close site the latest features predating the defences, which included a circular posthole building, were thought to be either Romano-British or middle Anglo-Saxon. The only datable find was a Romano-British sherd.[208] Similarly, layers 45–47 (which Ellis interpreted as a 'possible primary bank' which may have been 'associated with the ditch excavated in 1972 beneath the later rampart'), included sherds of Romano-British pottery and a bronze coin, unidentifiable but probably of the same date.[209]

Two sherds of Anglo-Saxon pottery were found immediately to the rear of the Period 1 rampart. In layer 49 there was 'a sherd of middle to late-Saxon pottery of a type recognized at Oxford and dating from the eighth or ninth to the eleventh centuries'.[210] It was also described as a sherd 'which Maureen Mellor commented was "very similar" to Oxford fabric B dated late eighth or early ninth century to early eleventh century'.[211] The layer (37) which overlay 49, forming the bedding of 'stone feature' F38, included 'a sherd of local Saxon pottery dated to the late tenth or early eleventh centuries'.[212] This was also described as 'Winchcombe limestone-tempered pottery'.[213] Both layers also contained Romano-British sherds.

As Ellis rightly noted, '49 is not sealed by the rampart and gives a strict *terminus post quem* only to F38.'[214] In an earlier discussion he commented that, 'To the south the tail of layer 43 was recorded as layer 49.'[215] This is potentially misleading, since it could be understood as meaning that 49 was an integral part of the rampart and that a sherd found in it would therefore give to its construction, if not a firm *terminus post quem*, then at least a loose one. However, an examination of Fig. 26 shows that 49 cannot be safely regarded as part of the *in situ* rampart, but instead is probably a spread caused by weathering of the rear of the Period 1 rampart or by slumping or deliberate removal of some of its make-up onto the ground surface behind it. But whatever the exact cause of its formation it must be regarded as an unsealed layer into which a small sherd could have been introduced after its deposition. Consequently the single sherd retrieved from 49 must be treated for dating purposes in the same way as the coin of Edward the Martyr from Wainwright's site at Tamworth has been. While the possibility that it had been originally included in the rampart's make-up cannot be discounted, for the reason given above it must not be treated as if it had been.

The layers added in order to heighten the Period 1 rampart produced no finds apart from an unidentifiable but probably Romano-British bronze coin.[216] A posthole, F163, which was said to have been stratigraphically later than the circular posthole building F150 and which may have been of the same period as the heightened rampart, contained a sherd of 'local late-Saxon pottery'.[217]

A *terminus post quem* for a local collapse of the stone wall which was added to the front of the Period 2 rampart was provided by a silver penny, dated to 1180x9, which was found 'at the foot of the...wall F15 on its north side overlain by layer 11', the latter being collapsed masonry

from the wall.[218] This *terminus* also applies to the ditch F7 which cut 9–11 and which 'may represent the south side of a later medieval ditch...relating either to the town or to the abbey or to both.'[219] From 11 itself came 'two small sherds of Gloucester early medieval ware...dated 11th to 13th century.'[220]

On the Junior School site the fills of F64, the so-called 'pre-rampart ditch', contained sherds of Romano-British pottery but nothing else.[221] The same is true of the layers and features associated with the two phases of the Period 2 rampart. Nothing post-Roman was found lower in the stratigraphical sequence than layer 4, which was a deep deposit of red-brown clays on the rear of the rampart and mainly indistinguishable from 7 below it (Figs 28–9). This contained some thirteenth-century pottery, which Ellis thought to be 'presumably intrusive as a result of manuring and ploughing'.[222]

No significant dating evidence was found on the Almsbury Farm site; and none of the three sites produced any radiocarbon dates.

Winchcombe: discussion

Ellis commented that the sections across the Back Lane defences showed that they were 'typologically Saxon',[223] and stressed that 'a progression from a timber- and/or turf-revetted bank to a stone-fronted rampart is fundamental' to prevailing models of the development of late Anglo-Saxon defences.[224] He also pointed out that the Winchcombe ones conformed to other diagnostic features 'such as a flat-topped profile, a rearward revetment and the use of branches in the body of the rampart', and that differences between what different excavations found should not be a surprise 'in view of the evidence of sectional construction of these defences at Lydford, Devon', a method suggested by M. Biddle to be in general use.[225] He concluded that the timber-revetted, *i.e.* Period 2, Phase 1, rampart 'may well be of the same date as the other Mercian defences in the Midlands' (*i.e.*, in his opinion, early tenth-century), and considered that the addition of the stone wall, 'like the parallel additions elsewhere, cannot be closely dated', observing that a date in the late tenth or early eleventh century was probable, 'in line with that suggested for these additional defences elsewhere'.[226] In all of this Mr Ellis's opinions carry conviction.

His views on the Period 1 features were understandably more cautious. He acknowledged that they were likely to be of middle Anglo-Saxon date and could be defensive, and that they were similar to features found underlying the late ninth-/early tenth-century defences at Hereford and Tamworth; but because of their close proximity to the minster, he suggested that they might merely have marked the north boundary of its precinct, originating as part of a *vallum monasterii* and eventually being used as the base for the late Anglo-Saxon defences through the area concerned.[227] This is a possibility which must be taken seriously, since the Anglo-Saxon minster and its associated buildings doubtless lay within a clearly defined enclosure.[228] However, there are two reasons why the Period 1 features are more likely to belong to a defensive circuit than to a minster's boundary earthwork. The first is the very fact of their similarity to the features found in a stratigraphically identical position at Hereford and Tamworth, where in both cases the latter are highly unlikely to have bounded an ecclesiastical precinct. The reconsideration of the first-stage defences at Tamworth which has been presented here makes their degree of similarity even greater than Ellis may have imagined.

The second reason is the probability that in the middle Anglo-Saxon period the minster's land did not extend northwards as far as the line of the defensive circuit. In and after the late medieval period Winchcombe's main west-east street – Gloucester Street, which continues to the east as High Street, then Hayles Street – passes immediately to the south of St Peter's parish church and, a short distance to the east of it, the site of the Benedictine abbey church (Fig. 25); but it originally ran to the north of them as *Peticrueslane* and, beyond its junction with North Street, as Chandos Street (which is still in use today). In 1294 this former road was officially closed as a result of the abbot of Winchcombe's getting royal permission for him and his successors to 'shut off a certain road called *Peticrueslane* that runs westwards from the aforesaid town [*sc.* Winchcombe] between two gardens of the abbey in the said town, include it for the enlargement of the same gardens, and hold it, shut off and incorporated, for ever.'[229] This road, a length of which is still clearly visible as a hollow-way along the south boundary of the playing fields which lie north of St Peter's graveyard, is a long-distance through-route of very probably prehistoric origin, which together with North Street and its continuation (a road which was undoubtedly in use in the Roman period) formed the main axes of Winchcombe's Anglo-Saxon plan.[230] Accordingly, it seems likely that in the middle Anglo-Saxon period the minster complex would have been confined to the area in the south-west angle formed by their courses; and while the members of its community, or their reformed successors, certainly did acquire land in the north-west area, as the 1294 charter shows, it is most unlikely that their precinct extended beyond *Peticrueslane* until after it had been shut off and made into the church's private property. Indeed, until the laying out of Gloucester Street and the tenements which front onto it (which used *Peticrueslane* as their north boundary), it continued to be the main road into Winchcombe from the west.[231] There is, therefore, very little likelihood of the so-called Period 1 defences having had a different origin from that of their counterparts at Hereford and Tamworth.

Worcester

Worcester's defences

Although there has been no shortage of hypotheses offered about the route of Worcester's late Anglo-Saxon defences,

no substantive claim to have found direct archaeological evidence of them was made until 1988–9, when in excavations to the east of Deansway the remains of a west-east aligned rampart were uncovered. In 1998–9 what is almost certainly the ditch of the same defensive circuit was located on a site to the east of High Street.[232]

Deansway

A trench a little over 2 m. wide was extended northwards across the rampart's full width and as far as the south lip of an accompanying ditch (Fig. 34).[233] The excavation report concludes that it was built of 'a massive dump of soil, with lenses of clay and turf', and that it was *c.* 13 m. wide and perhaps at least 3 m. high, although only the lowest 1.5 m. of it survived. It is said to have been revetted at the front by an insubstantial wall, constructed in dry-stone fashion of re-used lias limestone and loose mortar, which survived to a height of 0.5 m. (Figs 35–6); timber lacing may also have been employed and there may have been a palisade along the top of the rampart, but the evidence was uncertain. Because of the wall's slightness the front edge of the rampart is thought more likely to have been steeply scarped than vertical. In front of the rampart, and separated from it by a 3 m. wide berm, was a ditch of which only the southernmost part lay within the excavation area, and which was therefore of unknown width and depth. A shallow linear feature found partly sealed below the stone revetment and partly lying in front of it is interpreted as a marking-out ditch.[234] There was no evidence of any earlier defences under the rampart, which was built across land which appeared to have been open pasture for many centuries.[235]

No significant dating evidence was recovered for the construction of the defences. The pottery and other identifiable artefacts found in their make-up and in stratigraphically earlier contexts were all Romano-British. By the late eleventh or early twelfth century (from which time onwards there was intensive occupation on their former site), the defences had already been substantially dismantled by piecemeal activity, and in some places had been completely levelled.[236] The excavators reasonably suggest that they are the ones which Æthelred and Æthelflæd are known to have built at Worcester prior to 900, but, surprisingly, they do not compare them with the other late ninth-/early tenth-century defences which are believed to have been excavated in western Mercia.[237] Their identification appears to have been based in part on similarities between the Deansway rampart and others of allegedly late ninth-century date which have been archaeologically examined in southern England, and in part on the knowledge that Worcester had defences by the end of the ninth century and that, since its post-Conquest ones evidently lay elsewhere, the Deansway rampart could not have belonged to the latter.[238]

In an initial phase of interpretation it was thought that there had been two phases of defences on the Deansway

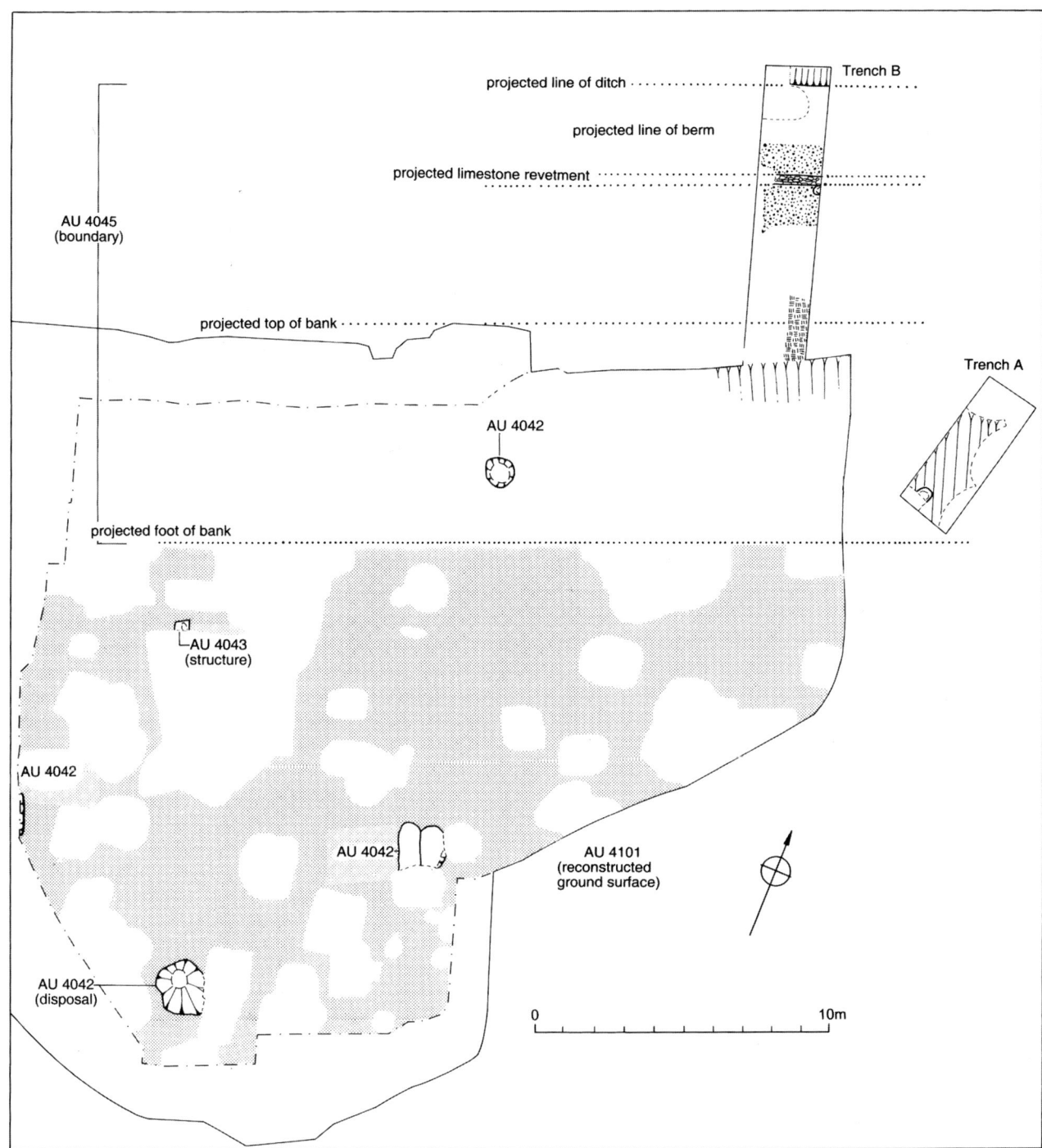

Figure 34. Deansway, Worcester: plan of Sites 4 and 5 in Period 7 (from the late ninth century to the late eleventh) showing (in Trench B) evidence for the late Anglo-Saxon rampart and ditch. (Originally published as H. Dalwood and R. Edwards, Excavations at Deansway, Worcester, 1988–89: Romano-British Small Town to Late Medieval City *(CBA Res. Rep., 139, 2004), fig. 136, on 222, and reproduced by permission of the Worcestershire Historic Environment and Archaeology Service and the Council for British Archaeology.)*

site, the first of which consisted of a bank and ditch, and in the second of which the limestone revetment was added and the bank enlarged; but this was subsequently rejected in favour of there having been only a single phase, 'on the grounds that there is insufficient clear evidence for two phases.'[239] It is arguable, however, that the excavators' initial interpretation was the correct one. There are several aspects of the evidence presented in the report which suggest that, as elsewhere, the stone phase was secondary and that it succeeded an initial one in which the rampart was frontally revetted in timber.

The excavation of the defences was considerably handicapped by a number of circumstances which must prevent a full understanding of their history on the Deansway site ever being achieved. The trench cut across them was only 2 m. wide; it had to be excavated in two separate parts; and within its area deep modern features were found to have removed a large amount of the rampart material which had escaped medieval dismantlement.[240] It is clear from the plans and section-drawing that this dismantlement had been extensive; indeed, a careful examination of the published line-drawings and plates offers clues that it may have been even greater than the report's authors suggest. Their reconstruction drawing of the rampart's revetment shows it with a 0.55 m. wide base, a vertical rear face, and a front face which tapers upwards to a very narrow top only *c*. 0.95 m. above the contemporary ground surface (Fig. 35); but there is no sign of this rear face in the section-drawing, which shows a deep, apparently homogeneous, layer of loose limestone rubble (9) extending southwards from the front edge of the rampart for at least 2 m., *i.e.* well beyond the line of the alleged rear face.[241] The latter is shown in the reconstruction drawing in a position which is on or immediately adjacent to the line of division in the trench's two-stage excavation, and it is very hard to dispel the suspicion that, coinciding as it does with the enforced break in the archaeological excavation, this edge cannot be relied on to have existed.[242]

If the revetment had no rear face on the suggested line, it may have been considerably more substantial than the report suggests. The stones shown in the published report's Figure 137 (Fig. 35) may well represent the *in situ* residue of a wall which had a near-vertical front face, subsequently robbed, and which was both wider and taller than the one illustrated in its Figure 138 (Fig. 35). It would, however, be unclear how large this residue was, since the information given about the surviving portion of revetment in the report's text and line-drawings can be re-interpreted as suggesting that some of it (and conceivably all) may be robbers' debris rather than surviving fabric. The north edge of the material which the section-drawing shows immediately overlying the front of the partly reduced rampart (Fig. 36: 15) may represent a robbing cut made some while after the initial phase of dismantlement, since it appears to cut down through layers (11–12) which presumably represent collapsed rampart make-up. It is

possible that the stone wall originally extended as far forwards as the north limit of layer 10.[243]

Finally, the feature identified as a marking-out ditch (3) and the two layers which it cuts (2) need to be considered.[244] An alternative interpretation of them would be that the layers formed the lowest part of the rampart's make-up and that the 'ditch' is all that was found within the excavation trench of a feature associated with an original timber revetment.[245] This new understanding of their role is prompted primarily by the difficulty of accepting the interpretation of the linear feature (3) as a marking-out ditch. If it had been one, it would surely have been dug from the surface of the ancient field soil on which the rampart was built (1); but instead it cuts through a couple of insubstantial layers which are reasonably thought to represent the first upcast from the ditch (2), and its wide flat bottom coincides with the field soil's surface. Consequently, it looks much more like a timber slot – or a feature subsequently dug to remove a timber – than a ditch, for which it has the wrong profile and, arguably, the wrong position in the stratigraphical sequence.

It is unclear if the feature survived to its full original depth, or if the work involved in building the limestone revetment removed its upper part.[246] Nor is it clear what precise structural role a horizontal timber of the sort envisaged would have played in an initial phase of the defences in which the front of the rampart was timber-revetted. The absence of any recognised postholes in its vicinity makes the suggested re-interpretation harder to sustain, since vertical posts would have been essential elements of a timber revetment. However, a circular feature situated close to the west edge of the trench, which is shown in part-outline in the published report's Figures 135 and 136 (Fig. 34) and as a soilmark in its Figure 139, may well be a posthole, and in an area as narrow as Trench B it would be unsurprising if no more than one such feature were present.[247]

City Arcade, High Street

A limited archaeological investigation in 1998–9 in advance of the construction of a new shopping arcade located what is almost certainly the ditch of the east arm of the late ninth-century defences. The small amount of shallow excavation permitted by the contractors showed that the ditch may have been at least 14 m. wide.[248] Only the top 2 m. of its fill could be examined, and it was impossible to establish the level from which the ditch had been cut.[249] There appeared to have been a long sequence of infilling, slumping and levelling comprising mainly dark loamy deposits interleaved with sandier material. Part of a layer containing limestone and mortar rubble which lay down the ditch's west side was thought likely to be derived from the slighting of a masonry revetment of the associated rampart, but otherwise no evidence of the latter was recovered.[250] The only dating evidence recovered from the ditch were residual Roman finds and some sherds of twelfth-century

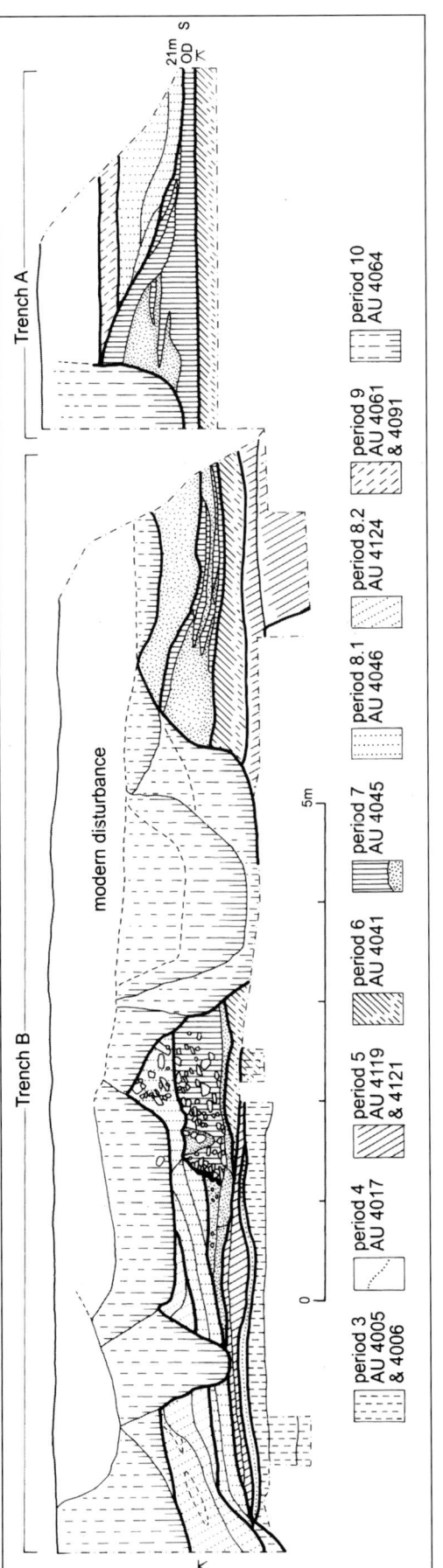
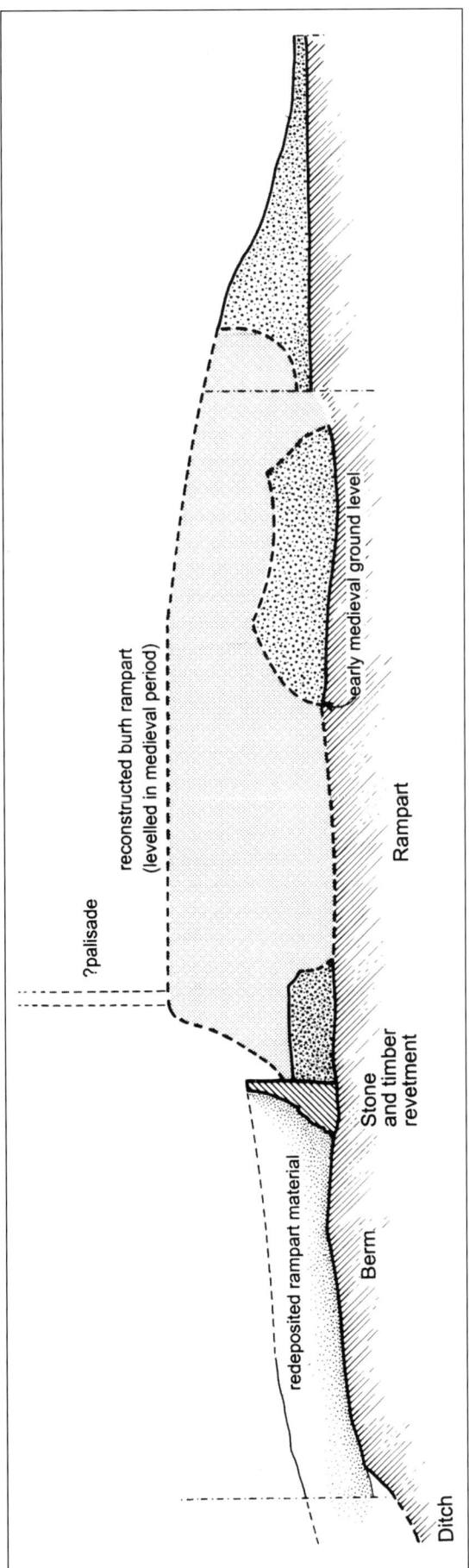

Figure 35. Deansway, Worcester (Site 5): the late Anglo-Saxon rampart and ditch as drawn in sectional view (above) and reconstructed schematically (below). (Originally published as H. Dalwood and R. Edwards, Excavations at Deansway, Worcester, 1988–89: Romano-British Small Town to Late Medieval City (CBA Res. Rep., 139, 2004), figs 137–8, on 223, and reproduced by permission of the Worcestershire Historic Environment and Archaeology Service and the Council for British Archaeology.)

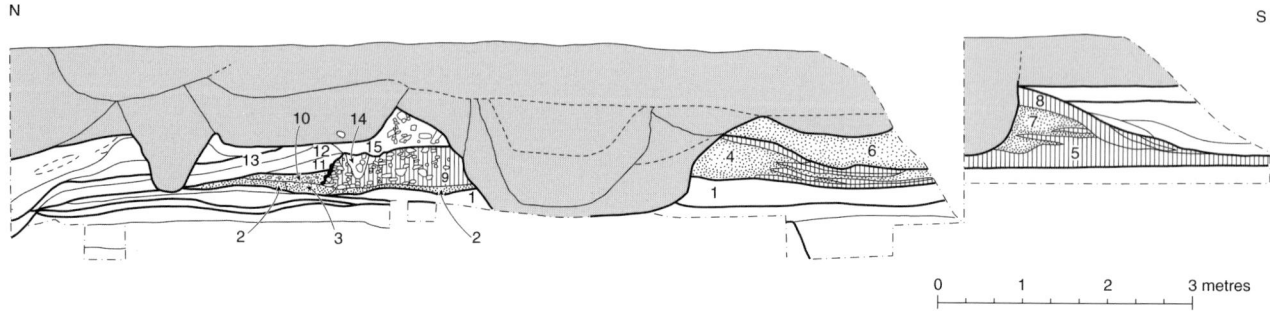

N   S

0   1   2   3 metres

Figure 36. A redrawing of the Deansway, Worcester (Site 5), section drawing (Fig. 35, top), with features and layers of Periods 6, 7 and 8.1 (fifth-twelfth centuries) being individually numbered. (Those of late fifteenth-century and later date are shown grey-tinted.)

pottery from its upper fills; but sherds identified as being of tenth- to eleventh-century date were recovered from layers in the vicinity of the ditch and were associated with its use and abandonment, and the excavators concluded that it had been completely backfilled by no later than the late twelfth or early thirteenth century.[251]

This ditch has probably been encountered on other occasions. Over 5 m. of stratification was found on the same line on a site *c.* 55 m. to the north during construction work at 37–8 High Street; and there are other reports of similarly deep deposits being found on its probable course.[252] It has also been suggested that P. Barker may have found a length of the same ditch *c.* 65 m to the south.[253]

Worcester: discussion

Discussion of the published evidence of two small portions of the apparently late Anglo-Saxon defences at Worcester must remain inconclusive. It has done no more than to offer an interpretation of the evidence from the Deansway site which is a reasoned alternative to the one offered in the published report. If it has any merit, it indicates that the defensive sequence at Worcester was much closer to that found at Hereford, Winchcombe and Tamworth than the report's authors suggest. But in one respect the sequence is without doubt entirely different, since it is plain that there were no earlier defences sealed below the ones excavated on the Deansway site, and nothing uncovered on the City Arcades site suggested that there were any there. If Worcester had serviceable defences in the middle Anglo-Saxon period, which is a strong likelihood on *a priori* grounds, they must have been based on its Romano-British ones. The south part of that circuit may also have formed the basis of what Æthelred and Æthelflæd built in the late ninth century, since the available evidence, such as it is, suggests that it was only to the north and north-east that their circuit took in a significant amount of new ground.[254]

Conclusions

The starting points of this study were two-fold. The first was an acute awareness that the albeit sparse and often very poorly recorded evidence for an early defensive circuit at Hereford, Tamworth and Winchcombe – characterised here as their first-stage defences – was being paid insufficient attention. A close re-examination of the evidence, including some not previously published, has shown that at Tamworth and Winchcombe these earliest defences were much more substantial than has been generally realised, and that they were built to a closely similar size and design. It has also reinforced the likelihood that the gravel rampart at Hereford (of which only the tail was found) was a third member of the same group.

The second starting point was strong concern about the basis of the widespread acceptance that the second-stage defences at Hereford, Tamworth and Winchcombe were of late ninth-/early tenth-century construction, and that those excavated much more recently at Worcester were being similarly labelled too hastily. It was proposed that, while the identifications may well be correct, to date they had been made on insufficiently good grounds, with most discussion of the individual instances having started from the premise that the defences belonged to this period on account of observed similarities with one or more of those found elsewhere in the west midlands and/or in southern England which were assumed to be of the same period, and also, in Worcester's and Tamworth's case, because of specific written evidence of the building of fortifications there by Æthelred and/or Æthelflæd. Because of the significant danger of circularity in these arguments it seemed that a fresh study of the evidence would be worthwhile, and that it should be one which determinedly ignored all preconceptions, even if and when it found itself plodding with laboriously didactic steps along a meandering route which tended ever closer to the very destination so nimbly attained by others' leaps of faith.

The study has shown that there can indeed be no doubt

about the close correspondence to each other of the second-stage defences at Hereford, Tamworth and Winchcombe. Their similar size and method of construction in both their initial timber phase and the subsequent masonry one have often been noted, as has their general correspondence to the defences excavated at a number of fortified places in southern England which are listed in the Burghal Hidage. None of the revisions proposed here to the published accounts of the second-stage defences has diminished the nature and extent of these similarities; and it has been proposed that Worcester's defences too shared the others' common characteristics, given that it has been shown here that they are likely to have had an initial phase in which timber was used to support the front of the rampart.

As a separate exercise the study has also reinforced the view that there are valid historical grounds for accepting that all four of these places had serviceable defences of recent construction by the early tenth century. For Worcester and Tamworth the evidence is explicit, referring to actual acts of fortification. For Hereford and Winchcombe it is merely implicit; but Hereford's recorded role in 914 as an important *burh* makes it virtually certain that it had well maintained defences then,[255] while Winchcombe's comparable contemporary importance and its possession of a mint by Edgar's reign suggest that it too would have been actively fortified by the early tenth century. It is, therefore, a virtual certainty that either the first-stage or the second-stage defences at Hereford, Tamworth and Winchcombe – and also those found at Worcester in the Deansway excavations, if they had a timber phase before the construction of the limestone revetment – were constructed in the late ninth and early tenth centuries.

This conclusion is easily reached; but when the question of which of the two stages was built at that time is approached strictly from first principles, it is much more of a challenge to choose the correct one. There are very good historical grounds for believing that these three places, and Worcester too, had had defences built there twice in the Anglo-Saxon period (in the period of the Mercian kings' overlordship in England and again in Æthelred's and Æthelflæd's time); but merely because incontrovertible evidence of three stratigraphically successive sets of defences has been found at Hereford, Tamworth and Winchcombe and because the latest of the three is demonstrably post-Conquest in each case, it does not automatically follow that the earlier two sets can only represent the Anglo-Saxon ones which we reckon to know about.

Nonetheless, in the present case there does appear to be just enough reliable evidence to enable us to identify the second-stage defences as those which were built in the late ninth and early tenth centuries, including the ones excavated at Worcester. Three main reasons for doing so can be given. The first one is, as others have pointed out, the significant similarity of their two-phase sequence – timber being replaced by masonry as the rampart's main support – to the defences excavated at Wareham,

Cricklade, Lydford and elsewhere in southern England.[256] This is the weakest of the reasons, however, because of the danger of over-reliance being put on a hypothesis built on another one; but it would be perverse to argue that these West Saxon defences are unlikely to have been built in the late ninth century merely because in our present state of knowledge we cannot prove that they were.

The second reason comprises the historical evidence for the establishment of a network of fortified settlements across the kingdom of Mercia during the period of its kings' greatest power in the eighth and early ninth centuries.[257] This provides an obvious context for the building of the first-stage defences at Hereford, Tamworth and Winchcombe – ones for which there is as yet no West Saxon analogue. The present study has established that they were of substantial construction and, in so far as the available evidence allows a reliable judgement to be made, that they were of a similar enough design to be products of a coherent scheme of fortification.

The third reason for identifying the second-stage defences as the product of Æthelred's and Æthelflæd's activities comprises the cumulative weight of the specific dating evidence relating to the four fortified places. No single piece of evidence, either written or archaeological, clinches the argument. However, the significant similarities of the defences at three of them make it legitimate to view the body of dating evidence as a whole; and its overall effect sits much more comfortably with the second-stage defences than with the first-stage ones. This effect is much enhanced if the rampart excavated at Worcester is seen as a two-phase one, since here alone there are no earlier defences beneath it, and the circumstantial evidence is particularly strong that the north arm of the documented late ninth-century defences was on the excavated rampart's line.[258]

Only Hereford has produced any specific dating evidence for the first-stage defences: the piece of carbonised timber recovered from one of the two corn-drying ovens on the Victoria Street site. In its recalibrated state it shows that it is almost certain (95.4%) that the oven was last fired in or after 668, and that it is twice as likely as not (68.2%) that it was last used in or after 714. This provides a *terminus post quem* for the entire defensive sequence, but between the abandonment of the oven and construction of the gravel rampart a timber building was erected and repaired at least once. Therefore, if the recalibrated radiocarbon date is a reliable one, it indicates that the first-stage, *i.e.* gravel, rampart is much likelier to have been created after the mid eighth century than before it; but there is enough uncertainty about the original determination's reliability to mean that no great weight can be placed on this conclusion. A date for the rampart in or after the second half of the eighth century might be thought to pose a problem in respect of the argument that the appearance of references to '*burh* work' in Mercian charters from the 740s onwards points to the existence of a kingdom-wide network of fortified places. However, until the late eighth century the Magonsæte may not have been brought fully enough under direct Mercian control for Hereford to be fortified, unlike a place such as Tamworth which was in the area of the 'original' kingdom of Mercia.[259]

For the most useful piece of direct dating evidence for the second-stage ramparts we must again rely, if somewhat reluctantly, on this piece of carbonised timber from the corn-drying oven on the Victoria Street site at Hereford. The recalibrated radiocarbon date, if reliable, gives a *terminus post quem* for the first-stage defences which, allowing for their use and subsequent decay, makes it very hard to envisage the second-stage rampart as having been built before the second half of the ninth century.[260] Of the other two radiocarbon dates from Hereford, one (for the timber lacing of the second-stage rampart) is still earlier than that for the carbonised timber, even after recalibration; and the other (for the burnt remains of timber buildings on the Berrington Street sites) has been shown to be irrelevant to the chronology of the defences.

Regrettably, the excavations at Tamworth, Winchcombe and Worcester produced no useful dating evidence for the second-stage defences. At the latter two sites the latest finds from relevant contexts were Romano-British; and although sherds of what was identified at the time as Anglo-Saxon pottery were found on a couple of sites at Tamworth, including three grass-tempered ones in the make-up of the rampart on the Brewery Lane site, they are now untraceable and the available information about them is insufficient to allow a useful date to be put on them. Accordingly, there is a strong temptation to say that if the silver cut half-penny of Edward the Martyr found on Wainwright's Albert Road site reached its findspot within the period 975–81,[261] and if this findspot was stratigraphically later than the second-stage rampart, then it provides – circumstantially, but not strictly – a *terminus ante quem* for the rampart's construction. However, too many assumptions are needed for this line of argument to be reliable, and we must accept that the coin cannot be used as evidence that the rampart is the one built in 913.

The same coin does, however, provide an unassailable *terminus post quem* of 975–8 for the rampart's refurbishment with stone.[262] This allows us to argue that it occurred in the reign of Æthelred II (975–1016), the most likely period for the western Mercian defences to be significantly renovated and strengthened.[263] By extension it suggests that a comparable refurbishment was undertaken at Hereford, Winchcombe and (as has been argued here) Worcester in the same period. These three places, however, have not produced any reliable dating evidence for the addition of their stone walls. The sherds from the 'decay levels' on the rear of the second-stage rampart on the Cantilupe Street site at Hereford have been shown to be inadmissable, as also has the radiocarbon determination for the bones from the same site. At Worcester, if the absence of eleventh-century and earlier pottery is a reliable indication of when settlement and dismantlement began in the area of Deansway sites 4–5,[264] the defences must have been established, and refurbished in stone, some considerable time before then.

Only Hereford produced evidence of a further refurbishment of the second-stage defences, with a secondary stone face being added in front of the main stone wall on the Cantilupe Street site and the rampart being heightened with dumps of gravel. If the bones found in layer 583 at Cantilupe Street were deposited before this secondary stone face was added, it is twice as likely as not (68.2%) to have been built in or after 1022 and very probably (94.8%) in or after 904.[265] This would comfortably allow it to be seen as part of what Harold did in 1056. However, this must be considered to be only a tentative conclusion, since 583 not only was not a sealed context but may still have been accumulating after the secondary stone face had been added, and there is also room for doubt about the reliability of the original radiocarbon determination.

It is strictly accurate to conclude that this re-examination of the evidence for the successive defences found at Hereford, Tamworth and Winchcombe has failed to establish the date of construction of any of them. Moreover, the considerable revision offered here of the published interpretation of Worcester's rampart will need to be accepted for it to become a useful analogue for the second-stage defences at the other three places. It would be unduly pessimistic to leave matters there, however, since to do so would involve giving full weight to every objection to a constructive interpretation which could be raised. On the balance of probabilities it must be safe to conclude several things. The first is that the first-stage defences found at Hereford, Tamworth and Winchcombe belong to the period of the Mercian kings' overlordship in England, even though their construction dates may differ by half a century or more in line with the slow but steady extension of direct Mercian rule into the kingdoms of their once independent neighbours such as the Hwicce and Magonsæte.

The second safe conclusion is that the second-stage defences at Hereford and Winchcombe, and also the rampart and ditch found in the Deansway area of Worcester, were built by Æthelred and Æthelflæd, and that Tamworth's equivalent ones are those which Æthelflæd built in 913.[266] Another conclusion, albeit a less safe one because of the uncertainty about what exactly was done at Worcester, is that these late ninth-/early tenth-century defences were all of a kind in so far as the local geology and the availability of timber allowed. The final safe conclusion is that stone revetments were added to three of the ramparts, and arguably to Worcester's too, and that, if this refurbishment was done systematically, all the west midlands examples can be dated to no earlier than the reign of Æthelred II (975–1016), the period in which Scandinavian armies tried to conquer England and eventually succeeded in doing so.

A great deal of the uncertainty surrounding the published results of the excavations which have been examined here arises from the unfortunately poor quality of the surviving evidence and the unsatisfactory conditions in which the work sometimes had to be done. It is no criticism of the excavators concerned to say that we are now ready for a new investigation of one of these defensive sequences, and that we are likely to benefit enormously from it in terms of our ability to understand the wider historical significance of the results. Among the several places in the west midlands where the full sequence can be expected to occur, one stands out as being likely to produce the best possible survival of evidence. An appropriately well funded excavation needs to be undertaken by an appropriately experienced team on the well preserved section of the defences at Winchcombe which lie immediately to the south of Back Lane.

Acknowledgements

The cost of this paper's publication has been met by a generous grant from the Marc Fitch Fund, which I gratefully acknowledge. I am also grateful to the following – for permission to reproduce, and in some cases redraw, published figures: Hal Dalwood and Rachel Edwards, Peter Ellis, Jim Gould, Philip Rahtz, Andy Richmond, Ron Shoesmith, and John Samuels and Dan Slatcher, and to English Heritage, the Council for British Archaeology, South Staffordshire Archaeological and Historical Society, Bristol and Gloucestershire Archaeological Society, Worcestershire Historic Environment and Archaeology Service, Derngate Holdings, and Sudeley Castle Estate Ltd; for permission to reproduce copyright photographs: Bob Meeson, and Staffordshire County Council; for funding for the preparation of line-drawings: the School of Historical Studies of the University of Birmingham, and the Council for British Archaeology; and for valuable discussions of specific issues and other assistance: Mark Blackburn, Andy Boucher, Nicholas Brooks, Vince Gaffney, Richard Holt, Robin Jackson, Bob Meeson, Christopher Bronk Ramsey, Ron Shoesmith, David Smith, Alan Vince, and Chris Wickham.

Notes

1. When Æthelflæd died.
2. S. Taylor (ed.), *The Anglo-Saxon Chronicle: a Collaborative Edition. Volume 4: MS B* (1983), 49–50; P. Stafford, "'The Annals of Æthelflæd': annals, history and politics in early tenth-century England', in J. S. Barrow and A. F. Wareham (eds), *Myths, Rulership, Church and Charters. Essays in Honour of Nicholas Brooks* (forthcoming).
3. D. Whitelock (ed.), *English Historical Documents. Volume I: c.500–1042* (second edn, 1979), 540–1 (no. 99). For Hereford and Winchcombe: below, 186–7, 224–5; for Shrewsbury: S. Bassett, 'Anglo-Saxon Shrewsbury and its churches', *Midland History*, 16 (1991), 1–23, at 1, 18–19. Also below, 230–2.
4. For Gloucester, below, 187; A. P. Garrod and C. M. Heighway, *Garrod's Gloucester: Archaeological Observations 1974–81* (1984), 3–6; N. Baker and R. Holt, *Urban Growth and the Medieval Church: Gloucester and Worcester* (2004), 76, 347. For Chester, the B manuscript of the Anglo-Saxon Chronicle, using an entry from the Mercian Register, reports that Chester was 'restored' (*geedneowad*) in 907, an act which John of Worcester's chronicle attributes to Æthelred and Æthelflæd: Taylor, *Anglo-Saxon Chronicle. MS B*, 49; R. R. Darlington and P. McGurk (eds), *The Chronicle of John of Worcester. Volume II: the Annals from 450 to 1066* (1995), 362–3. Also see M. Biddle, 'Towns', in D. M. Wilson (ed.), *The Archaeology of Anglo-Saxon England* (1976), 99–150, at 135 and n. 286; S. Ward, 'Edward the Elder and the re-establishment of Chester', in N. J. Higham and D. H. Hill (eds), *Edward the Elder 899–924* (2001), 160–6, at 162–4.
5. Full bibliographical references are given for Tamworth in notes 7, 70, 72, 96–7, 106, 109, 117, 120, 129, 132, 140, 143–4 and 149; for Hereford in notes 11 and 13; for Winchcombe in notes 173–4; and for Worcester in note 232.
6. *E.g.* C. A. R. Radford, 'Later pre-Conquest boroughs and their defences', *Medieval Arch.*, 14 (1970), 83–103, at 86–91, 102; R. P. Abels, *Lordship and Military Obligation in Anglo-Saxon England* (1988), 91–2; B. Yorke, *Wessex in the Early Middle Ages* (1995), 139; D. Hill, 'Gazetteer of Burghal Hidage sites', in D. Hill and A. R. Rumble (eds), *The Defence of Wessex. The Burghal Hidage and Anglo-Saxon Fortifications* (1996), 189–231, at 200. Others, however, have expressed a preference for the early tenth century, *e.g.* Biddle, 'Towns', 128, 137 (but also see below, note 262).
7. J. Gould, 'Third report on excavations at Tamworth, Staffs., 1968

– the western entrance to the Saxon borough', *Trans. Lichfield and South Staffs. Archaeol. and Hist. Soc.*, 10 (1968–9), 32–42, at 37. Also see P. Rahtz and R. Meeson, *An Anglo-Saxon Watermill at Tamworth* (CBA Res. Rep., 83, 1992), 4–5.
8. N. Brooks, 'The development of military obligations in eighth- and ninth-century England', in P. Clemoes and K. Hughes (eds), *England before the Conquest* (1971) 69–84; reprinted in N. Brooks, *Communities and Warfare* (2000), 32–47.
9. They may already have existed for some time by then. The earliest explicit reference to '*burh* work' is found in 749: P. H. Sawyer, *Anglo-Saxon Charters: an Annotated List and Bibliography* (1968), no. [hereafter S] 92; but its existence may be implied in a Kentish charter of 732: S 23; Brooks, 'Military obligations', 38–9. The fact that there are no known references to the obligation to perform '*burh* work' prior to 749 probably means, as Brooks argued (*ibid.*), that it had not been normal previously for those who held bookland to be exempted from it; or, not inconceivably, it might mean that there had been no prior requirement on them to be involved in the upkeep and manning of such fortified places (*i.e.* that exemptions began to be recorded only shortly after the obligation had been laid on the holders of bookland). In any case it certainly does not mean that the fortified places themselves must have been new then. For a discussion of the Mercian kings' use of fortifications as an essential element of statecraft: S. Bassett, 'Divide and rule? The military infrastructure of eighth- and ninth-century Mercia', *Early Medieval Europe*, 15 (2007), 53–85.
10. The importance of Winchcombe to the Hwiccian kings, and of both it and Tamworth to the Mercian kings, is well established: *e.g.* S. R. Bassett, 'A probable Mercian royal mausoleum at Winchcombe, Gloucestershire', *Antiquaries Jnl*, 65 (1985), 82–100; N. Brooks, 'The formation of the Mercian kingdom', in S. Bassett (ed.), *The Origins of Anglo-Saxon Kingdoms* (1989), 159–70, at 162 and refs cited there; S 1436; J. Blair, *The Church in Anglo-Saxon Society* (2005), 277–8. Reliable Anglo-Saxon sources for Hereford's history, however, are dominated by its cathedral; but Domesday Book shows that the king's interests were paramount there in 1086, and there are slight but significant indications of much earlier royal involvement: F. Thorn and C. Thorn (eds), *Domesday Book. 17: Herefordshire* (1983), section C; R. Shoesmith, *Hereford City Excavations, Volume 1: Excavations at Castle Green* (CBA Res. Rep., 36, 1980), 1–4; Blair, *Church*, 287–8.
11. R. Shoesmith, *Hereford City Excavations, Volume 2: Defences*

(CBA Res. Rep., 46, 1982); *idem, Hereford City Excavations, Volume 3: The Finds* (CBA Res. Rep., 56, 1985).

12. Shoesmith, *Defences*, 77.

13. A. Thomas and A. Boucher (eds), *Hereford City Excavations. Volume 4: 1976–1990. Further Sites and Evolving Interpretations* (2002), 184–6.

14. Shoesmith, *Defences*, 73–4. Æthelred appears to have been ruling by 881 and to have died in 911; Æthelflæd continued to rule until her death in 918: S. Keynes, 'King Alfred and the Mercians', in M. A. S. Blackburn and D. Dumville (eds), *Kings, Currency and Alliances* (1998), 1–45, at 19 and n. 84; J. M. Bately (ed.), *The Anglo-Saxon Chronicle: a Collaborative Edition. Volume 3: MS A* (1986), 64, 68; Whitelock, *English Historical Documents*, 211, 216.

15. Shoesmith, *Defences*, 74, 83–5.

16. *Ibid.*, 35, 76, and microfiche 1, E1–E7.

17. *Ibid.*, 34, 76–7; Biddle, 'Towns', 120–1; P. Rahtz, 'The archaeology of west Mercian towns', in A. Dornier (ed.), *Mercian Studies* (1977), 107–29, at 117; Abels, *Lordship*, 69; G. Halsall, *Warfare and Society in the Barbarian West, 450–900* (2003), 86.

18. Whether or not it was taken down for this reason, it seems best (*contra* Shoesmith, *Defences*, 49, 73) not to associate the date of its abandonment or dismantlement with that of the abandonment/dismantlement of the first-phase timber buildings excavated on the Berrington Street sites, even though all of them may indeed have been built at the same time: see below, 188–9.

19. Shoesmith, *Defences*, 77, and microfiche 1, E6.

20. *Ibid.*, 76.

21. *Ibid.*, 34, 36–8, 78–80.

22. *Ibid.*, 31, 34. On the Victoria Street site all evidence of this wall and of the front of the pre-Conquest ramparts was destroyed in the nineteenth century: *ibid.*, 35.

23. *Ibid.*, 34, 38–40, 80–82.

24. *Ibid.*, 34–5, 40–1, 82.

25. *Ibid.*, 35, 82–3.

26. *Ibid.*, 41, 82.

27. *Ibid.*, 17, 35, 42, 83–5; Thorn and Thorn, *Domesday Book. Herefordshire*, 2,8; H. C. Darby and I. B. Terrett (eds), *The Domesday Geography of Midland England* (1954), 103.

28. Shoesmith, *Defences*, 83–5, 94. This is the 'third-stage' rampart which has been previously referred to here.

29. R.C.H.M., 'Wareham West Walls', *Medieval Arch.*, 3 (1959), 120–38; D. M. Wilson and D. G. Hurst, 'Medieval Britain in 1965', *Medieval Arch.*, 10 (1966), 168–9; Radford, 'Later pre-Conquest boroughs'; C. A. R. Radford, 'Excavations at Cricklade 1948–1963', *Wilts. Archaeol. and Nat. Hist. Mag.*, 67 (1972), 61–111; Biddle, 'Towns', 124–34; J. Haslam, 'The towns of Wiltshire', in J. Haslam (ed.), *Anglo-Saxon Towns in Southern England* (1984), 87–147 at 107–10.

30. The eleven explicitly documented ones are Worcester, by *c.* 889x99 (S 223; Whitelock, *English Historical Documents*, 540–1), and, between 910 and 918, *Bremesburh*, *Bricg*, Chirbury, Eddisbury, Runcorn, *Scergeat*, Stafford, Tamworth, Warwick and *Weardburh* (Taylor, *Anglo-Saxon Chronicle. MS B*, 49–50 ('Mercian Register', *sub annis* 910, 912–15, 918)). The five for which the evidence is circumstantial are Chester, Gloucester, Hereford, Shrewsbury and Winchcombe: Taylor, *Anglo-Saxon Chronicle. MS B*, 48 (*sub anno* 915), 49 ('Mercian Register', *sub anno* 907); Bassett, 'Anglo-Saxon Shrewsbury', 1, 18–19; below, 224–5. For Æthelred and Æthelflæd: Keynes, 'King Alfred', 19–34; P. Stafford, 'Political women in Mercia, eighth to early tenth centuries', in M. P. Brown and C. A. Farr (eds), *Mercia. An Anglo-Saxon Kingdom in Europe* (2001), 35–49, at 44–9.

31. Worcester and Warwick may be named in the source known as the Burghal Hidage as representatives of, respectively, the western Mercian places fortified in the late ninth century by Æthelred and those fortified by Æthelflæd in the 910s, when her joint campaigning with her brother Edward necessitated what may have been a second programme of *burh* building. For the Burghal Hidage: Hill and Rumble (eds), *Defence of Wessex*, 18–35 and *passim*.

32. 'ða gemetton þa menn hie of Hereforda 7 of Gleawceastre 7 of þam neh<s>tum burgum 7 him wið gefuhtan': Taylor, *Anglo-Saxon Chronicle. MS B*, 48.

33. 'Cum cetera uero multitudine Herefordam rediens, uallo lato et alto illam cincxit, portis et seris muniuit': Darlington and McGurk, *John of Worcester*, 578–9.

34. Shoesmith, *Defences*, 34–5, 73, 82–3, 94.

35. *Ibid.*, 70–72; F. W. Shotton, D. J. Blundell and R. E. G. Williams, 'Birmingham University radiocarbon dates IV', *Radiocarbon*, 12 (1970), 385–99, at 394 (nos. 110–11, 159).

36. The dates given in Table 1 were supplied by Professor Christopher Bronk Ramsey, to whom I am most grateful for providing me with these new calibrations and with Fig. 6, and also for the following comment on the degree of reliability of the original dates: 'The time difference between the original measurements and the calibrations should not itself be relevant. The only question would be over the general reliability of dates measured at this time. Of course the dates...could be wrong, but this is not so very likely given this age range, the kind of material and wide uncertainties quoted. The difficulty for the probabilities essentially arises here, as I would say that there is a >5% chance that any of them might be wrong for unknown reasons.' (pers. comm., 12 March 2007).

37. Shoesmith, *Defences*, 31, 70 (Table 8), 71 (quotation), 72, and microfiche 1, C1.

38. *Ibid.*, 70–1.

39. F309 was one of two such ovens. Unlike the other one (F89) it did not directly underlie the gravel rampart. The two cannot be proved to have been in contemporary use, 'but it is considered that they were probably planned as a coherent double unit' (*ibid.*, 31). Both, moreover, were sealed by a deep continuous layer (30 = 73), and so F309 can be reliably accepted as having predated the gravel rampart.

40. Shoesmith, *Defences*, 77, and below, 191.

41. Shoesmith, *Defences*, 49, 71, 73, 97; R. L. Otlet and A. J. Walker, 'Harwell radiocarbon measurements III', *Radiocarbon*, 21 (1979), 358–83, at 373.

42. The radiocarbon date relates to the time at which the timber used in their construction/refurbishment was cut from a living tree.

43. Above, note 32.

44. 'and thus the radiocarbon date is somewhere between the date at which the branch started to grow and the date at which it was cut down': Shoesmith, *Defences*, 71. However, 'there was some contamination by modern rootlets', which had dried out and become 'difficult to see and remove by laboratory staff', which meant that a date had been produced which was 'liable to be too young': *ibid.*, 71.

45. *Ibid.*, 70.

46. *Ibid.*, 40, 71–2.

47. *Ibid.*, 71–2.

48. *Ibid.*, microfiche 1, G1.

49. Since 583 overlay three small mortar mixing pits it almost certainly did not begin to accumulate until after the wall had been added to the front of the rampart: *ibid.*, 40, 80.

50. It is shown abutting the front of the secondary stone face to a depth of *c.* 16 cm. (Fig. 7).

51. 'probable' because of the possibility, already noted, that 583 continued to accumulate after 629's construction.

52. Shoesmith, *Defences*, 71.

53. The layer also contained a sherd of 'West Midlands early medieval ware': *ibid.*, 40; below, 191, at note 58.

54. *Ibid.*, 73. It has recently been suggested that it was not used there until the late tenth or early eleventh century: A. Vince, 'West Midlands post-Roman research agenda: ceramics', *www.arch-ant. bham.ac.uk/wmrrfa/seminar4/Alan%20Vince-ADD.doc*, 1–19, at 1.

55. *Ibid.*, 72 That is to say, in reality they may have belonged to the fills of later features which, cutting down into the layers which their finders were excavating, had not been noticed, with the

result that the artefacts were mistakenly assumed to belong to the layers themselves. The suspicion that the sherds concerned were in later, unnoticed, features is reinforced by the pattern of pottery finds made in more recent excavations: A. Vince, 'The pottery', in Thomas and Boucher, *Hereford City Excavations*, 65–92, at 65–6.

56. Shoesmith, *Defences*, 73.
57. *Ibid.*, 73.
58. 'almost certainly', rather than 'certainly' because we cannot be certain that there was no pottery in use in Hereford before *c.* 950: above, note 54.
59. Shoesmith, *Defences*, Table 9 on 73.
60. Shoesmith, *The Finds*, 56–7. 'The current view is that red-painted Stamford ware was produced only for a short time in the late ninth century. There is little to add to the evidence presented by Kilmurry in her 1977 paper [K. Kilmurry, 'The production of red-painted pottery at Stamford, Lincs.', *Medieval Arch.*, 21 (1977), 180–6], apart from the realisation that the coin which helped date the kiln is likely to have been a Viking copy of an Alfred penny. However, this does not affect the date much: it would still be *c.* 880 to *c.* 899.' (Alan Vince, pers. comm.).
61. Shoesmith, *Defences*, 77. Elsewhere he estimated an even shorter life: 'A total period of use of less than 50 years would seem most likely': *ibid.*, 74. However, his thinking on this is likely to have been influenced by a reasonable expectation that the succeeding turf-and-clay rampart would have been built before the end of the same century.
62. 'there is a reasonable degree of probability that this defence was built during the middle part of the ninth century... It is unlikely to have been built at a later date than this but could have been earlier... The likelihood is that it is of pre-Alfredian date and it could be as early as the reign of Offa.' (*ibid.*, 77). Mr Shoesmith recently informed me that he no longer considered that a ninth-century date for its construction was likelier than one before 800 (pers. comm., 24 March 2004).
63. The quotations 'almost certainly' and 'very probably' are from Christopher Bronk Ramsey's written advice (pers. comm., 12 March 2007). For the sherd: Shoesmith, *Defences*, 40; *idem*, *The Finds*, 62–3 (Fabric G1). The ware, very probably made at Stafford, is now also known as 'Stafford-type ware': Vince, 'Ceramics', 7, where its dating is discussed.
64. *Calendar of Patent Rolls. AD 1216–25* (1901), 473.
65. *Calendar of Close Rolls. AD 1247–51* (1922), 534.
66. Darlington and McGurk, *John of Worcester*, 578–9; above, note 33.
67. A date in the late tenth or early eleventh century for the addition of stone walls to the ramparts erected in Wessex and western Mercia a century or more earlier has been more often proposed than any other one: *e.g.* C. A. R. Radford, 'The pre-Conquest boroughs of England, ninth to eleventh centuries', *Proc. Brit. Acad.*, 64 (1978), 131–53, at 139; Haslam, 'Towns of Wiltshire', 109; Yorke, *Wessex*, 139.
68. Another one, undertaken mechanically by R. Meeson on a site on Marmion Street, found nothing because of modern destruction: R. Meeson, 'The formation of Tamworth' (University of Birmingham, unpublished M.A. thesis, 1979), 119.
69. S 121; also referred to as a *vicus regius* in S 155; Gould, 'Third report', 37–38.
70. J. Gould, 'First report of the excavations at Tamworth, Staffs., 1967 – the Saxon defences', *Trans. Lichfield and South Staffs. Archaeol. and Hist. Soc.*, 9 (1967–8), 17–29, at 18. This is confirmed by *ibid.*, Figure 3 on 21, 'Plan of Area E', in which the main machine-cut trench is labelled as 'Excavation trench (top four feet removed mechanically)'.
71. *Ibid.*, 18.
72. *Ibid.*, 28; J. Gould, 'Tamworth, town defences (SK 205060)', *West Midlands Annual Archaeol. News Sheet*, 10 (1967), 16.
73. Gould, 'Third report', 33.
74. Gould, 'First report', 18.

75. *Ibid.*, 18.
76. Gould, 'Town defences'.
77. Gould, 'First report', 22–5.
78. Since no numbers appear on Fig. 9 to identify layers and there are only four letters (A, E, X, Y) to identify features, the layers and other features referred to in the text have been appropriately labelled on Fig. 10.
79. Gould, 'First report', 20.
80. It is unclear why Gould's section-drawing, 'Third report', Figure 2 (Fig. 14 here), excluded the area to the east of its east end, given that layer 6 is shown as continuing eastwards. It depicts part of the north edge of the machine-cut trench (C–D), with its west and east ends situated respectively 42 ft (12.80 m) and 32 ft (9.75 m) from the trench's west and east ends, and it would have been even more useful if it had been extended eastwards to the point beyond which modern features had removed all earlier layers and features.
81. Gould, 'First report', 20.
82. If so, its sides would have had closely similar angles of slope.
83. *Ibid.*, 20.
84. However, the small V-shaped feature, Z, found to the east of Y cannot be reliably interpreted.
85. Gould, 'First report', 18. Fig. 11 is reproduced with Bob Meeson's permission. In an undated latter of May 1995 he wrote, 'I have a slide which shows the depressions in the base of the "ditch" which led Jim [Gould] to speculate that "the ditch was possibly an early palisade trench" .. The conditions in the bottom of the "ditch" were very wet, the sand was extremely soft; as one of the two people who cleaned it out I would say that the interpretation of this feature as a palisade trench is plausible but not proven.'
86. *Ibid.*, 20.
87. Gould, 'Third report', 33, 35.
88. *Ibid.*, 35.
89. *Ibid.*, 37.
90. *Ibid.*, 35.
91. *Ibid.*, 35.
92. As opposed to having been caused by root action or even being geological anomalies.
93. Gould, 'Third report', Figure 3 (Fig. 16 here) helpfully shows in outline all the allegedly later features which he assigned to the second-stage defences. This inspires no confidence that any of the minor so-called 'pre-rampart' features shown there were of a different date from the other small ones to which they were adjacent.
94. *Ibid.*, Plate 1 (facing 32) corroborates this.
95. Gould, 'First report', 18 and Figure 4 (Fig. 12 here).
96. K. W. Sheridan, 'Orchard Street, Tamworth, Staffs. (SK 205041)', *West Midlands Annual Archaeol. News Sheet*, 15 (1972), 26. The rampart make-up 'survived to a height of 0.4 metres as a layer of dark heavy earth, probably decayed turf': K. W. Sheridan, 'Tamworth, Orchard Street, east side excavations 1972. A preliminary note', unpublished interim report (privately circulated), dated 20 November 1972. I am grateful to Bob Meeson for providing me with a copy of this report, which contains a plan. No section-drawing has been published or appears to have survived.
97. L. E. Webster and J. Cherry, 'Medieval Britain in 1972', *Medieval Arch.*, 17 (1973), 149. 'A closely packed arrangement of shallow postholes between the front two rows in the north part of the site is tentatively interpreted as a tower set into the rampart at this point': Sheridan, 'Orchard Street, Tamworth'.
98. *Ibid.*
99. Gould, 'First report', 23. Gould reported that on his Victoria Street site 'the rampart had been 28 ft wide whereas at the site of the 1967 excavations it was only 16 ft wide': Gould, 'Third report', 36. However, if the smaller 'postholes' which he believed to be part of the rampart's structure are considered unreliable, there is no reason why its width should have been significantly greater than it was on his other site. Gould's plan shows that the intermediate,

i.e. second, line of postholes on the Victoria Street site lay 10 ft (3.05 m.) to the rear of the front row (*ibid.*, Figure 4 on 38), which is very close to the distance between them – 9.5 ft (2.90 m.) – on the Brewery Lane site.

100. Above, 187; below, 225.

101. Sheridan, 'Tamworth, Orchard Street', 2.

102. *Ibid.*, 2 and plan on 4. This makes the identification even stronger, since post impressions were found in the wet sand at the bottom of the pre-rampart 'ditch' (X) on the Brewery Lane site: Gould, 'First report', 18.

103. No similar comparison can be made with what was found on the Lichfield Street site because there the relevant part of the east edge of the equivalent feature had been removed by a later post-pit.

104. Nothing can be usefully said about the structure of the second-stage rampart or about the putative tower in the absence of any published plans and sections. There is no mention of Tamworth's later medieval ditch in any of the three reports of this excavation.

105. 'Beneath the rampart was a forest of features cut into the natural sand and gravel. Some of these were clearly postholes and others probably the impressions of subsidiary posts driven down through the rampart above.': Sheridan, 'Tamworth, Orchard Street', 1. 'Beneath the rampart were three rows of postholes': Webster and Cherry, 'Medieval Britain in 1972'.

106. A. D. W. Richmond, 'An archaeological evaluation of the former Tamworth Hospital site' (unpublished report, Tempus Reparatum Field Services Department, 1996), unpaginated: §5.1.7.

107. *Ibid.*, §5.1.10.

108. However, the excavator's brief was a tightly defined one: *ibid.*, §1.5.1.

109. K. W. Sheridan, 'Ninth report of excavations at Tamworth, Staffs., 1972. A section through the north defences at Bell Inn Corner', *Trans. Lichfield and South Staffs. Archaeol. and Hist. Soc.*, 15 (1974), 54–7, at 57.

110. *Ibid.*, 55, 57.

111. 'In the eastern section was the remains of a timber post set into this clay and clearly associated with it': *ibid.*, 55. On the section-drawing (*ibid.*, Figure 2, reproduced here as Fig. 18), it is labelled as 'Decayed wood'.

112. *Ibid.*, 55. There may have been another, adjacent one at the opposite, *i.e.* west, edge of the trench. It was not recognised by the excavator, but its presence is suggested on Fig. 18 by a concentration of small stones in layer 3 at approximately the same distance behind the front of the rampart (Fig. 19: 'd'). Sheridan also suggested that a posthole *c.* 5.5 m. to the rear of 'a' (Fig. 18: b) was also part of its structure (*ibid.*, 57), but this is unconvincing.

113. *Ibid.*, 57.

114. *Ibid.*, 55.

115. The reason for this marked dislocation of their junction is unknown. Nothing similar is depicted in the other Tamworth section-drawings.

116. It is unclear if the sandy clay, 7, which covered it and spread beyond its rear, *i.e.* south, edge was a layer of occupation debris or had come from a collapse of rampart mark-up.

117. K. Sheridan, 'Seventh report of excavations at Tamworth, Staffs. A section through the northern defences excavated by Dr F. T. Wainwright in 1960', *Trans. Lichfield and South Staffs. Archaeol. and Hist. Soc.*, 14 (1973), 38–44.

118. *Ibid.*, 39.

119. *Ibid.*, 39.

120. D. M. Wilson and D. G. Hurst, 'Medieval Britain in 1960', *Medieval Arch.*, 5 (1961), 310; Sheridan, 'Seventh report', 39. Wainwright's description of 39 was 'Dark clayey soil – more like humus than clay; ?old turf line', which suggests that he believed that the rear face of the bank had weathered, producing a layer of soil tailing away from its edge on which turf had then grown. A brief note about the excavation, which was published anonymously but which is almost certain, on the basis of internal evidence, to have been written by Wainwright himself, states that, 'one of the fortunate incidents...was the find of an Anglo-Saxon

coin embedded in a paved road adjacent to and associated with the bank': anon., 'Tamworth (SK 206039)', *West Midlands Annual Archaeol. News Sheet*, 3 (1960), 8.

121. There are discontinuities to either side of both of the two northernmost baulks. One of them affects layers which are numbered 37 and 38 to the south of the baulk in question, but which are unnumbered to the north of it, where there is no line drawn to continue 38's surface. Consequently, it is impossible to relate reliably the robbing of the rear wall to the depositing of 38 onto the road surface.

122. 'The large ditch to the north is presumably of [late] medieval date to judge by its size': Sheridan, 'Seventh report', 39.

123. According to Wainwright's notes, 8 is 'Bottom of ditch', 13 is 'Undisturbed', and 7 is 'Reddish, clayey silt turning to black silt'; and layers 1–6 and 9–12 were all 'modern' deposits (*ibid.*, 38). Excavators of ditch sections often find it hard to distinguish between the natural subsoil through which a ditch was cut and an early fill of redeposited subsoil or, in some cases, even one of clean 'primary silt'.

124. Sheridan described it as a 'shallow depression' and, later, 'a pre-rampart ditch' and suggested that it 'possibly equates with the small pre-rampart ditch located by Gould beneath the tenth century western defences': *ibid.*, 39, 41.

125. *Ibid.*, 38.

126. *e.g.* Brewery Lane, Tamworth Hospital.

127. The 'red bank' and course of masonry were together numbered 20, 'Stones set in red bank': *ibid.*, 38.

128. Layers 18 and 19, respectively described as 'black, heaped up from behind' and 'black', were probably buried turf and topsoil, forming a continuation of 30, 39 and 44.

129. The excavation was apparently done entirely by machine: K. Sheridan, 'Sixth report of excavations at Tamworth, Staffs. (1971). A section of the Saxon and medieval defences, Albert Road', *Trans. Lichfield and South Staffs. Archaeol. and Hist. Soc.*, 14 (1973), 32–7, at 35.

130. *Ibid.*, 35.

131. *Ibid.*, 36. Above, 201 (for a width of 4.8 m. at Brewery Lane).

132. Even the postholes which he interpreted as having held timbers associated with the rampart (Fig. 22: b–g) were not found until the section was drawn: 'beneath it were a number of postholes, visible in section, but not uncovered in plan': K. W. Sheridan, 'Albert Road, Tamworth, Staffs. (SK 209043)', *West Midlands Annual Archaeol. News Sheet*, 14 (1971), 23.

133. Sheridan, 'Sixth report', 36.

134. What Sheridan labelled as 'Disturbance' on Fig. 22 may represent a later medieval operation which reduced the second-stage rampart and used its redistributed make-up to form the base of a new, much wider one.

135. *Ibid.*, 35–36.

136. *Ibid.*, 35.

137. *Ibid.*, 35. None of the materials through which the feature was cut looks likely to have produced 'fine silt and smooth rounded pebbles'.

138. Fig. 22 shows the feature to be completely filled with a layer (unnumbered but described as 'buried soil') directly underlying 6; but the majority of its fill is depicted as being a sand-free soil, which prompts the thought that it may be the same material as layer 6, notwithstanding the distinction made between them in Sheridan's section-drawing.

139. *Ibid.*, 36. The ditch's north edge and bottom were not found, but the angle of slope of its fills suggests a feature of a size consistent with that of the later medieval ditch (seen at its full width at Brewery Lane).

140. J. H. Barratt, 'Tamworth', *West Midlands Annual Archaeol. News Sheet*, 7 (1964), 10. I have copies of the photographs, made with Philip Rahtz's kind permission from ones in his possession.

141. *Ibid.*

142. A small part of one section was drawn: reproduced in Meeson, 'Formation of Tamworth', Figure 59 (between pp. 112–13). About

25 m. to the south another section was excavated by R. Meeson in 1977, but nothing was found on account of the extent of modern destruction: *ibid.*, 119.

143. C. Young, 'Brewery site, Tamworth (SK 210043)', *West Midlands Annual Archaeol. News Sheet*, 11 (1968), 21.

144. D. M. Wilson and D. G. Hurst, 'Medieval Britain in 1968', *Medieval Archaeol.*, 13 (1969), 239.

145. *Ibid.* The building material consisted of roof-slates, tiles and painted wall-plaster.

146. 'There was no standing rampart associated with the ditch, but 20 ft behind it were a number of horizontal timber features, either at right-angles or parallel to it. These could not be definitely associated with any phase, and may be the strapping of a rampart or [may be] occupation features.': *ibid.*

147. Young, 'Brewery site'.

148. Wilson and Hurst, 'Medieval Britain in 1968'. The claim that it had been entirely filled by the late thirteenth century is, however, unreliable: below, 213.

149. L. E. Webster and J. Cherry, 'Medieval Britain in 1978', *Medieval Arch.*, 23 (1979), 245.

150. *Ibid.*

151. Taylor, *Anglo-Saxon Chronicle. MS B*, 50; Whitelock, *English Historical Documents*, 212.

152. Shotton, Blundell and Williams, 'Radiocarbon dates', 394: Birm-109, given as BP 1541±80, *AD* 409.

153. They 'were identified by Mr J. G. Hurst as Saxon but belonging to anytime within that period.': Gould, 'First report', 22, 26 (nos. 2–4).

154. These were described as 'small scraps of very friable black pottery with much water-rounded quartz but very little bonding material': Gould, 'Third report', 35, 41 (no. 1).

155. 'One fragment of pottery 1 in. by 1 in., black with polishing on the outer surface and not hard fired': *ibid.*, 41 (no. 2).

156. 'This pottery was of a dark fabric, in some cases grass-tempered, and often with a reddish surface. One rim fragment was much thicker and of generally poorer quality than the others. The assemblage in general would fit a tenth century context.': Sheridan, 'Tamworth, Orchard Street', 2.

157. Richmond, 'Tamworth Hospital', §5.2.2; Sheridan, 'Ninth report', 54.

158. Sheridan, 'Sixth report', 36; Barratt, 'Tamworth'.

159. Wilson and Hurst, 'Medieval Britain in 1968'. On Meeson's site 'a black vesicular sherd came from the top of the silts' of the second-stage ditch 'below a thirteenth-century sealing layer': Webster and Cherry, 'Medieval Britain in 1978'.

160. Sheridan, 'Seventh report', 39; above, 207.

161. M. Dolley, 'The Anglo-Saxon coin', in Sheridan, 'Seventh report', 42–4; A. J. H. Gunstone, *Sylloge of Coins of the British Isles. 17. Ancient British, Anglo-Saxon and Norman Coins in Midlands Museums* (1971), Plate VII, no. 180.

162. Dolley, 'Anglo-Saxon coin', 44.

163. I am most grateful to Dr Blackburn for the following comment (pers. comm., 14 April 2004): 'I would broadly agree with Dolley, though today there is a more cautious approach to the chronology. We would not be so emphatic that the recoinage took place on a 6–yearly cycle at Michaelmas 979, though no one could really put it later than 980. The recoinages were pretty comprehensive, and probably complete within 6–12 months, as Dolley suggests. If the coin was a casual loss from circulation, I think that you could say that there is a 95% probability that it was lost by say 981. However, there is always that element of chance that the coin had been redeposited from an earlier level. As a piece of dating evidence it is pretty strong, but for proof one would like to have some corroboration that presumably does not exist.'

164. Only potentially, not certainly, because it would have been impossible to prove that the coin had not been 'introduced' into 39 until after that layer's deposition (but before the deposition of the stones).

165. Above, note 164

166. Notwithstanding strenuous efforts to do so. I am grateful to Suzy

Blake (Staffs. County Council), Jim Gould, Bob Meeson, David Symons (Birmingham City Museum and Art Gallery), and Sarah Williams (Tamworth Castle Museum) for their assistance and advice.

167. Sheridan, 'Tamworth, Orchard Street', 2.

168. Above, note 67.

169. Radford, 'Later pre-Conquest boroughs'; Haslam, 'Towns of Wiltshire'.

170. One may reasonably extend his argument to say that it had been either created or last cleaned out then. The earliest known documented reference to the later medieval defences is of 1294 (in Tamworth's court leet rolls, the earliest of which begins in 1288): H. Wood, *Tamworth Borough Records* (1952), 14; *idem, Borough by Prescription* (1958), 53.

171. 'Plan of the Manor of Sudeley...belonging to Lord Rivers' (1783) and 'Plan of the Separate Estates Part of the Demains of the Abbey of Winchcombe and Sudeley...belonging to The Rt Hon. Lord Fred. Montague' (undated but *c.* 1780): Gloucestershire Record Office [hereafter G.R.O.] D2579; Inclosure map of Greet and Sudeley Tenements (1815): G.R.O. Q/RI 159; Tithe Award map, 'Titheable lands in Sudeley; and in the Abbey Demesnes, and Langley, Sudeley Tenements and Coates in Winchcombe' (1848): G.R.O. GDR/T1/174.

172. Some corroboration of the importance of this line may come from John Leland's statement that, 'Avery parson of Dene tolde me... that the towne buyldinge was much toward Sudeley Castell, and that ther yet remayne sum tokens of a diche and the foundation of a wall...so that of old tyme it was a mighty large towne.': J. Leland, *The Itinerary of England and Wales in or about the Years 1535–1543*, ed. L. T. Smith (11 pts in 5 vols, 1964), ii, 220–1. Vineyard Street runs towards Sudeley Castle, and the putative course of the south arm of the defences lies immediately north of the entrance to the park within which the castle stands.

173. 'The bank is probably the one sectioned in the 1940s according to a letter in the 1962/3 correspondence in which a find of a bone implement of Saxon type is reported. There are no further details of the excavation.': P. Ellis, 'Excavations in Winchcombe, Gloucestershire, 1962–1972: a report on excavation and fieldwork by B. K. Davison and J. Hinchliffe at Cowl Lane and Back Lane', *Trans. Bristol and Gloucs. Archaeol. Soc.*, 104 (1986), 95–138, at 134.

174. J. Samuels and D. Slatcher, 'An archaeological evaluation at Almsbury Farm, Winchcombe, Gloucestershire' (unpublished report JSAC 543c/2000/04, John Samuels Archaeological Consultants, 2000).

175. 'We found all along the top of the bank traces of burnt wood': E. P. L. Brock, 'Excavation of the site of Winchcombe Abbey, Gloucestershire', *Jnl British Arch. Assoc.*, 49 (1893), 162–72, at 164. However, nothing similar was found in the excavations of 1963 and 1972, and it is likelier that the 'burnt wood' derived from natural vegetation than from a defensive feature.

176. A typescript report on Eric Gee's 1939 excavation, held by Cheltenham Art Gallery and Museum, refers to two phases of construction of the rampart and a robbed out stone wall associated with the latter phase. The record of the 1947 excavation (by either Norman Painting or Philip Styles) comprises only a handful of relatively uninformative photographs (Gloucestershire Record Office, 3530/6). I am very grateful to David Mullin and Timothy Grubb for these details.

177. Ellis, 'Excavations'.

178. *Ibid.*, 133.

179. *Ibid.*, 107.

180. *Ibid.*, 107.

181. *Ibid.*, 115.

182. 'The excavation record shows that the section across the rampart [at Convent Close] was not completely excavated, and that excavation was taking place at the very end of the time allotted for the excavation. The record is therefore an incomplete one.' (*ibid.*, 110–11). Moreover, 'Owing to lack of time, rampart features in

cutting A were not planned with the exception of F38, 39, 53 and 55.' (*ibid.*, 106).

183. *Ibid.*, 107. The 'ditch excavated in 1972' is F64 on the Junior School site.

184. *Ibid.*, 115.

185. Unlike at Tamworth it is not impossible to envisage F64 as a ditch; without knowing how firm the natural subsoil was, it cannot be said for certain that its sides were too steep for an open feature.

186. *Ibid.*, 112.

187. *Ibid.*, 116.

188. *Ibid.*, 117, Figure 11 on 118 ('Junior School 1972. Plan of period 2 features'). F63 and F90 are not shown on any of Ellis's section-drawings.

189. 'No postholes were recorded on the upper surface of F48A.' (*ibid.*, 110).

190. *Ibid.*, 110–11, 133.

191. *Ibid.*, 111–12.

192. *Ibid.*, 110.

193. Samuels and Slatcher, 'Almsbury Farm', 12–13, 23.

194. *Ibid.*, 12, 47.

195. *Ibid.*, 12.

196. See above, note 171.

197. Samuels and Slatcher, 'Almsbury Farm', 11.

198. *Ibid.*, Photos 3, 7 (unpaginated).

199. *Ibid.*, 11.

200. *Ibid.*, 16, 20–1.

201. *Ibid.*, 18.

202. *Ibid.*, 18, 48.

203. *Ibid.*, 24.

204. L. V. Grinsell, C. E. Blunt and M. Dolley, *Sylloge of Coins of the British Isles. 19: Ancient British Coins and Coins of the Bristol and Gloucestershire Mints* (1973), 105–9, at 107, and Plate IX; C. E. Blunt, B. H. I. H. Stewart and C. S. S. Lyon, *Coinage in Tenth-Century England: from Edward the Elder to Edgar's Reform* (1989), 257. For the relationship between mints and fortified places from Athelstan's reign onwards: F. L. Attenborough, *The Laws of the Earliest English Kings* (1922), 134–5, at cap. 14, 14.2 (which glosses cap. 14's use of *port* with *burh*).

205. R. C. Love, *Three Eleventh-Century Anglo-Latin Saints' Lives* (1996), lxxxix–cxxxix, 50–89; F. Wormald, *English Kalendars before AD 1100*, i (Henry Bradshaw Society Publications, vol. 72 for 1933), 22, 36, 64, and *passim*.

206. 'cum ibi firmauerit oppidum muro cinctum', which Love translates as 'when he established there a walled town': *Saints' Lives*, 66–7. For the date of composition: *ibid.*, xci.

207. The evidence for Winchcombe's importance to Coenwulf and his family, both actual and perceived, is set out and fully referenced in Bassett, 'Mercian royal mausoleum', 82–5.

208. Ellis, 'Excavations', 107.

209. *Ibid.*, 107.

210. *Ibid.*, 111.

211. *Ibid.*, 124.

212. *Ibid.*, 111.

213. *Ibid.*, 124.

214. *Ibid.*, 111.

215. *Ibid.*, 110.

216. *Ibid.*, 111.

217. *Ibid.*, 111. Illustrated on Ellis's Figure 5 ('Convent Close 1963. Plan of features'), *ibid.*, 108.

218. *Ibid.*, 112.

219. *Ibid.*, 112.

220. *Ibid.*, 124.

221. *Ibid.*, 115.

222. *Ibid.*, 117, 120, 124.

223. *Ibid.*, 132, citing Biddle, 'Towns', 128, and Radford, 'Pre-Conquest boroughs', 149.

224. Ellis, 'Excavations', 132.

225. *Ibid.*, 132, citing Wilson and Hurst, 'Medieval Britain in 1965', 168, and Biddle, 'Towns', 128.

226. *Ibid.*, 133, citing Radford, 'Pre-Conquest boroughs', 150.

227. Ellis, 'Excavations', 132. A *vallum monasterii* was an earthwork or wall which enclosed a minster and associated structures: Blair, *Church*, 196–8.

228. It is reasonable to assume that it stood on or close to the site of one or other of the churches which succeeded it: Bassett, 'Mercian royal mausoleum', 85–9.

229. 'quod ipse quandam viam, que se ducit a villa predicta versus occidentem, inter duo gardina eiusdem Abbatis in eadem villa, que vocatur Peticrueslane, obstruere, et ad elargacionem eorundem gardinorum includere, et illam obstructam et inclusam tenere possit sibi et successoribus suis, imperpetuum.': D. Royce (ed.), *Landboc sive Registrum Monasterii Beatae Mariae Virginis et Sancti Cenhelmi de Winchelcumba* (2 vols, 1892–1903), ii, 105–6; Bassett, 'Mercian royal mausoleum', Figures 1–2 and 86–7.

230. Before the late twentieth-century renumbering of many major roads Gloucester Street, High Street and Hayles Street were part of the A46 trunk road from Bath to the north-east coast via Leicester. More locally the road passes through Stroud, Cheltenham, Winchcombe, Broadway and Stratford-upon-Avon, usually running along the foot of the Cotswold scarp, but deviating from it in the vicinity of Winchcombe. Its course in the south-west midlands is not recognised in I. D. Margary, *Roman Roads in Britain* (third edn, 1973), but it is referred to as a *herepað* (military road, highway) in a boundary statement attached to a grant, made in 777x9 by Offa and Ealdred to the minster at Bishop's Cleeve, of land nearby at *Timbingctun*: W. de G. Birch, *Cartularium Saxonicum* (3 vols, 1885–93), i, 340–2 (no. 246), at 342; S 141. There is a convenient map of the mid twentieth-century course of the A46 at *http://www.sabre-roads. org.uk/roadlists/f99/46.shtml*. The north-south road of which part is perpetuated in the line of North Street ran from the Romano-British 'small town' at Wycomb in Andoversford (and ultimately from Cirencester) to Alcester, another such 'small town'. Today it is intermittently followed north of Winchcombe by the B4078 (as far as Sedgeberrow) and then much more consistently by the A435, crossing the River Avon at Evesham. For the road's route between Cirencester and Andoversford: Margary, *Roman Roads*, 145–6 (*i.e.* his road 55 and one of the minor roads which branched off it).

231. An analysis of Winchcombe's plan shows that most of its medieval streets and its main property boundaries conform to a rectilinear layout based on the place's two axial through-routes (above, note 230). Gloucester Street, however, stands out as being notably at variance with this dominant trend, and may represent a new road which was laid out between *Peticrueslane* and the main street along the south edge of the prominent spur of Lower Lias clay on which the Anglo-Saxon settlement sat. Its course appears to have been designed to accommodate as many tenements of equal width as possible. The earliest known reference to the road, as the *Strata Regia communis*, is of 1236: Royce, *Landboc*, i, n. 2 on p. xcvii. If it does represent a planned addition to the townscape, it was probably designed to take traffic from *Peticrueslane* to the abbey's market-place on High Street. The aftermath of the great fire of *c.* 1150 (*ibid.*, i, pp. xvii, 83) would have provided an appropriate occasion for its creation, if it did not already exist then.

232. M. O. H. Carver (ed.), 'Medieval Worcester', *Trans. Worcs. Archaeol. Soc.*, third series, 7 (1980), 3–5; N. Baker *et al.*, 'From Roman to medieval Worcester: development and planning in the Anglo-Saxon city', *Antiquity*, 250 (1992), 65–74, at 72; H. Dalwood and R. Edwards, *Excavations at Deansway, Worcester, 1988–89: Romano-British Small Town to Late Medieval City* (CBA Res. Rep., 139, 2004); S. Griffin, R. Jackson, *et al.*, 'Excavation at City Arcade, High Street, Worcester', *Trans. Worcs. Archaeol. Soc.*, third series, 19 (2004), 45–109. For the most recent discussion of the full extent of the pre-Conquest defences: Baker and Holt, *Gloucester and Worcester*, 133–4, 165–8, 172–3, 176–7, 184, 189, 347–50.

233. Dalwood and Edwards, *Deansway*, 55–6, 219–22.

234. *Ibid.*, 55, 219.

235. *Ibid.*, 52.

236. *Ibid.*, 65, 203, 226.

237. Birch, *Cartularium Saxonicum*, ii, 221–2 (no. 579); S 223; translated in Whitelock, *English Historical Documents*, 540–1. The report contains no reference to the excavations done at Hereford, Winchcombe and Tamworth, of which the authors appear unaware.

238. Dalwood and Edwards, *Deansway*, 22–3, 59. In addition, a lease by Bishop Wærferth in 904 of, among other lands, a *haga* in Worcester states that its west boundary was on the River Severn and that its north one was 28 rods long and lay 'along the north wall eastwards' ('bi þæm norð wealle east wardes xxviii roda lang'): S 1280; Birch, *Cartularium Saxonicum*, ii, 266–7 (no. 608), *i.e.* that it lay in the north-west corner of the late ninth-century *burh*. The *haga*'s location has been plausibly argued by Baker and Holt to have lain to the north of Copenhagen Street, to the west of Bridport and to the south of Grope Lane, which itself runs just to the south of the projected course of the Deansway rampart and ditch: *Gloucester and Worcester*, 174–7. However, since their argument starts from the premise, albeit a reasonable one, that the *weall* in question is the rampart which Æthelred and Æthelflæd are known to have built at Worcester prior to 900 and, secondly, that it was located on Deansway Site 5, the evidence of the 904 lease cannot be used to corroborate the excavators' identification of the latter. Nor can the use of the word *weall* be taken to indicate that the rampart was already frontally revetted in stone since it was used in Old English sources for earthen walls as well as stone ones, and also for palisades, *e.g.* S. Irvine (ed.), *The Anglo-Saxon Chronicle: a Collaborative Edition. Volume 7: MS E* (2004), 9 (entry for AD 189).

239. Dalwood and Edwards, *Deansway*, 22–3, 59.

240. *Ibid.*, 207–8 and Figure 137; below, note 242. The modern features were so extensive along the trench's western side that almost none of the rampart and revetment was visible in section: *ibid.*, Figures 136, 139 and Mr Robin Jackson, pers. comm. (The section illustrated in *ibid.*, Figure 140, is the eastern one, notwithstanding the caption's claim that it is east-facing.) Figure 139 shows shuttering along the interface between the two separately excavated parts of the trench.

241. *Ibid.*, Figures 137–8.

242. 'A real problem existed here in the manner in which the trench had to be excavated. Namely, the south end was excavated first up to as far as the shuttering. This was recorded, then backfilled, and the northern part opened as a separate exercise. This had to happen as the trench lay across an access corridor for contractors on the site. Thus there is effectively a split in the record which... lay more or less on the critical wall line.' (Robin Jackson, pers. comm.). The exact line of division may be depicted as a broken line bisecting Trench B in *ibid.*, Figure 134.

243. Figure 137 shows a feature (Fig. 35:14) with a side which could be construed as being continued upwards by the south 'edge' of layer 12, but with no corresponding continuation of its south side. It is identified as a posthole, but only in the online fiches (*http://ads.ahds.ac.uk/catalogue/library/cba/rr139fiche*, Table 39 on 120, where it is unnumbered), and can be seen, if indistinctly, in Figure 136 (Fig. 34), but both its position in the stratigraphical sequence and its function must be considered unresolved.

244. *Ibid.*, 219. Only one of these two layers (Fig. 36: 2; numbered CG 5014 and 5015 in the online fiches (ref. in note 243), Table 39 on 119) is shown on Fig. 35.

245. The feature is not shown on any of the plans (unless it is on *ibid.*, Figure 134), and it had yet to be excavated when *ibid.*, plate Figure 139 was taken.

246. The rubble layer shown on Figure 137 (Fig. 35; Fig. 36: 10) definitely lay up against the front of the limestone revetment, 'thus suggesting it is associated with demolition/decay rather than construction' (Robin Jackson, pers. comm.).

247. This feature appears not to be mentioned in the report's text, neither in the hard copy nor in the 'Activity unit tables' to be found in the online fiches (ref. in note 243) However, the long narrow feature shown in outline as cutting into the rampart along

248. Griffin, Jackson *et al.*, 'City Arcade', 60.

249. The ditch's minimum depth was established largely by observation of the sides of deep late medieval pits, from auguring and boreholes, and by digging test pits: *ibid.*, 45, 48, 60–1. The published section-drawing (*ibid.*, Fig. 9 on 62) does not distinguish between its separate fills.

250. *Ibid.*, 61–3. The discussion of the cartographic and other documentary evidence for the site and its environs takes no account of the rampart, which would have been a significant feature of the local landscape for as long as the ditch itself was: *ibid.*, 101–3.

251. *Ibid.*, 61–3, 75, 101.

252. *Ibid.*, 101; L. Richardson, 'Messrs Marks and Spencer Ltd: geology and archaeology of the site', *Trans. Worcs. Naturalists Club*, 11.3 (1958–9), 141–6, at 142; *idem*, 'The Shambles (rear of Littlewoods)', *ibid.*, 11.4 (1960–1), 224. It is possible that excavation on the Marks and Spencer site revealed the lowest two courses of the limestone wall which revetted the front of the late ninth-century rampart. They lay 75 ft (*c.* 23 m.) east of the High Street frontage, were 3 ft (*c.* 0.9 m.) wide, and are referred to as 'pitched masonry [which] I think is the remains of the foundation for a wall': Richardson, 'Marks and Spencer', 145–6. (However, this depends on the alleged wall's alignment as having been from NNW to SSE, not from WNW (*sic*) to SSE as reported: *ibid.*, 146).

253. P. Barker, 'Excavations on the Lich Street development site, 1965–6', *Trans. Worcs. Archaeol. Soc.*, third series, 2 (1969), 44–56, at 51; Baker and Holt, *Gloucester and Worcester*, 172–3.

254. For the use which the late ninth-century defences made of the Romano-British ones: Baker and Holt, *Gloucester and Worcester*, Figure 6.11 on 167, 172–3, 184, 349. For the putative locations of defences built by Mercian kings in the eighth and/or early ninth century: Bassett, 'Divide and rule?', 77–81.

255. D. Whitehead pointed out that the Anglo-Saxon Chronicle's entry for 893 refers to the summoning of king's thegns from 'every fortified place [*of ælcere byrig*] east of the Parret, and both west and east of Selwood, and also north of the Thames and west of the Severn', and argued from it that Hereford must have had its turf-and-clay rampart by then: 'The historical background to the city defences', in Shoesmith, *Defences*, 13–24, at 14; Taylor, *Anglo-Saxon Chronicle. MS B*, 42 (*sub anno* 894).

256. Above, note 29.

257. Brooks, 'Military obligations'; Bassett, 'Divide and rule?', 57–9, 81–3.

258. Baker and Holt, *Gloucester and Worcester*, 174–7.

259. The same can be said with greater confidence of Winchcombe, given the much better evidence available for its slow but inexorable subjugation by the Mercians in the course of the eighth century: S. Bassett, 'In search of the origins of Anglo-Saxon kingdoms', in *idem* (ed.), *Origins of Anglo-Saxon Kingdoms*, 3–27, at 6–17. The key location for any future attempt to date the first-stage defences has to be Tamworth, the only place in 'original' Mercia where such defences have been found or indeed where they can be authoritatively predicted to have existed.

260. As Shoesmith himself argued: *Defences*, 80.

261. Which Dolley and Blackburn believe to be 95% certain: above, 211–12.

262. This suggests that the addition of a stone wall to the newly constructed earthwork defences at Towcester as early as 917 was, as Biddle suggested, an exceptional and therefore noteworthy activity: Bately, *Anglo-Saxon Chronicle. MA A*, 68; Biddle, 'Towns', 137.

263. Just as it is considered to be for the West Saxon ones: above, note 6.

264. Dalwood and Edwards, *Deansway*, 61.

265. See above, note 63.

266. The long delay before Tamworth was fortified may have arisen from its having been in Danish hands from the late 870s until some time in the first half of 913.

The Significance of Old English *Burh* in Anglo-Saxon England

Simon Draper

English place-names containing OE burh *are common and may be interpreted in several different ways, from prehistoric fortifications to medieval manors and towns. In all these definitions, the underlying root meaning is generally assumed to be 'stronghold' or 'fortification', but archaeological and documentary evidence discussed in this paper argues instead for a more basic association with ditched enclosures. In particular, a link is found between some* OE burh *place-names and enclosures surrounding high-status settlements of Middle and Late Saxon date.*

Introduction: Old English *Burh* in English Place-Name Studies

Old English *burh* is generally counted by place-name scholars as one of the most important 'habitative' (*i.e.* denoting settlement) elements in English place-names: indeed, Barrie Cox listed it among the five such elements 'important in the formation of English place-names during the period *c.* AD 400 to 730'.[1] It occurs in a variety of place-name types across the country (major, minor and field-names) and in a wide range of spellings, including 'borough', 'brough' and 'burgh'. Perhaps the commonest form, however, is 'bury', representing the dative singular form of *burh*, which is *byrig*. It occurs either on its own as a simplex or, more commonly, as a suffix compounded with a personal name or descriptive element; for example, Aylesbury, 'Ægel's *burh*', or Westbury, 'west *burh*'.[2] *Burh* is also found as the first element in a handful of compounds, including *burh-stede*, '*burh* site', and *burh*-stow, '*burh* place', although the most numerous is *burh-tun*, '*burh* farm/settlement', which will receive special attention below.[3]

Although it is evident that *burh* has its roots in the verb *beorgan*, 'to protect, shelter',[4] the basic topographical meaning of the element remains obscure. Most place-name scholars suggest the gloss 'fortification', but one suspects that this has more to do with *burh*'s best-known associations with prehistoric hillforts and Late Saxon fortified towns, rather than actual etymology. In truth, little detailed research has been carried out into the variety of physical features referred to in *burh* place-names.

There exists no dedicated national or regional survey and only A.H. Smith's 1956 discussion gives any sense of the full range of possible topographical associations, from 'ancient pre-English earthwork or encampment' to 'Roman station or camp', 'fortified house or manor' and 'market town'.[5]

All too often, authors are left unsure as to the significance of *burh* in individual place-names. In the absence of any clear evidence, most accept the traditional defensive interpretation of the element, speculating on the existence of a hitherto undiscovered fortification, prehistoric or later in date, in the immediate vicinity. In my opinion, this is to ignore a more fundamental association of *burh* place-names with man-made enclosures, defensive or otherwise, which is discernable in the archaeological record. Through an examination of evidence from a variety of sites across England, I aim to show not only that the primary meaning of *burh* was 'enclosure', but also that some of these enclosures performed important social and legal functions in the Middle and Late Saxon periods, defining monastic, seigneurial and urban settlements.

Old English *Burh* as enclosure: The archaeological evidence

Prehistoric and Roman Earthworks

Perhaps the clearest archaeological association between *burh* place-names and man-made enclosures may be seen in the earthwork circuits of prehistoric and Roman

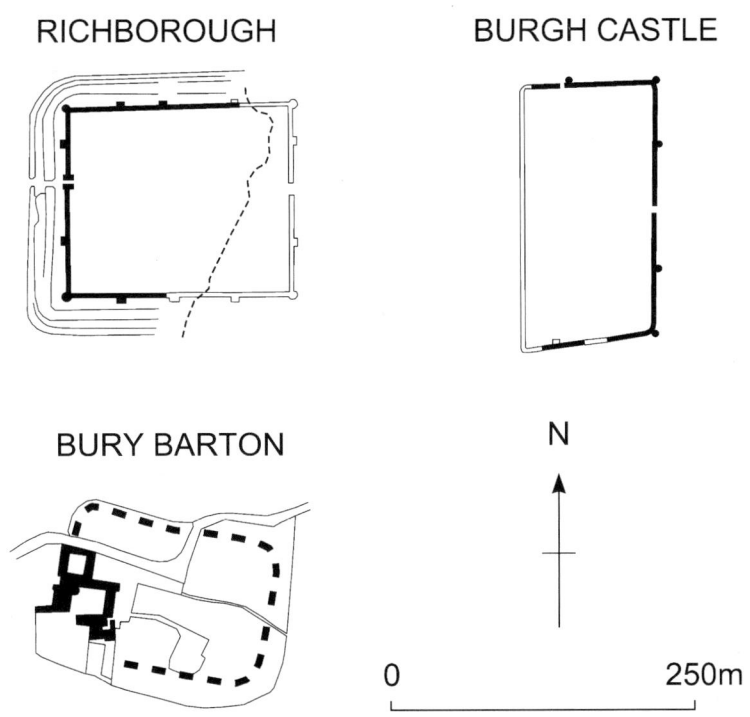

RICHBOROUGH

BURGH CASTLE

BURY BARTON

N

0   250m

Figure 1. Roman rectilinear enclosures indicated by place-names containing OE *burh. After Maxfield 1989 and Todd 1985.*

forts. Margaret Gelling has described the use of *burh* in connection with Roman military sites as a mainly northern English phenomenon: 'rare, possibly not known, in the south'.[6] Whilst it is certainly true that many of the better-known examples occur in northern and eastern counties – Brough (Cumbria), Aldborough (North Yorkshire), Richborough (Kent) and Burgh Castle (Norfolk), for example – we should not overlook evidence from Devon, where the place-names Woodbury, Broadbury, Bury Barton and Old Burrow have all convincingly been associated with Roman forts, fortlets or signal stations.[7] Clearly, the Roman military significance of *burh* place-names extends well beyond the geographical limit proposed by Gelling and, in each case, such sites are revealed on the ground by well-defined, sub-rectangular enclosures (Fig. 1).

More common across England are the hundreds of Iron Age hillforts and promontory camps known by place-names containing the element *burh*. In Wiltshire alone there are twenty-seven examples,[8] several of which, including Yarnbury and Rybury, display impressive circuits of concentric earthen ramparts (Fig. 2). Even where nothing is visible on the ground today, a place-name containing *burh* may sometimes betray the presence of a 'lost' prehistoric earthwork enclosure. Such has proved to be the case at both Woodbury in Wiltshire (Wadbury in 1323) and Berber Hill in Devon (Berberry in 1841), where

aerial photography has helped to identify two previously unknown Iron Age hillforts.[9]

The question of how these hillforts gained their *burh* place-names has been considered by Ian Burrow, working in Somerset.[10] One possibility examined is that the calling of a hillfort *burh* indicated that it continued to be occupied into the early medieval period. 'The weight of opinion is against such a view', Burrow concluded, but it is nevertheless striking that two hillforts in the county named Cadbury, 'Cada's *burh*' – South Cadbury and Cadbury Congresbury – have yielded important archaeological evidence for post-Roman activity.[11] Perhaps a more plausible explanation is that the term *burh* was applied by Old English speakers to anywhere in the landscape where prominent earthwork enclosures were still visible. One such place was Yarborough (Lincolnshire), which derives its name from *eorth-burh*, 'earth *burh*'.[12] Here, the 'earth *burh*' in question was a small sub-rectangular earthwork, known as Yarborough Camp, which lent its name to and formed the focal place of Yarborough wapentake.[13]

One last point relevant to this discussion is that *burh* was not solely associated with earthwork enclosures with a military or defensive function. In Glamorgan, Matthew Griffiths has considered the thirteenth-century place-name Blakeberege, 'black *burh*', concluding that it referred directly to the earthworks of a Romano-

British farming settlement, which were evidently still prominent when the name was coined.[14] A small late prehistoric or Romano-British enclosed farmstead in Alton (Wiltshire), meanwhile, appears to account for the boundary marks *eorth byrig*, 'earth *burh*', and *ealdan burh*, 'old *burh*', which are recorded in charters of 903 and 957 respectively.[15]

Monastic Sites

The use of *burh* in connection with early monasteries and minster churches has long been suspected by Anglo-Saxon historians. Sir Frank Stenton, in a paper first published in 1943, commented on its use in place-names describing Middle Saxon religious foundations, especially those seemingly established by noble women; for example, Beage in the case of Bibury (Gloucestershire) and Flæde at Fladbury (Worcestershire).[16] Tetbury (Gloucestershire), which preserves the female name Tette, is variously described in charters as *Tettan byrig* and *Tettan monasterium*, and Stenton writes; 'there is other evidence that *burh* and monasterium could be used interchangeably. Westbury on Trym in Gloucestershire appears as *Uuestburg* in an original charter of Offa, and as *Westmynster* in a document of 804 … The usage presumably refers to the enclosure which surrounded the monastic buildings'.[17]

Despite the perceptiveness of Stenton's observations, it is only in recent years that archaeological and topographical evidence has been sought to support this association. John Blair in particular has identified a number of Anglo-Saxon minster towns where curvilinear enclosures, each encompassing the historic church site, are preserved in current property boundaries. One such example is Bampton (Oxfordshire), where excavations in the 1980s confirmed the presence of a substantial ditch, 4 m wide and containing eleventh-century pottery, on the line of the projected enclosure.[18] Other curvilinear enclosures are to be found in towns bearing *burh* place-names and notable examples include Charlbury (Oxfordshire) and Kintbury (Berkshire) (Fig. 3). Lambourn (Berkshire), which is also shown in Figure 3, displays a particularly distinctive oval street pattern and was referred to as both a minster and *byri hæme tun*, 'home farm belonging to the *burh*', in a charter of *c.* 1033.[19] Further *burh* place-names that may perhaps be explained by the presence of an Anglo-Saxon monastic enclosure include Tisbury (Wiltshire), Congresbury (Somerset), Tilbury (Essex) and Alberbury (Shropshire).[20] These locations would surely repay future archaeological and topographical survey.

Another place that would certainly benefit from detailed archaeological investigation is Thornbury, near Binsey (Oxfordshire) (Fig. 3).[21] Thornbury (*Thornbiri*, 'thorn *burh*', in its late twelfth-century form) has long been regarded as a holy site, due to its historical association with the legend of the eighth-century St Frideswide. Today, a medieval chapel of St Margaret stands within a prominent

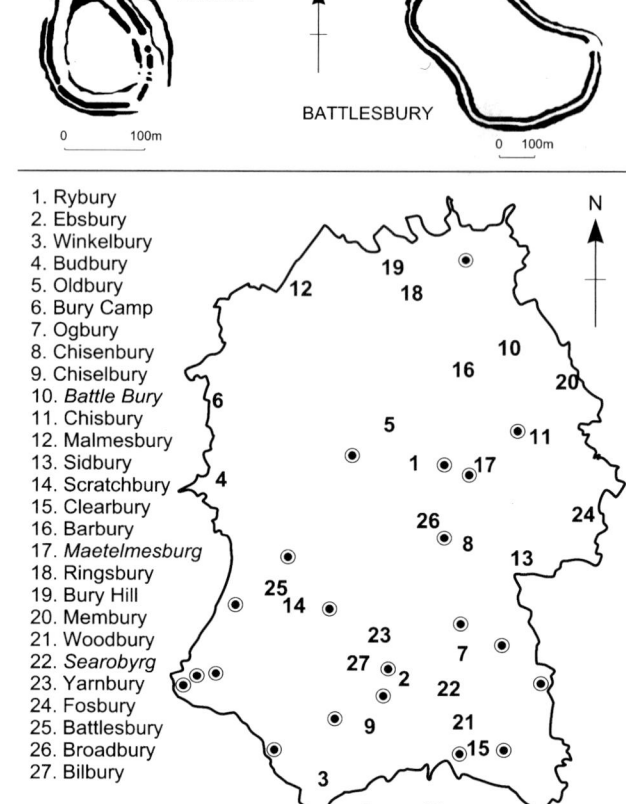

Figure 2. OE burh *and Iron Age hillforts in Wiltshire. Rybury and Battlesbury, after Field, Brown and McOmish 2005 and McOmish, Field and Brown 2002.*

oval ditched enclosure and this has prompted John Blair to speculate that a small monastic cell or retreat-house was once located here, perhaps during Frideswide's own lifetime.[22] Unfortunately, small-scale excavations carried out in 1987 on the enclosure ditch failed either to confirm or deny this hypothesis, but a stratified sherd of Anglo-Saxon organic-tempered pottery, found sealed underneath the primary fill of the ditch, nevertheless demonstrated that it had been in use during the Early or Middle Saxon period. Further fieldwork within the enclosed area itself is now needed if Blair's ideas are to be fully tested, but the use (or re-use) of Thornbury as an eighth-century monastic enclosure remains a distinct possibility.

Whilst clear archaeological evidence for Middle Saxon occupation may be lacking at Thornbury, it is undoubtedly present at Flixborough (Lincolnshire) (*Flichesburg* in 1086, 'Flik's *burh*') and Burrow Hill (Suffolk) (*Insula de Burgh* in 1594), where unusually large metalwork assemblages have also confirmed these settlements as 'productive' sites, linked into early medieval networks of production and trade.[23] In both cases, it is reasonable to suggest that the *burh* place-names record the presence of these high-

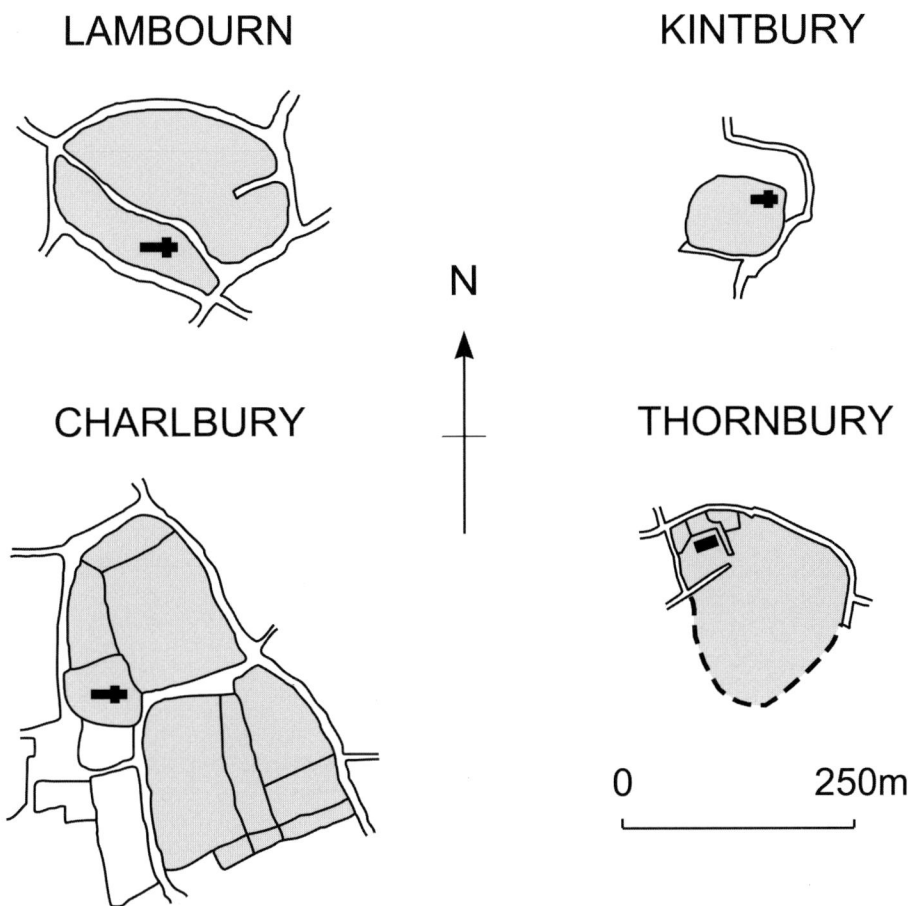

Figure 3. Potential Anglo-Saxon minster enclosures associated with place-names containing OE burh. *After Blair 1988a, 1988b and Astill 1984.*

status Anglo-Saxon settlements, or more accurately the enclosures that once surrounded them.[24] Nevertheless, the question remains; were they monastic settlements, similar to those discussed above, or secular sites, representing the estate centres of kings or aristocrats?

This is a debate that has occupied many minds in recent years. Whilst John Blair in particular has argued for Flixborough's interpretation as a monastic site, largely on the basis of finds of writing styli and other objects indicative of 'minster culture',[25] Chris Loveluck has argued instead for its primary secular function, albeit with periods of clerical and ecclesiastical activity.[26] Burrow Hill's interpretation by its excavator as a monastery founded by the East Anglian royal family has similarly come in for criticism.[27] In recent years, however, sound advice has been offered by Tim Pestell, who warns that 'we have, perhaps, become too obsessed with the idea of identifying and categorising site types'.[28] In reality, there is little to separate Anglo-Saxon monastic settlements archaeologically from secular estate centres: both produce

artefactual evidence for production and trade, both were engaged in document production and both are frequently characterised by major boundary enclosures meriting the descriptive element *burh*. In cases where there is no supporting documentary evidence, then, it is perhaps best to keep an open mind.

Royal and Aristocratic Residences

Bearing in mind the high degree of similarity between Anglo-Saxon ecclesiastical and secular high-status settlements, it is perhaps not surprising that *burh* developed a Middle English form bury, which was used of numerous later medieval manor houses in the Midlands and Home Counties in particular.[29] The predecessors of these manors, many of which were enclosed by moats, were Anglo-Saxon royal and aristocratic residences. More often than not, these too were situated within substantial ditched enclosures. Notable examples revealed by excavation include the great enclosure of the Middle Saxon royal 'palace' of Milfield

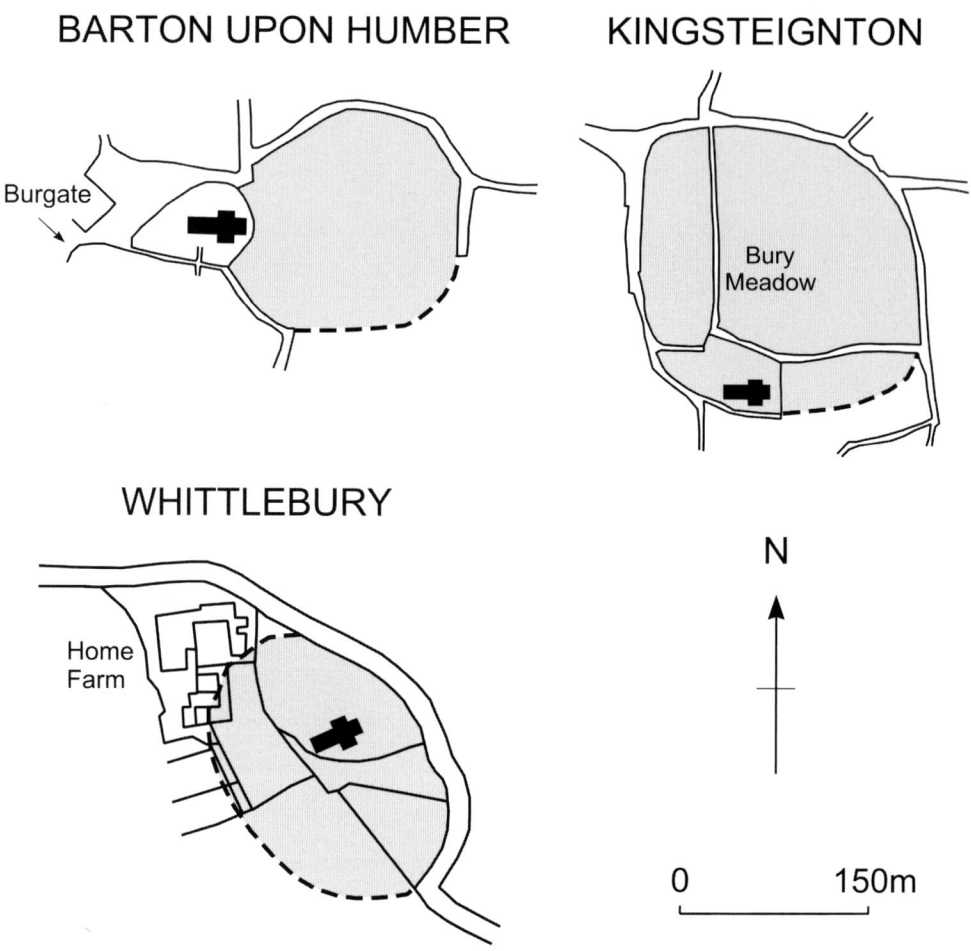

BARTON UPON HUMBER

Burgate

KINGSTEIGNTON

Bury
Meadow

WHITTLEBURY

Home
Farm

N

0   150m

Figure 4. Potential Anglo-Saxon manorial enclosures associated with place-names containing OE burh. *After Rodwell and Rodwell 1982, Weddell 1987 and Jones and Page 2001.*

(Northumberland) and the smaller oval-shaped enclosures at the Late Saxon lordly residences of Faccombe Netherton (Hampshire), Goltho (Lincolnshire) and Trowbridge (Wiltshire).[30] That these enclosures were also known by the term *burh* is suggested by a variety of evidence and three locations that deserve our particular attention are Barton upon Humber (Lincolnshire), Kingsteignton (Devon) and Whittlebury (Northamptonshire).

At Barton upon Humber, a large oval enclosure, measuring *c.* 210 × 160 m, has been revealed to the east of the Anglo-Saxon church of St Peter (Fig. 4). Excavations conducted here between 1978 and 1984 not only confirmed that the enclosure ditch had been dug before 900, but also that the area within and around the enclosure had seen occupation throughout the Anglo-Saxon period.[31] Although various interpretations have been placed on the site, from monastery to Saxon fort and even Danish camp,[32] the consensus of modern opinion now favours an Anglo-Saxon secular function as an aristocratic residence and estate centre.[33] Perhaps more important for us,

however, is the street-name Burgate, which is to be found immediately west of the enclosure. This derives either from the compound *burh-geat*, '*burh* gate', or from Old English/Old Norse *burh-gata*, '*burh* street'.[34] Given that the parallel street to Burgate is Priestgate, the argument for the latter interpretation is perhaps stronger. The best translation is therefore 'street leading up to the *burh*' and this is indeed an accurate description of its spatial relationship to the ditched enclosure.

Kingsteignton was, as the name suggests, the focus for a large Domesday royal estate and there is further evidence – not least its 'river name + *tun*' place-name – to suggest that it also held this status in the later Anglo-Saxon period.[35] In addition, the existing morphology of Kingsteignton village preserves the outline of a sub-circular enclosure with a diameter of *c.* 225 m (Fig. 4). At its heart sits Bury Meadow, where excavations conducted in 1985 revealed ditches of Middle or Late Saxon date.[36] On the basis of the available evidence, it is tempting to suggest that both the *burh* place-name and distinctive village topography betray the existence of an Anglo-Saxon royal residence, surrounded by an imposing ditched (and probably also fenced) enclosure. Confirmation of this is still dependent on any future archaeological research, but the circumstantial evidence is certainly promising.

The place-name Whittlebury, 'Witela's *burh*', may too preserve a record of an enclosed Anglo-Saxon royal residence. A royal legislative assembly (*witan*) is recorded as having taken place here *c.* 930 and, as Peter Sawyer reminds us, such assemblies 'were occasionally held in towns but most ... seem to have been in royal residences in the countryside'.[37] With this in mind, it is intriguing to note that research in Whittlebury, conducted as part of the Whittlewood Project, has yielded clear field evidence for an oval enclosure in the village, measuring *c.* 250 × 125 m, which encompasses the parish church (Fig. 4).[38] This has recently been confirmed as an Iron Age enclosed settlement, perhaps a hillfort,[39] but its position at the heart of the medieval village of Whittlebury does suggest a later re-use. Whilst a monastic function for the enclosure cannot be ruled out (although there is no specific evidence for the existence of a minster here), it is equally likely, particularly in light of the documentary evidence, that it surrounded a royal residence – perhaps a royal hunting-lodge, from which the visiting members of the *witan* could ride out into the adjacent Whittlewood Forest.

Many more Anglo-Saxon royal and aristocratic residences throughout England are likely to be commemorated in major and minor place-names containing the element *burh*. Burystead in Raunds (Northamptonshire), whose name preserves the compound *burh-stede*, 'site of a *burh*', has yielded archaeological evidence for Late Saxon occupation and it may represent the *caput* of Raunds' second Domesday manor, Furnells being the other.[40] The frequent proximity of fields and streets bearing names such as 'The Bury', 'Bury Croft' and 'Berry Lane' to the historic core of villages and towns, meanwhile, should also be noted: W.G. Hoskins' example of The Bury in Thorverton (Devon) is a single case in point.[41]

Particular attention, however, should be paid to place-names containing the compound *burh-geat*, '*burh* gate'.[42] Some academic confusion has surrounded the archaeological significance of this term, but both Barry Cunliffe and Guy Beresford are confident that such features were present at the Late Saxon manorial sites of Portchester (Hampshire) and Goltho (Lincolnshire) in the form of elaborate gateways or gate-towers, which controlled access in and out of the enclosed manorial compound – the *burh*.[43] David Parsons has also interpreted the tower of All Saints Church, Earls Barton (Northamptonshire), as a secular aristocratic gate-tower (a *burh-geat*) that later had a church tacked on, whilst Ann Williams has made a similar observation concerning the tower-nave at St Peter's, Barton upon Humber.[44]

Another compound place-name that deserves special attention is 'Kingsbury', from *cyninges-burh*, 'king's

burh'.[45] Kingsbury in St Albans (Hertfordshire) is first mentioned in the tenth century, when it was occupied by the king's ministers and fishermen.[46] Its location within the city has been the subject of some debate, but Rosalind Niblett has recently suggested that the *burh* in question lay within the Roman walls of *Verulamium*.[47] Kingsbury Field in Old Windsor (Berkshire), meanwhile, has been thought to mark the site of a ninth-century royal palace. Close by, a large mill and a stone building were revealed by archaeological excavation, both of which were apparently destroyed and then replaced in the early tenth century.[48] Similar royal residences may also have existed within Calne, Marlborough and Wilton in Wiltshire, all of which have streets named Kingsbury.[49] Each of these towns was in royal ownership in 1086, whilst Kingsbury Square in Wilton was the findspot for the Wilton hanging bowl – an item that is likely to have had a very wealthy and powerful owner in the decades or centuries following its manufacture, perhaps in *c.* 450.[50] A comparable place-name to 'Kingsbury' is *Earlesburgh*, 'earl's *burh*', which was noted by an antiquarian in connection with the area off Marygate in York and is likely to record the location of the eleventh-century manorial compound of the ruling Anglo-Scandinavian earls of Northumbria.[51]

Towns

Traditionally, the coining of the sense 'town' for *burh* has been ascribed to the late ninth and early tenth centuries, when the West Saxon king Alfred and his son Edward established a network of fortified proto-urban centres, which came to be known by both contemporaries and modern-day historians as *burhs*. In recent years, however, archaeology has revealed that towns of a different sort – unenclosed coastal trading settlements, known as *wics* – were present in England during the preceding Middle Saxon centuries. These were often twinned with enclosed royal and ecclesiastical settlements near by, many of which came to be known by *burh* place-names and later grew to become important urban centres.

Canterbury (Kent) is a case in point (Fig. 5). The area within the Roman walls of *Durovernum* continued to be occupied throughout the post-Roman period and was called *Cantwaraburg*, 'the *burh* of the people of Kent', by the mid eighth century.[52] At this time, Canterbury was a flourishing royal and ecclesiastical centre, its abbey church of SS Peter and Paul having been founded with royal patronage by St Augustine *c.* 598. The majority of eighth-century trade, however, took place at the undefended coastal settlement of Fordwich, 'ford *wic*', some 3 km to the northeast, and, as Tim Tatton-Brown has proposed, it is likely that the two settlements were closely linked.[53] With the advent of Viking raids in the mid ninth century, many of the traders from Fordwich may well have sought refuge within the walls of Canterbury and various charters from the ninth and tenth centuries refer to the *innan burhwara* and the *utan burhwara, i.e.*

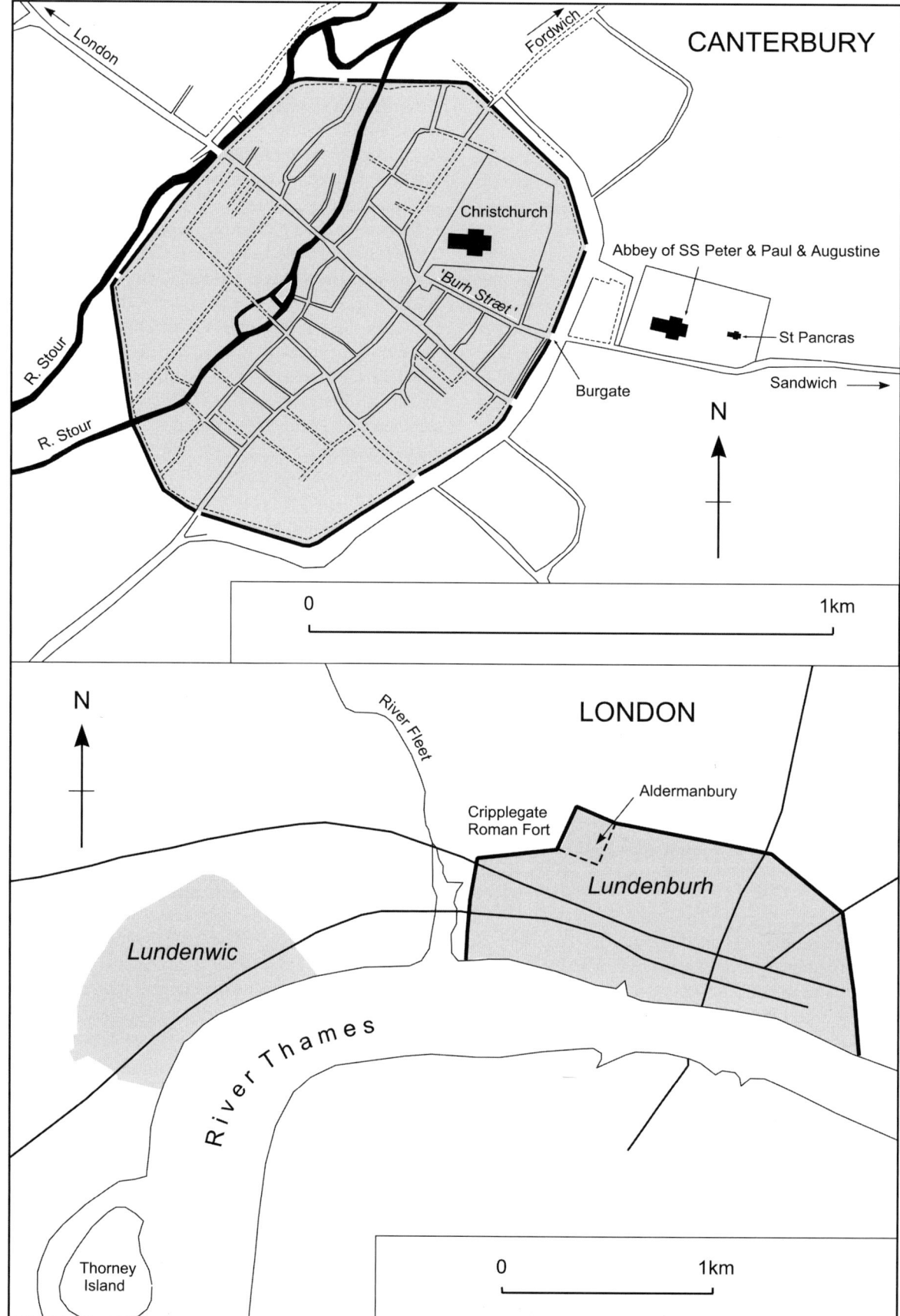

Figure 5. Old English burh *and enclosed urban settlements: Canterbury and London. After Tatton-Brown 1988 and Cowie 2004.*

the people who lived inside and outside the *burh*.[54] In case we are left in any doubt that the *burh* in question was the enclosure formed by the Roman town walls, the Late Saxon town contained a *burh stræt*, '*burh* street', named in a charter of 1002, which led up to the re-used Roman gateway known as Burgate (Fig. 5).[55]

Richborough, also in Kent, offers another example of a royal estate centre with a *burh* place-name, albeit unattested in the pre-Conquest period,[56] which was enclosed within the walls of a Roman fort (*Ritupis*) (Fig. 1) and linked with a trading *wic* (Sandwich, 2 km to the south) at an early date: indeed, several finds of sceattas and pennies of King Offa at Richborough have confirmed its status as an eighth-century 'productive site'.[57] Perhaps the most well known example of a Middle Saxon trading *wic* and an administrative *burh* occurring in close proximity, however, is to be found in London (Fig. 5). Here, recent archaeological investigations have established the identity of the twin settlements referred to in various eighth- and ninth-century documentary sources as *Lundenwic* and *Lundenburh*.[58] International trade took place in the unenclosed riverside settlement of *Lundenwic*, at modern Aldwych and the Strand, whilst the former Roman walled town of Londinium to the east became *Lundenburh*. That the *burh* referred to in *Lundenburh's* place-name was the enclosure formed by the Roman town walls is not in doubt, but it is interesting to note also that an area within the oblong circuit of the Roman fort at Cripplegate attracted the place-name Aldermanbury, '*burh* of the alderman'. This location has traditionally been favoured as the site of King Offa's eighth-century royal palace, but recent archaeological work has cast doubt on this assumption.[59] Nevertheless, the name Aldermanbury still hints at some former importance for this *burh* within a *burh*.

Like Fordwich and Sandwich, *Lundenwic* succumbed to both the fear and reality of Viking attack in the ninth and tenth centuries and was abandoned in favour of the more defensible *Lundenburh*, which developed over time to become the medieval city of London. An important date, however, in the birth of the city was 886, when King Alfred recaptured *Lundenburh* from the Danes and set about creating new streets and markets within a strong defensive circuit.[60] *Lundenburh* now became a *burh* in its Late Saxon urban and military sense and it only missed out on being recorded in the early tenth-century text known as the Burghal Hidage because it was on the northern, Mercian bank of the River Thames, rather than in Wessex to the south.[61]

The thirty-three places listed as *burhs* in the Burghal Hidage represent locations chosen by the West Saxon kings prior to 914 to be fortified local centres in a network of defences against the Vikings that extended across the whole of Wessex. Some of these places, such as Winchester (Hampshire) and Exeter (Devon), were already important settlements, but received a burst of urban planning. Others, however, including Halwell (Devon) and Chisbury (Wiltshire), were simply existing Iron Age hillforts, which

were soon abandoned after a short period of reoccupation. A third category, of which Cricklade (Wiltshire) and Oxford are good examples, were effectively established *de novo* as new towns. The principal factor uniting all these *burhs* was their situation within strong ditched enclosures. Those at Winchester, Cricklade and Oxford have been subject to recent archaeological investigation and were rectilinear in plan, comprising single (Oxford), double (Winchester) and perhaps even triple (Cricklade) sets of ditches, which, at Winchester, were up to 1.7 m deep and 8.2 m wide.[62] It is surely these impressive earthwork enclosures that prompted use of the term *burh*.

Interestingly, none of the known West Saxon burghal forts gave rise to *burh* place-names: this is presumably because the locations chosen already had well-established local nomenclature. Even Avebury (Wiltshire), which Andrew Reynolds has interpreted as a 'lost' ninth-century burghal fort,[63] is more likely to have gained its name in an earlier century, in recognition of an enclosure surrounding a Middle Saxon royal manor or minster, rather than any Late Saxon military stronghold.[64] Nevertheless, Avebury does possess a highly regular settlement plan that may well bear witness, as Reynolds also suggests, to a failed Late Saxon urban enterprise.

Such tenth- and eleventh-century 'new towns' sprang up across England and that they occasionally led to a change of place-name in favour of one incorporating the element *burh* is arguably illustrated by the cases of Peterborough (Cambridgeshire) and Bury St Edmunds (Suffolk), whose names were coined *c.* 1000 to replace *Medeshamstede* and *Beadriceswyrð* respectively.[65] Newbury (Berkshire) too was a 'new town' founded *c.* 1080 by Ernulf de Hesdin on the site of a rural vill listed in the Domesday Book as *Ulvritone*. Recent excavations have revealed its earliest burgage plots on Bartholomew Street and Cheap Street.[66] Unlike Winchester or Oxford, there is no evidence that eleventh-century Newbury was ever fortified to any significant degree. What this surely tells us is that the term *burh* had recently undergone another semantic shift. Whilst it had earlier described the defensive circuits that were needed to protect developing urban centres, it now referred to the urban settlements in their own right, giving the medieval Latin term *burgus*, 'town', and providing us with our modern word 'borough'.

Old English *Burh* as 'enclosure': An historical perspective

So far, I have outlined the archaeological and topographical evidence for the root meaning of *burh* as 'enclosure' and its semantic development over time to become associated with Anglo-Saxon minsters, manors and towns. Now, it is necessary to examine the use of *burh* in a selection of pre-Conquest histories, chronicles, laws and tracts, in order to see whether the interpretations presented thus far are reflected here too.

Turning first to English texts compiled before 750,

including notably the works of Bede, it is interesting to note, as John Blair has done, that of the ten *burh* place-names recorded, 'seven are minsters: Bangor, *Cnobheresburg*, Coldingham (*Colodesburg*), Fladbury, Glastonbury, Malmesbury and Tilbury'.[67] Clearly, then, the monastic association of the element *burh* was well established by the early eighth century, but it was not the only type of settlement being referred to by the term at this date. Two of the remaining three *burh* place-names were towns within Roman wall circuits – London (*Lundenburh*) and Canterbury. As James Campbell has observed, these two cases represent something of an exception to Bede's general rule that OE *ceaster*/Latin *civitas* denoted a place known to have had a significant Roman past, whilst OE *burh*/Latin *urbs* was reserved for an important settlement with no notable Roman heritage.[68] One possible explanation for this, however, is the fact that both *Lundenburh* and Canterbury had trading *wic* settlements closely associated: perhaps the term *burh* was used in these cases to stress the enclosed nature of settlement within the Roman walls, in stark contrast to their daughter settlements near by.

The tenth and final *burh* place-name to be documented in England before 750 was Bamburgh (Northumberland). This was the principal seat of the Anglo-Saxon kings of Northumbria and its construction as a royal citadel, supposedly by King Ida in the sixth century, is also recorded in the late Peterborough manuscript of the *Anglo-Saxon Chronicle*: 'first enclosed by a stockade and thereafter by a wall'.[69] Here, then, is a clear statement that a royal dwelling should be enclosed and a further insight into the layout of a royal residence is provided by the description of another event in the *Anglo-Saxon Chronicle* – the murder of King Cynewulf in his *burh* at the unidentified *Merantun* by the *ætheling* Cyneheard.[70] From the narrative, it is clear that the site was enclosed, as Cyneheard's forces are noted as having to lock its gates against an army of the king. What is seemingly being described here is an enclosed manorial site, not dissimilar to those discussed above at Barton upon Humber and Goltho. The *burh* referred to is the enclosure itself, whilst the gates mentioned are surely those of a *burh-geat*, *i.e.* a gatehouse or gate tower, such as those discussed above at Portchester and Earls Barton.[71]

The various law-codes of the Anglo-Saxon kings also shed some light on the nature of an enclosure surrounding a high-status dwelling. In the Laws of Ine (688–726), we read of the crime of *burh-bryce*, 'breaching a *burh*', which is defined in the following terms: '120 shillings compensation shall be paid for breaking into the fortified premises (*burh*) of the king or [those of] a bishop within his sphere of jurisdiction; [for breaking into those] of an *ealdorman* 80 shillings; into those of a king's *thegn* 60 shillings; into those of a nobleman who holds land 35 shillings'.[72] What is interesting about this law is the tacit implication that only noblemen, *i.e.* those holding the rank of *thegn* or above, owned enclosures around their

dwellings that could be referred to by the term *burh*. Indeed, when the law of *burh-bryce* was reiterated in the Laws of Alfred (871–99), the crime of breaking through the enclosure of a free peasant (*ceorl*) was described not as *burh-bryce*, but as *edor-bryce*, 'breaching a hedge or fence'.[73] A *burh*, then, was clearly an enclosure that was more substantial than a mere hedge or fence and it is possible that the word was used in contrast to the terms *worð* and *worðig*. Law 40 of the Laws of Ine states that 'a commoner's premises (*ceorles worðig*) shall be fenced both winter and summer',[74] and this leads us to the logical conclusion that, whilst a *burh* was an impressive ditched enclosure associated with a high-status site, a *worð* was a less substantial fenced enclosure, owned and maintained instead by a free peasant.[75]

Further detail concerning the construction and maintenance of a manorial *burh* may be gleaned from two eleventh-century legal tracts, entitled *Rectitudines singularum personarum* ('On the Rights and Ranks of People') and *Gerefa* ('The Reeve'). According to *Rectitudines*, the superior peasants, known as *geneatas*, were required to perform a number of public services for their lord, including 'to build and fence the *burh*', whilst 'to make good the hedges' of the *burh* was among the duties that a good reeve must perform, as described by *Gerefa*.[76] Evidently, fences and hedges were common means of defining the *burh*, but that it was also ditched, as the examples identified through archaeology and topographical analysis attest, is indicated by the mid-eleventh-century manorial survey of Tidenham (Gloucestershire), which stipulates that each lesser peasant (*gebur*) must 'fence and dig one pole of the *burh-hege*'.[77]

The term *burh-geat* also occurs in two pre-Conquest legal tracts. The eleventh-century 'promotion law' (*Geþyncðo*) contains the following passage setting out the means by which a *ceorl* could obtain the rank of *thegn*: 'and if a *ceorl* prospered, that he possessed fully five hides of land of his own, [church and kitchen] a bell and a *burh-geat*, a seat and special office in the king's hall, then was he henceforth entitled to the rights of a *thegn*'.[78] The late tenth- or early eleventh-century tract entitled *Be Griðe* ('On Peace'), meanwhile, defines the king's personal peace as extending 'from his *burh-geat*'.[79] What these texts both seem to be suggesting is that the *burh-geat*, *i.e.* the gate tower or gatehouse, was an essential and highly important part of an Anglo-Saxon manorial complex, marking its legal threshold and symbolizing the status of its inhabitants. In light of this evidence, we should expect to find many more such structures in the archaeological record at sites of known pre-Conquest manorial status.

Turning finally to documentary evidence relating to the use of the term *burh* in its Late Saxon military and urban senses, it is necessary to consider briefly the Anglo-Saxon public service of *burhbot* ('boroughwork'). This obligation to build and maintain fortifications, which was levied on all land, is first recorded in Mercian charters of the mid eighth century, but it came into its own in Wessex in the second half of the ninth century, in response to the Viking threat.[80] The text known as the Burghal Hidage essentially provides us with a detailed calculation of the *burhbot* arrangements for the West Saxon kingdom as they were in the years around 900, together with a list of the principal forts.[81] In the Grately Laws of Æthelstan (924–39), meanwhile, under the heading *Be burhbot*, 'on boroughwork', in some manuscripts, we read that 'every fortress (*burh*) shall be repaired by a fortnight after Rogation days'.[82]

Many of the Alfredian forts in Wessex, however, were also flourishing urban settlements and it is undoubtedly simplistic to separate out the military and civil functions of central places regarded as *burhs* in the Late Saxon period. This point is particularly apt when considering the significance of the passage in the Peterborough manuscript of the *Anglo-Saxon Chronicle* describing the change of name for what is now Peterborough from *Medeshamstede* to *Burch* (*i.e. Burh*), following the construction of a wall around its monastery.[83] Whilst it is possible to interpret this episode from a solely military perspective, regarding the provision of the wall as 'a practical defence at such times',[84] we should not lose sight of the fact that the century 950–1050 saw planned urban development at numerous monastic settlements across England.[85] Indeed, it is perhaps just as likely that Peterborough's wall and change of name reflected new-found urban status, particularly since Peterborough is known to have had a pre-Conquest mint.[86] The use of the term *burh* in Late Saxon England, then, was almost certainly multi-layered and we should not be restricted by the narrow definitions of our modern words 'town', 'monastery' and 'fortress'.[87]

'Burton' place-names

Before moving to a conclusion, it is necessary to address one last aspect of *burh* that has caused a great deal of academic debate in recent years – its significance when compounded with the element *tun*, 'farm/settlement', either in its nominative (*burhtun*), genitive (*byrhtun*) or dative (*byrigtun*) forms, usually giving the modern names Burton and Bourton. Such 'Burton' place-names are distributed widely across England, although with notable concentrations in the Welsh Marches and Lincolnshire (Fig. 6).[88] They have attracted numerous interpretations. Margaret Gelling and Barrie Cox have both opted for a strictly military explanation, regarding them as evidence for networks of forts operational during the conquests and expansion of the various Anglo-Saxon kingdoms in the Middle Saxon centuries.[89] John Blair instead prefers to see such places as farms adjoining minster churches, 'using *burh* in its specifically monastic sense'.[90] Ann Williams, however, has suggested the meaning 'defensible house', carrying the manorial sense of *burh*.[91]

Given the wide variety of uses outlined in this article for the element *burh* in Anglo-Saxon England, it would clearly be naïve to insist that *burhtun* and its variants had only one specific connotation. Nevertheless, there

is one piece of evidence, largely overlooked until now, which I believe sheds important new light on the term's archaeological and historical significance – its frequent occurrence in proximity to notable Anglo-Saxon estate centres and/or minster settlements, either in royal or ecclesiastical ownership. Great and Little Bourton in the historic parish of Cropredy (Oxfordshire) is a notable case in point. Cropredy was a major estate centre held by the bishop of Lincoln at the time of Domesday and, as John Blair has argued, it is also likely that it possessed an important pre-Conquest minster church associated with the cult of St Freomund.[92] Other examples are too numerous to list here, but include Bourton (Berkshire), which lies adjacent to the royal estate centre and minster settlement of Shrivenham, Burton upon Stather (Lincolnshire), which is only 2.5 km south of Flixborough, and Bourton (Shropshire), which is situated within the historic parish of Much Wenlock – a minster site since the seventh century and associated with St Mildburh.[93]

As Margaret Gelling's gazetteer of 'Burton' place-names reveals, the majority of such places went unrecorded before the thirteenth or fourteenth centuries;[94] a fact that, in the light of the evidence presented above, can best be explained in terms of their likely secondary development within larger landholdings, much in the same way as the widespread 'Bartons', 'Berwicks' and 'Kingstons' of Anglo-Saxon England.[95] In conclusion, therefore, it is likely that the primary meaning of *burhtun* was 'farm dependent on a *burh*', using *burh* in either its monastic or manorial context. I can find little supporting evidence for the military sense of *burh* in such place-names, as claimed by Gelling and Cox. One final caveat that we would be wise to bear in mind, however, is Rosamond Faith's suggestion that some 'Burton' place-names may in fact preserve the compound *gebura-tun*, 'farm of the *geburs*', rather than *burhtun*.[96] One case where this is perhaps likely is Black Bourton, near Bampton (Oxfordshire). In the words of John Blair, '*gebur* (boor) is the standard late Anglo-Saxon term for a lowland inland peasant, and in some counties Domesday uses it as equivalent to *colibertus*, 'freed-man'; in the Oxfordshire folios these only occur at Bampton, where there were 17 *buri* as well as 40 *villani* and 13 *bordarii*'.[97]

Conclusion

English place-names containing *burh* have long been regarded as amongst those most useful to the modern archaeologist. However, academic discussion of the element has until now focussed almost entirely on its association with fortified sites of prehistoric or Late Saxon date. What this paper has set out to achieve is a wider recognition of the many other historical and archaeological associations that *burh* acquired during the course of the Anglo-Saxon period, all of which can be shown to correlate with significant ditched, fenced, hedged or even walled enclosures on the ground. Furthermore, the

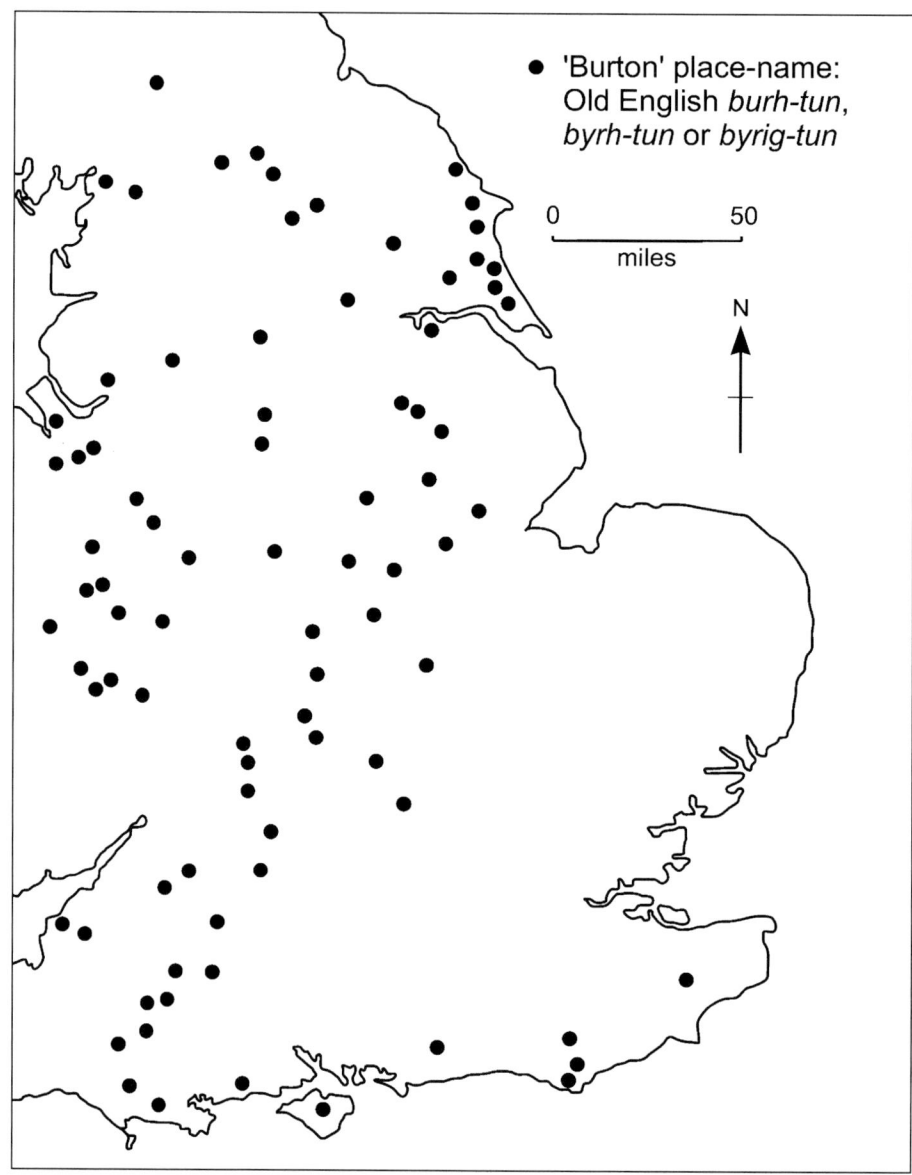

Figure 6. Distribution map of 'Burton' place-names. After Gelling 1989.

importance of these associations cannot be overstressed. Current research identifies Middle Saxon royal manors and minsters as major catalysts in the processes of urban, economic and territorial development in England,[98] whilst the construction of smaller manorial compounds in the Late Saxon period is rightly regarded as a key factor in the explanation of the processes of nucleation and planning in villages and towns.[99] In a growing number of cases, excavation and fieldwork is establishing the link between *burh* place-names and Anglo-Saxon settlement enclosures and, based on the evidence assembled and discussed above, it is clear that many more places so named will one day yield similar archaeological evidence

for their origins. As such, a large proportion of place-names containing *burh* across England are potentially of enormous value to those investigating the origins of medieval settlements and they are surely deserving of future targeted research.

Acknowledgements

I would especially like to thank Mick Aston, Chris Gerrard and Barry Lane for their many useful thoughts and observations. All figures were drawn from the originals by the author. Any errors or inaccuracies are my own.

Notes

1. Cox 1976, 66
2. Mills 1998, 19, 122
3. Smith 1956, 62
4. Hume 1974, 66
5. Smith 1956, 58–62
6. Gelling 1997, 146
7. Griffith 1984a; Silvester and Bidwell 1984; Maxfield 1985; Todd 1985; Weddell, Reed and Simpson 1993
8. There are forty-eight hillforts in the county, so fifty-six per cent have place-names containing Old English *burh*.
9. Crawford 1929; Bersu 1940; Griffith 1984b. See also Griffith 1986 for a wider discussion of Old English *burh* place-names and prehistoric enclosures in Devon.
10. Burrow 1981, 47–54
11. *Ibid.*, 13. See also M. Gelling in Rahtz, Woodward, Burrow, Everton, Watts, Leach, Hirst, Fowler and Gardner 1992, 5.
12. See Gelling 1997, 147–8, for a consideration of other Old English *eorth-burh* names in England.
13. Leahy 2003, 150–2
14. Griffiths 1983
15. S 368; S 647; Chandler 2003, 7–8; Reynolds 2005, 175
16. Stenton 1970, 317–21. See Sims-Willliams 1990 for the historical background to these monasteries.
17. *Ibid.*, 320–1
18. Blair 1998
19. Barker 1982, 106
20. Sims-Williams 1990, 93; Blair 2005, 250
21. Blair 1988a; 1994, 67–8
22. Blair 1988a, 3
23. Loveluck 1998; 2001; Fenwick 1984. For 'productive' sites in general, see Pestell and Ulmschneider 2003.
24. A portion of what is interpreted as a Middle Saxon boundary ditch has been revealed at Flixborough: Loveluck 1998, fig. 3. Tim Pestell, meanwhile, has speculated that the island location of Burrow Hill, surrounded by water on all sides, may account for the monastic 'enclosure' here: Pestell 2004, 52. For the occurrence of enclosed settlements in Anglo-Saxon England as a whole, see Reynolds 2003.
25. Blair 1996, 9; 2005, 204–12
26. Loveluck 1998, 159; 2001, 121
27. Fenwick 1984, 40–1; Pestell 2004, 52, 61–2, 73
28. Pestell 2003, 137
29. Smith 1956, 59; Gelling 1997, 143; Williams 1992, 222
30. Scull and Harding 1990; Fairbrother 1990; Beresford 1987; Graham and Davies 1993
31. Rodwell and Rodwell 1982
32. *Ibid.*, 308–10; Cox 1994, 42–6; Bryant 1994, 73–7
33. Williams 1992, 234–5; Reynolds 2003, 117
34. Cox 1994, 44. See below for further discussion of Old English *burh-geat*.
35. Weddell 1987, 75–81. For the significance of 'river name + Old English *tun*' place-names, see Everitt 1986, 72–3.
36. Weddell 1987, 89
37. Attenborough 1922, 169; Sawyer 1983, 277
38. Jones and Page 2001, 22
39. Dyer, Jones and Page 2002; Mark Page *pers. comm.*
40. Cadman 1983, 121–2; Youngs, Gaimster and Barry 1988, 265. See Williams 1992, 236, however, for a note of caution.
41. Hoskins 1955, 51
42. Examples include Boreat (Dorset), Buckhatch (Essex) and Burgate (Hampshire, Suffolk and Surrey): Smith 1956, 62.
43. Cunliffe 1976, 303; Beresford 1987, 30–7. The Watergate at Portchester, which was re-built in the Late Saxon period, may represent the *burh-geat* here, rather than the tower S18.
44. Audouy, Dix and Parsons 1995; Williams 1992, 234–5. See also Renn 1994.

45. 'Kingsbury' place-names can be found in Greater London, Warwickshire and Somerset. Conisbrough (South Yorkshire) has the same meaning, although its first element is **ON** *konungr*, 'king': Mills 1998, 95, 206.
46. Saunders and Havercroft 1978, 1
47. Niblett 2001, 11
48. Astill 1984, 79
49. Haslam 1984
50. Youngs 1998; Draper 2006, 49
51. Hall 1988, 235–6
52. Ottaway 1992, 112–15; Ekwall 1960, 85; Campbell 1979, 36
53. Tatton-Brown 1988. Fordwich first appears on record as *Fordeuuicum* in a charter, dated 675, of King Hlothhere; S 7.
54. S 1215; S 1506; Brooks 1984, 28. See also Tatton-Brown 1988, 228.
55. S 905; Tatton-Brown 1988, fig. 10.3
56. The Old English *burh* element in Richborough's place-name is first recorded in the form *Ratteburg'* in 1197; Gelling 1997, 56. This does not necessarily mean, however, that it was not known by the term Old English *burh* at a much earlier date.
57. Tatton-Brown 1988, 217, 226; Rigold and Metcalf 1984, 258–61
58. Hobley 1988; Vince 1990
59. Cowie 2004, 203; *contra* Hobley 1988, 73–4
60. Hobley 1988, 76–80
61. This is not to say that Mercia did not develop urban *burhs* of its own. Excavations at Hereford have suggested that town planning here anticipated the layout of many West Saxon *burhs* by several decades; Shoesmith 1982. See also Blair 2005, 287–90, for a discussion of eighth-century Mercian town planning.
62. Biddle 1976, 128; Haslam 2003; Blair 1994, 146–52
63. Reynolds 2001; Pollard and Reynolds 2002, 204–10
64. Draper 2006, 103
65. *ASC* 963 E, Swanton 2000, 117; Ekwall 1960, 78, 364
66. Astill 1984, 79–80; Vince, Lobb and Richards 1997
67. Blair 2005, 250. See also Cox 1976, 47.
68. Campbell 1979, 34–43
69. *ASC* 547 E, Swanton 2000, 17
70. *ASC* 755, Swanton 2000, 47–9
71. The word Old English *bur*, 'bower', is used in some manuscripts to describe one of the buildings at *Merantun*; *ASC* 755 AA²DE, Swanton 2000, 47.
72. Ine 45, Attenborough 1922, 50–1
73. Alfred 40, Attenborough 1922, 82–3; Bosworth and Toller 1898, 239
74. Ine 40, Attenborough 1922, 48–9
75. For two recent surveys of Old English *worð* place-names, see Costen 1992 and English 2002.
76. Liebermann 1898, 445, 454–5; Douglas and Greenaway 1953, 813; Swanton 1993, 26
77. S 1555; Douglas and Greenaway 1953, 817; Robertson 1956, 204–7. Old English *burh-hege* is a general term for a substantial enclosure that could be fenced or walled, as well as a hedged in our modern sense of the word; see Williams 1992, 227–8.
78. Liebermann 1898, 456; Whitelock 1955, 432. The words in square brackets appear only in the *Textus Roffensis* version.
79. Liebermann 1898, 390; Williams 1992, 226
80. Brooks 1996, 129; Blair 2005, 287
81. See Hill and Rumble 1996 for a detailed discussion of the Burghal Hidage.
82. II Æthelstan 13, Attenborough 1922, 134–5
83. *ASC* 963 E, Swanton 2000, 117
84. Swanton 2000, 117
85. Blair 2005, 330–41
86. Dolley 1952
87. For a further spiritual dimension to the military and urban senses of Old English *burh*, see Swanton 1987, 142; Blair 2005, 247–51.
88. Gelling 1989, 153

89. *Ibid.*; Gelling 1992, 119–22; Cox 1994
90. Blair 2005, 251
91. Williams 1992, 224
92. Blair 1994, 66–7, 75–6
93. Astill 1984, 57–8; Blair 2005, 301–2; Sims-Williams 1990, 98–9

94. Gelling 1989, 149–53
95. See Faith 1997, 36–47, for a discussion of these place-names.
96. *Ibid.*, 80
97. Blair 1994, 141
98. See, for example, Blair 2005, 246–90.
99. See, for example, Faith 1997, 153–77.

Abbreviations

S = Sawyer, P. 1968. *Anglo-Saxon Charters: An Annotated List and Bibliography*, R. Hist. Soc. Guides and Handbooks, 8, London: R. Hist. Soc.

Bibliography

Astill, G. 1984. 'The towns of Berkshire', in J. Haslam (ed.), *Anglo-Saxon Towns in Southern England*, 53–86, Chichester: Phillimore.

Attenborough, F. 1922. *The Laws of the Earliest English Kings*, Cambridge: Cambridge University Press.

Audouy, M., Dix, B. and Parsons, D. 1995. 'The tower of All Saints' Church, Earls Barton, Northamptonshire: its construction and context', *ArchJ*, **152**, 73–94.

Barker, K. 1982. 'The early history of Sherborne', in S. Pearce (ed.), *The Early Church in Western Britain and Ireland*, 77–116, BAR British Series, 102, Oxford: BAR.

Beresford, G. 1987. *Goltho: The Development of an Early Medieval Clayland Manor, c. 850–1150*, English Heritage Archaeological Report, 6, London: English Heritage.

Bersu, G. 1940. 'Excavations at Little Woodbury, Wilts.', *Proc. Prehist. Soc.*, **6**, 30–111.

Biddle, M. 1976. 'Towns', in D. Wilson (ed.), *The Archaeology of Anglo-Saxon England*, 99–150, London: Methuen.

Blair, J. 1988a. 'Thornbury, Binsey: a probable defensive enclosure associated with St Frideswide', *Oxoniensia*, **53**, 3–20.

Blair, J. 1988b. 'Minster churches in the landscape', in D. Hooke (ed.), *Anglo-Saxon Settlements*, 35–58, Oxford: Blackwell.

Blair, J. 1994. *Anglo-Saxon Oxfordshire*, Stroud: Alan Sutton.

Blair, J. 1996. 'Palaces or minsters? Northampton and Cheddar reconsidered', *ASE*, **25**, 97–121.

Blair, J. 1998. 'Bampton: an Anglo-Saxon minster', *Current Archaeol.*, **160**, 124–30.

Blair, J. 2005. *The Church in Anglo-Saxon Society*, Oxford: Oxford University Press.

Bosworth, J. and Toller, T. 1898. *An Anglo-Saxon Dictionary*, Oxford: Oxford University Press.

Brooks, N. 1984. *The Early History of the Church of Canterbury*, Leicester: Leicester University Press.

Brooks, N. 1996. 'The administrative background to the Burghal Hidage', in D. Hill and A. Rumble (eds), *The Defence of Wessex: The Burghal Hidage and Anglo-Saxon Fortifications*, 128–50, Manchester: Manchester University Press.

Bryant, G. 1994. *The Early History of Barton upon Humber*, 2nd edit., Barton upon Humber: Workers' Educational Association, Barton upon Humber Branch.

Burrow, I. 1981. *Hillfort and Hilltop Settlement in Somerset in the First to Eighth Centuries AD*, BAR British Series, 91, Oxford: BAR.

Cadman, G. 1983. 'Raunds 1977–1983: an excavation summary', *MA*, **27**, 107–22.

Campbell, J. 1979. 'Bede's words for places', in P. Sawyer (ed.), *Names, Words and Graves: Early Medieval Settlement*, 34–54, Leeds: School of History, University of Leeds.

Chandler, J. 2003. *Devizes and Central Wiltshire*, East Knoyle: Hobnob Press.

Costen, M. 1992. 'Huish and worth: Old English survivals in a later landscape', *ASSAH*, **5**, 65–83.

Cowie, R. 2004. 'The evidence for royal sites in Middle Anglo-Saxon London', *MA*, **48**, 201–9.

Cox, B. 1976. 'The place-names of the earliest English records', *JEPNS*, **8**, 12–66.

Cox, B. 1994. 'The pattern of Old English *burh* in Lindsey', *ASE*, **23**, 35–56.

Crawford, O. 1929. 'Woodbury: two marvellous air photographs', *Antiquity*, **3**, 452–5.

Cunliffe, B. 1976. *Excavations at Portchester Castle Vol. 2: Saxon*, Reports of the Research Committee of the Society of Antiquaries of London, 33, London: Society of Antiquaries.

Dolley, R. 1952. 'A new Anglo-Saxon mint – Medesham*stede*', *BNJ*, **27**, 263–5.

Douglas, D. and Greenaway, G. (eds) 1953. *English Historical Documents, Vol. 2, 1042–1189*, London: Eyre and Spottiswoode.

Draper, S. 2006. *Landscape, Settlement and Society in Roman and Early Medieval Wiltshire*, BAR Brit. Ser. 419, Oxford: Archaeopress.

Dyer, C., Jones, R. and Page, M. 2002. 'The Whittlewood Project', *Med. Settlement Research Group Annual Report*, **17**, 42.

Ekwall, E. 1960. *The Concise Oxford Dictionary of English Place-Names*, 4th edit., Oxford: Oxford University Press.

English, J. 2002. 'Worths in a landscape context', *Landscape Hist.*, **24**, 45–51.

Everitt, A. 1986. *Continuity and Colonization: The Evolution of Kentish Settlement*, Leicester: Leicester University Press.

Fairbrother, J. 1990. *Faccombe Netherton: Excavations of a Saxon and Medieval Manorial Complex*, British Museum Occasional Paper, 74, London: British Museum.

Faith, R. 1997. *The English Peasantry and the Growth of Lordship*, Leicester: Leicester University Press.

Fenwick, V. 1984. 'Insula de Burgh: Excavations at Burrow Hill, Butley, Suffolk, 1978–81', *ASSAH*, **3**, 35–54.

Field, D., Brown, G. and McOmish, D. 2005. 'Some observations on change, consolidation and perception in a chalk landscape', in G. Brown, D. Field and D. McOmish (eds), *The Avebury Landscape: Aspects of the Field Archaeology of the Marlborough Downs*, 1–11, Oxford: Oxbow.

Gelling, M. 1989. 'The place-names Burton and variants', in S. Hawkes (ed.), *Weapons and Warfare in Anglo-Saxon England*, 145–53, Oxford: Oxford University Committee for Archaeology.

Gelling, M. 1992. *The West Midlands in the Early Middle Ages*, Leicester: Leicester University Press.

Gelling, M. 1997. *Signposts to the Past: Place-Names and the History of England*, 3rd edit., London: Phillimore.

Gover, J., Mawer, A. and Stenton, F. 1939. *The Place-Names of Wiltshire*, EPNS, 16, Cambridge: Cambridge University Press.

Graham, A. and Davies, S. 1998. *Excavations at Trowbridge, Wiltshire, 1977 and 1986–1988*, Wessex Archaeology Report, 2, Salisbury: Wessex Archaeology.

Griffith, F. 1984a. 'Roman military sites in Devon: some recent discoveries', *Devon Archaeol. Soc. Proc.*, **42**, 11–32.

Griffith, F. 1984b. 'Aerial reconnaissance in Devon in 1984: a preliminary report and the discovery of a hillfort', *Devon Archaeol. Soc. Proc.*, **42**, 7–10.

Griffith, F. 1986. '*Burh* and *Beorg* in Devon', *Nomina*, **10**, 93–103.

Griffiths, M. 1983. 'A note on *Blakeberege*', *Archaeologia Cambrensis*, **132**, 126–32.

Hall, R. 1988. 'The making of Domesday York', in D. Hooke (ed.), *Anglo-Saxon Settlements*, 233–48, Oxford: Blackwell.

Hall, T. 2000. *Minster Churches in the Dorset Landscape*, BAR British Series, 304, Oxford: Archaeopress.

Haslam, J. 1984. 'The towns of Wiltshire', in J. Haslam (ed.),

Anglo-Saxon Towns in Southern England, 87–148, Chichester: Phillimore.

Haslam, J. 2003. 'Excavations at Cricklade, Wiltshire, 1975', *Internet Archaeology*, **14**, at http://intarch.ac.uk/journal/issue14/haslam_index (accessed 15 July 2005).

Hill, D. and Rumble, A. (eds) 1996. *The Defence of Wessex: The Burghal Hidage and Anglo-Saxon Fortifications*, Manchester: Manchester University Press.

Hobley, B. 1988. 'Lundenwic and *Lundenburh*: two cities rediscovered', in R. Hodges and B. Hobley (eds), *The Rebirth of Towns in the West, AD 700–1050*, 69–82, CBA Research Report, 68, London: CBA.

Hoskins, W. 1955. *The Making of the English Landscape*, London: Hodder and Stoughton.

Hume, K., 1974. 'The concept of the hall in Old English poetry', *ASE*, **3**, 63–74.

Jones, R. and Page, M. 2001. 'Medieval settlements and landscapes in the Whittlewood area: interim report 2001–2', *Med. Settlement Research Group Annual Report*, **16**, 15–25.

Leahy, K. 2003. 'Middle Anglo-Saxon Lincolnshire: an emerging picture', in T. Pestell and K. Ulmschneider (eds), *Markets in Early Medieval Europe: Trading and 'Productive' Sites, 650–850*, 138–54, Bollington: Windgather Press.

Liebermann, F. 1898. *Die Gesetze der Angelsachsen*, Vol. 1, Halle: Max Niemeyer.

Loveluck, C. 1998. 'A high-status Anglo-Saxon settlement at Flixborough, Lincolnshire', *Antiquity*, **72**, 146–61.

Loveluck, C. 2001. 'Wealth, waste and conspicuous consumption: Flixborough and its importance for Middle and Late Saxon rural settlement studies', in H. Hamerow and A. MacGregor (eds), *Image and Power in the Archaeology of Early Medieval Britain*, 78–130, Oxford: Oxbow.

Maxfield, V. 1985. 'Excavations at Ashbury in 1983 with a note on Broadbury Castle', *Devon Archaeol. Soc. Proc.*, **43**, 51–8.

Maxfield, V. (ed.) 1989. *The Saxon Shore, A Handbook*, Exeter Studies in History, 25, Exeter: University of Exeter Press.

McOmish, D., Field, D. and Brown, G. 2002. *The Field Archaeology of the Salisbury Plain Training Area*, Swindon: English Heritage.

Mills, A. 1998. *Dictionary of English Place-Names*, 2nd edit., Oxford: Oxford University Press.

Niblett, R. 2001. 'Why Verulamium?', in M. Henig and P. Linley (eds), *Alban and St Albans*, 1–12, British Archaeological Association Conference Transactions, 24, Leeds: Maney.

Ottaway, P. 1992. *Archaeology in British Towns from the Emperor Claudius to the Black Death*, London: Routledge.

Pestell, T. 2003. 'The afterlife of 'productive' sites in East Anglia', in T. Pestell and K. Ulmschneider (eds), *Markets in Early Medieval Europe: Trading and 'Productive' Sites, 650–850*, 122–37, Bollington: Windgather Press.

Pestell, T. 2004. *Landscapes of Monastic Foundation: The Establishment of Religious Houses in East Anglia, c. 650–1200*, Anglo-Saxon Studies, 5, Woodbridge: Boydell.

Pestell, T. and Ulmschneider, K. (eds) 2003. *Markets in Early Medieval Europe: Trading and 'Productive' Sites, 650–850*, Bollington: Windgather Press.

Pollard, J. and Reynolds, A. 2002. *Avebury: The Biography of a Landscape*, Stroud: Tempus.

Rahtz, P., Woodward, A., Burrow, I., Everton, A., Watts, L., Leach, P., Hirst, S., Fowler, P. and Gardner, K. 1992. *Cadbury Congresbury 1968–73. A Late/Post-Roman Hilltop Settlement in Somerset*, BAR British Series, 223, Oxford: BAR.

Renn, D., 1994. '*Burhgeat* and *gonfanon*: two sidelights from the Bayeux Tapestry', *ANS*, **16**, 177–98.

Reynolds, A. 2001. 'Avebury: a late Anglo-Saxon *burh*?', *Antiquity*, **75**, 29–30.

Reynolds, A. 2003. 'Boundaries and settlements in later sixth to eleventh-century England', *ASSAH*, **12**, 98–135.

Reynolds, A. 2005. 'From *pagus* to parish: territory and settlement in the Avebury region from the Late Roman period to the Domesday Survey', in G. Brown, D. Field and D. McOmish (eds), *The Avebury Landscape: Aspects of the Field Archaeology of the Marlborough Downs*, 164–80, Oxford: Oxbow.

Rigold, S. and Metcalf, D. 1984. 'A revised check-list of English finds of sceattas', in D. Hill and D. Metcalf (eds), *Sceattas in England and on the Continent*, 245–68, BAR British Series, 128, Oxford: BAR.

Robertson, A. 1956. *Anglo-Saxon Charters*, Cambridge: Cambridge University Press.

Rodwell, W. and Rodwell, K. 1982. 'St Peter's church, Barton upon Humber: excavation and structural study', *AntJ*, **62**, 283–315.

Saunders, C. and Havercroft, A. 1978. 'Excavations in the city and district of St Albans 1974–76', *Hertfordshire Archaeol.*, **6**, 1–77.

Sawyer, P., 1968. *Anglo-Saxon Charters: An Annotated List and Bibliography*, R. Hist. Soc. Guides and Handbooks, 8, London: R. Hist. Soc.

Sawyer, P. 1983. 'The royal *tun* in pre-Conquest England', in P. Wormald, D. Bullough and R. Collins (eds), *Ideal and Reality in Frankish and Anglo-Saxon Society*, 273–99, Oxford: Basil Blackwell.

Scull, C. and Harding, A. 1990. 'Two early medieval cemeteries at Milfield, Northumberland', *Durham Archaeol. Jnl*, **6**, 1–29.

Shoesmith, R. 1982. *Hereford City Excavations Volume 2*, CBA Research Report, 46, London: CBA.

Silvester, R. and Bidwell, P. 1984. 'A Roman site at Woodbury, Axminster', *Devon Archaeol. Soc. Proc.*, **42**, 33–58.

Sims-Williams, P. 1990. *Religion and Literature in Western England, 600–800*, Cambridge: Cambridge University Press.

Smith, A. 1956. *English Place-Name Elements*, Vol. 1, EPNS, 25, Cambridge: Cambridge University Press.

Stenton, F. 1970. 'The place of women in Anglo-Saxon society', in D. Stenton (ed.), *Preparatory to Anglo-Saxon England*, 314–24, Oxford: Oxford University Press.

Swanton, M. 1987. *English Literature Before Chaucer*, London: Longman.

Swanton, M. (ed.) 1993. *Anglo-Saxon Prose*, 2nd edit., London: Dent.

Swanton, M. (trans. and ed.) 2000. *The Anglo-Saxon Chronicles*, 2nd edit., London: Phoenix Press.

Tatton-Brown, T. 1988. 'The Anglo-Saxon towns of Kent', in D. Hooke (ed.), *Anglo-Saxon Settlements*, 213–32, Oxford: Blackwell.

Todd, M. 1985. 'The Roman fort at Bury Barton, Devonshire', *Britannia*, **16**, 49–56.

Vince, A. 1990. *Saxon London: An Archaeological Investigation*, London: Seaby.

Vince, A., Lobb, S. and Richards, J. 1997. *Excavations in Newbury, Berkshire, 1979–1990*, Wessex Archaeology Report, 13, Salisbury: Wessex Archaeology.

Weddell, P. 1987. 'Excavations within the Anglo-Saxon enclosure at Berry Meadow, Kingsteignton, in 1985', *Devon Archaeol. Soc. Proc.*, **45**, 75–96.

Weddell, P., Reed, S. and Simpson, S. 1993. 'Excavation of the Exeter-Dorchester Roman road at the River Yarty and the Roman fort ditch and settlement site at Woodbury, near Axminster', *Devon Archaeol. Soc. Proc.*, **51**, 33–134.

Whitelock, D. (ed.) 1955. *English Historical Documents, Vol. 1, c. 500–1042*, London: Eyre and Spottiswoode.

Williams, A. 1992. 'A bell-house and a *burh-geat*: lordly residences in England before the Norman Conquest', in C. Harper-Bill and R. Harvey (eds), *Medieval Knighthood 4*, 221–40, Woodbridge: Boydell.

Youngs, S. 1998. 'Medieval hanging bowls from Wiltshire', *Wiltshire Archaeol. and Nat. Hist. Soc. Mag.*, **91**, 35–41.

Youngs, S., Gaimster, D. and Barry, T. 1988. 'Medieval Britain and Ireland in 1987', *MA*, **32**, 225–314.

The Distribution of the 'Winchester' Style in Late Saxon England: Metalwork Finds from the Danelaw

Jane F. Kershaw

The 'Winchester' style captures the foliate and zoomorphic motifs characteristic of English art from the mid-tenth to eleventh centuries. Traditionally, the style has been seen as a southern English phenomenon, closely tied to the reformed monastic communities in which it was thought the style originated. New finds of metalwork, largely recovered through metal-detecting, encourage a re-evaluation of the style's distribution and significance. Discoveries of strap-ends and other dress items in the 'Winchester' style show that the style permeated much further north and east than was thought. These items demonstrate that the style was applied to an array of secular artefacts, of varying quality. This paper outlines the appearance of the style on common dress items and fittings, revealing the widespread distribution of 'Winchester' style metalwork within the Danelaw. It presents evidence for the production of the style within the Scandinavian area of settlement and relates its appearance and use to broader questions of social and cultural identity.

Introduction

The 'Winchester' style refers to the art produced under the influence of monastic reform in Anglo-Saxon England from the mid-tenth to eleventh centuries. Although chiefly used to describe a distinct type of illuminated manuscript, the term can also refer to ornamentation adorning contemporary stone and ivory carvings and metalwork. Traditionally, the Winchester style has been viewed as a southern English phenomenon, predominantly produced within an ecclesiastical milieu. It is the argument of this paper that new finds of metalwork, uncovered through recent excavation and metal-detecting and recorded by the Portable Antiquities Scheme (PAS), significantly alter this picture. It is now apparent that the Winchester school crossed the Danelaw boundary and appeared on secular dress accessories, most notably strap-ends. This has implications for our understanding of both the Winchester style and its context and distribution, and social and cultural interaction within the Danelaw. In particular, a study of Winchester-style metalwork contributes to the increasing scholarly interest in how the form, decoration and distribution of material culture was used by inhabitants of the Danelaw to construct and express social identity.[1]

Traditional Approaches to the Winchester Style

Illuminated manuscripts in the Winchester style are distinguished by a number of stylistic and technical features, many, but not all, of which derive from Continental traditions. Most recognizable is the appearance of heavy borders filled with florid Carolingian-derived acanthus leaves, which frame expertly drawn, colourful figures.[2] The figures themselves are also Continental in origin, inspired by models from Rheims and Metz, with fluttering drapery and occasionally enlarged hands.[3] Outline drawing is a further feature of this school, alongside elaborate initials decorated with foliage, interlacing stems and biting animal heads, a motif familiar in Anglo-Saxon art of the ninth century.[4] Classic Winchester-style ornamentation is seen in a number of tenth-century manuscripts, but it is in the *Benedictional of St Æthelwold*, produced in Winchester itself around 971–984, with its acanthus-filled gold bar frames and vividly coloured figures, that the culmination of the style is best seen.[5]

There has been some debate about whether the term 'Winchester School' is a misnomer for a style with a much broader southern inspiration and spread. This is particularly the case concerning the provenance of Winchester-decorated manuscripts, which have been linked to monastic houses in the south, south-west and east of England, including Canterbury, Ely, Bury St Edmunds and Glastonbury.[6] More recently the provenance of other media in the style has also come under scrutiny, particularly by Hinton, who has called into doubt evidence that has traditionally ascribed textiles, paintings and metalwork to the monastic see.[7] Few scholars, however, including Hinton, deny the overall influence of Winchester on artistic developments in tenth- and eleventh-century English art and many have confirmed the West Saxon capital as the true home and focal point of the style.[8]

Winchester-style ornamentation has been identified not just on illuminated manuscripts but on a wide variety of other media, some of which is only gradually coming to light. Zarnecki has drawn attention to the acanthus motifs typical of the School used to decorate church capitals and bases, as in the chancel arch of St Mary's Church in Bibury, Gloucestershire, highlighting rare examples of manuscript-inspired stone carving.[9] Figural carvings in ivory have received the most scholarly attention. As early as 1924, Brøndsted recognized an early eleventh-century walrus crozier handle found at Alcester, Warwickshire, as displaying relief-carved acanthus leaf and animal figures characteristic of the School.[10] A number of miniature walrus ivory carvings have also been demonstrated to be in the Winchester style.[11] Perhaps the most famous of these, a triangular panel depicting two addorsed angels with enlarged hands and fluttering drapery, has figures which are closely paralleled in the Charter of the New Minster, from Winchester.[12]

From this brief description of some of the more traditional objects displaying Winchester ornamentation, it is clear that they share two of the key characteristics of the illuminated manuscripts: they have a southern distribution, arguably reflecting a Winchester focus, and come from a predominantly ecclesiastical milieu, hardly surprising since the art was intimately associated with Benedictine-inspired monastic reform. The southern provenance of the Winchester style and its role in bringing a new spirit to English monasticism has, on the whole, set the tone for scholars' understanding and interpretation of the art form. It is this understanding which, I argue, needs to be revised in light of recent finds of metalwork.

In contrast to the distinctive figural styles of the ivories and manuscripts, metalwork in the Winchester style is principally identified through the display of Carolingian-derived foliage, which, on more elaborate examples, is inhabited with confronted pairs of naturalistic birds or quadrupeds.[13] The repertoire of Winchester-style metalwork can encompass a variety of motifs, but characteristic of the School is symmetrically-arranged foliage executed in openwork and high relief with open, bifurcating tendrils ending in lobed volutes and a central stem which springs from an inverse animal mask.[14] Inhabited foliage motifs contain animals or birds with long necks, backward-turned heads and biting or gaping jaws.[15] Recent finds of metalwork of Carolingian date from Germany suggest that the treatment of these

motifs, including the inhabited vine scroll and bird motifs, may have developed from Continental rather than Insular sources and firmly root the cultural origins of the Winchester style, as it appeared on metalwork, in Carolingian traditions.[16]

Metal objects in the Winchester style have yet to receive the attention commanded by manuscripts and ivories. Indeed, twenty years ago, the tenth and eleventh centuries were thought to represent a 'massive lacunae' in surviving metalwork.[17] Before the advent of metal-detecting, metalwork that had survived in England had come predominantly from urban or church-based excavations, and had been overwhelmingly ecclesiastical in nature. In 1964, David Wilson was able to identify only a handful of metal objects that displayed acanthus motifs in the late tenth-century Winchester style, most of which were liturgical items with a Continental provenance. Among these items were mounts from a crozier at Cologne Cathedral, with classic Carolingian-derived foliates, and the frame of a portable alter, now in the Musée de Cluny, with figures close in style to the figures of St Peter and St Michael in the New Minster *Liber Vitae*, produced at Winchester around 1031.[18] A cruet, or small jug, with panels depicting pairs of birds with biting, upward-turned beaks, first discussed by Kendrick, and three copper-alloy censer covers, now in the British Museum, were also included in Wilson's small corpus.[19]

Examples of secular metalwork in the Winchester style have, until recently, been much rarer. A small group of secular, utilitarian items with Winchester-style ornamentation was identified by Kendrick over sixty years ago. Three strap-ends and a mount shared common decorative motifs typical of the style which, Kendrick argued, firmly placed them in a tenth-century tradition.[20] Other objects now assigned to the Winchester style include a small number of artefacts which are entirely without zoomorphic elements, but which retain the typical acanthus design. A strap-end from a burial at Bowcombe Down on the Isle of White, originally identified erroneously as a late-Roman artefact, belongs to this category, as does a quadrangular bronze mount from Southampton.[21] A copper-alloy strap-end displaying uninhabited foliage from Meols in Cheshire offers a further antiquarian example of this category.[22]

More recent finds from excavations have slightly expanded this small catalogue. An oval copper-alloy mount recovered from Shakenoak villa in Oxfordshire, originally published as Romano-British, is now thought to date to the tenth or eleventh century on account of its symmetrically-placed bipeds and foliage.[23] An elaborate series of relief-decorated strap-ends with Winchester-style decoration have been uncovered from the extensive excavations at Winchester itself.[24] These strap-ends display both inhabited and uninhabited foliage but among the group is an item from a mid-tenth century grave believed to be the finest example of all strap-ends decorated in the style.[25] It displays very finely executed pierced openwork with stylized foliage and paired, symmetrical biting birds, which can be compared to the creatures and foliage in the border of the dedication page in a copy of Bede's *Lives of Cuthbert*, produced in the south-west of England in the 930's.[26] Two other strap-ends from Winchester, both with uninhabited symmetrical plant patterns, and a buckle with roughly applied paired birds, reflect simplified versions of the Winchester style and post-date the examples with inhabited foliage.[27]

Three out of the four objects in Kendrick's corpus come from eastern England: the mount from Thetford, and the Ixworth and Wilbury Hill strap-ends, from Suffolk and Hertfordshire respectively.[28] By and large, however, the Winchester style as depicted on known items of metalwork appears to have a southern distribution, with the finest examples of the style coming from Winchester itself.[29] It is perhaps not surprising then that scholars have characterized ornamental Winchester-style objects as, like the manuscripts, a purely southern English phenomenon. Wilson saw the motifs on objects produced by the Winchester School as 'a style of south-east England in the first half of the tenth century' with metalwork from this period virtually absent in the north and sculpture at northern ecclesiastical centres such as Durham displaying little in the way of tenth-century ornament.[30]

The boundary with the area of Scandinavian settlement in England, the Danelaw, was thought to mark the most northern and easterly limits of the Winchester style. In spite of his own evidence for the presence of the Winchester style in the east of England, Kendrick argued that the Viking presence actively stifled the development of 'Christian' art which had flourished 'in the victorious West Saxon districts of England from which the Danes had been expelled'. There was no doubt in Kendrick's mind that, had there not been such a settlement, 'the acanthus would have flourished…and there would have been a Northumbrian 'Winchester' style. It was the Vikings who put back the clock'.[31]

Recent Discoveries of Winchester-style Metalwork from the Danelaw

Such views are now increasingly undermined by new finds of metalwork from regions which were once part of the Danelaw. These stray finds, recovered by metal-detecting and recorded by the Portable Antiquities Scheme, require that we re-examine earlier assumptions about the Winchester style. Small, utilitarian, secular items of metalwork, predominantly strap-ends but also single examples of a mount and hooked-tag, reveal a northern and easterly rural distribution within the Danelaw. They bear testimony to the versatility and widespread popularity of the Winchester style in late Saxon England and are suggestive of the broad qualitative range of artefacts to which the style was applied.

Gabor Thomas' doctoral thesis first drew attention to the easterly spread of his Class E, category 1 Winchester type strap-ends, dated on stylistic grounds to the tenth-century.[32] He noted seventeen examples of this tongue-shaped type, which displayed either pure Winchester acanthus foliage, inhabited foliates or devolved, stylised scroll, found north of the Danelaw, a concentration greater than that from the 'traditional heartland' of the style.[33] In addition to providing evidence that the Winchester style circulated in the Danelaw, Thomas has raised the possibility that it was also manufactured there.[34] The following discussion of finds now recorded on the PAS database largely confirms Thomas' findings and offers an interpretation of their importance in the context of Scandinavian settlement in the Danelaw.

It is, of course, important to highlight the problems inherent in interpreting metal-detected finds. Different land-use patterns between eastern and western England have resulted in a wealth of finds being recorded from the eastern counties of Norfolk, Suffolk and Lincolnshire, where most land is arable and metal-detecting widespread, but significantly fewer from central and western England, where pastoral farming is the norm. As we shall see, Winchester-style objects within the Danelaw reveal very clearly this eastern bias. Further, metal-detected items are stray finds recovered from the topsoil (or ploughsoil) and thus lack an archaeological context and associated stratigraphy possessed by items uncovered in urban or rural settlement excavations. In some cases, their find-spots are not precisely recorded, and make reference only to a find locale of one square kilometer. Nonetheless, as chance finds, metal-detected items also benefit the overall archaeological record, balancing out the bias towards traditional areas of focus: burials, settlements and hoards.[35]

In addition to the strap-ends recorded by Thomas in 2000, sixty-five further items decorated in the Winchester School style have been found in the Danelaw territories from metal-detecting activity alone: twenty-seven from Norfolk, sixteen from Lincolnshire, nine from Suffolk, three finds from both Cambridgeshire and Nottinghamshire, two from Leicestershire and Northamptonshire and single finds from Hertfordshire, Bedfordshire and Derbyshire (Fig. 1). The vast majority of these finds, sixty-three, are strap-ends, with one hooked-tag and one mount. The corpus is substantially expanded when antiquarian discoveries, artefacts in Historic Environment Records (HERs) – formerly known as Sites and Monuments Records (SMRs) – and finds from excavations are taken into account. An antiquarian find of a bone strap-end from Leicester and excavated strap-ends from Middle Harling and Thetford in Norfolk and the Lloyd's Bank and Coppergate areas of York, together with a brooch also excavated at Thetford, clearly display the Carolingian-inspired Winchester style but have not been considered here.[36] A number of strap-ends appear on regional HERs, some of which are also published in county archaeological journals.[37]

This essay is, however, concerned predominantly with stray finds recently recorded by the Portable Antiquities

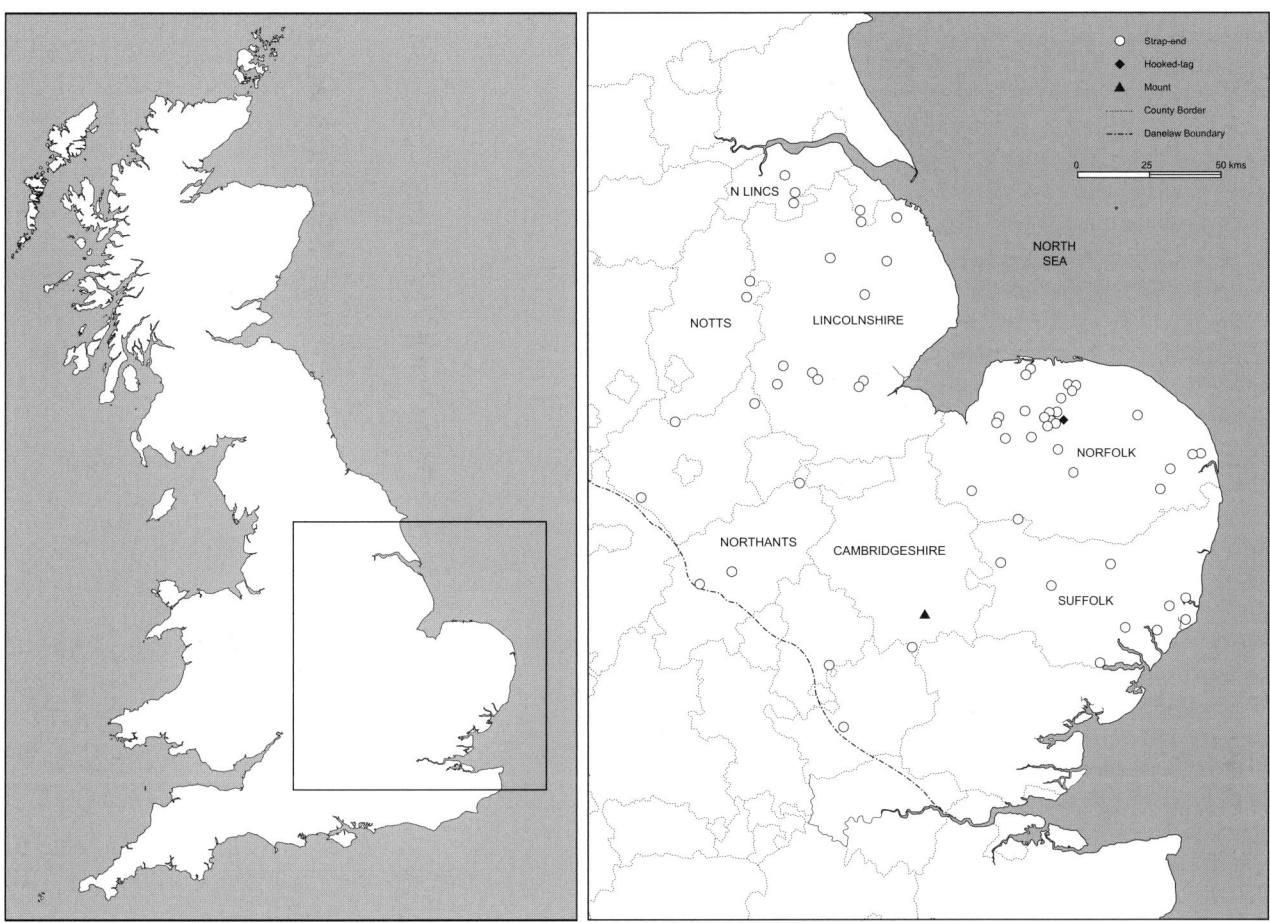

Figure 1. Map showing the distribution of Winchester-style metalwork within the Danelaw

Scheme. The items are displayed and illustrated on the Scheme's database (available at www.finds.org.uk) and are referred to here by their PAS 'Find-ID'. Where good quality illustrations or digital photographs of the objects exist, they have been included although, regrettably, many images displayed on the PAS database are not suitable for publication. It should also be emphasized that objects recorded by the Scheme are not necessarily representative of the wider corpus of Danelaw finds and that the total number of such items is much larger than current PAS records suggest.

The Danelaw finds make up a diverse group and display the full repertoire of Winchester-style motifs. Finds can have double- or single-sided decoration, be cast in copper- or lead-alloys, executed in both openwork and high-relief and can have plain or embellished surfaces. Although many items are now worn or corroded, it is clear that they display varying levels of artistic skill and craftsmanship. A small number of finds are artistically accomplished, with masterful examples of Winchester-style acanthus foliates, occasionally inhabited by naturalistic birds or animals. Most examples, however, lack the zoomorphic element and display only a heavily debased and schematic tree

scroll pattern. There are also a number of rare and 'one off' finds, discussed further below.

A small group of strap-ends from the Danelaw comprise finds with refined and skillful Winchester-style ornament, although none can be said to parallel the high caliber of decoration found in Anglo-Saxon manuscripts in the manner of the finest strap-end from the Winchester group. The most complicated Winchester-style inhabited-foliage design in the Danelaw corpus appears on an incomplete copper-alloy strap-end from Tunstall, Suffolk (SF4115, Fig. 2). On both the front and back of this object, back-to-back birds with backwards-angled wings flanking a central rosette sit on branches stemming from a central trunk. Below them, two lower branches run around the back of a quadruped, probably a lion, depicted in profile with its head turned backwards and its tail in its mouth. While the top arrangement on this strap-end is typical of the Winchester School, the profiled lion may be Romanesque in inspiration. If this were the case, the Tunstall find could be one of the latest strap-ends in the Winchester series and only the second artefact of its type to show Romanesque influence; the other example, also with a profiled lion-like creature, comes from Hindolveston in Norfolk.[38]

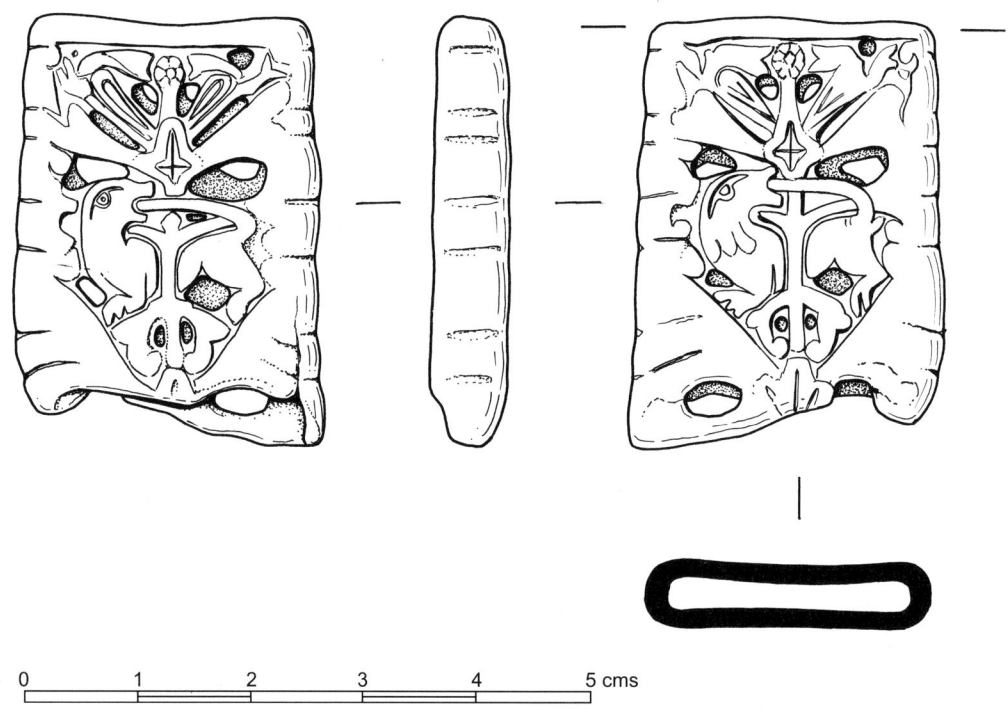

Figure 2. Strap-end from Tunstall, Suffolk (drawing by Donna Wreathall, copyright Suffolk County Council)

Another strap-end with inhabited foliage comes from Hinckley in Leicestershire (LEIC-0C2B81, Fig. 3). This object has scalloped edges, a central stem issuing from a basal bulb and a spherical protrusion at the terminal. Bifurcating tendrils of fleshy acanthus leaves emanate from both ends. Positioned in the middle is a pair of confronted animal heads, with rounded ears, small bored eyes and triangular-shaped faces. These cat-like masks are addorsed in typical Winchester-style fashion and their treatment can be paralleled on a number of other Winchester-style pieces, including one of the liturgical bronze censer covers, from London Bridge, and an unprovenanced bone comb, both discussed in detail by Wilson.[39] The animal heads are also paralleled by those on another Leicestershire object, a bone strap-end from Highcross Street in Leicester. This object depicts four full-face animal masks, two with contorted bodies emanating from a central inverted mask and the others with deeply drilled eyes and issuing tendrils.[40] The Hinckley strap-end demonstrates that Danelaw finds depict motifs which fit well into the known repertoire of Winchester-style ornament, and suggests that some elements of the style could be common to both ecclesiastical and secular metalworking traditions.

Other strap-ends with inhabited foliage include a number of cast lead examples. The terminal end of a fragmentary lead strap-end from Hibaldstow in Lincolnshire depicts a pair of confronted birds with conjoined beaks (NLM-

Figure 3. Strap-end from Hinckley, Leicestershire (photo courtesy of the Portable Antiquities Scheme) Actual length 40mm.

419320). Another lead object, from Hatcliffe in North East Lincolnshire, displays a pair of addorsed birds perched either side of a veined central stem (NLM5373). Little detail survives on the birds' heads or bodies but it appears as if foliage springs from their wings to scale the sides of the front panel and terminates at the attachment-end, itself decorated by a row on punched-dots. Another strap-end belonging to this group is a complete item from Lissington, another Lincolnshire find (LIN-D17C35, Fig. 4). The Lissington strap-end, although somewhat crudely executed, displays classic Winchester-style inhabited foliage, namely a pair of confronted lizard-like creatures positioned within symmetrically-arranged bifurcating acanthus foliates, which emanate from a central spine.

Other strap-ends depict well-executed Winchester-style foliates without the zoomorphic element. Characteristic of the ornament on this group of finds is a clearly defined central stem springing from an inverse animal mask or plain trefoil feature and off-shooting tendrils ending in scrolled terminals, most features of which are seen on strap-end 1060 from Winchester.[41] An incomplete copper-alloy item from Barton-le-Clay in Bedfordshire is perhaps the most elegant of such finds in the Danelaw corpus (BH-7E3CD7, Fig. 5). It has scalloped edges and double-sided moulded decoration consisting of an inverse animal mask protruding from the terminal, central spine and open tendrils. Although no animals or birds inhabit the foliage, a zoomorphic influence in the pattern of the tendrils, emphasized by a complex openwork pattern, is discernable. A further Danelaw find decorated with fine Winchester-style foliates comes from Hindringham in Norfolk (NMS-F7A7C1). Although

worn, this item has double-sided counter-relief decoration consisting of two sets of pendant cinqefoils with elongated foliates and is, unusually, gilded.

Far more numerous among Danelaw finds are strap-ends with classic Winchester-style features in devolved or simplistic forms. The ornament on this group of artefacts is a simplified version of plant scroll decoration and lacks zoomorphic features. It is identifiable chiefly through a symmetrical and regular openwork pattern, a good example of which is seen on an elongated strap-end from Silk Willoughby, Lincolnshire (NLM 4546, Fig. 6). The animal-head masks on these objects are often missing, or, in some instances, substituted by plain, raised triangular features (for instance, SWYOR-7DF7B5). Typically, the central stem is only subtly, if at all, defined. The acanthus scrolls are also debased, the ends appearing simply as a series of opposed sub-rectangular bosses running parallel along the edge of the strap-end, good examples of which can be seen on terminal fragments from Honnington in Lincolnshire and Croxton Kerrial in Leicestershire (NLM4781; NLM6142).

On some examples, however, the foliate motifs are more developed. On a strap-end from Nottinghamshire, for instance, these appear as bifurcating tendrils which emanate from two bulbs along the central spine (LEIC-15A500). On other finds foliate motifs are given extra emphasis by leaf- or crescent-shaped openwork perforations, as on an example from Pitsford, Northamptonshire (NARC2638, Fig. 7). Although these are clearly devolved items, the more elaborate examples have double-sided moulded decoration and were clearly meant to be seen on both sides. Plant decoration and engraving in a symmetrical layout is present on both sides of a now-broken strap-end from Burnham Market, Norfolk, and an example from Seething, also in Norfolk (NMS97; NMS-1D99B4). Artefacts from this group could also be embellished and examples of gilded strap-ends are discussed further below.

Figure 4. Strap-end from Lissington, Lincolnshire (photo courtesy of the Portable Antiquities Scheme)

Figure 5. Strap-end from Barton-le-Clay, Bedfordshire (photo courtesy of the Portable Antiquities Scheme)

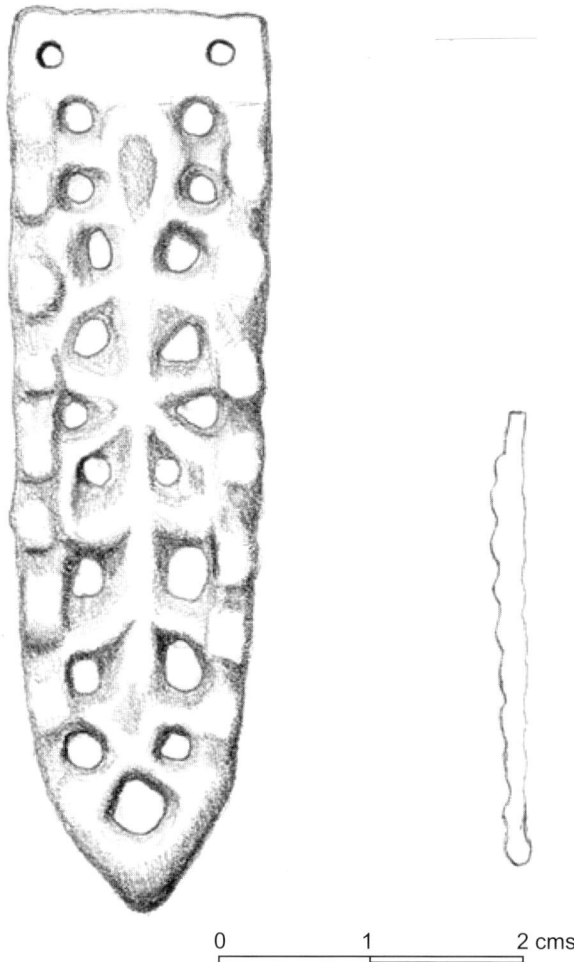

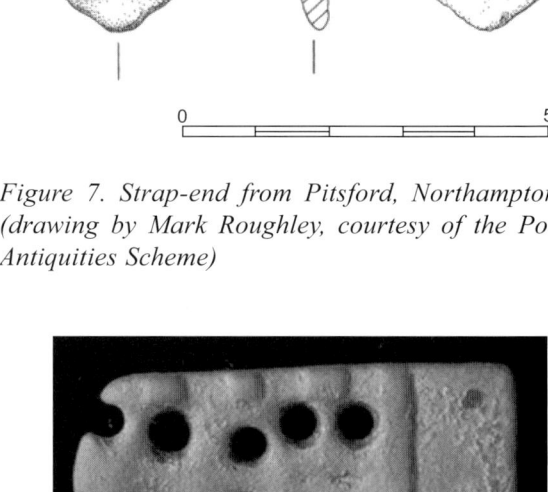

Figure 7. Strap-end from Pitsford, Northamptonshire (drawing by Mark Roughley, courtesy of the Portable Antiquities Scheme)

Figure 6. Strap-end from Silk Willoughby, Lincolnshire (drawing by Marina Elwes, courtesy of the Portable Antiquities Scheme)

Figure 8. Strap-end from Mautby, Norfolk (photo courtesy of the Portable Antiquities Scheme)

It should be apparent, therefore, that while this group of finds display only stylised and debased motifs, they were not necessarily 'low quality' pieces.

The worn nature of these stray finds can make it difficult to judge just how competently a strap-end was originally rendered. On an item from Suffolk, for instance, a series of piercings in imitation of an openwork design are irregularly spaced, though this may be because they were set around a now-indiscernible motif (SF-F83BF8). However, a small number of Danelaw finds do seem to display a further level of debased ornament. The Winchester style as it appears on these items is entirely schematic; it is recognizable chiefly through crude circular openwork patterns, sometimes only roughly symmetrical in layout, and occasionally by the remains of raised bosses representing tendril ends, as on a strap-end from Mautby in Norfolk (NMS-70301, Fig. 8). On a rectangular fragment of a strap-end from Gunthorpe in Norfolk the raised bosses have been subject to a further

debasement and appear simply as notches around the edge of the decorated panel and attachment end (NMS-89DD25). The openwork pattern on this item is crudely cast, consisting of three roughly oval-shaped perforations. On the face of the strap-end, punched ring designs appear at random in between the openwork apertures, a common feature on strap-ends with schematic renderings of the Winchester style.

Strap-ends with embellished surfaces

With six strap-ends cast in lead and the remaining artefacts in copper-alloy, Winchester-style strap-ends from the Danelaw belong to the large category of 'base-metal' dress items thought to be widespread in tenth- and eleventh-century England.[42] Some examples, however, show traces of gilding, a technique which re-gained some popularity in the tenth-century, perhaps because of the influx and

Figure 9. Hooked-tag from Whissonsett, Norfolk. Copyright The Trustees of the British Museum.

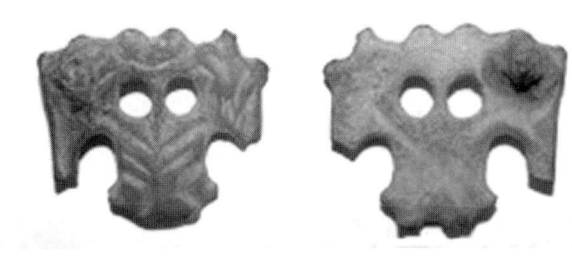

Figure 10. Mount from Great Shelford, Cambridgeshire. Image courtesy of the Portable Antiquities Scheme

influence of gilded Carolingian strap-ends around this time.[43] Of the fifty-seven copper-alloy strap-ends recorded by the PAS, three show traces of gilding, although many finds are now so corroded that evidence of original gilding is unlikely to survive (NMS-F7A7C1; NMS657; LEIC-0C2B81, Fig. 3).

Further examples of embellished strap-ends not recorded by the PAS include a strap-end from Shipdam in Norfolk, recorded on the county's HER, and one of the strap-ends included in Kendrick's catalogue.[44] The latter object, from Ixworth, originally had silver inlay in its surface ornament, in the bird's wings and plant decoration, although now only slight traces are visible.[45] Several of the known Winchester-style objects with liturgical significance also bear traces of silver gilding or plating and, in the tradition of later ninth-century Anglo-Saxon metalwork, niello inlay.[46] The evidence provided by the newly discovered strap-ends indicates that such embellishment was not limited to ecclesiastical items, but was also employed on personal dress accessories. This is of note given that finds from excavations have largely given the impression that

common late Saxon dress attachments, including strap-ends and hooked-tags, were undecorated.[47]

The hooked-tag and mount

A hooked-tag and mount are the only two other artefact types with Winchester-style decoration to have been uncovered by metal-detecting from the Danelaw and recorded by the PAS, although a brooch with Winchester-style birds, discussed below, was found during the Thetford excavations. While there are other parallels for the mount, the recently-discovered hooked-tag from Whissonsett in Norfolk is notable not only for being the only known example of a hooked tag with Winchester-style decoration, but also for being the only cast silver item in the style from the Danelaw (PAS-E897A3, Fig.9). The tag, a British Museum Treasure, comprises a circular plate and perforated projection lug, although its hook is missing.[48] The plate has an incised border ring which surrounds a central domed stud and four radiating arms with expanded ends forming a cross-like motif. Each arm contains a semi-circular basal bulb and fleshy, bifurcating acanthus leaves, accentuated by the use of niello inlay. The motif is a simplified version of the Winchester-style scroll and firmly places the tag in the tenth century. The tag, probably used as a dress fastener, is a remarkable piece for demonstrating that the Winchester style adorned artefacts of precious metals in the Danelaw at a time when personal dress items in silver and gold were extremely rare.

A mount from Great Shelford in Cambridgeshire, perhaps from a stirrup-strap, survives only as a fragment but may have originally been rectangular or square in form, as indicated by a surviving rivet in the upper right corner (CAM-D45F73, Fig. 10). The upper surface of the Great Shelford fragment depicts in moulded relief a trefoil feature, central stem and foliates. Only two complete openwork perforations remain, around which the decoration is somewhat difficult to decipher. It is clear, however, that the fragment depicts stylised foliates characteristic of the Winchester School. The mount from Thetford noted by Kendrick is a reminder that this item is not unique among Danelaw finds.[49] Other mounts bearing Winchester-style decoration are also known south of the Danelaw. Mounts from Shakenoak and Southampton have already been mentioned, although a more recent detector find from the Winchester area with pairs of back-to-back interlacing creatures set within a bifurcating plant with scrolled tendril ends portrays the most complex design.[50] These mounts would have had varying functions; they could have been attached to dress straps, pieces of equestrian equipment or even items of furniture. Such items, together with the hooked-tag, suggest that the Winchester Style was applied to a broad range of artefact types and hint at the versatility and appeal of the style.

Production and Distribution

The distribution of these artefacts clearly shows a concentration in the most easterly counties, with only a few finds recorded from the more westerly Hertfordshire, Leicestershire, Nottinghamshire and Derbyshire (Fig. 1). The entirely rural distribution of these finds is also marked; there is no evidence of clustering around urban centres in Norfolk or Lincolnshire, where finds are most numerous and where evidence of such clustering is most likely to be revealed. However, given that excavated finds indicate that the Winchester style was known in urban locations, this pattern is probably the result of low levels of recovery and recording of metal-detected finds from modern built-up areas, and does not suggest that the Winchester style was confined to the rural Danelaw.

Gabor Thomas's research on ninth- and tenth-century Anglo-Scandinavian strap-ends from the Danelaw has shown that finds from the eastern Danelaw display a much wider variety of cultural and artistic influences compared to finds from the rest of the Scandinavian settlement area.[51] Thomas has identified an eclectic range of strap-ends circulating in the eastern Danelaw, including Scandinavian examples with Borre-style ring-knot designs, Anglo-Scandinavian hybrids with Insular versions of a Borre-style motif and examples paralleled by finds from the Irish Sea region, all of which have a clearly eastern distribution with few or no finds coming from areas such as West or South Yorkshire, Nottinghamshire, Staffordshire and Leicestershire.[52]

While we must question the extent to which the current distribution pattern reflects accurately the contemporary spread of Winchester-style artefacts within the Danelaw, it may also be that York served as the epicenter for Anglo-Scandinavian cultural interaction within the region. While there is evidence in York and its immediate hinterland for the presence and manufacture of Hiberno-Norse-type strap-ends with incised roundels and panels of interlace, very few of these items have been found between the Irish Sea coast and the Yorkshire region, although metal-detected finds from this area overall are less frequent than finds from other eastern counties.[53] Nonetheless, neither excavations of rural settlements nor metal-detecting activity has located a significant number of items with hybrid cultural influences in this upper Midland band. Few artefacts have been uncovered at Wharram Percy in east Yorkshire where Mid-Saxon occupation is believed to have given way to Scandinavian settlement, or at what may be a Scandinavian farmstead at Simy Folds, Upper Teesdale, although this is fairly typical for the acidic soils of upland sites.[54] The presence of two Norse bells at another upland, potentially Scandinavian, farmstead at Cottam in the Yorkshire Wolds is a very rare indication of cultural and trading links between the western and eastern Scandinavian communities not focused at York, although the close proximity of Cottam to York may suggest trade via the Scandinavian capital.[55] It should, perhaps,

be expected that York acted as the catalyst for cultural integration given similar evidence for long-distance trade and artistic assimilation in other Viking-Age urban settlements, such as Dublin.[56] This impression is confirmed when we take into account evidence for the manufacture of Winchester-style ornament within the Danelaw.

Evidence for the production of Winchester-style objects in late Saxon England is sparse. No moulds for strap-ends decorated in the Winchester style survive.[57] The discovery in recent years of a small number of undecorated strap-ends in copper- and lead-alloys, including an item from Coddenham in Suffolk, may attest to the general production of strap-ends in rural locales (SF-3D3311). This piece has a single rivet hole and a plain tag tapering towards the end, and may well be a model or unfinished strap-end. There is, however, nothing to suggest that such an item could have been used in the manufacture of Winchester-style items in particular. Indeed, Winchester-style strap-ends display integrally cast openwork designs or designs in high relief, probably executed during the initial stages of production.

It is conventional to cite decorated strap-ends and jewellery in lead or lead alloys such as pewter as archaeological evidence for manufacturing. These items are often interpreted as trial pieces or models, used in the serial production of artefacts in copper-alloys.[58] Such interpretations seem reasonable given that the bulk of the finds, including items from Hibalstow in Lincolnshire and Congham in Norfolk, are fragmented artefacts bereft of the attachment appendages required for use (NLM-419320; NMS168). This assumption is, however, more difficult to sustain in the light of complete finds with surviving and functioning attachment ends. Two lead strap-ends mentioned above, from Hatcliffe and Lissington in Lincolnshire, retain attachment panels with the remains of pierced rivet holes which would have enabled each object to be attached to a belt (NLM5373; LIN-D17C35, Fig. 4). Such fittings indicate that that these objects were not casting models, but were meant to be worn and used.

The Lissington and Hatcliffe strap-ends are just two among several recent finds of Anglo-Saxon and Anglo-Scandinavian dress items in lead which retain their attachment lugs and clearly functioned as dress accessories.[59] Several Jelling-style lead disc brooches retain remains of pin-lugs and catchplates, and, in some cases, traces of original iron pins, as do a number of late Saxon disc brooches of English manufacture.[60] Kevin Leahy has recently catalogued a number of lead strap-ends and brooches from the area of Anglo-Saxon Lindsey in North Lincolnshire, many of which have the remains of attachment appendages or pierced rivet holes.[61] Given such examples, we must remain open to the possibility that some lead artefacts, rather than being tools in a manufacturing process, were intended to be worn.

Given that we can no longer assume that lead dress items were mere models, we must turn to other evidence for the production of Winchester-style pieces. Several

Figure 11. Die or patrix from Sporle with Palgrave, Norfolk. Scale 2:1. Drawing by Susan White. Copyright Norfolk County Council

recent finds suggest that the Winchester style both circulated in the rural Danelaw, and was produced there. A copper-alloy strap-end from Osleston and Thurvaston in Derbyshire has symmetrical openwork decoration in the shape of a plant motif and belongs to the group of strap-ends with stylised versions of Winchester-style foliage (WMID-4EF045). However, although it is complete, no rivet piercings are discernable on its attachment end and one of its eight openwork perforations is filled in, raising the possibility that the artefact was unfinished when it was lost or discarded.

More concrete evidence for the production of the motif in the eastern counties rests on two further finds. The first is a rectangular bronze die or patrix, recovered from Sporle with Palgrave in Norfolk with early Winchester-style decoration (Fig. 11). The die is decorated in relief with a central bifurcated stem supported by three basal lobes, a feature of Carolingian art. Flanking the stem is a pair of profiled birds with lentoid-shaped eyes, gaping jaws and pelleted wings. They appear in a circular arrangement; their heads look down, their wings curve under their bodies and their clawed feet, continuing this curvature, come round to touch their beaks. Such an arrangement hints at an early date and finds parallels in the restricted pose of ninth-century Trewhiddle-style creatures.[62] The pattern fills the entire decorative surface, indicating that the die's margin or border is missing.[63]

The pattern on this die would have been imprinted onto the surface of a thin foil, probably of silver, which would then have been applied to the surface of copper-alloy artefacts. There is little doubt that it would have been used to create high quality, finely embellished pieces. The decorative layout of the die is arranged horizontally and it therefore would not have been used to create patterns on strap-ends, which depict perpendicular foliage designs flowing either upwards or downwards. Nonetheless, the die, with its lobed features and restricted birds, raises the possibility that Winchester style circulated in East Anglia at an early stage, perhaps in the early tenth century, and may hint at local production around this date.

Further evidence for the manufacture of Winchester-style

metalwork in the Danelaw rests on a single fragmentary mould for a trefoil brooch found at Blake Street, York, in the heart of the old Roman fortress (Fig. 12). This item is exceptional in depicting Winchester-style foliage and animal masks on a mould for a trefoil brooch, a brooch-type introduced to England from Scandinavia in the Viking Age.[64] Animal masks of the type seen on the Canterbury and London Bridge censer covers can be seen both at the junction of the two surviving arms and in the centre of each arm below a pair of inward-looking birds, another Winchester prototype.[65] This too may be an early Winchester piece, as the trefoil brooch was a type which circulated in the Danelaw in the late ninth and tenth centuries. Although no brooch from this mould survives, the mould was found with a crucible, suggesting manufacture at a site on or near its location spot.

Other artefacts recovered from the city certainly suggest that dress items in Scandinavian styles were manufactured in York. A lead-alloy matrix with Borre-style decoration and a bird-head suspension loop found at Blake Street could have been used to create pendants similar to Danish examples found in the Tolstrup hoard.[66] Two disc brooches depicting devolved versions of the Scandinavian Jelling-style backwards-looking animal are also known from the city and were probably produced there.[67] A clear mixing of Scandinavian and Anglo-Saxon decoration is also evident on some finds. A copper-alloy tenth-century strap-end found during the St Mary Bishophill excavations has a characteristic Anglo-Saxon form but a modified version of the Scandinavian Borre-style ring-chain.[68] A strikingly similar find uncovered from Coppergate suggests these items were produced locally.[69] In light of this evidence, the production of a Winchester-style trefoil brooch at York would be just one of a number of culturally hybrid artefact types manufactured in the heart of the Scandinavian kingdom.

Chronology and Development

The evidence for both devolved and well crafted Winchester motifs on strap-ends from the Danelaw gives the impression that the Danelaw finds were not simply southern English examples which strayed north and east, but a semi-independent group, which was clearly inspired by Winchester models, but which adapted the Winchester style in an appropriate manner. Without an associated stratigraphy, a precise dating of these objects is problematic. The strap-ends with inhabited foliage from the Winchester series date to the mid-tenth century by their associations with graves and house structures, and may therefore be considered contemporary with the latest phases of the Borre and Jelling styles as they appeared in England.[70] It has been suggested, however, that the series continued with simple, uninhabited renderings of the style into the early-mid eleventh-century, when the later Scandinavian Ringerike style was current in southern England.[71] The find contexts of the plainer strap-ends and buckle from Winchester suggest a chronology consistent with such a time frame.[72]

If it is the case that the zoomorphic element received less emphasis as the style evolved, most Danelaw examples, with plain symmetrical openwork patterns, would date to the late tenth or early eleventh centuries. None of the metal-detected finds can, however, be dated on anything other than stylistic grounds. Unfortunately, the few Winchester-style artefacts recovered from excavations within the Danelaw come either from only broadly datable contexts or contexts which have yielded no chronological information.[73]

The die from Norfolk and the trefoil mould from York have already been mentioned as potentially early Winchester-style pieces on account of their associated art styles and morphological attributes and it is notable that both display clear zoomorphic elements. It may be possible to identify further instances of early and late stages of the Winchester style on the strap-ends themselves. Early versions of the style, like Carolingian designs, tend to show flat, dense and fleshy acanthus leaves, rather than the more spindly, open tendrils typical of most of the Danelaw finds.[74]

Such renderings are discernable on a rectangular copper-alloy strap-end from Weeting with Broomhill in Norfolk with a simple folded metal construction (SF3658). The ornament on this item is neither moulded nor carved in openwork, but engraved, and consists of luxuriant acanthus leaves ending in rounded lobes on either side of a plain central longitudinal band. Unusually, the strap-end also has two centrally positioned rivet holes, which may suggest its re-use as a mount. At the other end of the chronological scale, the strap-end from Tunstall already mentioned (Fig. 2) on which the Winchester style was paired with Romanesque-influenced designs may date to the mid-eleventh century or later on account of its late artistic affinities. While dating objects on a stylistic basis alone does not offer a precise chronology, there seems to be evidence both for the early manufacture of the Winchester style in the Danelaw and for the style remaining a popular artistic idiom in the eastern counties for several generations.

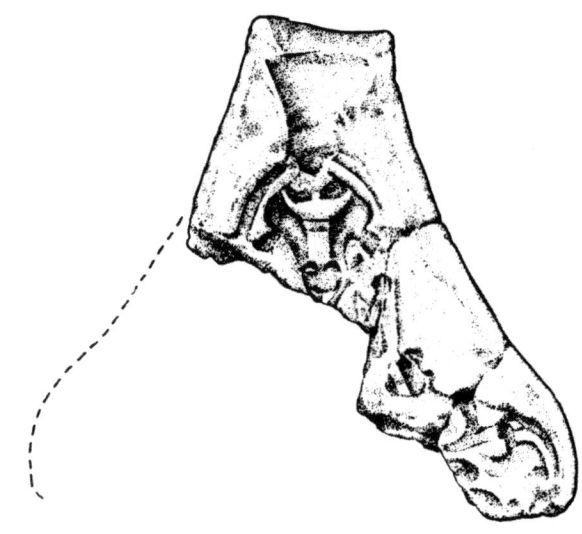

Figure 12. Trefoil brooch mould from Blake Street, York. Copyright York Archaeological Trust. Max. l c. 100m

Social and Cultural Implications

The Winchester style can no longer be considered an ecclesiastical motif present only on items with liturgical significance. Its appearance on strap-ends and other dress items is testimony to its use on secular and personal accessories. Nor can it be considered a style only of southern England, for the distribution of Winchester-style finds from the Danelaw clearly demonstrates that the style was not confined to 'English' England. What, then, did the Winchester style mean and communicate? Who wore it and for what purpose?

Recent interpretations of Viking-Age material culture have demonstrated ways in which Scandinavian and Anglo-Scandinavian metalwork from the Danelaw can inform our views of, for instance, contemporary settlement patterns, wealth and social status, and cultural and trade contacts.[75] Of increasing interest is the value of metalwork, specifically its form and decoration, in elucidating aspects of social identity and cultural interaction.[76] Work by Caroline Paterson in particular has demonstrated how the appearance of the Scandinavian Borre and Jelling styles on items of metalwork produced in England may be studied to reveal processes of cultural exchange and assimilation in mixed Anglo-Scandinavian communities.[77] Paterson's analysis is underpinned by modern theoretical approaches to material culture, which emphasize the role of artefacts as both embodying and shaping the identity of their makers and wearers.[78] Such approaches see variability in artefact style as a means of communicating aspects of social identity, such as gender, age and regional or political affiliations. In some circumstances, the selective use of objects is thought to facilitate social and cultural interaction.[79]

Items with Winchester-style decoration recovered

from the Danelaw may help further elucidate the inter-relationships between incoming and native populations. Several objects recorded through excavation suggest that the Winchester style occurred on items of mixed cultural or regional forms and styles. A pewter plate brooch recovered during excavations at Mill Lane, Thetford, demonstrates that the Winchester style was applied to brooch forms of Continental origin.[80] While the straight-edged, rectangular shape of the brooch has Carolingian parallels and the foliage is representative of the true Carolingian acanthus, the naturalistic bird motifs are later in date and drawn from the canon of the Winchester School. The pair of profiled birds, with speckled necks, clearly defined wings and tail-feathers and raised heads bear a striking resemblance to the confronted birds on the strap-ends with inhabited foliage from the Winchester series.[81]

There is further evidence for the incorporation of Scandinavian design elements into Winchester-style objects south of the Danelaw. A gilt silver strap-end and rectangular decorative plaque from the Old Minster, Winchester, combine Jelling and Winchester motifs. The strap-end, in typical Saxon tongue-shaped form, depicts an animal with Jelling-esque spiral hips but an acanthus-shaped tongue.[82] On the plaque, the divisions of decorative panels are Swedish in origin, the contorted creatures Scandinavian and the foliage classically Winchester style.[83]

Ornament on other artefacts is suggestive of the fusion of the later Scandinavian Ringerike style with Winchester motifs. This is, to a certain extent, to be expected given the close similarities between the styles, and there has been some debate about the relative influence of the Winchester School on the development of the Scandinavian style, which flourished in the south of England under the patronage of King Cnut and his dynasty from the early eleventh century.[84] Ringerike-style foliates, with their long, drawn out, clustered tendrils and tightly-curled scrolls, together with the interlacing snakes typical of the style, are seen in isolated forms on a variety of media, including sculpture and metalwork, from the south of England.[85]

The style could, however, also occur alongside Winchester-style birds and foliage on individual objects. Interspersed flourishes of Ringerike animals and tendrils are seen in a small number of manuscripts in the Winchester style and both styles appear on decorative panels of an unprovenanced bone comb.[86] The fusion of Winchester and Ringerike styles also occurs on a small number of items of metalwork, including some with a Scandinavian provenance and place of manufacture. Symmetrical acanthus foliage and bird motifs found in the Winchester repertoire transfuse with Ringerike tendrils on a pair of gilt bronze stirrup plates found in a barrow grave in Velds in Denmark and on an elaborate gilt silver sword guard from Dybäck in southern Sweden, both of which have been discussed at some length elsewhere.[87] Of course, the socio-political and regional contexts in which the Ringerike style was produced in England vary greatly from those in which the

Borre and Jelling styles flourished; when Kendrick wrote of the Viking rejection of the Winchester acanthus he was speaking not of the Scandinavians in the court of Cnut, but of the Danish settlers of the late ninth and tenth centuries.[88] Nonetheless, the integration of the Ringerike style with that of the Winchester School is a clear indication that the Winchester style continued to appear in amalgamated forms on culturally hybrid items, in both England and the Scandinavian homelands, into the eleventh century.

The combination of different artistic motifs may simply reflect heightened levels of cultural contact in culturally and ethnically mixed communities. It may, however, also suggest that metalwork provided a medium through which meaningful expressions relating to identity were made. Inhabitants of the Danelaw may have chosen to fuse together Winchester motifs with other regional styles in order to portray mixed cultural or regional identities. Perhaps the Winchester style was adopted and altered by Scandinavian settlers in an attempt to integrate with the existing population, taking on local fashions. Caroline Paterson's work has demonstrated that Scandinavian settlers quickly abandoned dress artefacts of Scandinavian origin which had long been out of fashion in England, such as pendants, yet retained types which could be more easily assimilated into native costume, such as disc brooches.[89] Hybrid forms could also have been created by the English living under Scandinavian rule, possibly to gain social or political advantage.

Significantly, metalwork displaying other forms of hybrid Anglo-Scandinavian and Hiberno-Scandinavian styles largely share with Winchester-style metalwork a widespread distribution in East Anglia and Lincolnshire.[90] A prolific disc brooch series from the region reflects a similar fusion of Anglo-Saxon and Scandinavian art. Although their Borre-style knotwork designs are Scandinavian in inspiration, their flat form and single attachment lug reflect insular production.[91] Some strap-ends depict Scandinavian design elements rendered in an Insular style. Examples from Walsingham and Blo Norton in Norfolk, for instance, display a ring-chain motif surrounding central lozenges, a devolved form of the Borre-style ring-knot motif.[92] The presence in Lincolnshire, Suffolk, East and North Yorkshire of double-sided strap-ends with interlace decoration and a distinctive animal-head terminal incorporating rounded eyes further reflects cultural contact, in these instances between the eastern Danelaw and Scandinavian communities around the Irish Sea littoral. Although this type derives from ninth-century Irish models, some examples from the Danelaw also have Borre-style decoration, revealing an amalgamation of different art styles.[93]

Most finds from the Danelaw are, however, purely Winchester in inspiration. These items encompass a broad qualitative range, making any assessment of the overall status of the Danelaw corpus problematic. The silver hooked tag and Jelling-Winchester-style strap-end from the Old Minster, and perhaps also items on which the die from Norfolk was used, indicate that precious metals could be adorned with the style on either side of the Danelaw border. Such items must be considered 'high-status'. The appearance of fine, technically-accomplished examples, some with gilded surfaces, double-sided decoration and unique combinations of art styles also suggests highly-skilled craftspeople freely incorporated Winchester forms and motifs into high quality objects in the Danelaw.

In the past, the base-metal composition of new metalwork finds of late Saxon date has led to interpretations that the owners of such items were poor or low-status, able only to afford mass-produced artefacts at the lower-end of the market.[94] The worn nature of many of these finds, interpreted as evidence that such items were in use for a long time, has added to this view, as has their predominantly rural distribution.[95] Certainly, the crude execution and simplified designs of several of the Danelaw finds suggests that the Winchester style occurred on objects of more lowly status, as well as on precious metals.

It is, however, well-known that, in this period, dress accessories in precious metals were increasingly replaced by those in copper and lead alloys. As Hinton has suggested, the decline in the quality and elaboration of dress fittings in the tenth century may reflect changing attitudes among the elite to the display of wealth through personal adornment, rather than a decline in resources.[96] The recovery of Winchester-style strap-ends from recent urban excavations together with the rural find-spots indicated by PAS records, establishes that the style circulated in both the town and countryside. While the Danelaw finds clearly belong to the base-metal repertoire of tenth-century metalwork, they do not necessarily reflect the low social-standing of their owners and wearers. The Winchester style seems to have been appropriate on both items worn to 'mark out' an elite group and on those intended for everyday use by rural and urban populations.

The meaning of the Winchester style, associated neither with specific cultural nor social groups, remains enigmatic. We cannot be certain whether it was adopted by the native English, by newly arrived Scandinavians, or both, and no doubt all inhabitants of the Danelaw were familiar with it. It seems to have been a genuinely popular style, which enjoyed a widespread circulation in the towns and countryside of both the Danelaw and Wessex. It was also adaptable and applied to a wide range of artefact types with varying degrees of skill and artistry. It was just one of an assorted range of cultural and regional styles available to consumers of metal dress items in the Danelaw. The style's easterly distribution highlights the eclecticism of metalwork styles present in the Danelaw in the tenth and early eleventh centuries; an eclecticism which hints at the

potentially complex social and political circumstances within which choices relating to expressions of affiliation and identity were made.

Conclusion

An analysis of Winchester-style metalwork from the Danelaw poses more questions than it can answer, but this new corpus of finds clearly demonstrates the need for a revision of our understanding of the development and distribution of the style. We can now state with confidence that, in contrast to traditional characterizations of the Winchester style as a southern English and ecclesiastical phenomenon, the art of late Anglo-Saxon England and of monastic reform, permeated the Scandinavian area of settlement. It appeared on secular dress fittings right across rural East Anglia and Lincolnshire, and probably over the wider Danelaw. Although the precise chronology of the style is unknown, evidence for both early and late expressions of the style indicate that it was a long-lived and familiar motif in the Danelaw in the tenth and eleventh centuries. There is, furthermore, sound evidence for its manufacture both in the rural Danelaw, and in the capital of the Scandinavian kingdom, arguably the focus of artistic and cultural interaction.

In attempting to define the meaning and significance of the Winchester style within the Danelaw we are on shakier ground. The Winchester style could be expressed with its full inhabited foliage motifs or in devolved and schematic designs, and appeared on artefacts in both silver and lead-alloys. While most artefacts considered here represent stylized, debased forms of the style, a number of unusual and high-status finds hint at the wide-ranging and varied nature of the Danelaw corpus. The style appears on artefacts in a 'pure' form akin to the examples from Winchester itself, but it also reflects the opportunities available for cultural exchange, and appears on culturally-hybrid items alongside motifs of Scandinavian and Carolingian origin. This study has demonstrated that the Winchester style was popular, versatile and long-lived, and flourished on secular dress fittings north of the Danelaw in the tenth and eleventh centuries.

Acknowledgements

I would like to thank the anonymous reviewer for his/her many useful comments on the original draft of this paper, and my supervisor, Professor Helena Hamerow, for her support and encouragement in bringing this paper to publication.

Notes

1. Hadley and Richards 2000
2. Backhouse *et al.* 1984, pl. XV
3. Wamers 1987, 107; Saunders 1928, 20
4. Saunders 1928, 19, 25–7; Wormald 1945; 1971
5. Backhouse *et al.* 1984, no. 37
6. Wormald 1945, 131–3; Parkes 1976
7. Hinton 1990a, 32–3; 1996
8. Hinton 1996, 216; Saunders 1928, 16; Kendrick 1949, 1; Deshman 1977; Wilson 1984, 160
9. Zarnecki 1979; see too examples noted by Wilson 1984, 195–200
10. Brøndsted 1924, 263 Fig. 187
11. Wilson 1984, 190–5
12. Wilson 1984, 190–3 Fig. 241; Backhouse *et al.* 1984, no. 114
13. Backhouse *et al.* 1984, 88
14. Kendrick 1938, 380–1
15. Wamers 1987, 107
16. Wamers 1987
17. Backhouse *et al.* 1984, 88
18. Wilson 1964, 43; Backhouse *et al.* 1984, no. 76
19. Kendrick 1938; Wilson 1964, nos. 9, 44, 56, 147
20. Kendrick 1938, 380–1 pl. LXXIV
21. Hillier 1855, plate 4 Fig. 2; Wilson 1975, pl. XXIIb
22. Bu'Lock 1960, 13 Fig. 4f
23. Hinton 1990b, 495; Backhouse *et al.* 1984, no. 79
24. Hinton 1990b, 494–500 figs. 124–125
25. Wilson 1969
26. Hinton 1990b, Fig. 124; Backhouse *et al.* 1984, no. 83
27. Hinton 1990b, Fig. 125 1060 and 1061, 512 Fig. 129 1101
28. Kendrick 1938, 380
29. Hinton 1990b, 498–9 1057 and 1056
30. Wilson 1984, 160, 200
31. Kendrick 1941, 125, 130–1
32. Thomas 2000a, 249–50; Thomas 2001, 42
33. Thomas 2000a, 108–9, 249
34. Thomas 2000b, 241
35. *Ibid.*, 238
36. Backhouse *et al.* 1984, no. 133; Rogerson and Archibald 1995, Fig. 41.75; Rogerson and Dallas 1984, Fig. 111.28; MacGregor 1982, Fig. 46; Mainman and Rogers 2000, Fig. 105 10421; Youngs 2004, pl V SF161
37. See, for instance, Gurney 2002, Fig. 6G; 2003, Fig. 6B; Martin *et al.* 2001, 66
38. Thomas 2004, Fig. 4 no. 32
39. Wilson 1964, no. 44; 1960, pl. VIIc
40. Backhouse *et al.* 1984, no. 133
41. Hinton 1990b, Fig. 125
42. Hinton 1975, 176–8
43. Thomas 2000a, 165
44. Gurney 2002, 160 Fig. 6G; Kendrick 1938, 380–1 pl. LXXIV
45. Backhouse *et al.* 1984, no. 81
46. Hinton 1975, 203–5; Wilson 1984, 158–60; Backhouse *et al.* 1984, nos. 72–3, 75–6
47. Hinton 1990a, 32

48. Youngs 2001
49. Kendrick 1938, pl. LXXIV
50. Hinton 1996, Fig. 4
51. Thomas 2000b, 244
52. *Ibid.* 244–6; Thomas 2001, 44–6
53. Thomas 2000b, 246 Fig. 20
54. Richards 1997; Coggins *et al.* 1983
55. Haldenby 1990, Fig. 6.1; 1994 Fig. 3.1; Richards 2000, 305 Fig. 29
56. Wallace 1987
57. Hinton 1990a, 32
58. Thomas 2000b, 241; Coatsworth and Pinder 2002, 73–6
59. Mainman and Rogers 2000
60. *Ibid.* See on the PAS LIN-FC1347, SF7482
61. Leahy 2007, pers. comm
62. Webster and Backhouse 1991, 220–1; Youngs 1998
63. Youngs 1998
64. Petersen 1928, 93–114
65. Roesdahl *et al.* 1981, YMW14
66. *Ibid.* YMW13
67. *Ibid.* YD12 and YD13
68. Wilson 1965b, Fig. a; Thomas 2001, 44
69. Roesdahl *et al.* 1981, YD38
70. Hinton 1990b, 497–8; Wilson 1977
71. Hinton 1990b, 497–8; Wamers 1987, 107
72. Hinton 1990b, 499–500, 512
73. Youngs 2004, pl. V SF161; Rogerson and Archibald 1995, Fig. 41.75; Rogerson and Dallas 1984, 69 no. 28; MacGregor 1982, 89 no. 451
74. Wamers 1987, 107–8
75. Margeson 1996; 1997; Thomas 2000b; Leahy and Paterson 2001
76. Thomas 2000b, 252
77. Richardson 1992, 1993; Paterson 2002
78. Wobst 1977; Weissner 1989; Shennan 1989, 17–22
79. Thomas 2000b, 252; Jones 1997, 106–9
80. Youngs 2004, pl.V SF161
81. Youngs 2004, 38; Hinton 1990b, Fig. 124
82. Wilson 1965a, Fig. 7
83. *Ibid.*, Fig. 8
84. Wilson and Klindt-Jensen 1966, 142; Wilson 1984, 209–10; Horn Fugelsang 1980, 77
85. Horn Fugelsang 1980, 47–51, 63–5, 68–9
86. Wilson 1984, 209; Fugelsang 1980, 70–5; Wilson 1960 pl. VII
87. Backhouse *et al.* 1984, nos. 96, 98; Wilson 1964, 45–6, 50; 1975, 205, 248
88. Kendrick 1941, 130–1
89. Paterson 2002
90. Thomas 2000b
91. Richardson 1993, 20
92. Margeson 1996, 54
93. Thomas 2000b, 247–9 Fig. 22
94. Richardson 1993, 37; Margeson 1996, 48; 1997, 6–7
95. Margeson 1996, 55
96. Hinton 1975, 178–80; 1978, 141–3

Bibliography

Backhouse, J., D. Turner and L. Webster 1984. *The Golden Age of Anglo-Saxon Art, 966–1066*. London: British Museum

Brøndsted, J. 1924. *Early English Ornament: the sources, development and relation to foreign styles of pre-Norman ornamental art in England*. London and Copenhagen: Hachette

Bu'Lock, J. D. 1960. 'The Celtic, Saxon and Scandinavian Settlement at Meols in Wirral', *Trans. of the Historical Society of Lancashire and Cheshire* 112, 1–28

Coatsworth, E. and M. Pinder 2002. *The Art of the Anglo-Saxon Goldsmith: Fine metalwork in Anglo-Saxon England, its practice and practitioners*. Woodbridge: Boydell Press

Coggins, D. *et al.* 1983. 'Simy Folds: an early medieval settlement site in Upper Teesdale, County Durham', *Medieval Arch* 27, 1–26

Deshman, R. 1977. 'The Leofric Missal and tenth-century English art', *Anglo-Saxon England* 6, 145–174

Gurney, D. ed. 2003. 'Archaeological Finds in Norfolk 2002', *Norfolk Archaeology* 44 pt. 2, 356–368

Gurney, D. ed. 2002. 'Archaeological Finds in Norfolk 2001', *Norfolk Archaeology* 44 pt. 1, 149–162

Hadley, D. M. and J. D. Richards eds. 2000. *Cultures in Contact: Scandinavian Settlement in England in the Ninth and Tenth Centuries.* Turnhout: Brepols

Haldenby, D. 1990. 'An Anglian site on the Yorkshire Wolds', *Yorkshire Archaeological Jnl* 62, 51–63

Haldenby, D. 1994. 'An Anglian site on the Yorkshire Wolds- part III', *Yorkshire Archaeological Jnl* 66, 51–6

Hillier, G. 1855. 'Excavations at Brightstone and Bowcombe Downs', *Jnl of the British Archaeological Assoc.* 11, 34–40

Hinton, D. 1975. 'Late Anglo-Saxon metal-work: an assessment', *Anglo-Saxon England* 4, 171–80

Hinton, D. 1978. 'Late Saxon Treasure and Bullion', in Hill, D. (ed), Æthelred the Unready. Oxford: British Archaeological Reports 59, 135–58

Hinton, D. 1990a. 'The Medieval Gold, Silver, and Copper-Alloy Objects from Winchester', in Biddle, M. (ed.), *Object and Economy in Medieval Winchester,* vol. 1. Oxford: Clarendon Press, 29–35

Hinton, D. 1990b. 'Relief-decorated Strap-Ends', in Biddle, M. (ed.), *Object and Economy in Medieval Winchester,* vol. 2. Oxford: Clarendon Press, 494–500

Hinton, D. 1996. 'A "Winchester-style" mount from near Winchester', *Medieval Arch* 40, 214–7

Horn Fugelsang, S. 1980. *Some Aspects of the Ringerike Style. A phase of eleventh-century Scandinavian art.* Odense: Odense University Press

Jones, S. 1997. *The Archaeology of Ethnicity.* London: Routledge

Kendrick, T. D. 1938. 'An Anglo-Saxon cruet', *The Antiquaries Jnl* 18, 377–381

Kendrick, T. D. 1941. 'The Viking taste in pre-Conquest England', *Antiquity* 15, 124–141

Kendrick, D. T. 1949. *Late Saxon and Viking Art.* London: Methuen

Leahy, K. and Paterson, C. 2001. 'New light on the Viking Presence in Lincolnshire: the artefactual evidence', in Graham-Campbell, J. (ed.), *Vikings and the Danelaw: Selected papers from the proceedings of the Thirteenth Viking Congress, Nottingham and York, 21–30 August 1997.* Oxford: Oxbow, 181–202

MacGregor, A. 1982. *Anglo-Scandinavian Finds from Lloyds Bank, Pavement, and Other Sites.* York, Council for British Archaeology

Mainman, A. J. and Rogers, N. S. H. (eds.) 2000. *Craft, Industry and Everyday Life: Finds from Anglo-Scandinavian York.* York: Council for British Archaeology

Margeson, S. 1996. 'Viking settlement in Norfolk: a study of new evidence', in Margeson, S., Ayers, B., and Heywood, S. (eds.), *A Festival of Norfolk Archaeology.* Huntstanton, Norfolk and Norwich Archaeological Society, 47–57

Margeson, S. M. 1997. *The Vikings in Norfolk.* Norwich: Norfolk Museums Service

Martin, E., Pendleton C., Plouviez J., Thomas G., and Geake, H. 2001. 'Archaeology in Suffolk 2000', *Proceedings of the Suffolk Institute of Archaeology and History,* 40 pt. 1, 65–81

Paterson, C. 2002. 'From Pendants to Brooches: the exchange of Borre and Jelling style motifs across the North Sea', *Hikuin* 29, 267–76

Parkes, M. B. 1976. 'The paleography of the Parker manuscript of the Chronicle, laws and Sedulius, and historiography at Winchester in the late ninth and tenth centuries', *Anglo-Saxon England* 5, 149–171

Petersen, J. G. T. 1928. *Vikingetidens Smykker.* Stavanger, Dreyers Grafiske Anstalt

Richards, J. D. 1997. 'Anglian and Viking Settlement in the Yorkshire Wolds.' *Papers of the Medieval Europe Brugge Conference* 6. Zellik, Instituut voor het Archeologisch Patrimonium, 233–42

Richards, J. D. 2000. 'Identifying Anglo-Scandinavian Settlements', in Hadley and Richards (eds.) 2000, 295–310

Richardson, C. 1993. The Borre Style in the British Isles and Ireland:

a reassessment, Unpublished M Litt thesis. University of Newcastle

Richardson, C. 1992. 'Form, function and assimilation: the impact of the Borre Style in the British Isles', *Medieval Europe,* Pre-Printed Papers, vol. 5, 121–23. York: University of York

Roesdahl, E. (ed.) 1981. *The Vikings in England: and in their Danish homeland.* London: Penshurst

Rogerson, A. and Archibald, M. 1995. *A Late Neolithic, Saxon, and Medieval Site at Middle Harling, Norfolk.* East Anglian Archaeology 74. London & Norwich: British Museum & Norfolk Museums Service

Rogerson, A. and Dallas. C. 1984. *Excavations in Thetford 1948–9 and 1973–80. East Anglian Archaeology* 22. Gressenhall: Norfolk Archaeological Unit

Saunders, O. E. 1928. *English Illumination.* Firenze and Paris: Pantheon-Casa Editrice, Pegasus Press

Shennan, S. 1989. *Archaeological Approaches to Cultural Identity.* London: Unwin Hyman

Thomas, G. 2000a. A New Survey of Late Anglo-Saxon and Viking-Age Strap-Ends from Britain. Unpublished PhD. thesis. University of London

Thomas, G. 2000b. 'Anglo-Scandinavian Metalwork from the Danelaw: Exploring Social and Cultural Interaction', in Hadley and Richards (eds.) 2000, 237–255

Thomas, G. 2001. 'Strap-ends and the identification of regional patterns in the production and circulation of ornamental metalwork in late Anglo-Saxon and Viking-Age Britain', in Redknap, M. (ed.), *Pattern and Purpose in Insular Art: Proceedings of the Fourth International Congress on Insular Art: held at the National Museum and Gallery, Cardiff 3–6 September 1998,* 39–49

Thomas, G. 2004. Late Anglo-Saxon and Viking-Age strap-ends 750–1100: Part II. The Finds Research Group AD 700–1700, *Datasheet* 33

Wallace, P. 1987. 'The Economy and Commerce of Viking Age Dublin', in Düwel, K. *et al.* (eds.), *Untersuchungen zu Handel und Verkehr der vor- und frühgeschichtlichen Zeit in Mittel- und Nordeuropa.* Göttingen, Vandenhoek & Ruprecht, 200–45.

Wamers, E. 1987. 'A tenth-century metal ornament from Mainz, West Germany', *Medieval Arch* 31, 105–9

Webster, L. and Backhouse, J. (eds.) 1991. *The Making of England: Anglo-Saxon Art and Culture, AD 600–900.* London: British Museum Press

Weissner, P. 1989. 'Style and the changing relations between the individual and society', in Hodder, I. (ed.), *The Meaning of Things.* London: Harper Collins, 56–63

Wilson, D. M. 1960. 'An Anglo-Saxon ivory comb', *The British Museum Quarterly* 23, 17–19

Wilson, D. M. 1964. *Anglo-Saxon Ornamental Metalwork, 700–1100, in the British Museum.* London: Trustees of the British Museum

Wilson, D. M. 1965a. 'Late Saxon Metalwork from the Old Minster, 1964', in Biddle, M. (ed.), 'Excavations at Winchester, 3rd Interim Report', *The Antiquities Jnl* 45, 262–3

Wilson, D. M. 1965b. 'Two 10th-Century Bronze Objects', *Medieval Arch* 9, 154–6

Wilson, D. M. 1969: 'A Late Saxon strap-end', *The Antiquaries Jnl* 49, 326–9

Wilson, D. M. 1975. 'Tenth-Century Metalwork', in Parsons, D. (ed.), *Tenth-Century Studies. Essays in Commemoration of the Millennium of the Council of Winchester and Regularis Concordia,* London and Chichester: Phillimore, 200–207

Wilson, D. M. 1977. 'The dating of Viking Art in England', in Lang, J. (ed.), *Anglo-Saxon and Viking-Age Sculpture and its Context: Papers from the Collingwood Symposium on insular sculpture from 800 to 1066.* Oxford: British Archaeological Reports, 135–144

Wilson, D. M. 1984. *Anglo-Saxon Art from the Seventh Century to the Norman Conquest.* London: Thames and Hudson

Wilson, D. M. and Klindt-Jensen, O. 1966. *Viking Art.* London: Allen and Unwin

Wobst, H. M. 1977. 'Stylistic Behaviour and Information Exchange', in Cleland, C. (ed.), *For the Director: Research essays in honor of James B. Griffin*. Ann Arbor: University of Michigan, 317–42

Wormald, P. 1945. 'Decorated Initials from English Manuscripts from 900–1100', *Archaeologia* 91, 107–136

Wormald, P. 1971. 'The 'Winchester School' before St Æthelwold', in Clemoes P. and Hughes, K. (eds.), *England before the Conquest. Studies in primary sources presented to Dorothy Whitelock*. Cambridge: Cambridge University Press, 305–14

Youngs, S. 1998. Report on a die from Sporle, Norfolk, for the British Museum. Medieval and Late Antiquities record 2846

Youngs, S. 2001. 'Whissonsett, Norfolk: Anglo-Saxon silver-gilt hooked tag (M+ME 436)', *Treasure Annual Report*. London: Department for Culture, Media and Sport, no.57, 40–1

Youngs, S. 2004. 'Lead alloy brooches' in Wallis, H. *et al.* (ed.), *Excavations at Mill Lane, Thetford, 1995. East Anglian Archaeology* 108. Gressenhall: Norfolk Archaeological Unit, 38–40

Zarnecki, G. 1979. *Studies in Romanesque sculpture*. London: Dorian Press

Anglo-Saxon Studies in Archaeology and History 15, 2008

Warriors, Heroes and Companions: Negotiating Masculinity in Viking-Age England

D. M. Hadley

Detailed analysis of the construction of gender identities has transformed our understanding of many aspects of early medieval society, yet the study of the Vikings in Britain has largely remained immune to this branch of scholarship. In responding to this lacuna, this paper examines the gendered dimension of the funerary record of the Scandinavians in England in the ninth and tenth centuries, and suggests that the emphasis on masculine display, in both the burial and the sculptural record, is not merely a quirk of survival, but rather it has much to reveal about the negotiation of lordship in the context of conquest and settlement.

Introduction

For a generation of scholars gender has been an important analytical category. It is, as a result, now widely recognised that femininity and masculinity were not immutable organic categories, but that they were socially constructed, historically contingent and diverse. The plurality and fluidity of gender identities are increasingly being elucidated, as are the multifarious contexts in which they were constructed and contested. Gender is now also understood as a primary signifier of power in society, and as a mechanism of social inclusion and exclusion. The study of gender has accordingly transformed our understanding of many aspects of early medieval society.[1] However, the study of Scandinavian settlement in Britain in the ninth and tenth centuries has largely failed to absorb the insights of this generation of scholarship. A chapter in Christine Fell's volume *Women in Anglo-Saxon England* and Judith Jesch's book *Women in the Viking Age* both offered invaluable wide-ranging, interdisciplinary surveys of the role of women during the period of Scandinavian raids and settlement, but they were written at a time when researchers were principally concerned with increasing the visibility of women in the past, rather than with engaging in the construction of gender identities.[2] In developing the work of these two pioneers, and in seeking to respond to subsequent advancements in gender studies, this paper explores aspects of masculine identity in the context of Scandinavian conquest and settlement in England.

This focus on masculinity requires some justification, since it may, admittedly, appear unnecessary. It is certainly difficult to dissent from the opening sentiment of Jesch's book that 'Vikings are irredeemably male in the popular imagination', and they are scarcely less male in academic preoccupations.[3] Yet, as is often the case when discussion of men dominates historical discourse, men tend to be, in the words of John Tosh, 'everywhere but nowhere', and the importance of disaggregating the generality that is 'men' has recently been stressed.[4] Studies of the multiplicity of medieval masculinities have been greatly influenced by the sociologist R.W. Connell's elaboration of the concept of 'hegemonic masculinities', in which attention is drawn to the ways in which societies often legitimize a dominant form of masculinity, to which few men are able or permitted to aspire, and which serves to marginalise or subordinate other masculinities and femininities.[5] The performative quality of masculinity has also been stressed in recent research, influenced in particular by Judith Butler's observation that 'gender is an identity tenuously constituted in time … through a stylised repetition of acts', and many recent studies have subsequently explored the ways in which early medieval gender identities were constructed through, for example, clothing, gesture, and ritualised actions, including burials.[6] The present paper explores the role of funerary practices as a medium of social display in the wake of Scandinavian conquest and settlement in England, contending that they were contexts through which elite masculinity was renegotiated. Yet, as we shall see, despite the emphasis on masculine funerary display, ultimately it was to be within the contexts of families that Anglo-Scandinavian acculturation was achieved.

Masculinity and the Scandinavian burial rite in England *c.* 900

The burials of Scandinavian settlers in England have proved notoriously elusive, with the diagnostic evidence of cremations and inhumations accompanied by grave goods found at only *c.* 30 sites (Fig. 1).[7] The scarcity of such burials has been regarded as perplexing, especially in the light of the extensive Scandinavian influence on place-names and language, and it has frequently been understood as the result of the paucity of excavated burial sites of the ninth and tenth centuries and of the Scandinavian habit of burying their dead in pre-existing cemeteries, which, it has been stated, 'may explain the relative scarcity of Viking burials in England, since most of their burial places have remained in use down to the present day'.[8] Given the perceived limitations of the data set, the interpretive load borne by this funerary record has largely been restricted to mapping areas of Scandinavian settlement.[9] Recently, however, the social and political messages conveyed by these Scandinavian burials have begun to be explored, and it is worth briefly rehearsing these arguments before considering the gendered dimensions of this burial record.

Martin Biddle and Birthe Kjølbye-Biddle have argued that the late ninth-century funerary complex at Repton (Derbyshire), the site of a major Mercian royal monastery, was created in the context of Scandinavian political and military conquest. A small number of burials accompanied by grave goods were excavated near to the church, along with a former mausoleum containing the remains of at least 264 individuals, which was sealed by a low mound surmounted by a stone kerb. According to an antiquarian account, this deposit incorporated a central warrior burial; it was subsequently disturbed and this claim could not, thus, be confirmed archaeologically, but a number of artefacts, including an iron axe, seaxes, knives and a fragment of a sword, may have accompanied such a burial. The excavators have suggested that the putative central burial may have been for someone of royal status, perhaps Ivar *beinlauss*, one of the leaders of the viking 'great army' active in England from 865 and who died in the 870s, and was buried, according to saga evidence, in a mound. They have interpreted this funerary strategy as 'a ruthless assertion by the Vikings of their own ancient religion'.[10] Situated on a bluff overlooking the River Trent, this burial complex was certainly a highly visible symbol of the great army's occupation of an important Mercian royal and cult centre over the winter of 873–4, although whether it involved obliteration of the old order or, as Julian Richards prefers, a degree of accommodation, in which the new order was 'invested with the authority of the past', is debatable.[11] Nearby at Heath Wood, Ingleby

(Derbyshire) Richards has excavated part of a prominent hill-top cemetery consisting of 59 barrows, thrown up over cremated human and animal remains, from which Scandinavian-type metal items have been recovered. This cemetery is unique, and Richards suggests that it was created at a time of military activity, with those responsible for the site seeking to underpin a precarious position through 'a statement of religious, political and military affiliation', and one which was overtly pagan.[12] The funerary displays at Repton and Heath Wood represent different, if equally dramatic, responses to the circumstances of raiding and the early phases of conquest, and it has been suggested that the groups responsible were engaged in an ideological 'dialogue' with each other.[13] Whether or not this was the case, it is plausible that the statements of conquest made by these groups through funerary displays were intended for an indigenous as well as a Scandinavian audience, and this is probably true of many other Scandinavian-type burials, which were often in conspicuous locations, such as near churches or under mounds.[14]

These recent discussions are important advances in our appreciation of the burial record not simply as a conservative reflection of traditional Scandinavian practices, but as a flexible medium through which socio-political statements relating to group identity and conquest were conveyed. What has, however, largely escaped comment is the gendered dimension of the funerary record; yet the emphasis on masculine display is striking.[15] Almost all of these Scandinavian-type burials were of adults, and most were seemingly provided for men, or at least – given that osteological sexing has not been reliably performed on some of the skeletons from older excavations – contained items with strong masculine associations. These comprise, in particular, swords, shields, spurs, axes, military belt fittings and riding equipment. Examples include seven or eight inhumations accompanied by swords and other weapons, spurs, buckles, a whetstone and also the beam and pans of a set of scales discovered beneath the church at Kildale (Yorkshire); a burial encountered in the churchyard at Wensley (Yorkshire) accompanied by a sword, spear, knife and sickle; and an inhumation accompanied by a sword, spearhead, an axe, shield, gold buckle and Carolingian-style strap-end within a stone cist underneath a mound at Beacon Hill, Aspatria (Cumberland).[16] A burial at Hesket-in-the-Forest (Cumberland) produced a sword, a horse bit, an axe head, buckles, spearheads and a pair of spurs, and another at Claughton Hall, Garstang (Lancashire) contained a sword, spearhead, and a Carolingian baldric mount.[17] In addition, swords recovered from churchyards, such as Farndon (Nottinghamshire), Ormside (Cumberland) and Rampside (Lancashire), have been interpreted as having been disturbed from Viking-Age graves.[18] In contrast, female graves of Scandinavian type are rare and comparatively less well-furnished. The few examples include a female accompanied by oval brooches, an iron knife and key or

Figure 1. Map of Scandinavian burials. After J. D. Richards, Viking Age England *(2nd edn, Stroud, 2000), fig. 63, with the addition of recently-discovered sites.*

latch-lifter and a decorated bronze bowl from Adwick-le-Street (Yorkshire), and a female wearing a necklace of beads and silver pendants and accompanied by a knife from Saffron Walden (Essex).[19] In a small cemetery excavated recently at Cumwhitton (Cumberland) there were two female graves, one containing a jet bracelet and a belt fitting, and the other accompanied by an iron knife, a bead and a wooden chest with a weaving baton, although a pair of oval brooches founded prior to excavation by metal detectorists may also have originally formed part of this grave assemblage.[20] The discovery of a pair of oval brooches near to a sword at Santon Downham (Norfolk)

may have come from a grave, but the circumstances of discovery are poorly recorded.[21] Finally, the grave of a female at Repton, in a later phase than the other furnished burials, included an iron knife and a strike-a-light, but these artefacts scarcely distinguish it from burials with occasional small items that can be found across the country in the ninth and tenth centuries.[22]

There are several reasons for suggesting that this burial record represents more than the simple transference to England of normal Scandinavian funerary practices, and that burial strategies were deliberately modified in response to the circumstances of conquest and the processes of making claims to land and status in newly-occupied territories. First, a recent survey of cemeteries dating to *c.* AD 800–1000 in southern Sweden (much of which was part of the Danish territories in the Viking Age) revealed that around half of burials had been accorded gendered assemblages of grave goods, typically with weapons in male graves and jewellery in female graves, but that the number of feminine burial assemblages was roughly three times that of masculine assemblages.[23] A similar pattern of greater visibility of feminine grave assemblages in ninth-century Jutland and the Danish islands has also been noted, although in those regions elaborately-furnished graves are generally rare before the tenth century.[24] In contrast, a study of ninth-century cemeteries in the Sogn district of western Norway revealed around three times more masculine than feminine assemblages.[25] In other parts of Norway, however, a more even distribution of masculine and feminine assemblages has been noted.[26] In this context, and even taking into account the evidence from the Sogn district, the overwhelmingly masculine display in the funerary record of the settlers in England is striking. Second, this masculine emphasis in England contrasts with the situation in other regions of Scandinavian settlement, such as the Scottish Isles, where female and, to a lesser extent, juvenile and infant burials of Scandinavian type are considerably more numerous, and there are roughly similar numbers of burials with masculine and feminine assemblages of grave goods, many of which are considerably more elaborate than most of the examples from England.[27] Third, other indications that deliberate choices were made about burial display in the context of settlement include the fact that Scandinavian practices such as boat burials have not been securely identified in England, but they do occur in both the Scottish Isles and the Isle of Man.[28] Thus, among the Scandinavian settlers in other parts of the British Isles, funerary displays signalling Scandinavian identity were apparently more distinctive and expressed more broadly in the burials of all members of the community than was the case in England.[29] In contrast, analysis of the admittedly limited funerary record from England suggests a disproportionate emphasis on masculine display, which was often allied to Anglo-Saxon strategies of social display through the location of burials in the vicinity of churches.[30]

What significance can we attach to these masculine displays? That they were more nuanced than simply reflecting the military status of the deceased is suggested by recent discussions of the mnemonic qualities of early medieval grave goods. Howard Williams, for example, has argued that the significance of weapons in burials derived from not only their association with male violence, which was an integral component of masculine identity, but also from their symbolism of social status and ancestral associations, and also their connections with particular deities, and links with smiths, who in Germanic mythology were imbued with mythical, sometimes shamanic, qualities.[31] Similarly, Elisabeth van

Houts has demonstrated the ways in which the memories of individuals and events were often associated in the minds of early medieval chroniclers and will-makers with particular artefacts, which she has described as 'pegs for memory'. Swords, she observes, were prized ancestral heirlooms because of 'the memorial value attached to these weapons and the stories they generated'.[32] In this respect the presence among the burial assemblages of the Scandinavians of such items as Carolingian belt fittings and Anglo-Saxon swords and coins warrants further consideration.[33] Although it is impossible to know whether they had been acquired through warfare, purchase or inheritance, it is quite likely that such artefacts evoked particular associations with battles fought and past adventures.

Yet grave goods might also be chosen for their contemporary resonance. This is suggested, in part, by evidence that viking armies raiding in Frankia apparently prized Frankish military apparel, leading Charles the Bald in 864 to prohibit the sale of Frankish swords to the Northmen, who were apparently also keen to acquire Frankish horse-fittings.[34] Anne Pedersen has argued that the appearance of riding equipment in southern Scandinavian burials in the tenth century 'may reflect a way of life comparable to or at least attempting to emulate western European court life', suggesting that burial strategies could be employed to make contemporary political statements.[35] The burial record of the Scandinavians in England also has similarities with the coinage minted for Scandinavian kings in England in the late ninth and early tenth centuries, which likewise incorporated complex combinations of Anglo-Saxon, Carolingian, Christian and secular influences.[36] Mark Blackburn has argued that the designs of these coins were deliberately chosen as if to convince the kings of other realms, including Wessex and Frankia, that the new Scandinavian polities were 'within the civilised community of Christian states'.[37] Furthermore, the readiness with which Guthrum, one of the leaders of the great army, took up the trappings of Anglo-Saxon kingship, including baptism; the minting of coinage on which he employed his baptismal name, Æthelstan; and the issuing of written legislation in collaboration with King Alfred, suggests that at least some of the Scandinavians were adept at adopting new forms of lordly behaviour.[38] We may quibble over whether lavishly furnished burials would have been understood as the attributes of a 'civilised' people by the Anglo-Saxons, but their contents, as also the locations of some near to churches, suggest that they were created by Scandinavian communities looking beyond the confines of the warband of which they were, or had been, a part. For their part, although the Anglo-Saxons may have long since given up burying their dead with lavish assemblages of grave goods, they would surely have understood elements of the symbolic repertoire of these funerary displays. In sum, it can be suggested that among the Scandinavian settlers, masculine funerary display was simultaneously employed as a focal point for the construction of ancestral memories and as a medium for mediating the processes of conquest.

Restricting Masculinity in the Burial Rite

This masculine emphasis was, however, only one part of the processes of conquest and acculturation. Despite oft-repeated comments to the contrary (see *Introduction*, above), it is becoming increasingly difficult to avoid the conclusion that the burials of the majority of the settlers and their descendants must be found among the thousands of largely unfurnished late ninth- and tenth-century burials known from England. Burials of this date continue to be excavated at a regular rate, but the corpus of elaborately furnished burials has, with few exceptions, remained fairly static over recent decades, suggesting that the comparatively limited scale of furnished burials is a real phenomenon.[39] This is, indeed, a deduction that is beginning to be supported by stable isotope analysis (see below), revealing the presence of individuals born in Scandinavia among the unfurnished burials of cemeteries in northern and eastern England.[40] Among the majority of ninth- and tenth-century burials neither gender nor age normally determined the form of burial accorded an individual, and family status seems to have been an important factor determining burial provision, for the Scandinavians as much as the local population.[41] Consideration of this broader funerary landscape reinforces the impression that the burials of only certain Scandinavian males were elaborated as part of the process of conquest, and that only for a few of these was warrior status articulated in death.

This differential treatment is most strikingly demonstrated by considering the male burials excavated at Repton. Grave 511 was a lavishly-furnished burial containing a sword in a wooden scabbard lined with fleece and covered with leather, a necklace with two beads and a Thor's hammer, two buckles (one from a belt, the other for a suspension strap for the sword), two knives, a key, the tusk of a wild boar and the humerus of a jackdaw or raven, possibly in a bag or box.[42] The warrior status of the male interred in this grave was evidently being emphasized. Moreover, the Thor's hammer on his necklace and the bird bone, possibly evoking the god Odin who was associated with ravens in Scandinavian mythology, suggest that the powers of the gods were also being invoked for this man.[43] In contrast, the adjacent and subsequent male burial (grave 295) contained only an iron knife.[44] But for its location, this adjacent burial might not have entered the corpus of Scandinavian burials, since occasional examples of burials with knives are not unknown in many regions of later Anglo-Saxon England.[45] However grave 295 was clearly part of the same funerary display as grave 511. The two burials were covered with a single stone setting, while a 30 cm-square post-hole centrally placed at the east end of the two graves suggests that they were jointly marked

above ground.[46] That these two individuals were both of Scandinavian origins has recently been suggested by the application of stable isotope methods. This involves analysis of the oxygen and strontium isotopes laid down in teeth during childhood that derive from drinking water, which is regionally varied according to local geology, and which can reveal the regions in which individuals spent their early years.[47] This evidence demonstrates, thus, that neither Scandinavian origins, nor burial within a larger funerary display with a fellow Scandinavian, invariably qualified a man for elaborate weapon burial.

There are several possible reasons for the disparity between the funerary provision for the two men, including their relative social status and age, since the occupant of grave 511 was *c*. 35–45 years at death, while his companion was *c*. 17–20 years. As the excavators have asked, 'Do we see here an older warrior buried with his companion, his weapon-bearer?'.[48] Alternatively, having buried one of their number with an elaborate weapon display, perhaps it was not thought appropriate or necessary to consign another set of weapons to the ground, with status for the second interment being conferred, instead, through proximity of burial to the warrior display. The absence of elaborate display in the grave of the younger man is purely a matter for speculation, but it was certainly not because he had never fought, since he appears to have died from a cut to the right side of the skull and generalized trauma on his skeleton suggest that 'he had experienced great physical strain'.[49] In contrast, while his elevated social status may have determined the funerary treatment of the older male, the manner of his death may also have been a factor. He had been struck on the head, possibly being killed by the thrusting of a sharp object through the orbital socket. He had also experienced a massive sword blow to the head of the left femur, in an attack apparently made while he was on the ground, and cut marks on the lower vertebrae have been interpreted as possible evidence of disembowelling. This man had died violently, probably while in a vulnerable position, and the injury to his groin is notable, perhaps indicating that his genitals had been mutilated.[50] It is tempting to suggest that the emasculation – both metaphorical and literal – of this warrior in the manner of his death was a factor necessitating more elaborate funerary provision, and greater emphasis on masculine warrior prowess, than was afforded the male in the adjacent grave. The fate of the older man may also explain the presence of the tusk of a wild boar, with its known amuletic properties, placed between his thighs.[51]

An axe-head discovered among the burials to the south of the crypt at Repton may have been disturbed from a grave, as perhaps was an iron spearhead found to the north of the crypt, however aside from graves 511 and 295 only three other burials reportedly contained grave goods. These comprised a gold ring and five silver pennies (grave 529), a copper-alloy ring (grave 83), and a knife and a strike-a-light from the aforementioned female burial (grave 203) in a later generation.[52] These have been labeled as viking burials by their excavators, and the skeletal remains of the male buried in grave 529 have, indeed, yielded a Scandinavian isotopic signature.[53] The male aged *c.* 50 years in grave 83, wearing a copper-alloy ring on the third finger of his left hand, was buried to the south of the chancel adjacent to a male aged *c.* 20 years, and there is an interesting parallel here with graves 511 and 295 on the north side of the church; each was interred in their own coffin but they were apparently buried simultaneously in a large pit.[54] Double graves of adult males are very rare in ninth- and tenth-century cemeteries in England,[55] and the presence of two among the earliest generation of Scandinavian settlers in England may tentatively be interpreted as emphasizing male comradeship, which was certainly an important motif among Scandinavian armies, according to the evidence of skaldic poetry and the inscriptions on Scandinavian runestones.[56]

It is apparent that for the majority of the Scandinavians buried at Repton warrior status was not the crucial identity being expressed in their burial provision, nor was 'Scandinavianness' being overtly articulated in all but a handful of graves. Nonetheless, burial near to a warrior, including grave 511 and the putative central burial in the former mausoleum, may have been important for conveying messages about the status and ethnic identity of the other Scandinavians who were buried at Repton. It is certainly not uncommon in the early medieval period for status to be conveyed by burial near to prominent graves, reflected in, for example, the Christian desire for burial near to the bodies of saints (*ad sanctos*).[57] Similarly, in the seventh century the most elaborate burials, frequently incorporating masculine grave assemblages and commonly under mounds, were often the focal point for clusters of other, less well-furnished burials.[58] Status for the latter was conferred through place, rather than manner, of burial. Nick Stoodley has argued that the restriction of the most elaborate burial displays in seventh-century Wessex mainly to males, in contrast to the practices of the fifth and sixth centuries when masculine and feminine displays were more equally found, was 'a direct consequence of the increasing stratification within society' which saw 'profound changes to the expression of gender as reflected through the burial rite'.[59] A similar restriction among the Scandinavian settlers in England *c.* 900 of the most elaborate funerary provision to a select group of males, around which other burials clustered, is perhaps also a product of conquest and social competition as the settlers competed to establish their authority. Warrior status may have been aspired to by many men, but was afforded in death to only a few, and this need not, as the evidence of grave 295 at Repton demonstrates, have derived solely from actual experience of fighting.

Masculine imagery on funerary sculptures of the tenth century

In the tenth century there was a proliferation of stone sculptures in the regions of Scandinavian settlement, especially northern England, a small proportion of which incorporated armed men. While precise dating is difficult, it is generally thought that most of the sculptures with such images date to the earlier to mid-tenth century, and thus they probably largely post-date the furnished burials already discussed.[60] These 'warrior' images are diverse, and this suggests considerable experimentation by sculptors. Some of these armed men are depicted on horseback, as at Sockburn (Fig. 3), Chester-le-Street, Gainford, Hart (County Durham), Brompton (Yorkshire) and Crowle (Lincolnshire).[61] Others are standing, as on sculptures from Weston (Fig. 4), Middleton (Yorkshire) and Norbury (Derbyshire), while yet others are seated, as, for example, on another shaft from Middleton (where the sitting position is indicated by the foreshortened lower legs and the pellets above the shoulders which were possibly part of a chair) (Fig. 3) and on a shaft at Nunburnholme (Yorkshire).[62] Some of the men have only one weapon, such as Middleton 1 and Great Stainton (County Durham), while others have two or more, for example, Middleton 2 and 5 and Sockburn 7. Many are helmeted and some carry shields, such as Sockburn 3 and 5 and Alstonfield (Staffordshire) (Fig. 3).[63] A few appear to be engaged in combat, or possibly hunting (such as Sockburn 14) (Fig. 2) or even jousting (as at Neston (Cheshire)), but most are inactive, such as the figure on Middleton 2 who is surrounded by, but not holding, his weapons (Fig. 3), and the figure on the Weston sculpture whose weapons hang down rather than being brandished (Fig. 4).[64] It is likely that workshops and individual sculptors were important in driving artistic styles, and Richard Bailey's study of the use of templates permits identification of the same sculptor or workshop behind warrior images at both Sockburn and Brompton, while two different warrior images at Middleton were constructed with the same template. The influence of the patron can, however, sometimes be discerned in evidence that single workshops, even individual sculptors, produced diverse monument forms.[65]

There are clearly similarities between the array of artefacts found in the more elaborate male graves and those depicted on the sculptures, yet the latter are seemingly related much more closely to the processes of integration and acculturation. The martial imagery on sculptures was firmly incorporated into Christian schema, and warriors are commonly juxtaposed with cross-heads, as on Middleton 2, and sometimes occur alongside ecclesiastical figures, such as evangelists and priests, as on shafts from Nunburnholme and Brompton.[66] Given these settings it is possible that the warrior images themselves sometimes possessed Christian connotations. It has, for example, been suggested that weapons might sometimes

Figure 2. Sculptures with figural art: a) a priest (Brompton, Yorkshire); b) men armed with spears on horseback (Gosforth, Cumberland); c) a man with a shield on horseback (Chester-le-Street, County Durham); d) a man wearing a helmet and armed with a shield and spear (Sockburn, County Durham); e) eight figures in a boat bearing shields (on the left-hand side) and eight or ten standing figures also bearing shields (right-hand side), between which stands a figure raising one arm (Lowther, Westmorland); f) figure on horseback carrying a spear (Baldersby, Yorkshire)

have served symbolically as 'weapons of faith', and that the mounted horsemen may have derived in some way from Christian models.[67] However, as Bailey points out, when we find the horsemen engaged in the aristocratic pursuit of hunting or even jousting, as on a stone at Neston, a Christian model seems unlikely, and it need not be assumed that warrior figures could only find a place if they had specific Christian overtones.[68] Indeed, since such stones first aroused academic curiosity, there has been increased understanding that there is no necessary contradiction between Christianity and the aristocratic, martial ideal. As an analogy, Patrick Wormald argued that the Anglo-Saxon poem *Beowulf*, with its mixture of pagan rites, secular subject matter and biblical references, could have been created and enjoyed within a monastic setting because of the 'aristocratic environment of early

English Christianity'. Similarly, it can be suggested that warrior imagery on tenth-century stone sculptures reveals that the Church had once again strategically adapted itself to the aristocratic environment.[69]

Yet, although military deeds could find a place within an ecclesiastical context, there were undoubtedly those who disapproved. To continue the *Beowulf* analogy, there are hints that although heroic tales were known among monastic communities they were also frowned upon; Alcuin condemned the hearing of 'the songs of pagans' in monastic communities in a letter to the bishop of Lindisfarne *c.* 797, asking 'What hath Ingeld to do with Christ?'.[70] Similar misgivings may have been expressed at the sculptures with their secular imagery, perhaps fuelled by the recent, on-going and probably not always entirely straightforward processes of conversion of the Scandinavian settlers, which doubtless resulted in churchmen being faced with a wide range of behaviour in the name of Christianity.[71] In areas of Scandinavian settlement the Church had undoubtedly suffered badly, both through direct attacks and the loss of land, and in many regions had probably struggled to be re-established. In this respect, it is significant that ecclesiastics are depicted more commonly on tenth-century sculptures than on those of an earlier date, perhaps indicating a greater need to reinforce their presence than in the past.[72] The sculptures thus appear to have been a medium in which the competing (male) influences in local society were articulated and negotiated, and they hint at the complexity of the processes of acculturation.

Whatever the Christian connotations of the sculptures, it is difficult to deny that armed figures must also have conveyed messages about the status and attributes of the person for whom they were commissioned. It is plausible to suggest that at least some of the warrior images were depictions of real men, perhaps serving as memorials to them. Indeed, a fragmentary inscription on a shaft from Crowle indicates that it was a commemorative stone, perhaps to one or more of the three men depicted, while the name Eadmund was inscribed, possibly as a secondary addition, above the armed warrior on horseback depicted on a shaft at Chester-le-Street (Fig. 2).[73] We should, however, remember that possession, use and deposition of weapons and armour were not unproblematic in the Anglo-Saxon period. In the society evoked in *Beowulf* weapons and armour, including helmet, spear and sword were certainly the markers of members of a warrior aristocracy, yet in reality possession of weapons alone is unlikely to have been sufficient to maintain status.[74] For example, the well-known early eleventh-century compilation on status (*Geþyncðo*) commented that even if a *ceorl* possessed a helmet, byrnie (mail) and sword he was not worthy of thegnhood unless he also had the requisite amount of land; that all thegns were necessarily well-equipped for battle is also to be doubted.[75] This clause from *Geþyncðo* serves as a reminder of the potential tensions over elite status, and this should caution against reading the military images on sculptures as necessarily confident images of lords; they may have been as much attempts to convince local society of the status of the patron or the person commemorated, although undoubtedly they had resources to have been able to have commissioned this sculpture.

It would be hazardous to attach significance to the distinctions in military apparel depicted on various sculptures, not least because some are by any standards crude products. The warriors are often depicted in constricted spaces with limited room for elaboration, and the impression conveyed by the weaponry would doubtless have been enhanced by the application of gesso and paint which does not now survive.[76] Nonetheless, the extent to which a man was armed would certainly have mattered in this society. At a later date, for example, the Bayeux Tapestry seems to differentiate between men with only spear and shield and those fully armed.[77] Weapons were also important constituents of later Anglo-Saxon heriot payments, a duty paid to a lord, often the king, upon death, and which were diverse and gradually increasing during the tenth century. Nicholas Brooks has suggested that heriots may find their origins in the abandonment of the deposition of weapons in graves, arguing that previously there may have been tension between the requirement to equip the dead and the demands of lords for armed retainers.[78] If so, for a short time in northern England these tensions may have re-emerged given the Scandinavian inclination to bury weapons with the dead, and also to deposit them in bogs and rivers, especially as the settlers began to be acculturated to Anglo-Saxon norms of lordly behaviour.[79] We do not know whether heriots were paid in the regions of Scandinavian settlement in the immediate aftermath of conquest, but in the later tenth century heriots were less onerous in the Danelaw than in southern England, and Brooks suggests that either the Danelaw nobility were less well-armed or that kings were less able to exact such heavy payments.[80] Either way, when assessing the significance of weaponry on funerary sculptures we should bear in mind the potential tensions surrounding the possession of weapons and their fate upon the death of individuals in tenth-century northern England.

The armed men on tenth-century sculptures in northern England have attracted surprisingly little comment, but implicit in such commentary as there has been is that they arose out of the changed circumstances of a turbulent era and reflect the prominence of men in tenth-century aristocratic society.[81] Yet although the importance of weapons, armour and hunting to lordly status was scarcely an innovation, there is nothing inevitable about the appearance of such images on sculpture. There were few precedents among earlier sculptures, and the Scandinavians did not bring a widespread tradition of sculptural production with them, nor was figural art apparently common in their other artistic mediums.[82] Moreover, elite men fulfilled many roles in this era, and the emphasis on military apparel suggests that it was either particularly important to the status of the patrons and those depicted, or that this martial aspect of their identity was in some sense contentious. In a recent study of aristocratic masculinity in the ninth century, Janet L. Nelson has drawn attention to the dilemmas faced by elite males who had to negotiate the competing expectations of secular power and Christian models for behaviour, which included both physical and sexual self-constraint; in a number of cases rejection of the sword and sword-belt became a 'symbolic object of rejection' for men who were tormented by these contrasting demands.[83] We do not know who commissioned the sculptures incorporating armed men, but in considering their significance we would be advised to keep in mind that the period of Scandinavian settlement presented many challenges to elite men, of both Scandinavian and indigenous origins, as the era witnessed many battles (the clashing of swords is a repeated motif in the panegyric to the English victors at the battle of Brunanburh in 937 incorporated in the Anglo-Saxon Chronicle),[84] caused considerable political disruption, doubtless caused massive amounts of land to change hands, and brought together two differing religious belief systems which valorized competing dimensions of masculine behaviour. In this context, perhaps it is not surprising that a new demand to depict the attributes of aristocratic masculinity on sculpture emerged. It is also striking that these warrior images emerged at the periphery of royal authority, reinforcing the impression that they were less confident images of an established regime than the mechanism by which a new social order was reinforced.

There are also parallels to be drawn between the iconography of the figural sculpture and another medium of lordship, the coinage minted in York under Scandinavian rule in the early tenth century. The latter, while overwhelmingly assimilated to Christianity and Anglo-Saxon forms, also periodically incorporated items with secular connotations, including a sword, bow and arrow and a banner of the type displayed on a battle field, while other images, such as Thor's hammers and ravens, had links with battle as well as with Norse mythology.[85] Some of the most striking innovations in coinage occurred in the wake of regime changes. These include the inclusion of a hammer and a bow and arrow on the coins minted for Ragnall, who seized York *c.* 919, after which a sword was incorporated into the pre-existing St Peter's coinage, and the appearance of a raven on the coins of Olaf Guthfrithson, who captured York in 939, and is presented on his coinage in Norse as *cununc* (ON *konungr*) rather than Latin *rex*, in what Richard Hall has described as 'propaganda coinage'.[86] Thus, both sculpture and coinage were intermittently employed to display the attributes of lordship; in the case of coinage, which is more closely datable, this can be linked to times of considerable political change, and this may also have been a factor accounting for the sporadic appearance of warrior imagery on sculpture.

Depictions of Sigurd the dragon-slayer and Wayland the Smith were also innovations on tenth-century sculpture, although the stories from which they derive were previously known in England.[87] Richard Bailey has argued that such heroic scenes were not, as once thought, intended as celebrations of pagan culture, but were rather used to convey Christian truths.[88] For example, there are potential parallels between the Eucharist and Sigurd's enlightenment through consumption of the dragon's blood, which may have been made explicit when the lower part of an image of a mass priest on a sculpture from Nunburnholme was recut by another sculptor, who was also responsible for the addition of various ecclesiastical scenes, to make way for two figures interpreted as representing the Sigurd legend.[89] Indeed, while much later Norse poems and sagas elaborate an extensive train of events in the story

of Sigurd, and various versions of the story circulated, it is consistently the dragon-killing, heart-roasting and consumption of the blood that appear on sculptures in both the British Isles and post-conversion Scandinavia, perhaps precisely because these elements of the story can be incorporated into a Christian context.[90] Parallels also seem to have been drawn between the Wayland legend and Christian themes, as, for example, on the Leeds (Yorkshire) shaft where Wayland's flight is accompanied by Christian imagery of flight, including winged angels and St John's eagle (Fig. 3).[91] Recently Victoria Thompson has drawn attention to the links between Sigurd (whose foster-father was a smith) and Weland (the legendary smith) and Old English glosses on Biblical descriptions of Christ, in which he is transformed from an artisan into a smith, and she suggests that the two heroic figures may also have served iconographically as 'types of Christ'.[92] Yet while acknowledging these Christian connotations, we should not underestimate the capacity of those who commissioned sculptures to have purposefully requested images capable of eliciting diverse responses, and thus for heroic figures to have served simultaneously as commemorations of Scandinavian traditions, as didactic aids in the processes of conversion, and as reflections of masculine aspirations.[93]

Women and the Family in Viking-Age England

The marginality of women in the symbolic language of sculpture is highlighted by rare exceptions, including the shaft from Weston on which a male brandishing his sword is grabbing or protecting a woman (Fig. 4), and a similar scene from Kirklevington (Yorkshire). On a sculpture at Lowther (Westmorland) a figure stands between two ships of shield-bearing warriors, which Bailey has suggested may be a scene from the legend of 'Hildr and the Everlasting Battle', given the similarities with a panel on a picture-stone from Lärbo St Hammers (Gotland), where the central figure is more obviously female; if so, the Lowther sculpture depicts woman as the nemesis of man, given Hildr's legendary role in provoking perpetual warfare.[94] While male ecclesiastical figures, saints and Christ continue to be depicted, Mary all but disappears from the sculptural repertoire until the end of the tenth century. This seems surprising given that she was potentially an appropriate image for circumstances of conversion, playing, of course, a crucial role in man's redemption.[95] In contrast, Mary does appear in the iconography and runic inscriptions on stone sculptures produced in Scandinavia following conversion. Birgit Sawyer has suggested that Mary may have had a particular appeal for female converts, and that she was consistently depicted as a mother rather than as a virgin, perhaps 'due to the high esteem in which fertility had been held in pagan Scandinavia'.[96] Thus, the absence of Marian imagery from the period of Scandinavian conversion in

Figure 3. Sculptures with warrior and heroic images: a) mounted warriors (Sockburn, County Durham) (Length 63.5 cm); b) the flight scene from the heroic story of Wayland the Smith (Leeds, Yorkshire) (height of section shown 82.5 cm); c) an armed warrior (Sockburn, County Durham) (height 48 cm); d) an armed warrior on a sculpture from Middleton (Yorkshire) (height 56 cm)

England is especially striking.

The paucity of feminine display on sculpture is as striking as it is in the burial record, but it is unlikely to be explained by a virtual absence of female settlers. Two entries in the *Anglo-Saxon Chronicle* reveal that the raiders were sometimes accompanied by women and children. For example, in 893 the viking fortress at Benfleet (Essex) was captured, including 'both goods, and women and also children', and subsequently 'the *wif* [variously translated as 'wife' or 'woman'] and two sons' of the leader of the viking army, Hæsten, were taken to King Alfred, while the *Chronicle* entry for 895 reports that 'the Danes had placed their women in safety in East Anglia'.[97] Continental chronicles convey a similar impression. For example, when converting to Christianity under the sponsorship of a Frankish king, both Harald Klak in 826, and Weland in 862, were said by contemporary chroniclers to have been accompanied by their wives, while the early tenth-century chronicler Regino of Prüm records that in 873 a band of raiders arrived in the deserted city of Angers 'with women and children'.[98] Scandinavian women were, then, clearly present during the period of raiding and settlement. Their role in the acculturation process, and doubtless also that of their Anglo-Saxon counterparts, has also recently been highlighted in analyses of the burgeoning corpus of metalwork recovered (mainly by metal-detectorists) from eastern England, which reveals innovative combinations of Anglo-Saxon and Scandinavian styles and forms, especially on female dress-accessories.[99]

Whatever the roles that women played during the Viking Age, the burial and sculptural evidence suggests that in the turbulent circumstances of conquest and assimilation to a new culture, emphasis was placed on masculine display and on conveying the masculine attributes and appeal of Christianity. There are grounds for suggesting that a major dynamic in the settlement context was the incorporation of elite men into the new social and religious order. Indeed, there are hints in the written record of the importance, if not always the success, of marriage of Scandinavian men with indigenous women. Most famously, negotiations at Tamworth (Staffordshire) in 926 between King Athelstan of Wessex and King Sihtric of York were sealed by the marriage of the latter to Athelstan's sister.[100] A later medieval source records that prior to the battle of *Brunanburh* in 937, an alliance between Olaf Guthfrithson, from the Norse ruling dynasty in Dublin, and King Constantine of the Scots, was sealed by the marriage of Olaf to Constantine's daughter, and it would be unsurprising if there were many more examples of inter-marriage between Scandinavian men and indigenous women than the chronicles record.[101] The contracting of political marriages between members of rival groups was standard fare in early medieval Europe, and in the eleventh century the followers of both Cnut and William the Conqueror employed the strategy of marriage with indigenous women as a means of legitimizing claims to land.[102] Does this dynamic offer another explanation for the overwhelmingly masculine emphasis of the figural imagery? Roughly contemporary slate sculptures from the Isle of Man incorporate runic inscriptions that offer tantalizing evidence for their production within the context of inter-marriage between Norse men and local women. Examples include the inscription on Kirk Michael III in which the commemorated is a woman with a Celtic name with a Norse-named husband.[103] Despite the frequency with which women are mentioned on these sculptures, the iconography remains resolutely masculine: for example, on Kirk Andreas II the inscription commemorates a woman, yet the associated imagery relates to hunting.[104] In the absence of comparable inscriptions on the English sculptures it is difficult to take this argument further, and the sculptures were probably not commissioned solely by those of Scandinavian origins. The stone sculptures of diverse form and decoration were evidently produced in the context of cultural and ethnic assimilation, changing religious affiliations, and the emergence of new types of local lordship, and given the evidence, admittedly limited, of the importance of marriage strategies among the Scandinavian settlers, it can be hypothesized that sculptures were also commissioned within the context of marriages and families.

The proliferation of stone sculptures in the tenth century derives from secular lords exercising a novel form of conspicuous display at what were frequently newly founded churches. Sculptures were probably sometimes, perhaps often, intended to serve as markers of the status of the whole family, and not simply of the individual over whose grave they were placed. At rural churches, in particular, it is rare to find more than one or two such monuments,

Figure 4. A tenth-century sculpture from Weston (Yorkshire) depicting a warrior with his sword in one hand, while with the other hand he grabs, pushes or perhaps protects a woman. On the reverse of this sculpture the warrior is depicted alone with his sword and battle-axe (height of section shown 22 cm)

even among churches extensively excavated or renovated.[105] The so-called hogback monuments of the tenth century, which were possibly grave covers, are typically house-shaped monuments, often depicting a roof or even a door, and while there has been debate about possible prototypes of this monument among early shrines it would surely not be too great a leap to believe that these house-shaped monuments also symbolised, and were created within the context of, the family.[106] Later Anglo-Saxon wills indicate that the prospect of death typically focussed attention on the family, including disposal of family property, provision for heirs, obligations of future generations with regards to property and commemoration, and the property and welfare of the souls of already-deceased family members, and it is consequently plausible that stone monuments were also part of a family-oriented response to death.[107] In this context, we should acknowledge the historically-attested role of aristocratic women in commemorating the dead and in the preservation of dynastic memory in the early medieval period, and the part they played in the transmission of cultural and artistic traditions through their marriages into new families.[108] It is a moot point whether such women commissioned sculptures, but their role in reinforcing claims to status through support of their male kin is perhaps hinted at occasionally on sculptures; for example, a fragmentary stone from Sockburn depicts a women proffering a horn to a man, in a scene that is reminiscent of depictions of Valkyries welcoming dead heroes into Valhalla on picture-stones from Gotland.[109] The role that women played, or at least were valorized for, in the society of northern England following the Scandinavian settlements is perhaps best demonstrated by the imagery on one of the most complex stone monuments of all. On the great cross at Gosforth, a female figure from Norse mythology identified as Sigyn tends to her husband, the god Loki, holding a vessel to catch the snake venom as it drips onto him; on the other side of the monument a female figure depicted in typically Scandinavian fashion with pigtail and trailing dress tends to the crucified Christ, and she has been identified as Mary Magdalen, a symbol of the converted heathen.[110] Here for once we see acknowledgement of the role of women in religious observation, the family and the conversion process, but it is a role that was normally hidden behind the masculine display that was more normally utilized to represent lordship, constrained as it doubtless was by expectations of the symbolic qualities of lordship. The career of Æthelflaed of the Mercians is the best-documented reminder of the fact that women undertook many more roles in the Viking Age than they were acknowledged for in the medium of stone sculpture.

Conclcusions

This paper has suggested a new reading of the funerary practices that emerged in the wake of the Scandinavian conquests and settlements of the later ninth and tenth centuries. This evidence suggests that Scandinavian modes of behaviour were transformed in the wake of contact with, and acculturation to, Anglo-Saxon society, and, in the case of the sculptural evidence, indigenous lords and the Church appear to have been flexible and innovative in their responses to the newcomers. Expressions of Scandinavian

identity in a funerary context were constructed with an emphasis on masculine display. Weapon burials were constructed for a select group of elite Scandinavian men who conquered and settled in parts of northern and eastern England; but they should no longer be presented as wholly representative of Scandinavian funerary strategies. To do so, as the recent proliferation of studies of medieval masculinities have observed, is to permit the manifestation of elite masculinity to stand for the experiences of all men. As in many other circumstances of conquest and social change in the early medieval period, a renegotiation of elite masculine status occurred, prompting the display of new forms of masculine symbolism, as part of the processes of ameliorating social disruption and staking claims to land and status.[111] Ultimately, however, it was to be within the context of families, marriage and conversion to Christianity that Anglo-Scandinavian acculturation occurred, and it is thus not surprising that secular images of masculine prowess were sporadic and short-lived, since they represent innovative responses to abnormal circumstances.

Acknowledgements

I would like to thank Dr Jane Hawkes and Dr Sally Smith for their comments on an earlier draft of this paper, and for their numerous suggestions for improvements. I am also grateful for the feedback provided by the graduate seminar of the Department of Medieval History, University of Birmingham; participants in the Semana de Estudios Medievales de Estella (July, 2007); and members of the audience at a session of the 42nd International Congress on Medieval Studies at Western Michigan University organised by Dr Christina Lee entitled 'Swords make the man: gender and material culture in the Viking Age'. The illustrations were drawn by Oliver Jessop. The images in Fig. 2 are reproduced by permission of the Corpus of Anglo-Saxon Stone Sculpture at the University of Durham; the photographers were J. Crook (Baldersby) and T. Middlemass.

Notes

1. Nelson 1997a; Smith 2004
2. Fell 1984, 129–47; Jesch 1991
3. Ibid., 1
4. Tosh 1994, 180
5. Connell 1995, 76–81; Hadley 1999, 4–8; Smith 2004, 9, 18–19
6. Butler 1990, 140; Hadley 1999, 14–16; Smith 2004, 16–17; Stoodley 1999; Gilchrist 1994
7. Graham-Campbell 1980; Graham-Campbell 2001; Richards 2002
8. Morris 1981, 77
9. Reviewed in Halsall 2000, 259–61
10. Biddle and Kjølbye-Biddle 2001, 60–85
11. Richards 2001, 101
12. Richards, Jecock, Richmond and Tuck 1995, 65–6; Richards 2001, 101–02
13. Richards et al 1995, 65–8; Richards 2001, 102
14. Richards 2002, 157–9; Griffiths 2004, 131–8

15. This was first noted in Halsall 2000, 270; see also Hadley 2004, 214
16. Richards 2002, 160; Edwards 1998, 8–10
17. Ibid., 14–16, 19; for other examples see Richards 2002; Graham-Campbell 2001; Hadley 2006, 239–46
18. Edwards 1998, 17–18, 21–2; Graham-Campbell 2001, 106–8
19. Speed and Walton Rogers 2004; Graham-Campbell 2001, 114
20. Pitts 2004
21. Graham-Campbell 2001, 110–11
22. Biddle and Kjølbye-Biddle 2001, 65; Hadley 2006, 246–53
23. Svanberg 2003, 22
24. Randsborg 1980, 121–33
25. Dommasnes 1982, 76
26. Dommasnes 1991, 67 citing an unpublished survey by M. Høgestøl
27. Graham-Campbell and Batey 1998, 113–42
28. Ibid., 118–22, 135–8; Bersu and Wilson 1966
29. The significance of this contrast is discussed in Hadley in press a

30. Richards 2002, 160–65; Hadley 2006, 242–3
31. Williams 2005, 264–7
32. van Houts 1999, 93–120, at 110 for the quotation
33. Edwards 1998, 9, 16–17; Biddle and Kjølbye-Biddle 2001, 65; Halsall 2000, 264–5, 268–9
34. Nelson 1997b, 37–8
35. Pedersen 1997, 182
36. Blackburn 2001; Blackburn 2004
37. Blackburn 2001, 136
38. Hadley 2006, 29–34
39. Ibid., 246–53
40. MacPherson 2006, 130, 159–60; the results of isotope analysis on skeletal remains from Riccall (Yorkshire) cited in Hadley 2006, 254 have since been withdrawn by the laboratory (Jo Buckberry, pers. comm.)
41. Hadley and Buckberry 2005, 141–2, 145; Hadley in press b
42. Biddle and Kjølbye-Biddle 2001, 60–5
43. As suggested in Richards 2003, 388
44. Biddle and Kjølbye-Biddle 2001, 65
45. Hadley 2006, 248
46. Biddle and Kjølbye-Biddle 2001, 60
47. Budd, Millard, Chenery, Lucy and Roberts 2004, 127–41
48. Biddle and Kjølbye-Biddle 2001, 60, 65
49. Ibid., 65
50. Ibid., 61; Richards 2003, 388
51. Ibid.
52. Biddle and Kjølbye-Biddle 2001, 65–6
53. Budd *et al.* 2004, 137–8
54. Biddle and Kjølbye-Biddle 2001, 65
55. Hadley in press c
56. Jesch 2001, 187–94, 216–35
57. James 1989, 29
58. Stoodley 1999, 101–06
59. Ibid., 104–05
60. Bailey and Cramp 1988, 28–31; Lang 1991, 28–43; Lang 2001, 66–8; Everson and Stocker 1999, 147–51
61. Cramp 1984, 53–4, 81–2, 93, 138, 140–1; Everson and Stocker 1999, 147–51
62. Bailey 1997, 93–4; Lang 1991, 181–6, 189–93
63. Ibid., 182–6; Cramp 1984, 136–8; Bailey 1997, 84
64. Cramp 1984, 140–1; Bailey 1997, 85, 9304; Lang 1991, 182–4
65. Bailey 1980, 242–9, 254–5
66. Lang 1991, 189–93; Lang 2001, 66–8
67. Thompson 2004, 148–52
68. Bailey 1997, 85
69. Wormald 1978; Bailey 1997, 85
70. Wormald 1978, 42–9
71. Abrams 2000, 143–7
72. Bailey 1980, 102, 161, 231–3; Cramp 1984, 68–71; Bailey and Cramp 1988, 81; Lang 1991, 88–9; Lang 2001, 36
73. Ibid.; Cramp 1984, 53–4
74. Brooks 1978, 82–3
75. Brooks 1978, 83
76. Bailey 1980, 25–7
77. Brooks 1978, 85
78. Ibid., 90–3
79. On ritual deposits of weapons in Viking-Age England see Halsall 2000, 274
80. Brooks 1978, 85–90
81. Bailey 1997, 84–5
82. Cramp 1984, 20; Biddle and Kjølbye-Biddle 1985; Bailey and Cramp 1988, 61–72, 125; Lang 1991, 83–4; Bailey 1997, 66–9. On Scandinavian art in this period see Wicker 2003
83. Nelson 1999, at 138 for the quotation
84. ASC 939, Whitelock 1979, 219
85. Blackburn 2004, 333–5
86. Hall 1994, 20
87. Lang 1976; Bailey 1980, 103–4, 116–17
88. Bailey 1997, 85–93
89. Lang 1991, 189–93
90. Bailey 1980, 116–25
91. Lang 1976, 90–1; Bailey 1980, 104
92. Thompson 2004, 163–8
93. On heroic imagery as masculine ideals more broadly see Lees 1994b
94. Bailey 1997, 94; see also Jesch 1991, 128–9
95. Hawkes 1993, 259–60; Hawkes 2003, 366–8
96. Sawyer 2000, 140–1
97. ASC 892, 895, Whitelock 1979, 203–05
98. Jesch 1991, 104–5
99. Leahy and Paterson 2001, 191–7; Hadley 2006, 127
100. ASC 926, Whitelock 1979, 218
101. Ibid., 283
102. Williams 1986, 14; Williams 1995, 199–202
103. Holman 1996, 137–41
104. Ibid., 103–04; Margeson 1983, 99
105. Stocker 2000, 180–2, 199–200
106. Bailey 1980, 85–100; Lang 1984; Stocker 2000, 198–9; Hadley 2004, 320
107. Crick 2000, 195–205
108. van Houts 1999, 65–120; Sawyer 2000, 46–51, 65–6, 92–7, 111–16
109. Bailey 1981, 92–3; Cramp 1984, 136–7
110. Bailey 1997, 88–9
111. Hadley 2004, 323; Smith 2004, 19

Bibliography

Abrams, L. 2000. 'Conversion and assimilation', in D. M. Hadley and J. D. Richards (eds), *Cultures in Contact: Scandinavian settlement in England in the ninth and tenth centuries*, 135–53, Turnhout: Brepols.

Bailey, R. N. 1980. *Viking Age Sculpture in Northern England*, London: Collins.

Bailey, R. N. 1981. 'The hammer and the cross', in E. Roesdahl (ed.), *The Vikings in England and in their Danish Homeland*, 83–94, London: Anglo-Danish Viking Project.

Bailey, R. N. 1997. *England's Earliest Sculptors*, Toronto: Pontifical Institute of Medieval Studies.

Bailey, R. N. and Cramp, R. 1988. *Corpus of Anglo-Saxon Stone Sculpture, Volume 2. Cumberland, Westmorland and Lancashire North-of-the-Sands*, Oxford: Oxford University Press.

Bersu, G. and Wilson, D. M. 1966. *Three Viking Graves in the Isle of Man*, Society for Medieval Archaeology Monograph, 1, London: SMA.

Biddle, M. and Kjølbye-Biddle, B. 1985. 'The Repton stone', *Anglo-Saxon England*, 14, 233–93.

Biddle, M. and Kjølbye-Biddle, B. 2001. 'Repton and the "great heathen army", 873–4', in J. Graham-Campbell, R. A. Hall, J. Jesch and D. N. Parsons (eds), *Vikings and the Danelaw. Select Papers from the Proceedings of the Thirteenth Viking Congress*, 45–96, Oxford: Oxbow.

Blackburn, M. 2001. 'Expansion and control: aspects of Anglo-Scandinavian minting south of the Humber', in J. Graham-Campbell, R. A. Hall, J. Jesch and D. N. Parsons (eds), *Vikings and the Danelaw. Select Papers from the Proceedings of the Thirteenth Viking Congress*, 125–41, Oxford: Oxbow.

Blackburn, M. 2004. 'The coinage of Scandinavian York', in R. A. Hall (ed.), *Aspects of Anglo-Scandinavian York*, 325–49, The Archaeology of York, 8, York: CBA.

Brooks, N. P. 1978. 'Arms, status and warfare in late-Saxon England', in D. Hill (ed.), *Ethelred the Unready*, 181–103, BAR British Series, 59, Oxford: British Archaeological Reports.

Budd, P., Millard, A., Chenery, C., Lucy, S. and Roberts, C. 2004. 'Investigating population movement by stable isotope analysis: a report from Britain', *Antiquity*, **78**, 127–41.

Butler, J. 1990. *Gender Trouble: Feminism and the Subversion of Identity*, London: Routledge.

Connell, R. W. 1995. *Masculinities*, Cambridge: Polity.

Cramp, R. 1984. *Corpus of Anglo-Saxon Stone Sculpture, Volume 1. County Durham and Northumberland*, Oxford: Oxford University Press.

Crick, J. 2000. 'Posthumous obligation and family identity', in W. O. Fraser and A. J. Tyrell (eds), *Social Identity in Early Medieval Britain*, 193–208, London: Leicester University Press.

Dommasnes, L. H. 1982. 'Two decades of women in prehistory and in archaeology in Norway. A Review', *Norwegian Archaeological Review*, **25** (1), 1–14.

Dommasnes, L. H. 1991. 'Women, kinship and the basis of power in the Norwegian Viking Age', in R. Samson (ed.), *Social Approaches to Viking Studies*, 65–74, Glasgow: Cruithne.

Edwards, B. N. J. 1998. *Vikings in North-West England*, Lancaster: Centre for North-West Regional Studies.

Everson, P. and Stocker, D. 1999. Corpus of Anglo-Saxon Stone Sculpture, Volume 5. Lincolnshire, Oxford: Oxford University Press.

Fell, C. 1984. *Women in Anglo-Saxon England, and the Impact of 1066*, London: British Museum.

Gilchrist, R. 1994. *Gender and Material Culture: the archaeology of religious women*, London: Routledge.

Graham-Campbell, J. 1980. 'The Scandinavian Viking-Age burials of England – some problems of interpretation', in P. Rahtz, T. Dickinson and L. Watts (eds), *Anglo-Saxon Cemeteries 1979*, 379–82, BAR British Series, 82, Oxford: British Archaeological Reports.

Graham-Campbell, J. 2001. 'Pagan Scandinavian burial in the central and southern Danelaw', in J. Graham-Campbell, R. A. Hall, J. Jesch and D. N. Parsons (eds), *Vikings and the Danelaw. Select Papers from the Proceedings of the Thirteenth Viking Congress*, 105–23, Oxford: Oxbow.

Graham-Campbell, J. and Batey, C. 1998. *Vikings in Scotland: an archaeological study*, Edinburgh: Edinburgh University Press.

Griffiths, D. 2004. 'Settlement and acculturation in the Irish Sea region', in J. Hines, A. Lane and M. Redknap (eds), Land, Sea and Home, 125–38, *Society for Medieval Archaeology Monograph*, **20**, Leeds: SMA.

Hadley, D. M. 1999. 'Introduction: medieval masculinities', in D. M. Hadley (ed.), *Masculinity in Medieval Europe*, 1–18, London: Longman.

Hadley, D. M. 2004. 'Negotiating gender, family and status in Anglo-Saxon burial practices, *c.*600–950', in L. Brubaker and J. M. H. Smith (eds), *Gender in the Early Medieval World. East and West, 300–900*, 301–23, Cambridge: Cambridge University Press.

Hadley, D. M. in press a. 'Britain and Ireland in the long ninth century, *c.*790–900: Scandinavian settlement', in P. A. Stafford (ed.), *Blackwell Companion to British History, Volume 1 The Early Middle Ages*, London: Blackwell.

Hadley, D. M. in press b. 'Engendering the grave in later Anglo-Saxon England', in *Proceedings of the Chacmool Conference*, Calgary: Calgary University Press.

Hadley, D. M. in press c. 'Social and physical difference in and beyond the Anglo-Saxon churchyard', in J. L. Buckberry and A. K. Cherryson (eds), *Later Anglo-Saxon Burial, c.650 to 1100AD*, Oxford: Oxbow

Hadley, D. M. and Buckberry, J. L. 2005. 'Caring for the dead in late Anglo-Saxon England', in F. Tinti (ed.), *Pastoral Care in Late Anglo-Saxon England*, 121–47, Woodbridge: Boydell.

Hall, R. A. 1994. *Viking Age York*, London: Batsford.

Halsall, G. 2000. 'The Viking presence in England? The burial evidence reconsidered', in D. M. Hadley and J. D. Richards (eds), *Cultures in Contact: Scandinavian settlement in England in the ninth and tenth centuries*, 259–76, Turnhout: Brepols.

Hawkes, J. 1993. 'Mary and the cycle of Resurrection: the iconography of the Hovingham panel', in M. Spearman and J. Higgitt (eds), *The Age of Migrating Ideas: early medieval art in Britain north of the Humber*, 254–60, Edinburgh: National Museums of Scotland.

Hawkes, J. 2003. 'Sermons in Stone: the Mysteries of Christ in Anglo-Saxon Sculpture', in M. O. H. Carver (ed.), *The Cross Goes North: Processes of Conversion in Northern Europe, AD 300–1300*, 351–70, Woodbridge: Boydell.

Holman, K. 1996. *Scandinavian Runic Inscriptions in the British Isles: their historical context*, Trondheim: Norwegian University of Science and Technology.

James, E. 1989. 'Burial and status in the early medieval West', *Royal Hist. Soc. Trans.*, 5th ser., **39**, 23–40.

Jesch, J. 1991. *Women in the Viking Age*, Woodbridge: Boydell.

Jesch, J. 2001. *Ships and Men in the Late Viking Age: the vocabulary of runic inscriptions and skaldic verse*, Woodbridge: Boydell.

Lang, J. T. 1976. 'Sigurd and Weland in pre-Conquest carving from northern England', *Yorkshire Arch Jnl*, **48**, 83–94.

Lang, J. T. 1984. 'The hogback: a viking colonial monument', *ASSAH*, 3, 85–176.

Lang, J. T. 1991. *Corpus of Anglo-Saxon Stone Sculpture, Volume 3. York and Eastern Yorkshire*, Oxford: Oxford University Press.

Lang, J. T. 2001. *Corpus of Anglo-Saxon Stone Sculpture, Volume 6. Northern Yorkshire*, Oxford: Oxford University Press.

Lees, C. 1994a. 'Introduction', in C. Lees (ed.), *Medieval Masculinities*, xv–xxv, Minneapolis: University of Minnesota Press.

Lees, C. 1994b. 'Men and Beowulf', in C. Lees (ed.), *Medieval Masculinities*, 129–48, Minneapolis: University of Minnesota Press.

MacPherson, P. 2006. *Tracing Change: an isotopic investigation of Anglo-Saxon childhood diet*, unpublished PhD thesis, University of Sheffield.

Margeson, S. 1983. 'On the iconography of the Manx crosses', in C. Fell, P. Foote, D. M. Wilson and R. Thomson (eds), *The Viking Age in the Isle of Man*, 95–106, London: Viking Society for Northern Research.

Morris, C. 1981. 'From sword to plough', in E. Roesdahl (ed.), *The Vikings in England and in their Danish Homeland*, 69–77, London: Anglo-Danish Viking Project.

Nelson, J. L. 1997a. 'Family, gender and sexuality in the Middle Ages', in M. Bentley (ed.), *Companion to Historiography*, 153–76, London: Routledge.

Nelson, J. L. 1997b. 'The Frankish Empire', in P. H. Sawyer (ed.), *The Oxford Illustrated History of the Vikings*, 19–47, Oxford: Oxford University Press.

Nelson, J. L. 1999. 'Monks, secular men and masculinity, *c.* 900', in D. M. Hadley (ed.), *Masculinity in Medieval Europe*, 121–42, London: Longman.

Randsborg, K. 1980. *The Viking Age in Denmark: the formation of state*, London: Duckworth.

Pedersen, A. 1997. 'Similar finds – different meanings? Some preliminary thoughts on the Viking-age burials with riding equipment in Scandinavia', in C. K. Jensen and K. Høilund Nielsen (eds), *Burial and Society*, 171–83, Aarhus: Aarhus University Press.

Pitts, M. 2004. 'Cumbrian heritage', British Arch, 79, 28–31.

Richards, J. D. 2001. 'Boundaries and cult centres: viking burial in Derbyshire', in J. Graham-Campbell, R. A. Hall, J. Jesch and D. N. Parsons (eds), *Vikings and the Danelaw*, 97–104, Oxford: Oxbow.

Richards, J. D. 2002. 'The case of the missing Vikings: Scandinavian burial in the Danelaw', in S. Lucy and A. Reynolds (eds), *Burial in Early Medieval England and Wales*, 156–70, Society for Medieval Archaeology Monograph, 17, London: SMA.

Richards, J. D. 2003. 'Pagans and Christians at the frontier: Viking burial in the Danelaw', in M. O. H. Carver (ed.), *The Cross Goes North: processes of conversion in northern Europe AD 300–1300*, 383–95, Woodbridge: Boydell.

Richards, J. D. 2004. 'Excavations at the Viking Barrow cemetery at Heath Wood, Ingleby, Derbyshire', *Antiquaries Jnl*, **84**, 23–116.

Richards, J. D., Jecock, M., Richmond, L. and Tuck, C. 1995. 'The viking barrow cemetery at Heath Wood, Ingleby, Derbyshire', *Medieval Arch*, **39**, 51–70.

Sawyer, B. 2000. *The Viking-Age Rune-Stones*, Oxford: Oxford University Press.

Smith, J. M. H. 2004. 'Introduction: gendering the early medieval world', in L. Brubaker and J. M. H. Smith (eds), *Gender in the Early Medieval World. East and West, 300–900*, 1–19, Cambridge: Cambridge University Press.

Speed, G. and Walton Rogers, P. 2004. 'A burial of a viking woman at Adwick-le-Street, South Yorkshire', *Medieval Arch*, **48**, 51–90.

Stocker, D. 2000. 'Monuments and merchants: irregularities in the distribution of stone sculpture in Lincolnshire and Yorkshire in the tenth century', in D. M. Hadley and J. D. Richards (eds), *Cultures in Contact: Scandinavian settlement in England in the ninth and tenth centuries*, 179–212, Turnhout: Brepols.

Stoodley, N. 1999. 'Burial rites, gender and the creation of kingdoms: the evidence from seventh-century Wessex', *ASSAH*, 10, 99–107.

Svanberg, F. 2003. *Death Rituals in South-East Scandinavia AD 800–1000*, Lund: Almqvist and Wiksell.

Thompson, V. 2004. *Death and Dying in later Anglo-Saxon England*, Woodbridge: Boydell.

Tosh, J. 1994. 'What should historians do with masculinity? Reflections on nineteenth-century Britain', *Hist. Workshop Jnl*, **38**, 179–202.

van Houts, E. 1999. *Memory and Gender in Medieval Europe, 900–1200*, Basingstoke: Macmillan.

Whitelock, D. (ed. and trans.) 1979. *English Historical Documents, Volume I, c. 500–1042*, 2nd edit., London: Eyre Methuen.

Wicker, N. 2003. 'The Scandinavian animal styles in response to Mediterranean and Christian narrative art', in M. O. H. Carver (ed.), *The Cross Goes North: processes of conversion in northern Europe AD 300–1300*, 531–49, Woodbridge: Boydell.

Williams, A. 1986. '"Cockles among the wheat": Danes and English in the western midlands in the first half of the eleventh century, *Midland Hist.*, **11**, 1–22.

Williams, A. 1995. *The English and the Norman Conquest*, Woodbridge: Boydell.

Williams, H. 2005. 'Keeping the dead at arm's length: memory, weaponry and early medieval mortuary technologies', *Jnl of Social Arch.*, **5** (2), 253–75.

Wormald, P. 1978. 'Bede, "Beowulf" and the conversion of the Anglo-Saxon aristocracy', in R. Farrell (ed.), *Bede and Anglo-Saxon England*, 32–95, BAR British Series, 46, Oxford: British Archaeological Reports.